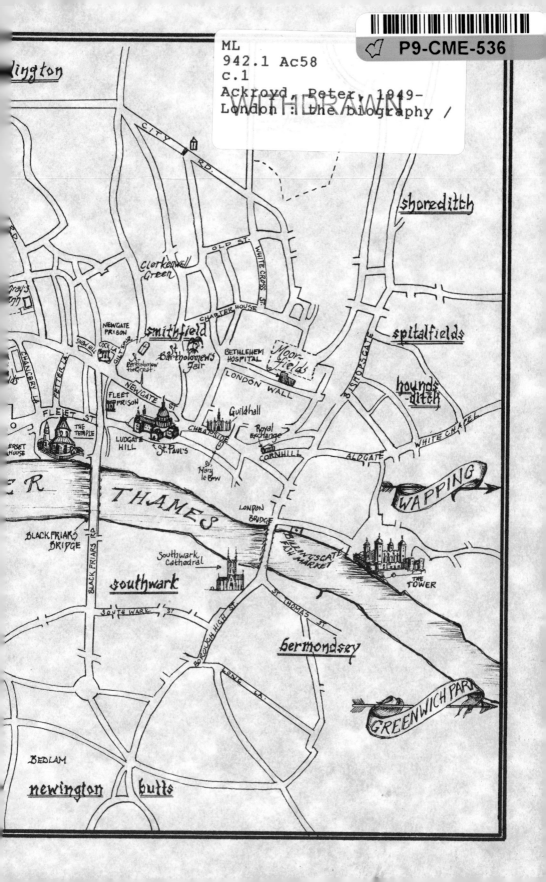

London

THE BIOGRAPHY

London

THE BIOGRAPHY

Peter Ackroyd

NAN A. TALESE

DOUBLEDAY

New York   London
Toronto   Sydney   Auckland

PUBLISHED BY NAN A. TALESE

an imprint of Doubleday
a division of Random House, Inc.
1540 Broadway, New York, New York 10036

DOUBLEDAY *is a trademark of Doubleday*
a division of Random House, Inc.

First published in the United Kingdom by Chatto & Windus, London.

Book design by Ellen Cipriano
Maps designed by Pamela Talese

Library of Congress Cataloging-in-Publication Data
Ackroyd, Peter, 1949–
London : the biography / Peter Ackroyd.—1st ed.
p. cm.
Includes bibliographical references (p. 761) and index.
1. London (England)—Description and travel. 2. London (England)—
Social life and customs. I. Title.

DA684.25 .A28   2001
942.1—dc21
2001027153

ISBN 0-385-49770-9

For Iain Johnston
and
Frederick Nicholas Robertson

❧

Contents

The Late Medieval City

Onward and Upward

Trading Streets and Trading Parishes

A London Neighbourhood

London as Theatre

Pestilence and Flame

After the Fire

Crime and Punishment

Voracious London

London as Crowd

The Natural History of London

Night and Day

London's Radicals

Violent London

Black Magic, White Magic

A Fever of Building

London's Rivers

Under the Ground

Victorian Megalopolis

Refashioning the City

Cockney Visionaries

List of Illustrations

Chronology

994 Siege of London by Danish forces

1013 The second siege of London, by conquering Sweyn

1016 Third siege of London by Cnut, repulsed

1035 Harold I elected king by Londoners

1050 The rebuilding of Westminster Abbey

1065 Dedication of Westminster Abbey

1066 The taking of London by William the Conqueror

1078 The building of the White Tower

1123 Rahere establishes St. Bartholomew's

1176 The building of a stone bridge

1191 The establishment of a London commune

1193–1212 The first mayor of London, Henry Fitz-Ailwin

1220 Rebuilding of Westminster Abbey

1290 Expulsion of the Jews; Eleanor Crosses set up at Chepe and Charing Cross

1326 The London revolution: deposition of Edward II

1348 The Black Death kills one-third of London's population

1371 Charterhouse founded

1373 Chaucer living above Aldgate

1381 Wat Tyler's revolt

1397 Richard Whittington first elected mayor

1406 Plague in London

1414 The Lollard revolt

1442 The Strand is paved

1450 Jack Cade's revolt

1476 The establishment of Caxton's printing press

1484 The sweating sickness in London

1485 Henry VII enters London in triumph after the Battle of Bosworth

1509 Henry VIII ascends the throne

1535 Execution of Thomas More on Tower Hill

1535–9 The spoilation of London's monasteries and churches

1544 Wyngaerde's great panorama of London

1576 The building of the Theatre in Shoreditch

1598 Publication of Stow's *Survey of London*

1608–13 The construction of the New River

1619–22 The building of Inigo Jones's Banqueting House

1642–3 The construction of earthen walls, and forts, against the king's army

1649 Execution of Charles I

1652 The emergence of the coffee house

1663 The building of a theatre in Drury Lane

1665 The Great Plague

1666 The Great Fire

1694 The foundation of the Bank of England

1733 The covering of the Fleet River

1750 The building of Westminster Bridge

1756 The construction of the New Road

1769 The building of Blackfriars Bridge

1769–70 Wilkite agitation in London

1774 The London Building Act

1780 The Gordon Riots

1799 The establishment of the West India Dock Company

1800 The foundation of the Royal College of Surgeons

1801 London's population reaches one million

1809 Gas-lighting instituted in Pall Mall

1816 Radicals meet at Spa Fields: riots in Spitalfields

1824 National Gallery founded

1825 Nash rebuilds Buckingham Palace

1829 London Metropolitan Police Force founded

1834 Houses of Parliament destroyed by fire

1836 University of London established

1851 The Great Exhibition opened in Hyde Park

1858 The "great stink" leads to Bazalgette's sanitary engineering

1863 The opening of the world's first underground railway

1878 The advent of electric lighting

1882 The emergence of the electric tram-car

1887 "Bloody Sunday" demonstrations in Trafalgar Square

1888 The appearance of Jack the Ripper in Whitechapel

1889 The establishment of the London County Council

1892 The beginning of the Blackwall Tunnel under the Thames

1897 The emergence of the motor-omnibus

1901 Population of London reaches 6.6 million

1905 Epidemic of typhus. Aldwych and Kingsway opened to traffic

1906 Suffragettes demonstrate in Parliament Square

1909 The opening of Selfridge's department store

1911 The siege of Sidney Street

1913 The inauguration of the Chelsea Flower Show

1915 The first bombs fall on London

1926 The General Strike

1932 The building of Broadcasting House in Portland Place for the BBC

1935 The inauguration of the Green Belt

1936 The battle of Cable Street

1940 The beginning of the London Blitz

1951 The Festival of Britain on the South Bank

1952 The great smog

1955 The opening of Heathrow Airport

1965 The abolition of the London County Council; creation of the Greater London Council

1967 The closure of the East India Dock; the building of Centre Point

1981 The Brixton riots; the establishment of the London Docklands Development Corporation

1985 Broadwater Farm riots

1986 Completion of M25 ringway; abolition of GLC; the "big bang" in the Stock Exchange

1987 The building of Canary Wharf

2000 Mayoral elections

Acknowledgements

The author and publisher are grateful to the following for permission to reproduce illustrative material which appears in the text pages: Bibliothèque Nationale, Paris, 587; British Library, 43; Folger Shakespeare Library, Washington, D.C., 81; Guildhall, 383, 455, 471, 529, 751; Imperial War Museum, 721; Magdalene College, Cambridge, 191; Museum of London, 5, 89, 121, 135, 219, 237, 297, 403, 551, 613, 661, 735.

The author and publisher are grateful to the following for permission to reproduce copyright material: Italo Calvino, *Invisible Cities* (Secker & Warburg and the Wylie Agency (UK) Ltd.); Sally Holloway, *Courage High* (HMSO); Mike and Trevor Phillips, *Windrush: the Irresistible Rise of Multi-Racial Britain* (HarperCollins); *Virginia Woolf, The Diaries*, ed. Anne Oliver Bell (the Executors of the Estate of Virginia Woolf, The Hogarth Press and Harcourt Brace).

The jacket and endpapers show details from the following paintings and photographs:

Front cover: *London from Southwark*, c.1630, British School; *The Great Wheel, Earl's Court Exhibition*, 1890, by Charles Wilson; *Curds and Whey Seller,*

Cheapside, c.1730, British School; *Coombe and Co's Brewer's, St. Giles*, c.1875, by Alfred and John Bool © Museum of London; Canary Wharf from the Isle of Dogs; Thames Barrier © Matthew Weinreb; inside flap: *The Crawlers*, c.1876, by John Thomson © Museum of London; Lloyds of London © Matthew Weinreb; back cover: *May Morning*, c.1760, by John Collet; *Allen's Tobacconist Shop*, c.1841, by Robert Allen; *A Shop in Macclesfield Street, Soho*, 1883, by Henry Dixon; *Suffragette Demonstration in Trafalgar Square*, c.1908, © Museum of London; Simpson's of Piccadilly; John Lewis, Oxford Street © Matthew Weinreb; inside flap: *Westminster Bridge from the River Looking South*, c.1750, British School; *Railway Maintenance Gang, St. Pancras*, c.1900, by Rev. John Galt © Museum of London; spine: *Regent Street*, c.1886, anon. © Museum of London; endpapers: *Seven Phases in the Evolution of Old London Bridge* © Museum of London.

Cartography on endpapers by Pamela Talese.

While the publishers have made every effort to trace the owners of copyright, they will be happy to rectify any errors or omissions in further editions.

The City as Body

he image of London as a human body is striking and singular; we may trace it from the pictorial emblems of the City of God, the mystical body in which Jesus Christ represents its head and the citizens its other members. London has also been envisaged in the form of a young man with his arms outstretched in a gesture of liberation; the figure is taken from a Roman bronze but it embodies the energy and exultation of a city continually expanding in great waves of progress and of confidence. Here might be found the "heart of London beating warm."

The byways of the city resemble thin veins and its parks are like lungs. In the mist and rain of an urban autumn, the shining stones and cobbles of the older thoroughfares look as if they are bleeding. When William Harvey, practising as a surgeon in St. Bartholomew's Hospital, walked through the streets he noticed that the hoses of the fire engines spouted water like blood from a cut artery. Metaphorical images of the Cockney body have circulated for many hundreds of years: "gob" was first recorded in 1550, "paws" in 1590, "mug" in 1708 and "kisser" in the mid-eighteenth century.

Harvey's seventeenth-century hospital was beside the shambles of Smithfield, and that conjunction may suggest another image of the city. It is fleshy and voracious, grown fat upon its appetite for people and for food, for

goods and for drink; it consumes and it excretes, maintained within a continual state of greed and desire.

For Daniel Defoe, London was a great body which "circulates all,
exports all, and at last pays for all." That is why it has commonly been portrayed in monstrous form, a swollen and dropsical giant which kills more
than it breeds. Its head is too large, out of proportion to the other members;
its face and hands have also grown monstrous, irregular and "out of all
Shape." It is a "spleen" or a great "wen." A body racked with fever, and
choked by ashes, it proceeds from plague to fire.

Whether we consider London as a young man refreshed and risen from
sleep, therefore, or whether we lament its condition as a deformed giant, we
must regard it as a human shape with its own laws of life and growth.

Here, then, is its biography.

Some will object that such a biography can form no part of a true history. I admit the fault and plead in my defence that I have subdued the style of my enquiry to the nature of the subject. London is a labyrinth, half of stone and half
of flesh. It cannot be conceived in its entirety but can be experienced only as
a wilderness of alleys and passages, courts and thoroughfares, in which even
the most experienced citizen may lose the way; it is curious, too, that this
labyrinth is in a continual state of change and expansion.

The biography of London also defies chronology. Contemporary theorists have suggested that linear time is itself a figment of the human imagination, but London has already anticipated their conclusions. There are many
different forms of time in the city, and it would be foolish of me to change its
character for the sake of creating a conventional narrative. That is why this
book moves quixotically through time, itself forming a labyrinth. If the
history of London poverty is beside a history of London madness, then the
connections may provide more significant information than any orthodox
historiographical survey.

Chapters of history resemble John Bunyan's little wicket-gates, while all
around lie sloughs of despond and valleys of humiliation. So I will sometimes
stray from the narrow path in search of those heights and depths of urban experience that know no history and are rarely susceptible to rational analysis.
I understand a little, and I trust that it will prove enough. I am not a Virgil
prepared to guide aspiring Dantes around a defined and circular kingdom. I
am only one stumbling Londoner who wishes to lead others in the directions
which I have pursued over a lifetime.

The readers of this book must wander and wonder. They may become lost upon the way; they may experience moments of uncertainty, and on occasions strange fantasies or theories may bewilder them. On certain streets various eccentric or vulnerable people will pause beside them, pleading for attention. There will be anomalies and contradictions—London is so large and so wild that it contains no less than everything—just as there will be irresolutions and ambiguities. But there will also be moments of revelation, when the city will be seen to harbour the secrets of the human world. Then it is wise to bow down before the immensity. So we set off in anticipation, with the milestone pointing ahead of us *"To London."*

Peter Ackroyd
London
March 2000

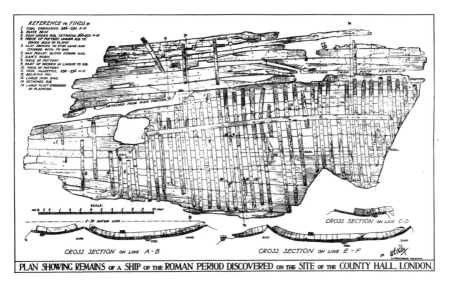

PLAN SHOWING REMAINS OF A SHIP OF THE ROMAN PERIOD DISCOVERED ON THE SITE OF THE COUNTY HALL, LONDON.

The relics of past ages have been found beneath many areas of London;
they are the foundations upon which it rests.

CHAPTER I

The Sea!

❧

If you were to touch the plinth upon which the equestrian statue of King Charles I is placed, at Charing Cross, your fingers might rest upon the projecting fossils of sea lilies, starfish or sea urchins. There is a photograph of that statue taken in 1839; with its images of hackney cabs and small boys in stove-pipe hats the scene already seems remote, and yet how unimaginably distant lies the life of those tiny marine creatures. In the beginning was the sea. There was once a music-hall song entitled "Why Can't We Have the Sea in London?," but the question is redundant; the site of the capital, fifty million years before, was covered by great waters.

The waters have not wholly departed, even yet, and there is evidence of their life in the weathered stones of London. The Portland stone of the Customs House and St. Pancras Old Church has a diagonal bedding which reflects the currents of the ocean; there are ancient oyster shells within the texture of Mansion House and the British Museum. Seaweed can still be seen in the greyish marble of Waterloo Station, and the force of hurricanes may be detected in the "chatter-marked" stone of pedestrian subways. In the fabric of Waterloo Bridge, the bed of the Upper Jurassic Sea can also be observed. The tides and storms are still all around us, therefore, and as Shelley wrote of London "that great sea . . . still howls on for more."

London has always been a vast ocean in which survival is not certain. The dome of St. Paul's has been seen trembling upon a "vague troubled sea" of fog, while dark streams of people flow over London Bridge, or Waterloo Bridge, and emerge as torrents in the narrow thoroughfares of London. The social workers of the mid-nineteenth century spoke of rescuing "drowning" people in Whitechapel or Shoreditch and Arthur Morrison, a novelist of the same period, invokes a "howling sea of human wreckage" crying out to be saved. Henry Peacham, the seventeenth-century author of *The Art of Living in London*, considered the city as "a vast sea, full of gusts, fearful-dangerous shelves and rocks," while in 1810 Louis Simond was content to "listen to the roar of its waves, breaking around us in measured time."

If you look from a distance, you observe a sea of roofs, and have no more knowledge of the dark streams of people than of the denizens of some unknown ocean. But the city is always a heaving and restless place, with its own torrents and billows, its foam and spray. The sound of its streets is like the murmur from a sea shell and in the great fogs of the past the citizens believed themselves to be lying on the floor of the ocean. Even amid all the lights it may simply be what George Orwell described as "the ocean bottom, among the luminous, gliding fishes." This is a constant vision of the London world, particularly in the novels of the twentieth century, where feelings of hopelessness and despondency turn the city into a place of silence and mysterious depths.

Yet, like the sea and the gallows, London refuses nobody. Those who venture upon its currents look for prosperity or fame, even if they often founder in its depths. Jonathan Swift depicted the jobbers of the Exchange as traders waiting for shipwrecks in order to strip the dead, while the commercial houses of the City often used a ship or boat as a weather-vane and as a sign of good fortune. Three of the most common emblems in urban cemeteries are the shell, the ship and the anchor.

The starlings of Trafalgar Square are also the starlings who nest in the cliff faces of northern Scotland. The pigeons of London are descended from the wild rock-doves who lived among the steep cliffs of the northern and western shores of this island. For them the buildings of the city are cliffs still, and the streets are the endless sea stretching beyond them. But the real confluence lies in this—that London, for so long the arbiter of trade and of the sea, should have upon its fabric the silent signature of the tides and waves.

And when the waters parted, the London earth was revealed. In 1877, in a characteristically grand example of Victorian engineering, a vast well was taken down 1,146 feet at the southern end of Tottenham Court Road. It travelled hundreds of millions of years, touching the primeval landscapes of this city site, and from its evidence we can list the layers beneath our feet from the Devonian to the Jurassic and the Cretaceous. Above these strata lie 650 feet of chalk, outcrops of which can be seen upon the Downs or the Chilterns as the rim of the London Basin, that shallow saucer-like declivity in which the city rests. On top of the chalk itself lies the thick London clay which is in turn covered by deposits of gravel and brick-earth. Here, then, is the making of the city in more than one sense; the clay and the chalk and the brick-earth have for almost two thousand years been employed to construct the houses and public buildings of London. It is almost as if the city raised itself from its primeval origin, creating a human settlement from the senseless material of past time.

This clay is burned and compressed into "London Stock," the particular yellow-brown or red brick that has furnished the material of London housing. It truly represents the *genius loci*, and Christopher Wren suggested that "the earth around London, rightly managed, will yield as good brick as were the Roman bricks . . . and will endure, in our air, beyond any stone our island affords." William Blake called the bricks of London "well-wrought affections" by which he meant that the turning of clay and chalk into the fabric of the streets was a civilising process which knit the city with its primeval past. The houses of the seventeenth century are made out of dust that drifted over the London region in a glacial era 25,000 years before.

The London clay can yield more tangible evidence, also: the skeletons of sharks (in the East End it was popularly believed that shark's teeth might cure cramp), the skull of a wolf in Cheapside, and crocodiles in the clay of Islington. In 1682 Dryden recognised this now forgotten and invisible landscape of London:

> Yet monsters from thy large increase we find
> Engender'd on the Slyme thou leav'st behind.

Eight years later, in 1690, the remains of a mammoth were found beside what has since become King's Cross.

London clay can by the alchemy of weather become mud, and in 1851 Charles Dickens noted that there was so "much mud in the streets . . . that it would not be wonderful to meet a Megalosaurus, forty feet long or so, waddling like an elephantine lizard up Holborn Hill." In the 1930s Louis-Ferdinand Céline took the motor buses of Piccadilly Circus to be a "herd of mastodons" returning to the territory they had left behind. In *Mother London* Michael Moorcock's late twentieth-century hero sees "monsters, by mud and giant ferns" while crossing the footbridge alongside the Hungerford railway bridge.

The mammoth of 1690 was only the first primeval relic to be discovered in the London region. Hippopotami and elephants lay beneath Trafalgar Square, lions at Charing Cross, and buffaloes beside St. Martin-in-the-Fields. A brown bear was discovered in north Woolwich, mackerel in the old brickfields of Holloway and sharks in Brentford. The wild animals of London include reindeer, giant beavers, hyenas and rhinoceri which once grazed by the swamps and lagoons of the Thames. And that landscape has not entirely faded. Within recent memory the mist from the ancient marshes of Westminster destroyed the frescoes of St. Stephen's. It is still possible, beside the National Gallery, to detect the rise of ground between the middle and upper terraces of the Thames in the Pleistocene era.

This was not, even then, an unpeopled region. Within the bones of the King's Cross mammoth were also found pieces of a flint hand-axe which can be dated to the Palaeolithic period. We can say with some certainty that for half a million years there has been in London a pattern of habitation and hunting if not of settlement. The first great fire of London was started, a quarter of a million years ago, in the forests south of the Thames. That river had by then taken its appointed course but not its later appearance; it was very broad, fed by many streams, occluded by forests, bordered by swamps and marshes.

The prehistory of London invites endless speculation and there is a certain pleasure to be derived from the prospect of human settlement in areas where, many thousands of years later, streets would be laid out and houses erected. There is no doubt that the region has been continually occupied for at least fifteen thousand years. A great gathering of flint tools, excavated in Southwark, is assumed to mark the remains of a Mesolithic manufactory; a hunting camp of the same period has been discovered upon Hampstead Heath; a pottery bowl from the Neolithic period was unearthed in Clapham. On these ancient sites have been found pits and post-holes, together with human remains and evidence of feasting. These early people drank a potion similar to mead or beer. Like their London descendants, they left vast quantities of rubbish everywhere. Like them, too, they met for the purposes of worship. For many thousands of years these ancient peoples treated the great river as a divine being to be placated and surrendered to its depths the bodies of their illustrious dead.

In the late Neolithic period there appeared, from the generally marshy soil on the northern bank of the Thames, twin hills covered by gravel and brick-earth, surrounded by sedge and willow. They were forty to fifty feet in height, and were divided by a valley through which flowed a stream. We know them as Cornhill and Ludgate Hill, with the now buried Walbrook running between. Thus emerged London.

The name is assumed to be of Celtic origin, awkward for those who believe that there was no human settlement here before the Romans built their city. Its actual meaning, however, is disputed. It might be derived from *Llyn-don*, the town or stronghold (*don*) by the lake or stream (*Llyn*); but this owes more to medieval Welsh than ancient Celtic. Its provenance might be *Lain-don*, "long hill," or the Gaelic *lunnd*, "marsh." One of the more intriguing speculations, given the reputation for violence which Londoners were later to acquire, is that the name is derived from the Celtic adjective *londos* meaning "fierce."

There is a more speculative etymology which gives the honour of naming to King Lud, who is supposed to have reigned in the century of the Roman invasion. He laid out the city's streets and rebuilt its walls. Upon his death he was buried beside the gate which bore his name, and the city became known as *Kaerlud* or *Kaerlundein*, "Lud's City." Those of sceptical cast of mind may be inclined to dismiss such narratives but the legends of a thousand years may contain profound and particular truths.

The origin of the name, however, remains mysterious. (It is curious, perhaps, that the name of the mineral most associated with the city—coal—also has no certain derivation.) With its syllabic power, so much suggesting force or thunder, it has continually echoed through history—*Caer Ludd, Lundunes, Lindonion, Lundene, Lundone, Ludenberk, Longidinium*, and a score of other variants. There have even been suggestions that the name is more ancient than the Celts themselves, and that it springs from some Neolithic past.

We must not necessarily assume that there were settlements or defended enclosures upon Ludgate Hill or Cornhill, or that there were wooden track-ways where there are now great avenues, but the attractions of the site might have been as obvious in the third and fourth millennia BC as they were to the later Celts and Romans. The hills were well defended, forming a natural plateau, with the river to the south, fens to the north, marshes to the east, and another river, later known as the Fleet, to the west. It was fertile ground, well watered by springs bubbling up through the gravel. The Thames was easily navigable at this point, with the Fleet and the Walbrook providing natural harbours. The ancients trackways of England were also close at hand. So from earliest time London was the most appropriate site for trade, for markets, and for barter. The City has for much of its history been the centre of world commerce; it is perhaps instructive to note that it may have begun with the transactions of Stone Age people in their own markets.

All this is speculation, not altogether uninformed, but evidence of a more substantial kind has been discovered in later levels of London earth. In those long stretches of time designated as the "Late Bronze Age" and the "Early Iron Age"—a period spanning almost a thousand years—shards and fragments of bowls, and pots, and tools, were left all over London. There are signs of prehistoric activity in the areas now known as St. Mary Axe and Gresham Street, Austin Friars and Finsbury Circus, Bishopsgate and Seething Lane, with altogether some 250 "finds" clustered in the area of the twin hills together with Tower Hill and Southwark. From the Thames itself many hundreds of metal objects have been retrieved, while along its banks is to be found frequent evidence of metal-working. This is the period from which the great early legends of London spring. It is also, in its latter phase, the age of the Celts.

In the first century BC, Julius Caesar's description of the region around London suggests the presence of an elaborate, rich and well-organised tribal civilisation. Its population was "exceedingly large" and "the ground thickly studded with homesteads." The nature and role of the twin hills throughout this period cannot with certainty be given; perhaps these were sacred places, or perhaps their well-defined position allowed them to be used as hill-forts in order to protect the trade carried along the river. There is every reason to suppose that this area of the Thames was a centre of commerce and of industry, with a market in iron products as well as elaborate workings in bronze, with merchants from Gaul, Rome and Spain bringing Samian ware, wine and spices in exchange for corn, metals and slaves.

In the history of this period completed by Geoffrey of Monmouth in 1136, the principal city in the island of Britain is undoubtedly London. But according to modern scholars his work is established upon lost texts, apocryphal embellishments and uninformed conjecture. Where Geoffrey speaks of kings, for example, they prefer the nomenclature of tribes; he dates events by means of biblical parallel, while they provide indicators such as "Late Iron Age"; he elucidates patterns of conflict and social change in terms of individual human passion, where more recent accounts of prehistory rely upon more abstract principles of trade and technology. The approaches may be contradictory but they are not necessarily incompatible. It is believed by historians of early Britain, for example, that a people known as the Trinovantes settled on territory to the north of the London region. Curiously enough, Geoffrey states that the first name of the city was Trinovantum. He also mentions the presence of temples within London itself; even if they had existed, these palisades and wooden enclosures would since have been lost beneath the stone of the Roman city as well as the brick and cement of succeeding generations.

But nothing is wholly lost. In the first four decades of the twentieth century there was a particular effort by prehistorians to discover something of London's supposedly hidden past. In books such as *The Lost Language of London*, *Legendary London*, *Prehistoric London* and *The Earlier Inhabitants of London*, tokens and traces of a Celtic or Druidic London were thoroughly examined and were found significant. These studies were effectively killed off by the Second World War, after which urban planning and regeneration became more important than urban speculation. But the original works survive, and still repay close study. The fact that existing street names may betray a Celtic origin—Colin Deep Lane, Pancras Lane, Maiden Lane, Ingal Road among them—is, for example, as instructive as any of the material "finds" recorded on the site of the ancient city. Long-forgotten trackways have guided the course of modern thoroughfares; the crossroads at the Angel, Islington, for example, marks the point where two prehistoric British roads intersected. We know of Old Street leading to Old Ford, of Maiden Lane crossing through Pentonville and Battle Bridge to Highgate, of the route from Upper Street to Highbury, all following the same ancient tracks and buried paths.

Yet there is no more suspect or difficult subject, in the context of this period, than Druidism. That it was well established in Celtic settlements is not in doubt; Julius Caesar, who was in a position to speak with some authority on the subject, stated that the Druid religion was founded (*inventa*) in Britain and that its Celtic adherents came to this island in order to be educated in its mysteries. It represented a highly advanced, if somewhat insular, religious culture. Of course we might speculate that the oak woodland to the north of the twin hills provided a suitable site for sacrifice and worship; one antiquary, Sir Laurence Gomme, has envisaged a temple or sacred space upon Ludgate Hill itself. But there are many false trails. It was once generally agreed that Parliament Hill near Highgate was a place for religious assembly, but in fact the remnants which have been discovered there do not date from prehistory. The Chislehurst caves in south London, once reputed to be of Druid origin connected in some fashion with the observation of the heavens, are almost certainly of medieval construction.

It has been suggested that the London area was controlled from three sacred mounds; they are named as Penton Hill, Tothill and the White Mound, otherwise known as Tower Hill. Any such theory can readily be dismissed as nonsense, but there are curious parallels and coincidences which render it more interesting than the usual fantasies of latter-day psychogeographers.

It is known that in prehistoric worship a holy place was marked by a spring, a grove and a well or ritual shaft.

There is a reference to a "shrubby maze" in the pleasure gardens of White Conduit House, situated on the high ground of Pentonville, and a maze's avatar was a sacred hill or grove. Close at hand is the famous well of Sadlers Wells. In recent days the water of this well flowed under the orchestra pit of the theatre but, from medieval times, it was considered holy and was tended by the priests of Clerkenwell. The site of the high ground in Pentonville was also once a reservoir; it was until recently the headquarters of the London Water Board.

Another maze was to be found in the area once known as Tothill Fields in Westminster; it is depicted in Hollar's view of the area in the mid-seventeenth century. Here also is a sacred spring, deriving from the "holy well" in Dean's Yard, Westminster. A fair, similar to the pleasure gardens upon White Conduit Fields, was established here at an early date; the first extant reference is dated 1257.

The sites are, therefore, comparable. There are other suggestive coincidences. On old maps, "St. Hermit's Hill" is a noticeable feature of the area beside Tothill Fields. To this day, there is a Hermes Street at the top of the Pentonville Road. It is perhaps also interesting that in a house on this site dwelled a physician who promoted a medicine known as the "Balsam of Life"; the house was later turned into an observatory.

On Tower Hill there was a spring of clear bubbling water, reputed to possess curative properties. A medieval well exists there, and traces of a Late Iron Age burial have been uncovered. There is no maze but the place has its own share of Celtic legends; according to the *Welsh Triads* the guardian head of Bran the Blessed is interred within the White Hill to safeguard the kingdom from its enemies. London's legendary founder Brutus, also, was supposed to have been buried on Tower Hill, in sacred ground that was used as an observatory until the seventeenth century.

The etymology of Penton Hill and Tothill is reasonably certain. *Pen* is the Celtic signifier for head or hill, while *ton* is a variant of *tor/tot/twt/too*, which means spring or rising ground. (Wycliffe applies the words *tot* or *tote*, for example, to Mount Zion.) Those of a more romantic disposition have suggested that *tot* is derived from the Egyptian god Thoth who is of course reincarnated in Hermes, the Greek personification of the wind or the music of the lyre.

Here, then, is the hypothesis: London mounds, which bear so many similar characteristics, are in fact the holy sites of Druid ritual. The maze is the sacred equivalent of the oak grove, while the wells and springs represent the worship of the god of the water. The London Water Board was, then, well situated. Pleasure gardens and fairs are more recent versions of those prehistoric festivals or meetings which were held upon the same ground. So antiquaries have named Tothill, Penton and Tower Hill as the holy places of London.

It is generally assumed, of course, that Pentonville is named after an eighteenth-century speculator, Henry Penton, who developed the area. Can one place assume different identities, existing in different times and in different visions of reality? Is it possible that *both* explanations of Pentonville are true simultaneously? Might Billingsgate be named after the Celtic king Belinus or Belin, as the great sixteenth-century antiquary John Stow would have it, or after a Mr. Beling, who once owned the land? Can Ludgate really bear the name of Lud, a Celtic god of the waters? Certainly there is room for contemplation here.

It is equally important to look for evidence of continuity. It is likely that there was antiquity of worship among the Britons long before the Druids emerged as the high priests of their culture, and in turn Celtic forms of ritual seem to have survived the Roman occupation and subsequent invasions by the Saxon tribes. In the records of St. Paul's Cathedral the adjacent buildings are known as "*Camera Dianae*." A fifteenth-century chronicler recalled a time when "London worships Diana," the goddess of the hunt, which is at least one explanation for the strange annual ceremony that took place at St. Paul's as late as the sixteenth century. There, in the Christian temple erected on the sacred site of Ludgate Hill, a stag's head was impaled upon a spear and carried about the church; it was then received upon the steps of the church by priests wearing garlands of flowers upon their heads. So the pagan customs of London survived into recorded history, just as a latent paganism survived among the citizens themselves.

One other inheritance from prehistoric worship may also be considered. The sense of certain places as being powerful or venerable was taken over by the Christians in the recognition of "holy wells" and in such ceremonies of territorial piety as "beating the bounds." Yet the same sensibility is to be found in the writings of the great London visionaries, from William Blake to Arthur Machen, writings in which the city itself is considered to be a sacred place with its own joyful and sorrowful mysteries.

In this Celtic period, which lurks like some chimera in the shadows of the known world, the great legends of London find their origin. The historical record knows only of warring tribes within a highly organised culture of some sophistication. They were not necessarily savage, in other words, and the Greek geographer Strabo describes one Briton, an ambassador, as well dressed, intelligent and agreeable. He spoke Greek with such fluency that "you would have thought he had been bred up in the lyceum." This is the proper context for those narratives in which London is accorded the status of a principal city. Brutus, in legend the founder of the city, was buried within London's walls. Locrinus kept his lover, Estrildis, in a secret chamber beneath the ground. Bladud, who practised sorcery, constructed a pair of wings with which to fly through the air of London; yet he fell against the roof of the Temple of Apollo situated in the very heart of the city, perhaps on Ludgate Hill itself. Another king, Dunvallo, who formulated the ancient laws of sanctuary, was buried beside a London temple. From this period, too, came the narratives of Lear and of Cymbeline. More powerful still is the legend of the giant Gremagot who by some strange alchemy was transformed into the twins Gog and Magog, who became tutelary spirits of London. It has often been suggested that each of this characteristically ferocious pair, whose statues have stood for many centuries within the Guildhall, guards one of the twin hills of London.

Such stories are recorded by John Milton in *The History of Britain*, published a little more than three hundred years ago. "After this, *Brutus* in a chosen place builds *Troia nova*, chang'd in time to *Trinovantum*, now *London*: and began to enact Laws; *Heli* beeing then high Priest in *Judaea*: and having govern'd the whole Ile 24 Years, dy'd, and was buried in his new *Troy*." Brutus was the great-grandson of Aeneas who, some years after the fall of Troy, led the exodus of Trojans from Greece; in the course of his exilic wanderings he was granted a dream in which the goddess Diana spoke words of prophecy to him: an island far to the west, beyond the realm of Gaul, "fitts thy people"; you are to sail there, Brutus, and establish a city which will become another Troy. "And *Kings* be born of thee, whose dredded might shall aw the World, and Conquer Nations bold." London is to maintain a world empire but, like ancient Troy, it may suffer some perilous burning. It is interesting that paintings of London's Great Fire in 1666 make specific allusion to the fall of Troy. This is indeed the central myth of London's origin which can be found in the sixth-century verses of "Tallisen," where the British are celebrated as the living remnant of Troy, as well as in the later poetry of Edmund Spenser and of Alexander Pope. Pope, born in Plough Court beside Lombard Street, was of course invoking a visionary urban civilisation; yet it is one highly appropriate for a city first vouchsafed to Brutus in a dream.

The narrative of Brutus has been dismissed as mere fable and fanciful legend but, as Milton wrote in the judicious introduction to his own history, "oft-times relations heertofore accounted fabulous have bin after found to contain in them many foot-steps, and reliques of something true." Some scholars believe that we can date the wanderings of the apparently legendary Brutus to the period around 1100 BC. In contemporary historiographical terms this marks the period of the Late Bronze Age when new bands or tribes of settlers occupied the area around London; they constructed large defensive enclosures and maintained an heroic life of mead-halls, ring-giving and furious fighting which found expression in later legends. Segmented glass beads, like those of Troy, have been discovered in England. In the waters of the Thames was found a black two-handled cup; its provenance lies in Asia Minor, with an approximate date of 900 BC. So there is some indication of trade between western Europe and the eastern Mediterranean, and there is every reason to suppose that Phrygian or later Phoenician merchants reached the shores of Albion and sailed into the market of London.

Material evidence of an association with Troy itself, and with the region of Asia Minor in which that ancient doomed city resided, can be found elsewhere. Diogenes Laertius identified the Celts with the Chaldees of Assyria; indeed the famous British motif comprising the lion and the unicorn may be of Chaldean origin. Caesar noted, with some surprise, that the Druids made use of Greek letters. In the *Welsh Triads* there is a description of an invading tribe who have travelled to the shores of Albion, or England, from the region of Constantinople. It is suggestive, perhaps, that the Franks and Gauls also claimed Trojan ancestry. Although it is not altogether out of the question that a tribe from the region of fallen Troy migrated to western Europe, it is more likely, perhaps, that the Celtic people themselves had their origins in the eastern Mediterranean. The legend of London, as a new Troy, is therefore still able to claim some adherents.

At the beginning of any civilisation there are fables and legends; only at the end are they proved to be accurate.

One token of Brutus and his Trojan fleet may still remain. If you walk east down Cannon Street, on the other side from the railway station, you will find an iron grille set within the Bank of China. It protects a niche upon which has been placed a stone roughly two feet in height, bearing a faint groove mark upon its top. This is London Stone. For many centuries it was popularly believed to be the stone of Brutus, brought by him as a deity. "So long as the stone of Brutus is safe," ran one city proverb, "so long shall London flourish." Certainly the stone is of great antiquity; the first reference to it was discovered by John Stow in a "fair written Gospel book" once belonging to Ethelstone, an early tenth-century king of the West Saxons, where certain lands and rents are "described to lie near unto London stone." According to the *Victorian County History* it originally marked the very centre of the old city, but in 1742 was taken from the middle of Cannon Street and placed within the fabric of St. Swithin's Church opposite. There it remained until the Second World War; although a German bomb entirely destroyed the church in 1941, London Stone remained intact. It is constructed of oolite which, as a perishable stone, cannot be assumed to have survived since prehistoric times. Yet it has been granted a charmed life.

There is a verse by the fifteenth-century poet, Fabyan, which celebrates the religious significance of a stone so pure that "though some have it thrette . . . Yet hurte had none." Its actual significance, however, remains unclear. Some antiquaries have considered it to be a token of civic assembly, connected with the repayment of debts, while others believe it to be a Roman *milliarium* or milestone. Christopher Wren argued, however, that it possessed too large a foundation for the latter purpose. A judicial role is more likely. In a now forgotten play of 1589, *Pasquill and Marfarius*, a character remarks: "Set up this bill at London Stone. Let it be doone sollemly with drom and trumpet" and then again "If it please them these dark winter nights to stikke uppe their papers uppon London Stone." That it became a highly venerated object is not in doubt. William Blake was convinced that it marked the site of Druid executions, whose sacrificial victims "groan'd aloud on London Stone," but its uses were perhaps less melancholy.

When the popular rebel Jack Cade stormed London in 1450, he and his followers made their way to the Stone; he touched it with his sword and then exclaimed: "Now is Mortimer"—this was the name he had assumed—"lord of this city!" The first mayor of London, in the late twelfth century, was Henry Fitz-Ailwin de Londonestone. It seems likely, therefore, that this ancient object came somehow to represent the power and authority of the city.

It sits now, blackened and disregarded, by the side of a busy thoroughfare; over and around it have flowed wooden carts, carriages, sedan chairs, hansom cabs, cabriolets, hackney cabs, omnibuses, bicycles, trams and cars. It was once London's guardian spirit, and perhaps it is still.

It is at least a material remnant from all the ancient legends of London and of its foundation. For the Celtic people these narratives comprised the glory of a city once known as "Cockaigne." In this place of wealth and delight the traveller might find riches and blessed happiness. This is the myth that established the context for later legends, such as those of Dick Whittington, as well as those unattributable proverbs which describe London's streets as "paved with gold." Yet London gold has proved more perishable than London Stone.

CHAPTER 2

The Stones

A section of the original London Wall, with medieval additions, can still be seen by Trinity Place just north of the Tower of London; part of the Tower itself was incorporated within the fabric of the wall, demonstrating in material form William Dunbar's claim that "Stony be thy wallys that about thee standis." It was almost ten feet wide at its base, and more than twenty feet in height; besides these relics of the wall by Trinity Place can be seen the stone outline of an inner tower which contained a wooden staircase leading to a parapet which looked east across the marshes.

From here the spectral wall, the wall as once it was, can be traversed in the imagination. It proceeds north to Cooper's Row, where a section can still be seen in the courtyard of an empty building; it rises from a car park in the basement. It goes through the concrete and marble of the building, then on through the brick and iron of the Fenchurch Street Station viaduct until an extant section rises again in America Square. It is concealed within the basement of a modern building which itself has parapets, turrets and square towers; a strip of glazed red tiling bears more than a passing resemblance to the courses of flat red tiles placed in the ancient Roman structure. For a moment it is known as Crosswall and passes through the headquarters of a company named Equitas. It moves through Vine Street (in the car park at No. 35 is a security camera on the ancient line of the now invisible wall), towards Jewry Street, which itself follows the line of the wall almost exactly until it meets Aldgate; all the buildings here can be said to comprise a new wall, separating west from east. We find Centurion House and Boots, the chemist.

The steps of the subway at Aldgate lead down to a level which was once that of late medieval London but we follow the wall down Duke's Place and into Bevis Marks; near the intersection of these two thoroughfares there is now part of that "ring of steel" which is designed once more to protect the city. On a sixteenth-century map Bevis Marks was aligned to the course of the wall, and it is so still; the pattern of the streets here has been unchanged for many hundreds of years. Even the lanes, such as Heneage Lane, remain. At the corner of Bevis Marks and St. Mary Axe rises a building of white marble with massive vertical windows; a great golden eagle can be seen above its entrance, as if it were part of some imperial standard. Security cameras once more trace the line of the wall, as it leads down Camomile Street towards Bishopsgate and Wormwood Street.

It drops beneath the churchyard of St. Botolph's, behind a building faced with white stone and curtain-walling of dark glass, but then fragments of it arise beside the church of All Hallows-on-the-Wall, which has been built, in the ancient fashion, to protect and bless these defences. The modern thoroughfare here becomes known, at last, as London Wall. A tower like a postern of brown stone rises above 85 London Wall, very close to the spot where a fourth-century bastion was only recently found, but the line of the wall from Blomfield Street to Moorgate largely comprises late nineteenth-century office accommodation. Bethlehem Hospital, or Bedlam, was once built against the north side of the wall; but that, too, has disappeared. Yet it is impossible not to feel the presence or force of the wall as you walk down this straightened thoroughfare which can be dated to the later period of the Roman occupation. A new London Wall then opens up after Moorgate, built over the ruins of the Second World War. The bombs themselves effectively uncovered long-buried remnants of the ancient wall, and stretches both of Roman and medieval origin can still be seen covered with grass and moss. But these old stones are flanked by the glittering marble and polished stone of the new buildings that dominate the city.

Around the site of the great Roman fort, at the north-west angle of the wall, there now arise these new fortresses and towers: Roman House, Britannic Tower, City Tower, Alban Gate (which by the slightest substitution might be renamed Albion Gate) and the concrete and granite towers of the Barbican which have once more brought a sublime bareness and brutality to that area where the Roman legions were sequestered. Even the walkways of this great expanse are approximately the same height as the parapets of the old city wall.

The wall then turns south, and long sections of it can still be seen on the western side sloping down towards Aldersgate. For most of its course from Aldersgate to Newgate and then to Ludgate, it remains invisible, but there are suggestive tokens of its progress. The great beast of classical antiquity, the Minotaur, has been sculpted just to its north in Postman's Park. The mottled and darkened blocks of the Sessions House beside the Old Bailey still mark the outer perimeter of the wall's defences, and in Amen Court a later wall looking on the back of the Old Bailey is like some revenant of brick and mortar. From the rear of St. Martin's Ludgate we cross Ludgate Hill, enter Pilgrim Street and walk beside Pageantmaster Court, where now the lines of the City Thames Link parallel those once made by the swiftly moving River Fleet, until we reach the edge of the water where the wall once abruptly stopped.

The wall enclosed an area of some 330 acres. To walk its perimeter would have taken approximately one hour, and the modern pedestrian will be able to cover the route in the same time. The streets beside it are still navigable and, in fact, the larger part of the wall itself was not demolished until 1760. Until that time the city had the appearance of a fortress, and in the sagas of Iceland it was known as Lundunaborg, "London Fort." It was continually being rebuilt, as if the integrity and identity of the city itself depended upon the survival of this ancient stone fabric; churches were erected beside it, and hermits guarded its gates. Those with more secular preoccupations built houses, or wooden huts, against it so that everywhere you could see (and perhaps smell) the peculiar combination of rotten wood and mildewed stone. A contemporary equivalent may be seen in the old brick arches of nineteenth-century railways being used as shops and garages.

Even after its demolition the wall still lived; its stone sides were incorporated into churches or other public buildings. One section in Cooper's Row was used to line the vaults of a bonded warehouse while, above ground, its course was used as a foundation for houses. The late eighteenth-century Crescent by America Square, designed by George Dance the Younger in the 1770s, for example, is established upon the ancient line of the wall. So later houses dance upon the ruins of the old city. Fragments and remnants of the wall were continually being rediscovered in the nineteenth and twentieth centuries, when the succeeding phases of its existence were first seen steadily and as a whole. On the eastern side of the wall were found in 1989, for example, eight skeletons of late Roman date turned in different directions; there were also unearthed the skeletons of several dogs. This is the area known as Houndsditch.

It is often believed that the Roman wall first defined Roman London, but the invaders were in command of London for 150 years before walls were built and, during that long stretch of time, the city itself evolved in particular—sometimes bloody, sometimes fiery—stages.

In 55 BC a military force under the command of Caesar invaded Britain, and within a short time compelled the tribes around London to accept Roman hegemony. Almost a hundred years later the Romans returned with a more settled policy of invasion and conquest. The troops may have crossed the river at Westminster, or Southwark, or Wallingford; temporary encampments may have been established in Mayfair, or at the Elephant and Castle. It is important for this account only that the administrators and commanders finally chose London as their principal place of settlement because of the strategic advantages of the terrain, and the commercial benefits of this riverine location. Whether the Romans occupied an abandoned settlement, its tribal occupants having fled on wooden trackways into the swamps and forests, is not known. It seems likely, in any event, that the invaders understood the significance of the site from the beginning of their occupation. Here was an estuary, served by a double tide. So it became the central point for seaborne trade in the south of Britain, and the focus for a network of roads which have survived for almost two thousand years.

The outlines of that first city have been revealed by excavation, with two principal streets of gravel running parallel to the river on the eastern hill. One of these streets skirted the bank of the Thames, and can still be traced in the alignment of Cannon Street and Eastcheap; the second road, some hundred yards to the north, comprises the eastern stretch of Lombard Street as it approaches Fenchurch Street. Here are the true origins of the modern city.

And then there was the bridge. The wooden Roman bridge was located approximately one hundred yards east of the first stone London Bridge, spanning the area west of St. Olav's Church in Southwark and the foot of Rederes (Pudding) Lane upon the northern bank; the exact date of its foundation cannot now be known but it would have seemed a majestic and even miraculous construction, not least to the native peoples who had settled under the Romans. Half the legends of London arose upon its foundations; miracles were performed, and visions seen, upon the new wooden thoroughfare. Since its sole purpose was to tame the river, it may then have harnessed the power of a god. Yet that god may have been enraged at the stripping of its riverine authority; thus all the intimations of vengeance and destruction invoked by the famous rhyme "London Bridge is broken down."

It is not clear whether Londinium was first used as a Roman military camp. Certainly it soon became a centre of supplies. In its first stages we must imagine a cluster of small dwellings with clay walls, thatched roofs and earthen floors; narrow alleys ran between them, with a series of streets connecting the two main thoroughfares, filled with the smells and noises of a busy community. There were workshops, taverns, shops and smithies crowded together while, beside the river, warehouses and workshops were grouped around a square timber harbour. Evidence for such a harbour has been found in Billingsgate. Along the thoroughfares, which every traveller to London used, there were taverns and tradesmen. Just beyond the city were round huts, in the old British style, which were used as places for storage, while on the perimeter of the city were wooden enclosures for cattle.

Only a few years after its foundation, which can be approximately dated between AD 43 and 50, the Roman historian, Tacitus, could already write of London as filled with *negotiatores* and as a place well known for its commercial prosperity. So in less than a decade it had progressed from a supply base into a flourishing town.

Negotiatores are not necessarily merchants but men of *negotium*; business and negotiation. They can be described as traders and brokers. Thus the line of continuity—it might almost be called the line of harmony—can still be traced. The shining buildings which now stand upon the Roman wall contain brokers and dealers who are the descendants, direct or indirect, of those who came to London in the first century. The City has always been established upon the imperatives of money and of trade. That is why the headquarters of the procurator, the high Roman official who controlled the finances of the province, were erected here.

London is based upon power, therefore. It is a place of execution and oppression, where the poor have always outnumbered the rich. Many terrible judgements of fire and death have visited it. Barely a decade after its foundation a great fire of London utterly destroyed its buildings. In AD 60 Boudicca and her tribal army laid waste the city with flame and sword, wreaking vengeance upon those who were trying to sell the women and children of the Iceni as slaves. It is the first token of the city's appetite for human lives. The evidence of Boudicca's destruction is to be found in a red level of oxidised iron among a layer of burnt clay, wood and ash. Red is London's colour, a sign of fire and devastation.

There was at least one other tribal attack upon the Roman city, at the end of the third century, but by that time the city and its defences were strong. Immediately after the Boudiccan assault the work of rebuilding was begun. If you were to stand now at the great crossroads in the City, where Gracechurch Street divides Lombard Street from Fenchurch Street, you would be facing the main entrance of the Romans' public forum, with shops and stalls and workshops on either side. The new forum was constructed of ragstone from Kent, carried by boat up the Medway, and, with its plastered surfaces and its roofs of red tiles, was a small fragment of Rome placed upon an alien soil.

Yet the influence of Roman civilisation was enduring in more than one respect. The chief cashier's office in the eighteenth-century Bank of England was based upon the design of a Roman temple, very like the basilica situated to the left of the early forum. Throughout the centuries London has been celebrated or denounced as a new Rome—corrupt or mighty, according to taste—and it can safely be said that part of its identity was created by its first builders.

London began to grow and flourish. A greater forum, and a greater basilica, were built upon the same site in the late first century; the basilica itself was larger than St. Paul's, Wren's seventeenth-century cathedral on Ludgate Hill. A great fort was built to the north-west, where the Barbican now stands. There were public baths, and temples, and shops, and stalls; there was an amphitheatre where the Guildhall now rests, and just south of St. Paul's a racing arena: by the strange alchemy of the city a name, Knightrider Street, has survived for almost two thousand years.

We can find evidence of further survival in the line, if not the name, of other streets. At the corner of Ironmonger Lane and Prudent Passage, traces of a Roman road passing from east to west have been uncovered together with the alignment of structures against it; at least seven successive buildings, all apparently engaged in the same kind of industrial activity, were erected upon that same alignment. There was an interval of destruction caused by fire, and then a gap of some five hundred years, until new buildings were erected upon the base of the old Roman road in the early ninth century. By the twelfth century, when the name of Ironmonger Lane enters recorded history, the buildings still followed the northern edge of the street laid out more than a thousand years before. The same buildings were in use until the seventeenth century, providing evidence of perhaps unequalled continuity in the life of the city.

We can cite many of the ancient streets in this vicinity—Milk Street, Wood Street, Aldermanbury among them—as the visible remnants of a Roman street horizon. It is suggestive, also, that the great markets of London at Cheapside and East Cheap lay until recent years on the thoroughfares established by the Romans on their first arrival. In the space of fifty years, by the end of the first century, London had acquired its destiny. It became the administrative and political capital of the country as well as its trading centre. The focus of communication and commercial activity, it was governed by imperial laws concerning trade, marriage and defence, laws that survived the passing of the Romans themselves. It was in all essentials a city-state with its own independent government, albeit in direct relationship to Rome; that independence, and autonomy, will be found to mark much of its subsequent history.

During the strongest period of its growth, at the end of the first century, the city would have possessed some thirty thousand inhabitants. There were soldiers, and merchants, and businessmen, artisans and artists, Celts and Romans, all mingled together. There were grand houses for the wealthier merchants and administrators, but the standard house of most Londoners was a form of cubicle or bed-sitting-room, its walls painted or decorated with mosaic. Sometimes, we can even hear the people speak.

There are surviving letters dealing with matters of finance and of trade, as might be expected, but there are also less formal communications. "Primus has made ten tiles. Enough! . . . Austalis has been taking off on his own every day for the last fortnight . . . for shame! . . . London, next door to the temple of Isis . . . Clementinus fashioned this tile." These are the earliest known words of a Londoner, scratched upon pieces of tile or pottery and fortuitously preserved among all the ruins that have been heaped over the city's earth. More pious memorials have also been found, with inscriptions for the dead and invocations to the gods. The stamps for the labels of an optician have been uncovered, proffering remedies for running eyes, for inflammation and for dim sight.

Our own sight of the past may be cleared a little if we are able to reconstruct the scattered evidence of the remains. A great hand of bronze, thirteen inches long, was found beneath Thames Street; a head of the Emperor Hadrian, again more than life-size, in the waters of the Thames itself. So we may imagine a city adorned with great statues. Fragments of a triumphal arch have been recovered, together with stone frescoes of goddesses and gods. This is a city of temples and monumental architecture. There were public baths also, and one lay in North Audley Street quite a long way outside the City. When workmen of the late nineteenth century discovered it in an underground arched chamber, it was still half-filled with water. Votive statues and daggers, sacred urns and silver ingots, swords and coins and altars, all express the spirit of a city in which trade and violence were not divorced from a genuine religious spirit. But there is significance, also, in the smallest detail. More than a hundred styli have been found at the bottom of the Walbrook River, where countless busy clerks simply threw used pens out of the window. It is an image of bustling life which would not be inappropriate in any period of London's history.

Yet the security and prosperity of London are not at this early date so certain. Like an organic being London grew and developed outwards, always seeking to incorporate new territory, but it also suffered periods of weariness and enervation when the spirit of the place hid its head. We may find tokens of just such a change by those same eastern banks of the Walbrook where the clerks of the empire tossed their pens into the water. Here was discovered, in 1954, the remains of a temple devoted to Mithras and subsequently to other pagan deities. It was not uncommon for Roman Londoners to embrace a variety of faiths; there is good evidence, for example, that the beliefs of the original Celtic tribes were incorporated into a peculiar Romano-Celtic form of worship. But the Mithraic mystery cult, with its rites of initiation and the secrets of its arcane ritual, seems at least in theory to presage a more disturbed and anxious city.

The most resourceful period of Roman London lay in the years spanning the first and second centuries, but these were followed by an uneven period combining development and decline. That decline was in part associated with the two great titular spirits of London, fire and plague, but there was also a steady alteration of imperial rule as the empire itself weakened and decayed. In approximately AD 200, some fifty years before the temple of Mithras was erected, the great wall was constructed around London. It speaks of an age of anxiety, but the very fact of its erection suggests that the city still had formidable resources of its own. Large areas within the wall were unoccupied, or used for pasture, but there were fine temples and houses in the more fashionable district close to the river. The first London mint was established in the third century, testifying once again to the city's true nature. In that century, too, a riverine wall was constructed to complete the city's defences.

What, then, was the nature and activity of the citizens themselves in the last decades of Roman London? They would be largely of Romano-British descent, and there were occasions when they were ruled by a British "king." But London has from its inception always been a mixed city, and the streets would have been filled with the inhabitants of many nations including the native Celtic tribes who, over three hundred years, had naturally grown accustomed to the new order. This Roman city spanned a period as long as that from the late Tudors to the present day, but we have in general only the silent evidence of scattered cups and dice, bath scrapers and bells, writing tablets and millstones, brooches and sandals. How can we make these objects live again?

There were of course, in the passages of this long history, periods of turbulence and warfare. Many have gone unrecorded, but one or two powerful incidents survive. The darkness breaks and a scene presents itself, frozen for a moment, throwing into further confusion and mystery the historical process of which it is a part. A Roman leader named Allectus sailed to Britain in order to put down a local rebellion; having defeated the rebels he set up his headquarters in London. A Celtic chieftain, Asclepiodotus, in turn marched against the imperial victor; outside the city there was a great battle in which the British were successful. The remaining Roman troops, fearing massacre, fled within the walls and closed the gates. Siege engines were brought, and a breach was made in the defences; the Celts poured in and the leader of the last legion begged for mercy. It was agreed that the Romans could withdraw and take to their ships but one tribe or group of tribesmen reneged on the agreement: they fell upon the Roman soldiers, decapitated them in ritual Celtic style and, according to the narrative of Geoffrey of Monmouth, threw their heads into "a brook in the city . . . in Saxon, Galobroc." Many skulls were, in the 1860s, found in the bed of the long-buried Walbrook River. The rest is silence.

But we cannot from the evidence of this single anecdote assume that the history of London is one of warring tribes against a common Roman enemy. All the evidence suggests otherwise and instead intimates a degree of mingling, maintained by mutual trade, that encouraged an almost unbroken continuity of commerce and administration. There would by now be something of a London type, perhaps with that particular "muddy" complexion which became characteristic in later years. No doubt the citizens spoke a Latin patois which included native elements, and their religious beliefs would have been equally mixed and idiosyncratic. The Mithraic temple is only one example of a mystery religion—predominantly the reserve of merchants and professional administrators—but the Christian faith was not unknown. In AD 313 a certain Restitus attended the Council of Arles in his capacity as Bishop of London.

The city's economic activity was equally mixed and practical; the commercial and military quarters were still in active operation, but the archaeological evidence suggests that many public buildings were allowed to fall into disuse and earth was laid over once inhabited sites for the purposes of farming. It may seem odd to have farms and vineyards within the walls of the city but, even as late as the time of Henry II, half of London was open ground with fields, orchards and gardens adorning it. There is also evidence, in the third and fourth centuries, of quite large stone buildings which were conceivably farm-houses. We might then have the paradox of rural landowners within the city itself. Certainly the city was still formidable enough to withstand the attentions of marauding tribes; in AD 368 the Attacotti laid waste to much of Kent without daring to make an onslaught upon London itself.

But in 410 Rome withdrew its protecting hand; like the hand found beneath Thames Street, it was of bronze rather than of gold. There are reports of raids against the city by Angles and Saxons, but there is no record of any great collapse or transition. There is, however, some evidence of decay. There was once a bath-house in Lower Thames Street which, in the early fifth century, was abandoned. The glass was shattered, and the wind destroyed the roof; then at a later date, after the collapse of the roof, the walls of the eastern range of buildings were systematically demolished. Found among the debris was a Saxon brooch, dropped by a woman while clambering over these alien ruins.

The arrival of the Saxons has been dated to the beginning of the fifth century when, according to the historian Gildas, the land of Britain was licked by a "red and savage tongue." Within certain cities "in the midst of the streets lay the tops of lofty towers, tumbled to the ground, stones of high walls, holy altars, fragments of human bodies." But in fact the Angles and the Saxons were already living in the London region, and it is clear from the archaeological evidence that by the late fourth century troops of Germanic origin were guarding London as legionnaires under the imperial banner.

It was once assumed, however, that the arrival of the Saxons resulted in the destruction and desertion of the city itself. In fact there was no fiery carnage in the London area from which Rome retreated. On several sites has been found a layer of "dark earth" which was believed to indicate dereliction and decay, but contemporary experts have suggested that levels of dark soil may point to occupation rather than destruction. There is other evidence of the continuous habitation of London during that period once known as the "dark ages." In one of those extraordinary instances of historical survival, it has been shown that the provisions of London law in the Roman period—particularly in terms of testamentary provisions and property rights—were still being applied throughout the medieval period. There was, in other words, a continuous administrative tradition which no Saxon occupation had interrupted.

The old chronicles assert that London remained the principal city and stronghold of the Britons. In the histories of Nennius and Gildas, Geoffrey of Monmouth and Bede, it is regularly cited as an independent town which is also the home of the British kings; it is the place where sovereigns were made and acclaimed, and it is the site where the citizens were called together in public assembly. It is also the chief place of defence when, on various occasions, the Britons fled within the safety of the walls. It is the seat of the British and Roman nobility, as well as representing one of the great sees of the Christian realm. The ancient British kings—Vortigern, Vortimer and Uther among them—are depicted as reigning and living in London.

Yet in these early chronicles the distance between factual interpretation and fanciful reconstruction is short. In these accounts, for example, Merlin makes many prophecies concerning the future of the city. Another great figure who exists somewhere within the interstices of myth and history is also to be found in London: King Arthur. According to Matthew of Westminster, Arthur was crowned by the archbishop of London. Layamon adds that he entered London after his investiture. The mark of this urban civilisation was its sophistication; Geoffrey of Monmouth, for example, celebrates the affluence and courtesy of Arthur's subjects as well as the "richness" of decorative art everywhere apparent. In Malory's great prose epic, derived from several original sources, known as *Le Morte d'Arthur*, there are many references to London as the principal city of the realm. At a time of foreboding after the

death of Uther Pendragon, "Merlyn wente to the Archebisshop of Caunter-
bury and counceilled hym for to sende for all the lordes of the reame and alle
the gentilmen of armes that they shold to London come" and gather "in the
grettest chirch of London—whether it were Powlis or not the Frensshe
booke maketh no mencyon." In later books the Feir Maiden of Astolat is laid
beside the Thames, Sir Launcelot rides from Westminster to Lambeth across
the same river, and Guenevere "cam to London" and "toke the Towre of
London."

The less controversial documents of historians and chroniclers add detail
to this picture of legendary munificence. Ecclesiastical records reveal that a
synod was held, either in London or Verulamium, in 429; since the assembly
was called to denounce the heresies of a British monk, Pelagius, it is clear that
there was still a thriving religious culture in the regions bordering upon
London.

Some twelve years later, according to a contemporaneous chronicle, the
provinces of Britain accepted Saxon domination. Although that source is
silent on the fate of London, it seems to have retained its independence as a
city-state. By the middle of the sixth century, however, the city can be assumed to have accepted Saxon rule. Large parts of the walled area were employed as pasture, and the great public buildings were no doubt used as
marketplaces, or stockades for cattle, or as open spaces for the wooden
houses and shops of a population living among the monumental ruins of what
was already a distant age. There is a wonderful Saxon poem on the material
remnants of just such a British city; they are *enta geweorc*, the "works of giants," the shattered memorials to a great race which passed away *hund
cnect*—a hundred generations ago. In the description of broken towers and
empty halls, of fallen roofs and deserted bath-houses, there is a combination
of sorrow and wonder. There are intimations here, also, of another truth. The
stone fabric of this ancient city has been dissolved by *wyrde* or "destiny," and
age; it has not been violently attacked or pillaged by marauders. The Saxons
were not necessarily destroyers, therefore, and this poem displays a genuine
reverence for antiquity and for a *beohrtan burg*, "bright city," where heroes
once dwelled.

We can infer, in turn, the lineaments of Saxon London. A cathedral
church was built here, and the palace of the king was maintained on a site now
claimed by Wood Street and Aldermanbury. Seventh-century records mention a "king's hall" in London, and two centuries later it was still known as
"that illustrious place and royal city"; the location of the royal palace beside

the old Roman fort in the north-west of the city suggests that its fortifications had also been maintained. But there is even more striking evidence of continuity. One of the most important archaeological discoveries of recent years has been that of a Roman amphitheatre upon the site of the present Guildhall; this is exactly the location where the Saxons were known to hold their folkmoots, in an area always specified as being to the north-east of the cathedral. It seems certain, therefore, that the Saxon citizens used the ancient Roman amphitheatre for their own deliberations; it throws a suggestive and curious light upon their relationship to a remote past, that they should sit and argue upon stone rows erected more than two centuries before. It is no less suggestive, of course, that the modern Guildhall is erected upon the same site. There is evidence, at the least, for administrative permanence. It seems very likely, in turn, that the great walled city was known as the centre of authority and of power.

This would help to explain the location of the thriving Saxon town, Lundenwic—*wic* meaning "marketplace"—in the area now known as Covent Garden. A typical Saxon community, in other words, had grown up just beyond the walls of the powerful city.

We may imagine several hundred people, living and working in an area from Covent Garden to the Thames. Their kilns and pottery have lately been found, together with dress pins and glass beakers, combs, stone tools and weights for their looms. A butchery site has been excavated in Exeter Street, off the Strand, and farm buildings in Trafalgar Square. All the evidence suggests that a flourishing commercial area was, therefore, surrounded by small settlements of farmers and labourers. The names and sites of Saxon villages are still to be heard within the districts of a much greater London, Kensington, Paddington, Islington, Fulham, Lambeth and Stepney among them. The very shape and irregular street line of Park Lane are determined by the old acre strips of the Saxon farmers. Long Acre, too, reflects that pastoral tradition. It was an extended community, therefore, and it may have been of Lundenwic—rather than of London—that Bede spoke when he described it as situated "on the banks of the Thames . . . a trading centre for many nations who visit it by land and sea."

Documents dated 673–85 are concerned with the trade regulations to be observed by the men of Kent when they barter in Lundenwic. Gold coins stamped "LONDUNIU" were being used in the same period, so that there was no necessary disparity between administrative London and commercial Lundenwic. Similarly a continual process of assimilation and absorption was maintained between erstwhile Britons and Saxon settlers, achieved by inter-marriage and peaceful commerce. The evidence for this lies in the most reliable of sources, language itself, since many old British words are to be found in "Saxon" English. Among them are "basket," "button," "coat," "gown," "wicket" and "wire," so it can be surmised that skill in textile and wicker-work can best be attributed to the Britons. Another English word testifies to the mixed nature of London: the name Walbrook is derived from *Weala broc*, "brook of the Welsh," which suggests that there was still a defined quarter for the "old Britons" in their ancient city.

Bede had said that "Londuniu" was the capital of the East Saxons, but over the period of middle Saxon rule the city seems to have accepted the authority of any king who was dominant within the region—among them kings of Kent, Wessex and Mercia. It might almost be regarded as the commercial reward for any successful leader, together with the fact that the walled city was also the traditional seat of authority. Given this changing pattern of sovereignty, however, it is not perhaps surprising that the main source of continuity lay within the Christian Church. In 601, four years after the arrival of Augustine, Pope Gregory proclaimed London to be the principal bishopric in all Britain; three years later Ethelbert of Kent erected the cathedral church of St. Paul's. There follows a bare chronicle of ecclesiastical administration. In the year when St. Paul's was erected Augustine, Archbishop of Britain, consecrated Mellitus as bishop of London; the citizens then formally became Christian but, thirteen years later, Mellitus was expelled after a change of royal rule. The innate paganism of London, for a while, reasserted itself before being eventually restored to the Roman communion.

And then came the Danes. They had plundered Lindisfarne and Jarrow before turning their attention to the south. The *Anglo-Saxon Chronicle* records that in 842 there was "great slaughter in London," a battle in which the Vikings were beaten back. Nine years later they returned and, having pillaged Canterbury, sailed up the Thames and with a fleet of 350 ships fell upon London. The city wall along the river may well have been already in ruinous condition but, even if the Saxons had been able to mend it, the defences were not enough to withstand the army of invaders. London was entered and pillaged. Many of the citizens may already have fled; those who remained were put to the sword, if Viking custom was followed, and their huts or shops consigned to the flame. Some historians have considered that the events of 851 marked a decisive moment in London's history, but this is perhaps to misunderstand the nature of a city which is perpetually rising from flame and ruin. Indeed it has been defined throughout its history by such resurrections.

The invaders returned sixteen years later. Their great army moved through Mercia and East Anglia intent upon capturing Wessex; in 872 they built a camp near London, no doubt to protect their warships along the river, and it seems likely that their purpose was to control London and the Thames basin in order to exact tribute from neighbouring kingdoms. Certainly they occupied the city itself, which was used as a military garrison and storage base. Here they remained for fourteen years. This was not a bare ruined city, therefore, as some have suggested, but once more a busy centre of administration and supply. The Norse commander, Halfdere, minted his own silver coinage which, interestingly enough, is based upon Roman originals. The tradition of literal money-making in London had been preserved since that distant period, testifying once again to the organic continuity of its financial life. Coins were minted in London for Alfred, in his role as client king of Wessex. The native inhabitants may not have been as fortunate as Alfred; from the evidence of coin hoards buried in the first year of Norse occupation, the richer citizens ran for their lives along with every other Englishman who was able to flee.

Then, in 883, Alfred engaged in some form of siege, mustering an English army outside the walls of the city. London was the great prize, and three years later Alfred obtained it. It was, in fact, in the city itself that his sovereignty over the whole region was formally advertised, when "all the English people that were not under subjection to the Danes submitted to him." London was still the emblem of power, in other words, even after its occupation by the Norsemen. The Danes sued for peace and were allocated territory to the east of the River Lea. London became a frontier town, therefore, and Alfred initiated a scheme of resettlement and fortification. The walls were restored, the quays rebuilt, and all the activities of Lundenwic brought within the defences of the revived city; it is at this point that Lundenwic passes into history as Aldwych, or "old market-town."

London had once more become new, since Alfred instituted a scheme of works which might qualify as an early attempt at city planning. He built a road, just within the walls, from Aldgate to Ludgate; the outline of it still exists in the streets of the modern City. The alignments of new streets were plotted close to the wharves of Queenhithe and Billingsgate. He re-established London and rendered it habitable.

Certainly the city was powerful and formidable enough to withstand

Viking assaults in succeeding years; the *burgwara*, or citizens, even marched out against them in 893 and 895. On that later occasion Londoners sallied forth to destroy or plunder the enemy ships. The fact that the Vikings were unable to retaliate against London suggests the effectiveness of its defences.

The restoration of London's life and power might not have been all of Alfred's doing, although his native genius as a planner of cities suggests that he played a prominent role. He had given lordship of London to his son-in-law, Ethelred, and had granted lands within the walls to religious and secular magnates. There then grew up that curious division or subdivision of land which is manifest today in the various wards and parishes of the City. An area of London ground might have been defined by streams, or by the course of Roman remains, but once apportioned to an English lord or bishop it became his especial *soke* or territory. Churches, of wood or of limestone and sandstone, were erected to bless and protect each well-defined area of London's earth; these sacred edifices in turn became the focal point for small communities of tradesmen, artificers and others.

The early tenth century was a period of peace, although the citizen army of London assisted Alfred in his efforts to free those British regions still held under the Danelaw. The historical records describe only the succession of Mercian kings to the overlordship of London. In 961 there was a great fire, succeeded by an outbreak of plague fever; the cathedral church of St. Paul's was destroyed in the conflagration, and once more we witness the periodic fate and fatality of the city. There was another great fire twenty-one years later, and in the same year three Viking ships attacked the coast of Dorset. The succeeding years were marked by a series of Viking attacks upon the prosperous city; no doubt the London Mint, with its reserves of silver, was a particular attraction. But the defences, restored by Alfred, were strong enough to withstand a number of incursions; in 994 the Danes sent a force of ninety-five ships into the Thames in order to blockade and assault the city, but they were driven back by London's army. According to the *Anglo-Saxon Chronicle* these citizens visited upon the Danes "more slaughter and harm than they ever supposed that townsmen could inflict." It is important to recognise, in the course of these battles and sieges, that London itself had acquired its own army and therefore a measure of independent power; it possessed the characteristics of a kingdom or a sovereign state which, for many centuries, it never wholly lost.

So the soldiers of London continually resisted the Danes, and there are records of them seizing the alien ships and rowing them back to the city.

They marched to Oxford to assist their countrymen and, although the Viking raids occasionally swept within the vicinity of their walls, the city stood firm. Indeed London still maintained its position as a flourishing port, and in 1001 an Icelandic poet recorded his impressions of the quayside where merchants from Rouen, Flanders, Normandy, Liège and other regions paid a fixed toll upon their goods; they brought in wool, and cloth, and planks, and fish, and melted fat; a small ship paid a toll of one halfpenny, and in turn the mariners bought pigs and sheep for their journey homewards.

In 1013 the Danish leader, Sweyn, commanded a full invasion force of Scandinavian warriors and marched upon London "because therein was King Aethelred." The "citizens would not yield," according to the *Anglo-Saxon Chronicle*, "but resisted with full battle." It was not enough, however, and after a long siege they surrendered their city to the Danes. The reigning monarch fled but in the following year he returned with a most unlikely ally, Olaf of Norway. Olaf's Norsemen manoeuvred their ships close to London Bridge, tied them to its wooden piles with ropes and cables, then, assisted by the tide, strained at the wooden supports until they were dislodged and the bridge itself fell into the Thames: a notorious episode in the history of that great thoroughfare. In recent years iron axes and swords have been found at this point in the river. An Icelandic saga suggests that "the citizens, seeing their river occupied by the enemy's navy so as to cut off all intercourse that way with the interior provinces, were seized with fear." Since they were being relieved of a temporary and alien king this is perhaps open to debate, but the loss of the bridge was indeed a serious impediment to commerce and communications. Yet the saga ends happily, or at least with an encomium—"And thou hast overthrown their bridges, oh! thou storm of the sons of Odin! skilful and foremost in the battle. For thee it was happily reserved to possess the land of London's winding city." Olaf himself was eventually beatified, and in London were erected six churches to venerate his memory, one by the southeastern corner of the bridge which he had once destroyed. St. Olave in Hart Street, where Samuel Pepys worshipped, still stands.

During the next three years the English and the Norse were engaged in a series of sieges and battles and assaults; in this protracted warfare London remained the single most important site of power and authority. After the death of Aethelred in 1016, "all the councillors who were in London and the citizens chose Edmund as king," again according to the *Anglo-Saxon Chronicle*, which suggests that there was some kind of folkmoot where the king was chosen and saluted. When Cnut eventually won the crown in 1016 he extracted tribute from the whole nation, but London was obliged to render one-eighth of the entire amount.

Meanwhile, a Danish population, trading peacefully, settled outside the walls in the area once occupied by the Saxons. The church of St. Clement Danes, at the mouth of the Strand, marks the site of their occupation; it is even possible that a tribal community of Danes had lived and worked here for several generations, but it was in the time of Cnut that the wooden church was turned to stone. It is also believed to be the burial place of Harold Harefoot, the son of Cnut, and there is a runic monument which proclaims the fact that three Danish leaders also "lie in Luntunum." So once more we have evidence of a flourishing market-centre dependent upon the walled city. William of Malmesbury suggests that "the citizens of London," after long familiarity with the Danes, "had almost entirely adopted their customs"; this suggests a renewed history of assimilation.

One custom was thoroughly absorbed. There was once a stone cross close by the church of St. Clement Danes, which marked a place of power and ritual. Here an open court assembled, and it was "at the Stone Cross" that manorial dues were paid; for one piece of land in the vicinity, payment was given in horseshoes and iron nails. It is sometimes believed that this is an obscure remembrance of a pagan rite, but it has also become a modern one. In the early twenty-first century there is still a ritual of presenting six horseshoes and sixty-one hobnails in the Court of Exchequer, within the Law Courts close to the site of the old cross itself, as part of rent due to the Crown.

So the Danes, and the Londoners, flourished during a period in which the historical narratives record only the actions of "the citizens of London" or "the army of London" as an independent and effectively self-governing community. When the pale-skinned and devout Edward (afterwards "the Confessor") was anointed, the *Anglo-Saxon Chronicle* records that "all men chose him for king in London." A legal statute in fact defined London "qui caput est regni et legum, semper curia domini regis" as the source of law and royal rule.

CHAPTER 3

Holy! Holy! Holy!

dward the Confessor left a memorial more enduring than his family's fortunes; he retired to a palace, and established a monastery, in Westminster.

There had been a church there since the second century, but London antiquarians have suggested that there was once a pagan shrine to Apollo on the same site. Certainly a Roman sarcophagus, and a section of floor mosaic, have been found in the immediate vicinity. It was an area of great importance, in any case, since Westminster—or more particularly Thorney Island upon which Parliament and the abbey now rest—marked the spot where the road from Dover was united with Watling Street which proceeded northward. At low tide it was possible to cross the river here, and to ride along the great Roman ways. Yet topography is not simply a matter of road alignments. Tothill Fields beside Westminster was part of a ritualised area of power and worship; a document of 785 describes it as "that terrible place which is known as Westminster," "terrible," in this context, meaning sacred or holy terror.

It is not inappropriate, therefore, that the founding of Westminster Abbey is enwrapped in dreams and visions. The night before the hallowing of the first Saxon church here, in the seventh century, St. Peter himself appeared to a fisherman and was ferried across the river from Lambeth; the ven-

erable figure crossed the threshold of the new church and all at once it was illuminated by a light brighter than a thousand candles. So began the history
of the church of St. Peter. Edward the Confessor was in turn granted a dream,
or vision, which persuaded him to build a great abbey. It became the repository of sand from Mount Sinai and earth from Calvary, a beam from the holy
manger of Jesus and pieces of his cross, blood from Christ's side and milk
from the Virgin Mary, a finger from St. Paul and hair from St. Peter. Almost
a thousand years later, in this place, William Blake was granted a vision of
monks chanting and proceeding down the central aisle. A century before the
poet's sighting, Edward the Confessor also reappeared: a chorister came
upon the broken coffin of the venerable king and drew from it a skull. So the
sainted king had turned into a death's head. It is perhaps an appropriate story
for an abbey which has become London's city of the dead, where the generations of kings and leaders and poets lie in silent communion as a token of
that great mystery where past and present are mingled together. It is the
mystery, and history, of London.

West Smithfield, after the foundation of St. Bartholomew-the-Great in the
early twelfth century, witnessed as many miracles as any similar plot in Rome
or Jerusalem. Edward the Confessor, in a prophetic dream, was informed that
Smithfield had already been chosen by God as a place for his worship;
Edward journeyed there the next morning and foretold that the ground
should be a witness to God. In the same period three men from Greece came
on pilgrimage to London, for already it had the renown of a sacred city; they
approached Smithfield and, falling prostrate upon the ground, prophesied
that there would be constructed a temple which "shall reach from the rising
of the sun to the going down thereof."

"The Book of the Foundation" of that great church of St. Bartholomew,
from which these words are taken, was written in the twelfth century; it has
much material for contemplation, but it also contains evidence relating to the
piety of London and of Londoners. The founder of the church, Rahere, was
on a journey in Italy when in a dream he was taken up by a beast with four
feet and two wings to a "high place" where St. Bartholomew appeared to him
and addressed him: "I, by the will and command of all the High Trinity, and
with the common favour and counsel of the court of heaven, have chosen a
spot in the suburb of London at Smithfield." Rahere was to erect there a
tabernacle of the Lamb. So he journeyed to the city where, in conversation
with "some barons of London," it was explained that "the place divinely

shown to him was contained within the king's market, on which it was lawful neither for the princes themselves nor for the wardens of their own authority to encroach to any extent whatever." So Rahere sought an audience of Henry I in order to explain his divine mission to the city; the king graciously gave Rahere title to the spot which was at that time "a very small cemetery."

Rahere then "made himself a fool" in order to recruit assistants in the great work of building. He "won to himself bands of children and servants, and by their help he easily began to collect together stones." These stones came from many parts of London, and in that sense the narrative of construction is a true representation of the fact that St. Bartholomew's was a collective work and vision of the city; it became, in literal form, its microcosm.

So the church rose, and many priests gathered to live "under regular rule" with the founder as prior. Beginning with its first foundation, when "a light sent from heaven gleamed over the church and remained over it for the space of an hour," there were so many miraculous events within its walls that the chronicler declares that he will mention only those which he himself has witnessed. Wolmer, a cripple who supported himself "on two little stools he dragged behind him," was carried to St. Bartholomew's in a basket and, falling before the altar, was healed. A "certain woman of the parish of St. John" had her "enfeebled" limbs cured, and Wymonde that was dumb began to speak. Many of these miracles occurred on the day of the Feast of St. Bartholomew, so there was a continual awareness of sacred time in the city as well as sacred place. Miraculous cures were also performed in the "hospital of the church," now St. Bartholomew's Hospital. So St. Bartholomew's is a temple of the holy spirit which has endured for almost nine hundred years.

When some citizens of London were on a long voyage to "the remote ends of the world," they were threatened with shipwreck; but they comforted each other with the words: "what do we with little faith fear who have the good Bartholomew, the accomplisher of so many great marvels, set nigh to us in London? . . . He will not hide the bowels of his mercy from his fellow citizens." In the oratory of the church was "an altar hallowed to the honour of the most blessed and perpetual Virgin Mary"; here the Virgin appeared to one lay brother and declared: "I will receive their prayers and vows and will grant them mercy and blessing for ever."

That oratory survives still, but it is by no means an object of pilgrimage. St. Bartholomew's Church is now largely ignored, set back from the circular road which connects the meat market to the hospital and which forms the perimeter of the old Bartholomew Fair. Yet Bartholomew himself might still be considered as one of the sacred guardians of the city and, even at the beginning of the twenty-first century, there are ten streets or roads which bear his name.

London was once a holy city, therefore, and of Smithfield we read: "Awful, therefore, is this place to him that understands, here is nothing else but the house of God and the gate of heaven to him that believes." This invocation is echoed by other visionaries and mystics of London; here, in the very grimy and malodorous streets of the city, the "gate of heaven" can be opened.

There are in London many holy wells of healing, although most were long ago filled in or demolished. The ancient well of St. Clement lies beneath the Law Courts; Chad's Well is buried beneath St. Chad's Street. The well of Barnet was covered first by a workhouse and then by a hospital, so its air of healing was not thoroughly dispelled; in the same spirit the curiously named but efficacious Perilous Pond lay beside St. Luke's Hospital in Old Street. A healing well that was guarded by monks, near Cripplegate, is still recalled by the name of Monkwell Street, while Black Mary's Well has been transformed into the area still known as Bagnigge Wells beside Farringdon Road. The only ancient well still to be seen is the Clerk's Well, now protected by a glass window a few yards north of Clerkenwell Green: here for many centuries were staged miracle plays as well as more secular bouts of wrestling and jousting. The holy well of Shoreditch—commemorated by Holy Well Row and Holy Well Lane—marks the site of one of the first English theatres, erected in 1576 by James Burbage, more than twenty years before the Globe. Sadler's Well was also a pleasure garden and, later, a theatre. So the holy spirit of the wells, in a fashion appropriate to London, turned into theatre.

Hermits were often chosen to be the guardians of the wells, but their principal stewardship was of the gates and crossroads of the city. They collected the tolls, and dwelt in the very bastions of London Wall. In a sense, then, they were the protectors of London itself, professing by their vocation that this was a city of God as well as a city of men. This was the theory, at least, but it is clear that many were hermits by device rather than by profession; the author of *Piers the Plowman*, William Langland, condemned them as "Grete lobyes and longe that loth were to swynke" or impostors who were simply unwilling to work. In 1412, for example, William Blakeney was convicted at the Guildhall for going about "barefooted and with long hair, under the guise of sanctity." Nevertheless the picture of London surrounded, as it were, with hermits who lived in their small stone oratories keeping vigils and reciting orisons is an arresting one.

The figure of the hermit has another significance also; the stories of the city, throughout the centuries, have been filled with lonely and isolated people who feel their solitude more intensely within the busy life of the streets. They are what George Gissing called the anchorites of daily life, who return unhappy to their solitary rooms. The early city hermits may therefore be regarded as an apt symbol for the way of life of many Londoners. An extension of that hermitic spirit can be traced in the four churches of St. Botolph, which guarded four of the city's gates; Botolph was a seventh-century Saxon hermit, who was especially associated with travellers. So the wanderer and the interior exile are seen as part of the same short pilgrimage among the streets of London.

But those streets can also be filled with prayer. There was in Marylebone, before the redevelopment of Lisson Grove, a Paradise Street approached by Grotto Passage; in the immediate vicinity were Vigil Place and Chapel Street. Perhaps here we have evidence of an ancient hermitage, or sacred spot, linking the city to eternity. In the immediate vicinity of St. Paul's are to be found Pater Noster Row, Ave Maria Lane, Amen Court and Creed Lane: here we may usefully imagine a procession through various streets in which particular prayers or responses were chanted. So the old churches of London maintain their ancient presence and seem periodically to relive their histories.

That is why the area around St. Pancras Old Church, for example, still remains desolate and dreary. It has always been an isolated and somewhat mysterious place—"Walk not there too late," counselled one Elizabethan topographer. It is the traditional terminus for murderers, suicides and those who were killed while fighting duels at Chalk Farm, but no true resting place: the corpses are continually being dug up and reburied. The last great removal occurred in 1863 when the railway lines of St. Pancras Station were laid through the site. The tombstones were placed against a great tree, the roots of which curl among them; from a distance it would seem that the headstones are indeed the fruit of that tree, ripe and ready to be gathered. Among these ancient memorials will be some to the Catholic dead; it was for them a holy place. St. Pancras is believed to be the first Christian church in England, established by Augustine himself, and is reported to contain the last bell which was able to toll during the Mass. Pancras has therefore been construed as Pangrace; a more likely derivation, associated with the saintly boy named Pancras, is Pan Crucis or Pan Cross—the monogram or symbol of Christ himself. So we have a Vatican historian, Maximilian Misson, asserting that "St. Pancras under Highgate, near London . . . is the Head and Mother of all Christian Churches." Who could imagine the source of such power in the wasteland north of King's Cross Station?

It has its bells, like the other London churches. The bells of St. Stephen, Rochester Row, were named "Blessing," "Glory," "Wisdom," "Thanksgiving," "Honour," "Power," "Might" and "Be Unto Our God For Ever and Ever Amen Alleluiah."

We do not necessarily need the evidence of the famous nursery rhyme to realise that the bells were a familiar and friendly presence in the life of Londoners:

> You owe me five farthings,
> Say the bells of St. Martin's.
> When will you pay me,
> Say the bells at Old Bailey.

In 1994 the Meteorological Office reported that, before the sound of motorcars entered the already crowded streets, the bells of St. Mary-le-Bow in Cheapside "would have been audible all over London." In a true sense, then, every Londoner was a Cockney. Yet the East End may lay an especial claim to that honorific, perhaps, since the oldest business in that area is the Whitechapel Bell Foundry which was established in the fifteenth century. Citizens used to bet which parish could make its bells heard at the greatest distance and it was said that bell-ringing was a salutary way of keeping warm in winter. It was sometimes surmised that at the Last Judgement the angels would peal the bells of London, rather than sound their trumpets, in order to convince the citizens that the day of doom had truly arrived. The bells were part of the sound and texture of its life. When the protagonist of George Orwell's *1984* recalls the famous song with its mention of St. Clement's and St. Martin's, Bow and Shoreditch, he seems to "hear the bells of a lost London that still existed somewhere or other, disguised and forgotten." Some of the bells of that lost London can still be heard.

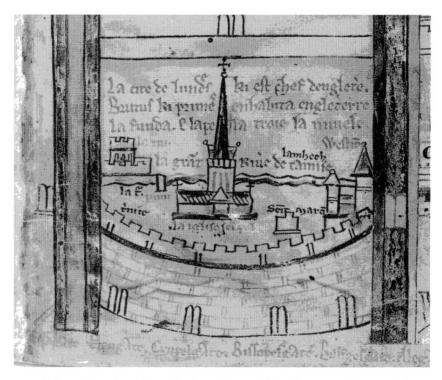

A map of London, drawn by chronicler and illuminator Matthew Paris in 1252; it shows the Tower, St. Paul's and Westminster.

$\mathcal{Y}ou \; \mathcal{B}e \; \mathcal{A}ll \; \mathcal{L}aw \; \mathcal{W}orthy$

n the last month of 1066, William, Duke of Normandy, marched down St. Giles High Street before turning south to Westminster. He had already savaged Southwark and now intended to lay siege to London Wall by Ludgate, which was then the principal entrance to the city. It was commonly said at the time that London "neither fears enemies nor dreads being taken by storm" because of its defences but, in fact, after some form of secret treaty or negotiations, certain Saxon nobles opened the gate. William's troops made their way to St. Paul's and Cheapside but then "*in platea urbis*"—an open space or wide street—they were attacked by a group, or perhaps even an army, of citizens who refused to countenance the entry of the foreign leader. A late eleventh-century chronicler, William of Jumieges, records that the Norman forces at once "engaged them in battle, causing no little mourning to the City because of the very many deaths of her own sons and citizens." Eventually the Londoners capitulated. But their action demonstrates that they considered themselves to dwell in an independent city which could withstand foreign invasion. On this occasion they were mistaken, but for the next three hundred years Londoners would assert their sovereignty as members of a city-state.

The Battle of London, however, was over. Eleven bodies have recently been recovered just south-west of Ludgate, with some suggestion that they had been dismembered, while a hoard of several thousand coins of that period was found by the Walbrook.

The new monarch's primary task was to subjugate the city. Work began on three military stockades at various points on the perimeter wall—Montfichet Tower, Baynard's Castle and against the south-east section of the Wall, a structure that has since become known as the "Tower of London." But the Tower never belonged to London and was considered by the citizens to be an affront or threat to their liberty. In *The Making of London*, Sir Laurence Gomme contemplates their displeasure when "they heard the taunts of the people who said that these walls had been built as an insult to them, and that if any one of them should dare to contend for the liberty of the city he would be shut up in them and consigned to imprisonment."

After a great fire in 1077 which, like its predecessors, seems to have devastated much of the city, a stone tower was built in place of the original fortification; it took more than twenty years to complete, and pressed labour from the neighbouring shires was used in its construction. It was called the White Tower, and rose some ninety feet in the air to emphasise its power over the city. Elaborate rituals were drawn up in order to formalise the presence of London's leaders in the Tower for judicial or administrative purposes, but it remained outside their jurisdiction. Built of alien material, cream-coloured Caen stone from Normandy, it was a visible token of foreign rule.

William was also graciously pleased to grant a "Charter" to London, on a tiny parchment less than six inches in length. It is written in Anglo-Saxon and French. Addressed to "the chiefs of the city" it granted to London "rights" that the city already possessed and had had since the days of Roman domination. "I do you to know that I will that you be all law worthy that were in King Edward's day," runs the translation. "And I will that every child be his father's heir after his father's day. And I will not endure that any man offer any wrong to you. God keep you."

It may seem innocuous but, as Gomme suggests in *The Governance of London*, it represents "an entirely new constitutional factor in the history of London." Londoners were to be allowed to live under the rule of law that the city itself had established. The king was asserting his sovereignty over the ancient governance of London.

William had, however, recognised the one central fact—that this city was the key both to his own fortunes and to those of the country he had conquered. That is why he had inaugurated the transition of London from the status of an independent city-state to that nation's capital. In 1086 the Domesday Survey left London uninspected, no doubt on the ground that the complex financial and commercial activity within the city could not usefully be considered as part of the king's revenue. At the same time the Norman king and his successors initiated an inspired plan of public works in order to emphasise the central place of London in the new politics. The cathedral of St. Paul was rebuilt and William's successor, his son William Rufus, began the construction of Westminster Hall; a number of monastic houses and nunneries, together with priories and hospitals, were also erected in this period so that London and its environs were the site of prolonged and continual construction. The building and rebuilding, have been maintained ever since. The area around the Roman amphitheatre, for example, was cleared in the early twelfth century. In the same area the first guildhall was completed by 1127, and a second built in the early fifteenth century.

The earliest form of public administration was the folkmoot, which met three times a year, in the Roman amphitheatre and then latterly by St. Paul's Cross. There was also a more formal court, known as the hustings. These institutions were of the greatest antiquity, dating to Saxon and Danish times when the city was autonomous and self-governing. The territorial divisions of London, still in existence, were also of very early date. By the eleventh century the principal unit of territory had become the ward, which was led and represented by an alderman. The ward was more than a collection of citizens administering their own streets and shops; it was also a unit of defence and attack, with a midsummer inspection when, according to an official document dating from the reign of Henry VIII, "ev'y alderman by hymself musteryd hys owne warde yn the fields, vewyng theym in harnes and sawe that ev'y man had a sworde and a dagger and suche as were not meate to be archars were turnyd to pykes." As late as the fourteenth century a clerk could term London a *respublica*, and in this account of a carefully marshalled citizen army it is possible to trace the force and antiquity of the republican ideal.

But if the ward boundaries were the most significant within the city, they were not necessarily the most distinctive. Beneath the ward were the precincts with their own assemblies, and below them the individual parishes with their self-governing vestries. The city embodied a series of intricately related authorities, and that network of affiliations and interests has materially affected its life. Throughout the nineteenth century, for example, there

were continual complaints about the rigidity and stubbornness of the city authorities. This resistance to change was the legacy of a thousand years, affecting and obscuring the capital as powerfully as its coal-smoke and its fog.
It is also the setting in which succeeding events are best understood.

William the Conqueror's successor, William Rufus, was characterised by his attempt to impose ever more extortionate taxes and dues and tolls on the citizens. In his struggles with the Norman barons ensconced in England, it was
also Rufus's custom to send prisoners to be executed in London; it was a token of its role as capital, perhaps, but also of the king's authority.

After the death of Rufus in 1100, his brother, Henry I, hastened to the
city in order to be acclaimed as the new sovereign. The records of his reign
include a list of aldermen, from 1127, which displays so comprehensive a mixture of English and French names that a thoroughly ordered and working association between citizens who were now properly "Londoners" can be
assumed. In fact the study of the names of Londoners becomes of extreme
interest and significance in this period, as Old English names are gradually
supplanted by those of French origin. Surnames were by no means universal,
but were attached to a person because of locality or occupation—Godwinus
Baker was thus distinguished from Godwin Ladubur (moneyer) and God-
wyn Turk (fishmonger) or Godwinne Worstede (mercer) and Godwynne
Sall (hatter). Other citizens were identified by patronymics or, more commonly, by nicknames. Edwin Atter's name meant Edwin of the sharp tongue
while Robert Badding's implied an effeminate man; Hugh Fleg was "wide
awake," Johannes Flocc had woolly hair, John Godale sold good ale while
Thomas Gotsaul was honest.

Even as they associated with each other in trade and commerce, however,
the relationship of the citizens with the king became more problematic. For
him, the city was predominantly a place to be "farmed" for revenue; the
reason why Henry rarely interfered in the life of London was simply that he
needed it to prosper in order to benefit from its wealth.

After Henry's death in 1135, the dynastic struggles of the various
claimants to the throne were directly affected by the loyalties and allegiances
of Londoners; Henry's nephew Stephen, Count of Blois, claiming the right of
succession, promptly "came to London, and the London folk received
him . . . and hallowed him king on midwinter day." So says the *Anglo-Saxon
Chronicle*, and another ancient source adds that the "Alderman and wise folk
gathered together the folkmoot, and there providing at their own will for the

good of the realm unanimously resolved to choose a king." The citizens of London had, in other words, formally elected a king for the entire country. It is not clear what Stephen promised or granted the city, in return, but from this time forward it takes the first place in national affairs with a degree of independence which suggests that London is almost self-governing.

The coronation of Stephen, however, was not in itself enough. The landing in 1139 of his rival, Henry's daughter the Empress Matilda, and his own capture at the Battle of Lincoln in 1141, meant that London was forced to choose again. A great conference was held at Winchester in order to consider the royal claims of Matilda, and a speech in her favour by Stephen's own brother was concluded with the following significant remarks: "We have despatched messengers for the Londoners, who, from the importance of their city in England, are almost nobles, as it were, to meet us on this business; and have sent them a safe-conduct." They arrived on the following day, saying that they had been sent *a communione quam vocant Londoniarum*—"from the community, or commune, of London." This testimony from William of Malmesbury is the clearest possible evidence of the city's significance. As the nation divided in baronial wars, London had ceased to be a capital and had once again become a city-state. The events of Matilda's short subsequent reign reinforce this impression. She tried to curb the power of London and unwisely demanded money from its richest citizens. That is why, when Stephen's own queen, Maud, approached London, its inhabitants rushed into the streets, according to *Gesta Stephani*, with weapons "like thronging swarms from beehives" in order to support her. Matilda fled from the irate citizenry, and never regained the throne.

A proviso must be entered here, if only to dispel the impression of thorough independence. When the national policy was disrupted by dynastic struggle, then London naturally took the lead. But in a peaceful well-ordered kingdom the citizens, equally naturally, accepted the authority of the sovereign. So it was that the reign of Henry II, Matilda's son and Stephen's successor, marked a slight diminution of the city's authority. In his charter the king granted to Londoners "all their liberties and free customs which they had in the time of Henry my grandfather," but the royal sheriffs conducted much of the administration under the king's direct control.

The murder of Thomas à Becket in the winter of 1170 at Canterbury, for example, ought to have been a matter for Londoners. The archbishop was known to his contemporaries as "Thomas of London" and for many centuries he was the only Londoner to be canonised; his theatricality and flamboyance were also characteristic of the city. But there is no evidence of any popular support for his cause among Londoners. Perhaps he is one of those striking figures in the city's history who move beyond their immediate context into eternity.

Yet it was Becket's own twelfth-century biographer, William Fitz-Stephen, who celebrated the more earthly values of the city in that period. His account is written in the new style of urban *encomia*, since the formation of flourishing cities and the conduct of their citizens were then at the centre of European debate, but Fitz-Stephen's depiction is nevertheless remarkable for its enthusiasm. It is also highly significant as the first general description of London.

He describes the sound or "clatter" of the mills, turned by streams in the meadows of Finsbury and Moorgate, as well as the shouts and cries of the market vendors who "have each their separate station, which they take every morning." There were many wine shops close by the Thames, to accommodate the local artisans as well as traders who came to the docks; there was also a large "public eating-house," where servants could purchase bread and meat for their masters or where the local vendors could sit and eat. Fitz-Stephen also depicts the "high and thick wall" which surrounded and protected all this activity, with its seven double gates and northern towers; there was also a great fortress to the east, "the mortar used in the building being tempered with the blood of beasts," and two "strongly fortified" castles on the western side. Beyond the walls were gardens and vineyards, the mansions of the noble and the powerful interspersed among them. These great houses were generally in the western suburbs, where Holborn is now situated, while to the north were meadows and pastures which bordered upon "an immense forest" of which Hampstead and Highgate are the only remnants. Just beyond the city wall, on the north-western side, was a "smooth-field" now known as Smithfield where horses were sold every Friday. In paddocks close by, oxen and pigs were also slaughtered and sold. The same activity had taken place in precisely the same area for almost a thousand years.

Fitz-Stephen's account is distinctive for the emphasis he lays upon the energy, combativeness and vivacity of the citizens. There were games of football every evening in the fields outside the city, when the young men were watched and cheered by their teachers, parents or fellow apprentices; upon each Sunday, at the same time, there were games of combat when they rode against one another "with lances and shields." Even in its sports London had a reputation as a violent city. At Easter a tree was fixed into the middle of the Thames with a target hung upon it; a boat was rowed hard against it, carrying a young man with a lance. If he missed the target he fell into the river, to the amusement of the spectators. In the coldest days of winter, when the marshland of Moorfields froze, the more sportive citizens would sit upon great blocks of ice, which were pulled along by their friends; others fashioned skates from the shin bones of animals. But again there was an element of competition and violence in their pursuit; they skated towards each other until "either one or both of them fall, not without some bodily hurt" and "very frequently the leg or arm of the falling party" was broken. Even the lessons and debates of schoolboys were characterised in combative terms, with a steady stream of "scoffs and sarcasms." It was a world of bear-baiting and cock-fighting, somehow consonant with Fitz-Stephen's report that London could raise an army of 80,000 men, a world of violence and laughter mingled with what Fitz-Stephen terms "abundant wealth, extensive commerce, great grandeur and magnificence." His is a portrait of a city celebrating its destiny.

It was a time, therefore, of prosperity and growth. The docks were expanding, as the waterfront was continually reclaimed and extended in order to accommodate the Flemings and the French and the Hanseatics as well as the merchants from Brabant and Rouen and Ponthieu; there was trade in fur, wool, wine, cloth, grain, timber, iron, salt, wax, dried fish and a hundred other commodities to feed, clothe and support an ever increasing population. Most of this population was itself busily engaged in commerce: the furriers of Walbrook, the goldsmiths of Guthrun's Lane, the butchers of East Cheap, the shoe-makers of Cordwainer Street, the mercers in West Chepe, the fish-mongers in Thames Street, the woodmongers of Billingsgate, the candle-stick-makers of Lothbury, the ironmongers of Old Jewry, the cutlers of Pope's Head Alley, the prayer-bead-makers of Paternoster Row, the vintners of Vintry, all of them involved in perpetual trade.

The city was indeed a much noisier place than it is now, filled with continual cries of porters and water-bearers as well as the general uproar of wagons and bells, of blacksmiths and pewterers beating out their wares, of porters and apprentices, of carpenters and coopers working alongside each other in the same small area of lanes and alleys. There was of course the smell as well as the noise, concocted from tanneries and breweries, slaughter-houses and vinegar-makers, cook-houses and dung-heaps as well as the ever flowing tide of refuse and water which ran down the middle of the narrower streets. All this created a miasma of deep odours which could not be dispersed by even the most violent wind. It was further enriched by the increased use of coal by brewers and bakers and metal-forgers.

Throughout this period, too, there was a continual process of building and rebuilding; not one part of the city was untouched by this expansion as new shops and "sleds" or covered markets, churches and monasteries, houses of stone and timber were constructed. When these layers of the city were ex-cavated there lay revealed foundations of chalk and ragstone, chalk cesspits, arches of Reigate stone, building rubble, beechwood piles, oak timbers and threshold beams as well as the various impressions of walls, drains, floors, vaults, wells, rubbish-pits and stake holes. They were evidence of protracted and productive activity.

There was also constant activity in the "suburbs," or fields just outside the walls. In the twelfth century the great priories of Clerkenwell and Smith-field, St. John and St. Bartholomew, were established, while in the succeed-ing century the religious houses of Austin Friars, St. Helen, St. Clare and Our Lady of Bethlehem were also founded. The church of St. Paul's was rebuilt, and the monastic hospital of St. Mary Spital erected. The white friars and the black friars completed their great religious houses within twenty years of each other in the west of the city. This was the part of London in which there was the most heavy investment, with vacant land being sold on the promise of immediate development while buildings and tenancies were continually being subdivided into more profitable units. Yet the grandest work in all the rebuilding was that of London Bridge. It rose in stone and became the great highway of commerce and communication which has remained upon the same site for almost nine hundred years.

On either side of the southern entrance to that bridge, there now rear two griffins daubed in red and silver. They are the totems of the city, raised at all its entrances and thresholds, and are singularly appropriate. The griffin was the monster which protected gold mines and buried treasure; it has now flown out of classical mythology in order to guard the city of London. The presid-ing deity of this place has always been money. Thus did John Lydgate write of London in the fifteenth century: "lacking money I might not spede." Alexander Pope repeated his sentiments in the eighteenth, invoking, "There, London's voice: 'Get Money, Money still!' "

"The only inconveniences of London," Fitz-Stephen wrote, "are, the im-moderate drinking of foolish persons, and the frequent fires." In this he was prophetic as well as descriptive. Other observers at a slightly later date in the twelfth century, however, were more critical. One Yorkshire writer, Roger of Howden, reported that the sons of the wealthier citizens would assemble at night "in large gangs" in order to threaten or assault anyone who passed by. A monk from Winchester, Richard of Devizes, was more colourful in his condemnation: for him London was a place of evil and wrong-doing, filled with the worst elements of every race as well as native pimps and braggarts. He referred to the crowded eating houses and taverns, where dicing and gambling were customary. It is perhaps significant that he also mentioned *theatrum*, "the theatre," which suggests that the London appetite for drama was already being satisfied in forms other than those of the mystery or miracle plays staged at Clerkenwell. (The "first" theatres of 1576, the Theatre and the Curtain, may well descend from lost originals.) The monk also provided an interesting survey of the city's population, comprising in part "pretty boys, effeminates, pederasts." They are joined by "quacks, belly-dancers, sorceresses, extortioners, night-wanderers, magicians, mimes" in a panoply of urban life that would be celebrated, rather than condemned, in other centuries by writers as diverse as Johnson and Fielding, Congreve and Smollett. It is, in other words, the permanent condition of London.

William Fitz-Stephen noted that "The city is delightful indeed, when it has a good governor." The word itself might be construed as "leader" or "master," and has generally been taken to refer to the king. Yet in the years immediately succeeding his chronicle, the term is susceptible to other interpretations. There came a moment, in the last decade of the twelfth century, when it was shouted abroad that "Londoners shall have no king but their mayor!" This short-lived revolution was the direct consequence of a king's absence on crusade in Palestine and Europe. Richard I had come to London for his coronation and was anointed on the first Sunday in September 1189 "that was marked unlucky in the calendar"; indeed it proved "very much so to the Jews in London, who were destroyed that day." These cryptic words describe a mass slaughter—called by Richard of Devizes a "holocaust"—which has generally been scantily treated by historians. It has often been said that the principal culprits were those who owed money to the Jews, but it is hard to overestimate the savagery of the London mob; it represented a violent and ruthless society where the metaphor for the native population was that of bees swarming in angry clusters. The multitude are "busie Bees," according to the sixteenth-century author of *The Singularities of the City of London*; their clamour, according to Thomas More in the same period, was "neyther loude nor distincke but as it were the sounde of a swarme of bees." On this occasion the mob of bees stung the Jews and their families to death.

In the absence of the king on his religious wars, the leaders of London once more became the ascendant voice of England. The animus and will of Londoners were materially strengthened by the fact that Richard's represen-tative, William Longchamp, established himself in the Tower and began to erect new fortifications around it. It was a symbol of authority which was un-welcome. When Richard's brother, John, aspired to the crown in 1191, the citizens of London assembled at a folkmoot in order to pronounce upon his claims; at this significant moment they agreed to accept him as king as long as he in turn recognised the inalienable right of London to form its own com-mune as a self-governing and self-elected city-state. To this John agreed. It was not a new title but for the first time it was accepted by the reigning monarch as a public organisation "to which all the nobles of the kingdom, and even the very bishops of that province, are compelled to swear." These are the words of Richard of Devizes, who considered the new arrangement to be nothing other than a "tumor" or swelling-up of the people which could have no good consequences.

The connotations of the word "commune" are, from the French example, generally considered to be radical or revolutionary, but this particular revo-lution was instigated by the richest and most powerful of the London citizens. It was in fact, and in effect, a civic oligarchy comprising the most influential families—the Basings and the Rokesleys, the Fitz-Thedmars and the Fitz-Reiners—who styled themselves aristocrats or *"optimates."* They were a governing elite who took advantage of the political situation in order to re-assert the power and independence of the city which had been curtailed by the Norman kings. So we read in the great chronicle of the city, *Liber Albus*, that "the barons of the city of London shall choose for themselves each year a mayor from among themselves . . . provided always that when so elected he shall be presented unto his lordship the king, or in the king's absence unto his justiciar." Thus the mayor and his governing council of *probi homines*, the "honest men" of aldermanic rank, attained formal rank and dignity. The honour of becoming the first mayor of London goes to Henry Fitz-Ailwin of Londenstone, who remained in office for twenty-five years until his death in 1212.

It was not long after the authority of the mayor and commune was es-tablished that a sense of tradition entered the affairs of London: it is almost as if it had reacquired its history at the same time that its old powers were restored. Communal archives and records were deposited in the Guildhall, together with wills, charters and guild documents; from this period, too, issues a great spate of laws and mandates and ordinances. London had thereby acquired an administrative identity which animated such later bodies as the Metropolitan Board of Works and the London County Council of the nineteenth century as well as the Greater London Council of the twentieth. Here is the evidence of organic development which has not faded in time.

The administration of the city also began to demand the full-time employment of clerks, notaries and lawyers. An extraordinarily detailed code of civic legislation was established, and courts were instituted to deal with various misdemeanours. These courts also exercised general supervision over the condition of the city, such as the state of London Bridge and the creation of a water supply, with the various wards supervising matters of local sanitation, paving and lighting. The wards were also responsible for public safety as well as health, with twenty-six separate forces of police who were classified as "unpaid constables . . . beadles or bellmen, street keepers, or watchmen." Extant records show that this was by no means a sinecure: we may estimate the population of London in the late twelfth century at approximately forty thousand, many of whom were not disposed to obey the precepts of authority and good order imposed by the *optimates*.

When in 1193 the citizens of London were asked to provide money for the ransom of the absent king, his brother's brief rebellion having been effectively suppressed, there were many who resented the imposition. When Richard himself returned to London in the following year he was greeted with great ceremony, but then proceeded to milk the revenues of the city with methods ever more exacting; he is once supposed to have stated that "he would sell London if he could find a buyer," which scarcely endeared him to the already hard-pressed citizens. It seems likely that those artisans and merchants beneath the level of the *optimates* carried the heaviest burden, and in 1196 a revolt of these Londoners was led by William Fitz-Osbert "of the long beard." The beard was long but the rebellion was short. He seems to have had the support of a large number of citizens, and has been variously described as a demagogue and a defender of the poor. These are not in fact incompatible descriptions; but his insurrection was put down in a ruthless and violent manner which was entirely characteristic of the city. Fitz-Osbert sought sanctuary in St. Mary-le-Bow, on Cheapside, but the city authorities summarily removed him and hanged him with eight others at Smithfield in the sight of his erstwhile supporters. But the significance of the brief tumult was in the fact that a group of citizens had refused to obey the royal officials and merchant princes who controlled the city. It was the harbinger of necessary and inevitable change, as the population began to assert its own place in the general polity.

Yet the central area of tension, and possible conflict, still lay between city and king. The death of Richard I in 1199, and the elevation of John, did nothing to alleviate what seems to have been an instinctively anti-monarchical trend in London politics. It was the familiar story of the citizens being forced to pay increasing taxes or "tallage" to cover the king's expenditure. The mayor and the most powerful citizens attempted to maintain a spirit of co-operation, if only because many of them were involved with the king's household and would not necessarily benefit from his eclipse. But there was a growing disaffection within the commune. It would seem that King John, despite earlier promises, had abrogated certain rights and properties to himself, which prompted the thirteenth-century chronicler Matthew Paris to conclude that the citizens had almost turned into slaves. Yet the elective capacity of the folkmoot could still be asserted. In 1216 five wealthy Londoners gave 1,000 marks to the French prince, Louis, in order that he might travel to the city and be consecrated as king in place of John. The civic ritual of coronation proved unnecessary, however, when John died in the autumn of that year. London sent Louis home again, with more money, and welcomed the young Henry III, John's nine-year-old son, as its rightful sovereign.

We may walk the streets of London during the long reign of Henry III (1216–72). There were great houses as well as hovels, fine stone churches against which were erected wooden stalls for passing trade. The contrast of fair and foul can be put in another context with the statistic that, out of forty thousand citizens, more than two thousand were forced to beg for alms. The richer merchants constructed halls and courtyards while the poorest shopkeepers might live and work in two rooms ten feet square; the more affluent citizens owned fine furniture and silver, while those of straiter means possessed only the simplest pottery and kitchen utensils together with the tools of their trade.

One examination of a murder, when a young man killed his wife with a knife, incidentally provides a household inventory of the "middling" sort. The unfortunate pair lived in a house of wooden construction with two rooms, one above the other, and a thatched roof. In the lower room which opened upon the street there were a folding table and two chairs, with the walls "hung about with kitchen utensils, tools and weapons." Among them were a frying pan, an iron spit and eight brass pots. The upper room was reached by means of a ladder—here were a bed and mattress, with two pillows. A wooden chest held six blankets, eight linen sheets, nine tablecloths and a coverlet. Their clothes "which were laid in chests or hung upon the walls" consisted of three surcoats, one coat with a hood, two robes, another hood, a suit of leather armour and half a dozen aprons. There were a candlestick, two plates, some cushions, a green carpet, and curtains hung before the doors to keep out the draughts. There would also have been rushes on the floor, not included in any inventory. It was a small, but comfortable, residence.

Those in poorer situations lived in rooms built within tenements which could be found down the narrow alleys between wide thoroughfares. The upper floor of these small houses was known as the "solar," which protruded into the street itself so that little of the sky could be seen between two overhanging solars. Many of the smaller houses had been built of wood with thatched roofs, still reflecting the appearance of Saxon or early Norman building; London retained in part the atmosphere of a much earlier city, with tribal or territorial connotations. Yet after the many fires that visited the city, particularly a great conflagration in 1212, ordinances compelled householders to build their walls of stone and their roofs of tiles. Broken tiles from this period have been found in cesspits, wells, cellars, rubbish dumps and the foundation stones of roads. So there was a general process of transition, not perfectly managed, in which new stone and old timber stood side by side.

The condition of the streets themselves can be ascertained from the extant documents of the period. In the pleas and memoranda of the Guildhall, for example, we read of the master of Ludgate putting dung into the Fleet to such an extent that the water was stopped in certain places; a common privy is "diffectif" and "the ordur therof rotith the stone wallys." The taverners of St. Bride's parish put their empty barrels, and slops, into the street "to nusauns of all folk ther passyng." There were complaints about defective paving in Hosier Lane, while in Foster Lane the fourteen households had the habit of casting from their windows "ordure & vrine, the which annoyet alle the pepol of the warde." The cooks of Bread Street were indicted for keeping "dung and garbage" under their stalls, while a great stream of "dong and water and other diverse filth" was known to pour down Trinity Lane and Cordwainer Street by Garlickhithe Street, and descend between the shops of John Hatherle and Richard Whitman before discharging itself into the Thames. A

dung-hill in Watergate Street beside Bear Lane "is noyowse to all the commune people, kasting out in-to this lane ordour of Prevees and other orrible
sightis." There are reports of stinking fish and bad oysters, of common steps
in disrepair and of thoroughfares being blocked up, of areas or "pryue
places" where thieves and "money strumpettes" congregate.

But some of the best evidence for the condition of the streets comes in the
many regulations which were, from the evidence of the courts, being continually flouted. Stallholders were supposed to set up their stands only in the
middle of the street, between the two "kennels" or gutters on either side. In
the narrower thoroughfares the kennel ran down the middle of the street, thus
effectively forcing pedestrians to "take the wall." The scavengers and rakers
of each ward were ordered "to preserve, lower and raise the pavements, and
to remove all nuisances of filth"; all such "filth" was taken by horse and cart
down to the river where it was carried off in boats built for the purpose.
Special arrangements were made for carting off the noisome stuff from the
sites of butchery—the shambles, the Stocks Market and the market at East
Cheap—but there were always complaints of foul odours. In More's *Utopia*
(1516) the killing of animals takes place outside the city walls; his pointed recommendation is evidence of the real disgust which many citizens felt about
the proximity of this trade.

In the *Liber Albus* there are also instructions that pigs and dogs be not allowed to wander through the city; more curiously, perhaps, it was decreed
that "barbers shall not place blood in their windows." No citizen was allowed
to carry a bow for firing stones, and no "courtesans" were permitted to dwell
within the city walls. This last ordinance was persistently flouted. There were
elaborate regulations about the building of houses and walls, with special
provisions applied for neighbours' disputes; once again the impression is of a
close compacted town. In the same spirit of good order it was decreed that the
owners of the larger houses should always possess a ladder and a barrel of
water in case of fire; since it had been ordained that tile rather than thatch
should be the standard material of the roofs, the aldermen of each ward had
the power to come with a pole or hook in order to remove any offending
straw.

It is indicative of the close watch kept upon all citizens that there were
also regulations about private and social arrangements. Every aspect of life
was covered by an elaborate network of law, ordinance and custom. No
"stranger" was allowed to spend more than one day and a night in a citizen's
house, and no one might be harboured within a ward "unless he be of good

repute." No lepers were ever allowed within the city. No one was permitted to walk abroad "after forbidden hours"—that is, after the bells or curfew had been sounded—unless he or she wished to be arrested as a "night-walker." It was also forbidden that "any person shall keep a tavern for wine or for ale after the curfew aforesaid . . . nor shall they have any persons therein, sleeping or sitting up; nor shall anyone receive persons into his house from out of a common tavern, by night or by day."

The curfew itself was rung at nine o'clock in the summer months, earlier in the darkness of winter. When the bell of St. Mary-le-Bow in Cheapside rang curfew, followed by the bell of St. Martin's, St. Laurence's and St. Bride's, the taverns were cleared, the apprentices left their work, the lights dimmed as rush or candle were put out, the gates of the city were locked and bolted. Some of these apprentices believed that the clerk of St. Mary-le-Bow kept them at work too long by ringing too late and, according to John Stow, a rhyme was issued against

> Clerke of the Bow bell with the yellow lockes
> For thy late ringing thy head shall have knocks.

To which the offending clerk responded:

> Children of Cheape, hold you all still,
> For you shall have the Bow bell rung at your will.

This exchange testifies to the close relationship between all the members of the city so that everyone, for example, knew the bell-ringer with yellow hair. But the most striking image is perhaps that of the dark and silent city, barricaded against the outer world.

That silence was sometimes punctuated by screams, shouts and cries. It was the citizens' duty to "raise hue and cry" against any transgressor of the peace, for example, and any citizen "who comes not on such hue and cry raised" was heavily fined. London was a city where everyone was watching everyone else, for the sake of the spirit of the commune, and there are numerous reports of neighbours "crying shame" at the ill treatment of an apprentice or the abuse of a wife.

Yet it is to be expected that, in a mercantile culture, the greatest body of law should be concerned with commercial transactions. There are many hundreds of regulations in this period, controlling every aspect of trading life. It was ordered that the vendors of certain products like cheese and poultry "shall stand between the kennels in the market of Cornhulle so as to be a nuisance to no one" with other trades distributed in various sites in the city. No vendor could "buy any victuals for resale before prime rung at St. Paul's." From the twenty regulations applying to bakers alone, it might be noted that a baker of "tourte" or pan-baked bread was not permitted to sell white bread; every baker also was commanded to leave "the impression of his seal" upon each loaf of bread. It was decreed that "all kinds of fish brought into the City in closed baskets shall be as good at bottom of the basket as at the top," and that "no stranger ought to buy of a stranger."

Fishermen laboured under hundreds of regulations about what they could catch, how they could catch, and where they could catch; the size and mesh of their nets were carefully measured. There was also an elaborate system of tolls and taxes, so that "Every man who brings cheese or poultry if the same amounts to fourpence halfpenny shall pay one halfpenny. If a man on foot brings one hundred eggs or more he shall give five eggs. If a man or woman brings any manner of poultry by horse and lets it touch the ground" he or she will pay more. It was an intricate system but its purpose was simply to ensure that the inhabitants of the city were adequately fed and clothed. It attempted both to pre-empt the extortionate demands of those who bought and sold, and to protect the rights of the citizens to trade in the city at the expense of "aliens" or "strangers." The regulations had a further primary purpose, in the efforts to systematise trading so that there was little possibility of false measures, adulterated food or shoddy manufactures.

It is in the context of this thriving, colourful and energetic city that we can trace specific events which reveal the dangerous condition of the streets. In court records of the period we read of unnamed beggar women collapsing and dying in the street, of occasional suicides and constant fatal accidents— "drowned in a ditch outside Aldersgate . . . fell into a tub of hot mash." We learn that "A poor little woman named Alice was found drowned outside the City wall. No one is suspected . . . a certain Elias le Pourtour, who was carrying a load of cheese, fell dead in Bread Street . . . a girl of about eight years old was found dead in the churchyard of St. Mary Somerset. It was believed that she was thrown there by some prostitute. No one is suspected." Suicide in this age of piety, was considered a token only of madness. Isabel de Pampesworth "hanged herself in a fit of insanity" in her house in Bread Street. Alice de Wanewyck "drowned herself in the port of Dowgate, being

non compos mentis." Drunkenness was general, and there are continual references to citizens falling from their solars to the ground, falling down steps
into the Thames, falling off ladders. The reports of these, and other fatalities,
are to be found in *The London Eyre of 1244* edited by Chew and Weinbaum.
Other incidents are redolent of the period. "A certain man named Turrock"
was found dead but "it was found that three men were lying in the deceased's
bed when he died .. and they are in mercy," the last phrase denoting that they
had been acquitted of any charge. In another instance "Roger struck Maud,
Gilbert's wife, with a hammer between the shoulders and Moses struck her in
the face with the hilt of his sword, breaking many of her teeth. She lingered
until the feast of St. Mary Magdalen, and then died."

This litany of death and disaster highlights the crude violence of the city
streets; tempers are short, and life is held very cheap. "Henry de Buk killed a
certain Irishman, a tiler, with a knife in Fleet Bridge Street, and fled to the
church of St. Mary Southwark. He acknowledged the deed, and . . . abjured
the realm. He had no chattels." The quarrel of three men in a tavern by Milk
Street led to a fatality when one was attacked with an "Irish knife" and a
"misericord," a merciful knife which was meant to guarantee a quick exit
from this life; the fatally wounded man reached the church of St. Peter in
Cheapside, but none of the bystanders offered to assist him.

The various trade guilds openly fought against each other in the streets;
a group of goldsmiths, for example, fell upon a saddler and proceeded to lay
open his head with a sword, chop off his leg with an axe and generally be-
labour him with a staff; he died five days later. When apprentices of the law
rioted by Aldersgate, a citizen "amused himself" by shooting into the crowd
an arrow which killed an unfortunate bystander. A "love-day," designed to
reconcile the coppersmiths and ironsmiths, turned into a general and murderous riot. When a group of unruly men entered a tavern one of the customers enquired, "Who are these people?" and was promptly killed with a
sword. There were continual fights in the street, ambushes and arguments
over nothing—or over "goat's wool" as it was known. Games of "dice" or
"tables" frequently ended in drunken fights, while it is clear that some of the
owners of dicing taverns were engaged in wholesale fraud. It is a curious but
instructive fact that the officers of the ward or parish were quick to tend to the
religious needs of the maimed or dying, but there were few attempts to administer any form of medical treatment by physician or barber-surgeon. The
injured were generally left to recover, or die, as providence intended.

There were many assaults upon women; in the transcripts there are cases of female Londoners being beaten or kicked to death, or callously murdered in premeditated fashion. Lettice accused Richard of Norton, vintner, of "raping and deflowering her" but the case did not proceed to trial. Wife-beating was common and went largely unremarked; but the brutalised women themselves could then in turn become brutal. A drunken woman started howling out insults to certain builders who were working on the corner of Silver Street—she called them "tredekeiles," which might be translated as "lousy slobs," and promptly started a fight in which one man was stabbed in the heart. Women could also be exponents of justice, rough even by London standards: when a Breton murdered a widow in her bed, "women of the same parish come owte with stonys and canell dong, and there made an ende of hym in the hyghe strete."

The aldermen and watch of each ward had other duties which cast an intriguing light upon the customs of medieval London. They were instructed, for example, to arrest anyone wearing a "visor or false face" in the streets; to be masked was to be considered a criminal. The Court Rolls suggest that they were also given power to remove the doors and windows from any house of dubious reputation; there is a record of their "entering the house of William Cok, butcher, in Cockes Lane and tearing away eleven doors and five windows with hammers and chisels." It is significant that the name, trade and street of the offender are conflated in characteristic medieval manner; it is an indication of how one activity, in this case the slaughter of poultry, can imbue an entire area of the city. Other incidents may also be representative, although less violent. The watch arrested certain apprentices who had filled a barrel with stones and then rolled it downhill from Gracechurch Street to London Bridge "to the great terror of the neighbours."

There were more salacious, or intimate, events noted in the judicial records of a slightly later date; in their striking immediacy we might almost be in the same chamber with these early Londoners. "Will'm Pegden saieth that one Morris Hore broughte one Cicell and the saide Colwell had the vse of the bodie of the saide Elizabeth and the saide Alice Daie burned [gave a venereal disease to] the saide Cicell . . . And then the saide Alice daie came vppe Imediatlie, and lepped vppon the bed & said Cicell with hir kissinge together, and laying hir legges so broade that a yoked sow might go betwene."

The crimes could be egregious, but the punishments had a distinctively communal aspect. It has often been suggested that the officials of the medieval city were more lenient than their successors in the seventeenth and eighteenth centuries, and there is a partial truth to this. Punishments such as amputation were often commuted. But the civic spirit could be violent indeed, at least when it was threatened, and there are many records of hanging or beheading for offences against the city's peace. The fatal penalty was almost always imposed upon rebels and upon those offenders who had in some other way touched the king's majesty; one man was hanged, for example, for tampering with the royal seal. The heads of rebels and traitors were boiled and placed upon London Bridge, sometimes adorned with a crown of ivy as a final theatrical touch in the drama of punishment. At times of tension or disorder within the city, also, the mayor and aldermen resorted to capital punishment as the most expeditious way of controlling the populace. Murder was always a hanging offence (except when committed by a woman who could prove herself to be pregnant) but, in more peaceful time, the prison and the pillory were the common remedies for crime. Walter Waldeskef was charged "with being addicted to playing knucklebones at night"; he was described in the report as "a night walker, well dressed and lavish of his money, though no one knew how he got his living." In the year after his arrest he was stabbed in Lombard Street and died in the church of St. Swithin at Walbrook. Agnes de Bury was imprisoned "for selling old fur on Cornhill," while Roger Wenlock was committed to prison "for selling beer at 2d a gallon." John Mundy, baker, "was set vpon the pyllery in Cornhill for makyng and sellyng of false breed," and in the same month Agnes Deynte was also put in the pillory for selling "false mengled buttur." Many and various frauds were also detected and punished. One baker cut a hole upon his moulding board; when the customer brought in his dough to be cooked, part of it was removed by a member of the baker's family crouched beneath the counter. In another instance a former servant of a law officer, dismissed, travelled to various taverns and pretended to confiscate ale; the good tavern wives paid him to leave them alone. Eventually he was caught, and placed in the pillory.

Some of the punishments were more exotic. Bawds and "whore-mongers" had their hair shaved, leaving a two-inch fringe upon the heads of men and a small clump upon the heads of women. They were taken to their respective pillories by minstrels, the female pillory being known as a "thew," where they became the target of the honest citizens' anger or high spirits. If a woman was found to be a prostitute "let her be taken from the prison unto Aldgate" while wearing a hood of striped cloth and carrying a white taper in her hand; the minstrels once more led her to the pillory and, after the ritual abuse, she was marched down Cheapside and through Newgate to take up guarded lodgings in Cock Lane by West Smithfield.

Those consigned to the pillory for fraudulent manufacture or for selling shoddy goods had the items of their trade burned before them. John Walter had sold false measures of coal; he was condemned to stand in the pillory for an hour "with his sakkis brent [burnt] under him." The journey to this place of obloquy was accompanied by other diversions: the culprit sometimes was forced to ride backwards on a horse, the tail towards him, and crowned with a fool's cap. When one priest was found *in flagrante delicto* he was paraded through the streets with his breeches down and his clerical robes carried before him. Sir Thomas de Turberville, traitor, was taken through the streets of London dressed in a striped coat and white shoes; he was tied to a horse while around him rode six officials dressed all in red as emblems of the devil. Punishment becomes a form of festivity; in a relatively small and enclosed city, it turns into a celebration of communal feeling.

Yet harshness—one might almost call it savagery—was never very far from the surface, and can best be exemplified by the destination for London criminals who were spared the pillory or the noose: Newgate. During the coroner's inquests of 1315–16, sixty-two of the eighty-five corpses under investigation had been taken from Newgate Prison. That is why there were many desperate attempts to break out of what was, essentially, a house of death. On one occasion the prisoners forced their way on to the roof "and faught ageyn the Citizens and kept the gate a greate while," reinforcing the point that it was Londoners themselves who were essentially their guards and captors. It is perhaps appropriate, then, that one of the first extant texts in London English, written in the middle of the thirteenth century, should be entitled "The Prisoner's Prayer."

There was essentially only one escape from the wrath of the citizens, and that was the plea of sanctuary. A felon who could avoid capture, and take refuge in one of the many churches, was safe there for forty days. A watch was always placed around the church, in case of a sudden escape, and a body of citizens would have been encamped there day and night. Other places of sanctuary were Southwark, south of the river, and the east side of the Tower; where the power of the city stopped, in other words, the criminal was free. This is another indication of the self-sufficiency of the city, even if on such occasions it might have preferred a wider jurisdiction. During the course of sanctuary the prisoner often made a confession to the officers of the law and, at the end of the forty days, he or she was forced to "abjure the realm" and flee into exile. The status of the outcast was then announced at the folkmoot.

So from ancient deeds and coroners' inquests, chancery rolls and chancery warrants, calendars of inquisitions and court records, we can summon up the spirit of medieval London in the streets, lanes and alleys that survive even still. But if this urban society was often characterised by violent confrontation so, too, was its political culture.

For much of the thirteenth century the record is one of riots, and massacres, and street-fighting. During this period London was in almost perpetual conflict with the reigning monarch, Henry III, while the aspiring leadership of the city was divided between the *optimates* and the *populares*—the old commercial magnates who had comprised the oligarchical commune of the city, as against the representatives of the crafts and trades who were beginning to feel their power. The situation was further complicated by the fact that the magnates tended to be royalist in their sympathy while the *populares*, sometimes also known as the *mediocres*, instinctively supported the barons of the realm with whom the king was in open conflict. London, once more, was the key. Whoever controlled the city was close to controlling the kingdom. The periodic baronial wars had this further consequence; there were parties and families within the city who maintained different allegiances, so that the national struggle was played out in miniature within the streets of London. It was truly the epitome of all England.

A traffic "lock" or jam on Ludgate Hill, sketched by the French artist
Gustave Doré towards the close of the nineteenth century.

CHAPTER 5

Loud and Everlasting

London has always been characterised by the noise that is an aspect of its noisomeness. It is part of its unnaturalness, too, like the roaring of some monstrous creature. But it is also a token of its energy and of its power.

From its earliest foundation London rang with the hammers of artisans and the cries of tradesmen; it produced more noise than any other part of the country, and in certain quarters, like those of the smiths and the barrel-makers, the clamour was almost insupportable. But there were other noises. In the early medieval city, the clatter of manufacturing trades and crafts would have been accompanied by the sound of bells, among them secular bells, church bells, convent bells, the bell of the curfew and the bell of the watchman.

It might be surmised that the effect of the bells ended with the Reformation, when London ceased to be a notably pious Catholic city, but all the evidence suggests that the citizens continued to be addicted to them. A German duke entered London on the evening of 12 September 1602, and was astonished by the unique character of the city's sound. "On arriving in London we heard a great ringing of bells in almost all the churches going on very late in the evening, also on the following days until 7 or 8 o'clock in the evening. We were informed that the young people do that for the sake of exercise and amusement, and sometimes they lay considerable sums of money as a wager, who will pull a bell longest or ring it in the most approved fashion. Parishes spend much money in harmoniously-sounding bells, that one being preferred which has the best bells. The old Queen is said to have been pleased very much by this exercise, considering it as a sign of the health of the people." This account is taken from *The Acoustic World of Early Modern England* by Bruce R. Smith, which offers an intimate version of London's history. There is some suggestion here that the harmony of the bells is in some sense intended to demonstrate the harmony of the city, with the attendant "health" of its citizens, but there is also an element of theatricality or bravura intrinsic to London and Londoners. Indeed there is almost a kind of violence attached to their liking of loud sound. Another German traveller, of 1598, wrote that Londoners are "vastly fond of great noises that fill the ear, such as the firing of cannon, drums, and the ringing of bells, so that it is common for a number of them . . . to go up into some belfry, and ring the bells for hours together for the sake of exercise." A chaplain to the Venetian ambassador similarly reported that London boys made bets "who can make the parish bells be heard at the greatest distance." To the element of display are added aggression and competition.

It is perhaps not surprising, therefore, that the very definition of the Londoner should be adduced in terms of loud noise. A Cockney was one who was born within the sound of the bell of St. Mary-le-Bow, in Cheapside, which according to John Stow was "more famous than any other Parish Church of the whole Cittie or suburbs." Fynes Moryson, in 1617, announced that "Londiners, and all within the sound of Bow-Bell, are in reproach called Cocknies, and eaters of buttered tostes." Bruce R. Smith has suggested that "cockney" in fact derives from the "cock-shaped weathervane" which once surmounted the belfry of St. Mary-le-Bow and that the Londoners' identification with the sound came from their own "loud loquaciousness" or "boastfulness."

As the city grew, so did its level of noise. By the beginning of the fifteenth century, according to Walter Besant's *London*, "there was no noisier city in the whole world"; it could be heard from Highgate and from the Surrey hills. Dekker in *The Seven deadly Sinnes of London* evokes something of the incessant din—"hammers are beating in one place; Tubs hooping in another, Pots clinking in a third, water-tankards running at tilt in a fourth." Here noise itself is associated with energy, and specifically with the making of money. Sound was intrinsic to the trades of the carpenters and the coopers, the blacksmiths and the armourers. Other occupations, such as dockers and porters, the loaders and unloaders by the wharves, actively employed noise as an agent of business; it was the only way of affirming or expressing their role within the commercial city.

Certain areas produced particular noises. The metal foundries of Lothbury, for example, produced "a loathsome noise to the by-passers, that hath not been used to the like" and the quarter of the blacksmiths was permeated "with the noise of and sound of their hammers & anuiles." There was also the general circumambient noise of the London streets where, according once more to Thomas Dekker, "carts and Coaches make such a thundring" and where "in the open streetes is such walking, such talking, such running, such riding, such clapping too of windowes, such rapping at Chamber doores, such crying out for drink, such buying vp of meate, and such calling vppon Shottes, that at every such time, I verily beleeue I dwell in a Towne of Warre." Images of violence and assault spring unimpeded from the experience of London sound. In 1598 Everard Guilpin wrote a verse satire upon "the peopled streets" of London, which he depicts as a "hotch-potch of so many noyses . . . so many severall voyces." Here the heterogeneity of London is seen as an aspect of its noise. Yet without the perpetual hum of traffic and machines which seems to characterise the noise of contemporary London streets, individual voices would have been heard more clearly. The wooden and plaster houses on either side of the main thoroughfares acted as an echo-chamber, so that one of the characteristics of the sixteenth-century city would be a continual babble of voices making up one single and insistent conversation; it might be termed the conversation of the city with itself.

There were certain places where the voices reached such a pitch and intensity that they could also be characterised as a London sound. The interior of St. Paul's Cathedral was known for its particular timbre. To quote once more from Bruce Smith's account, "the noyse in it is like that of Bees, a strange humming or buzze, mixt of walking, tongues, and feet: It is a kind of still roare or loud whisper." The Royal Exchange, where merchants from all over the world congregated, was "vaulted and hollow, and hath such an Eccho, as multiplies euery worde that is spoken." At the centre of commerce there is a great reverberation, as if the conduct of finance could only take place within thunder. Then, in the taverns to which the dealers and merchants retired, "men come here to make merry but indeed make a noise." So, in the places of power and speculation, the insistent sound is that of raised male voices. Samuel Johnson once remarked upon the subject of taverns, "Sir, there is no other place where the more noise you make, the more welcome you are." It is a suggestive observation, with its implications of theatricality and aggression as part of the London experience; the more "noise" you make, the more you become a true inhabitant of the city. In the theatres, too, there was unabated noise, with the hucksters and the criers and the huddled throng; everybody talking together, breaking nuts, and crying out for ale.

On the streets outside were the bells, the wagons, the cries, the barking dogs, the squeaking of shop signs blowing in the wind. But there was another sound, relatively unfamiliar to Londoners of later generations. It was that of rushing water. The sixteenth-century city was crossed by streams and rivers. The sound of water from fifteen conduits mingled with the noise of the Thames and its lapping tides, audible along all the lanes and thoroughfares which led to the river. Great wheels were used to pump water from the Thames into small wooden pipes, and their endless grinding and reverberation added materially to the overwhelming noise of the city.

In 1682 it was still the same endless sound, like a great shout perpetually renewed. "I lie down in Storms," Sir John Oldham announced in that year, "in Thunders, rise." He evokes the "Din" of the "restless Bells" as well as

Huzza's of Drunkards, Bellmen's midnight Rhimes
The noise of Shops, with Hawkers early Screams.

The allusion here is to a city that is always wakeful; there is no end to its activity, neither at night nor at day, and it lives continually. In the seventeenth century, too, London was still a city of animals as well as people. Samuel Pepys was disturbed one night by a "damned noise between a sow gelder and a cow and a dog." The noise of horses, cattle, cats, dogs, pigs, sheep and chickens, which were kept in the capital, was confounded also with the sound of the great herds of beasts being driven towards Smithfield and the other open markets; London consumed the countryside, or so it was said, and the noise which accompanied its devouring appetite was everywhere apparent.

It has often been observed how foreigners, or strangers, were astonished and perplexed by the noise of London. On one level it was regarded as representative of London's "license," where the boundary between anarchy and freedom remained ambiguous. In a city filled with an implicitly egalitarian spirit, each inhabitant was free to occupy his or her own space with endless noisy expressiveness. In Hogarth's engraving of 1741, *The Enraged Musician*, a foreign visitor is assailed by the sound of a sow-gelder (perhaps a descendant of the one who annoyed Pepys), by howling cats, a girl's rattle, a boy's drum, a milkmaid's cry, a ballad-seller's plaintive call, a knife-grinder and a pewterer at their respective trades, a carillon of bells, a parrot, a wandering "haut-boy" or oboe player, a shrieking dustman and a barking dog. The significance of these heterogeneous images is that they are all striking and familiar London types. Hogarth is here celebrating the noises of the city as an intrinsic aspect of its life. It is the prerogative of Londoners to make noise; therefore, noise is a natural and inevitable part of their existence in the city. Without that right, for example, many of the vendors and street-sellers would perish.

Those who came to the city as visitors were not of course necessarily able to share Hogarth's implicit enthusiasm for this native uproar. In Tobias Smollett's novel of 1771 Humphry Clinker is dismayed by its nocturnal aspects. "I start every hour from my sleep, at the horrid noise of the watchmen bawling the hour through every street and thundering at every door," thus illustrating the fact that time itself can be imposed with a shout. In the morning, too: "I start out of bed, in consequence of the still more dreadful alarm made by the country carts, and noisy rustics bellowing green peas under my window." Commerce, as well as time, must be understood in raucous terms. Joseph Haydn complained that he might fly to Vienna "to have more quiet in which to work, for the noise that the common people make as they sell their wares in the street is intolerable." Yet there were others who so wished to enter the spirit of London that they rejoiced in the clamour and embraced it like a lover. "The noise," Boswell wrote upon his first arrival in London in 1762, "the crowd, the glare of the shops and signs agreeably confused me." He arrived in the capital by way of Highgate, from which eminence he would already have heard the noise. "Let anyone ride down Highgate Hill on a summer's day," Laetitia Landon wrote in the early nineteenth century, "see the immense mass of buildings spread like a dark panorama, hear the ceaseless and peculiar sound, which has been likened to the hollow roar of the ocean, but has an utterly different tone . . . then say, if ever was witnessed hill or valley that so powerfully impressed the imagination with that sublime and awful feeling, which is the epic of poetry." So the noise of the city partakes of its greatness.

This sense of disturbing, almost transcendental, sound was essentially a discovery of the nineteenth century when London represented the great urban myth of the world. Its noise became an aspect of its mightiness, and horror; it became numinous. In 1857 Charles Manby Smith, in the paradoxically entitled *The Little World of London*, described it as "that indefinable boom of distant but ever-present sound which tells that London is up and doing, and which will swell into a deafening roar as the day grows older [and] now rises faintly but continuously upon the ear." The "roar" here suggests the presence of some great beast, but more significant is this sense of a continuous, distant sound as if it were a form of meditation or self-communing. We read in the same narrative of "the uninterrupted and crashing roar of deafening sounds, which tell of the rush of the current of London's life blood through its thousand channels—a phenomenon, however, of which the born Londoner is no more unpleasantly conscious than is the Indian savage, cradled at the foot of a cataract, of its everlasting voice." This is an interesting image, which identifies London itself with some kind of natural force; at the same time it covertly admits savagery among the citizens, in a locale both untamed and untamable.

From three miles' distance, in what was then an "outlying" suburb soon to be drawn within the vortex of the city, the sound of London is "like the swell of the sea-surge beating upon a pebbly shore when it is heard far inland." Here is a haunting impression of proximity to the great city. That perpetual sound was variously compared to Niagara, in its persistence and remorselessness, and to the beating of a human heart. It is intimate and yet impersonal, like the noise of life itself. That same intuition was vouchsafed to Shelley who wrote of

> London: that great sea whose ebb and flow
> At once is deaf and loud, and on the shore
> Vomits its wrecks, and still howls on for more.

The adjectives "deaf" and "loud" summon up an image of pitiless activity; the verb "howls" one of fear, pain and rage in equal measure. The noise is one of greed and helplessness, as if it were in a perpetually infantile state. Its noise is ancient, but always renewed.

A celebrated American of the nineteenth century, James Russell Lowell, has written: "I confess that I never think of London, which I love, without thinking of that palace which David built for Bathsheba, sitting in hearing of one hundred streams—streams of thought, of intelligence, of activity. One other thing about London impresses me beyond any other sound I have ever heard, and that is the low, unceasing roar one hears always in the air; it is not a mere accident, like a tempest or a cataract, but it is impressive, because it always indicates human will, and impulse, and conscious movement; and I confess that when I hear it I almost feel as if I were listening to the roaring loom of time. "

Here, then, is a further sense of the numinous. London becomes the image of time itself. The great "streams" of thought and intelligence never cease; to change the metaphor, they resemble cosmic winds. But is the sound of the city also the sound of time itself? The noise would then be striated by the shuttling of the future into the past, that instantaneous and irremediable process that takes place in a "present" moment that can never really be glimpsed or known. The sound is then one of vast loss, the "howl" of which Shelley writes. In the phrase of T.S. Eliot, a poet whose vision of time and eternity sprang directly from his experience of London, "All time is unredeemable." London is unredeemable, too, and we may also think of its noise as comprising a vast mass of subjective private times continually retreating into non-existence.

Even in the middle of that maelstrom, however, it was possible to pick out and to remember specific London sounds which belonged to that place and to no other in the nineteenth century. There were the notes of the "German band," with their horn and trombone and clarionet; there was the lament of the barrel organ and the barrel piano; there was the cry of "Lucifers" from an old man bearing a tray of matches. There was the rumble of the scavenger's cart drawn by great horses "adorned with tiaras of tinkling bells." There was the incessant clatter of horses' hooves which, when they departed, left London bereft. "I shall miss the 'orses' feet at night, somethin' shockin'," one Cockney lady put it, *"they was sech comp'ny like."* There was of course the continual noise of wheels, endlessly turning with their own resistless momentum. "To the stranger's ear," a journalist wrote in 1837, "the loud and everlasting rattle of the countless vehicles which ply the streets of London is an intolerable annoyance. Conversation with a friend whom one chances to meet in midday is out of the question . . . one cannot hear a word the other says." Jane Carlyle, having settled in London with her husband Thomas, asked a correspondent in 1843: "Is it not strange that I should have an everlasting sound in my ears, of men, women, children, omnibuses, carriages, glass coaches, street coaches, wagons, carts, dog-carts, steeple bells, door-bells, gentlemen-raps, twopenny post-raps, footmen-showers-of-raps, of the whole devil to pay." It is as if the whole world had broken in upon her. That same sense emerges in a book entitled *Memories of London in the*

1840s where the constant roar of traffic was described "as if all the noises of all the wheels of all the carriages in creation were mingled and ground together into one subdued, hoarse, moaning hum."

Wooden paving was laid upon many of the main thoroughfares in the 1830s—Oxford Street and the Strand being two particular examples—but nothing could really withstand the encroaching noise of the city. In *The Strange Case of Dr. Jekyll and Mr Hyde* (1886) R. L. Stevenson writes of "the low growl of London from all round." In a life of Tennyson it is remarked that the poet "always delighted in the 'central roar' of London." "This is the mind," he told his son, "that is a mood of it." Charlotte Brontë heard that "roar" and was deeply excited by it. In each instance the presence of a living thing is being registered, perhaps with some disquiet; it is one great life comprising the sum of individual lives so that, at the end of *Little Dorrit*, the little heroine and her husband "went quietly down into the roaring streets, inseparable and blessed; and as they passed along in sunshine and shade, the noisy and the eager, and the arrogant and the froward and the vain, fretted and chafed, and made their usual uproar." Those who are "blessed" are silent, like strangers in the city, but the "eager" and the restless maintain their uproar. Or, rather, the sound of London is transmitted through them.

It has changed during the course of the twentieth century. Those at the beginning recall the noise of horse-driven vans and the apoplectic roar of the omnibuses mingled with the strangely peaceful and satisfying sound of horses' hooves. It is perhaps not surprising that the writers who dwelled in the city in the first decades of the twentieth century, should instil an enchantment in those noises; it is as if they were aware of their imminent destruction.

In 1929, according to the *Journal of the London Society*, a deputation from the British Medical Association had visited the Ministry of Health to suggest that "city noise" was "a menace to public health." Instead of the sound of London being celebrated as a token of life itself, or at least of the energy of the city, it was now being construed as injurious and unwelcome. It had become more uniform and monotonous so that, two years later, a report noted that "people are beginning to rebel against this disturbing, wearying factor in their lives." It had also become more impersonal and, in response to its dehumanising potential, the measurement of the "decibel" was introduced. Various sources of what was now considered a nuisance were reported. It offers an odd contrast with Hogarth's print of *The Enraged Musician*, surrounded by human sources of sound, to note that the new disturbers of the peace in the 1930s included the pneumatic street drill, the motor horn, building construction, and the railway steam-whistle described as "harsh and grating." Much attention was paid to the "unnatural" quality of London noise—"a riveter is equal to 112 decibels, whereas thunder can register only 70"—thus reintroducing the old notion of a city intrinsically opposed to natural laws of growth and development. It was also suggested that the sound of London had a wholly deleterious effect upon "the brain and nervous system," creating fatigue, inattention and general weariness.

D.H. Lawrence had a peculiar intuition of this change in the city's noise. He had considered it, in the first decade of the twentieth century, as an expression of "the vast and roaring heart of all adventure" with the emphasis upon "roar" or "uproar" as a token of exhilaration; but then the traffic had become "too heavy." This was also the gist of official reports, so that the novelist can be presumed to have touched upon an authentic alteration. "The traffic of London used to roar with the mystery of man's adventure on the seas of life" but now "it booms like monotonous, far-off guns, in a monotony of crushing something, crushing the earth, crushing out life, crushing everything dead."

The reiterated note of monotony is entirely characteristic of descriptions of modern London sound. Virginia Woolf described the noise of traffic as "churned into one sound, steel blue, circular" which adequately conveys the artificiality or impersonality of the circumambient noise. In recent years, too, there have been reports of a low humming sound which can be discerned everywhere. It is an accompaniment of fluorescent light, perhaps, or of the vast electronic systems working continuously beneath the surface of the city; it is now the low-level "background" noise which masks other sounds. The noise of cars and cooling systems has changed the air of London in every sense, principally by dulling down the variety and heterogeneity of sound. The great roar of nineteenth-century London is today diminished in intensity but more widespread in its effects; from a distance it might be recognised as an incessant grinding sound. The image would no longer be that of a sea but, rather, of a machine. The beating "heart" of London can no longer be credited with human or natural attributes.

The sound of voices, once such an intrinsic aspect of the street, has now been marginalised—except for the individual voice responding to the call of the mobile telephone, in a manner louder and more abrupt than that of ordinary conversation. Yet two aspects of these changing soundscapes have remained constant. Native Londoners have for many centuries been known to talk louder than their contemporaries, with a marked tendency towards shouting. London has become one unyielding and unending shout. There is a second characteristic noise. If you stand in Lombard Street at any time of the day, for example, that narrow thoroughfare like others in the vicinity echoes to hurrying footfalls. It has been a continuous sound for many hundreds of years, in the very centre of the City, and it may be that the perpetual steady echo of passing footsteps is the true sound of London in its transience and in its permanence.

CHAPTER 6

Silence Is Golden

et, on Sundays and public holidays, Lombard Street falls quiet. Throughout the old City, silence returns.

The history of silence is one of London's secrets. It has been said of the city that its most glorious aspects are concealed, and that observation is wonderfully well fitted to account for the nature of silence in London. It comes upon the pedestrian, or traveller, suddenly and unexpectedly; it momentarily bathes the senses, as if going from bright light into a darkened room. Yet if London sound is that of energy and animation, silence must therefore be an ambiguous presence within city life. It may offer peace and tranquillity, but it may also suggest absence of being. It may be a negative force. The city's history is striated with moments of silence: the silence of the surrounding country when the anonymous poet of *London Lickpenny* leaves Cheapside in 1390, the silence of the civic assembly when Richard III was first proposed as king in 1483, the silence of desolation after the Fire in 1666.

There was the silence of sixteenth-century London, after the day's last cry at the stroke of midnight:

Looke well to your locke,
Your fier and your light,
And so good-night.

Of course the London night was not wholly quiet. What London night ever is, or ever will be? It is the contrast that is significant, in an almost theatrical sense, because it marks an interdiction upon the natural ardour of the citizens. In that sense the silence of London is indeed unnatural. There is a mid-seventeenth-century poem by Abraham Cowley which intimates that, on the departure of all the wicked and the foolish, the city would become "a solitude almost," the implied silence suggesting here that noise and bustle are indistinguishable from sinfulness or folly. In that sense London could never be a silent city.

The absence of noise has also been marked as yet another contrast in an endlessly contrasting place. An eighteenth-century traveller observed that in the smaller streets off the Strand, running down to the Thames, there was "so pleasing a calm" that it struck the senses. This is a constant refrain. When the American connoisseur of antiquity, Washington Irving, wandered through the grounds of the Temple, off Fleet Street, "strangely situated in the very centre of sordid traffic," he entered the silence of the chapel of the Knights Templar. "I do not know a more impressive lesson for the man of the world," he wrote, "than thus suddenly to turn aside from the high way of busy money seeking life and sit down among these shadowy sepulchres, where all is twilight, dust and forgetfulness." Here silence becomes an intimation of eternity, with the suggestion that London once emerged from a great silence and will one day return to it.

The great *locus solus* of silence, amid the overbearing noise of nineteenth-century London, acquired therefore an almost sacred status. Another American writer of that century, Nathaniel Hawthorne, entered it, having gone astray in Holborn. He walked "through an arched entrance, over which was 'Staple Inn' . . . but in a court opening inwards from this was a surrounding seclusion of quiet dwelling houses . . . there was not a quieter spot in England than this. In all the hundreds of years since London was built, it has not been able to sweep its roaring tide over that little island of quiet." Silence has derived its power here by being able to withstand the sound of London, and in the process has itself acquired a kind of immensity—"there was not a quieter spot in England."

Dickens knew the same courtyard well and employed it in *The Mystery of Edwin Drood*. "It is one of those nooks, the turning into which out of the clashing street imparts to the relieved pedestrian the sensation of having put cotton in his ears and velvet soles on his boots. It is one of those nooks where a few smoky sparrows twitter in smoky trees, as though they called to one an-

other, 'Let's play at country.' " There is almost a theatrical aspect to this silence, therefore, as if it had been tainted by the artificiality of London. It is
not a natural silence but a "play," one of a series of violent contrasts which
the inhabitants of London must endure. It is in that sense wholly ambiguous;
it may provoke peaceful contemplation, or it may arouse anxiety.

When Hawthorne continued his pilgrimage to the centres of silence—a
journey by an antiquarian determined to prove that "modern" London had
not obtained full mastery over the silent past—he entered the precincts of
Gray's Inn. "It is very strange to find so much of ancient quietude right in the
monster city's very jaws," he wrote, confirming his intuition that noise is a
consequence of inattention or ignorance. It is silence which partakes of the
past, and redeems the present. "Nothing else in London is so like the effect of
a spell, as to pass under one of these archways, and find yourself transported
from the jumble, rush, tumult, uproar, as if an age of weekdays condensed
into the present hour, into what seems an eternal Sabbath." So silence is the
equivalent of the holy days of rest. Silence is the sound of *not* working, *not*
making money.

But this again is ambiguous since the Sunday of London was known for its
altogether dismal aspect, gloomy and generally disheartening. So does silence
itself partake of this dreariness? In London the absence of noise, and activity,
may be peculiarly enervating. Gabriel Mourey, a French traveller of the nineteenth century, remarked that on a Sunday "it is like a dead city; all trace of life
and activity of the past six days has vanished." Everyone noticed the change. It
was "horrible," and manifested a contrast which no other place on earth could
afford. Once more the uniqueness of this sudden transition is being emphasised,
so that even silence itself reflects the magniloquence of nineteenth-century
London.

Yet there are other forms of silence which seem to presage activity. The
author of *The Little World of London* recognised, and heard, them all. There
was the moment of early dawn, a brief period of stillness before the distant
noise "of horses' hooves and grinding wheels" marked the awakening of the
city into life. And then, at night, "a dead sepulchral silence seems to reign in
the deserted thoroughfares, where but a few hours ago the ear was distracted
by every variety of sounds." This "stillness so sudden and complete . . . has
a solemn suggestiveness," containing within itself the idea of death as the
"sudden and complete" surcease. The nature of the nineteenth-century city
was such that it invited and provoked such "solemn" contemplation, pre-

cisely because it included the elements of life and death within itself. This is not the silence of the countryside, in other words, where repose seems natural and unforced. The silence of London is an active element; it is filled with an obvious absence (of people, of business) and is therefore filled with presence. It is a teeming silence.

That is why it can actually awake the sleeper. An inhabitant of Cheapside was asked by a London reporter how he knew when it was past two in the morning. "He will tell you, as he has told us, that the silence of the City sometimes wakes him at that hour." Silence can sound like an alarm. Henry Mayhew noted the "almost painful silence that everywhere prevailed" in certain deserted London alleys, as if the absence of sound provoked mental or physical suffering. Silence can also be associated with what the poet James Thomson described as "the Doom of a City." Many images abound of silent stone. The City at night, "the city of the dead" as it has been called, has been seen to resemble "a prehistoric forest of stone." One writer within the great volumes of *London*, edited by Charles Knight and published in 1841, contemplated the city "with its streets silent and every house untenanted—how should we be excited and thrilled by so touching a sight!" The advent of this silence strangely excites him, as if it represents the erasure of all human energy.

The silence of the nineteenth-century city can induce an almost spiritual sense of transcendence; Matthew Arnold wrote some lines in Kensington Gardens, where peace and silence prevailed over "men's impious roar" and the "city's hum":

Calm Soul of all things! make it mine
To feel, amid the city's jar,
That there abides a peace of thine,
Man did not make, and cannot mar.

So the "soul of all things" is to be recognised within this silence. Charles Lamb considered it to be a token of all lost and past things, while others believed it to be an emanation or manifestation of that which is secret and hidden. The silence then becomes another aspect of what a contemporary critic has described as "London's unknowability." Certainly, in the nineteenth and twentieth centuries, there was an obscure fascination for what Julian Wolfreys in *Writing London* has called "the hidden court, the forgotten square, the unobserved portico" as if the mystery of London exists within its silence. It is the mystery which Whistler observed in his *Nocturnes*, and which generations of Londoners have encountered in silent streets and strange byways.

Fountain Court, in the Temple, is one such sacred spot that has survived until the beginning of the twenty-first century; its solace seems to be unchanging. The silence of Tower Hamlets cemetery, in the middle of the East End, is also profound and permanent; there is silence in the square by St. Alban the Martyr, off busy Holborn, and there is a sudden silence in Keystone Crescent off the Caledonian Road. There is the silence of Kerry Street in Kentish Town, of Courtenay Square off Kennington Lane, of Arnold Circus in Shoreditch. And then there is the silence of the outer suburbs, waiting to be born within the encroaching and approaching noise of London.

Perhaps these quarters of silence are necessary for the harmony of the city itself; perhaps it needs its antithesis in order properly to define itself. It is like the quiet of the dead upon whom London rests, the silence as a token of transience and eventual dissolution. So oblivion and wakefulness, silence and sound, will always accompany each other in the life of the city. As it is written in that great urban poem of the late nineteenth century, *The City of Dreadful Night*,

> Thus step for step with lonely sounding feet
> We travelled many a long dim silent street.

A Tudor depiction of the market of East Cheap; note the number of
butchers' shops, in a city where meat was at a premium.

CHAPTER 7

This Companye

※

he visitation of "the death" in the last months of 1348 destroyed 40 per cent of London's population. Perhaps 50,000 people died within the city. A decade later, one-third of the land within the walls remained uninhabited. It was called "the great pestilence" as well as "the death," and reoccurred with extraordinary virulence eleven years later. London (like most other European cities) remained under the threat of bubonic plague for the rest of the century. It was not an urban disease but it flourished in urban conditions; it was transmitted by rats, living in the straw and thatch of medieval dwellings, as well as by close respiratory proximity.

Yet London seems inured to disaster, and there is no evidence of any discontinuity in the history of this period. It was said that in the city itself there were not enough living to bury the dead but, for those who survived, the disease offered an unparalleled opportunity to thrive and flourish. Many, for example, became prosperous as a result of unexpected inheritance; while, for others, the demand for labour meant that their worth was greater than they had imagined. The late fourteenth century was a time when many families, those of labourers and merchants alike, moved from the neighbouring provinces to the great city in order to make their fortunes. From this period dates the apocryphal history of Dick Whittington, which once more spread the story of London as "Cockaigne" or the realm of gold.

The real Richard Whittington was a member of the mercers' guild, and London's history cannot properly be understood without also understanding the nature of those fraternities which combined the regulation of work with religious observances and parish duties. London may not have been recognised as a "city of god" upon the earth, but there were many late medieval theorists who believed that the city itself was the pattern of human existence as well as an emblem of human harmony.

There seem to have been trading guilds since the time of the Saxons, *gegildan*, later known as "frith guilds," which also possessed military or defensive functions. In the twelfth century certain traders, such as the bakers and the fishmongers, were allowed to collect their own taxes without being "farmed" or tolled by the royal administration. As part of a complementary, if not directly connected, process we find the various trades congregating in separate areas; the bakers were ensconced in Bread Street, while the fishmongers might be found in Friday Street (good Catholics ate no meat on Fridays).

The growth of craft guilds, located in a specific area, cannot be distinguished from the parish guilds of the same vicinity. The tanners who pursued their noisome craft along the banks of the River Fleet, for example, were accustomed to meet at their own "fraternity" in the Carmelite house in Fleet Street. By the late thirteenth century there were approximately two hundred fraternities in which craft regulation and religious observance were mingled. In the church of St. Stephen, Coleman Street, for example, three fraternities are recorded; while at St. James Garlickhythe there was a "litel companye" of joiners. It was a typically late medieval arrangement, which effectively allowed a self-regulating and self-sustaining community to prosper within the context of a rapidly developing city. In the early fourteenth century was issued a royal charter in which it was formally announced that no man might join a specific craft without the recommendation and security of six other members of that craft; a further stipulation decreed that only members of a craft might be admitted to the freedom of the city. Only citizens, in other words, could belong to a trade guild. In this fashion the guilds acquired enormous economic power within the city. One ordinance, for example, required that ale or beer could be bought only from freemen enfranchised in and inhabiting London.

But in London economic power in turn purchased political and social pre-eminence so that, in 1351 and again in 1377, the crafts themselves elected the Common Council of the city. It ought to be remembered, also, that there were "many craftes" and "mochel smale poeple" who would simply have met for business in their local church. The religious and social constraints of these trading "mysteries"—the word has no sacred significance, but comes from the French *métier*—are also implicit within the ordinances of the guilds themselves which emphasised the importance of honesty and good reputation. The rules of the fraternity of St. Anne at St. Laurence Jewry, for example, demanded that "yif any of the company be of wikked fame of his body and take othere wyues than his owene or yif he be a sengle man and be holde a comone lechour or contecour or rebell of his tonge" then he is to be admonished. After three such warnings, if unavailing, he is to be expelled so that "godemen of this companye ne be nat sclaundered bi cause of hym."

There are other aspects of these guild ordinances which reveal the very condition of the time. It is noted in the same rules that anyone who "vse hym to lye longe in bedde & atte risyng of his bed ne wil nat worcke to wynne his sustenaunce & kepe his house & go to the tavernne to the wyn to the ale to wrastelynge to schetynge," "schal be put of for euermore of this companye." Clearly the enjoyment of drink and what might now be termed "spectator sport" was not considered compatible with good working practice; the same admonitions against urban amusements were made by Daniel Defoe in his seventeenth-century manual on London trade. In a similar spirit there are injunctions against any who acquire an "euel name" as "theft or commune barettour or comune questmonger or meyntenour of quereles"; the guilds were here condemning those who breached public peace, as if the act of quarrelling or disputing might itself be construed as sinful in a community whose harmony was maintained only with great difficulty. The emphasis here is upon good standing, and the avoidance of shame among equals; it is typical of the regulations which "smale poeple" devised in order to protect their "good name" and therefore assist them in the remorseless pressure to move "upward" in the hierarchy of trades. That is why the ordinary workmen or "journeymen" sometimes tried to combine against their employers, but the city authorities were generally able to prevent any "union" of the lower workers. There came a time when the victualling and manufacturing trades were indeed engaged in bitter dispute about precedence and power, but it was essentially only a further stage in the continual restless and dissatisfied movement of those "lower" trades and professions who gradually pushed themselves forward into the social and political life of the city. This is the true history of London which lives and moves beneath the incidents and events of public record.

But no account of medieval London would be complete without an understanding of the elaborate and complicated manner in which the Church itself remained the single most disciplined and authoritative director of the city's affairs. In the simply material sphere, the administrators of the Church were the biggest landlords and employers both within and without the walls. Many thousands of people, both secular and spiritual, owed their livings to the great abbeys and monastic foundations of the city, but these large communities also owned ancient lands and manors beyond the jurisdiction of the city itself. The bishop of St. Paul's, for example, owned the manor of Stepney which stretched to the boundaries of Essex on the east and to Wimbledon and Barnes on the south-west; the canons of that establishment possessed thirteen other manors, ranging from Pancras and Islington to Hoxton and Holborn. This territorial power is a direct expression of secular, as well as spiritual, authority which dates from a very early period indeed; during the steady disintegration of Romanised England, and the dissolution of Roman London, these magnates of the Church had already become the true governing class of the country. The bishop of each province had taken on "the mantle of the Roman consul" and, in default of other public institutions, the parish church and the monastery became the centre of all organised activity. That is why the earliest administrative records of London emphasise the power of the Church authorities. In 900 we read that "the bishop and the reeves who belong to London make, in the name of citizens, laws which were confirmed by the king," and it was customary for priors and abbots also to become aldermen. There was no distinction between secular and spiritual power because both were seen as intrinsic aspects of the divine order.

London itself was a city of churches, containing a larger number than any other city in Europe. There were more than a hundred churches within the walls of the old City, sixteen alone devoted to St. Mary, and it can reasonably be inferred that many were originally of Saxon date and of wooden construction. In *London* Walter Besant has noted that "there was no street without its monastery, its convent garden, its college of priests, its friars, its pardoners, its sextons and its serving brothers." This may seem exaggerated but, although not every lane and alley contained a monastery or a convent garden, a look at any map will show that the main thoroughfares did indeed harbour religious institutions great and small. Beside the 126 parish churches there were thirteen conventual churches, including St. Martin's le Grand and the Priory of St. John of Jerusalem; there were seven great friaries, including the Carthusian friars of Hart Street; there were five priories, among them St. Bartholomew the Great in Smithfield and St. Saviour's in Bermondsey; there were four large nunneries and five priests' colleges. Of the hospitals and refuges, for the sick and the indigent, we have records of seventeen in areas as diverse as Bevis Marks and Aldgate, Charing Cross and St. Laurence Pountney (among them a refuge for the insane at Barking, and thus the phrase "barking mad"). This is not to mention the chantries, the church schools and the private chapels. It is a further indication of the sanctity of London that in the thirteenth and fourteenth centuries there was continual reconstruction of these sacred edifices. The piety of Londoners is not in doubt.

The evidence of medieval wills in London is of some consequence, and in the last testaments of John Toker, vintner (1428), of Robert Ameray, cordwainer (1410), of Richard Whyteman, wax-chandler (1428), and Roger Elmesley, wax-chandler's servant (1434), there are tokens of a simple but profound piety. In the details of these testaments there is all the paraphernalia of ordinary London life, with bequests of towels and spoons, beds and blankets; Roger Elmesley left an iron rack for roasting eggs as well as some peacock feathers and "my roller for a towell," but his main wish was that he be buried "vnder the stone with-oute the Dore of the porche" of St. Margaret Pattens in Little Tower Street. He was concerned also with the spiritual destiny of his godson, to whom he left "a prymmer for to serve god with," as well as "a litel cofur to putte in his smale thynges." All of these wills mention sums of money to be given to the poor, or the imprisoned, or the sick, on condition that these disadvantaged would then pray for the soul of the departed. John Toker the vintner, for example, gave various bequests to the priests of St. Mildred's in Bread Street "forto praie for my soule" with other moneys to be paid to the prisoners of "Ludgate, Marchalsie Kyngesbenche," as well as to the "pore folk lying sike in the spitell of our lady with-oute Bisshopes-gate, Oure lady of Bedlem, Oure lady of Elsingspitel, of Seynt Bathilmewys in Smythfeeld, And seint Thomas in Sowthwerk." Many of these institutions exist today, albeit in altered form, while others linger only in the folk memory of London. John Toker left to his apprentice Henry Thommissone "my mancion that is cleped the Mermaid in Bredstreet" which is the very same tavern where Shakespeare and Jonson were supposed to have drunk. The history of London is a palimpsest of different realities and lingering truths.

The patron saint of the medieval city was a seventh-century monk who ruled as the bishop of London: Erkenwald was the spiritual leader of the East Saxons for eighteen years and, after his death, many miracles were vouchsafed on his behalf. The wooden cart or litter upon which Bishop Erkenwald would travel through the streets of London, when age and sickness prevented him from walking through his diocese, became the centre of a cult. Fragments and splinters of this vehicle were credited with curative properties, and the litter was enshrined behind the main altar of St. Paul's with the relics of the saint himself. The physical remains of Erkenwald were sealed within a leaden casket which was fashioned "in the form of a gabled house or church," thus rendering in sacred space the physical topography of the city itself.

The cult of Erkenwald survived for many centuries, testifying once more to the piety or credulity of the citizens. There was a miracle at Stratford, where now an industrial park is sited by the River Lea, as well as many other reported wonders in the thoroughfares around St. Paul's itself. It was in fact something of a miracle that the physical remains of St. Erkenwald survived the various fires that visited the cathedral, most notably the great fire of 1087, after which the relics were placed in a silver shrine befitting *Lundoniae maxime sanctus*, "the most holy figure of London." We read of the servants of the abbey moving the body of the saint to yet another great shrine clandestinely by night, since its exposure during the day would have created hysteria among the crowd assembled. This devotion was not of the populace alone. Even in the early sixteenth century the shrine of St. Erkenwald was an object of pilgrimage to the most successful lawyers of London who, on being nominated as serjeants of law, would walk in procession to St. Paul's in order to venerate the physical presence of the saint.

Legends of dead saints may seem of little relevance, but they were part of the very texture of London life. The citizens when they first carried Erkenwald's body to the cathedral, declared: "We are like strong and vigorous men who will . . . undermine and overturn cities heavily fortified with men and weapons before we will give up the servant of God, our protector . . . we ourselves intend that such a glorious city and congregation should be strengthened and honoured by such a patron." There is indeed an Erconwald Street in the western part of the twenty-first-century city. So we may still name him as the patron saint of London, whose cult survived for over eight hundred years, before entering the temporary darkness of the last four centuries.

.   .   .

The medieval city can be understood in a variety of ways, therefore, whether in terms of its violence or its devotion, its commercial imperatives or its spiritual precepts. The bells of the church tolled the end of each trading day, and the traders' weights were tested and measured at the market cross. Could we say that the administrators of the Church in London were thoroughly secularised? Or that the citizens, avid for trade and capable of great savagery, were thoroughly spiritualised? The question lends absorbing interest to the lives of medieval Londoners. Perhaps the perpetual press of business and of domestic routine was viewed in the terms of eternity. Perhaps there was so much savagery because life itself, in contrast to the immortal soul, was considered to be relatively worthless. The city then becomes the true home of fallen humankind.

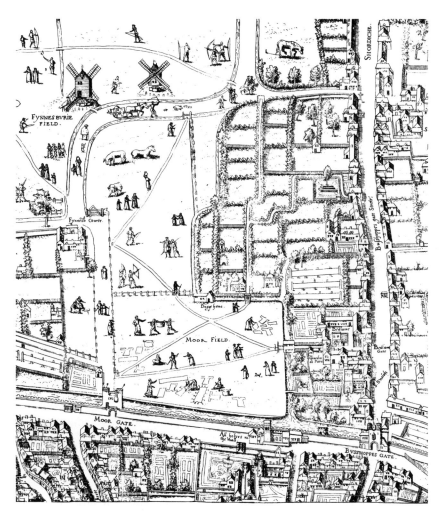

A mid-sixteenth-century map of Moorfields, north of London. Some women
dry linen upon the ground, while the citizens engage in archery. The line of
Bishopsgate Street marks the accelerating growth of the city.

CHAPTER 8

Rather Dark and Narrow

*J*ohn Stow, *the great sixteenth-century antiquarian,* offered the most vivid and elaborate description of Tudor London. He wrote of new streets and new buildings continually springing up beyond the walls and, within the city itself, of "encroachments on the highways, lanes, and common grounds." Where once there had been sheds or shops, in one of which an old woman used to sell "seeds, roots and herbs," there were now houses "largely built on both side outward, and also upward, some three, four or five stories high." Growth is the continual condition of the city, but one which Stow himself lamented when it encroached upon the ancient topography of the place which he had known as a child in Cordwainer Lane.

We can follow John Stow down Butchers' Alley, beside St. Nicholas Shambles and Stinking Lane, where he discoursed on the rising price of meat. In the old days, he said, a fat ox was sold for 26*s* 8*d* "at the most" and a fat lamb for a shilling, but "what the price is now I need not to set down." In such local touches, Stow stands alone among the chroniclers of the city. It was said that "he reporteth *res in se minutas,* toys and trifles, being such a smell-feast that he cannot pass by Guildhall, but his pen must taste of the good chear therein." But that is what makes him such an excellent London surveyor, and such a characteristic Londoner. In his *Survey of London*, he provides a detailed and immediate account of the lanes and alleys which he had known all his life.

He was born in 1525 and came from at least two generations of tallow chandlers who resided in Threadneedle or Threeneedle Street; Thomas Cromwell, Henry VIII's familiar councillor, encroached upon his father's garden there, and Stow ruefully noted "that the sudden rising of some men causeth them in some matters to forget themselves." Little is known of any formal education which Stow may have received, although it is likely that he attended one of London's free grammar schools. He himself recalled how he used to walk to a farm belonging to the nuns of the Minories where "I myself have fetched many a halfpenny worth of milk," thus indicating that there was grazing land by the very walls of the city. But of other juvenile incidents he is silent. It is known that he took up the profession of a tailor, however, and established himself in a house by the well at Aldgate close to the farm where he had bought milk as a child, but his true labours had not yet begun.

Antiquarian studies seem to be an instinctive London passion, and Stow remains their greatest exemplar. It is appropriate that his first work should be an edition of Chaucer; that fine London poet was Stow's original pursuit before he turned to the city which nourished his genius. He began the study of London records, primarily kept in the Guildhall, as a "fee'd chronicler"; we may imagine him among slips of parchment, manuscript rolls and broken-backed volumes, trying to decipher the history of his city. In one of his first volumes, *A Summarie of Englyshe Chronicles*, he wrote that "It is now eight years since I, seeing the confused order of our late English Chronicles, and the ignorant handling of ancient affairs, leaving mine own peculiar gains, consecrated myself to the search of our famous antiquities." This might suggest that he had abandoned his trade as a tailor in order to devote himself to historical study, but extant documents show that he maintained his business for some time. He complained about being called a "prick-louse," an invidious catchphrase for those who sewed as a profession, and he testified that a neighbour threw stones and tiles at his apprentice.

The "antiquities" were all around him. A few yards from his own house, between Billiter Lane and Lime Street, were buried a wall and gate of stone "about two fathoms deep" under the ground. They had been discovered after demolition work in 1590; Stow investigated the curiosity, and believed the old stonework to date from the reign of King Stephen some 450 years before. The ground of London was always rising, built again and again upon the ash and rubble of its previous incarnations. Stow walked everywhere, and once confessed that his labours "cost many a weary mile's travel, many a hard-earned penny and pound, and many a cold winter night's study." He was tall and lean, "of a pleasant and cheerful countenance; his sight and memory were good; very sober, mild, and courteous to any that required his instructions."

There was much to instruct since, in the early sixteenth century, London would indeed have been an antiquarian's delight. Stow often mentions the presence of great houses "of old time built upon arched vaults, and with gates of stone" which date from the eleventh and twelfth centuries; there would still have been extant walls, pillars and pavements from the Roman period. Much of the brick and masonry of that early time had been pillaged for modern re-building, but there is no doubt that there would have been evidence of the first century in succeeding periods of London's history. Yet much also was being destroyed even as Stow continued his survey. The Reformation of faith, inaugurated by Henry VIII, wreaked a sudden transformation upon the buildings as well as the beliefs of London. The fabric of the Roman communion, to which the citizens had so fervently attached themselves, was shattered; the uncertainty and bewilderment of Londoners were in turn embodied in the changing fabric of the city itself where monasteries and chantry chapels and lady chapels were vandalised or broken. The dissolution of the abbeys, churches and monastic hospitals in particular meant that the entire city was in a fevered period of demolition and construction. Parts of it would have resembled a vast building site, while other areas were left to slow neglect and in Stow's words became "sore decayed."

London was in many respects a place of ruins. Stow notes the remains of an "old court hall" in Aldermanbury Street, now "employed as a carpenter's yard." A mayor's great house in Old Jewry became in turn a synagogue, a house of friars, a nobleman's house, a merchant's house, and then a "wine tavern" known as the Windmill. A chapel became a "warehouse and shops towards the street, with lodgings over them," bishops' houses were turned into tenements, and so on. Other documentary sources reveal that a Cistercian house was pulled "clean down" and in its place were erected storehouses, tenements and "ovens for making ship's biscuit." The convent of the Poor Clares, known as the Minories, was destroyed to make way for storehouses; the church of the Crutched Friars became a carpenter's shop and a tennis court; the church of the Blackfriars was turned into a warehouse for the carts and properties of the "pageants." (It is perhaps appropriate that on this same site rose the Blackfriars Playhouse.) St. Martin's le Grand was pulled down and a tavern built upon its remains.

There are many other examples, but the salient point remains that after the Reformation much of late Tudor London was in a ruined condition, with walls and gateways and ancient stone windows to be glimpsed among the shops and houses which lined the lanes and thoroughfares. Even in the area outside the walls, where the palaces of the bishops and nobles had led down from the Strand towards the river, the grand houses were, according to the Venetian ambassador, "disfigured by the ruins of a multitude of churches and monasteries."

Yet even in the midst of lamentation there was also renovation. In Goldsmiths Row, between Bread Street and Cheapside Cross, Stow extols the shops and dwellings—built just thirty-five years before his birth—which are "beautified towards the street with the Goldsmith's arms . . . riding on monstrous beasts, all of which is cast in lead, richly painted over and gilt." A fifteenth-century traveller, Dominic Mancini, noted, in the same area, "gold and silver cups, dyed stuffs, various silks, carpets, tapestry." These are the true tinctures of Tudor London. An old church may be pulled down, but in its place Stow remarks that there has been erected "a fair strong frame of timber . . . wherein dwell men of divers trades." An old cross is removed, and on the same site is constructed a glistening water-conduit. An aristocratic dwelling is converted into a market "for the sale of woollen baize, watmols [coarse wool], flannels and such like." A stone building of great antiquity is gradually taken down and in its place are erected "divers fair houses."

This is the trade, and energy, of Tudor London. Stow himself, quint-essential Londoner as he is, cannot prevent himself from enumerating the gardens, the mills, the houses of stone and timber, the taverns, the conduits, the stables, the yards, the hostelries, the markets, the tenements and guild halls which comprise the city's life.

The older versions of the grand London house, established around a separate hall and courtyard, were no longer appropriate to the new conditions of the city; they were built over, or encroached upon, by smaller dwellings in streets which were already acquiring a reputation for being "rather dark and narrow." Even the mansions of the wealthy merchants were now more compact, with a shop and warehouse on the ground floor, a hall and parlour on the first floor and the other living quarters above; it was not uncommon for such a house to rise to five or six storeys, with two rooms on each level, in the customary timber and mortar fashion. Such was the premium upon space in the bustling city that cellars and garrets were utilised as dwellings for the poor. Estimates of population can only be approximate but there are figures of 85,000 by 1565, rising to 155,000 by 1605; this does not include those who lived in "the liberties" or within "the bars," which would increase the figures by more than 20,000. It represents, to use a perhaps anachronistic phrase, a population explosion.

The price of property had risen so steeply that no one would willingly demolish even the smallest shop or house. So the growth of the city meant that the ancient ditches, used for both defence and refuse, were now filled in and covered over and became the site of more properties. The main roads leading to the city gates were "improved" and paved, so that within a very short time shops and houses were erected beside them. The road to Aldgate, for example, was, according to Stow, "not only fully replenished with buildings outward" but "also pestered with divers alleys on either side to the bars." Even the fields beyond the city, where once the younger citizens had shot their arrows or walked among the streams, had "now within a few years made a continual building throughout of garden houses and small cottages, and the fields on either side turned into garden plots, tenter yards, bowling alleys, and such like."

The overcrowding became so serious that, in 1580, Elizabeth I issued a proclamation "perceiving the state of the city of London (being anciently termed her chamber) and the suburbs and confines thereof to increase slowly, by access of people to inhabit the same" so that there was no chance of sustaining "victual food, and other like necessaries for man's life, upon reasonable prices, without which no city can long continue." There was further cause for alarm concerning the overpopulation within the city itself "where there are such great multitudes of people brought to inhabit in small rooms, whereof a great part are seen very poor, yea, such as must live begging, or by worse means, and they heaped up together, and in a sort smothered with many families of children and servants in one house or small tenement." This is one of the earliest accounts of overcrowding in London, and can be considered the first extended version of a description which has haunted the city ever since. The queen's remedy was to prohibit "any new buildings of any house or tenement within three miles from any of the gates of the said city of London." It has been suggested that this was the first venture at a "green belt" around London, a surmise which would at least have the merit of emphasising the historical continuity within all apparently "modern" plans for the city, but it was more likely to be an attempt to protect the trading and commercial monopoly of the citizens within the walls who did not relish the appearances of trades and shops beyond their jurisdiction.

Another aspect of the proclamation is also of some significance, in that passage where the monarch and her city advisers prohibit "any more families than one only to be placed, or to inhabit from henceforth in any house that hereto fore hath been inhabited." The idea of one family occupying one house was indeed the stated purpose behind much of the city's development in the seventeenth and eighteenth centuries; it has even been considered a peculiarly London solution. It is peculiar to the city because it is historical in spirit; as S.E. Rasmussen put it in *London: The Unique City*, the Elizabethan remedy represented a "conservative clinging to the medieval form of housing." In a similar spirit new building was only allowed if it were raised "on old foundations." Here we have an inkling of that continuity, and sense of permanence, which London still exemplifies.

It did not, however, work. Within three years of Elizabeth's proclamations the city authorities were lamenting the continual increase in sheds, lodgings and tenements outside the walls. There were further edicts and orders issued at regular intervals throughout the reign of her successors; none of them was ever obeyed, and none of them was in the least successful at controlling the growth of the city.

The truth is that the growth of London could not, and cannot, be controlled. It spread to the east along the high street of Whitechapel, and to the west along the Strand. It spread north to Clerkenwell and Hoxton; to the south, Southwark and its environs became "pestered," to use Stow's word, with places of popular resort, taverns, brothels, pleasure grounds and theatres. In turn the Inns of Court, clustered in the "suburbs" of Holborn between the city and the royal palaces of Westminster, were extended and embellished.

Yet the quality of transport from suburb to city was not always of the best. In the latter years of the reign of Henry VIII the high road between the Temple "and the village of Charing," now known as the Strand, was noted in the Rolls of Parliament to be "full of pits and sloughs, very perilous . . . very noyous and foul, and in many places thereof very jeopardous to all people passing and repassing, as well on horseback as on foot." More modern forms of transportation, however, were not necessarily welcomed. The introduction of hackney coaches, known as "chariots" or "whirlicotes," led Stow to reflect that "the world runs on wheels with many whose parents were glad to go on foot."

The state of traffic in the capital was a source of constant complaint in the sixteenth century, as it has become for each generation. Stow again noted "the number of cars, drays, carts and coaches, more than hath been accustomed, the streets and lanes being straitened, must needs be dangerous, as daily experience proveth"—dangers not tempered when coachmen lashed their horses forward without checking what was behind them and inebriated drivers quarrelled frequently and violently in the street over who had right of passage. And there was the noise "where even the very earth quakes and trembles, the casements shatter, tatter, and clatter."

There was, however, a significant improvement in the conditions of urban living at least for those who could afford the new "luxuries" of city life. There were pillows and bedding where there had once lain a log and a straw pallet; even the poorer citizens dined off pewter rather than wood and the "middling" households might boast of wall-coverings, brass, soft linen, cupboards garnished with plate, jars and pots made from green glazed earthenware. There was also a fashion for brick and stone chimneys, which in turn had an effect both upon the appearance and atmosphere of London.

The city had forfeited some of its independence to Parliament and to the sovereign, even to the extent of accepting Henry VIII's recommendations for the mayoralty, but in turn it had become the recognised capital of a unified nation. The municipal ideal had been displaced by a national ideal—and how could it not be so in a city which was now largely populated by immigrants? The new arrivals came from every area of England, Cornwall to Cumberland (it has been estimated that one-sixth of all Englishmen became Londoners in the second half of the sixteenth century), and the number of foreign immigrants rose at an accelerating pace, making the city truly cosmopolitan. So high was the mortality, and so low the birth rate, that without this influx of traders and workers the population would in fact have steadily declined. Yet instead it continued to expand, with brewers and book-binders from the Low Countries, tailors and embroiderers from France, gun-makers and dyers from Italy, weavers from the Netherlands and elsewhere. There was an African or "Moor" in Cheapside who made steel needles without ever imparting the secret of his craft. Fashion followed population, just as the populace followed fashion. In the reign of Elizabeth I (1558–1603) there was a surfeit of silk shops, selling everything from gold thread to silk stockings, and at the time of her accession it was reported that no country gentleman could "be content to have eyther cappe, coat, doublet, hose or shirt . . . but they must have their geare from London."

If London had become the centre of fashion, it had also become the centre of death. Mortality was higher than in any other part of the country, the two great harvesters being the plague and the sweating sickness. In poorer parishes life expectancy was only between twenty and twenty-five years, while in the richer it rose to thirty or thirty-five years. These fatal infections confirm the evident truth that sixteenth-century London remained a city of the young. The greatest proportion of the citizens were under the age of thirty, and it is this actuarial statistic which helps to explain the energy and restlessness of urban life in all its forms.

The most striking example comes from within the turbulent body of the apprentices, a peculiarly London phenomenon of young men who were bound by strict articles of agreement and yet managed to retain a high-spiritedness and almost feverish buoyancy which spilled over into the streets. They "wold ether bee at the taverne, filling their heads with wine, or at the Dagger in Cheapeside cramming their bellies with minced pyes; but above al other times it was their common costome, as London prentises use, to follow their maisters upon Sundays to the Church dore and then to leave them, and hie unto the taverne." There are reports of various fights and "affrays," the common victims being foreigners, "night-walkers," or the servants of noblemen who were considered to take on the airs of their superiors. A declaration, in 1576, warned apprentices not to "misuse, molest, or evil treat any servant, page, or lackey of any nobleman, gentleman, or other going in the streets." There were often disturbances after football matches and three young men were put in the local prison for "outrageously and riotously behaving themselves at a football play in Cheapside." But drunken high spirits could turn into something more violent, and threatening. Apprentices as well as artisans and children took part in the "evil May-day" riots of 1517, in which the houses of foreigners were ransacked. In the last decade of the sixteenth century there were still more outbreaks of riot and disorder but, unlike other continental cities, London never became unstable or ungovernable.

The accounts of foreign travellers suggest the unique status of London in this period. A Greek visitor reported that the treasures in the Tower were "said to exceed the anciently famed wealth of Croesus and Midas," while a Swiss medical student reported that "London is not said to be in England, but rather

England to be in London." There was a standard guided tour for visitors, who were first taken to the Tower and the Royal Exchange before being escorted to the west, with Cheapside, St. Paul's, Ludgate and the Strand viewed, before a magnificent arrival at Westminster and Whitehall. The roads were unpaved in parts, but a journey on horse was still sometimes preferable to that upon the Thames. Giordano Bruno, spy and magician, has left a graphic account of his attempts to hire the services of a wherry. He and his companions, wishing to travel to Westminster, spent a great deal of time looking for a boat and vainly crying out "Oars!" At last a boat arrived with two elderly boatsmen—"After much question and reply as to whence, where, why, how and when, they brought the prow to the foot of the stairs." The Italians believed they were at last on their way to the destination but then, after about a third of the journey had been completed, the boatsmen began to row towards the shore. They had reached their "station," and would go no further. This is a small incident, of course, but it reveals the rudeness and obstinacy which was seen by strangers to be characteristic of London behaviour. Just as typical, perhaps, is Bruno's arrival on the shore only to find a footpath thick with mud where he was forced to journey through "a deep and gloomy hell."

Other reports emphasise both the violence and xenophobia of ordinary Londoners. A French physician, in London between 1552 and 1553, observed that "the common people are proud and seditious . . . these villains hate all sorts of strangers" and even "spit in our faces." Gangs of apprentices were also likely to set upon foreigners in the street, and one traveller saw a Spaniard being forced to take refuge in a shop from a mob after he dared to wear his national costume. The Swiss medical student was in that respect perhaps too kind when he mentioned that "the common people are still somewhat coarse and uncultured . . . and believe that the world beyond England is boarded off."

Yet the city also lives in its details gathered in these foreign accounts. One traveller noted that it was remarkable for the number of kites which were "quite tame" and wandered through the streets as if they owned them; they were the city's scavengers and the butchers threw out offal for them to consume. The number of butchers' shops was matched only by the number of taverns. A passion for privacy was also noted, with individual dwellings separated from their neighbours by walls of stone; the same conditions applied in the taverns themselves, where wooden partitions were set up "so that one table cannot overlook the next." It may be that in a teeming and overcrowded city such attempts at privacy were natural or inevitable, yet they also represent a significant and permanent aspect of the London character.

In other accounts "between meals one sees men, women, and children always munching through the streets." The same children, when not eating apples and nuts, could be seen "gathering up the blood which had fallen through the slits in the scaffold" after a beheading on Tower Hill. The executioner on this occasion wore a white apron "like a butcher." We seem to have come full circle in a city dominated by violence, blood, meat and continual consuming appetite.

CHAPTER 9

Packed to Blackness

There was once a *Dark Lane*, in the medieval city; a tavern was erected there, known as the Darkhouse. That narrow thoroughfare was then renamed Dark House Lane, and is to be seen on eighteenth-century maps of London. On the same site there now stands Dark House Wharf, which is dominated by the headquarters of the Bank of Hong Kong. This building is clad in dark blue steel and dark, tinted glass. So does the city maintain its dark secret life.

Dust, mud, soot, slime and smut were the objects of continual dissatisfaction. "Though a chamber be never so closely locked up," John Evelyn complained in the seventeenth century, "men find at their return all things that are in it evenly covered with a black thin soot." In the same century a Venetian chaplain described "a sort of soft and stinking mud which abounds here at all seasons, so that the place more deserves to be called *Lorda* (filth) than *Londra* (London)." The "filth of the city" was also depicted as being "rich and black as thick ink." In the eighteenth century the road outside Aldgate "resembled a stagnant lake of deep mud," while in the Strand the puddles of filth were three or four inches deep so that they "fill coaches when their windows happen not to be up, and bedaub all the lower parts of the houses." If they were not strewn with mud, the streets were filled with dust. Even in the mid-nineteenth century, according to the *Quarterly Review*, there was not a man or woman in London "whose skin and clothes and nostrils are not of necessity more or less loaded with a compound of powdered granite, soot, and still more nauseous substances." It was said that St. Paul's Cathedral had a right to be blackened because it was built with a tax upon sea coal, but it was hard upon the animals of the city which were similarly affected by the smoke and dirt; the feathers of the redstarts and the martins were suffused with soot, while the dust of London was believed to clog the breathing and dull the senses of the omnipresent spiders. All creatures were affected and, as a late twentieth-century character in Iris Murdoch's novel *The Black Prince* puts it, "I could feel the thick filth and muck of London under my feet, under my bottom, behind my back."

Yet it is more than material filth. There is a drawing of Fish Street Hill by George Scharf, executed in the late 1830s, as accomplished and as detailed as all his work. But in the foreground a vast shadow obscures the people and the house-fronts; it is in fact the outline of the Monument, otherwise concealed from sight, but in that shadow Scharf has somehow managed to depict something of the nature of London itself. It has always been a shadowy city.

As James Bone, the author of *The London Perambulator*, remarked in 1931, it resides in "the appearance of great shadows where there can be no shadows, throwing blackness up and down." This is also the London vision of Verlaine, who writes of "*l'odieuse obscurité . . . quel deuil profond, quelles ténèbres!*" within "*la monstrueuse cité.*" Much of the slate used in London building is striated by what geologists term "pressure shadows" but they are inconspicuous beside the blackened surfaces of Portland stone. One foreign traveller remarked that the streets of London were so dark that the citizenry seemed to delight in playing "hide and seek" with the light, like children in a wood, while in the summer of 1782 Charles Moritz noted that "the houses in general struck me as if they were dark and gloomy." The gloom affected him profoundly: "At that moment I could not in my own mind compare the external view of London with that of any other city I had ever before seen."

There were almost a score of Dirty Alleys, Dirty Hills and Dirty Lanes in the medieval city; there were Inkhorn Courts and Foul Lanes and Deadman's Places. Lombard Street in the City, at the centre of capitalist imperialism, was a notoriously dark street. At the beginning of the nineteenth century its brick was so blackened with smoke that the walls resembled the mud in the road. Today, in the twenty-first century, it is still just as narrow and just as dark, its stone walls constantly echoing to the sound of hurried footsteps. It is still close to what a century ago Nathaniel Hawthorne called "the black heart of London." Hawthorne's compatriot Henry James also noticed the "deadly darkness" but he revelled in it as if he were a "born Londoner." In the 1870s Hippolyte Taine simply found the darkness "horrible"; the houses from a distance looked "like ink-stains on blotting paper" while from a closer vantage the "tall, flat straight façades are of dark brick." The darkness of London seems to have entered Taine's soul with his crepuscular invocations of "a bone-black factory" which is a London dwelling, of "porticoes foul with soot . . . every crevice inked in . . . long ranks of blind windows . . . the fluting of the columns full of greasy filth, as if sticky mud had been set flowing down there."

There were others who were intimate with this darkness. In his account of nineteenth-century Whitechapel, Charles Booth, the sympathetic chronicler of *The Life and Labour of the People of London*, mentions that the tables of the poor are "fairly black" with thick swarms of flies congregating on every available surface while, in the streets outside, at the level of the hip, "is a broad dirty mark, showing where the men and lads are in the constant habit of standing."

Charles Booth's images of disease and torpor somehow increase the darkness of the capital, as the very embodiment of those shadows which the rich and powerful cast upon the dispossessed and the disadvantaged. The effect of the industrial revolution, although less noticeable in London than in some of the northern manufacturing towns, deepened those shadows. The growth of factories as well as small workshops, and the increasing demand for coal in a city which by the beginning of the eighteenth century was already the manufacturing centre of Europe, only intensified London's characteristic darkness.

In another sense its darkness suggests secrecy, and the titles of many accounts of the city confirm that sense of concealment, among them *Unknown London, its Romance and Tragedy*, *The London Nobody Knows* and *London in Shadow*. And yet that secrecy is of its essence. When Joseph Conrad described the city "half lost in night," in *The Secret Agent* (1907), he was echoing Charles Dickens's remark seventy years before in *Sketches by Boz* that "the streets of London, to be beheld in the very height of their glory, should be seen on a dark dull murky winter's night." The tone is ironic but the meaning is by no means so. In his last completed work Dickens returned to it in his description of "a black shrill city . . . a gritty city . . . a hopeless city, with no vent in the leaden canopy of its sky." Darkness is of the city's essence; it partakes of its true identity; in a literal sense London is possessed by darkness.

CHAPTER 10

Maps and Antiquarians

*T*he history of London is represented by the history of its maps. They can be seen as symbolic tokens of the city, and as attempts to picture its disorder in terms of fluent and harmonious design. From the first great copperplate map of the mid-sixteenth century to the "Underground" map of the late twentieth century, the mapping of London represents an attempt to understand the chaos and thereby to mitigate it; it is an attempt to know the unknowable.

That is why the first map, from which John Stow himself borrowed, has always been a source of wonder and curiosity. It is inscribed upon copper plates by an unknown hand, but all the evidence suggests that this carefully prepared map was commissioned by Queen Mary I. In its complete form (only three fragments remain) it would have been some eight feet in width and five feet in depth, covering the entire area of city and suburbs. It is in certain respects extraordinarily detailed: the very scales of Leadenhall Market are depicted, together with the dog-kennels in some of the gardens; the position of a tree or the number of buckets by a well are faithfully recorded; shirts and bed linen lie stretched out to dry in Moor Field, while games of musketry and archery are conducted in the neighbouring pastures. The churches and monastic remains are also visible, many of them rendered in such detail that we may distinguish between wood and stone. When Shakespeare's John of Gaunt compared the sea around England with "a moat defensive to a house," we now know that his audience, coming to the Theatre, by Shoreditch, had passed just such a moated house on the road out of London through Finsbury Fields. Since this copperplate is also the original upon which most other maps of sixteenth- and early seventeenth-century London are based, in its lineaments we may find the most lucid and significant outline of the city.

In certain respects, however, the map inevitably strays from accuracy. The actual warren of passages and alleyways is ignored in order to display the principal lanes and streets; the city has in that respect been cleansed. The number and variety of houses are also neglected in order to create a more uniform and pleasing appearance. The citizens depicted at work or at play are in turn of an unnatural size, suggesting that the cartographer wished to emphasise the human dimension of the city. Nevertheless it is a beautiful feat of engraving, and it is no accident that it did become the source and inspiration for maps completed some years later.

One coloured map of mid-Tudor London, for example, which is known as the "Braun and Hogenberg," is a smaller copy of the great original. Here the city is given compact form and, although it is by no means a spiritualised shape, it is in instinctive harmony with its surroundings; the skiffs and wherries ply their river trade in graceful formation, while the main thoroughfares themselves seem to mimic the natural passage of the water. It depicts the "fair city" of contemporary report, but it also has one other significant aspect; in the foreground, quite out of proportion, stand four Londoners. An older man is dressed in the robes of a merchant, with cap and fur-trimmed coat, while upon his right hand stands his apprentice wearing a short coat like a doublet as well as sword and buckler; the merchant's wife is dressed in a simple blue gown over a Spanish farthingale while her maid is plainly attired in gown and apron. These are modest figures but they stand upon a hill above London as the true representatives of the city. The map itself can be seen as an advertisement of London's mercantile power, with the vessels on the Thames behind the four Londoners depicting its status as a port.

In similar spirit the two great "panoramas" of London, before the Fire of 1666 utterly destroyed its appearance, take the river as the leading spirit of their design. Anthony van den Wyngaerde's riverine views of the mid-seventeenth century have been eclipsed by Hollar's panorama of 1647, but Wyngaerde's study has the merit of showing the bustling life of the Thames. Some row, while others fish. Travellers wait at Stargate Horse Ferry, while others make their way up Southwark High Street towards London Bridge.

Of course Hollar's more powerfully executed engraving is perhaps the most beautiful and harmonious of all London panoramas. In his work, London has become a world city of which the horizons are scarcely visible. The artist takes his stand upon the roof of St. Mary Overie by Bankside, so that in the foreground of the engraving are great clusters of roofs and house-fronts by the entrance to London Bridge. The chimneys and windows, the rooftops of tile and wood, suggest the massive presence of a city already congregating by its southern mouth; on the Thames there are almost eighty great vessels as well as innumerable smaller craft, the river itself forming a great sheath of light and space which lends London a monumental aspect. There are more intimate details on the southern bank where, among the throng of roofs and chimneys, Hollar has opened up two short vistas of the streets. A dog can be seen, a man on horseback, couples wandering, here and there a solitary figure, all fixed for ever as part of the pattern of London. From Hollar's high vantage a walled garden can be observed and, beyond it, two circular buildings labelled "The Globe" and "Beere bayting" respectively. Beyond them lie fields, where horses are grazing. On the other side of the Thames there is a forest of rooftops and church spires; although that of St. Paul's had been destroyed by a thunderstorm some eighty years before, the cathedral church still dominates the skyline of the city. It rises above the streets and wharves, where people can be seen working or waiting for transport. There is continuous building eastwards from the Tower to Shadwell, while the line of the city is prolonged westward to Whitehall. The effect is that of great activity caught in majestic perspective, with the city arrayed in glory. The panorama is completed by various classical deities who, as it were, introduce and applaud the scene from the wings; the figure of Apollo hovers just above St. Paul's.

It is perhaps the finest ever representation of London, and certainly the greatest image of the city before the Great Fire of 1666. Later maps by Norden, as well as Newcourt and Faithorne, in style and spirit reflect the first great copperplate map. Similarly, the familiar map of the London Underground today still completes and complements the one first designed with such clarity of purpose in 1933. The original Underground map bears only approximate relation to the location of lines and stations, but it is so aesthetically pleasing that its lineaments have never been changed.

In 1658 Wenceslaus Hollar completed a further etching, of the western aspect of the city. We observe that still more areas of fields and stiles and country lanes have been replaced by squares and piazzas and dwellings. Some of these houses are several storeys high, others on a smaller scale, but all reflect a pleasing symmetry which did not in fact exist. Another theme obtrudes, at least in retrospect. The streets and open areas are devoid of figures or any depiction of active life—the city had already grown too large to register even the symbolic presence of its citizens—and so it seems like some great empty place waiting silently for its destruction in the Great Fire.

The extent of that destruction can be see in another engraving by Hollar; it was completed in 1667, and depicts the razed city as more than four hundred acres of whitened contours. The ruins of the churches, prisons and main public buildings are sketched in, but the rest is empty space encroached upon by dark clusters of building which had escaped the flames.

Within days of that Fire, however, various speculative maps of a new London were being completed. These were visionary schemes. To a certain extent they resemble the structure of planned cities such as Paris and New York which were to be laid out grandly in the nineteenth century. Many of these seventeenth-century designs for London incorporated grid systems of intersecting thoroughfares, with great avenues linking majestic public edifices. Wren and Evelyn conceived of a humane and civilised city built upon a preordained pattern, while some of their contemporaries presented mathematically ingenious systems of roads and squares. These noble plans could not work, and they did not work. The very nature of the city defeated them: its ancient foundations lie deeper than the level at which any fire might touch, and the spirit of the place remained unscathed.

London is not a civilised nor a graceful city, despite the testimony of the maps. It is tortuous, inexact and oppressive. It could never be laid out again with mathematic precision, in any case, because the long history of streets and estates meant that there was a bewildering network of owners and landlords with their own especial claims or privileges. This is a social and topographical fact, but it in turn suggests a no less tangible aspect of London. It is a city built upon profit and speculation, not upon need, and no mayor or sovereign could withstand its essential organic will.

That is why the map of reconstructed London, published ten years after the Fire, shows the city restored approximately to its original state. One new thoroughfare has been built, the new King Street and the new Queen Street leading to the Guildhall from the river, but the congerie of streets around it—Milk Street, Wood Street, Aldermansbury, Old Jewry, and all the rest—have

sprung up again. Thoroughfares were widened after more stringent fire pre-
cautions and building regulations were applied, but the essential topography
of the neighbourhood was revived.

There was one other change. The surveyors of this post-Fire map, John
Ogilby and William Morgan, had declared that they would chart "all Bye-
streets and Lanes, all Courts and Allies, all Churches and Church-yards" by
scientific principles of "Mesuration and Plotting" with theodolites and "cir-
cumferentors." So for the first time the city became susceptible to scientific
measurement, with the result that it could no longer be depicted as an aesthetic or harmonious whole. Paradoxically it then became fragmented,
chaotic, unknowable. The twenty sheets of this topographical survey are
covered by rectangles and numbers—"i 90 . . . B69 . . . C54"—which are designed to expedite identification, but the general effect is one of bewildering
complexity. When London is seen in terms of abstract size and measurement,
it becomes unimaginable.

There was, instead, a vogue for guidebooks which rendered London intimate
and identifiable—among them Couch's *Historical Remarques and Observations*
of 1681, de Laune's *The Present State of London* and Colsoni's *Le Guide de
Londres* of 1693. They were complemented by such volumes as *The Antiquities of London and Westminster*, with accounts of the town-ditch, the gates, the
schools, hospitals, churches and wards.

By the eighteenth century there was an efflorescence of those books
which emphasise "whatever is most remarkable for GRANDEUR, ELE-
GANCE, CURIOSITY OR USE." There were others designed to aid visitors, or new residents, as to the way in which they should conduct themselves
in the city. One, for example, suggests that should a carrier of a sedan chair
behave unmannerly, "take the Number of the Chair, as you do of a Hackney
Coach, and complaining at the office abovementioned, the Commissioners
will correct their Insolence." *The London Adviser and Guide* of 1790 offers
similar advice, with the note that common people will be charged one shilling
for swearing in the street and that every gentleman will face the higher
penalty of five shillings. The number of convictions is not mentioned.

The next attempt at a comprehensive cartography, undertaken by John
Roque, in 1783, emphasises the problems that were now inevitably encountered; trigonometrical measurements of the streets did not align with actual measurements, and street names were thoroughly confused. The project
took seven years to finish and, in the process, Roque himself came close to

bankruptcy. The plan itself was of enormous size and the publishers suggested that it be placed on a "Roller" so that "it will not interfere with any other Furniture." Yet it is by no means a complete survey. It omits certain smaller or inconsiderable features, place names are missing, and there has been no effort to include individual buildings. This is hardly surprising in a map covering some ten thousand acres of built land, and the publishers were tactful enough to encourage subscribers to point out "Inaccuracies and Omissions." So it remains in many respects an impressionistic survey, with the actual lanes, tenements and shops reduced to a fine grey shading; it has an "enduring enchantment," according to the authors of *The History of London in Maps*, but it is the enchantment of distance.

At the end of the eighteenth century the largest map ever printed in England conveyed what seemed to be, even then, the immensity of London. Richard Horwood's map was ninety-four feet square, and contained street numbers as well as names and houses. The project continued for nine years but four years after its publication Horwood, tired and careworn, died at the age of forty-five. Some of the inevitable difficulties he encountered can be measured by changes in four different editions. Within the space of thirteen years the fields adjacent to Commercial Road were gradually filled with houses and terraced streets. In the space of twenty years the number of houses in Mile End had tripled. The persistent and steady growth of London, in a sense, had killed its map-maker.

Horwood's aim was largely utilitarian. The enterprise was sponsored by the Phoenix Fire Insurance office, one of the city's most significant institutions, and was advertised as indispensable "in bringing Ejectments or Actions, in leasing or conveying Premises etcetera." In that, it proved successful, if only because every subsequent attempt at conveying the specific houses or buildings of the city was engulfed by its sheer immensity. The first Ordnance Survey of London completed in 1850, for example, comprised some 847 sheets; it was greatly reduced for publication but then proved to be on too small a scale to be useful for travellers and inhabitants alike. This and later maps of mid- and late Victorian London simply display lines of streets linked together, with shading used indiscriminately to represent the shops, offices, houses, tenements and public buildings.

These are the direct predecessors of the contemporary *A to Z* gazetteer in which hundreds of pages are needed to chart a city which cannot be recognised or understood in terms of one central image. The begetter of the *A to*

Z, Phyllis Pearsall, entranced by London's immensity, compiled the first edition in the mid-1930s by "rising at five and walking for 18 miles per day." She covered 3,000 miles of streets, and completed 23,000 entries which she kept in shoeboxes beneath her bed. Michael Hebbert, the author of *London*, has revealed that the maps "were drawn by a single draughtsman, and Pearsall herself compiled, designed and proof-read the book." No publisher was interested, however, until she delivered copies on a wheelbarrow to a W.H. Smith buyer. By the time of her death, in 1996, the number of London streets had risen to approximately 50,000.

The nineteenth-century city, already seeming too vast for comprehension, was sometimes plotted in terms of theme or subject. There were "cab-fare maps" outlining the distance which could be travelled for a certain fare, maps of street improvements with the renovated thoroughfares outlined in vivid red, maps of the "modern plague of London" which marked each public house with a red spot, and maps displaying the incidence of death by cholera. Maps of the underground railway, of trams, and of other forms of modern transport soon followed so that London became a city of maps, one laid upon another like an historical palimpsest. It never ceased to grow and, in the process, glowed perpetually with various colours—those of death, alcohol and poverty competing with those of improvements and railways.

"Up to this time," *Henry James* wrote in 1869, "I have been crushed under a sense of the mere magnitude of London—its inconceivable immensity—in such a way as to paralyse my mind for any appreciation of details." Yet for the true antiquarian of London those details live and survive within the memory, beyond the reach of any plan or survey. "In my youth," John Stow wrote in the sixteenth century, "I remember, devout people, as well men as women of this city, were accustomed oftentimes, especially on Fridays, weekly to walk that way [to Houndsditch] purposely there to bestow their charitable alms; every poor man or woman lying in their bed within their window, which was towards the street, open so low that every man might see them." It is a distinct and striking image, in a city of spectacle and ritual. And then again: "I remember within this fifty four years Malmsey not to be sold more than one penny halfpenny the pint." Memory here must complete the task of observation, if only "to stop the tongues of unthankful men, such as used to ask, Why have ye not noted this, or that? and give no thanks for what is done."

Stow remains the guardian spirit of all those Londoners who came after him, filled with their own memories of time passing and time gone. There is Charles Lamb wandering through the Temple in the early 1820s, noting "what an antique air had the now almost effaced sun-dials, with their moral inscriptions, seeming coevals with that Time which they measured"; these were "my oldest recollections." A decade later Macaulay spoke of a coming time when the citizens of London, "ancient and gigantic as it is, will in vain seek, amidst new streets, and squares, and railway stations for the site of that dwelling" which was in their youth the centre of their lives or destinies. Leigh Hunt, in *The Town* of 1848, observed of the city, "nor perhaps is there a single spot in London in which the past is not visibly present to us, either in the shape of some old buildings or at least in the names of the streets." At the very beginning of the nineteenth century a London journalist known as "Aleph" wandered down Lothbury, recalling its previous "tortuous, dark vista of lofty houses" lit only by oil-lamps; since Aleph's journey it has changed many times, yet it still remains unique and identifiable, most particularly with its recurrent "darkness" and "loftiness."

It has been said that no stone ever leaves London but is reused and redeployed, adding to that great pile upon which the city rests. The paradox here is of continual change and constant underlying identity; it is at the core of the antiquarian passion for a continually altering and expanding city which nevertheless remains an echo chamber for stray memories and unfulfilled desires. That is perhaps why, as V.S. Pritchett noted in the late 1960s, "London has the effect of making one feel personally historic." "It is strange," he once wrote, "that although London wipes out its past, the Londoner does not quite forget." Every journey through the streets of London can then become a journey into the past, and there will always be Londoners who thrill to that past like an obsession. In the early 1920s another London visionary, Arthur Machen, walked through Camden Town and found himself witnessing like a revenant the city of 1840, with pony gigs and dimly lit interiors, all of it conjured up by the sudden glimpse of a "little coach-house and the little stables; and all a vision of a mode of life that has passed utterly away."

Until recent years it was possible to find inhabitants of Bermondsey who were, in the words of one reporter, "enthralled by the history of their borough." It is a genuine London passion. Where Thomas Hardy could hear "the voice of Paul" in ancient stones exhibited within the British Museum, Londoners hear the voices of all those who came before them in the smallest houses and meanest streets. Charles Lamb remembered a cashier in the

South-Sea House, Mr. Evans, who was eloquent "in relation to old and new London—the site of old theatres, churches, streets gone to decay—where Rosamond's pond stood—the Mulberry Gardens—and the Conduit in Cheap." The author of *Highways and Byways in London*, Mrs. E.T. Cook, stood upon Westminster Bridge in a winter's twilight, when "as the light faded, and the mist rose, I seemed to lose the forms of the modern buildings, and to see, as though in a vision, the 'Thorney Isle' of the dim past." Yet even as this early twentieth-century observer sees intimations of the eighth century, her meditations are broken by a beggarwoman's plea for money. "I ain't got a place ter sleep in this night. Gawd knows I ain't, dear lydy." Past and present collide in a thousand different forms. When Rose Macaulay visited the wilderness of a bomb-site in the Second World War, she had an intimation of "the primeval chaos and old night which had been before Londinium was." In the preceding century Leigh Hunt observed that St. Paul's Churchyard was "a place in which you may get the last new novel, and find remains of the ancient Britons and of the sea." Despite his fear of the city's immensity Henry James himself experienced "the ghostly sense, the disembodied presences of the old London." There is a foot-tunnel under the Thames, linking Greenwich with the Isle of Dogs, which seems to harbour something of its mystery; for Stephen Graham, the author of the lachrymose *London Nights*, it "told of an enigma which would never be solved; the enigma of London's sorrow, her burden, her slavery."

There have always been solitary Londoners meditating upon the past, musing, even, upon civilisations which like their own had fallen into decay and dissolution. Edward Gibbon sat alone in his lodgings in Bond Street and, to the sound of rattling coaches, reflected upon the fall of Rome. The young John Milton sat up half the night in his bed-chamber in Bread Street, his candle glimmering at the window, while he dreamed of ancient London and its founders. There have been such men in every generation, men who have spent "their lives in the disquisition of venerable ANTIQUITY concerning this city." One of the first, Fabyan, a sheriff and alderman of London, wrote a *Chronicle or Concordance of Histories* of which the first edition was published in 1485. Among other topics he compiled a chronology of the successive weathercocks upon St. Paul's. Arnold's *Chronicle, or Customs of London* appeared in 1521 where among a record of the charters of the city can be found "an estimate of the livings of London" and a recipe "to pickle sturgeon."

The work of Stow himself was successively edited and corrected by Munday, Dyson and Strype who also considered themselves the faithful recorders of London, "being birthplace and breeder to us." They were followed by William Stukeley, who found evidence of Julius Caesar's camp by Old St. Pancras Church and traced the line of Roman roads through eighteenth-century London. He "appears to have had all the quiet virtues and gentle dispositions becoming an antiquarian—one living in the half-visionary world of the past," as so many other Londoners have done. He died in Queen Square and by his particular direction was buried in the forlorn churchyard of East Ham.

The most elaborate and extensive antiquarian studies, however, can be dated from the middle decades of the nineteenth century. It was the time of encyclopaedic surveys, including the six great volumes of *Old and New London* edited by W. Thornbury and E. Walford. There are literally hundreds of other volumes chronicling the "curiosities" and "celebrities" of what had become the largest and wealthiest city in the world. This was also the period in which were completed various histories of London, a tradition which was maintained into the early twentieth century by Sir Walter Besant, the founder of "the People's Palace," whose memorial can now be viewed beneath Hungerford Railway Bridge. It was Besant who remarked, on his death-bed, "I've been walking about London for the last thirty years, and I find something fresh in it every day," an observation which could be confirmed by almost any admirer of London.

By the 1870s, at the time when urban chroniclers were extolling the size and variety of the new city, there were others who, like their predecessors in earlier centuries, mourned the passing of the old. The Society for Photographing Relics of Old London was established in 1875, as a direct result of the threat of demolition of the Oxford Arms in Warwick Lane, and its work was complemented by such books as *London Vanished and Vanishing* and *Unknown London*. There were individual writers, many of them journalists from London newspapers, who explored the vestiges of the past concealed in old courts and antique squares. Their labours were in turn continued in the twentieth century by books such as *London's Secret History*, *The Vanished City* and *Lost London*. The city has always provoked sensations of loss and transitoriness.

Yet antiquarianism can take many forms. At the turn of the twentieth century Sir Laurence Gomme, a great administrative historian, wrote a series of volumes which suggested, even if they did not entirely prove, that London had retained a territorial and judicial identity since the time of the Roman oc-

cupation. The permanent and unchanging nature of London was, thereby, affirmed in the very face of change. Gomme's work was in a sense complemented by that of Lewis Spence whose *Legendary London* connected the
history of the city with the tribal patterns of the Celts as well as the magic of
the Druids.

Their contributions to the history of London have been sadly neglected
or derided, partly as a result of the more precise and "scientific" record of the
city's growth maintained by the various London archaeological societies
whose own work has proved invaluable. A more fundamental challenge came
from the numerous sociologists and demographers who in the postwar years
were more concerned with rebuilding and with new forms of urban planning.

Antiquarianism might itself be considered outmoded, therefore, except
for one curious ceremony which is conducted every year at the church of St.
Andrew Undershaft. Here rests John Stow's tomb, with a memorial figure of
the Tudor antiquarian resting upon it. He holds a quill pen in his hand and
every year, at the beginning of April, the Lord Mayor of London and a distinguished historian proceed to the memorial where a new quill is placed in
Stow's stone hand. So the city honours one of its greatest citizens, with the
changing of the quill a solemn token of the fact that the writing of London's
history will never come to an end.

The merry Milk Maid
la Femme au Lait

The London milkmaid, as portrayed by Marcellus Laroon in the mid-seventeenth century; milkmaids were generally Welsh and seldom merry. The silver plate on her head was part of Mayday festivities.

Where Is the Cheese of Thames Street?

In the nineteenth century, old clothes were sold by male Jews. The largest number of bakers, in the same century, came from Scotland, while London barbers were characteristically city-born. Brick-makers were of London, too, while their labourers were "almost exclusively Irish." "Navvies" sprang from Yorkshire and Lancashire, while a large proportion of shoe-makers arrived from Northampton. Sugar-refining and the trade in toys were once almost entirely in the hands of Germans, who confined themselves to Whitechapel and its environs. Most butchers and fishmongers, of Smithfield and Billingsgate respectively, were London-born but cheesemongers characteristically arrived from Hampshire and dairymen from Wales; the Welsh "milk-maid" was once a regular sight of the capital. Linen drapers came from Manchester, and only a small proportion of their assistants were Londoners; most came from the counties of Devon and Somerset. In each case members of the same profession tended to form distinct enclaves of habitation and employment.

The same segregation has always been part of London's trade. Thus in the seventeenth century opticians tended to congregate in Ludgate Street, pawn-brokers in Long Lane, booksellers in St. Paul's Churchyard. In the eighteenth century cheese was to be found in Thames Street, and playing cards along the Strand. Signs for shops and taverns were on sale in Hoop Alley, Shoe Lane, where the sign-painters kept large stocks ranging from teapots to white harts and red lions. Bird-sellers were located in Seven Dials, coach-makers in Long Acre, statuaries in Euston Road, clothiers in Tottenham Court Road and dentists along St. Martin's Lane.

Yet sometimes a street will shake off old associations and change its trade. Catherine Street was once known as the quarter for pornographic book-dealers, despite the fact that the saint's name is derived from the Greek for "purity," but then in the early decades of the nineteenth century it changed its trade to eating-houses, newsvendors and advertising agents. The Strand was notable for its publication of newspapers before that industry moved eastwards to Fleet Street, and then eastwards again to the newly resurgent Docklands.

Certain parishes were identified by the trades which were continued within them; there were poulterers in St. George's, lace-men in St. Martin's, artists in Holy Sepulchre without Newgate and timber merchants in Lambeth. Wheelwrights were to be found in Deptford, millers in Stratford and saddlers at Charing Cross.

Trades sometimes delayed their departure even when the streets themselves were pulled down. "Very curious it is to mark," Walford wrote in *Old and New London*, "how old trades and old types of inhabitants linger about localities." He gave the example of the silversmiths in Cranbourn Street; the street was demolished, together with the adjacent Cranbourn Alley, when suddenly shops in the recently created New Cranbourn Street were "overflowing with plates, jewellery and trinkets."

The segregation of districts, within London, is also reflected in the curious fact that "the London artisan rarely understands more than one department of the trade to which he serves his apprenticeship," while country workmen tend to know all the aspects of their profession. It is another token of the "specialisation" of London. By the nineteenth century the divisions and distinctions manifested themselves in the smallest place and in the smallest trade. In Hoxton there grew up the industry of fur- and feather-dressing, for example, and in *East London* Walter Besant observed that "the number of their branches and subdivisions is simply bewildering"; "a man will go through life in comfort knowing but one infinitesimal piece of work . . . a man or woman generally knows how to do one thing and one thing only, and if that one piece of work cannot be obtained the man is lost for he can do nothing else."

So these workers become a small component of the intricate and gigantic mechanism which is London and London trade. A map of the "industrial quarters of north-east London, 1948" shows well-defined patches of light blue for "Camden Town instruments" and the "Hackney clothing quarter" as well as the "South Hackney shoe area." A dark blue area shows the "Aldersgate clothing quarter" close to the "Shoreditch printing quarter" which is bordered on the north by "furniture quarter" and on the south by "East End clothing quarter." These areas, comprising many small industries and businesses, were described in *The Times London History Atlas* as "the successors of long-established crafts which originated in the medieval city." Then, as if in imitation of the conditions of the city's medieval origin, other more outlying areas began to specialise in certain trades. Hammersmith and Woolwich were known for engineering and metals, Holborn and Hackney for their textiles.

Certain other professions migrate together, flocking over the centuries to new territories as if by instinct or impulse. It is well known that doctors and surgeons now cluster in Harley Street. But in the eighteenth and early nineteenth centuries notable medical practitioners inhabited Finsbury Square, Finsbury Pavement, Finsbury Place and Finsbury Circus, while the younger or less affluent doctors took lodgings in the immediate vicinity. They all migrated in the 1840s and 1850s, and Finsbury became a "socially deserted district." There was a similar movement in the manufacture of hats. They were made in an area of Bermondsey known as "the Maze," between Bermondsey Street and Borough High Street, together with Tooley Street, but then some unknown migratory instinct pushed "the grand centre of hat manufacture" further westward until it came to reside by the Blackfriars Road; why Bermondsey should thus be abandoned is unknown although it would be fair to guess that it was the result of some hidden mechanism involved in commerce. By some similar process the business of furniture-making removed from Curtain Road, Shoreditch, to Camden Town.

The phenomenon of trading streets and trading parishes can also be recognised on a larger urban scale, with the employment of "land use" maps; these demonstrate that the whole area was once divided into regions marked "built up area," "clay pits (unproductive)," "market garden," "pasture," "mixed farming" and "grain rotations" in a remarkably fluent pattern of organisation. A map of eighteenth-century food markets shows a similar natural pattern, as if the very topography of London was determined by silent and invisible lines of commerce.

Why have the furniture dealers of Tottenham Court Road, still operating in that street after 150 years, in recent times been joined by shops selling electronic apparatus? Why have the clock-makers of Clerkenwell been supplemented by design consultancies and advertising companies? Why has Wardour Street, the home of antique bric-à-brac, now become the centre of the film industry? An intervening period in the late nineteenth century, when Soho became the centre of music publishing, may help to account for the transition but it does not explain it. Like much else in London there is no surviving rhyme or reason to elucidate its secret and mysterious changes.

A depiction of the "rookery" of St. Giles parish, in 1800; it was perhaps even more noisome and squalid than this sketch suggests. Note the pig.

CHAPTER 12

The Crossroads

he bells of St. Giles-in-the-Fields, according to a church report, "are in very fair condition, and, in spite of their great age, work very well." They are more than three hundred years old, and yet are still heard every Thursday lunchtime. But the history of this London parish stretches back much further.

In familiar and almost characteristic fashion, there was a Saxon church on the site of the present St. Giles. Drury Lane, once known as "via de Aldwych," was the main road leading towards Watling Street from the settlement of Lundenwic, or Covent Garden; at its northern end was a village cross and a chapel administered by "John of good memory." Upon this site, in the first years of the twelfth century, were established a chapel and a hospital for lepers; they were dedicated to St. Giles, himself the patron saint of lepers. The establishments lay among fields and marshes, their contagion kept apart from the city. But St. Giles was also the intercessionary saint for beggars and cripples, for those afflicted with misery or those consigned to loneliness. He himself was lame but refused to be treated for his disability in order that he might practise self-mortification all the more fervently.

The invocation of sorrow and loneliness, first embodied in the twelfth-century foundation, has never entirely left this area; throughout its history it has been the haunt of the poor and the outcast. Vagrants even now roam its streets and close to the church there is still a centre for the homeless.

The grounds belonging to the hospital, which eventually became the parish of St. Giles, are now roughly delineated by the triangle of Charing Cross Road (formerly Hog Lane and, even earlier, Eldestrate), New Oxford Street and Shaftesbury Avenue. It remained a refuge for lepers until the fifteenth century, when it seems that it also made provision for the very poor and the infirm; it was, in the words of a London County Council survey, a "peculiarly London institution." A village sprang up beside the refuge, with small shops catering to the needs of the inmates; Gervasele Lyngedrap (linen-draper) is one of the late medieval merchants mentioned in the hospital records. At the time of the Reformation the establishment was dissolved, and the chapel transformed into the parish church of St. Giles-in-the-Fields. The first post-Catholic building was erected in 1631, but by that time the nature of the district had changed. Always an ambiguous and ill-defined area, hovering between city and country, in the ninth century it had been on the Saxon high-way and, as London grew more prosperous, its trade and traffic had in-creased; there were taverns and hostels for travellers. Another kind of wanderer arrived when, by proclamation of Elizabeth in 1585, many foreigners were ejected from the city itself and settled in the vicinity. These in turn were followed by the vagrant and the impoverished. Meanwhile, the position of St. Giles, outside the city and close to Westminster, attracted various notables who built grand houses among pasture grounds recreated as gardens. By the seventeenth century St. Giles was known for its startling con-trasts between rich and poor, the latter clustering to the south of what is now New Oxford Street. It remained in that unsettled state for several centuries. "Numbers of the habitations seem calculated for the depth of misery," one chronicler of the parish wrote in the nineteenth century, "others for the ex-tremes of opulence."

It functioned, then, as both entrance and exit; it greeted arrivals and har-boured those who had been expelled from the city. It was in every sense a crossroads. A gallows and, later, a "cage" or "pound" were placed on the spot where now Tottenham Court Road, Charing Cross Road, Oxford Street and New Oxford Street meet. Beneath St. Giles Circus, as it is called, exists the crossroads of the "Northern" and "Central" lines of the Underground system. St. Giles has also been the crossroads between time and eternity. "For a shroud for a poor woman that dyed in the cage," reads one notation in the churchwarden's account. Even after the gallows had been removed, in the late fifteenth century, St. Giles was still the guardian of the threshold to death; all malefactors on their way to the "Tyburn tree" halted at the aptly named "Resurrection Gate" of St. Giles-in-the-Fields where they were given a bowl of ale to comfort them on their journey. It might almost be described as a local celebration, since St. Giles was remarkable for nurturing the hangmen of the day, as well as being the second largest source of those who were hanged. In the words of an old lyric: "St. Giles' breed, better hang than seed."

That final drink upon the rite of passage was appropriate in another sense, also, since the parish was celebrated or condemned, according to taste, for the number of taverns and the incidence of drunkenness. The White Hart, established in the thirteenth century, survives in name at least by the corner of Drury Lane, but many others have crumbled to dust—the Maidenhead in Dyot Street, the Owl Bowl in Canter's Alley, the Black Bear, the Black Jack, the Black Lamb, the Vine and the Rose. The Maid in the Moon, off Drury Lane, has now been curiously succeeded by the Moon Under Water along the Charing Cross Road. There is another connection with alcohol; the present Grape Street is aligned with the old vineyard of the hospital.

This is also the neighbourhood where William Hogarth set *Gin Lane*. The tradition of the last drink or "the St. Giles bowl," according to John Timbs, the author of the nineteenth-century *Curiosities of London*, had "made it a retreat for noisome and squalid outcasts." But no description can match the outrage and despair of the eighteenth-century engraving. Hogarth has established the essential spirit of the place where vagrants still sit in small groups drinking ale from cans—the emaciated young man, the drunken woman with syphilitic sores, the suicide, the hasty burials *in situ*, the child about to fall to its death, all these reflect in exaggerated detail the reality of St. Giles as a centre of death-dealing drink but they are also uncannily prophetic of the early nineteenth-century slums known as the "Rookeries" which would arise on the identical spot some fifty years later.

Another calamity was visited by drink upon St. Giles-in-the-Fields in 1818. A great vat of the Horseshoe Brewery, situated just north of the crossroads, exploded and released approximately ten thousand gallons of beer; stalls, carts and walls were washed away in the flood and the beer quickly filled the cellars of the vicinity, drowning eight people. Gin Lane and Beer Lane met in confluence.

The cellars that proved so fatal have their own history. "To have a cellar in St. Giles" was a catchphrase for squalor and misery. As early as 1637 the churchwardens' accounts refer to "the great influx of poor people into this parish . . . persons that have families in *cellars*, and other abuses." These lower rooms acquired their reputation for foulness because of the locality itself: St. Giles-in-the-Fields was known for being "damp and unwholesome." A parliamentary Act of 1606 had condemned Drury Lane and its environs as "deepe foul and dangerous to all who pass those ways." A report by Christopher Wren complained of its "noisomnesse," as it was surrounded by marshland, conduits and open ditches; and in the same period an inquiry at Westminster complained that the area "was very much overflowed with water" and had become "exceeding miry, dirty and dangerous."

It was dangerous in more than one respect since, from Drury Lane and the little courts beside it, emerged that pestilence which became known as the Great Plague of London. In the last weeks of 1664 the first people to be visited by that contagion were living at the northern end of the lane, opposite the Cole Yard where the fourteen-year-old Nell Gwynne dwelled. The outbreak "turned people's eyes pretty much to that quarter," as Daniel Defoe put it in his *Journal of the Plague Year*, and the sudden increase of burials in the parish led everyone to suspect "that the plague was among the people at that end of the town." So this unlucky spot was the source of the great distemper which threatened to destroy the greater part of London's citizens before being purged by fire. Many of the houses were closed down, and in his diary for 7 June 1665 Samuel Pepys noticed "much against my will" the red crosses daubed upon the wooden doors. The area was in a curious way blamed for the virulent disease—"that one parish of St. Giles at London hath done us all this mischief" Sir Thomas Peyton wrote—and it seems likely that its ambiguous status as a resort for the wretched and the outcast was now responsible for its dire reputation. The refuse of the city were, in a most threatening form, coming back into the city.

Yet this was not the end of St. Giles's unhappy history. Waves of poor settlers generally inhabited its large buildings which over the years were converted into tenements and cellars. It is not too fanciful to suggest that the spirit of St. Giles himself influenced the journey of the poor to the parish of St. Giles since, as a direct consequence of its earlier history as a hospital, it was known for the scale of its charitable relief. The mid-seventeenth-century accounts of the parish note: "Gone to *Tottenham-court Meg*, being verie sicke, 1s. 0d. . . . Geven to the *Ballet-singing Cobler* 1s. 0d. . . . Gave to *old Fritz-wig* 0s. 6d. . . . P^d a year's rent for *Mad Bess* £1 4s. 6d." There are many references to relief granted for "poore plundered Irish," to families "that came oute of Ireland," and in fact that nation was to maintain its hold upon the area for two centuries. But the French also came, and those expelled from the city for vagrancy, as well as black servants reduced to beggary who were known as "St. Giles blackbirds." In this quarter there emerged a tradition of mendicity which it has not wholly exorcised; as early as 1629 there were calls for "idle persons" to be taken up and within a generation complaints that the parish was the resort of "*Irish* and aliens, *beggars*, and dissolute and *depraved characters*." Three generations later the area was considered to be "overburthened with poor." The whole history of London vagrancy can be understood by proper attention to this small territory.

Most poignant, perhaps, is the unhappy fate of individuals who appear in the annals of poor relief. In the mid-eighteenth century "Old Simon" lived with his dog under a staircase in a ruined house within Dyot Street; a contemporary description of him by J.T. Smith in *Book for a Rainy Day* is similar to that which could be given of late twentieth-century vagrants: "He had several waistcoats, and as many coats, increasing in size, so that he was enabled by the extent of the uppermost garment to cover the greater part of the bundles, containing rags of various colours, and distinct parcels with which he was girded about, consisting of books, canisters containing bread, cheese, and other articles of food; matches, a tinder-box, and meat for his dog." The presence or companionship of a dog seems to be a permanent characteristic of the London vagrant.

"Old Jack Norris, the Musical Shrimp Man" lived, some seventy years later, in the same street (now renamed George Street). A beggar, engaged in the "cadging ramble" under the guise of selling shrimps, he starved to death or, as the jury put it, "died by the visitation of God." There was Anne Henley, who in the spring of 1820 died in her 105th year in Smart's Buildings. "She used to sit at various doors in Holborn to sell her pincushions. She was short in stature, mild and modest in her deportment, cleanly in her person and generally wore a grey cloak."

At the time of writing, a large woman, with a shaved head, sits on New Oxford Street between Earnshaw Street and Dyott Street (which has reacquired its old name); she carries bags filled with newspapers and talks to herself continually, but she never asks for money. It is not clear why she should choose each day the same very public position, unless we were to surmise that the old lure of Dyott Street has not been wholly lost in the rebuilding of the area. A young man, with close-cropped hair and steel-rimmed glasses, sits and begs near the corner of Dyott Street. On St. Giles High Street, between Earnshaw Street and Dyott Street, the steps and doorway of a disused office block are used by middle-aged men who beg money for "a cup of tea." St. Giles is indeed still a haven for beggars and vagrants, among them the woman who sits surrounded by pigeons in a urine-stained corner off High Holborn, and the old man who is always drunk but never begs by the Dominion Theatre where once the brewery stood. Vagrant youths beg from passers-by around the corner of the theatre. They lie in sleeping bags directly across the road from the YMCA hostel, emphasising that the place of transients in the life of St. Giles has never faded.

On the threshold of St. Giles, where the great road of High Holborn passes the entrances of Southampton Row and Proctor Street, vagrants can always be seen singly or in groups as if they were guardians of the area. They also linger in the churchyard of St. Giles-in-the-Fields, whiskered, red-faced, dirty, drinking spirits like the generations who came before them.

In this spirit of individual narrative we can note the end of the characteristically short lives in this neighbourhood, as recounted in the parish record, like those of "Elizabeth Otley, and one Grace, who were killed by the fall of a chimney in *Partridge-alley* . . . one Farmer's child in the *Cole-yard*, drowned in a tub of water . . . a dead man, being thrust in the eye by a footman . . . one Goddid White, that drowned herself . . . a girl in *Hogg Lane*, that hanged herself . . . the deathe of a childe that parte of the limbes were bitt off by a dog or cat, at my Lord of Southampton's house, in *Long-fielde* . . . a male child murdered, and layed at the backside of the *King's Head* inne . . . indictment against Priscilla Owen, for biting her husband's finger, which occasioned his death."

There is another way of describing its inhabitants. In pictorial narratives they are seen as emblematic of a certain urban type, whose depraved or drunken character leads inevitably to an early demise through illness or upon the gallows. Death, then, becomes once more the province of St. Giles. The fatal stages of Hogarth's *Harlot's Progress* are set in Drury Lane, and in a neighbouring night-cellar the "Idle Apprentice" is arrested for murder before being dispatched to the gallows. Another of Hogarth's infamous characters, Tom Nero in *Four Stages of Cruelty*, is a St. Giles charity boy. He also ends upon the gallows. Death was rife within the parish in another sense, since St. Giles had the second greatest rate of mortality in the entire city.

The poor can also become the creatures of another narrative device, when their lives are retold by those with a taste for neo-Gothic sensationalism or prurience. Charles Dickens was repeatedly drawn to this area, either alone or in the company of police inspectors, and immortalised one of its most celebrated thoroughfares in his "Reflections upon Monmouth Street." Tobias Smollett wrote of "two tatterdemalions from the purlieus of St. Giles, and between them both was but one shirt and a pair of breeches." In 1751 Henry Fielding, another great London novelist, published his own account of infamous proceedings in St. Giles where "men and women, often strangers to each other, lie promiscuously, the price of a double bed being no more than three-pence, as an encouragement for them to lie together: That as these places are adapted to whoredom, so are they no less provided for drunkenness, gin being sold in them all at a *penny* a quartern . . . in one of these houses, and that not a large one, he [Mr Welch, high constable of Holborn] hath numbered fifty eight persons of both sexes, the stench of whom was so intolerable, that it soon compelled him to quit the place." Drink, sex and smell are here mingled in a heady compound designed to titillate the senses of those fortunate enough to be able otherwise to avoid the area; these are precisely the scenes and scents which Fielding could not have presented within any of his official fiction but in the guise of sober reportage he could indulge his novelistic appetite for the "filth" and "noisomness."

It is not necessary to emphasise that the lives of the St. Giles poor were indeed wretched, and that there were dirty houses of assignation in the parish; but it ought also to be remembered that the great London novelists, such as Dickens and Fielding, created a strange shadow-play of urban imagery. Their own occluded or obsessive characters mingled with the darker forces of the city to create a theatrical and symbolic London which has on many occasions supplanted the "reality" of various areas.

The most sensational accounts of St. Giles-in-the-Fields were reserved for the first decades of the nineteenth century. This was the time of the Rookeries, an island of cellars and tenements roughly bounded by St. Giles High Street, Bainbridge Street and Dyott Street. Within this unfortunate triangle, before New Oxford Street was constructed to lay waste the slums, were Church Lane, Maynard Street, Carrier Street, Ivy Lane and Church Street together with a congregation of yards and courts and alleys which turned the area into a maze used both as a refuge and as a hiding-place for those who dwelled there. "None else have any business there," wrote Edward Walford in *Old and New London*, "and if they had, they would find it to their interest to get out of it as soon as possible."

"The Rookeries" were also known as "Little Dublin" or "The Holy Land" because of the Irish population which dwelled there. But there were thieves, coiners, prostitutes and vagrants as well as labourers, road-sweepers and street-sellers. The lanes here were narrow and dirty, windows of decaying tenements were stuffed with rags or paper, while the interiors were damp and unwholesome. The walls were sagging, the floors covered in dirt, the low ceilings discoloured by mould; their smell was altogether indescribable. Thomas Beames, in *The Rookeries of London*, described how these sinister streets were "crowded with loiterers . . . women with short pipes in their mouths and bloated faces and men who filled every intermediate occupation between greengrocer and bird-catcher." Its inhabitants were also "squalid children, haggard men with long uncombed hair, in rags . . . wolfish looking dogs." Behind some of the most populous and busy streets in the capital were these areas of stale inactivity and impoverished languor; it was one of the many permanent and formidable contrasts within the city. The night lodgings here were known colloquially as "beggar's operas" because of the drink and tumult which were encouraged.

For many generations there was also an annual carnival of beggars in the vicinity. In fact only sex and drink could make the conditions bearable. An official report in 1847 states that one room in a house "was occupied by only three families in the day but as many as could be got into it at night." More than twenty people were often found in one small space, together with the wares which they sold in the street, oranges, onions, herrings and watercress being the favoured articles. In one alley behind Church Street there was a chamber like "a cow house" where "seventeen human beings eat, drunk and slept." In this fearful place "the floor was damp and below the level of the court."

Once again the peculiar dampness or fetidness of the parish is emphasised, the "noisomness" of which Wren and others had complained. The area was filled with vermin of every description and, in these conditions, there were innumerable cases of fever, cholera and consumption. Thomas Beames found a young man with a fatal consumptive cough—"he was quite naked, had not a rag to his back, but over him was thrown a thin blanket, and a blue rug like a horse cloth—these he removed to let us see there was no deception." In many cases of mortal disease "those stricken were left to die alone, untended, unheeded, "they died and made no sign" . . . without a word which betokened religious feeling on their lips, without God in the world . . ." Nobody was beside them to murmur "St. Giles, protect them!," because the presiding saint may be said to have fled the vicinity. The Irish behaved in a reckless and violent manner because they believed that they had entered a "heathen city." "The Rookeries" embodied the worst living conditions in all of London's history; this was the lowest point which human beings could reach before death took hold of them, and to the Irish it seemed that the city and its inhabitants were already given over to the devil.

They were given over to the landlord, however, and not to the devil. London is established upon commercial profit and financial speculation, and the pattern of its housing has followed similar imperatives. It has grown largely from speculative building, advancing in succeeding waves of investment and profit-taking while being momentarily stilled in periods of recession. The parish of St. Giles was a particularly interesting case of exploitation. A small group of individuals owned the housing stock of the area—eight people, for example, owned about 80 per cent of the houses in the Church Lane quarter—and they in turn let out the streets one by one. A person for an agreed sum rented a street by the year and then let out certain houses on a weekly return, while the proprietor of each house rented out separate rooms. The person who rented a room would then take money from those who inhabited a corner of it. It represents an absolute hierarchy of need, or desperation, in which no one assumed responsibility for the dreadful conditions which prevailed. They were instead blamed upon the "Irish" or the vices of the "lower orders" who somehow were seen to have brought their unhappy fate upon themselves. The caricatures of Hogarth, or of Fielding, damn the victims rather than their oppression.

There also emerged the "mob" of St. Giles, an undifferentiated mass of common human beings who posed a threat to order and security. In one armed raid upon "an Irish ken," as reported in Peter Linebaugh's *The London Hanged*, "the whole district had become alarmed, and hundreds came pouring down upon us—men, women, and children. Women, did I say!—they looked fiends, half naked." Here the demonic language of the heathen city is applied to the tormented themselves. But if we look more closely at this "mob," it will perhaps become more variegated and more interesting. It was often assumed that, because St. Giles was a haven for transients, it was therefore inhabited by a wholly transient population. But in fact the evidence of the settlement and examination books of the period reveals that the population was relatively stable and the movement in the parish took place only within sharply defined boundaries; the poor, in other words, clung to their neighbourhood and had no desire to move outside it. When later redevelopment of the area removed many parts of "the Rookeries," their inhabitants migrated to adjacent streets where they lived in even more overcrowded circumstances. It is in fact a general characteristic of Londoners that they tend to conduct their lives in a relatively restricted area; it is still possible to find people in Hackney or Leytonstone, for example, who have never "gone West" and, similarly, inhabitants of Bayswater or Acton who have never travelled to the eastern portions of the city. In the case of the paupers of St. Giles-in-the-Fields, that territorial imperative was very strong; they lived and died within the same few square yards with their own network of shops, public houses, markets and street contacts.

The great social topographer Charles Booth described St. Giles-in-the-Fields as the repository of "ordinary labour" but this term, like "mob," hardly does justice to the nature of employment in this quarter of outcast London. There were knife-grinders and street-singers, dealers in vegetables and makers of door mats, dog-breakers and crossing sweepers, bird dealers and shoemakers, hawkers of prints and sellers of herring. More exotic trades, too, flourished in the neighbourhood.

Until 1666, when houses were built upon it, the southern region of the parish was a wasteland known as Cock and Pye Fields. It was not properly urbanised until 1693, however, when seven streets were laid out to meet at a central pillar and thereby form a star. This area was known as the Seven Dials. Perhaps the symbolic dimension of this late seventeenth-century development materially encouraged the presence of the astrologers who assembled here. There was Gilbert Anderson, "a notorious quack" who lived beside the inn called the Cradle and Coffin, in Cross Street; there was Dr. James Tilbury at the Black Swan by St. Giles-in-the-Fields, who sold the herb spoonwart supposedly mingled with gold; W. Baynham, who resided a few yards away at "the Corner house over against the upper end of *St. Martin's Lane* near the *Seven Dials, St. Giles*," was able to inform his customers "*Which shall win in Horse or Foot races*"; again "near the *Seven Dials* in St. Giles, Liveth a Gentlewoman, *the seventh daughter of a Seventh Daughter*" who could divine the result of pregnancies and lawsuits: "SHE ALSO INTERPRETS DREAMS." Another famous quack and alchemist lived "by St. Giles Church, where you may see over the door a printed paper," where he promised to reveal the workings of "Sulphur and Mercury," and there was the notorious Jack Edwards who lived "in Castle-street in the Parish of St. Giles-in-the-Fields" where he sold medicines, pills and potions for the treatment of humans and animals alike. All of them can be found in *The Quacks of Old London* by C.J. Thompson.

These examples of what we might now term alternative medicine are taken from the seventeenth and early eighteenth centuries, but the neighbourhood has never lost its oblique reputation for occultism and strange practice. In succeeding years the Freemasons, the Swedenborg Society, the Theosophical Society and the Order of the Golden Dawn have established themselves in the same parish. A few hundred yards from Monmouth Street is the Atlantis Bookshop, which remains the most celebrated depository of occult literature in England. Here again may be another example of that territorial imperative, or *genius loci*, which keeps inhabitants and activities in the same small area.

Jack Edwards was a ballad singer as well as a doctor, and the ballads of Seven Dials were as notorious as the events and people whom they commemorated. James Catnach of Monmouth Court was the first begetter and promoter of the broadsides, songs and pamphlets which circulated through the streets of eighteenth-century London. They cost a penny each, hence the term "catchpenny" as a tribute to his marketing skills. He was forced to take the coppers to a bank, however, because no one else would touch them in case of infection springing off the metal. The reputation of Seven Dials was always dark and disturbed, although Catnach himself remedied his own position by boiling the pennies in potash and vinegar so that they became bright once more.

There were five other printers of ballads in the immediate vicinity of St. Giles, publishing street literature with titles such as "Unhappy Lady of Hackney," "Letter Written by Jesus Christ," "Last Dying Speech of . . ." These broadsides were, for the people of London, the real "news" passing from hand to hand; in many instances it was disruptive or polemical news, concerning events which affected the citizens themselves. There was one mid-eighteenth-century ballad, for example, which was issued from Seven Dials and which concerned the local workhouse—"The Workhouse Cruelty, Workhouses turn'd Gaols, and Gaolers Executioners." The death of "one Mrs. Mary Whistle" in the institution became the subject of popular resentment. There were also ballad complaints about the conditions of paupers and beggars, many left to die in the very same streets from which the ballads were issued. In that sense St. Giles-in-the-Fields, perhaps because of its raging population and its awful mortality, acted as an alternative source of authority. That made it a suitable haven for "coiners" who were in effect issuing another kind of money, in the process helping to disrupt the system of commerce and finance which cast so palpable a shadow over the impoverished inhabitants of this area.

It is appropriate, also, that the parish should be the haunt of prostitutes and a harbour of "night houses." The courts and lanes adjoining Drury Lane were the most notorious for the trade and it was here, in his *London Labour and the London Poor* published between 1851 and 1862, that Henry Mayhew recorded the statement of one woman "over forty, shabbily dressed and with a disreputable unprepossessing appearance." Mayhew's accounts are a remarkable and affecting source of street life as well as street anecdote. His veracity and accuracy have sometimes been questioned, largely because he was part of a generation of mid-Victorian writers who tended to sensationalise or fictionalise the events and inhabitants of the "great wen." But the general tenor and candour of Mayhew's transcriptions can be trusted, as in this unhappy woman's story: "I lodge in Charles Street, Drury Lane, now. I did live in Nottingham Court once and Earl Street. But, Lord, I've lived in a many places you wouldn't think, and I don't imagine you'd believe one half. I'm always a-chopping and a-changing like the wind as you may say . . . I don't think much of my way of life. You folks as has honour, and character, and feelings, and such, can't understand how all that's been beaten out of people like me. I don't feel. *I'm used to it* . . . I don't suppose I'll live much longer, and that's another thing that pleases me. I don't want to live, and yet I don't care enough about dying to make away with myself. I arn't got that amount of feeling that some has, and that's where it is." Mayhew declares that "she had become brutal," but in fact the city had brutalised her.

Her fatalism, however, has not necessarily been shared. D.M. Green, in *People of the Rookery*, remarked that because of its dreadful conditions St. Giles contained "the seeds of revolution." It is a curious chance, then, that in 1903, the Second Congress of the Russian Social Democratic Party should take place on Tottenham Court Road itself; it was organised by Lenin, and resulted in the separation of Bolsheviks from Mensheviks. As the author of *Lenin in London*, Lionel Kochahs, has put it, "It is almost true to say that Bolshevism as a political party was actually founded in Tottenham Court Road." So the parish of St. Giles-in-the-Fields did indeed contain those "seeds" of violent social disruption, even if it were a species of instinctive and distant revenge.

. . .

The area around St. Giles was, in the language of the period, a "sore" or "abscess" that might poison the whole body politic, with the unspoken assumption that it must in some way be purged or cauterised. So between the years 1842 and 1847 a great thoroughfare known as New Oxford Street was run through it, leading to wholesale demolition of the worst lanes and courts with an attendant exodus of the poor inhabitants—although most of them moved only a few streets further south. The language of the body was once more used by contemporary moralists who characteristically celebrated the fact that "one huge filthy mass" had been dispersed. Yet the heady atmosphere of the place was by no means removed; the exiled poor simply lived in conditions worse and more overcrowded than before, while the premises and shops of the new street remained unlet for some years. It was still a damp, dismal and "noisome" place to which few new residents could be attracted. And so it stands today. New Oxford Street is one of the least interesting thoroughfares in London, with no character except the somewhat dubious one of being dominated by the high-rise block of Centrepoint. The building towers above the site of the old "cage" and gallows, and may perhaps be considered a fitting successor to them. It is an area now without character or purpose, the home of computer suppliers, an Argos superstore, some indistinguishable and undistinguished office buildings, and shops designed for the trade of passing tourists. There are still the vagrants lingering in the recesses of the area as a token of its past, but where there was once life and suffering there is now a dismal quiet from which St. Giles himself can offer no deliverance.

The Puppethow.

Vol. II page 3.

Pub June 29 1801 by I Marshall N° 4 Aldermary Ch Yd Lon

"Punch and Judy" arrived early in London and could be seen on the streets until recent times. Street entertainers have haunted the city since the thirteenth century, and perhaps before.

CHAPTER 13

Show! Show! Show! Show! Show!

how! Show! Show! Show! Show! This was the cry of a seventeenth-century city crowd, as recorded in Ned Ward's *London Spy*. There were indeed many shows to be seen on the London streets, but the greatest fair of all was held at Smithfield. It was known as Bartholomew's Fair.

Smithfield itself began as a simple trading area, for cloth in one place and cattle in another, but its history has always been one of turbulence and spectacle. Great jousts and tournaments were held there in the fourteenth century; it was the ritual place for duels and ordeal by battle; it was the home of the gallows and the stake. That festive nature was also evident in less forbidding ways. Football matches and wrestling contests were commonly staged and the appropriately named Cock Lane, just beyond the open ground, was the haunt of prostitutes. Miracle plays were also part of its entertainment.

The trading market for cloth had become outmoded by the middle of the sixteenth century but "the privileges of the fair" were still retained by the city corporation. So, instead of a three-day market, it was transformed into a fourteen-day festival which resounds through the plays and novels of succeeding centuries with the cry of "What do you lack? What is it you buy?"

From the beginning of its fame there were puppet-shows and street performers, human freaks and games of dice and thimble, canvas tents for dancing or for drinking, eating-houses which specialised in roast pork.

This was the fair which Jonson celebrated in his play of the same name. He notes the sound of rattles, drums and fiddles. Here on the wooden stalls were laid out mousetraps and gingerbread, purses and pouches. There were booths and toyshops. Displayed "at the sign of the Shoe and Slap" was "THE WONDER OF NATURE, a girl about sixteen years of age, born in Cheshire, and not above eighteen inches long . . . Reads very well, whistles, and all very pleasant to hear." Close by was exhibited "a Man with one Head and two distinct Bodies," as well as a "Giant Man" and "Little Fairy Woman" performing among the other freak shows and theatrical booths. There were puppies, whistling birds and horses for sale; there were ballads cried out, with bottled ale and tobacco being constantly consumed. Cunning men cast nativities, and prostitutes plied their trade. Jonson himself noted small details, too, and watched as the cores of apples were gathered up for the bears. As one of his characters puts it, "Bless me! deliver me, help, hold me! the Fair!"

It continued, curiously enough, during the Puritan Commonwealth, no doubt with the primary motive of venting the steam of the more unruly citizens, but flourished after the Restoration of 1660 when liberty and licence came back into fashion. One versifier of the period notes masquerades dramatising "*The Woman of Babylon, The Devil and The Pope,*" as well as shows of dancing bears and acrobats. Some acts came year after year: there was the "Tall Dutchwoman" who made annual appearances for at least seventeen years, together with the "Horse and no Horse, whose tail stands where his head should do." And there were always rope-walkers, among them the famous Scaramouch "dancing on the rope, with a wheelbarrow before him with two children and a dog in it, and with a duck on his head," and the notable rope-dancer Jacob Hall "that can jump it, jump it." Perhaps the most celebrated of all the acts, however, was that of Joseph Clark, "the English Posture Master" or "Posture Clark" as he was known. It seems that he could "put out of joynt almost any Bone or *Vertebra* of his Body, and to re-place it again"; he could so contort himself that he became unrecognisable even to his closest friends.

And so the fair went on, as all fairs do. There was even a Ferris wheel, known then as a "Whirligig" (later an "Up and Down") where, according to Ned Ward in *The London Spy* (1709), "Children lock'd up in Flying Coaches who insensibly climb'd upwards . . . being once Elevated to a certain height come down again according to the Circular Motion of the Sphere they move in."

The general noise and clamour, together with the inevitable crowd of pickpockets, finally proved too much for the city authorities. In 1708 the fortnight of the fair was reduced to three days at the end of August. But if it became less riotous, it was no less festive. Contemporary accounts dwell upon the drollery of "merry Andrews," otherwise known as Jack Puddings or Pickled Herrings; they wore a costume with donkey's ears, and accompanied other performers with their fiddles. One of the more famous fools was a seller of gingerbread nuts in Covent Garden; since he was paid one guinea a day for his work at Bartholomew Fair, "he was at pains never to cheapen himself by laughing, or by noticing a joke, during the other 362 days of the year."

Alongside the merry Andrews leapt the mountebanks who sold miracle cures and patent medicines to those credulous enough to purchase them. In an illustration by Marcellus Laroon one such is dressed as a harlequin from *commedia dell'arte* with a monkey tied to a rope beside him. His voice, too, might be heard among the general noise and tumult—"a rare cordial to strengthen and cheer the Heart under any Misfortune . . . a most rare dentifrice . . . good to fortifie the stomach against all Infections, Unwholesome damps, malignant effluvias." And so the fair rolled on. It is perhaps appropriate, amid the noise and excitement, that in 1688 John Bunyan collapsed and died at the corner of Snow Hill and Cock Lane.

If there was one central character, however, it was that of Punch, the uncrowned monarch of "puppet-plays, hobby-horses, tabors, crowds, and bagpipes." He had emerged upon the little stage by the end of the seventeenth century, announced by a jester and accompanied by fiddle, trumpet or drum. He is not a uniquely London phenomenon, but he became a permanent entertainer at the fairs and streets of the city; with his violence, his vulgarity and his sexual innuendo he was a recognisable urban character. "Often turning towards a tightly packed bend of girls, he sits himself down near to them: My beautiful ones, he says, winking roguishly, here's a girl friend come to join you!" With his great belly, big nose and long stick he is the very essence of a gross sexual joke which, unfortunately, in later centuries became smaller, squeakier, and somehow transformed into entertainment for children. There is a watercolour by Rowlandson, dated 1785, which shows a puppet-play with Punch in action. George III and Queen Charlotte are driving to Deptford, but the attention of the citizens is drawn more towards the wooden booth where Punch is beating the bare buttocks of his wife. He was often conceived as a "hen-pecked" husband but, here, the worm has turned. Rowlandson's work is of course partly conceived as a satire against the royal family, but it is filled with a greater and all-encompassing urban energy.

Within Bartholomew Fair itself there was a complete erasure of ordinary social distinctions. One of the complaints against it lay in the fact that apprentice and lord might be enjoying the same entertainments, or betting at the same gaming tables. This is entirely characteristic of London itself, heterogeneous and instinctively egalitarian. It is no coincidence, for example, that at the time of the Fair an annual supper was held in Smithfield for young chimney-sweeps. Charles Lamb has immortalised the occasion in one of his essays, "The Praise of Chimney Sweepers," where he reports that "hundreds of grinning teeth startled the night with their brightness" while in the background could be heard the "agreeable hubbub" of the Fair itself. It might be argued that there is no true egalitarianism in the gesture, and that such solemn festivities merely accustom the little " 'weeps" to their dismal fate. This might then be considered one of the paradoxes of London, which consoles those whom it is about to consume.

Punch is also advertised in Hogarth's print of *Southwark Fair*. Known as "the Lady Fair," it was held in the streets around the Borough in the month after Bartholomew Fair. But since Hogarth announced his engraving as "The Fair" and "the Humours of a Fair" we may safely assume that he is portraying a characteristic and familiar London entertainment. Here Punch is mounted upon a stage horse which picks the pocket of a clown; above him, there is a poster announcing "Punches Opera" which depicts the large-nosed figure wheeling his wife in a barrow towards the open mouth of a dragon.

Elsewhere in this fair a motley group of performers stands upon a wooden balcony where a painted cloth announces "The Siege of Troy is here"; the entertainers have been identified as part of Hannah Lee's theatrical company, and one of their advertisements has in fact survived. "To which will be added, a New Pantomime Opera . . . intermixed with Comic scenes between Punch, Harlequin, Scaramouch, Pierrot and Columbine. N.B. We shall begin at Ten in the Morning, and continue Playing till Ten at Night." It was a long day at the fair.

On each side of the players there are various feats of acrobatics; a tightrope-walker spans two wooden buildings, while a rope-flyer descends precipitously from the tower of St. George the Martyr. In another corner of

the fair a wooden stage has collapsed, and the actors fall upon stalls selling
china and upset a table where two gamblers are playing at dice. There are
dwarves, conjurors and waxworks, performing dogs and monkeys; a girl
beats a drum while a mountebank sells his medicine; a pickpocket plies his
trade while another kind of performer swallows fire. One customer can be
seen gazing into the aperture of a wooden peep-show and does not notice
that, by his side, a man is being arrested by a bailiff.

Bartholomew Fair itself became the arena for fictional characters whose authors used it as the setting of their adventures, but perhaps the most famous
account is autobiographical in nature. In the seventh book of his *Prelude*
Wordsworth memorialised his youthful residence in London in the 1790s,
and chose Bartholomew Fair as one of its emblems with its "anarchy and din
Barbarian and informal"—a word which we might better translate as form-
less. It was

Monstrous in colour, motion, shape, sight, sound

filled with

chattering monkeys dangling from their poles,
. . . And children whirling in their roundabouts . . .
The Stone-eater, the Man that swallows fire

It is clear that the entertainments had not changed throughout the eighteenth
and early nineteenth centuries, but Wordsworth's particular response to its
barbaric "din" and shapelessness is an example of his general attitude towards
the city itself. The fair becomes, in fact, a simulacrum of London. The first
lines of Pope's *Dunciad* make a similar point by extolling:

The Mighty Mother, and her Son who brings
The Smithfield Muses to the ear of Kings

It is a symbol of disorder and anarchy, threatening to overwhelm the values
of a humanised and civilised London with all its vulgar paraphernalia of
"shews, machines, and dramatical entertainments, formerly agreeable only to
the taste of the Rabble." The egalitarian energies of the city, therefore, are

treated with the gravest mistrust by those who wrote for smaller London circles.

At the time of Wordsworth's visit the Fair was gradually being extended until, by 1815, it had spread up along one side of St. John's Street and, in the other direction, had almost reached the Old Bailey. It had also become a place of danger and lawlessness with gangs of thieves, known as "Lady Holland's mob," who "robbed visitors, beat inoffensive passers-by with bludgeons, and pelted harmless persons." These were no longer the festivities of the eighteenth century, and were certainly not to be endured in the more respectable climate of the mid-nineteenth. Bartholomew Fair could never have lasted long into the Victorian era, and in 1855 it passed away without much sign of public mourning.

Yet Wordsworth had divined, in the spectacle of the Fair, a permanent aspect of London life. He recognised and recoiled from an innate and exuberant theatricality, which was content to manifest sheer contrast and display with no interior or residual meaning. In this book of *The Prelude*, "Residence in London," he remarks:

> On Strangers of all ages, the quick dance
> Of colours, lights and forms, the Babel din

It is the play of difference, characterised by mobility and indeterminacy, which disturbs him. Within a few lines he notes "Shop after Shop, with Symbols, blazon'd Names . . . fronts of houses, like a title page" as if the city harboured endless forms of representation, not one of which is superior to any other. He records the ballads hanging upon the walls, the huge advertisements, the "London Cries" and the stock urban characters of the "Cripple . . . the Bachelor . . . the military Idler," as if they were all part of some great and endless theatre.

Yet it is at least possible that he did not fully understand the very reality which he so vividly describes—these "shifting pantomimic scenes," these "dramas of living Men," this "great Stage" and "public Shows," the spectacles and the showmen, may indeed represent the true nature of London. Its theatricality therefore leads to "Extravagance in gesture, mien, and dress," just as in all the streets and lanes the citizens were "living shapes"; even the roadside beggar wears "a written paper" announcing his story. Thus all may be, or seem, unreal. Wordsworth believed that he saw only "parts," in every sense, and could derive no "feeling of the whole." He may have been mistaken.

Wordsworth was correct about the essential theatricality of the city, but it may also be considered from another vantage. It may become a cause for celebration. Charles Lamb, that great Londoner, extolled his city as "a pantomime and masquerade . . . The wonder of these sights, impels me into night-walks about her crowded streets, and I often shed tears in the motley Strand from fulness of joy at so much life." Macaulay wondered at the "dazzling brilliancy of London spectacles," while James Boswell believed it to comprise "the whole of human life in all its variety"; for Dickens it was the "magic lantern" which filled his imagination with the glimpse of strange dramas and sudden spectacles. For each of these Londoners, whether by birth or adoption, the theatricality of London is its single most important characteristic.

The crowd that gathered to see the inauguration of the first underground railway, in 1863, was compared in newspaper accounts "to the crush at the doors of a theatre on the night of a pantomime," and Donald J. Olsen, the author of *The Growth of Victorian London*, has compared the speed and scale of city transport in that period to the "magical transformation of the pantomime continually being translated into life." That is why London has always been considered to be the home of stock theatrical characters—the "shabby genteel," the "city slicker," the "wide boy." In print-shop windows of the mid-eighteenth century there were caricatures of London "types," while the more fashionable citizens of the same period dressed up in costume for masques and disguisings.

The most famous pictorial series displaying London characters, Marcellus Laroon's *The Cryes of the City of London Drawne after the Life*, published in 1687, reveals many professions and trades where the actual principle was that of acting. Many beggars put on a masquerade for the benefit of their passing audience, but Laroon himself chose a particular female vagrant to exemplify what he called "The London Beggar." He did not give her name, but in fact she was known as Nan Mills who, according to the most recent editors of his work, was "not only a good physiognomist but an excellent mimic . . . and could adapt her countenance to every circumstance of distress." There is no reason to doubt that she was also poor, and conscious of her degradation. Here, too, is part of the mystery of London where suffering and mimicry, penury and drama, are aligned with each other to a degree where they become indistinguishable.

The rituals of crime have, in London, also taken on a theatrical guise. Jonathan Wild, the master criminal of mid-eighteenth-century London, declared that "The mask is the *summum bonum* of our age" while the marshalmen, or city police of a slightly later date, were costumed in cocked hats and spangled buttons. There were more subtle disguises available to the detective of the city. One is reminded of Sherlock Holmes, a character who could have existed only in the heart of London. According to his amanuensis, Holmes "had at least five small refuges in different parts of London, in which he was able to change his personality." The mysteries of Dr. Jekyll and Mr. Hyde, too, could be conducted only through "the swirling wreaths" of London fog where character and identity may suddenly and dramatically be obscured.

If crime and detection rely upon disguise, so London punishment had its own theatre of judgement and of pain. The Old Bailey itself was designed as a dramatic spectacle, and was indeed compared with "a giant Punch and Judy show" where the judges sat within the open portico of a Sessions House which resembled a theatrical backdrop.

Yet since Punch, who in the end manages to hang the hangman Jack Ketch, is the epitome of disorder it is likely that his spirit would also be found in noisome circumstances. The cellar floor of the Fleet Prison was known as "Bartholomew Fair," while in the chapel of Newgate there were galleries where spectators were invited to watch the antics of those condemned to die who deliberately entertained their audience with acts of outrageousness or defiance. We read, for example, of one John Riggleton who "made a practice of sneaking up to the Ordinary [prison clergyman] when his eyes were fast shut in prayer and shouting out loud in his ear." This of course is the role of the pantaloon in pantomime.

The theatre did not end in the prison chapel, but continued upon the little stage where the execution took place. "The upturned faces of the eager spectators," wrote one contributor to *The Chronicles of Newgate*, "resembled those of the 'gods' at Drury Lane on Boxing Night." Another witness remarked upon the fact that, just before the execution, there was a roar of " 'Hats off!' and 'Down in front!' as at a theatre." There was one peculiarly theatrical episode at the execution in 1820 of Thistlewood and his "Cato Street" companions for treason; according to the traditional sentence, they were to be hanged and then beheaded. "When the executioner had come to the last of the heads, he lifted it up, but, by some clumsiness, allowed it to drop. At this the crowd yelled out, '*Ah, Butter-fingers!*' " This small episode manifests the peculiar temperament of the London crowd, combining humour and savagery in equal measure.

The witnesses at executions were not the only inhabitants of London to appreciate the virtues of urban theatre. Inigo Jones's construction of the Banqueting House in 1622 was, in the words of John Summerson's *Georgian London*, "really an extension of his stage work"; the same might be said of his other great urban projects. In a similar spirit, two hundred years later, John Nash disguised a concerted effort at town planning, dividing the poor of the east from the wealthy of the west, by creating streets and squares which represented the principles of "picturesque beauty" by means of scenic effects. George Moore commented that the "circular line" of Regent Street was very much like that of an amphitheatre, and it has been noted that the time of Nash's "Improvements" was also the period of the great panoramas and dioramas of London. Buckingham Palace, as viewed from the end of the Mall, seems nothing more than an elaborate stage-set while the House of Commons is an exercise in wistful neo-Gothic not unlike the elaborate dramas to be seen in the patent theatres of the period. The latest Pevsner guide notes that the clearing banks of the City of London "were built to impress inside and out," while much of the architecture of the 1960s "took the expressive potential of concrete to a theatrical extreme."

That central spirit of London has been divined by artists as well as architects. In the work of Hogarth the streets are delineated in terms of scenic perspective. In many of his prints, perhaps most notably in his delineation of the Fair, the division between performers and spectators is for all practical purposes invisible; the citizens fulfil their roles with even more animation than the stage actors, and there are more genuinely dramatic episodes among the crowd than upon the boards.

Some of the more famous portraits of London also borrow their effects from the theatre of the period. It has been remarked, for example, how Edward Penny's painting of *A City Shower* is taken from a scene from David Garrick's *The Suspicious Husband*. One of the greatest painters of mid-nineteenth-century cityscapes, John O'Connor, was also an accomplished painter of theatrical scenery. The editors of the most comprehensive volume upon the subject, *London in Paint*, go so far as to suggest that "further research will be carried out into this vital link between the two professions" of urban painter and theatrical designer. They may not be two professions, however, but one.

. . .

It would seem that everyone in London wore a costume. From the earliest period the city records reveal the vivid displays of rank and hierarchy, noting garments of coloured stripes and gowns of rainbow hues. When the dignitaries of the city attended the first day of Bartholomew Fair, for example, they were expected to wear "violet gowns, lined," but the emphasis on colour and effect was shared by all manner of London citizens. In fact in such a crowded city people could be recognised only by their costume, the butcher by his "Blue-Sleeves and Woollen Apron" or the prostitute by "Hood, Scarf and Top-Knot." That is why at the Fair, when costumes change, all social hierarchy is undermined.

A shopkeeper of the mid-eighteenth century would advertise the traditional worth of his wares "with his hair full-powdered, his silver knee and shoe buckles, and his hands surrounded with the nicely-plaited ruffle." In the early twentieth century it was noted that the bank messengers and fishboys, waiters and city policemen, still wore mid-Victorian costume as if to display their antique deference or respectability. In any one period of London's history, in fact, it is possible to detect the presence of several decades in the dress and deportment of those in the streets.

Yet disguise can also be a form of deception; one notorious highwayman escaped Newgate "dressed up as an oyster-girl," while a character in *Humphry Clinker*, Matthew Bramble, noticed how mere journeymen in London went around "disguised like their betters." In turn Boswell delighted in "low" impersonation, dressing up and taking on the role of a "blackguard" or soldier in order to pick up prostitutes and generally to entertain himself in the streets and taverns of the city. Boswell was entranced by London precisely because it allowed him to assume a number of disguises and thus escape from his own identity. There was, as Matthew Bramble had written, "no distinction or subordination left," which accounts precisely for the combination of egalitarianism and theatricality that is so characteristic of London.

London is truly the home of the spectacle, whether of the living or of the dead. When in 1509 the cadaver of Henry VII was carried along Cheapside, a wax effigy of his royal person, dressed in the robes of state, was placed upon the hearse. The wagon was surrounded by priests and bishops, weeping, while the king's household of six hundred persons followed in procession with lighted candles. It was the kind of funeral parade at which London has always excelled. The funeral of the Duke of Wellington in 1852 was no less ornate and sumptuous, and a contemporary account describes the event in highly theatrical terms—"the effect is novel and striking" with the mass of shade relieved by colour, particularly that of "a Grenadier Guardsman, his scarlet uniform strongly contrasting with the sable decorations around him."

On the arrival of foreign monarchs, or upon the birth of princes, or after news of success in wars, the city decked itself out in colourful pageants. When Catherine of Aragon entered London in 1501 she was greeted by painted wooden castles built upon stone foundations, columns and statues, fountains and artificial mountains, mechanical zodiacs and battlements. It is impossible to overestimate the thirst for spectacle among Londoners through many centuries. When Henry V returned from Agincourt in 1415 he saw two gigantic figures placed upon the entrance to London Bridge; on the bridge itself "were innumerable boys representing the angelic host, arrayed in white, with glittering wings, and their hair set with sprigs of laurel"; the conduit on Cornhill was covered by a pavilion of crimson cloth and, on the king's approach, "a great quantity of sparrows and other small birds" were set free. At the conduit in Cheapside there were virgins, dressed entirely in white, "who from cups in their hands blew forth golden leaves on the king." An image of the sun, "which glittered above all things," was placed upon a throne and "round it were angels singing and playing all kinds of musical instruments." In succeeding reigns the conduits of Cornhill and Cheapside were arrayed with trees and caves, artificial hills and elaborate streams of wine or milk; the streets themselves were draped with tapestries and cloth of gold. As Agnes Strickland, an early biographer of Elizabeth I, remarked upon these manifestations, "The city of London might, at that time, have been termed a *stage*." A German traveller similarly observed that, at the coronation of George IV, the king "was obliged to present himself, as chief actor in a pantomime" while the royal costume "reminded me strikingly of one of those historical plays which are here got up so well."

There is another kind of drama which seems close to the life of the city. The streets provided a permanent arena, for example, in which any "patterer" or chanting trader could attract an inquisitive audience. The stages of sixteenth-century theatres were built to face the south, so that more light might fall upon the players, but we may imagine the actions and deportment of less professional actors to be similarly lit upon the crowded thoroughfares of London. Historical scenes were dramatised by street performers. There are extant photographs of actors in nineteenth-century street theatre; they seem poor, and perhaps grimy, but they wear spangling tights and elaborate costumes against garishly painted backdrops. In the early twentieth century, too, scenes from the novels of Dickens were played out on open carts on the very sites where those scenes were set.

Dickens may have appreciated such a gesture, since he turned London itself into a vast symbolic theatre; much of his dramatic imagination was formed by visiting the playhouses which abounded in his youth, particularly the penny gaffs and the small theatrical "houses" around the Drury Lane Theatre. In one of them he saw a pantomime and "noticed that the people who kept the shops, and who represented the passengers in the thoroughfares, and so forth, had no conventionality in them, but were unusually like the real thing." He is adverting to the fact that ordinary Londoners, mainly of the younger generation, paid to be allowed to act in that season's latest urban drama or pantomime. In *Vanity Fair* his contemporary, Thackeray, noted two London boys as having "a taste for painting theatrical characters." In a similar spirit almost every street of London was once the object of dramatic curiosity, from *A Chaste Maid of Cheapside* to *The Cripple of Fenchurch Street*, from the *Boss of Billingsgate* to *The Lovers of Ludgate*, from *The Devil of Dowgate* to *The Black Boy of Newgate*. The audience found in them what they also found in *Bartholomew Fair*, a theatre which reflected the nature of their lives as well as the nature of the city itself. These plays were generally violent and melodramatic in theme, but that is precisely why they offered a true image of teeming city life.

London life itself could in turn become street theatre, even if it were sometimes of a tragic and inadvertent kind. The poor, and the outcast in particular, can claim no privacy and, as Gissing noted in his novel *The Nether World* (1889), "their scenes alike of tenderness and of anger must for the more part be enacted on peopled ways" where their shouts and muttered words could plainly be heard.

CHAPTER 14

He Shuld Neuer Trobell the Parish No More

✳

"Out you rogue, you hedge-bird, you pimp . . . Does't so, snotty nose? Good lord, are you snivelling? You were engendered on a she-beggar in a barn." These lines from *Bartholomew Fair* evoke something of the flavour of London speech, even if they do not catch its particular accent and intonation.

London speech has been variously described both as harsh and as soft, but the predominant characteristic is that of slackness. W. Matthews, author of *Cockneys Past and Present*, suggests that "Cockneys avoid movement of the lips and jaw as far as possible"; M. MacBride, author of *London's Dialect*, makes the same point, after examining microsegments and terminal contour peaks, nuclei and junctures, by declaring that "the Cockneys avoid, as far as possible, any unnecessary movements of the articulating organs." In other words, they are lazy speakers. One more obvious point might also be made. If the Cockney voice is indeed "harsh," it is perhaps because Cockneys have always inhabited a harsh and noisy city where the need to be heard above the roar of "unresting London" is paramount.

There are many famous examples of what became known as Cockney—a "piper" rather than a "paper," "Eye O pen" rather than "High Holborn," "wot" not "what." There are also very familiar constructions—"so I goes . . .

and he goes" is now more common than "so I says . . . and he says," but the immediacy is still there. "Innit?" or "Ennit?" are now more favoured than "Ain't it?.," and memorable phrases such as " 'E didn't 'alf 'it 'er, 'e did" or "You ain't seen nuffin" or "nuffink" can still be heard in certain regions of the East End. Other Cockneyisms, however, have not survived the middle decades of the twentieth century. "For why?" is uncommon, as is "summut." Even "blimey" is fading out of discourse. Certain Cockneyisms—familiar perhaps from the novels of Dickens—are now of distant vintage. "Wery" instead of "very," "wulgar" rather than "vulgar," are quite out of use, although the device was always more popular in fiction than upon the streets; the same might be said of "Hexcuse" rather than "excuse." In the early decades of the twentieth century you might hear a stall-keeper shouting out: "Plees to reckleck [please recollect] that at this 'ere stall you gets . . ."; but no longer. It would once have been possible to hear the following sentence from a Cockney waiter—"There are a leg of mutton, and there is chops"—but that particular construction appears to have gone out of favour. Some words have simply shifted allegiance; in the mid-nineteenth century Cockneys would tend to employ "Ax" rather than "Ask," but that ellipsis is now in use predominantly among black Londoners. One construction is still current—"paralysed, like" or "fresh, like"—even though it has been part of the London tongue for at least two centuries. A more substantial point can be made in this context, too, since there is clear evidence that Cockney English has not changed in its essentials for over five hundred years.

Its history is significant, therefore, if only to demonstrate once more the essential continuities of London life. Cockney has always represented an oral rather than a written culture, sustained by an unbroken succession of native speakers, but for many centuries there was no standard London speech. The legacy of the Old English tongue left a variety of identifiable dialects among the citizens of early medieval London; we can trace south-eastern speech, south-western speech and East Midland speech. West Saxon was the language of Westminster, because of the historical connection between the reigning sovereign's household and Winchester, while the predominant language of the city itself was East Saxon; hence the connections throughout the centuries between the London dialect and the Essex dialect. "Strate" in London was "strete" at Westminster. There was no standard or uniform pronunciation, in other words; it would have differed even from parish to parish.

There were other forms of speech, too, which rendered the language of the city more heterogeneous and polyglot. One linguistic survey of the registers of London English, from the last decade of the thirteenth century to the beginning of the fifteenth, reveals a vast range of sources and borrowings. In the previously unstudied archives of London Bridge, generally dealing with the employment of Thames fishermen, there are elements of Old English, Anglo-Norman and medieval Latin as well as Middle Dutch and Middle Low German; this might be considered merely the work of educated clerks transcribing the rough tongue into a more polished and formal style, but in fact all the evidence suggests that there was a truly "mixed" or "macaronic" style caused by "the interaction between different registers of London English." The author of *Sources of London English*, Laura Wright, has also pointed out that Londoners "who used French and Latin habitually in their work would in all probability retain the terminology of these languages even when discussing or thinking about their work in English." We do not need to imagine Thames fishermen, however, speaking classical Latin. Their Latin would have been some form of argot or patois which included terms inherited from the time of the Romans. The addition of French is predictable enough, after the Conquest, when all these tongues became part of the fabric of living speech.

There were, however, broad patterns of change. During the fourteenth century the dominant East Saxon voice of London was displaced by that from the Central and East Midlands; there is no single reason for this shift, although it is likely that over several generations the more wealthy or educated merchant families had emigrated from that region into the city. There was in the same period another essential linguistic change, when this different and apparently more "educated" language inaugurated a slow process of standardisation. By the end of the fourteenth century there had emerged a single dialect, known as "London English," which in turn became what the editor of the *Cambridge History of the English Language* calls "modern literary Standard English." Writing standards were progressively set by the scribes of Chancery, too, with their emphasis upon correctness, uniformity and propriety.

So the East and Central Midland dialect became the language spoken by educated Londoners and increasingly the language of the English generally. What happened, then, to the East Saxon dialect which had previously been the native tongue of the native Londoner? To a certain extent it was displaced but, more importantly, it was demoted. One of the central prejudices against its use lay in the fact that it had always been spoken and rarely, if ever, written down. Thus these "vocal cries" were filled with "Incongruities and Bar-

barism." By the sixteenth century this difference between "standard" and what had become "Cockney" English was well enough understood to be the subject of critical attention, but the salient fact was its survival.

The vestry records of the late sixteenth and early seventeenth centuries show that Cockney was not only well established but already exhibited certain permanent features. Thus "the abbot of Westmynster and the monks reprevyed . . . Mr. Phipp who was chosen constable in which complaint he made appear his imbecility . . . yt was erecktyde by most voysses . . . without the least predyges of the paryshe . . . he wold nott church a woman owt-sept she wold com at vi in the mornyng." Then there were the double negatives: "he shuld neuer trobell the parish no more . . . not otherwysse to be ussyd at noo tyme"; in a seventeenth-century stage play this is parodied as "Were you never none of Mister Moncaster's scholars?" Here again we can hear them talking: "Att this vestry it was ffurder menshoned whether the parishe would be pleased to Accept of Mr. Gardener for to bee a Lecterrer . . . greytt necklygence of our pyssheners." In diaries of the sixteenth century, particularly that of Henry Machyn, there are phonetic spellings that catch the very accent and intonation of these early Cockneys: "anodur" for "another" and "alff" for "half." Vestmynster, Smytfeld, Hondyche and Powlles Cross are mentioned together with Honsley heth and Bednoll Grene. One of Machyn's entries concerns a sudden bolt of lightning, when "on of servand was so freyd that ys here stod up, and yt wyll never come down synes." A diligent investigator has also found many devices, used by Cockneys of the sixteenth and seventeenth centuries, which are still familiar; among them are "Stren" instead of "Strand," "sattisfectory" instead of "satisfactory," "texes" instead of "taxes," "towled" instead of "told," "owlde" instead of "old," "chynes" not "chains," "rile" instead of "rail," "suthe" instead of "south," "hoathe" instead of "oath," "orfunt" instead of "orphan," "cloues" instead of "clothes," "sawgars" instead of "soldiers," "notamy" instead of "anatomy," "vill" instead of "will," "usse" instead of "house," " 'im" instead of "him." Certain key words and phrases have also survived the centuries, among them "sav'd 'is bacon," bouze (drink), poppet (girl), elbow-grease (energy), paw (hand), swop (exchange) and tick (credit). The central point is clear: the Cockney speech of the twenty-first century is in many respects identical to that of the sixteenth century. As an oral tradition, it has never died.

Cockney of the sixteenth and seventeenth centuries was also reproduced on stage, as well as in written reports, but at this early date it was parodied rather than mocked. Mistress Quickly, the garrulous hostess of the Boar's

Head in East Cheap in the second part of Shakespeare's *Henry IV*, might stand as an emblem for the more strident Cockney females. "I was before Master Tisick, the debuty, t'other day; and, as he said to me, 'twas no longer than Wednesday last, 'I' good faith, neighbour Quickly,' says he; Master Dumbe, our minister, was by then; 'neighbour Quickly,' says he, 'receive those that are civil; for' said he, 'you are in an ill name.' " It might be the voice of Mrs. Gamp, almost three centuries later. Shakespeare must have heard these elisions, repetitions and asides whenever he walked through the streets of the city.

Fielding was another wonderful observer of London life in the first decades of the eighteenth century; he heard the voices, too, and reproduced them with great precision. "It would be the hiest preasumption to imagine you eggnorant of my loave. No, madam, I sollemly purtest," writes Jonathan Wild to an assumed admirer, ". . . I have not slept a wink since I had the hapness of seing you last; therefore hop you will, out of Kumpassion . . ."

It is the same accent identified by Smollett at a slightly later date. "Coind sur, Heaving the playsure of meating with you at the ospital of anvilheads [invalids], I take this lubbertea of latin you know . . ." There is more than humour here; there is also a sense of farce and singularity which in no way condemns the Cockney speakers for their mannerisms. In the same spirit the dramatic vitality and sympathy, to be found in Shakespeare, emerge in these other urban writers. Smollett practised for a while as a surgeon in Downing Street, and Fielding as a judge in Bow Street; they knew all the voices. Their connection with London speech also throws a suggestive light upon the observations of Karl Friedrich Schinkel, writing in his journal of 1826, that for "a man of letters who endeavours to cultivate, however modestly, the medium of Shakespeare and Milton . . . London must ever have a great illustrative and suggestive value, and indeed a kind of sanctity."

Writers of a later generation were more concerned with polite taste and the maintenance of "good" English as the medium of enlightenment. In that context the Cockney accent becomes absurd, and deplorable. So, in dramas of the mid-eighteenth century, it is lampooned. "I have heard, good Sir, that every Body has a more betterer and more worserer Side of the Face than the other . . . It is the onliest way to rise in the world . . . all them kind of things." Soon enough there were treatises and educational manuals which condemned the vulgarity and incorrectness of Cockney speech; their prejudice was strengthened with the proliferation of board schools and religious schools where, in the context of national education, the Cockney speaker was considered "uneducated" and illiterate. Since "London English" had become the standard of "proper" English, so in turn the native dialect of London was all the more strongly condemned. It became the mark of error and vulgarity.

The figure of the Cockney, however, never disappeared. The term itself has been considered one of derision. "Cockney" is generally supposed to derive from the medieval term "cokenay" or cock's egg; in other words an unnatural object or freak of nature. There is another, equally derisory, explanation. A Londoner, on his first visit to the country, is supposed innocently to have asked, "Does a cock neigh too?" But there is also the possibility of more agreeable origins. One historian has suggested that it comes from the Latin term *coquina*, or "cookery," and derives from the time when London was considered the great centre of cook-shops. It may also come from the Celtic myth of London as "Cockaigne," a place of milk and honey, of whom the Cockneys are the true inhabitants. Yet even this origin has been held against them. By the fifteenth century the term was synonymous with "a milksop . . . an effeminate fellow" and in the sixteenth century was "a derisive appellation for a townsman as a type of effeminacy, in contrast to the hardier inhabitants of the country." Sometimes he or she seems to be an image of pity, then, as in Dickens's reproduction of the crossing-sweeper's conversation—"a sov'ring as waw give me by a lady in a wale as sed she was a servant and as come to my crossin' one night as asked to be showd this 'ere ouse." But there are many Cockney characters in Dickens who retain their exuberance and vitality. There is Ikey in "A Passage in the Life of Mr. Watkins Tottle," from *Sketches by Boz*, who has the very model of a Cockney manner: "He seed her several times, and then he up and said he'd keep company with her . . . the young lady's father he behaved even worser and more unnatural . . . So then he turns round to me and says . . . and wasn't he a trembling, neither." Dickens was a master of the spoken word and throughout his fiction he evinces his command of the London dialect. It might even be said that the nineteenth century was the one in which Cockneys and Cockneyisms really flourished. They were no longer the city merchants or innkeepers of the seventeenth-century drama or the aspiring (if vulgar) neighbours of the eighteenth-century novel; they were considered to be members of a distinctive and extensive group.

The rise of rhyming slang, for example, can be dated to the first decades of the nineteenth century, when there emerged phrases such as "apples and pears" for "stairs" and "trouble and strife" for "wife." Back-slang, or the reversal of words, also appeared at this time. Thus is "yob," for example, slang for "boy."

In the same century, too, the Cockney fully emerged as an identifiable if not always lovable character. Writers including Pierce Egan, Henry Mayhew and G.A.H. Sala—whose careers span the entire century—copied a recognisable idiom in such phrases as "She's a bloody rum customer when she gets lushy" or "They doesn't care nothink for nobody" or "She tipp'd him a volloper right across the snout."

The literature of Cockney in the nineteenth century is for all practical purposes endless, but it found one specific focus in the language of the music hall. Performers such as Albert Chevalier, Dan Leno, Marie Lloyd and Gus Elan gave Cockney idiom artistic form and direction; it allowed the genuine outflow of communal feeling with songs such as "My Shadow is My Only Friend" and "I Wonder What It Feels like to be Poor." They are the true songs of London. The routines of the "halls" encouraged much elaboration and ingenuity, also, so that it can fairly be said that the standard of Cockney was set by the 1880s. Certainly this was the period that witnessed the emergence of what may still be called modern Cockney.

Its most fastidious exponent was, perhaps, Bernard Shaw's Eliza Doolittle: "There's menners f'yer. Te-oo banches o' voylet trod into the mad . . . Ow eez yee-ooa san, is 'e?" The last sentence—"Oh he's your son, is he?"—is indicative of Shaw's skill at phonetic reproduction, but it is not always easy upon the ear or eye. Other examples of twentieth-century Cockney may be more amenable. "The other dye I 'appened ter pick up a extry 'alf-thick-un throo puttin' money on my opinyun of the Gran' Neshnal. Well, nar, the fancy tikin' me, I drops in on a plice as were a cut above whart I patterinizes as a yooshal thing." This dates from 1901, and then twenty-one years later we have the following: "Vere was a bloke goin' dahn Tah'r Bridge Road, an' ve Decima Stree' click se' abaht 'im. Vey dropped 'im one . . . "

Pronunciations like "relytions" (relations), "toime" (time), "owm" (home), "flahs" (flowers), "inselt" (insult), "arst" (asked), "gorn" (gone), "I done it" (I did it), have become standard. Certain words and phrases have changed. "Smashin'," for example, has become "blindin' " or "brilliant." Other words have been retrieved. "Mate" or "mite" went quite out of fashion, but then returned through the intermediary of Australian television soap opera. But in general terms construction and intonation have remained the same. A speaker from the 1960s—"He did not say nothing . . . so he come in and just as he come in . . . Right in the corner it was . . . Of course they was cursing . . . So—any way—I give one look . . . I seen them . . . Them days"—does not differ radically from any Cockney speaker of the early twenty-first century.

One proviso ought to be entered, however. There are still speakers of modern or standard Cockney but among younger Londoners it has become milder or at least more subdued; this may be the result of better formal education, but is perhaps more closely related to the general diminution of local or native dialects as a result of mass "media" communications.

Yet it is still a remarkable record of continuity; native London speech has survived all the incursions of intellectual fashion, educational practice or social disapproval and has managed to retain its vitality after many centuries of growth. Its success reflects, and indeed may even be said to embody, the success of the city itself. Cockney grew, like London, by assimilation; it borrowed other forms of speech, and made them its own. It has taken words from Dutch and Spanish, Arabic and Italian, French and German; it has borrowed the cant of thieves and the argot of prison. Since the city itself has on many occasions been described as a prison, it is fitting that the language of the Cockney should in part be the language of the convict, from "nark" to "copper." Given the general and persistent violence of London life, also, it is not altogether surprising that the London dialect has taken many words and phrases from the boxing ring including "kisser," "conk," "scrap" and "hammer." Other terms have come from the army and navy, where Cockneys served, and in recent decades Americanisms have also been assimilated. Thus the language thrives.

Cockney has other characteristics which also serve to define the life of the city. It benefits from an extraordinary theatricality; it is filled with a magniloquence and intensity not unconnected to braggadocio. In Machyn's diaries of the sixteenth century we encounter the same bravura which, with some modifications, can still be heard on the streets of London: "the goodlyest scollers as ever you saw . . . the greth pykkepus as ever was . . . ther was syche a cry and showtt as has not byne." This is also related to the Cockney tendency to mix up, or misunderstand, apparently impressive words in an effort to convince the hearer. A bathroom wall may be "covered in condescension" or an elderly person may suffer from "Alka-seltzer disease." Other observers have noted such phrases as "Yer a septic . . . collector of internal residue . . . jumbo sale . . . give 'im a momentum when he retires." The list is endless.

There is a certain cheerfulness and perkiness, too, which is as much a characteristic of the city as of the language. Londoners are fond of proverbs and of catchphrases, and of very harsh oaths which are a combination of comedy, aggression and cynicism. Their tongue has therefore been described as generally "crude and materialistic" but with precisely those characteristics it resembles and reflects the city in which it was fashioned.

Slang and catch-phrases are as old as the language itself. The streets of London have always been filled with slogans and catcalls. We can date some as far back as the fifteenth century. "Who put a turd in the boy's mouth?," "As bare as a bird's arse" and "God save you from the rain" are typical examples of street language. There were other expressions which had a specific urban origin. A famous performing horse, Morocco, for example, when asked by its owner to pick out the biggest fool in the audience, chose the comedian and jester Richard Tarleton, whose response, "God a mercy, horse," ran through London at the end of the sixteenth century. It could be used as a token of any kind of annoyance, but it had a comic touch because of its associations. "Oh good, Sir Robert, knock!" became in the seventeenth century a general cry of reproach among Londoners at some naughty deed; its derivation was the knock of a hammer to stop flagellation in Bridewell.

At the beginning of the nineteenth century, too, street slang appears and disappears for no particular reason. The word "quoz" was a great favourite, for example, and was capable of almost any meaning. According to Charles Mackay, in his *Memoirs of Extraordinary Popular Delusions*, it was a mark of incredulity, or hilarity, or condescension. "When a mischievous urchin wished to annoy a passenger, and create mirth for his chums, he looked him in the face and cried out '*Quoz*!' . . . Every alehouse resounded with *Quoz*; every street corner was noisy with it, and every wall for miles around was chalked with it." It was followed by another favourite phrase of street life, "What a shocking bad hat!," which was directed at almost anyone of distinctive appearance. This in turn was followed by the single word "Walker!," which was designed to cause maximum offence and "was uttered with a peculiar drawl upon the first syllable, and a sharp turn upon the last." It was used by young women to deter an admirer, by young boys mocking a drunk, or to anyone impeding the way. It lasted three or four months only, and was replaced by another piece of London slang which lasted an equally short period, "There he goes with his eye out." This was rivalled in its unfathomability by another popular phrase, "Has your mother sold her mangle?," which became a customary term of abuse among the Cockney population. Brevity and incomprehensibility are the two marks of popular favour. In the 1830s another phrase, "flare up," became literally the talk of the town.

"It answered all questions and settled all disputes," Charles Mackay wrote, ". . . and suddenly became the most comprehensive phrase in the English language." A man who had spoken out of turn, or who had drunk too much, or had been involved in a quarrel, had consequently "flared up." Its popularity lasted, again, for a short time, to be followed by "Does your mother know you're out?," addressed to anyone who looked a little too pompous or self-satisfied—as in the retort by the cab driver to the peer who resisted the attempt to be charged double.

There are other examples of this continual invention of new words or phrases which seem mysteriously to resound in the streets of London immediately after they have been coined by—who knows whom? It is almost as if they were invented by the city itself, and sent echoing down the alleys and thoroughfares in the litany of London generations: "I can come it *slap* . . . Would you be surprised to hear? . . . Go it! . . . Immensikoff! . . . It's naughty but it's nice . . . Whatcher me old brown son . . . Chase me . . . Whoa, Emma! . . . Have a banana . . . Twiggey-voo! . . . Archibald, certainly not . . . There's a lot of it about it . . . He's a splendid performer, I *don't* think . . . Can I do you now, sir . . . It's being so cheerful as keeps me going . . . See you later alligator . . . Shut that door." The most recent examples come respectively from music hall, radio and television—television, together with cinema and popular music, now being the most fruitful source of street slang.

The tradition continues, principally because it is an aspect of Cockney humour once known as "chaff." We hear in the eighteenth century of Londoners being sent into "convulsions" of laughter by prints of a couple yawning after sexual intercourse. The humour could also be of a more personal kind. Steele, in the *Spectator* of 11 August 1712, tells the story of an eighteenth-century gentleman who was approached by a beggar and politely asked for sixpence so that he might visit a tavern. "He urged, with a melancholy Face, that all his Family had died of Thirst. All the Mob have Humour, and two or three began to take the Jest." The "Humour" of "the Mob" here consists in the beggar implicitly mocking the gentleman, a form of burlesque which is the most common form of Cockney humour. Chimney-sweeps were dressed up as clergymen; shoe-blacks, "with their footstools on their heads," were driven around the "ring" of Hyde Park at the precise moment when the fashionable were about to parade. They were levelling distinctions, and parodying wealth or rank. William Hazlitt divined in *The Plain Speaker* of 1826 that "Your true Cockney is your only true leveller." He concluded that "Everything is vulgarised in his mind. Nothing dwells long enough on it to produce an interest; nothing is contemplated sufficiently at a distance to excite curiosity or wonder . . . He has no respect for himself, and still less (if possible) for you. He cares little about his own advantage, if he can only make a jest out of yours. Every feeling comes to him through a medium of levity and impertinence." This may represent too jaundiced an attitude, however, since the levelling humour is also related to the spirit of "fair play" which was said to be prevalent among the London crowd; one of the great Cockney expressions was "Fair play's a jewel." In this spirit the street urchins of the nineteenth century might innocently ask a gentleman, "Is the missus quite well?" Swift remembered a child declaring, "Go and teach your grandmother to suck eggs."

When street scavengers were confronted by the new "street-sweeping machines," "a brisk interchange of street wit took place, the populace often enough encouraging both sides." In similar fashion street fights, however spontaneous, took place according to rules well known to the London crowd. The same equalising spirit of London burlesque may also lie behind the permanent affection for cross-dressing among Cockneys. Theatrical transvestism has been prominent in London entertainments for centuries—from Mrs. Noah of the medieval pageants to the latest act in a London "drag" club. When in 1782 the actor Bannister played the character of Polly Peachum in *The Beggar's Opera*—itself a great emblem of London—one member of the audience "was thrown into hysterics which continued without intermission until Friday morning when she expired."

CHAPTER 15

Theatrical City

vidence for a Roman theatre, south-west of St. Paul's, is now very clear; it was located little more than 150 feet east of the Mermaid Theatre, which is situated by Puddle Dock. Further evidence can be found for a theatre at Whitechapel in 1567; it was just beyond Aldgate, with a stage some five feet high and a series of galleries.

This was in turn followed by the erection of the Theatre in the fields of Shoreditch. It was constructed of wood and thatch, well enough designed to merit the description of this "gorgeous playing-place erected in the Fields." Marlowe's *Doctor Faustus* and Shakespeare's *Hamlet* were performed here. Certainly it must have proved popular because, a year later, another theatre was built two hundred yards away; it was known as "The Curtain" or, latterly, "The Green Curtain" in deference to the colourful sign painted on its exterior. Theatres, like taverns and shops, were well illustrated to catch the attention of the citizens.

These two early theatres set the standard for those more famous playhouses which play so large a part in Elizabethan cultural history. These playhouses were always outside the walls of the city (unlike the "private" theatre of Blackfriars), and the two theatres in the northern fields were constructed upon land once belonging to Holywell Priory; as the name suggests, there

was a "holy well" in the immediate vicinity. It may be that they were deliberately sited close to the location where sacred plays had once been staged.
This might also account for the presence of a theatre in the old priory of the
Blackfriars. Londoners have always been aware of the topography of their
city and its environs, so that on many occasions and in many contexts the
same activity can be observed taking place in the same location. The situation
of the twelfth-century "theatrum" is not known, but it is at least reasonable
to suggest that it lay where the Rose, the Swan and the Globe eventually
emerged in the 1580s and 1590s.

There has been speculation about the origins of early theatre architecture, and some have supposed that it was established upon the pattern of the
yards of galleried inns where itinerant groups of minstrels or actors would
perform. They were known as "inn-playhouses"; there were two in
Gracechurch Street, the Bell and the Cross Keys, while another stood on
Ludgate Hill. The latter was known as the Belle Sauvage or the Bell Savage
and, like the others, soon acquired a distinctly unsavoury reputation. In 1580
an edict from the Privy Council commanded the officers of London "to thrust
out the Players from the City" and to "pull down the playing and dicing
houses within the Liberties" where the presence of actors encouraged "immorality, gambling, intemperance . . . Apprentices and Factions." The
theatre, then, may provoke that unrest which seems always to have been
present beneath the surface of the city's life. It also provided occasion for the
spread of those terrors of London, fire and disease.

Other theatrical historians have concluded that the true model of the
Elizabethan theatre was not the inn-yard but the bear-baiting ring or the
cockpit. Certainly these activities were not incompatible with serious drama.
Some theatres became bear-rings or boxing rings, while some cockpits and
bull-rings became theatres. There was no necessary distinction between these
activities, and historians have suggested that acrobats, fencers and rope-
dancers could also perform at the Globe or the Swan. Edward Alleyn, the
great actor-manager of the early seventeenth century, was also Master of the
King's Bears. The public arena was truly heterogeneous.

The popularity of Elizabethan drama characterises Londoners who attended it, both in their affection for colourful ritual and in their admiration of
magniloquence. The taste of the crowd for intermittent violence was amply
satisfied by the plays themselves, while the Londoners' natural pride in the
history of their city was recognised in those dramatic historical pageants

which were part of the diet of the playhouses. When Shakespeare places Falstaff and his company in East Cheap, he is invoking the life of the city which existed two centuries before. Spectacle and violence, civic pride and national honour, all found their natural home in the theatres of London.

There were, of course, familiar complaints. When Burbage attempted to reopen the theatre of Blackfriars in 1596, the "noblemen and gentlemen" who lodged in the old monastery buildings complained about the "vagrant and lewd persons" who would congregate there; they also declared that "the noise of the drums and trumpets" would hinder church services in the vicinity. When the Blackfriars was eventually reopened, visitors attending plays by Shakespeare or by Chapman were obliged to leave their coaches by the west end of St. Paul's or by the Fleet conduit, and proceed the rest of the way on foot; this was designed to prevent further tumult.

The Fortune Theatre in Golding Lane, now Golden Lane, was famous for its "inflamations" with "squibs . . . thunder . . . artificial lightning." The costs were a penny for standing room only, twopence for a chair and threepence for "the most comfortable seats which are cushioned." During the performance, according to Thomas Platter's *Travels in England*, "food and drink are carried around the audience."

During the Puritan Commonwealth the theatres were closed; it was said that the people had seen enough public tragedy and no longer required any dramatic version; instead theatrical entertainments were performed clandestinely or under cover of some other activity. The Red Bull Playhouse in Clerkenwell—only a few hundred yards to the north of Smithfield—remained open for rope-acts and the like, but also managed to make room for "drolleries" and "pieces of plays." So great was the appetite for these spectacles among ordinary Londoners that one contemporary wrote: "I have seen the Red Bull play-house, which was a large one, so full, that as many went back for want of room as had entered." There were continual complaints about plays and actors, even after various inhibitory proclamations of 1642 and 1648, so we may assume that the more spirited Londoners continued to find at least "pieces" of drama.

It might be thought then that the citizens would agree with one of their number, Samuel Pepys, who declared after the Restoration that the theatre was "a thousand times better and more glorious than ever before." He was referring to the newly licensed theatres of Dorset Gardens and Drury Lane, but the new theatres were nothing like the old; as Pepys went on to remark, "now all things civil, no rudeness anywhere." The drama had been refined, in other words, in order that it would appeal to the king, the court and those Londoners who shared the same values. Just as the "Cockney" dialect was now being denigrated, so the popular theatre of previous decades was dissolved.

And yet the more "Cockney" Londoners did also manage to attend the new plays; they were not necessarily welcomed in the boxes or the pit with the more prosperous citizens, but they took over the gallery from where they could shout insults or pelt fruit upon both stage and respectable audience. Cockney theatre-goers were only one aspect, however, of the generally partisan and inflammatory aspect of the urban audience. "Claques" would attend in order to cry up, or drown out, the latest production; fights would break out among the gentlemen "of quality," while there were often riots which effectively concluded all theatrical proceedings. Indeed the riots themselves were somewhat theatrical in appearance. When in the mid-eighteenth century David Garrick proposed to abolish "half-price" seats, for those who entered after the third of five acts (the whole performance beginning at six o'clock in the evening), the day appointed for that innovation found the Drury Lane Playhouse filled with a silent crowd. P.J. Grosley composed *A Tour of London* in 1772, and set the scene. As soon as the play commenced there was a "general outcry" with "fisty-cuffs and cudgels," which led to further violence when the audience "tore up the benches of the pit and galleries" and "demolished the boxes." The lion, which had decorated the king's box, was thrown upon the stage among the actors, and the unicorn fell into the orchestra "where it broke the great harpsichord to pieces." In his *London Journal* of 19 January 1763, Boswell remarks that "we sallied into the house, planted ourselves in the middle of the pit, and with oaken cudgels in our hands and shrill-sounding cat calls in our pockets, sat ready prepared."

Such behaviour in the capital's theatres continued well into the nineteenth century. A German traveller of 1827, Prince Pückler Muskau, later caricatured by Charles Dickens as Count Smorltork in *The Pickwick Papers*, reported that "The most striking thing to a foreigner in English theatres is the unheard-of coarseness and brutality of the audiences." The "Old Price" riots of 1807 lasted for seventy nights, and the private life of Edmund Kean—accused of being both a drunk and an adulterer—led to four nights of violent rioting in the playhouse of Drury Lane. What was termed "party spirit" did on more than one occasion prompt fights both among the spectators and the players. The presence of foreigners upon the stage was another cause of uproar; when the "Theatre Historique" arrived at Drury Lane from Paris, there was a general rush for the stage. Mobs surrounded the Theatre Royal in the Haymarket, in 1805, when a comedy entitled *The Tailors* caused offence among the fraternity. Professional boxers were brought into the auditorium by rival groups, as early as 1743, in order to slug it out. This was city drama, in every sense. And yet, in the city itself, the real drama was still performed upon the streets.

CHAPTER 16

Violent Delights

❦

As long as the city has existed there have been entertainers and entertainments, from the street ventriloquists who cast their voices into their hands to the "man with the telescope" who for twopence would allow you to look at the heavens on a summer's night. Performers balanced on the weathercock of St. Paul's steeple; there were midnight dog-shows and duels of rats; there were street jugglers and street conjurors, complete with pipes and drum; there were performing bears and performing monkeys dragged through the streets of London upon long ropes. In the late eighteenth century a pedlar exhibited a hare dancing upon a tambourine, while another entertainer displayed "a curious mask of bees on his head and face." In the early nineteenth century a crowd gathered around a booth labelled "Fantasina," while children examined a "Kelidascope." On Tower Hill there was set up an "ingenious contrivance" of many mechanical figures, with the legend "Please To Encourage the Inventor," while in Parliament Street a donkey pulled along a peep-show entitled "The Battle of Waterloo." There are now amusement arcades where there were once the windows of print-shops, and instead of the London Zoo there was once a "Menagerie" in Exeter Change along the Strand where the roaring of the beasts reverberated down the thoroughfare and frightened the horses.

There have always been wonders and curiosities. John Stow recorded the minute skills of a blacksmith who exhibited a padlock, key and chain which could be fastened around the neck of a performing flea; John Evelyn reported seeing "the Hairy Woman" whose eyebrows covered her forehead, as well as a Dutch boy who displayed the words "Deus Meus" and "Elohim" on each iris. In the reign of George II, it was announced that "from eight in the morning till nine at night, at the end of the great booth on Blackheath, a West of England woman 38 years of age, alive, with two heads, one above the other . . . She has had the honour to be seen by Sir Hans Sloane, and several of the Royal Society. Gentlemen and ladies may see her at their own houses as they please." The advertisement has been taken from a pamphlet entitled *Merrie England in the Olden Time*. So the unfortunate creature was taken to the London houses of the rich, to be inspected at closer hand. In the early nineteenth century "Siamese twins" were often exhibited, although such "monstrous couplings" had already been shown under other names in other centuries, and in the same period was displayed the "Anatomic Vivante" or "Living Skeleton" who at the height of five feet seven and a half inches weighed less than six stone. At another London exhibition, "the heaviest man that ever lived," weighing eighty-seven stone, also entertained the curious public. As Trinculo says upon first confronting Caliban, on that enchanted island strangely recalling London, "when they will not give a doit to relieve a lame beggar, they will lay out ten to see a dead Indian."

Fleet Street was once the home of London marvels other than those of newspaper "stories." The playwright Ben Jonson noticed "a new motion of the city of Nineveh, with Jonah and the whale, at Fleet Bridge." In 1611 "the Fleet Street mandrakes" were on show for a penny. A fourteen-year-old boy, only eighteen inches high, was to be seen in 1702 at a grocer's shop called the Eagle and Child by Shoe Lane; a Lincolnshire ox, nineteen hands high and four yards long, could be viewed at the White Horse nearby. There was the usual diet of giants and dwarfs; anything out of its due size and proportion was welcome in "disproportion'd London." There was also much interest excited by "automata" and other mechanical devices, as if they somehow imitated the motions of the city itself. It is curious to learn from the *Daily Advertiser* of 1742 that at the Mitre Tavern there was exhibited "a most curious Chaise that travels without Horses. This beautiful convenient Machine is so simply contriv'd, and easily manag'd as to travel upwards of forty Miles a Day."

In Fleet Street, too, were the waxworks. They were first exhibited by

Mrs. Salmon, the direct predecessor of Madame Tussaud, at the sign of the
Golden Salmon near Aldersgate; as the *Spectator* pointed out on 2 April 1711,
"it would have been ridiculous for the ingenious Mrs. Salmon to have lived
at the sign of the Trout." But she removed to Fleet Street, where her collection of 140 figures was the object of public admiration. On the ground floor
of her establishment was a toyshop, selling Punch dolls and cricket bats and
chessboards, while on the two upper floors stood replicas of John Wilkes,
Samuel Johnson, Mrs. Siddons and other London notables; the sign embla-
zoned across the house-front read, simply enough, "The Wax Work." Outside was the pale yellow wax image of Mother Shipton who, on the release of
a lever, would kick the unsuspecting pedestrian.

These figures, mobile or immobile, also served an apparently more
serious purpose. For many centuries the wax effigies of dead monarchs and
statesmen, coloured and "made up," were exhibited in Westminster Abbey.
Where once the effigy of the dead Elizabeth I, carried in procession at her funeral, elicited "general sighing, groaning and weeping," its decrepit condition in the mid-eighteenth century made her seem "half witch and half
ghoul." Yet the phrase "man of wax" was still in general circulation; it had no
disagreeable connotations then but, rather, meant a personage who one day
might be granted the honour of display in the Abbey.

Mrs. Salmon herself has long since sunk from view, but the waxworks of
Madame Tussaud survive in glory. Curiously enough, wax-workers have always been women, and Madame Tussaud herself can be credited with the invention of what *Punch* dubbed "the Chamber of Horrors." The present
establishment lies by the equally spectacular Planetarium.

Mayfair is named after the annual fair which took place on the north side of
Piccadilly; now only the prostitutes of Shepherd's Market bring an echo of its
past. But Haymarket has retained its old associations. Since the eighteenth
century it has been a street of entertainment, from the *Cats' Opera* of 1758 to
The Phantom of the Opera of the last decade of the twentieth century. In 1747
Samuel Foote, a famous actor and mimic, gave a series of comic lectures at
the Haymarket Theatre; in the theatre built upon the same site, in 1992, the
comic actor John Sessions gave a very similar performance. The persistent
energy of the city has its own momentum which defies rational explication.

It is a city always known for its vivacity and its restlessness. We learn
from Thomas Burke's *The Streets of London* that the citizens' "progress
through the streets is marked by impetuosity and a constant exertion of

strength." We learn further from Pierre Jean Grosley's *A Tour of London* in 1772 that "the English walk very fast; their thoughts being entirely engrossed by business, they are very punctual to their appointments, and those, who happen to be in their way, are sure to be sufferers by it; constantly darting forward, they justle them with a force proportioned to the bulk and velocity of their motion."

A century later a Parisian traveller noted that throughout London "there surges a bustling thrusting crowd such as our busiest boulevard gives no idea of . . . the cabs move twice as fast, watermen and 'bus conductors run a whole sentence to a single word . . . the last atom of value is extracted from every action and every minute." Even the entertainments were energetic, and at Greenwich "the rabble of London assemble on Easter Monday and roll down its green side, men and women promiscuously." Sexual licence and commercial energy are all mixed, to send the citizens whirling forward. A twentieth-century French traveller believed that in London "English legs move with greater velocity than ours. And this whirl carries even the ancient with it." The "whirl" is part flux and disorder, but it is also an aspect of the ceaseless movement of people, goods and vehicles. Tobias Smollett, in *Humphry Clinker*, noted only "rambling, riding, rolling, rushing, justling, mixing, bouncing, cracking, and crashing . . . All is tumult and hurry; one would imagine they were impelled by some disorder of the brain, that will not suffer them to be at rest." It does indeed on occasions appear to be a kind of fever. Maurice Ash, the author of *A Guide to the Structure of London* in 1972, when confronted with the continuous "hurrying to and fro," was tempted to conclude that there is no real business other "than the business of traffic itself"; the city, in other words, represents movement for its own sake. It is reminiscent of the scene of "shooting the bridge" out of George Borrow's *Lavengro* when a London boatman fearlessly navigated the rush of water through the middle arch of London Bridge "elevating one of his sculls in triumph, the man hallooing and the woman . . . waving her shawl." It is a picture of the intense vitality of London life.

When Southey asked a pastry-cook why she kept her shop open in harsh weather she replied that she would lose much custom, "so many were the persons who took up buns or biscuits as they passed by and threw their pence in, not allowing themselves time to enter." That pace has hardly slowed in a century, and one of the latest social surveys of London, *Focus on London 97*, reveals that "the economic activity rates for London have consistently been between 1 and 2 percentage points higher than those for the United Kingdom as a whole." This infinite motion has continued for more than a thousand years; fresh and ever renewed, it still partakes of antiquity. That is why the "whirl" and business of the streets comprise only an apparent disorder, and some observers have noticed a central rhythm or historical momentum which propels the city forward. This is the mystery—how can the endless rush itself be eternal? It is the riddle of London, which is perpetually new and always old.

There are days of rest, however, even in the turbulent city. It has often been remarked that Sunday is dreariest in London, of all cities, perhaps because restfulness and silence do not come easily or naturally to it. It was not always so. Londoners have characteristically used their holidays or holy days for "violent delights." From the early medieval period there have been archery and jousting, bowls and football—as well as the "hurling of Stones and Wood and Iron"—but the taste of the London crowd could also be less healthful. There were cock-fights and boar-fights, bull-baiting, bear-baiting and dog-baiting. The bears were given affectionate names, such as "Harry Hunks" or "Sacherson," but the treatment of them was vicious. One visitor to Bankside, in the early seventeenth century, watched the whipping of a blind bear "which is performed by five or six men, standing circularly with whips, which they exercise upon him without any mercy, as he cannot escape from them because of the chain: he defends himself with all his force and skill, throwing down all who come within his reach and are not active enough to get out of it, and tearing the whips out of their hands and breaking them." In the late seventeenth century we read of horse-baiting at Bankside where several dogs were set upon a "great horse"; it defeated its persecutors but then "the *Mobile* [mob] in the house cryed out it was a cheat, and thereupon began to untyle the house, and threatened to pull it quite down, if the Horse were not brought again and baited to death." This was the sport of the London crowd.

Bulls were baited with dogs, also, but they were sometimes maddened by having peas placed in their ears, or fireworks stuck on their backs. In the eighteenth century there was bullock-hunting in Bethnal Green, badger-baiting in Long Fields by the Tottenham Court Road, and ferocious wrestling matches at Hockley-in-the-Hole. This area, just across the Fleet from Clerkenwell, was one of the most dangerous and unruly in all London where "all sorts of rough games" were provided.

The more respectable seventeenth-century citizens were not necessarily amused by these diversions. Instead there were healthful "walks" in a number of carefully planned and plotted public areas. By the early seventeenth century Moorfields had been drained and laid out, creating "upper walks" and "lower walks," and a few years later Lincoln's Inn Fields were also designed for "common walks and disports." "Grays Inn Walks" were highly favoured and Hyde Park, although still a royal park, was open to the public for horse-racing and boxing. St. James's Park was designed a little later; here, in the words of Tom Brown, a contemporary journalist, "The green Walk afforded us varieties of discourses from persons of both sexes . . . disturbed with the noisy milk folks—crying—A Can of Milk, Ladies; A can of Red Cow's Milk, Sir."

But the true "nature" of London is not shrubbery or parkland, but human nature. At night beneath the shade of the trees, according to the Earl of Rochester, "Are buggeries, rapes and incests made" while Rosamond's Pond on the south-west side of St. James's Park became notorious for suicides.

In Spring Gardens were a bowling green and butts for target practice. In the New Spring Gardens, later Vauxhall Gardens, there were avenues and covered walks. Small green refreshment huts sold wine and punch, snuff and tobacco, sliced ham and quartered chicken, while ladies of doubtful morals sauntered among the trees with gold watches dangling from their necks as a token of their trade. The apprentices and their girls would visit Spa Fields in Clerkenwell or the Grotto Gardens in Rosoman Street, where they were encouraged to consume tea or ices or alcohol, to the accompaniment of song, music and generally "low" entertainment.

Much of that vigour has now vanished. The parks are now characteristically restful places within the noise and uproar of London. They attract those who are unhappy or ill at ease. The idle and the vagrant sleep more easily beneath the trees, together with those who are simply exhausted by the city. London parks have often been called the "lungs" of the city, but the sound is that of sleep. "It being mighty hot and I weary," Pepys wrote on 15 July 1666, "lay down upon the grass by the canalle [in St. James's Park], and slept awhile." It is a world of weariness which Hogarth depicted in an engraving that shows a London dyer and his family return from Sadler's Wells. The landscape behind them is one of sylvan charm but they are returning on the dusty road to the city. The plump and pregnant wife is dressed according to city fashion, and sports a fan with a classical motif upon it; but she is pregnant because she has cuckolded her husband, and the man himself looks tired and dejected as he carries an infant in his arms. Their two other children fight, and their dog looks at the canal which takes water from Islington into the conduits of London. Everything denotes heat and enervation, as an expedition out of London comes to its inevitable end. In more recent days, too, exhausted and fretful citizens still come back to London from their "outings" like prisoners returning to gaol.

CHAPTER 17

Music, Please

By the middle of the nineteenth century the pleasure gardens were outmoded, and their legacy lay in the concert rooms which sprang up within the city. In 1763 it was advertised that in the "great room" of Spring Gardens the seven-year-old Mozart would be seen "playing the Harpsichord in a Perfection it surmounts all . . . Imagination."

But formal music-making was not the only music of London. London's arias and laments began with the first street trader and have continued ever since. It has often been noted that the "low" culture of the native Londoner can revitalise and refashion the forces of traditional culture. The spectacle of the infant Mozart playing in a music room is complemented by Handel's remark that "hints of his very best songs have several of them been owing to the sounds in his ears of cries in the streets." In the city, "high" and "low" are inextricably mingled.

We hear the merchants of medieval Cheapside, singing out in *London Lickpenny* with "Strabery ripe" and "Cherryes in the ryse." "Here is Parys thred, finest in the land . . . Hot shepe's feete . . . Makerell . . . ryshes grene!" The costermonger sold "Costards!," which were big apples, but in later centuries the "coster," with his horse and cart, cried out, "Soles, oh! . . . Live haddick . . . Ee-ee-eels alive, oh! . . . Mackareel! mack-mack-mackareel!" So it continued, down other streets and other centuries. "Pretty Maids Pretty Pins Pretty Women . . . Buy My Great Eeels . . . Diddle Diddle Diddle Dumplens Ho . . . Any Card Matches or Savealls . . . Buy any Wax or Wafers . . . Old Shoes for Some Brooms . . . Buy a Rabbit a Rabbet . . . Buy a Fork or Fire Shovel . . . Crab Crab Crab any Crab . . . Buy my fat Chickens . . . Old Chairs to mend . . . Any Kitchen Stuff Have You Maids . . . 4 Pair For A Shilling Holland Socks . . . Buy My 4 Ropes of Hard Onyons . . . Any Work for John Cooper . . . New River Water."

Volumes have been written about these London cries, and we also have images of the tradespeople who uttered them. This identification was another way of deciphering the chaos of the city and of creating out of the poor or "lower order" a gallery of characters. The seller of cod, for example, wears an old apron, while the vendor of shoes sports a cape. The seller of dried hake carries the basket of that commodity upon her head, but the vendor of oranges and lemons carries her bounty at her waist. The Irish were known to sell rabbits and milk, the Jews old clothes and hare-skins, the Italians looking-glasses and pictures. The old woman selling fire-shovels dresses herself in an old-fashioned cone-shaped hat as a representation of the wintry months. Countrywomen entering the metropolis to sell their wares characteristically wore red cloaks and straw hats, while the countrymen wove flowers in their hair. Those who sold fish were generally the poorest, while women selling clothes were the most smartly dressed.

Yet the clothing of most street vendors bears the unmistakable mark of destitution, with worn and tattered dresses or coats. Many of these tradespeople were crippled or deformed and, as the editor of Marcellus Laroon's *The Cryes of the City of London Drawne after the Life*, Sean Shesgreen, has noted, "If they give one impression more than any other, it is a care-worn melancholy." Laroon's portraits are distinctly individual, unlike "types" or categories, and in his art we can see the lineaments of specific fate and circumstance. The distinctive features he depicted in the 1680s remain the silent token of many generations who have walked crying through the streets of the city.

Even as the poor trader died—or left some scanty stock to another—his or her cry was taken up like an echo. It was certainly true that, as Addison wrote in 1711, "People know the Wares they deal in rather by their Tunes than by their Words." The words were often indistinct or indistinguishable: the mender of old chairs was recognised by his low and melancholy note, while the retailer of broken glass specialised in a sort of plaintive shriek quite appropriate to his goods. But even the music itself might become confused and confusing. The vendor of shrimps could adopt the same tune as the vendor of watercress, and potatoes were sold with the same cry as that of cherries.

There was also in the passage of years, or centuries, the steady clipping or abbreviation of jargon. "Will you buy any milk today, mistress" became "Milk maids below," then "Milk below," then "Milk-o" and, finally, "Mieu" or "Mee-o." "Old clothes" became "Ogh clo" or "owld clo." "Salted hake" became "Poor Jake" or "Poor Jack"; then "Poor John" became the recognisable phrase for the vendors of dried cod. The chimney-sweep's cry became " 'we-ep" or " 'e-ep" and Pierce Egan, author of *Life in London*, recalled "one man from whom I could never make out more than *happy happy happy now*."

As London grew larger and noisier, the cries became louder—perhaps, even, more desperate and more hysterical. From a distance of half a mile, they were a low, steady and continuous roar much like a fall of water; they became a Niagara of voices. But in the middle of the city, they were a great turmoil of notes. London to foreign observers was "a distracted City" and Samuel Johnson noted that "The attention of a new-comer is generally first struck by the multiplicity of the cries that stun him in the street." Stun, stunner, stunning—it is a true London word. As the print salesman said of his wares placed in an upturned umbrella—"It'll show stunnin', and sell as yer goes."

The cries of the street-seller were joined by those of the "common criers" who announced such items of public news as "If any man or woman can tell any tydyngs of a grey mare, with a long mane and a short tayle . . ." There were the shopkeepers of Cheapside, Paternoster Row, East Cheap and a hundred other localities calling out continually "What do you lack . . . Will you buy . . ." The cry of the "mercury-women," "Londons Gazette here," was eventually superseded by that of the newsboy with his "Pa-a-par! ainy of the mornin' pipers." The horn of the sow-gelder plying his trade mingled with the bell of the dustman and the sound of the "Twancking of a brass Kettle or a Frying-pan" together with the myriad and unending sounds of the London traffic.

Today, street markets are still alive with chatter and patter; most of the cries have vanished, although even in the twenty-first century you might still hear the bell of the muffin-man or the horn of the knife-grinder and see the pony-and-trap of the "any-old-iron" or rag-and-bone man. There were also the barrow man with "Shrimps and winkles all alive-o," the lavender seller, and the "lilywhite" celery and watercress man who cried out, " 'Ere's yer salory and watercreases."

In the past there were also the ballad-singers and the street patterers and the peripatetic vocalists and the almanac vendors and the "flying stationers" who would take up their pitch on any corner and sell single sheets on juicy murders or fashionable songs.

Perhaps the oldest form was the broadside, a sheet printed on one side which bore the latest news and the newest sensations. From the earliest years of the sixteenth century this was the language of the street—"Sir Walter Raleigh His Lamentations! . . . Strange News from Sussex . . . No Natural Mother But a Monster . . ." Alongside these "headlines," as they might appropriately be called, were such broadside ballads as "A Maydens Lamentation For A Bedfellow Or I Can Nor Will No Longer Lye Alone . . . The Mans Comfortable Answer To The Mayden . . . This Maid Would Give Ten Shillings For A Kiss." These were the songs which were shouted down the streets and pasted on the walls. Their vendors did not expect to get paid for their voices but, instead, drew a crowd and then sold their wares for a halfpenny a sheet. There was of course an especial delight in "Last Dying Speeches" sold to the crowd at the very moment of execution by "flying patterers" otherwise known as "death hunters." In a city which lived upon rumour, sensation and sudden alterations of mass feeling, the crying out of news and the singing of popular ballads were the perfect forms of communication. The politic John Dryden was not able to compete with the political ballad, "Lillibullero," which outsold him in every sense, and another balladeer wrote: "Dryden thy Wit has catterwauld too long, / Now *Lero Lero* is the only song." Songs, like slogans and catchphrases, could sweep through the streets for days or weeks before being utterly forgotten.

Then new songs, together with an old ballad for company, would in turn become part of a "long song" which comprised several ballads printed together on a roll of paper. They might also come into the hands of the "pinner up" who fastened many hundreds of ballads on iron railings or an area of "dead wall." In the 1830s some eight hundred yards of wall on the south side of Oxford Street were used to display these song-sheets, until the arrival of shops and shop-fronts transformed the thoroughfare.

Yet some ballads retained their individual popularity for many years. "Willikins and his Dinah," "Billy Barlow" and "The Rat-Catcher's

Daughter" remained great favourites with the London crowd—the pretty daughter of the rat-catcher herself having "such a sweet loud voice, sir,/You could hear her all down Parliament Street/And as far as Charing Cross, sir." She was representative of those itinerant street-performers whose lives were often as pathetic and terrible as the ballads they sang. They performed mainly in the evening, sometimes accompanied by a flute or a cracked guitar, and were to be found upon every corner from the Strand to Whitechapel. Charles Dickens recalled his encounter with one such "itinerant singer" by the Upper Marsh on the south side of the river—"Singing! How few of those who pass such a miserable creature as this, think of the anguish of heart, the sinking of soul and spirit, which the very effort of singing produces!"

The ballad-singer had as a counterpart in the London streets the "running patterer" who cried out the romances and tragedies of the day. Henry Mayhew described their activities in his usual laconic style: "It is . . . a 'mob' or 'school' of the running patterers (for both these words are used) and consists of two, three or four men. All these men state that the greater the noise they make, the better the chance of sale." They would often take up positions in different parts of the street and pretend to vie with each other for attention, thus heightening interest in the latest crime, murder, elopement or execution. Once again, the requisite in the city is sheer volume of noise.

Commotion and rumour are certainly more important than "truth," if that commodity can ever actually be found in London, and the patterer often supplied his auditors with "cock"—politely described as a "pleasing fiction"—which was then sold as a "catchpenny." The offender was known as a "cock-crower" and sometimes advertised his false wares with a lurid picture, often incorporating the London motifs of blood and flame mounted upon a pole.

It would be unfair to scorn these products of native art. Joshua Reynolds confessed that he borrowed a motif from a woodcut he had found pinned to a dead wall; Walter Scott studied street literature, chapbooks and ballads to stimulate his interest in folk myth and history. It is important to emphasise once again how Cockney taste can enter and animate a more "refined" cultural tradition.

The voices of the running patterers and the itinerant singers were invariably joined by the often discordant airs of the street musicians. Hector Berlioz, visiting London in the mid-nineteenth century, wrote that "no city in the world" was consumed so much by music; despite his profession, he was concerned less with the melodies of the concert hall than with those of the barrel-organ, the barrel-piano, the bagpipes and the drums which filled the streets. As Charles Booth noted in his survey of the East End, "let a barrel organ strike up a valse at any corner and at once the girls who may be walking past, and the children out of the gutter, begin to foot it merrily. Men join in some-times, two young men together as likely as not," while an appreciative crowd watched the dancing.

There were German bands, as well as Indian drummers and blacked-up "Abyssians" who played violin, guitar, tambourine and castanets; there were glee singers, and minstrels (generally a couple) who could be heard crooning "Oh where is my boy tonight?" and "Will you meet me at the Fountain?" In the 1840s there was a blind musician who played the violoncello with his feet, and a crippled trumpeter who drove around in a dog-cart.

The cacophony was immense and yet, in one of those gradual but neces-sary transitions of London life, most of it has passed away leaving only buskers to entertain cinema queues and inventive players of illegal music in the underpasses of London's transport system.

CHAPTER 18

Signs of the Times

n eighteenth-century traveller remarked that "if towns were to be called after the first words which greeted a traveller on arrival, London would be called Damn it!" At the beginning of the twentieth century it would have been called "Bloody" and today "Fuckin'."

"Fucking" is one of the longest-serving terms of abuse, having been heard on the London streets since the thirteenth century, and it is perhaps no surprise that the prevalent adjective applied to the language of Londoners is "disgusting." The "disgust" is a response to that undertow of violence and anger which exemplifies life in the city, while such miseries as sexual abuse may have testified to the distaste which Londoners have had for their own fallen and once dirty condition. Contemporary standards of hygiene and more liberal sexual mores have not, however, materially diminished the "fucking" and "cunts" heard in the street. Perhaps modern Londoners are simply mouthing the words which the city itself has bequeathed to them.

In this context the obscene gesture should not be forgotten. In the sixteenth century a biting of the thumb represented aggression; this in turn led to the hat being cocked backwards and, in the late eighteenth century, "by a jerk of the thumb over the left shoulder." The thumb then moved to the tip of the nose to represent contempt, and by the twentieth century two fingers were raised in the air as a "V" sign. The arm and elbow were then employed in an upward thrust to suggest derision.

The hand gestures of the street could also be free of sexual innuendo. There was once, everywhere, a pointing hand on the palm of which a destination was offered—"please to go this way," whether to an eating-house or a toyshop. London was a city of signs. In 1762, according to Jenny Uglow's *Hogarth*, the "Society of Sign Painters" announced a "Grand Exhibition" of its products, and in some rooms off Bow Street were exhibited "Keys, Bells, Swords, Poles, Sugar-Loaves, Tobacco Rolls, Candles," all the "ornamental Furniture, carved in Wood." It was meant as a reproof to the more tasteful productions of the Society of Arts, but its comic variety was also a testimony to an ancient but still living tradition of street art.

Once a pole draped with red rags was the emblem of the barber-surgeon who was permitted to bleed customers on his premises, the pole itself a token of the wooden rod which the customer held to keep his arm steady. The red rag later turned into a red stripe, until it became the customary barber's pole of succeeding centuries. Almost every house, and certainly every trade, had its own sign so that the streets of the city were a perpetual forest of painted imagery: "Floure de Lice . . . Ravyns Head . . . Corniyshe coughs . . . The Chalice . . . The Cardinal's Hat." There were images of chained bears and of rising suns, of sailing ships and angels, of red lions and golden bells. There were also simple tokens of residence. Mr. Bell, for example, might hang the sign of a bell outside his house. But there were also well-known, if somewhat surprising, conjunctions in pub signs such as the Dog and Gridiron or the Three Nuns and a Hare. There were unusual attributions, too. As Addison pointed out, "I have seen a Goat set up before the Door of a Perfumer, and the French King's Head at a Sword-Cutlers's." Tom Jones, in Henry Fielding's novel of that name, takes up the litany: "Here we saw *Joseph's* Dream, the *Bull* and *Mouth*, the *Hen* and *Razor*, the *Ax* and *Bottle*, the *Whale* and *Crow*, the *Shovel* and *Boot*, the *Leg* and *Star*, the *Bible* and *Swan*, the *Frying Pan* and *Drum*." Adam and Eve represented a fruiterer, while the horn of a unicorn symbolised the shop of an apothecary; a bag of nails denoted an ironmonger, a row of coffins a carpenter. A sign of male and female hands conjoined might sometimes be completed by the message "Marriages performed within."

It was a question of reading the street, of making the right associations and connections in an environment which needed a thorough decoding to

mitigate its chaos and variety. Interpretative tracts, such as the elegantly titled *Vade Mecum for Malt Worms*, were also published. In 1716 John Gay
gave best expression to the situation, however, in "The Art of Walking The
Streets in London"—a theme taken up by many writers—with his portrait of
a stranger who "dwells on ev'ry Sign, with stupid Gaze/Enters the narrow
Alley's doubtful Maze."

There were also signs and plaques carved into the stone of London's
buildings. Small tablets marked newly laid-out streets—"This is Johns Street
Ano Dom 1685"—while corporate heraldry was employed in the "arms" of
a district or company affixed to various buildings; the symbol of St. Marylebone contains lilies and roses, because these were the flowers found in the
grave of St. Mary after whom the district is named. At a later date even the
lowly coal-hole covers were richly decorated, so that those who preferred to
look down upon the ground were still assaulted by symbols of dogs and
flowers. A nailed hoop upon a door or wall denoted the presence of fresh
paint, while a small bouquet of straw meant that building work was taking
place in the vicinity.

The city is indeed a labyrinth of signs, with the occasional but unnerving
suspicion that there may exist no other reality than these painted symbols
which demand your attention while leading you astray. As one commentator
said of the modern and brilliantly illuminated Piccadilly Circus, "it is a wonderful sight—unless you can read."

The signs of the city were distracting in another sense. They hung out so
far from the wall that they touched those on the opposite side of the street,
and they were sometimes so large that they blocked out sight of the sky. They
could also be dangerous; they were meant to be placed at least nine feet above
the level of the pavement, so that a horse and rider could pass beneath, but
the regulation was not always obeyed. They were very heavy and there were
occasions when the weight of sign and leaden support was too great for the
wall to which they were fixed—one "front-fall" of this kind in Fleet Street injured several people and killed "two young ladies, a cobbler, and the king's
jeweller." On windy days in the capital, the noise was ominous, their "creak-
ing Noise" a sure sign of impending "rainy Floods." So, in the same years as
the exhibition of street signs off Bow Street, the city authorities concluded
that they had become an impediment to the ever increasing traffic of the
streets and ordered that they be taken down. Ten years later came street numbers.

But all colour was not lost. The passion for street art simply changed its form, with the expansion of advertising. There had always been posters wrapped around the wooden posts of the street to publicise the latest auction or the latest play, but only after the demise of street signs did other forms of public art properly emerge. By the early nineteenth century London had "grown wondrously pictorial" with a variety of *papier-mâché* ornaments or paintings placed in shop windows to denote the trade of the occupant. An essay in *The Little World of London*, entitled "Commercial Art," lingers pleasurably on these *objets d'art*. Many coffee houses had a symbol of loaf and cheese together with cup; fishmongers painted the walls of their premises with "a group of fish in the grand style" all variously and picturesquely coloured, while grocers specialised in "conversation pieces" which portrayed various benevolent London matrons "assembled round the singing kettle or the simmering urn." Boots, cigars and sealing wax, in gigantic form, were also suspended over the doors of various premises, while the destruction of Pompeii seemed a fitting advertisement for a patent cockroach exterminator.

One great innovation of the nineteenth century was the advertising hoarding, and in some of the earliest photographs of London they can be seen lining the streets and the new railway stations offering everything from Pear's Soap to the *Daily Telegraph*. Advertising was in that sense very much part of the ideal of "progress," since the hoardings themselves had first been erected to protect the streets from the myriad building sites and railway improvements. Once posters had been enlarged to cover these wooden frames, then advertising images appropriate to the city itself—large, gaudy, colourful— began to emerge. There were certain popular sites, among them the north end of Waterloo Bridge and the dead wall beside the English Opera House in North Wellington Street. Here, according to Charles Knight's *London*, could be found "rainbow-hued placards vying in gorgeous extravagance of colour with Turner's last new picture . . . pictures of pens, gigantic as the plumes in the casque of the Castle of Otranto . . . spectacles of enormous size . . . Irishmen dancing under the influence of Guinness's Dublin Stout."

"A London Street Scene," painted by J.O. Parry in 1833, could serve as an introduction to any street scene over the last two centuries. A small blackened sweep-boy looks up in admiration as a poster for a new performance of *Otello* is placed over one advertising John Parry in *The Sham Prince*; there is a bill proclaiming "Mr. Matthews—At Home," "Tom & Jerry—The Christening—!!!!!!" and a narrow strip asking "Have You Seen The Industrious Fleas?" Thus the walls of the city become a palimpsest of forthcoming, recent and old sensations.

On a dead wall today, close to where I am now writing this book, and not far from the site of the 1833 painting, can be seen posters for "Armageddon," "To Heathrow in Fifteen Minutes," "Mr. Love Pants Is Coming," "Meltdown '98 Festival," "Drugstore—Sober—New Single Available," "Apostle" and "The Girl With Brains In Her Feet." More mysterious advertisements suggest that "There's A Revolution In Sight," that "The Magic Is Closer Than You Think," and that "Nothing Else Moves Me."

"Peripatetic placards" appeared on the streets in the 1830s. These were such a novel phenomenon that Charles Dickens interviewed one and, by describing him as "a piece of human flesh between two slices of pasteboard," created the phrase "sandwich man." George Scharf drew many of them, from a small boy in surtout overcoat holding a barrel inscribed "Malt Whiskey John Howse" to an old woman holding up a sign for "Anatomical Model of the Human Figure."

Then in characteristic London fashion the single placard-carriers were put together in order to create a kind of pageant or pantomime; a group of them were placed inside paste models of blacking pots, for example, and paraded in line to advertise the efficacy of "Warrens Blacking, 30 Strand," the very place where Dickens himself began his tortuous London childhood. Then arrived the advertisement as the horse-drawn gig, surmounted by an enormous hat or an Egyptian obelisk. The search for novelty was always intense and the passion for posters blossomed into the "electric advertisements" of the 1890s when "Vinolia Soap" was hailed in illuminated letters above Trafalgar Square.

Advertisements in lights soon began to move; at Piccadilly Circus could be seen a red crystal bottle pouring port into a waiting glass, and a car with turning silver wheels. Soon they were everywhere—above the ground, under the ground, and in the sky. The plethora of advertising in London helped fashion Huxley's vision of the future city in *Brave New World* where above Westminster "The electric sky-signs effectively shut off the outer darkness. 'Calvin Stopes and His Sixteen Sexophonists.'" Buses of the twenty-first century, perhaps beyond the purview of dystopian fiction, are now plastered with gaudy images like the pageant wagons of medieval London.

The pavement artists have had a less glorious career in the city. They commenced their work only when the streets were paved with stone rather than cobbles, and in that sense theirs is a recent London profession. There was a time when beggars scrawled their messages of supplication upon the stones—

"Can You Help Me Out" being a favourite expression—but the pavement artist supplied a variant in the 1850s with the chalked words "All My Own Work" or "Every Little Helps. I thank you." These street artists, or "screevers" as they were once called, had their own particular pitches. The corners of fashionable squares were considered to be ideal territory but Cockspur Street and the site opposite Gatti's restaurant in the Strand were favoured locales. There was also a line of such street artists along the Embankment, with twenty-five yards between each pitch. Many of these "screevers" were demoralised artists whose orthodox work had not prospered—Simeon Solomon's career as a Pre-Raphaelite painter had been applauded, for example, but he ended up as a pavement artist in Bayswater. Others were the homeless or unemployed who realised that they had a talent for the job; it required only coloured chalks and a duster, and a scene or portrait could be conjured upon the stone. Some specialised in portraits of contemporary politicians, or of sentimental domestic situations; one artist painted religious scenes along the Finchley Road, while in the Whitechapel Road another specialised in scenes of fire and burning houses. In all cases, however, they satisfied the taste of London by painting in the crudest and most garish tones, although by curious association they are related to the night sky above the city. In *The Highways and Byways of London*, Mrs. E.T. Cook reported that the sky behind the artists' lodging houses in Drury Lane or Hatton Garden would often be robed "in intense hues of orange, purple and crimson" as if mimicking their colours. George Orwell, in *Down and Out in Paris and London*, recalls the conversation of one screever, Bozo, whose pitch was close to Waterloo Bridge. He was walking with Orwell back to his lodgings in Lambeth, but was all the time looking up at the heavens. "Say, will you look at Aldebaran! Look at the colour. Like a—great blood orange . . . Now and again I go out at night and watch the meteors." Bozo had even engaged in correspondence with the Astronomer Royal on the subject of the sky above London, so that for a moment the city and the cosmos were intimately connected in the life of one wandering artist of the street.

But no account of London art can be complete without the history of its graffiti. One of the first is a curse by one Londoner upon two others, written in a Roman hand—Publius and Titus were "hereby solemnly cursed." It is matched by a late twentieth-century graffito recently recorded by the contemporary London novelist Iain Sinclair, "TIKD. FUCK YOU. DHKP," and suggests a characteristic of London street-writing. "For the stone shall

cry out of the wall," according to Habakkuk 2:11, and in London the cries are
frequently those of anger and hostility. Many are entirely personal, with no
meaning except to the one who carved or sprayed the words upon a wall, and
remain the most enigmatic features of the city; one moment of anger or loss
has been inscribed upon its surface, to become part of the chaos of signs and
symbols which exist all around. Outside Paddington station can be found
"Fume" everywhere together with "Cos," "Boz" and "Chop." "Rava" can
be seen upon the bridges of the south bank. "Great Redeemer, People's Lib-
erator" adorned Kentish Town Station in the 1980s. "Thomas Jordan cleaned
this window, and damn the job, I say—1815" was written on an ancient window and on a London wall a Thomas Berry scribbled "Oh Lord, cut them
with thy sword." As one exponent of the art of graffiti put it to Iain Sinclair,
"If you're going to be around the city all the time, you'd better put your name
up," which is the reason why people over many centuries have simply written down their names or initials on any tractable surface with the occasional
amendment of "was here" or more frequently "woz 'ere." It is a way of asserting individuality, perhaps, but it becomes immediately part of the anonymous texture of London; in that sense graffiti are a vivid token of human
existence in the city. They may be compared to footprints or handprints, laid
into cement, which become part of the city's fabric. Hand impressions have
been found in Fleet Road, Hampstead, as mysterious and poignant as symbols carved on ancient stones.

Sometimes graffiti have a relevance to the immediate locality—"James
Bone is a bad kisser" or "Rose Maloney Is A Thief"—where they serve as
silent messages, the written equivalent of drum-taps in the jungle. But there
are also more general admonitions. In one of his prose works Thomas More
quotes a fifteenth-century slogan written upon many walls—"D.C. hath no
P"—which can perhaps be deciphered with the help of More's summary that
it "toucheth the readiness that woman hath to fleshly filth, if she fall in drunkenness." One may surmise that D.C. denotes "drunken cunts" but the "P" is
mysterious.

Any particular year, over the last thousand, will provide its own litany of
curses, execrations and imperatives. In 1792, for example, these were some of
the graffiti: "Christ Is God . . . No Coach Tax! . . . Murder Jews . . . Joanna
Southcott . . . Damn the Duke of Richmond! . . . Damn Pitt!" In 1942 the
most prominent graffiti remained "Strike in the West Now!," and in the later
part of the century the two most formidable slogans were "George Davis Is
Innocent" and "No Poll Tax." The city seems almost to be speaking to itself

by means of these messages, in a language both vivid and cryptic. Some recent graffiti have been more reflective in tone—"Nothing Lasts" painted upon a brick wall, "Obedience Is Suicide" upon a bridge in Paddington, "The Tigers of Wrath Are Wiser than the Horses of Instruction" inscribed above "Rangers," "Aggro," "Boots" and "Rent Revolt" on the corner of Basing Street, Notting Hill Gate—the last being a potent example of the phenomenon of clustering. A wall may remain inviolate for many years but, as soon as one graffito is placed upon it, others ineluctably follow in competitive or aggressive display. Aggression can often be associated with sexuality. Many of these messages have an anonymous sexual intent which suggests isolation as well as desire—"Oh please don't cane me too hard master . . . 23/11 I am 30 I have a/place at Victoria SW/I love dressing up I am wearing/pink panties now."

The proper locale for these harsh and impersonal messages of love is, naturally enough, the public lavatory. It has become the principal source of all urban graffiti; here, in confinement and secrecy, the Londoner speaks to the entire city with words and signs that are as old as the city itself. One attendant told Geoffrey Fletcher, the author of *The London Nobody Knows*, that "the lavatory in Charing Cross Road was the place to go if you want the writing on the wall . . . make your blood run cold, it would." In fact London lavatories have been notorious for centuries, and in 1732 Hurlo Thrumbo printed at Bethlehem Wall, Moorfields, a compilation entitled *The Merry Thought or the Glass window and Bog House Miscellany*. We may extract from these some of the more salient and, perhaps, immortal epigrams. From the "bog-houses" of Pancras Wells comes

Hither I came in haste to shit
But found such excrements of wit
That to shew my skill in verse
Had scarcely time to wipe my arse.

There then ensues a dialogue or chorus of other costive notes in which "write" is frequently rhymed with "shite" and "London" with "undone." The anonymous authors' clothing is "undone," literally, in the London "bog-house"; but perhaps there is also a more plaintive suggestion that they have themselves been "undone" in London. From the "bog-house" by the Temple comes

No hero looks so fierce in fight
As does the man who strains to shite

and upon a tavern wall in Covent Garden

There's nothing foul that we commit
But what we write and what we shit.

Sometimes there is a grand riposte to this city scatology. "It is the vanity of degenerates," one Londoner inscribed, "to write their names here."

The other principal source of London graffiti has always been the prison house, from the inscription of Thomas Rose upon the wall of the Beauchamp Tower in the Tower of London—"Kept close/By those to whom he did no wrong. May 8th, 1666"—to the cell of a modern prison where one inmate has written "You may be guilty/But what must this/be like for those/who are not." These men also have been undone in London. Thomas Mehoe writes in 1581: "bi-tertvre-strange-my-trouth-was-tryed-yet-of-my-libertie-denied," with words painfully but carefully inscribed with an iron nail. They are still preserved within the Tower, and in that ancient prison are many carvings, crosses, skeletons, death-heads and hour-glasses carved as tokens or symbols of suffering. There are words which are supposed to provide comfort—"Hope to the end and have patience . . . Spero in Deo . . . patience shall prevail" which can be contrasted with the graffiti found in the modern London prison—"Home by May . . . This is where I spent most of my life . . . It was just one/time I never got away by someone who got caught . . . Treat me carefully/I'm seven years/bad luck." In many inscriptions the prison itself seems to be treated as an image of the world, or of the city, which will perhaps lend further significance to another graffito found upon a London wall—"I cant breathe."

CHAPTER 19

All of Them Citizens

here are other kinds of anonymity. Dickens knew of a woman, seen in the streets about the Strand, "who has fallen forward, double, through some affliction of the spine, and whose head has of late taken a turn to one side, so that it now droops over the back of one of her arms at about the wrist. Who does not know her staff, and her shawl, and her basket, as she gropes her way along, capable of seeing nothing but the pavement, never begging, never stopping, for ever going somewhere on no business! How does she live, whence does she come, whither does she go, and why?" Dickens saw her many times; he never knew her name, and she could not have seen the famous novelist as he passed her and, perhaps, looked back.

I used to pass a dwarf, dressed in old clothes and with wizened features, who in a hoarse voice would direct the traffic at the crossroads of Theobalds Road and Grays Inn Road; he was there every day and then suddenly, in the summer of 1978, he was gone. There was, even more recently, a young West Indian who would walk up Kensington Church Street dressed in silver foil and with balloons tied to his wrists. A gentleman, known colloquially as "The King of Poland," used to walk barefoot along the Strand in red velvet robes and with a wreath upon his head. He, too, vanished without warning.

These London particulars have their own locale and are rarely seen beyond it; they are the sprites or spirits of a specific place, and belong exclusively to the city. There was the "musical small-coal man" of Clerkenwell who, after his daily round was over, organised concerts in his lodgings in Jerusalem Passage; he died when as a practical joke a ventriloquist, known as "Talking Smith," pretended to be the voice of God proclaiming his doom. There was Lord Queensberry, "Old Q," who every day sat at the window of his house at 138 Piccadilly; although he had only one eye, he leered and winked at every pretty female who passed in the street. And there was "the afflicted girl—white faced and expressionless" who sat for many years close to the Horse-Shoe of Tottenham Court Road, "oblivious of time and inured to suffering through all the noise and tumult."

There were always such familiar faces in every locality. Today there are the lollipop men and women, helping children to cross the road, but until the early decades of the twentieth century the best known were the crossing-sweepers. Many crossing-sweepers remained at their posts—or on their particular "property," as it was called—for thirty or forty years. There was the bearded crossing-sweeper at Cornhill—"Sometimes I get insulted, only in words; sometimes I get chaffed by sober people." And there, at the corner of Cavendish Square, was Billy who could remember ancient riots—"The mob was carrying a quartern loaf dipped in bullock's blood, and when I saw it I thought it was a man's head; so that frightened me, and I run off." One elderly sweeper "kept" the narrow passage from Berkeley Street into Stratton Street, and wore an old huntsman's coat and hat. He once came into the police court as a witness, and the following exchange is recorded by Mayhew.

JUDGE: Are you a field-marshal?
WITNESS: No, my lord. I am the sweeper of the Lansdowne Passage.

There was "Sir" Harry Dimsdale of Seven Dials, according to *Old and New London*, "a poor diminutive creature, deformed and half an idiot" who hawked laces and threads at the turn of the nineteenth century; he followed the same routes, along Holborn or Oxford Street, and suffered the jeers of the children and the watermen who washed down the hackney-coach stands. He had only four or five teeth, but could bend a silver coin with them "when he could induce anybody to trust him with one." His favourite amusement was to torment children by pinching them or throwing them to the ground, but his chief pleasure was found in drink. He was "helplessly drunk every evening . . . howling in the frenzy produced by his fiery draughts or uttering the low, dismal plaint caused by hunger or pain." It is reported that his expression was one of "idiotcy, physical suffering and a propensity to mischief" but the mistress of his wretched lodgings—a back attic laid with straw—reported that at night she heard him praying. "Sir" Harry was known throughout London, and there is an extant engraving of him at the age of thirty-eight; but then he, too, suddenly disappeared. His is a curious story of suffering and isolation, but one with echoes and parallels in the modern city.

Other eccentric tradesmen led more amiable lives in the street. There was the famous character Peter Stokes, the "flying pie-man" of Holborn Hill in the early nineteenth century; as described by "Aleph" in *London Scenes and London People*, he "always wore a black suit, scrupulously brushed, dress coat and vest, knee breeches, stout black stockings, and shoes with steel buckles." This tradesman, with an expression "open and agreeable, expressive of intellect and moral excellence," would dash out of Fetter Lane on the stroke of twelve noon and run through the streets of the neighbourhood for the next four hours, dodging horses and wagons and coaches, incessantly crying "Buy! Buy! Buy!" He too was famous throughout London, and sat to an engraver with the basket of pies balanced neatly on his right arm.

Equally notable, in the streets of London, a little more than a century earlier, was "Colly Molly Puffe," a short hunch-backed man who also sold pastries. He preferred to balance his basket upon his head rather than his arm and, despite his frail form, he had a stentorian voice with which he sang out his wares. His cry was unmistakable, and he was to be seen at city parades or public hangings, always brandishing a big stick to ward off any thief or urchin who tried to steal his goods.

Tiddy Doll was a vendor of gingerbread in the Haymarket who wore ornate and brightly coloured dress, complete with feathered cap, and had the distinction of being drawn by Hogarth; he was so well known by Londoners that "once being missed from his usual stand . . . on the occasion of a visit which he paid to a country fair, a 'catch-penny' account of his alleged murder was printed and sold in the streets by thousands." His actual death was almost equally sensational: during a Frost Fair, when a festival was held upon the iced surface of the Thames, Tiddy Doll plunged through a sudden crack and was drowned.

There have been any number of London eccentrics and exhibitionists who achieved fame in the streets. There was a celebrated miser, Thomas Cook of Clerkenwell, who on his death-bed demanded his money back from the surgeon who had not cured him. There was a notorious doctor, Martin Van Butchell, who rode around the West End on a pony upon whose flanks he had painted spots. When at home in Mount Street he sold oranges and gingerbread on his doorstep and kept his first wife embalmed in the parlour. "He dressed his first wife in black, and his second in white," according to Edward Walford in *Old and New London*, "never allowing either a change of colour." He astonished his contemporaries by growing a beard—this at the end of the eighteenth century—and, equally astonishing to his fellow citizens, was "one of the earliest teetotallers."

Benjamin Coates first came to public notice in 1810 when he hired the Haymarket Theatre so that he might play Romeo for one night; he appeared on stage "in a cloak of sky-blue silk, profusely spangled, red pantaloons, a vest of white muslin, and a wig of the style of Charles II, capped by an opera hat." Unfortunately he had a "guttural" voice and the laughter which greeted his performance was increased by the fact that "his nether garments, being far too tight burst in seams which could not be concealed." He was known, ever after, as Romeo Coates and was often seen driving through the streets in a carriage manufactured in the shape of a sea shell. For sheer vigour and energy we may put him beside the engraver William Woolett who, each time he finished a new work, fired a cannon from the roof of his house in Green Street, Leicester Square.

Certain women also made a singular impression. There was the rich and learned Miss Banks who wore a quilted petticoat with "two immense pockets, stuffed with books of all sizes." When she wandered on her book-hunting expeditions through the streets she was always accompanied by a six-foot manservant "with a cane almost as tall as himself." In this state she was, again according to Walford, "more than once taken for a member of the balladsinging confraternity." Miss Mary Lucrine of Oxford Street kept the shutters of her windows barred and never left her lodgings for some fifty years, one of several London spinsters who closed themselves off from the anxiety and violence of the city.

Some Londoners became notorious through their diet. In the middle years of the seventeenth century Roger Crab of Bethnal Green subsisted on "dock-leaves, mallows or grasse" and plain water, while in the late twentieth century Stanley Green, wearing cap and blazer, paraded in Oxford Street with a banner proclaiming "Less Passion from Less Protein." For twenty-five years, crowds swirled about him, almost oblivious of his presence, engaged only in their usual uproar.

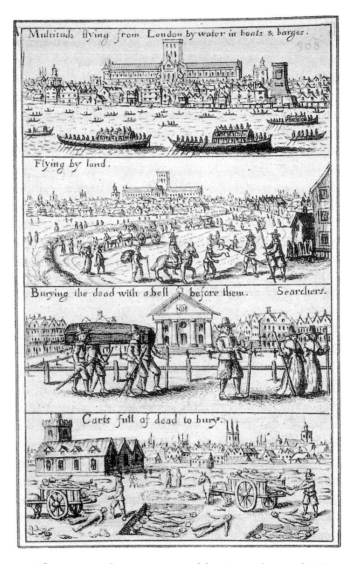

The causes and consequences of the Great Plague of 1665
were endlessly described, but most considered it to be
God's punishment upon a heathen city.

CHAPTER 20

A Plague Upon You

London is a city perpetually doomed. It has always been considered the Jerusalem about which the prophets were so clamant, and the words of Ezekiel have often been applied to curb its mighty spirit—"Say unto them which daub it with untempered mortar, that it shall fall . . . and a stormy wind shall rend it" (Ezekiel XIII: 11). In the fourteenth century John Gower lamented its approaching destruction, and in 1600 Thomas Nashe wrote that "London doth mourn, Lambeth is quite forlorn; Trades cry, woe worth that ever they were born . . . From winter, plague and pestilence, good Lord, deliver us!" In 1849 the Earl of Shaftesbury described London as the "City of the Plague," and one of the characters in George Orwell's *Keep the Aspidistra Flying* talks of "a city of the dead."

Much has been written about the nature of fear in London. James Boswell arrived in the city in 1762. "I began to be apprehensive that I was taking a nervous fever, a supposition not improbable, as I had one after such an illness when I was last in London. I was quite sunk." The editor's commentary upon Laroon's depiction of street traders emphasises the traces of anxiety upon their faces, in particular "hollow, frightened eyes." In the poem "London" William Blake's narrator wanders through the streets by the river, "And mark in every face I meet/Marks of weakness, marks of woe" together with the "Infants cry of fear . . . Soldiers sigh . . . Harlots curse . . . new-born Infants tear." In the illustration with which he has adorned the right-hand side of the poem, a child is warming itself beside a great fire which may itself be a token of calamity. In his account of the plague of 1664 and 1665, Daniel Defoe depicted the city itself torn by fever and nervous fear. It was said of Thackeray that "it seemed as if London were his disease, and he could not help telling all the symptoms" to which is appended the remark, "that is another sign of a true Londoner." In a poem by Thomas Hood, the stones of London cry out against a woman careering through the streets upon a horse—"Batter her! shatter her! Kick her brains out! Let her blood spatter her!"

There has always been so much to create anxiety in the city—the noise, the endless rush, the violence of the mob. London has been compared to a prison and to a grave. To the German poet, Heinrich Heine, "this over-driven London oppresses the fancy and tears the heart." Heckethorn's *London Memories* records that when in 1750 one soldier prophesied an earthquake "vast multitudes left London for the country, and the fields around were crowded with fugitives from the threatened catastrophe." The unfortunate seer was later confined to a madhouse. But the symptoms of fear have never materially diminished. In times of pestilence many citizens simply died of fright, and it has been remarked that in nineteenth-century discourse the word "gloom" emerges frequently. It is related to the fogs or "London particulars" of that century, but it seems also to have possessed an intimate and more unnerving significance. November was the month for London suicides and, when the fog was at its thickest, "people who experienced this phenomenon said it seemed as if the world was coming to an end." These last words were exactly those used by the inhabitants of Whitechapel Road, when a firework manufactory exploded. The phrase came readily and easily to the lips—as if, perhaps, there was some unconscious wish for this mighty cessation. Dostoevsky noted, after visiting the Great Exhibition in London, "And you feel nervous . . . a feeling of fear somehow creeps over you. Can this, you think, in fact be the final accomplishment of an ideal state of things? Is this the end, by any chance?"

Death has always been one of London's devices. "The Dance of Death" was painted on the wall of St. Paul's Churchyard, so that the people who thronged that church for business or amusement were always aware of their mortality. In June of 1557 the registrar of a parish records the following causes of death within that one month—"a swellynge . . . ague . . . consumption . . . thought [cough] . . . blody fluxe . . . poches [pox] . . . postum which brake . . . browce [bruise?] . . . famyne . . . consumed away." The bills of mortality in London, published every Thursday, include those who were "planet struck," or who suffered from "horseshoe head" or "rising of the lights," the latter now quite uninterpretable; there are entries on those "killed in the pillory" or who "died from want in Newgate." Even before the plague of 1665 and the Fire of 1666 *memento mori* motifs were "one speciality of the seventeenth century City churchyards." "Nobody is healthy in London," Mr. Woodhouse complains in *Emma*, "nobody could be." A character in Smollett's *Humphry Clinker*, Matthew Bramble, suffered certain symptoms in London "which warn me to be gone from this centre of infection." A century later London was described as the "Great Wen" or fleshy excrescence indicative of poor health.

There have always been epidemics and waves of death within the metropolis. The "Black Death" of 1348 killed approximately 40 per cent of London's population. Many were buried outside the walls in no-man's-land, otherwise known as Pardon Churchyard or Wilderness Row, now part of the Clerkenwell Road behind the Charterhouse. In the fifteenth and sixteenth centuries epidemics of the "sweating sickness" fell upon the capital on at least six occasions; that of 1528 "visited London with such violence that it carried off thousands in the space of five or six hours." The quagmires and open sewers of the city turned it into "a paradise for mosquitoes," thus causing the "ague" which is now known as malaria.

The plague came early to London; the first recorded instance is from the seventh century. Between the years 1563 and 1603 there were five severe attacks, in the latter year killing some 30,000 Londoners when "Feare and Trembling (the two Catch-polles of Death) arrest every one . . . no voyce heard but *Tue Tue*, Kill, Kill" and Watling Street was "like an empty Cloyster." No one was ever safe. No one was ever entirely well in a city "full of pits and sloughs, very perilous and noyous," dirty and filled with "corrupt savours." London itself had become a sink of disease. Yet nothing in its history could have prepared its citizens for the events which unfolded between the fated and fateful years of 1664 and 1666.

There had been intimations of catastrophe. In 1658 Walter Costello wrote that "if fire make not ashes of the city, and thy bones also, conclude me a liar for ever. Oh London! London!" In the following year a Quaker tract entitled *A Vision concerning London* contained the prophecy that "And as for the city herself, and her suburbs, and all that belonged to her, a fire was kindled therein; but she knew not how, even in all her goodly places, and the kindling of it was in the foundation of all her buildings and there was none could quench it." In his *Monarchy Or No Monarchy*, published in 1651, the London astrologer William Lilly inserted an hieroglyphical plate "representing on one side persons in winding streets digging graves; and on the other a large city in flames." Wenceslaus Hollar had noticed the vigour and energy of the citizens in 1647 but, on his return in 1652, "he found the countenances of the people all changed, melancholy, spight full, as if bewitched." Mother Shipton predicted a general conflagration, and a Quaker walked naked through Bartholomew Fair with a pan of fire and brimstone on his head as a prophecy. A man in a narrow passage by Bishopsgate convinced all those around him that a ghost there was making "signs to the houses, and to the ground" suggesting plainly that "abundance of people should come to be buried in that churchyard."

There is an area adjacent to Goswell Road known as Mount Mills. It is now an open space, used as a car park. It is unusual in this part of London to find what is essentially a patch of waste ground. The answer lies in its history. Here, according to Daniel Defoe in *A Journal of the Plague Year*, on "a piece of ground beyond Goswell Street, near Mount Mill . . . abundance were buried promiscuously from the parishes of Aldersgate, Clerkenwell, and even out of the city." It was a plague pit, in other words, where, during the Great Plague of 1664 and 1665, thousands were taken in "dead carts" and dumped in the loose soil.

It was comparable to the burial pit in Houndsditch, about forty feet in length, sixteen feet broad and twenty feet in depth, containing more than a thousand corpses. Some of the bodies "were wrapt up in linen sheets, some in rags, some little other than naked, or so loose that what covering they had fell from them in the shooting out of the cart." It was reported that the living, out of despair, sometimes flung themselves among the dead. The Pye tavern was very close to the Houndsditch pit itself and when, at night, the drunken heard the rumble of the dead cart and the noise of the iron bell they came to the window and jeered at anyone who mourned for the newly dead. They also uttered "blasphemous expressions" such as *There is no God* or *God is a devil*. There was one driver who "When he had any children in his dead cart could cry 'Faggots, faggots, five for sixpence' and take up a child by the leg."

The area of Mount Mills is waste ground still.

.   .   .

These reports are all taken from Defoe's chronicle. He was only six years old at the time of the visitation, and much of his evidence is anecdotal, but there are also contemporary accounts which furnish additional material for contemplation. Any observer willing to enter the city during the plague would first have noticed the silence; there was no traffic except for the dead carts, and all the shops and markets were closed. Those who had not fled had locked themselves within their houses, and the river was deserted. Any citizens who did venture upon the streets walked in the middle, down the kennel, away from the buildings; they also avoided chance meetings. It was so quiet that the rush of the water beneath the bridge could distinctly be heard throughout the old City. Great bonfires were placed at intersections and in the middle of main thoroughfares, so that the streets were filled with smoke as well as the miasma of the dead and dying. The life of London seemed to be over.

The plague had begun, in the parish of St. Giles, at the close of 1664. It is understood now that the infection was carried by the black rat, known also as *rattus rattus*, otherwise called the ship rat, or the house rat. These rats are old inhabitants of London, their bones being discovered in excavations of fourth-century Fenchurch Street. It is likely that they arrived from South Asia in Roman ships, and they have remained ever since. The severe cold of the early months of 1665 prevented any spread in the infection for a while, but from the beginning of spring the bills of mortality began to rise. By July the plague had entered the city from the western suburbs. It was a dry, hot summer without any wind. Grass grew in the abandoned streets.

John Allin, a clergyman, stayed in the city and sent many letters to those at a safe distance; they are reprinted in W.G. Bell's *Unknown London*. On 11 August he wrote: "I am troubled at the approach of the sicknesse neerer every weeke, and at a new burying place which they have made neer us." "They," indicating some indeterminate authority all the more pressing for being so vague, has always been part of the London vocabulary. Thirteen days later: "I am, through mercy, yet well in middest of death and that, too, approaching neerer and neerer: not many doores off, and the pitt open dayly within view of my chamber window." In the following week, at the beginning of September, he described "the dolefull and almost universall and continuall ringing and tolling of bells." So this was the noise that broke the silence. In the same letter he mentioned that his brother had left the house one morning and, on his return from the streets, had found "a stiffness under his eare, where he had a swelling that could not be brought to rise and breake, but choacked him; he dyed Thursday night last." Five days later Allin wrote of the distemper: "it is at the next doore on both hands of mee, and under the same roofe . . . These 3 dayes hath bene sea cole fyres made in the streets about every 12th doore, but that will not do the worke of stopping God's hand." His anxiety is palpable. It was not until the middle of September that some rain mitigated the appalling heat, but after that modest abatement the plague raged again.

John Allin told the story of six physicians who, believing that they had found a remedy, opened up an infected body—"it is said that they are all dead since, the most of them distractedly madd." Six days later there came report of "that word spoken by a child here concerning the increase of the Plague, until 18,317 dye in a weeke." The child died. Yet the rates began to fall. In the last week of February 1666, there were only forty-two deaths reported, whereas more than eight thousand died each week of September 1665.

Within the texture of Defoe's prose London becomes a living and suffering being, not the "abstract civic space" of W.H. Auden's poem. London is itself racked with "fever" and is "all in tears." Its "face" is "strangely altered," and its streets circulate "steams and fumes" like the blood of those infected. It is not clear whether the whole sick body of London is an emanation of its citizens, or whether the inhabitants are an emanation or projection of the city. Certainly its conditions were responsible for much death. In the great centre of trade and commerce, the process of buying and selling itself destroyed the citizens—"this necessity of going out of our houses to buy provisions was in a great measure the ruin of the whole city." The people "dropped dead in the very markets" in the act of trading. They would "just sit down and die" with the tainted coins still in their pockets.

There is another melancholy image which issues from the pages of Defoe. It is of a city where there "were so many prisons in the town as there were houses shut up." Metaphors of incarceration are persistent throughout London writing, but during the Great Plague there emerged vivid and literal examples of urban imprisonment. The symbolism of the red cross and the words "Lord have mercy on us" has not been wasted on mythographers of the city, but the measure of societal control has perhaps not been fully recognised. Of course many people escaped, often by the expedient of going over a garden wall or travelling along the roofs—even with some "watchmen" murdered to ensure liberty—but, in theory, each street and each house became a gaol.

One ordinance has remained in force for three centuries with the proclamation that "all the graves shall be at least six feet deep." All beggars were expelled. Public assemblies were banned. In a city which had shown its manic propensities in a thousand different ways, order and authority had to be imposed directly and harshly. Hence the turning of houses into prisons by "shutting up," a measure which even at the time was considered by many to be both arbitrary and pointless. But in a city of prisons it was the natural and instinctive response of the civic authorities.

By means of anecdote and circumstantial detail, Defoe provides a Londoner's vision of a city "quite abandoned to despair." It is clear from his report that the citizens very quickly reverted to superstition and apparently primitive belief. A genuine madness was in the streets, with prophets and interpreters of dreams and fortune-tellers and astrologers all terrifying "the people to the last degree." Many, fearful of sudden death, ran out into the streets to confess that "I have been a murderer" and "I have been a thief." At the height of the plague it was fully believed that "God was resolved to make a full end of the people of this miserable city," and as a result the citizens became "raving and distracted." Daniel Defoe knew London very well—perhaps better than any man living in his period—and he declared that "the strange temper of the people of London at that time contributed extremely to their destruction."

There were "conjurors and witches . . . quacks and mountebanks" who placed posters all over the city advertising their services and who dispensed pills and cordials and treacles and "plague waters" to the desperate. A list of cures was published at the "Sign of the Angell, neare the Greate Conduit in Cheapside," and it was possible for "An Excellent Electuary against the plague, to be drunk at the *Green Dragon* Cheape-side at Six-pence a pint."

London has always been a centre for healers and doctors, surgeons and magnetisers, of all descriptions. Perhaps its nervous fear has in turn promoted symptoms to be cured by "physic." In fourteenth-century London, calendars of saints, as well as various charts of astrology, were used to determine the efficacy of particular herbs. Ecclesiastics were the first surgeons. In the thirteenth century the papal authorities banned them for shedding blood. After that date, lay surgeons and physicians were ubiquitous. Not all of them had undergone the usual apprenticeship of ten years, however, and in the early sixteenth century it was proclaimed that "the science and cunning of physick and surgery" were being exercised by "smiths, weavers and women" who

Earlier Londoners admiring "London Stone," which has been considered alternately as a milestone or a symbol of civic power. It now lies almost unseen in Cannon Street.

John Stow: the great sixteenth-century antiquary whose *Survey* is the first complete and authentic description of London. His bust still survives in the church of St. Andrew Undershaft.

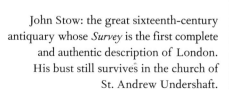

William I's charter: this small document marked the king's authority over London and its citizens, and was one of the first salvoes in the continual struggle between the monarchy and the city.

"Buy my fat chickens," "Fair lemons and oranges," "Knives, combs and inkhorns":
images of street sellers, drawn by Marcellus Laroon, c. 1687. They are
the ragged emblems of London life, confident or careworn, animated or
depressed, as the eternal crowd melts around them.

London, 1560. Note the Bankside bear-baiting arenas in the foreground.

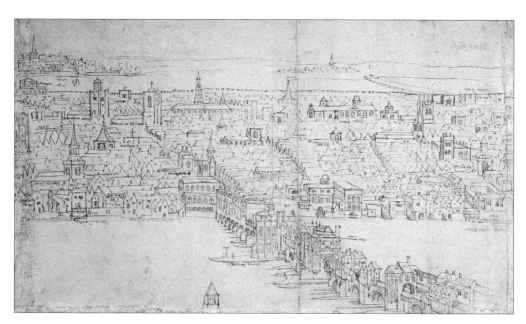

A panorama of London Bridge and the northern areas of London in the sixteenth century. The bridge was then a great thoroughfare, complete with shops, houses and public lavatories. Note the number of churches which Wyngaerde has depicted.

Hollar's panorama of London is one of the most striking and evocative images
of the seventeenth-century city before the Fire. The endless activity on
the river is a testimony to London's commerce, while the streets and
buildings are an emblem of its magnificence.

A view of old St. Paul's, completed by Hollar in the mid-seventeenth century.
This was the magnificent church quite destroyed in the Great Fire,
a reminder of all that London lost in that conflagration.

The Royal Exchange, forerunner of the Stock Exchange, as depicted by Hollar,
is packed with merchants and brokers; they are part of a commercial life which
was established as early as the Roman period and has continued ever since.

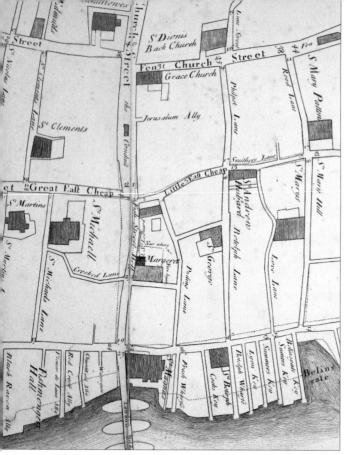

A detail of a map showing the devastation wreaked by the Great Fire of 1666. Even churches did not survive.

Rowlandson's depiction of a public hanging outside Newgate Prison. The rituals of executions provided unrivalled entertainment for the London crowd, and fresh anatomical specimens for the Royal College of Surgeons.

Seventeenth-century firemen at their trade; they were indispensable in a city notorious for fires, and their call of "Hi! Hi! Hi!" was as ubiquitous as the modern siren.

Moll Cut-Purse: an engraving of the most
notorious of the "roaring girls," those women
who wore masculine costume in order to confront
a male-dominated city on its own terms. The
animals and birds depicted were part of her own
private menagerie.

Newgate Prison showing the windmill which
supposedly helped provide air for the inmates.
The gaol was the most notorious within the city,
commemorated in songs, pamphlets and plays.
London writers of all periods have compared
the city to a prison, in implicit homage to
the pervasive power and presence of
that "hell on earth."

"The Modern Plague of London." A temperance map: each dot represents a public house. London is so large, and so diverse, that a thousand different maps or topographies have been drawn up in order to describe it. Here is a map of drunkenness in the city always notorious for its drunkards.

A photograph of the Café Monico, on Piccadilly Circus, in a period where horse-drawn vehicles competed with motor cars in the busy streets. Note that the age of advertising is in full swing.

used "sorcery and witchcraft" to effect their cures. It was believed, for example, that water drunk from the skull of a hanged man or the very touch of a dead man's hand were efficacious.

In seventeenth-century London, too, "quacks" or "healers" were in the ascendant and have been duly catalogued in Charles Mackay's volume of popular delusions and superstitions. When Valentine Greatraks, a "healer," moved to Lincoln's Inn Fields in the early 1660s, "Nothing was spoken of in London but his prodigies; and these prodigies were supported by such great authorities, that the bewildered multitude believed them almost without examination." Thus did another showman succeed in "*magnetising* the people of London." "Scurvy quacks" used spoonwart which grew by the banks of the Thames, while more noxious treatments such as "Spirit of Pearl" or "Essence of Gold" were also dispensed. There were "wise-women" and "wise-men" who examined urine (known as practitioners of "piss-pot science") or pored upon moles to discover the source of illness. The seventh child of a seventh child invariably entered the business, although many claimed that distinction without having attained it.

One William Salmon practised at the very gates of Bartholomew Hospital and claimed to have cured "Ambrose Webb at the *Three Compasses* in Westbury-street of a great bleeding at Nose; a youth, a son of William Ogben, a Taylor, near the *Black Boy* in Barnaby-street, of a long and tedious ague and madness . . . Nicholas Earl at the *Cup* in Long alley, of dropsy; Joan Ingram near the *Bear* in Moor Fields of the Gout, and Anthony Geasture at the *Cock* in Wapping of a consumption." The circumstantial detail is compelling. The advertisement also serves to elucidate the manner in which Londoners identified each other by citing location in terms of the nearest tavern.

There seems little doubt that William Salmon did indeed effect cures; like a modern psychiatrist, he was particularly effective at dispelling or exorcising that "melancholy" which was a recurring London condition. He was himself a London original, part showman, part sorcerer and part physician. He was born in the summer of 1644 and began life as "an assistant to a mountebank" before establishing his own career as the seller of "Elixir Vitae." He was also a popular educator, and in 1671 published *Synopsis Medicinae, or a Compendium of Astrological, Galenical and Chymical Physick* which passed through at least four editions. He wrote several other popular books, upon mathematics and drawing as well as medicine, but his most successful work was his *London Almanack* in which he prophesied in a manner to be later adopted or stolen by Old Moore. His practice across London can be traced with some accuracy—from Smithfield to Salisbury Court off Fleet Street, from there to the Blue Balcony by the ditch near Holborn Bridge and then on to Mitre Court beside Fleet Street. Like many Londoners he became a radical Dissenter; he joined a sect called the "New Religious Fraternity of Freethinkers" which assembled near the Leather-sellers' Hall. Then, at a somewhat late age, he began to practise anatomy. On his death in 1714 he left two microscopes and a library of over three thousand volumes.

Of course there were more genteel, if not more learned, practitioners of healing who came under the aegis of the Company of Barber Surgeons (they were later to split in two, becoming barbers *or* surgeons) or the College of Physicians. The latter institution, with a roof described as "the distant sight of a gilded pill," was in Warwick Lane, near Newgate Prison from which many of its anatomical subjects came. Anatomy lessons were its principal and compelling feature. They were conducted in a central chamber, used as the setting for Hogarth's *The Reward For Cruelty* in which the corpse of a wretched murderer, Tom Nero, is thoroughly anatomised and degraded. It was known as a "theatre," and indeed it became an intrinsic part of London spectacle. The taking of the corpses of the hanged for dissection and dispersal was an old custom—we read of the necessity of "a wax candle to look into the body"—but in later years the corpses were also used to test the properties of electricity. One recently deceased killer was "galvanised" in 1803, with the result that one of his eyes opened and he raised his right hand. It is reported by Charles Knight that the instructor "died that very afternoon of the shock." At an earlier date, in 1740, a specimen was about to be anatomised when "he threw his Hand in the Surgeon's face, and accidentally cut his Lips with the Lancet." After this escape from the knife he sat in a chair, groaning, and "in great Agitation"; eventually he recovered and "heartily" asked for his mother.

Hogarth's engraving is a swirling composition, in which the round complementarity of all parts evokes the circles of Tom Nero's life within the inferno of London; it also seems to demonstrate the connection between Nero's own cruelty and that of the physicians who are presently disembowelling him. The violence of the streets fashions Nero's character so that he becomes an emblem of the worst London "type." Yet he is not so different from the surgeon delightedly plunging a scalpel into his eye-socket. Hogarth based his portrait upon a surgeon named Dr. John Freke. In this city everything connects.

The skeletons of two famous malefactors, which once hung in the alcoves of the anatomical theatre, can still be seen in the museum of the Royal College of Surgeons. Jonathan Wild, the most notorious villain of eighteenth-century London, and William Corder, the killer of Maria Martin in the Old Red Barn murder, now hang together as part of a truly old-fashioned London spectacle. In the same gallery can be seen the Irish giant Charles Byrne, whose skeleton of seven feet ten inches has been placed beside the diminutive remains of Caroline Crachami who was only one foot ten and a half inches in height. They were London "freaks" and, in death, they still satisfy the taste for urban theatre.

The apothecaries of London, like the anatomists, were accustomed to stage management. They customarily wore black and it was almost mandatory that their shops, however humble, would contain a skull as well as a folio written in some ancient tongue. Here were sold herbs and powders, pills and electuaries, drugs and dentifrices, pomades and love-charms. In Camomile Street and Bucklersbury, in particular, all herbal remedies were to be found. In Smollett's *Roderick Random* (1748) there is a summary of the trading arts—"Oyster-shells he could convert into crab's eyes; common oil into oil of sweet almonds . . . Thames water into aqua cinnamoni . . . when any common thing was ordered for a patient, he always took care to disguise it in colour or taste, or both, in such a manner as that it could not possibly be known."

The drugs themselves came and went according to the fashion of the age. In the seventeenth century, these included moss, smoked horses' testicles, may dew and henbane. In the eighteenth century, we find nutmeg and spiders wrapped in their own silk. In the nineteenth century, we read of "Turkey rhubarb and sulphuric acid." In the early twentieth century, in the East End, there are reports of "Iron Jelloids, Zam Buk ointment, Eno's Fruit Salt, Owbridge's Lung Tonic, Clarke's Blood Mixture." Anderson's Scots Pills, first given to the world in 1635, "were still being sold in 1876."

In his account of the Great Plague Defoe emphasises the credulity of ordinary Londoners, who wore "charms, philtres, exorcisms, amulets" in order to ward off the encroaching disease. Some kept signs of the zodiac, or the written phrase "Abracadabra," in pockets and seals. They had reverted to the paganism that had dominated the city ever since the first wooden idol was carved in Dagenham (2200 BC).

There is a museum south of the river, off the Walworth Road, which contains the "Lovett Collection" of London charms, amulets and relics. It is the true home of urban superstition, with a range of artefacts which suggests that the city has absorbed all the traditions of magic and ritual from both native and immigrant populations. From the East End came, in 1916, "five uneven shaped stones on a string"; these were, according to the museum's catalogue, "hung on the corner of the bed to keep nightmares away." In the same year was deposited a "greyish white tubular bottle sealed at each end with thread. Mercury inside." This was used as a cure for rheumatism. A grey cat's skin was employed as a remedy for whooping cough, and a "leather slipper painted gold" was a symbol of good luck. From Clapham arrived a pincushion in the form of a domino piece, marked with seven dots. From east London came a key attached to a rope, as a talisman to safeguard the wearer against witches, as well as a necklace of amber and other gems worn in 1917 "to bring good health." Barking was the area in which to search for mandrake roots, which scream like a child when taken out of the ground. There are coins to bring wealth, iron pyrite acorns to prevent lightning strikes (the acorn from the tree of the thunder god), cows' hearts and rams' horns and donkeys' shoes to act as charms. The museum also contains the head of a London magician's wand or staff, engraved with Solomon's seal; it was carved in the fourteenth century, and then lost in the depths of the river. As recently as 1915, it was common practice, in the East End, to cut off some of the hair of a sick child. The hair was placed in a sandwich, and given to the first dog that was encountered; the illness then left the child and entered the body of the unfortunate animal. In the East End, too, it was customary for women and female children to wear blue glass beads around the neck "as a preventive charm against bronchitis"; these necklaces were sold in hundreds of small shops, "usually presided over by an aged woman," at the price of one halfpenny. It became a custom that the beads were eventually buried with the woman who had worn them. In the early twentieth century, too, young women all over London were visiting herbalists in order to purchase "tormentil root" or "dragon's blood"—gum from a Sumatran tree—as love philtres.

In a suggestive book written by Edward Lovett, *Magic in Modern London*, published in 1925, it is reported that sharks' teeth taken from the London clay were said to cure cramp. In Camberwell it was customary to cover a horseshoe with red cloth in order to ward off nightmares, while Mile End was known as the place where children could be "charmed" and healed. When market business was bad in the East End the trader would exclaim:

"Ah! I expect I forgot to bow to the new moon!" It is appropriate, in a city of commerce, that it was customary to call out "money" at the sight of a falling star. Strangely shaped stones were placed on London mantelpieces as a "votive offering," in the same manner that silver representations of limbs were hung in medieval city churches. A woman in Whitechapel told an investigator that, when moving house, it was customary to swing the cat around one room in order to induce it to stay. There are also interesting records of "cat sacrifice" in the walls of certain houses. Cauls in which children had been born were on sale for eighteen pence each as a safeguard against drowning but, at the time of the First World War, when the danger of death was very close, the price rose to £2. In London markets it was possible, until recent times, to buy neolithic stone axes or flint arrowheads as another precaution against thunderbolts.

London resembles a prison, and it is perhaps not surprising to discover that keys have always been an object of taboo. They were associated with magic and the presence of demons; thus "The art of lock-picking was known as the 'Black Art,'" according to Peter Linebaugh in *The London Hanged*, and "the most common lock-picking tool was called a 'charm.'" Keys were used to investigate suspected persons; the name was placed in the stem of a key and guilt was established if the key then moved or shook. The lodgings of prostitutes were often symbolised by "the drawing of a large key," and many ladies of the night wore keys around their neck as a symbol of their trade.

There is a suggestive eighteenth-century passage, connected with the storming of Newgate Prison. One rioter came back to his lodging house and announced: "I have got the keys of Newgate." At his subsequent trial, a fellow lodger was questioned by the magistrate about these keys. "You would not touch them for fear that they would contaminate you?" "I would not come near them."

Patients at Bedlam who refused to swallow their drugs had their mouths opened by a specially designed metal key.

At the time of the plague, spectres were seen in the thoroughfares of the city; indeed London has always been troubled by ghosts. A fine brick house on the south side of the churchyard in Clerkenwell was "seldom tenanted" because of its reputation. Number 7 Parker Street, off Drury Lane, had a name for "ill luck" and was eventually torn down. Another house in the same street, No.

23, was haunted by "fearful noises" in a corner where death had occurred. There was a haunted house in Berkeley Square which was "empty for a long time," and another in Queen's Gate.

P.J. Grosley, visiting the city in the eighteenth century, remarked upon "the great practical fear" of ghosts there, even while Londoners "make a jest of them in theory." Another stranger in the same period visited the theatres and noticed that the ghosts of Shakespearean drama provoked "surprise, fear, even horror . . . to such a degree, as if the scenes which they saw were real." It has often been remarked that, in a city of spectacle, Londoners find it difficult to distinguish theatre from reality but, more significantly, such reports suggest a surprising credulity. In the middle of the sixteenth century a young girl was found to have counterfeited a supernatural voice in a house near Aldersgate, "through which the people of the whole city were wonderfully molested." We must imagine flying rumour, and reports, and fear.

The London writer "Aleph" has another story. In the early months of 1762 it was firmly believed that, within a house in Cock Lane, that once "dingy, narrow, half-lighted street," there dwelled a ghost known as "Scratching Fanny" responsible for certain knockings and bangings. A young girl was believed to be possessed by this spirit, and "was constantly attended by mysterious noises, though bound and muffled hand and foot." Thousands of Londoners visited Cock Lane and the more genteel were permitted to visit the girl's bedroom, fifty at a time, "almost suffocating her from the stench." A committee of eminent Londoners was set up to investigate the claims—one of their number was the superstitious Samuel Johnson—and concluded that the girl "had some art of counterfeiting noises." Her father was put in the pillory at the end of Cock Lane, where "the populace treated him with compassion." And so the affair ended, after London had once again been "wonderfully molested." It is almost as if it were itself a spectral city, so filled with intimations of its past that it haunts its own inhabitants.

The "Islington Ghost" visited a patch of ground beside Trinity Church in Cloudesley Square causing "a wondrous commotion in various parts, the earth swelling and turning up every side"; Michael Faraday is supposed to haunt a telephone exchange in Bride Street which was once the chapel of his Sandemanian congregation. Lord Holland and Dan Leno, Dick Turpin and Annie Chapman, have variously been seen. Old hospitals and the city churches have proved fruitful ground for phantoms, and the stretch of Swains Lane in Highgate beside the cemetery has been the home of many "sightings." There is apparently a ghost in the Oriental Department of the British

Museum, and a phantom blackbird haunted a house in Dean Street for many generations. The daughter of the Earl of Holland, walking in Kensington Gardens, "met with her own apparition, habit and everything, as in a looking glass"; she died a month later. The rector of St. Bartholomew's, Smithfield, saw in his pulpit the ghost of a divine "in the black gown of Geneva . . . exhorting the unseen audience with the greatest fervour, gesticulating vehemently, bending first to the right and then to the left over the pulpit, thumping the cushions in front of him, and all the while his lips moving as though speech was pouring from him."

The Tower of London has of course been the natural haven of many spirits. Familiar figures have glided by, among them Walter Raleigh and Anne Boleyn. The latter was "seen" by three witnesses as a "white figure," and a soldier on duty at the door of the Lieutenant's Lodgings "fell in a dead faint." He was court-martialled but later acquitted. The ghost of a bear "issued from beneath the door" of the Jewel House, and the sentry who saw it died two days later. It might be recalled that there was indeed a menagerie, or a zoo, within the Tower itself. One of the most ambiguous apparitions was that vouchsafed to the Keeper and his wife; they were at table in the sitting room of the notorious Jewel House when "a glass tube, something about the thickness of my arm" hovered in the air. It contained some "dense fluid, white and pale azure . . . incessantly rolling and mingling within the cylinder." It approached the Keeper's wife who exclaimed "Oh Christ! it has seized me!" before it crossed the room and disappeared.

Other places have remained objects of London fear. It is believed the cries of drowned Jews, murdered in the great expulsion of 1290, can still be heard at low tide near Gravesend. The "Field of Forty Footsteps," which now lies beneath Gordon Square, was considered to be "charmed" or "blasted," according to taste. Here were once picked plantain leaves which were supposed to influence dreams but, more importantly, on the same spot two brothers killed each other in a duel. The imprint of their fatal footsteps was thought to have lingered, while the area of the killings could produce no grass. Southey did indeed decipher the outlines of seventy-six footsteps "the size of a large human foot about three inches deep" and in the summer of 1800, just before the area was built upon, Moser "counted more than forty."

Washington Irving observed the inhabitants of Little Britain, behind Smithfield and beside Aldersgate, in the 1830s. "They are apt to be rendered uncomfortable by comets and eclipses," he wrote in the guise of "Geoffrey Crayon,

gent," "and if a dog howls dolefully at night, it is looked upon as a sure sign
of death." He also listed the "games and customs" of the people. We may include here the ancient ceremony of beating the bounds, an act of parish as-
sertiveness which derives from the importance of beating the devil out of the
locality; once charity children were whipped at each boundary with white
willow wands, but in more recent years the particular walls are simply beaten
with sticks. There are altogether some fifty-six annual customs and ceremonies in the city, ranging from the "Swearing on the Horns" in Highgate to
"The Verdict of The Trial of the Pyx" in Goldsmiths' Hall, but the rituals of
May-day are the most enduring if not necessarily the most endearing.

In the first recorded ceremonies the "merry Milk Maids" of London
would carry upon their heads a "Pyramid" of "Silver plate" instead of their
usual pails; this may sound quaint, but the connotations of the practice were
more ritualistic and barbaric. The maids were hardly "merry"—they were
some of the most poorly paid and heavily worked of all city trades—and this
parade of silver plate, borrowed for the occasion from pawn-brokers, can be
seen as a token of their financial enslavement during the rest of the year. The
first of May was also a day of sexual licence and, in recognition of this lubri-
cious fact, young chimney-sweeps joined the maids in a later version of the
spectacle. Grosley reports that their black faces "are whitened with meal,
their heads covered with periwigs powdered as white snow, and their clothes
bedaubed with paper-lace; and yet, tho' dressed in this droll manner, their air
is nearly as serious as that of undertakers at a funeral." Chimney-sweeps, like
miners, have always been associated with the dark and promiscuous forces of
the world; hence their appearance on "May-day." But the young sweeps, with
their "serious" air, were also the most harshly treated of all London children.
Many were killed, burned or deformed in the exercise of the trade, which was
literally to climb up the flues of the chimneys and dislodge any soot or cinders. So their labour, and suffering, were paraded for one day of levity.

There is a painting of great interest, dated around 1730 and entitled *The
Curd and Whey Seller, Cheapside*; it depicts a blind girl sitting at the foot of
the conduit in that street, holding out her hand to three young sweeps. This
conduit was their usual haunt, and their expressions are of startling vivacity.
The faces of two of them are so blackened that only their eyes and mouths are
visible. They are all very small, and one of them seems to have a deformed
back. They do indeed seem like the grotesques of the city, with a suggestion
of threat or menace directed against the blind and very pale street-seller. It
can be suggested, therefore, that the procession of sweeps on May-day was a

re-enactment of their threat which was to be symbolically alleviated by laughter. Like all London rites, however, the ceremony gradually became more fanciful, with the introduction in the late eighteenth century of a "Green Man" covered in twigs and leaves. He was known as "Jack-in-the-Green" or simply "Green" and, accompanied by milkmaids and sweeps, was paraded in various parishes as some garish token of spring. May-day ceremonies were eventually taken over by street performers, before disappearing altogether.

Yet the superstitions of London have not wholly departed. The city itself remains magical; it is a mysterious, chaotic and irrational place which can be organised and controlled only by means of private ritual or public superstition. That great adopted Londoner, Samuel Johnson, felt obliged to touch every post in Fleet Street when he walked down that thoroughfare. In similar spirit, many London streets have refused to countenance a No. 13—among them Fleet Street, Park Lane, Oxford Street, Praed Street, St. James's Street, Haymarket and Grosvenor Street.

But the very line of a thoroughfare has, for some, a more numinous function. There have been many attempts to plot the trajectory of the city by means of "ley-lines" or "leys" which connect certain sites in straight alignment. One such line connects Highgate Hill in the north with Pollard's Hill in Norbury to the south, on the way touching a surprising number of churches and chapels. Efforts have been made to connect the various churches built by Nicholas Hawksmoor, or to align St. Pancras Old Church, the British Museum or the Greenwich Observatory within a significant topography. In one sense it marks a revival of the earth magic once practised by the Celtic tribes of this region, yet it also gives due recognition to the power of place.

This is the power that William Blake celebrated in his vision of Los treading through London "Till he came to old Stratford, & thence to Stepney & the Isle/of Leutha's Dogs, thence thro' the narrows of the River's side/And saw every minute particular." In those particulars, like the mournful days of the Great Plague, the life and history of the city can be revived.

CHAPTER 21

Painting the Town Red

ed is London's colour. The cabs of the early nineteenth century were red. The pillar boxes are red. The telephone boxes were, until recently, red. The buses are characteristically still red. The Underground trains were once generally of that colour. The tiles of Roman London were red. The original wall of London was built from red sandstone. London Bridge itself was reputed to be imbued with red, "bespattered with the blood of little children" as part of the ancient rituals of building. Red is also the colour of violence.

The great capitalists of London, the guild of the mercers, wore red livery. The *Chronicles of London* for 1399 describe "the Mair, Recourdour, and Aldermen off London in oon suyt, also in Skarlett," while a poem commemorating Henry VI's triumphal entry into London, in 1432, depicts "The noble Meir cladde in Reede velvette." The pensioners of the Chelsea Hospital still wear red uniforms.

Red was the colour used to mark street improvements on the maps of London, and to indicate the areas of the "well-to-do" or wealthy. "Red" was also the Cockney slang for gold itself. The London river-workers, who supported the mobs that poured through the streets in the spring of 1768, invented the red flag as a token of radical discontent.

Novelists have also identified the colour of red with the nature of the city. In *The Napoleon of Notting Hill* (1904), Chesterton's vision of a future London, a protagonist asks: "I was wondering whether any of you had any red about you" and then stabs his left palm so that "The blood fell with so full a stream that it struck the stones without dripping." This is a prelude to the success of "the red Notting Hillers" in that novel.

Red crosses were placed upon the doors of households shut up with the plague, thus confirming the symbolic association of the colour with that London disease which was once considered "always smouldering" like covered embers. The fire-fighters of London wore red jackets or "Crimson Livery Cloth." Their commander, dying in a great fire in 1861, performed one telling act—"pausing only for a moment to unwind the red silk Paisley kerchief from his neck." The colour is everywhere, even in the ground of the city itself: the bright red layers of oxidised iron in the London clay identify conflagrations which took place almost two thousand years ago. Yet there is one fire which has always remained in the memory of Londoners—a fire which, as John Locke noted, created "Sunbeams of a strange red dim light" which covered the whole of the city and could be seen even from his library in Oxford.

"The Great Fire of London" of 1666 was considered to be the greatest of fires, but in truth it was only one of a series of devastations. The fires of AD 60 and AD 125 destroyed most of the city, for example, creating what is described by archaeologists as a "fire destruction horizon." This is the horizon of the city itself. London burned in 764, 798, 852, 893, 961, 982, 1077, 1087, 1093, 1132, 1136, 1203, 1212, 1220 and 1227. R.S. Fitter, writing *London's Natural History* after the Second World War, noted that "The constant laying waste of large areas of the city must have made the aspect of medieval London often a good deal more like the blitzed London of 1945 than most people realise." James Pope-Hennessy, compiling a book on that wartime destruction, found in the ruins of London churches "a kind of continuity." He recalled that "The city fire of December 1940 did at one moment look like Pepys' famous description of the fire of 1666. The night sky, lit by a wavering orange glare, seemed to display an aura not at all unlike his 'bow of flame.' "

London seems to invite fire and destruction, from the attacks of Boudicca to those of the IRA. In the literature of the subject, there are references to particularly incandescent areas. Arthur Hardwick's *Memorable Fires in London* revealed Watling Street to be "the region in the heart of the City

[that] has always been a 'fiery' one." Aldersgate and Silver Street have "the reputation of the 'danger zone,' " while areas such as Cheapside and Bread Street have been repeatedly subject to flame. Wood Street, too, "has proved a notoriously fiery street"—perhaps because of its name—and mysterious fires have broken out in Paternoster Square. The area of St. Mary Axe was destroyed in 1811, 1883, 1940 and then again in 1993. It is significant, too, that, in the city of spectacle, theatres continually go up in flame; thirty-seven were destroyed in 130 years, from 1789 to 1919, providing an appropriately theatrical scene for those who flocked to watch them. The nature of London fires has also been conceived in theatrical terms. During one conflagration in Paternoster Square, in 1883, "the flames burst through the roof and brilliantly illuminated the City"; a fire two years later in the Charterhouse sent out a fiery glow "as though the sun shone over everything."

London Bridge has been destroyed by fire, as have the Royal Exchange, the Guildhall and the Houses of Parliament. In the nine years from 1833 to 1841 there were 5,000 fires in the city "yielding an average of 556 per annum, or about three in two days." In the city of 1833 there were some 750 fires; in the "Great London region" of 1993 occurred 46,000 "primary" and "secondary" fires. In 1833 there were approximately 180 chimney fires; in 1993 215 such events. More fires spring up in December, and fewer in April, than in any other months; Friday is the worst day of the week for conflagrations, and Saturday the best. The most hazardous time is ten in the evening, and the most benign seven in the morning. Some fires begin with arson, but most by accident—a great conflagration of 1748, consuming more than a hundred houses in the streets and passages by Exchange Alley and killing a dozen people, began "through the servant leaving a candle burning in the shed whilst she was listening to a band performing at the Swan Tavern." An engraving of the fiery ruins was promptly issued by a printer in Scalding Alley.

Yet fire can also reveal the forgotten or neglected history of the city. The site of Winchester Palace, on the south bank of the Thames, was first uncovered after a fire at Bankside Mustard Mills. The remains of a thirteenth-century barbican, or watch-tower, were revealed in 1794 after a fire in St. Martin's Court, Ludgate. Flame can recreate, therefore, as well as destroy. It is perhaps significant that, in London folklore, a dream of fire denotes "health and happiness" or "marriage with the object of the affections."

A nineteenth-century correspondent of *Le Temps* noticed that in comparison with Parisians, Londoners showed "astonishing promptitude" in their reaction to the call of "Fire! Fire!" It was the war cry of the city. In first-century London *vigiles* or "bucket boys" patrolled the city by night; already there was some fascination or mystery concerned with fire, since they were known for "their liveliness and devilry." Their organised system of watching decayed in succeeding centuries, but it can be inferred that the early medieval wards assumed responsibility for locating and putting out fires in their vicinity. The next attempt at precaution was the simple curfew or "*couvre-feu*"; on the ringing of the evening bell, resounding all over the eleventh-century city, all fires were supposed to be covered and the ashes raked. If a fire did rage, then the bells of the churches rang backwards to spread the alarm; it was as if the devil had suddenly re-emerged in the roar of the flames. Barrels of water were kept outside the larger houses and, by the twelfth century, there were elaborate regulations for the quenching of the flames and the pulling down of burning thatch.

In the fifteenth century it was decreed that each new sheriff and alderman, within a month of taking up office, "shall cause 12 new buckets to be made of leather for the quenching of fire." The successor of the humble bucket was "a kind of syringe or squirt," which was in turn followed by an early pumping device; this was pulled by the firemen, calling out their familiar cry of "Hi! Hi! Hi!," and has been termed "the first 'fire engine' to reach the streets of London." It was succeeded in the early seventeenth century by "an Engine or Instrument" which "with the help of tenne men to labor" could pump more water "than five hundred men with the helpe of Bucketts and laydels." This was the engine celebrated by Dryden, in *Annus Mirabilis*; he described the spectacle of the flames, and how "streets grow throng'd, and busy as by day." The impression, again, is of fire as some alternative sun flooding the streets with light. One of the earliest fire insurance companies named itself "The Sun," and its mark can still be seen on many houses. Fire by a sudden leap of metaphor then becomes the source of energy and power, as if it represented the sporadic and violent irruption of the city's own heated life. One of the greatest maps of London, "Horwood's Plan" of 1799, was dedicated to the Phoenix Fire office in Lombard Street which had risen soon after the fire of 1666; again it is a mark of the importance of those who deal with fire in the capital. Curiously enough, the first chief executive of the Phoenix was a Mr. Stonestreet.

Over the centuries the shouts of the firemen were replaced by handbells, then by mechanical and electric bells. Then came the siren, replaced in turn by a complex system of sound including the "two-tone," the "wail" and the "yelp." The first firemen themselves were placed in colourful regalia. One company, for example, was arrayed in "blue jackets with elaborate gold cuffs, and gold braiding" with "black knee-breeches, white stockings and gold garters"; on days of ceremony they marched with silver staffs and badges. They were themselves fired by duty—"hearts aglow," as Hilaire Belloc appropriately put it. Such was their prestige that the headquarters of many fire offices were described as "resembling in design highly-enriched palaces."

Two children pass the Phoenix Fire office in a novel by Edith Nesbit. "Fire?" one says. "For altars, I suppose?" Yes, for the great sacrificial altar of London.

Fire became one of the principal characteristics of the city. It was even known as "the Fire King." Throughout the eighteenth and nineteenth centuries the fires "grew in size and frequency" and, perhaps as a consequence, the crowds became larger. A conflagration at Tooley Street took more than a month to die away; the House of Commons was destroyed by fire in 1834, which provoked some of the most picturesque London paintings. The Westminster burning became, according to the authors of *London In Paint*, "the single most depicted event in nineteenth century London . . . attracting to the scene a host of engravers, water-colourists and painters," among them Constable and Turner. These artists recognised that in the heart of the flame they might also evoke the spirit and presence of the city itself. There are reports of great crowds assembling to view the destruction of the Crystal Palace in 1936, as well as of many dock fires and warehouse fires where "the ghost of Victorian" conflagrations was said to walk.

The consuming appetite for fire among the citizens did not diminish until the "blitz" of 1940. On the night of 29 December, the raid timed when the water of the Thames was at its lowest, some 1,500 fires were burning at the same time in the city. It was said then that the "Great Fire" had truly come again.

That Great Fire, one of the most formative events of the city's history, may be dated from 1 September 1666, when Pepys and his wife were "horribly frightened to see Young Killigrew come in [to a place of public resort] with a great many more young sparks." These "young sparks" represented the fiery youth of the city. Samuel and Elizabeth Pepys returned to their house in Seething Lane where, at three on the following morning, they were roused by a maid with news of a fire in the City. Pepys saw some flames at the lower end of a neighbouring street, and then went back to sleep. The fire had started one hour before at the house of the king's baker, Mr. Farryner, in Pudding Lane. At the later enquiry Farryner insisted that before retiring to bed he had "gone through every room, and found no fire but in one chimney, where the room was paved with bricks, which fire he diligently raked up in embers." The cause of the Great Fire was never discovered. It just happened.

The month of August had been unusually hot, "characterised by an extraordinary drought," so that the thatch and timber of the neighbouring buildings in the narrow streets and alleys were already "half-burned." The fire found friendly territory, in other words, and was further aided by a strong south-east wind; it was carried onward from Pudding Lane towards Fish Street and London Bridge, then down through Thames Street into Old Swan Lane, St. Lawrence Lane, and Dowgate. Everyone in a position to do so took to the water with boats, lighters and skiffs carrying the goods of their houses threatened by the flames. Pepys also took to the river, where with his face in the wind he was "almost burned with a shower of fire drops." He observed that most households took with them a pair of virginals. He also noticed that the "poor pigeons were loth to leave their houses, but hovered about the windows and balconies till they burned their wings and fell down."

The fire was now out of control, burning steadily to the north and to the west; Pepys eventually took refuge from the incendiary river in an alehouse on the other bank, and there "saw the fire grow . . . in corners, and upon steeples, and between churches and houses, as far as we could see up the hill of the City, in a most horrid, malicious bloody flame, not like the fire flame of an ordinary fire." It was then that he noticed the arch or bow of flame, about a mile in width (which Pope-Hennessy was to observe during the fire-raids of 1940).

That night the fire spread from Cheapside down to the Thames, along Cornhill, Tower Street, Fenchurch Street, Gracechurch Street and to Baynard's Castle. It had gone so far down Cheapside that it took hold of St. Paul's which, by chance, was surrounded by wooden scaffolding. John Evelyn, who walked among the streets even at this hour, noted that "the noise and cracking and thunder of the impetuous flames, the shrieking of women and children, the hurry of people, the fall of towers, houses, and churches, was like an hideous storm, and the air all about so hot and inflamed that at last one was not able to approach it."

The unprepared citizens were left bewildered; they made no attempt to put out the fires, and simply fled. Those who remained, of the "lower" sort, stole whatever they could take from the burning dwellings. Those who did not take refuge upon the river, itself now choked with smoke and deluged by "fire drops," went into the surrounding fields of Islington, Finsbury and Highgate, watched and wept.

By the following day, Monday, the fire had spread down Ludgate into Fleet Street and had burned down the Old Bailey; Newgate and Billingsgate were gone, while the molten lead from the roof of St. Paul's ran through the streets "glowing with fiery redness, so as no horse or man was able to tread on them." By now the smoke stretched for fifty miles, so that those leaving the city could travel for hours in its shadow.

That night several fires met together. One came down Cornhill, and one down Threadneedle Street; which, uniting together, in turn met two separate fires coming from Walbrook and Bucklersbury. John Evelyn remarked that "all these four, journeying together, break into one great flame at the corner of Cheapside, with such a dazzling light and burning heat, and roaring noise by the fall of so many houses together, that was very amazing." It was as if some ancient spirit of fire had reared its head in the very middle of the city.

By Tuesday the wind had abated, and the fire stopped at the top of Fetter Lane in Holborn. The deeds of the Mitre Tavern, at the other end of Fetter Lane, described a boundary by "the tree where the Fire of London divides." The fire was still raging in the north at Cripplegate and in the east by the Tower but the authorities, advised by Charles II, who had always evinced a strong interest in fire-prevention, were able to stop its growth by blowing up with gunpowder houses in its path.

On Thursday John Evelyn once more walked the streets of his city, now a ruin, "through the late Fleet Street, Ludgate Hill, by St. Pauls, Cheapside, Exchange, Bishopsgate, Aldersgate"—all gone. He found himself "clambering over heaps of yet smoking rubbish, and frequently mistaking where I was." This was also the experience of Londoners after the bombing raids of 1940; their city was suddenly unknown and unrecognisable. It had become an alien place, as if they had woken from some dream to encounter a quite different reality. "Nor could anyone have possibly known where he was," wrote Evelyn, "but by the ruins of some church or hall that had some remarkable tower or pinnacle remaining." The ground under his feet was so hot that he could hardly walk; the iron gates and bars of the prisons had all melted; the stones of the buildings were all calcined and rendered a brilliant white; the water left in fountains was still boiling while "subterranean cellars, wells and dungeons" were belching forth "dark clouds of smoke." Five-sixths of the city were thus consumed, the area of devastation encompassing a mile and a half in length and half a mile in breadth. Fifteen of the city's twenty-six wards were thoroughly destroyed and, in total, 460 streets containing 13,200 houses were razed. Eighty-nine churches had gone, and four of the seven city gates were reduced to ashes and powder. It was officially reported that only six people were killed, one a watch-maker in Shoe Lane where on excavation "his bones, with his keys, were found."

Perhaps the most notable image of this extraordinary fire was that from a clergyman, the Revd. T. Vincent, in a book entitled *God's Terrible Advice to the City by Plague and Fire*. He too had seen "the dreadful bow" of light across the city. He had witnessed the burning of the Guildhall "which stood the whole body of it together in view for several hours together after the fire had taken it, without flames, (I suppose because the timber was such solid oak), in a bright shining coal, as if it had been a palace of gold, or a great building of burnished brass."

In the aftermath of the Great Fire emerged a yellow-flowering plant known as London Rocket and, in 1667 and 1668, "it grew very abundantly on the ruins around St. Paul's"; it was seen again, in 1945, "just outside the City boundary." It is the true flower of fire. The Monument, erected on the site of the Fire's first emergence, is also a form of rocket or vehicle of fire; it was first proposed that a statue of the king, or a great phoenix, should be placed upon its summit. But it was eventually agreed that an urn of flames, known as "the Blaze," should furnish the column. Daniel Defoe deciphered the object as a great candle, with the urn as "handsome gilt flame!"

There were many representations of the events of those five days of fire, not least a series of long poems which can be found in an anthology entitled *London in Flames, London in Glory*. The burning city is severally compared to Rome, to Carthage, to Sodom and to Troy; the classical gods are depicted as wandering through the burning streets, together with Virgil and Jezebel, as the spectacle of flaming London conjures up images of dead or dying civilisations in past ages of the world. The painted images of the Fire were equally ostentatious, although some of them seem literally to have been sketched at the very time of the blaze itself. There are sober studies, including those of Hollar showing "A True and Exact Prospect of the Famous Citty of London" before the autumn of 1666 together with the same "As It Appeareth Now After the Sad Calamitie And Destruction by Fire"; it was sketched from the south bank of the river, and it is possible to see through the ruins right into Cheapside itself. But most works were in the style of "conflagration painting," according to *London in Paint*, which found their inspiration in "biblical or mythic city fires." Two of the most famous paintings, "after Jan Groffier the Elder," depict the towers and portcullis of Ludgate in flames as if it were the entrance to Hell itself; there may be another explanation for the appearance of Ludgate, however, since the area beside it was considered an "artists' quarter" in the middle of the seventeenth century. There are many small scenes and episodes reflected in these paintings: the woman running with wild face and arms outstretched from the encroaching fire, the man carrying a bundle of silver plate upon his head, the carts and horses being driven in a great crowd towards the open fields. But the most striking image is that of a man carrying a child on his shoulders against a backdrop of flame; it was re-employed by Blake, Doré, and other artists as a true representation of the mysteries and sufferings of London.

The Great Fire was not simply the inspiration, therefore, of contemporary artists. For over two hundred years it remained the most arresting image of the seventeenth century. Philippe Jacques de Loutherbourg, a great scenic designer in the London theatres, painted his own version at the end of the eighteenth century and in the following century the Great Fire was recreated every night at the Surrey Gardens.

But the conflation of the city and fire goes deeper than theatre or spectacle. To Panizzi, in the mid-nineteenth century, London had the appearance of a city that had somehow already been burned. In *Night and Day* Virginia Woolf describes it as "eternally burnt"; it seemed that "no darkness would ever settle upon those lamps, as no darkness had settled upon them for hundreds of years. It seemed dreadful that the town should blaze for ever in the same spot." In 1880 a Frenchman believed the entire capital to be "a temple of fire-worshippers"; his companion on this urban pilgrimage, Arthur Machen, went on to describe "all the fires of London reflected dimly in the sky, as if far away awful furnace doors were opened." Mirbeau talked of London in terms "of mystery, of the conflagration, of the furnace" while Monet, at the end of the nineteenth century, wished to depict the sun "setting in an enormous ball of fire behind Parliament." In some of that artist's paintings, in fact, London seems to breathe and live within an atmosphere of fire surrounding all streets and buildings with the same unearthly glow.

By the mid-nineteenth century the sky above London was notable for "the glowing atmosphere that hangs over the capital for miles"; the brick kilns on the perimeter of the city in that period created a ring as if of stage fire, while the great dust mountains inside the capital had the appearance of volcanoes. It was a city "where fires can scarcely be kept under" while, in twentieth-century terms, it is characterised as an "urban heat island." London was popularly known as the "Great Oven" and, in the 1920s, V.S. Pritchett confessed to the sensation of being "smoked and kippered" in the depths of the city. When the fire does eventually go out the city is forbidding, blackened and relentless, some charred monument of eternity filled with what Keats called "the Burden of Mystery."

It became clear, after the Great Fire, that fire itself must be controlled. The twin visitations of flame and plague had been interpreted by moralists as the handiwork of a God enraged by the sinfulness and dissipation of London. But there were others, including Christopher Wren and Edmond Halley, who began to question the wisdom of placing all responsibility for its disasters on fate or divine displeasure. The Royal Society had been established in London in 1660, and the two visitations prompted its members to find "scientific" or "objective" causes for such violent events. In the name of "Reason"—what is "simple, solid, sensible"—it was hoped that London consciousness might be changed so that, in future ages, such pestilences and conflagrations might be averted. The greatest effect of the Fire, paradoxically, was to promote the advancement of science. Even before the end of September 1666, according to a quotation in *London in Flames, London in Glory*, "Men begin now everywhere to recover their spirits again, and think of repairing the old and rebuilding a new City." Specifically it seemed an opportunity to exorcise "the rebellious Humours, the horrid Sacriledges . . . and gingling Extravagances" of the previous age. This refers to the civil war, and to the execution of Charles I, but it also suggests that extravagant piety and superstitious practice—precisely the citizens' responses to the plague, as documented by Defoe—were no longer permitted. It was to be a new city in every sense.

After the Fire

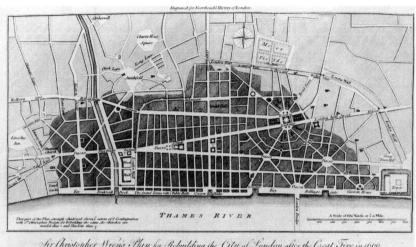

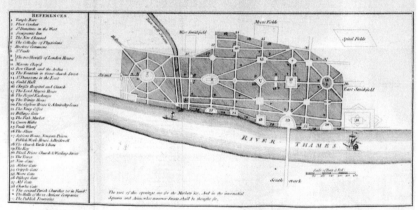

Two plans of a London reconstructed after the Great Fire of 1666, one by Christopher Wren and the other by John Evelyn. Their theoretical and hypothetical city had no chance against the twin forces of tradition and commerce which obstinately recreated London in its former image.

CHAPTER 22

A London Address

❧

$\mathcal{T}$he Great Fire had stopped by Fetter Lane which, for most of its existence, has been border territory. It runs from Fleet Street to Holborn, and the ancient route is now lined with twentieth-century air-conditioned office-blocks and some nineteenth-century survivals. In the stretch of Fetter Lane which leads directly out of Fleet Street, with, on the respective corners, a bookshop and a computer supplier, is Clifford's Inn, the oldest Inn of Chancery and once the most important edifice in the street. Rebuilt now, and partitioned into offices and apartments, it is situated beside a modern restaurant, the Café Rouge, and opposite a new drinking establishment called the Hogshead. The judicial air of the lane has not entirely disappeared, however, since beside Clifford's Inn is a building which contains the "Technology and Construction Court." This stretch of the lane is continually busy with traffic, in particular with taxis decanting into Fleet Street.

Upward from this site, towards Holborn, the lane divides and the eastern fork is turned into New Fetter Lane. But the old Fetter Lane still pursues its course northward, albeit now with difficulty. Its whole eastern side has been demolished, as the foundations of taller and greater buildings are sunk within the ever receptive London earth. The former Public Record Office is still visible, to the west of the statue of John Wilkes down Rolls Buildings, while closer to Holborn the Mucky Duck and the Printer's Devil have survived as public houses. Three mid-nineteenth-century houses remain, as if they were some ancient terrace preserving the memory of the street, and their ground floors are now occupied by coffee shops and sandwich bars.

And where did Fetter Lane get its name? John Stow, who knew it well, believed that "Fetter" was "so called of fewters (or idle people) lying there, as in a way leading to gardens." Others, however, have suggested that the word is derived from the Norman *defaytor* "defaulter." Some prefer another French origin in *foutre*, "blackguard." But there are other possibilities. Fetter may derive from the feuriers, or felt-makers, who are deemed to have inhabited the street in the fifteenth century. Or it may spring from the name of the landlord Viteri or Viter who lived there a century earlier. More ingenious antiquarians have in turn suggested that the name sprang from *fetor* or "offensive smell," on the face of it unlikely in an area surrounded by gardens and orchards—unless the fewters, or foutres, or defaytors, were in some way responsible for the stink. Another connection has been made with *frater*, "brother," which was a characteristic address between the men of law who frequented the area. A more simple connection has been made with the workshops of the street which manufactured *fetters* or lance vests for the Knights Templar who also congregated in the vicinity. The confusion and speculation will never be resolved, and the obscurity of Fetter Lane's derivation serves only to demonstrate the unknowability of many London names. It is as if the city was striving to conceal its origins. Yet, as G.K. Chesterton once remarked, "The narrowest street possesses, in every crook and twist of its intention, the soul of the man who built it, perhaps long in his grave. Every brick has as human a hieroglyph as if it were a graven brick of Babylon: every slate on the roof is as educational a document as if it were a slate covered with addition and subtraction sums." It might also be suggested that every object, every doorway, throws a light upon the ancient territory of which the present Fetter Lane is now the custodian.

A Roman urn filled with coins was found beneath the surface of the lane, confirming Stow's observation that an old Roman road had been located in the immediate vicinity. There was a wooden bridge over the Fleet here, too, so the early inhabitants of Fetter Lane and its environs had the advantage of living beside a swiftly flowing river. A ninth-century sword handle was also discovered within the depths of the lane. Its manufacture and material were of fine quality, indicating that it was employed for ceremonial rather than sanguinary purposes. It may then have some connection with a charter of 959 by which King Edgar of Wessex granted the neighbouring land to the monks of Westminster Abbey, one boundary of which was marked by a line parallel to Fetter Lane.

Throughout its history Fetter Lane acted as a boundary, or has been recorded as frontier territory; it was where the Great Fire stopped, and it marks the area where the City's influence ceases. It is also the area where two parishes, St. Andrew's, Holborn, and St. Dunstan's in the West, meet. We may find, in turn, that it has attracted those who live upon "the edge."

At the beginning of the fourteenth century its present contours emerged. In 1306 it was known as the "neu strete" but in 1329 it is styled as "a new lane called Faiteres Lane." The earliest records suggest, however, that it had already acquired an ambiguous reputation. There is a report on one "Emmade Brakkele, a harlot," living in Fetter Lane. A keeper of a house harbouring "prostitutes and sodomites" was noted as living in "fayters lane." Yet it must already have been a "mixed" neighbourhood in a thoroughly medieval spirit, since there is a tradition of an "Inne or Court" in "Fewter Lane" and the fact that Clifford's Inn was established here in 1345 suggests that some original foundations may have been maintained here even before Fetter Lane appeared in the public records. The religious establishments in the immediate vicinity will also have provided some measure of extra-mural control with St. Dunstan's to the south, St. Andrew's and Ely Place to the north. In 1349, John Blakwell, "Cetizen of London," purchased with his wife property in "Faytourslane," and Henry VI is recorded as collecting rents from the dwellings there. This in itself is not necessarily a guarantee of respectability, but these bare records suggest that throughout the medieval period it was a well-known and well-documented "subarbe" of London. By the early fifteenth century there was a famous tavern on the corner of Fetter Lane with Holborn, known as Le Swan on Le Hope, which contained rooms for travellers. There were complaints about its overhanging roof, and some "barriers which had been erected outside the inn and so distracted the roadway," but it survived until the middle of the eighteenth century under the revised name of the Black Swan. A few yards down the lane there now stands the Mucky Duck as a plaintive reminder of a more graceful presence.

On a mid-sixteenth-century map Fetter Lane is clearly marked with fifteen houses down its eastern side and twelve down its western; the topography may not be entirely accurate, but it is in contrast to "Liver Lane" (Leather Lane) to the north which proceeds among gardens and open fields.

At the northern end of Fetter Lane Barnard's Inn can be seen and, down towards Fleet Street, Clifford's Inn is already visible; a stone archway spanning
the lane, almost at its midway point, has also been marked. The map is less
than accurate in one respect, however, since it does not convey the continual
encroachment of new buildings in and around the lane itself; on land once
owned by St. Bartholomew's "ten tenements with gardens" were erected by
1555 and by 1580 a further thirteen "illegal new houses" had been constructed. Neither does the map reveal the narrow yards and alleys, like Fleur
de Lys Alley and Crane Court, which ran off the main thoroughfare and
which exist still.

Like other areas of London, it had its share in fires and executions. Both
entries to the lane were in fact customary sites for the gallows. There are
records of Catholic recusants, in 1590, being hanged and quartered at the
Fleet Street end; it is, according to one Catholic history, *Catholic London* by
W.D. Newton, "one of our sacred spots." The melancholy Catholic com-
poser John Dowland, who died in 1626, had been living in Fetter Lane. In
1643 two plotters against Parliament were hanged at the Holborn end,
having arranged their conspiracy in a lodging in the lane, and for two centuries this spot was often a place of execution. It has been the site of death in
more than one form, however. There was a distillery on the corner of Fetter
Lane and Holborn in the mid-eighteenth century; it was on the site of the
Black Swan, formerly Le Swan on Le Hope, and so had a long association
with drink. During the most violent days of the Gordon Riots in 1780, with
the mob's cry of "No Popery!" rising through the streets, it was rumoured
that the owner of the distillery was a Catholic. So it was ransacked and fired,
with fatal results. "The gutters of the street, and every crack and fissure in
the stones, ran with scorching spirit, which being dammed up by busy
hands, overflowed the road and pavement, and formed a great pool, into
which the people dropped down dead by dozens." This account is written by
Charles Dickens, who like many Londoners was obsessed with fiery death,
but his version is authenticated by several contemporary sources. So by
Fetter Lane "some stooped with their lips to the brink and never raised their
heads again, others sprang up from their fiery draught, and danced, half in
mad triumph, and half in the agony of suffocation, until they fell, and
steeped their corpses in the liquor that had killed them." Others, leaving the
distillery with their clothes on fire, actually rolled in the spirit mistaking it
for water until they "became themselves the dust and ashes of the flames

they had kindled, and strewed the public streets of London." They became part of Fetter Lane.

There have been other fires and explosions over the centuries. Curiously enough, one upon 10 April 1679 was believed to be the consequence of a "Papist Plot"; the hanging of the recusants, and the firing of the distillery, then become part of a morbid Catholic trinity. Then again, in 1583, just after the neighbouring church of St. Andrew's, Holborn, had been "new glazed" to remove all signs of popish superstition, a large explosion of gunpowder in Fetter Lane caused all its windows to shatter and fall. By use of gunpowder, too, the Great Fire was "quenched" in the vicinity. The Fire Court, established to adjudicate claims of ownership, sat in Clifford's Inn itself. So Fetter Lane became a famous boundary.

With its legal Inns beside its taverns, and its churches beside the houses of pimps, it always possessed an intermediary status. The more dubious healers lived here: in the seventeenth century one Bromfield at the Blue Balls in Plow Yard, Fetter Lane, advertised "Pills against all Diseases." Samuel Johnson's friend, a poor apothecary named Levett, met "a woman of bad character" by a coal-shed in Fetter Lane and was duped into marrying her. He was then nearly imprisoned for her debts, the whole story according to Johnson being "as marvellous as any page of the *Arabian Nights*." The lane was also the haunt of pawn-brokers, to which reference is made in one seventeenth-century drama, Barry's *Ram-Alley*:

Take thou these books
Go both to the broker's in Fetter Lane.

The allusion to books is appropriate in another sense since Fetter Lane has become associated with several London writers. Henry Peacham, the author of *The Art of Living in London*, dwelled here. Michael Drayton, the author of *Poly-Olbion*, lived at No. 184. Thomas Hobbes, according to John Aubrey's *Brief Lives*, "lived most part in Fetter-lane where he writ, or finished, his book *De Porpore*, in Latin and then in English." He preferred his Fetter Lane life to any in the country where "the want of learned conversation was a great inconvenience." John Dryden lived at the corner of Fetter Lane and Fleur-de-lys Court, in one of the houses newly fashioned after the Fire; he remained here for nine years, according to the *Dictionary of National Biography*, and for a while his neighbour across the street was another dramatist, Thomas Otway, who died of drink in an adjacent tavern. Charles Lamb attended school in an alley off the lane. Coleridge lectured in the lane and, at different times, Samuel Butler, Lionel Johnson and Virginia Woolf lived in Clifford's Inn. Lemuel Gulliver, the hero of Swift's novel, is also recorded as having dwelled in Fetter Lane.

One of the most notorious, if now least known, residents of Fetter Lane was Isaac Praisegod Barebone; he pursued his trade as a leather-seller on the corner of Fleet Street which by some atavistic remembrance may have prompted George Eliot, in the nineteenth century, to remark that Fetter Lane "had something about it that goes with the smell of leather." But Barebone was also a fiery and assiduous Anabaptist preacher who in the 1640s stirred up various tumults in the neighbourhood with his "disorderly preachment, pratings and prattlings." At Oliver Cromwell's instigation he entered Parliament as a member for the City of London; even though it was christened by its enemies as "Barebone's parliament," he did not speak in the chamber. He was imprisoned after the Restoration but, on his release, returned to his old parish; his burial is registered in St. Andrew's, Holborn, the church to the north of Fetter Lane.

But Barebone's presence was not the only element of dissent in that street. A group of sixteenth-century Puritans met in a carpenter's yard midway down the eastern side of the lane; during the reign of Mary, their persecutor, they prayed in a simple saw-pit, and in later years an anonymous pamphlet, *Our Oldest Chapel*, declared that the site was regarded by Dissenters "with feelings akin to veneration." It contrasts strangely with the "sacred spot" of Catholic veneration a few yards further south, where the gallows was situated on the corner of Fleet Street, and it is suggestive that one small London street can harbour contrasting spiritual memories.

In the reign of Elizabeth I (1558–1603) the Puritans were permitted to build a wooden temple on the site of the saw-pit; then the Presbyterians migrated to the location, and erected a brick chapel on the same spot. Their interest in Fetter Lane, like that of their nonconformist predecessors, lay in secrecy and seclusion. The chapel itself "could only be reached through a long narrow passage" known as Goldsmith or Goldsmith's Court; a seventeenth-century map of Fetter Lane reveals that there were a number of such courts and small yards aligned to it, so that its irrepressible life seemed to flow in all directions. The chapel was also concealed "by the continuous row of houses which even at that early date fringed the east of Fetter Lane" while upon the other side "tall buildings to the west . . . effectually masked it from the notice of any passer-by." So in the middle of London it was possible to find seclusion. Yet the London mob knew the byways of the city very well, and in 1710 the chapel was torched by rioters. It was rebuilt, but then adopted by the radical and sectarian Moravian Brethren who maintained their presence in the area for the next two centuries. The Wesleys worshipped here with the Brethren, and on the first day of 1739 John Wesley recorded that "the power of God came mightily upon us, insomuch that many cried out for exceeding joy, and many fell to the ground." So the "sudden effusion of the holy Ghost" had touched a small court in Fetter Lane, from where a "Revival . . . spread into other parts of England."

Other radicals and Dissenters were drawn to the same place. The conventicler Richard Baxter gave lectures in Fetter Lane; there was a Baptist congregation in Black Raven Passage, and another Dissenters' chapel in Elim Court between 104 and 107 Fetter Lane. A number of Moravians inhabited the area in "community houses," in Nevill's Court and elsewhere. They were living on the borders of orthodox faith, just as they were living on the borders of the city. Certain groups and people are undoubtedly attracted to a certain locality, the topography of which is strangely analogous to their own situation. That is why political, as well as religious, radicals were drawn to the same area. A "Jacobin" and member of the London Corresponding Society, Thomas Evans, established the centre of his operations in Plough Court, Fetter Lane. A public house in Fetter Lane, the Falcon, was also under surveillance as a centre for subversive political activity. Evans himself, who lived in Fetter Lane throughout the 1790s, laced his revolutionary zeal with strong drink, and financed his activities by selling ballads and pornography. In that, he was perfectly congruent with his equally ambiguous surroundings. He was elusive enough to have adopted numerous professions, among them pornographer, printer, coffee-house keeper and paint-colourer, all trades that were associated with Fetter Lane itself, so that in another sense he becomes as protean and as shiftless as the lane. Is it possible, then, that certain inhabitants acquire their identity, or temperament, from the circumstances of their immediate locale?

Other names can be enlisted in light of this radical connection. Tom Paine, whose *Rights of Man* became the unofficial bible of eighteenth-century radicalism, lived at No. 77 Fetter Lane. William Cobbett wrote and published his *Political Register* from No. 183 Fetter Lane. Keir Hardie lived at No. 14 Nevill's Court, off Fetter Lane, at the beginning of the twentieth century. For 6s 6d a week he lodged in one of the oldest houses in London, a "late-medieval, half-timbered five-storey tenement building"; so he was inhabiting the history of Fetter Lane, although perhaps unaware that Cobbett and Paine had trod the same street before him. As if in implicit homage to that past, the statue of John Wilkes, the great London radical, now stands at the place where Fetter Lane and New Fetter Lane converge. It has the incidental merit of being the only cross-eyed statue in London, adding to the ambiguous status of its locale.

In the nineteenth century the lane suffered a fate similar to many other streets of the period; it was overwhelmed by the size of London, seeming somehow to become smaller and darker. "Those who live in Fetter Lane and the adjoining streets," one church report stated, "are of the poorest and most irreligious class. The neighbourhood is simply a labyrinth of business premises." This was the condition of many streets close to the ancient centre of London. The Inns were demolished; in their place were constructed a workhouse and a great General Records Office. Of the buildings which were to be destroyed by that Office, an anonymous surveyor commented that "Those in Fetter Lane are principally occupied by persons not concerned in lucrative business, and it is believed that none of the leases are for a longer period than 21 years." It was always the character of Fetter Lane to have a migrant population. Except for the Moravian settlers, who knew that on this earth there is no abiding city, the pattern is one of transience.

And yet, in the city, there are always other patterns within the general pattern. In a street directory of 1828 there are no fewer than nine taverns listed; the relatively large number in so relatively short a street is an indication of early nineteenth-century London, but it also suggests elements of a mobile and perhaps anonymous population. In the commercial directory of 1841 there is a preponderance of printers, publishers, stationers, engravers and booksellers—some nineteen altogether—rivalled only by the proprietors of coffee houses, hotels and eating-houses. These are all trades reliant upon passing taste and what might be considered "news." It might be imagined, therefore, that Fetter Lane was not a stable or a settled place but one which participated in the City's usual uproar.

In a street directory of 1817 no fewer than three "oil and colour men" are listed. In the Post Office directory of 1845 are two painters and an "oil & colorman" and in 1856 an "oil and colour warehouse" appears; in one of his sketches, Charles Dickens describes a certain "Mr. Augustus Cooper, of

Fetter-lane" as "in the oil and colour line." Dickens may have discerned a remarkable coincidence of trade. Alternatively he was somehow divining the
spirit of the lane in his usual fashion. He also mentions that "over the way"
from Augustus Cooper was "the gas-fitters"; curiously enough in the directory for 1865 appears a "brass finisher & gasfitter." In that charmed urban
space where reality and imagination mingle it may also be noted that, in a
street where Lemuel Gulliver was a surgeon, two other surgeons are listed in
the 1845 directory.

A sketch of 1900, showing the west side of Fetter Lane, reveals that many
houses were of seventeenth-century date; but it is also clear that the thoroughfare was lined with ground-floor shops. One representative section, in a
street directory of 1905, manifested in sequence a butcher, a dairy, an ironmonger, a tool-maker, a watch-maker, an electric bell manufacturer, a pub, a
baker, a printer, a coffee house, another pub, another coffee house, a hairdresser and a map-mounter. Yet down the courts and alleys—Blewitt's
Buildings, Bartlett's Buildings, Churchyard Alley and many others—there
were tenants and lodgers who were often registered as "Poor," "Can't Pay"
or "Won't Pay" in the local rate books. In Nevill's Court, where Keir Hardie
lodged, once spacious houses were divided into tenements. Some predated
the Great Fire, while others were built immediately after the conflagration,
but they were characterised by small front gardens. In a report for the
London Topographical Society, in 1928, Walter Bell noted how well tended
these gardens were and suggested that "it is the poor man who keeps intact
for us this fragment of London's older self." In that sense the vicinity was re-
claiming its sixteenth-century identity, as a place of straggling courts and gardens. But in the early twentieth century "You rub your eyes and wonder. Can
this really be the City—this hidden place, where people live their lives, and
tend their flowers, and die? It is false that no one dies in the City."

In Fetter Lane they do not die; they move on. It is clear from the records
of the parish and the post office that businesses remained only for a short
period and then dissolved. At No. 83, over a period of seventy years, there
was in turn a razor-maker, an eating-house, a beer retailer, a coffee room, a
printer and a dairy man, all passing away into the fabric and texture of the
street. In the dwelling today, on the ground floor, can be found Tucker's
Sandwich Bar.

The pattern of small businesses persisted until the Second World War,
when in 1941 firebombs razed the area. When it arose again, Fetter Lane reasserted itself as a street of stationers, printers and cafés. But all the inhabi-

tants had gone. Now the remaining courts and alleys are lined with office accommodation and business premises, while in the lane itself the sandwich
bars are a present reminder of the coffee rooms and eating-houses which were
once so familiar a presence. But the principal sights, and sounds, are those of
demolition and rebuilding in this lane of perpetual change.

CHAPTER 23

To Build Anew

In 1666 many of the citizens immediately returned to the smoking ruins, in order to discover where their houses had once stood; they then laid claim to the area by erecting some kind of temporary shelter. On the very day that the Fire was extinguished Charles II was informed that "some persons are already about to erect houses againe in the Citty of London upon their old foundations."

Three days later the king issued a proclamation to the citizens in which he promised that rebuilding would proceed quickly but declared that no new work could begin until "order and direction" had been introduced. He then went on to formulate certain principles, the chief of which was that all new dwellings were to be built of brick or stone. Certain streets, such as Cheapside and Cornhill, were to "be of such breadth as may with Gods blessing prevent the mischief that one side may suffer if the other be on fire, which was the case lately in Cheapside." The monarch also showed some concern for the health of his subjects by declaring that "all those Trades which are carried on by smoak," such as brewers and dyers, should "inhabit together."

Certain schemes had already been propounded, most notably by Wren and Evelyn, in which the reconstruction of London was planned upon a grand and elaborate scale. Wren proposed a series of intersecting avenues on a European model; Evelyn's new city resembled a giant chessboard dominated by twelve squares or piazzas. None was accepted, none acceptable. The city, as always, reasserted itself along its ancient topographical lines.

But first the work of demolition had to begin. Those who had lost their trades, or who were otherwise unemployed, were called into city service; the ruins had to be levelled, and the debris carted away. The smoking streets must be cleared, and opened up, while the quays were once again made safe for trade. Makeshift markets were established on the perimeters of the city while the more enterprising bankers and merchants set up their businesses in the area by Bishopsgate which had not been touched by the flames. By the end of the year the tradesmen of the Royal Exchange, for example, had removed to Gresham College. There was in one sense a new, and exhilarating, atmosphere of freedom. Debts and property, mortgages and buildings, were destroyed by the Fire in equal measure. Yet, against this financial cleansing there must be put the loss of stock and of goods, the spices and the wine, the oil and the cloth, all destroyed in the warehouses and manufactories which contained them.

It was a sign of the city's vitality, however, that within a year the busy round of trade had been resumed. It was still the same city in another sense; thieves and footpads found the new conditions good for their own trade, and "there are many people found murdered and carried into the vaults among the ruins." This additional detail prompts further speculations. What happened to those prisoners who had, before the Fire, been inhabiting such "vaults"? Many of the compters and gaols were below the surface of the city, and it is hard to believe that all the prisoners were liberated and escaped with their lives. Is it not more likely that they burned or were suffocated to death? The stated mortality was six, but that extraordinarily low figure may in fact obfuscate the loss of life due to official negligence. Did many of those incarcerated escape as their prison bars melted? And what of the others?

A committee of six was established to direct the rebuilding of the city. One of its members was Christopher Wren who knew already that his idealised version of London was not to be achieved. A "Fire Court" was set up to adjudicate all the claims and disputes which arose over the ownership of land and property. By February of the following year Parliament had enforced what the commission suggested. Certain streets were widened but, not surprisingly, very few alterations were made. King Street was formed, and a small thoroughfare widened into Queen Street, so that the Guildhall could be approached directly from the Thames. A more noticeable change, however, was enforced upon the size and fabric of the houses themselves. They were to be built of brick or stone, as the king had declared, and there were to be four classes or types of houses "for better regulation, uniformity and gracefulness." Those on the principal streets were to be four storeys in height, for example, while in lanes and by-streets two storeys were considered sufficient. In other respects the old lines of the city were to be renewed.

Then the work began. The citizens and private householders were compelled to rely upon their own resources, while money for public works such as the rebuilding of the churches was funded by a tax on sea-coal. By the spring of 1667 the lines of the streets had been staked, and the entire country was advertised for "all persons who are willing to serve and furnish this City with timber, brick, lime, stone, glass, slates and other materials for building." Thus ensued one of the great changes in London's population.

It can be assumed that many of those who had lived in the city before the Fire did not return to the scene of devastation. Some migrated to the country districts, others travelled to the United States; in both instances the presence of relatives, and the possibility of work, affected their decision. But once the rebuilding of the city began, thousands of new people were drawn within its orbit. There were earth-movers and brick-makers, carters and moulders, who dwelled just outside the walls; in addition, hundreds of hawkers and traders moved into the city which had lost half of its markets and most of its shops. And there, of course, came the builders who took advantage of the situation to run up whole streets of houses. Roger North has described how the most celebrated of these speculators, Nicholas Barbon, eventually transformed part of London "by casting of ground into streets and small houses, and to augment their number with as little front as possible." Barbon understood the virtues of simplicity and standardisation—"It was not worth his while to deal little," he once remarked. "*That* a bricklayer could do." But the bricklayers had already been heavily employed.

Within two years of the Fire twelve hundred houses had been completed, and in the following year another sixteen hundred. It was not quite the rapid and vigorous process which some historians have assumed, and for some years London had all the aspects of a ruined city, yet gradually it was rising once again.

John Ogilby's map of 1677, only eleven years after the Great Fire, shows its new appearance. Most of the city has been rebuilt, although some of the churches are missing and a proposed development of the quays beside the Thames never occurred. The new brick narrow-fronted houses are drawn as square rectangles; already they are packed tightly together, making room for lanes and small alleys which thread among them. Many of these houses have small gardens or courtyards behind them, but the general impression is once more of dense and constricted life. If you were to walk eastwards down Leadenhall Street, one hundred yards from Billiter Lane to the junction with Fenchurch Street, you would pass on the left-hand side no fewer than seven small lanes or alleys—categorised by John Strype as "indifferent good" or "small, nasty and beggarly," which were either simple "dead-ends" or issued into tiny courtyards. Much of the area is shaded grey to mark small dwellings of brick and stone.

Ogilby's map reveals the steady spread of London. The area around Lincoln's Inn in the western district has been marked out for streets and houses; to the north, in Clerkenwell, there are already many new lanes and courts. Nicholas Barbon created Essex Street, Devereux Court, Red Lion Square, Buckingham Street, Villiers Street and Bedford Row. With his skills as a builder and developer, he was surpassed only by Nash in his influence upon the appearance of London. The pragmatism and financial opportunism of Barbon seem subtly to suit the nature and atmosphere of the city which he did so much to extend; both prospered together. Partly as a result of his activities, wealthier merchants and businessmen moved away from the smell and noise of the older trading areas. It was a means of escaping from the "fumes, steams and stinks of the whole easterly pyle."

Much of the development had in fact taken place before the Fire hastened its progress. The piazza of Covent Garden had been planned and rebuilt in 1631; it was followed by Leicester Fields four years later. The construction of Seven Dials linked the churches of St. Giles and St. Martin, both "in the fields." Great Russell Street was completed by 1670. In the year before the Fire Bloomsbury Square was laid out. By 1684 the process of western expansion had spread as far as Red Lion Square and St. James's Square.

The principle of these squares lay in the creation of what John Evelyn called a "little town," which in theory was not so different from the independent sokes of Anglo-Saxon London controlled by one great lord. In the seventeenth century a lord of the manor, such as Lord Southampton who owned Bloomsbury, might realise that there was money to be earned from his land. He himself would live in one of the residences upon his estate, but the rest was divided into units which were then leased to speculative builders, who constructed the housing before letting or re-leasing it. After ninety-nine years, the houses became the property of the landlord.

The other features of the squares lay in their civic aspect. They were, in the best circumstances, regarded as small communities with church and market attached to their development. It seemed to be a way of creating an attractive and humane city outside the old walls. When the squares were first erected they were considered to be, in Macaulay's words, "one of the wonders of England," combining convenience and gentility. The regularity and uniformity of these squares, so unlike the baroque vistas of Paris or of Rome, might have been derived from the example of old monastery courtyards or convent gardens with which London was once familiar. To walk through Queen Square, Russell Square, Torrington Square and Bedford Square was to sense that "the traditions of the Middle Ages had been handed down" and that the tranquillity of the ecclesiastical establishments had been carried westward.

Yet it is never wise to underestimate the atavistic elements of London life, even as it grows beyond all of its old boundaries. Expansion takes place in waves, with a sudden movement and roar succeeded by a calm. The city will on one occasion brush against an area, or on another colonise it wholly. Leicester Fields and Soho Square, for example, were already so close to the burgeoning capital that no attempt at creating a graceful public or communal space was ever made. In this context, too, it is important to note that the restless movement of the city was, in the words of John Summerson, established upon "the trade cycle rather than the changing ambitions and policies of rulers and administrators." For a while the city stopped to the west at what is now New Bond Street but what was then "an open field." Building had come to a temporary halt on the southern side of Oxford Street which was little more than "a deep hollow road, filled with sloughs" and bordered by hedges. Regent Street was then a "solitude" and Golden Square, previously employed as a plague pit, "was a field not to be passed without a shudder by any Londoner of that age."

The new squares did not necessarily remain models of civic or communal harmony for very long. Macaulay notes that by the end of the seventeenth century the centre of Lincoln's Inn Field "was an open space where the rabble congregated every evening" and where "rubbish was shot in every part of the area." St. James's Square became "a receptacle for all the offal and cinders, for all the dead cats and dead dogs of Westminster"; at one time "an impudent squatter settled himself there, and built a shed for rubbish under the windows of the gilded saloons." It is further evidence of the contrast and contrariness of London life, but it is also suggestive of a city which was even then established upon a basic brutality and offensiveness. It is tempting to think of the new squares as separate communities still surrounded by fields, for example, but in fact the fields themselves were being built upon. "At this end of town," one resident of Westminster complained, "whole fields go into new buildings and are turned into alehouses filled with necessitous people."

Where most of the developments of the western suburbs of London were conducted by means of leasehold arrangements and governed by Acts of Parliament, the extension of the eastern regions was confused and haphazard, governed as it was by ancient statutes of the manors of Stepney and Hackney which provided for only short "copyholds" of thirty-one years. Thus from the beginning the expansion of the city at the east end remained unplanned and underdeveloped. Wapping and Shadwell had taken shape ten years after the Fire, while Spitalfields was "almost completely built over" by the end of the century. Mile End was emerging as a populous district while the bankside from Ratcliffe to Poplar was a continuous mean street of houses and of shops.

The Ogilby map does not include the meaner streets of the east, nor the confused development of the west. Instead it reveals what in his poem, *Annus Mirabilis*, Dryden glorified as "a city of more precious mold."

More great then humane now, and more August,
New deified she from her fires does rise:
Her widening Streets on new Foundations trust,
And, opening, into larger parts she flies.

A view of Lambeth Palace, painted in the 1680s, reveals a distant prospect of Westminster and the Strand. It is altogether a model of elegance, with the spires of St. Clement Danes and St. Giles-in-the-Fields clearly visible together with stately representations of Durham House and Salisbury House. If the artist had turned his eyes only slightly to the east he would have seen, within the newly built city, the tower of the re-erected Royal Exchange which, as the financial centre of London, was naturally graced with the very first of the brand-new steeples. The great steeple of St. Mary-le-Bow had also been rebuilt, and was followed by that of St. Clement Eastcheap and St. Peter upon Cornhill, St. Stephen Walbrook and St. Michael Crooked Lane, as well as those of forty-seven other churches designed by Wren and his colleagues.

. . .

In Wren's visionary design of London, the great cathedral of St. Paul had been the central point from which the streets were to be extended, and he tried to hold fast to his original conception of its grandeur and immensity. He had found the old cathedral in ruins where, Pepys noted, "strange how the very sight of the stones falling from the top of the steeple do make me sea-sick." As late as 1674, eight years after the Fire, the ancient edifice had been neither replaced nor restored. London was still in part a ruined city. But Wren then began the task of demolishing the old walls with gunpowder and battering rams, and the first stone was laid in the summer of 1675. Thirty-five years later Wren's son, in the presence of his father the master architect, placed the highest stone of the lantern upon the cupola of the cathedral in order to mark its completion. "I build for eternity," Wren had said. Yet in that sentiment he was pre-empted by the poet, Felton, who predicted that nothing would last as long as the stones of Newgate.

A London hanging evoked by Rowlandson; the children in the crowd seem
delighted by the spectacle, and a mother carries her infant without the least
disquiet. It was often said, by foreigners, that Londoners did not fear death.

CHAPTER 24

A Newgate Ballad

ithin four years of the Great Fire Newgate Prison was near to completion, rebuilt with a design which the *London Encyclopaedia* describes as one of "great magnificence" and "sumptuousness." It was, in a sense, the very symbol of London. It had stood on the same site since the twelfth century and was, almost from its beginning, an emblem of death and suffering. It became a legendary place, where the very stones were considered "deathlike," and it has inspired more poems, dramas and novels than any other building in London. Its role as gateway also created elements of myth, since it was the threshold from which prisoners left the earthly city and were dispatched to Tyburn or Smithfield or the gallows just beyond the walls of Newgate itself. It became associated with hell, and its smell permeated the streets and houses beside it.

In the fourteenth and early fifteenth centuries Newgate Prison had begun to decay and to collapse upon itself; sixty-four prisoners died in an epidemic of "gaol fever" in 1419, while the various keepers were regularly charged with afflicting torture and unjust punishment upon the inmates. Jews falsely accused of circumcising Christian children, clippers and coiners, and murderers, were placed within deep underground dungeons where they were loaded with chains or confined in stocks. A bequest of money by Richard

Whittington ensured that the prison was completely rebuilt in 1423 but it soon reverted to its natural state of gloom and horror. Approximately three hundred prisoners were confined within the space of half an acre, in a building divided into three sides—the Master's side for prisoners who could pay for food and drink, the Common side for impecunious debtors and felons, and the Press Yard for "prisoners of note." It can be inferred, then, that the Common side was the site of hardship and indignity.

The keepers of Newgate had always been notorious for their violence and intemperance. In 1447 James Manning left the body of one of his prisoners in the thoroughfare "causing a nuisance and great danger to the King who was passing there"; when he refused to remove it after several warnings, and after his wife had spoken "shameful words," they were both taken to the compter. Two years later his successor was also imprisoned for "a dreadful assault" upon a female prisoner. So the keepers snuffed up the contagion of brutality as well as that of gaol fever. Perhaps the most famous of these gaolers, in the years before the Fire, was Andrew Alexander who in the reign of Mary I hurried his Protestant inmates to the fires of Smithfield with the words "Rid my prison! Rid my prison!" One favoured prisoner who played the lute for Alexander and his wife, who "do love music very well," was granted the best lodgings in the prison. But the conditions of the gaol could not be escaped—the "evil savours . . . threw the poor gentleman into a burning ague." Alexander offered to keep him in his own parlour "but it was near the kitchen, and the smell of the meat was disagreeable." The smell is pre-eminent in these accounts from *The Chronicles of Newgate* while, in the dungeons themselves, "there was turbulence, rioting, disorders."

Those who could afford liquor were continually drunk on "sherry sack . . . amber-coloured canary or liquorish Ipocras" while those imprisoned for their religious or political beliefs raved amid their shackles. "There are seditious preachings by fifth monarch men at Newgate," according to the records "and prayers for all righteous blood," while the prison was so overcrowded that the majority of prisoners had "an infectious malignant fever." It was "a place of infamy and great distress" where lice were the prisoners' "constant companions." One inmate was forced to lie in a coffin for a bed, while another spent fourteen days "without light or fire, living on half penny worth of bread a day." Here in 1537 eleven Catholic monks "were left, standing and chained to pillars, to die of starvation."

It was in this period that there first emerged the legend of the "Black Dog"—"a walking spirit in the likenesse of a blacke Dog, gliding up and

down the streets a little before the time of Execution, and in the night whilst
the Sessions continued." Some believed the creature to be an emanation of
the miseries of twelfth-century Newgate, when famine compelled certain
prisoners to cannibalism. Others surmised that it was a being which walked
"in the Name of Service and Office"; that it was, in other words, a phantom
created by the wickedness of the gaolers. By the early eighteenth century,
however, "Making The Black Dog Walk" was the phrase used to designate
"the prisoners' brutal treatment of new inmates." The present ivy-covered
wall at the bottom of Amen Court, close to the old Sessions House yard, is
supposed still to be the haunt of this malign spirit.

In the sixteenth century, however, the Black Dog was only one of the
many terrors of Newgate. An underground dungeon, known as "Limbo,"
was described as being "full of horrors, without light and swarming with vermin and creeping things." This was the condemned hold beneath the gates
which was "a most fearful, sad, deplorable place . . . They lie like swine upon
the ground, one upon another, howling and roaring—it was more terrible to
me than death." This is the constant refrain of those who had entered Newgate—"being more full of horror than death"—which of course marked one
of the entrances to London itself. When one prisoner, imprisoned for his religious beliefs, cried out: "I would not change my chain for my Lord Mayor's
great chain" he was in his agony making the connection between the sufferings of Newgate and the oppression of the city.

An anonymous drama of the early seventeenth century, *Dick of Devon-
shire*, contains the plea of a man as "loaden with gyves shackles & fetters" as
any thief that lay in Newgate, confirming the notion that it was a prison from
which it was impossible to escape. But it also became a symbol of brotherhood among thieves—"bothe shakeled in a fetter"—or, as Bardolph says to
Falstaff, "Two and two, Newgate fashion" and, in Dekker's *Satiro-mastix*:

> we'll walk arme in arme
> As tho' we were leading one another to Newgate.

It is in part a symbol of defiance under oppression and the prospect of death.
That is why one cry of the rogue or thief was "Newgate or Victory!" The
prison becomes the central token of authority and thus, as we shall see, the
first object of London rioters who were determined to destroy the order of
the city. In that capacity, too, it has often been the object of fire and flame,
with the Great Fire itself as a notable token of wrath or vengeance.

. . .

So it rose again in 1670, embellished and decorated in a manner appropriate to one of the city's greatest public monuments. There was even a bas-relief model of Richard Whittington's cat, and for a while the prison was known popularly as "the Whit"; no more lucid demonstration could be given of its intimate connection with London. It rose five storeys, spanning the entry to Newgate Street from Giltspur Street and the steep incline of Snow Hill. There were now five "sides" for various felons and debtors, together with a newly designed press room (the object of "pressing to death" was to extort confessions), condemned holds, a chapel and "Jack Ketch's kitchen."

On arrival the prisoners were fettered and "ironed," passing under the gate to be led to their appropriate dungeon; they passed, on the left, the keeper's house beneath which was the "hold" for those condemned to hang. A prisoner confined in this subterranean area, which did not perhaps differ very much from the dungeon before the Fire, is quoted in Anthony Babington's *The English Bastille* as saying that there were "some glimmerings of light . . . by which you may know that you are in a dark, opaque, wild room." Entered by a hatch, it was entirely constructed of stone with an "open sewer running through the middle" which diffused a "stench" that entered every corner. Fastened into the stone floor itself were hooks and chains to castigate and confine those who were "stubborn and unruly."

Immediately to the right of the gate was the drinking cellar. This was run by a prisoner who was allowed a profit on sales. Since it was also below ground it was lit by candles "placed in pyramidal candlesticks made of clay"; those inmates who could afford the prices were allowed to drink themselves into senselessness day or night, with gin variously known as "Cock-my-Cap," "Kill-Grief," "Comfort," "Meat-and-Drink" or "Washing-and-Lodging." One prisoner recalled that "such wretchedness abounds there that the place has the exact aspect of hell itself." Beyond this cellar tap-room, going along Newgate Street, were located a "stone hall" for common debtors and a "stone hold" for common felons. These were "virtually unlighted dungeons" strewn with "unutterable filth." "Trampling on the floor, the lice crawling under their feet made such a noise as walking on shells which are strewn over garden walks." The rest of the prison rose upward, for "master" prisoners and female prisoners.

So these were the quarters which greeted each new arrival, a place which no physician would enter. In the 1760s Boswell noticed the cells, "three rows of 'em, four in a row, all above each other. They have double iron windows, and within these, strong iron rails; and in these dark mansions are the unhappy criminals confined." These "dismal places" stayed with him all that day, "Newgate being upon my mind like a black cloud." Casanova, briefly imprisoned there, described it as an "abode of misery and despair, a hell such as Dante might have conceived." Wilhelm Meister, crossing the Press Yard on a tour of inspection, was "attacked as by a swarm of harpies and had no means of escaping but to throw a handful of half-pence amongst them for which they scrambled with all the fury of a parcel of wild beasts" while others "who were shut up, stretched forth their hands through the iron bars, venting the most horrible cries." This is the yard to which Daniel Defoe consigned Moll Flanders in his narrative of her adventures; since the author himself spent some time incarcerated in Newgate in 1703, his account bears the mark of genuine remembrance. It is "impossible to describe the terror of my mind, when I was first brought in, and when I looked round upon all the horrors of that dismal place . . . the hellish noise, the roaring, swearing and clamour, the stench and nastiness, and all the dreadful afflicting things that I saw there, joined to make the place seem an emblem of hell itself, and a kind of an entrance into it." In more than one passage, however, it is emphasised that the inmates by degrees grow accustomed to this hell so that it becomes "not only tolerable but even agreeable" with its inhabitants "as impudently cheerful and merry in their misery as they were when out of it." " 'It is natural to me now,' one female prisoner declares, 'I don't disturb myself about it.' " This is of course an astute observation of Newgate manners, but it might perhaps be construed in the wider context of London itself. In the company of this "crew" Moll herself "turned first stupid and senseless, and then brutish and thoughtless" until she becomes "a mere Newgate-bird, as wicked and as outrageous as any of them."

Some inmates were far from "thoughtless," however, and contrived many ingenious plans of escape. The great heroes of London have often been those who freed themselves from the constraints of Newgate. The greatest of them all, Jack Sheppard, escaped from confinement on six separate occasions; for two centuries he remained a type or symbol of those who elude the practices of oppression with effrontery and bravery as well as skill. It is worth noticing, for example, that a report of the Children's Employment Commission in the 1840s remarked that poor London children who had never heard of Moses or Queen Victoria had "general knowledge of the character and course of life of Dick Turpin, the highwayman, and more particularly of Jack Shepherd [*sic*], the robber and prison breaker."

Jack Sheppard was born in White's Row, Spitalfields, in the spring of 1702, and then placed in the Bishopsgate workhouse—built on the perimeter of the city, like Newgate itself—before being apprenticed to a carpenter in Wych Street. He broke free of his apprenticeship after six years of industry, even though he was within ten months of completing his terms, and turned to theft for his trade. In the spring of 1724 he was first imprisoned in the St. Giles Roundhouse, but was free within three hours after cutting open the roof and lowering himself to the ground with sheet and blanket. There "he joined a gathering throng" and made his escape through the lanes of St. Giles. A few weeks later he was arrested again, for a pickpocketing offence in Leicester Fields, and was incarcerated in the New Prison of Clerkenwell. He was taken to the "Newgate Ward" there and pinioned with links and fetters of great weight; he sawed through the fetters and somehow cut through an iron restraint before boring his way through an oaken bar some nine inches thick. The severed chairs and bars were afterwards kept by the prison authorities "to Testifie, and preserve the Memory of this extraordinary Event and Villain."

For three months he was at liberty before being found by the notorious criminal and "thief-taker," Jonathan Wild; Sheppard was now escorted to Newgate and, after being sentenced to death for three robberies, was consigned to the condemned hold. Even within that dreadful place, by some means or other, he managed to smuggle in a "Spike" and with that began to carve an opening in the wall (or perhaps ceiling); with the help of accomplices on the other side he was dragged out. It was the week of Bartholomew Fair, and he made his escape through the crowds of those going up Snow Hill and Giltspur Street into Smithfield. From there he travelled eastwards into Spitalfields, where he stayed at the Paul's Head; on an eighteenth-century map, like that of John Roque, it is still possible to track his route. It is in any case a potent image—of a prisoner almost miraculously escaping from incarceration to join the crowds celebrating their own temporary liberty among the booths and shows of Bartholomew Fair.

During the next few days, according to Peter Linebaugh's *The London Hanged*, he was seen by a "cobbler in Bishopsgate and a milkman in Islington." In Fleet Street he entered a watch-maker's shop and addressed the apprentice there, bidding him "stick to his Tools, and not use his Master to such ill Habits of working so late." He promptly robbed the premises, but was pursued and taken. Then, once again, he was led to Newgate and in a secluded gaol was "fastened to the floor with double fetters." Everyone came to see him, and everyone talked about him. He had become a true London sensation, the people "Mad about him" at a time of the greatest "idleness among Meckanicks that has been known in London." They had all gone to the taverns and ale-houses, in other words, to discuss the prodigy. When certain reverend gentlemen visited his cell he declared that they were "Ginger-bread Fellows" and that "One File's worth all the Bibles in the world." The pagan temper of the Londoner is here revealed. "Yes, sir, I am the Sheppard," he said while in confinement, "and all the jailors in the town are my flock." A file was found upon him and he was removed to the "Stone Castle" on the fifth storey where he was chained to the floor, his legs secured with irons and his hands cuffed. These instruments were inspected daily, and Sheppard himself was under regular supervision.

And then, wonderfully if not miraculously, he escaped again. Somehow he managed to slip his hands through his handcuffs, and with a small nail managed to loose one of the links in the chains about his legs; like some "posture master" from Bartholomew Fair he then squeezed through the great chains which held him. With a piece of this broken chain he worked out a transverse bar from the chimney and climbed upwards into the "Red Room," "whose door had not been unbolted for seven years." With a nail he freed its bolt in seven minutes and got into a passage which led to the chapel; then with a spike from one of the interior railings he opened four other doors which were all locked and bolted from the other side. On opening the final door he found himself on the outside of the prison, with the roofs of the city below him. Then he remembered his blanket. He had left it in his cell. He returned all the way to the "Stone Castle," through the chapel and down the chimney, in order to retrieve it. He returned to the outer air and, with the blanket spiked to the stone wall, slid down quietly.

Over the next few days, he disguised himself as a beggar and as a butcher, the two most familiar London types, while the streets around him were filled with ballads and broadsides proclaiming his latest escape. In the disguise of a foot porter he visited the printer of those "Last Dying Speeches" which, as he knew or guessed, would accompany his own journey to the scaffold. He robbed a pawn-broker in Drury Lane and, with the proceeds, bought a fashionable suit and a silver sword; then he hired a coach and, with that innate sense of theatre which never seemed to desert him, he drove through the arch of Newgate itself before visiting the taverns and ale-houses of the vicinity. Recaptured on that evening, two weeks after his escape, he was taken back to the prison from which he had effected such a remarkable exit, and constantly watched; when he was led to the court where the punishment of death was again pronounced, he was surrounded by "the most numerous Croud of People that ever was seen in London." He was sentenced to be hanged within a week. There were reports that he would break away at Little Turnmill along Holborn—and on the road to Tyburn a penknife was taken from him—but there was to be no reprieve from what Peter Linebaugh has called his "final escape."

It is an intensely private as well as a very public London story. We may infer that his youthful experience in the workhouse of Bishopsgate prompted his obsessive desire for escape, while it is likely that he somehow acquired his extraordinary skills while working as a carpenter's apprentice; certainly he would have learned the uses of files and chisels while practising upon wood. He was a violent and dishonest man, but his series of escapes from Newgate transformed the atmosphere of the city, where the prevailing mood became one of genuine collaborative excitement. To escape from the most visible and oppressive symbol of authority—that "black cloud" which pursued Boswell—was in a sense to be freed from all the restraints of the ordinary world. We might then equate the experience of the prison with the experience of the city itself. It is indeed a familiar and often an accurate analogy, and the history of Jack Sheppard suggests another aspect of it. He hardly ever left London, even with the opportunity and indeed the pressing necessity of doing so; after three days "on the run" in Northamptonshire, for example, he rode back to the city. After his penultimate escape from Newgate he returned to Spitalfields, where he had spent his earliest days. After his final escape he was determined to remain in London, despite the pleas of his family. He was in that sense a true Londoner who could not or would not operate outside his own territory.

He possessed other urban characteristics. After his escapes he disguised himself as a variety of tradesmen, and generally behaved in a thoroughly dramatic fashion. To ride in a coach through Newgate was a mark of theatrical genius. He was profane to the point of being irreligious, while his violence against the propertied interests was not inconsistent with the egalitarianism of the "mob." After one of his escapes a pamphleteer declaimed: "Woe to the

Shopkeepers, and woe to the Dealers in Ware, for the roaring Lion is abroad." So Jack became an intrinsic part of London mythology, his exploits celebrated in ballads and verses and dramas and fiction.

In 1750 the smell of Newgate had become pervasive throughout the neighbourhood. All its walls were then washed down with vinegar and a ventilation system was installed; seven of the eleven men working on that project were themselves infected with "gaol fever," which suggests the extent of the pestilence within. Five years later, the inhabitants of Newgate Street were still "unable to stand in their doorways" and customers were reluctant to visit the shops in the vicinity "for fear of infections." There were even directions for those who might come close to the criminals—"he should prudently empty his stomach and bowels a few days before, to carry off any putrid or putrescent substance which may have lodged in them."

The prison was rebuilt in 1770 by George Dance, and was described by the poet Crabbe as a "large, strong and beautiful building," beautiful, no doubt, because of its simplicity of purpose. "There is nothing in it," one contemporary wrote, "but two great windowless blocks, each ninety feet square." It was fired by rioters in 1780, and rebuilt two years later upon the same plan. It was in many respects now more salubrious and hygienic a prison than many others in London, but its ancient atmosphere lingered. A few years after the rebuilding, the new gaol "begins to wear a brooding and haunted air already." The old conditions also began to re-emerge within the prison and, in the early years of the nineteenth century, it was reported in *The Chronicles of Newgate* that "lunatics raving mad ranged up and down the wards, a terror to all they encountered . . . mock marriages were of constant occurrence . . . a school and nursery of crime . . . the most depraved were free to contaminate and demoralise their more innocent fellows."

The ministrations of Elizabeth Fry in 1817 seem to have produced some effect upon this "Hell above ground," but official reports in 1836 and 1843 from the Inspector of Prisons still condemned the squalor and the misery. Immediately before the first of these reports, Newgate was visited by a young journalist, Charles Dickens, who from childhood had been fascinated by the looming gatehouse of the dark prison; by his own account in *Sketches by Boz* he had often contemplated the fact that thousands of people each day "pass and repass this gloomy depository of the guilt and misery of London, in one perpetual stream of life and bustle, utterly unmindful of the throng of wretched creatures pent up within it." A "light laugh or merry whistle" can be heard "within one yard of a fellow-creature, bound and helpless, whose days are numbered" and who waits for execution. In his second novel, *Oliver Twist*, Dickens returns to those "dreadful walls of Newgate, which have hidden so much misery and such unspeakable anguish." Here Fagin sits in one of the condemned cells—Dickens notes that the prison kitchen is beside the yard where the scaffold is erected—and an engraving by George Cruikshank, drawn after a visit to one such "hold," shows a stone bench with a mattress across it. Nothing else is visible except the iron bars set in a thick stone wall, and the blazing eyes of the prisoner himself. The young Oliver Twist visits the condemned cell, through "the dark and winding ways" of Newgate, even though the gaoler has said that "It's not a sight for children." Dickens might be revisiting his own childhood, since his most formative early experience of London was of attending his father and family lodged in the Marshalsea Prison of Southwark. Perhaps that is why the image of Newgate always haunted him and why, towards the end of his life, at night, utterly wearied and demoralised, he returned to the old gaol "and, touching its rough stone" began "to think of the prisoners in their sleep."

Dickens was writing of a period when Newgate had ceased to be a general prison and was instead used to confine those who had been sentenced to death (as well as those waiting to be tried in the adjacent Central Criminal Courts), but a further refinement was added in 1859 when the prison was redesigned to house a series of separate cells where each inmate was held in silence and isolation. In a series of articles published in the *Illustrated London News* the prisoner awaiting a flogging is described as "the patient." The prison becomes a hospital, then, or perhaps the hospital is no better than a prison.

In this manner the institutions of the city begin to resemble one another. Newgate also became a kind of theatre when, on Wednesdays or Thursdays between the hours of twelve and three, it was open to visitors. Here sightseers would be shown casts of the heads of notorious criminals, as well as the chains and handcuffs which once held Jack Sheppard; they could at their wish be locked into one of the condemned cells for a moment, or even sit within the old whipping post. At the end of their tour they were conducted along "Birdcage" walk, the passage from the cells of Newgate to the Court of Sessions; here also they could read "curious letters on the walls" denoting the fact that the bodies of the condemned were interred behind the stone. The name of the walk is strangely reminiscent of a scene from Arthur Morrison's *A Child of the Jago* where an infant visits her father "before a double iron railing covered with wire netting" at Newgate—"carrying into later years a memory of father as a man who lived in a cage."

The last execution at Newgate took place at the beginning of May 1902, and three months later the work of demolition began. At a quarter past three in the afternoon of 15 August, according to the *Daily Mail* of the following day, "a piece of stone about the size of a foot fell on the pavement, and a hand with a chisel in it was seen working away in the breach. A little crowd soon gathered to watch the operations." It was noticed, too, that the "old pigeons, rough and grimy as the prison itself compared with the other flocks in London," fluttered about the statue of liberty on the pinnacle of the prison. These birds, at least, had no wish to leave their London cage.

Six months later an auction of Newgate relics was held within the prison itself. The paraphernalia of the execution shed sold for £5 15s 0d while each of the plaster casts of the famous criminals was "knocked down" for £5. Two of the great doors, and the whipping post for the "patients," may now be seen by the curious in the Museum of London. The Old Bailey now lies upon the ancient site.

CHAPTER 25

A Note on Suicide

any inmates committed "self-murder" within the walls of Newgate, but in London suicide assumes many forms. People have hurled themselves from the Whispering Gallery in the cathedral of St. Paul's; poisoned themselves in the solitude of London attics; and drowned themselves for love in the waters of St. James's Park. The Monument was another favourite location: the unhappy subject would throw himself or herself from the summit of the pillar and fall upon its base rather than the street. On 1 May 1765, according to Grosley's *A Tour of England*, "the wife of a colonel drowned herself in the canal in St. James's park; a baker hanged himself in Drury-lane; a girl, who lived near Bedlam, made an attempt to dispatch herself in the same manner." In the summer of 1862 "the Suicide Mania" became a topic of public attention. In that same century the Thames was wreathed with the bodies of the drowned.

London was the suicide capital of Europe. As early as the fourteenth century Froissart described the English as "a very sad race," which description applied particularly and even principally to Londoners. The French considered that the London vogue for suicides was owing to "the affectation of singularity," although a more perceptive observer believed that it was "from a contempt of death and a disgust of life." One Frenchman described the plight of London families "that had not laughed for three generations," and observed that citizens committed suicide in the autumn in order "to escape the weather." Another visitor remarked that self-slaughter was "no doubt owing to the fogs." He also suggested that beef was another essential cause, since "its viscous heaviness conveys only bilious and melancholic vapours to the brain"; his diagnosis has a curious resemblance to the folk superstition of Londoners, in which to dream of beef "denotes the death of a friend or relation." The modern connection between beef and "BSE" may be noted here.

It was also remarked by Grosley that "melancholy prevails in London in every family, in circles, in assemblies, at public and private entertainments . . . The merry meetings, even of the lowest sort, are dashed with this gloom." Dostoevsky observed the "gloom" which "never forsakes" the Londoner even "in the midst of gaiety." The wine sold in London taverns was also considered "to occasion that melancholy, which is so general." Even the theatre was held responsible for the unhappy distemper; one traveller described how the son of his landlord, after being taken to see *Richard III*, "leaped out of bed and, after beating the wainscot with his head and feet, at the same time roaring like one possessed, he rolled about the ground in dreadful convulsions, which made us despair of his life; he thought he was haunted by all the ghosts in the tragedy of Richard the Third, and by all the dead bodies in the churchyards of London."

Everything was blamed except, perhaps, for the onerous and exhausting condition of the city itself.

CHAPTER 26

A Penitential History

here have been more prisons in London than in any other European city. From the penitential cell in the church of the Knights Templar to the debtors' prison in Whitecross Street, from the Clink situated in Deadman's Place, Bankside, to the compter in Giltspur Street, London has been celebrated for its places of confinement. There was a prison in Lambeth Palace where early religious reformers, the Lollards, were tortured, and a roundhouse in St. Martin's Lane where twenty-eight "were thrust into a hole six-feet square and kept there all night," four of the women being stifled to death. New prisons were always being built, from the Tun in Cornhill at the end of the thirteenth century to Wormwood Scrubs in East Acton at the end of the nineteenth century. The prisoners were obliged to wear masks in the new "model prison" at Pentonville, while the "new prison" of Millbank was supposed to have been built as a "panopticon" whereby each cell and inmate could be individually scrutinised.

By the early seventeenth century the London prisons, like its churches, were celebrated in verse:

In *London* and within a mile I weene
There are of layles or Prisons full eighteene
And sixty Whipping-posts and Stocks and Cages.

The first prison mentioned in this sorrowful litany is the "Gatehouse" at Westminster, and it is followed by an encomium upon the Fleet Prison.

The Fleet was the oldest of them all, older even than Newgate, and had once been known as the "Gaol of London"; it was also one of the first of the medieval city's stone buildings. It was situated on the east side of the Fleet and surrounded by a moat with "tree clad banks" where now Farringdon Street runs down to the Thames. The lowest "sunken" storey was known as Bartholomew Fair, although the usual reports of brutality, immorality and mortality render it an ironic sobriquet. The prison was, however, most notorious for its "secret" and unlawful marriages performed by "degraded clergymen" for less than a guinea. By the early eighteenth century there were some forty "marrying houses" in taverns of the vicinity, with at least six known as the Hand and Pen. Women, drugged or intoxicated, could be taken there and married for their money; innocent girls could be duped into believing that they were lawfully joined. There was a watch-maker who impersonated a clergyman, calling himself "Dr. Gaynam"—or, perhaps, *gain them*. He resided in Brick Lane and it was his practice to walk up Fleet Street. Crossing Fleet Bridge "in his silk gown and bands," he was known for his commanding figure, and a "handsome though significantly rubicund face." In the locality he was named as the "Bishop of Hell."

On several occasions the Fleet Prison was itself consigned to the flames, the last notable fire taking place in 1780 when a mob—led, perhaps appropriately, by a chimney-sweep—mounted an incendiary assault upon it. It was rebuilt in its old form, with many of its more interesting details left intact. Along what is now Farringdon Street, for example, the wall of the gaol had one open grating with bars across it. Here was placed an iron box for alms and, from within, one chosen inmate would call out perpetually "Remember the poor prisoners." This was the prison in which was incarcerated Samuel Pickwick who, after speaking to those who lay there "forgotten" and "unheeded," muttered, "I have seen enough . . . My head aches with these scenes, and my heart too."

The Fleet Prison was demolished in 1846, but the site was not cleared for another eighteen years. Where once were walls and cells there emerged "blind alleys" which, even on summer days, were so narrow and crowded that they "are bleak and shadowed." The atmosphere of the ancient place lingered even after its material destruction.

It is likely that the Fleet inspired Thomas More's famous metaphor of the world as a prison, "some bound to a poste . . . some in the dungeon, some in the upper ward . . . some wepying, some laughing, some labouring, some playing, some singing, some chiding, some fighting." More eventually himself became a prisoner, too, but, before that time, as under-sheriff of London, he had sent many hundreds of Londoners to gaol. He consigned some to the Old Compter in Bread Street and others to the Poultry Compter near Bucklersbury; in 1555 the prison in Bread Street was moved a few yards northward to Wood Street, where one of the inmates might have been echoing the words of Thomas More. He is quoted in *Old and New London*: "This littel Hole is as a little citty in a commonwealth, for as in a citty there are all kinds of officers, trades and vocations, so there is in this place as we may make a pretty resemblance between them." The men consigned here were known as "rats," the women as "mice." Its underground passages still exist beneath the ground of a small courtyard beside Wood Street; the stones are cold to the touch, and there is a dampness in the air. Once a new prisoner drank from "a bowl full of claret" to toast his new "society," and now the Compter is on occasions used for banquets and parties.

The image of the city as prison runs very deep. In his late eighteenth-century novel *Caleb Williams*, William Godwin described "the doors, the locks, the bolts, the chains, the massy walls and grated windows" of confinement; he affirmed then that "this is society," the system of prison representing "the whole machine of society."

When Holloway Prison was opened in 1852 its entrance was flanked by two stone griffins which are, of course, also the emblems of the City of London. Its foundation stone carried the inscription "May God preserve the City of London and make this place a terror to evil doers." It is perhaps suggestive that its architect, James B. Banning, used the same principles of design in his work upon the Coal Exchange and the Metropolitan Cattle Market. There was a visible affinity between some of the great public institutions of the city.

In the 1970s V.S. Pritchett described London as "this prison-like place of stone" and in 1805 Wordsworth cursed the city as "A prison where he hath been long immured"; in turn Matthew Arnold in 1851 depicted it as this "brazen prison" where the inhabitants are "Dreaming of naught beyond their prison-wall." In 1884 William Morris added his own note to this vision of incarceration with his account of

this grim net of London, this prison built stark
With the greed of all ages

A mean lodging was his "prison-cell/In the jail of weary London." Keir Hardie, on returning to his native Ayrshire in 1901, wrote that "London is a place which I remember with a haunting horror, as if I had been confined there." A report on London prisoners themselves, in *London's Underworld* by Thomas Holmes, in the very same period as Keir Hardie's observations, notes that "the great mass of faces strikes us with dismay, and we feel at once that most of them are handicapped in life, and demand pity rather than vengeance." The conditions of poverty in the city were such that "the conditions of prison life are better, as they need to be, than the conditions of their own homes." So they simply moved from one prison to another. But gaol was the place, in Cockney idiom, "where the dogs don't bite."

There were also areas of "sanctuary rights" in London, apparent neighbourhoods of freedom over which the prisons failed to cast their shadows. These areas were once within the domains of great religious institutions, but their charm or power survived long after the monks and nuns had departed. Among them were St. Martin's le Grand and Whitefriars; they had been respectively the home of secular canons and of the Carmelites, but as sanctuaries from pursuit and arrest became in turn havens "for the lowest sort of people, rogues and ruffians, thieves, felons and murderers." One of the presumed murderers of the "Princes in the Tower," Miles Forest, took refuge in St. Martin's and stayed there "rotting away piecemeal." "St. Martin's beads" became a popular expression for counterfeit jewellery. The privileges of St. Martin's le Grand were abolished at the beginning of the seventeenth century, but the sanctuary of Whitefriars lasted for a longer period. The area became popularly known as "Alsatia" (named after the unhappy frontier of Alsace) because no parish watch or city officials would dare to venture there; if they did so, there was a general cry of "Clubs!" and "Rescue!" before they were seized and beaten. It is the area now marked by Salisbury Square and Hanging-Sword Alley, between Dorset Street and Magpie Alley.

Two other sanctuaries were connected with the coining of money. They were located by the Mints at Wapping and in Southwark, as if the literal making of money were as sacred as any activity which took place in monastery or chapel. In the mid-1720s legal officers attempted to infiltrate and expel the "Minters" of Wapping but were fought back. One bailiff was "duck'd in a Place in which the Soil of Houses of Office [lavatories] had been empty'd" while another was force-marched before a crowd with "a turd in his mouth." The connection between money and ordure is here flagrantly revealed.

Other sanctuaries still clung around the churches, as if the tradition of begging for alms had continued in a more dissipated form. The area which had once been dominated by Blackfriars was a notorious haunt of criminals and beggars. A sanctuary in the neighbourhood of Westminster Abbey was for centuries "low and disreputable," and Shire Lane beside the church of St. Clement Danes was known as Rogues' Lane. Here were houses known as "Cadgers' Hall," "The Retreat" and "Smashing Lumber," the last being a manufactory for counterfeit coin, wherein according to *Old and New London* "every room had its secret trap or panel . . . the whole of the coining apparatus and the *employés* could be conveyed away as by a trick of magic." In any alternative London topography, sanctuaries, like prisons, become highly specific sites of ill fame. Tread there who dares.

CHAPTER 27

A Rogues Gallery

If the places of crime and punishment do not necessarily change, but leave a steady mark, there may also be continuity among the criminals of London. We read of fourteenth-century forgers and blackmailers, and the coroners' inquests of 1340 reveal a long tally of "bawdy-house keepers, night-walkers, robbers, women of ill fame." The city was even then so filled with thieves that in this period the right of "infangthief" was given to the city authorities; it permitted them "to hang thieves caught redhanded (*cum manu opere*)" without trial by jury.

It was not until the sixteenth century, however, that the literature of London crime becomes extensive. The works of Robert Greene and Thomas Dekker, in particular, reveal an underworld of thieves and imposters which remains as old and as new as the city itself. Certainly the argot or cant of the thieves had very ancient roots, while some of its more expressive phrases endured well into the nineteenth century. "And bing we to Rome-vill, to nip a bung" can be translated as "Now let us travel to London, to cut a purse." How London acquired the name of "Rome-vill," long before it was ever compared to that imperial city, is something of a mystery. "Yonder dwelleth a queer cuffin. It were beneship to mill him"

("There lives a difficult and churlish man. It would be a very good thing to rob him").

The individuals, as well as their words, come to life in the pages of these old catalogues of crime—"John Stradling with the shaking head . . . Henry Smyth who drawls when he speaks . . . John Browne, the stammerer"—each of them engaged in some kind of fifteenth-century cheating trade. That trade, too, has survived. The game of cups, in which the spectator must choose which one conceals the ball, is still played on the streets of London in the twenty-first century; the fraud has now existed for over a thousand years in the capital.

In their record of "abraham men" (who pretended to be mad), "clapper dodgers" (who fished for goods from open windows) and "priggers of prancers" (horse thieves), Dekker and Greene may on occasions be guilty of over-emphasis; the streets of sixteenth-century London might not have been quite as violent or as perilous as they suggest. Nevertheless real criminality could be found in many specific areas. The neighbourhood of Chick Lane and Field Lane in Clerkenwell, for example, was always notorious. In Chick Lane itself there was a dwelling, once known as the Red Lion inn, which upon its demolition in the eighteenth century was discovered to be three centuries old; C.W. Heckethorn, in *London Souvenirs*, reveals that it contained "dark closets, trap-doors, sliding panels and secret recesses." One of these trap-doors opened upon the Fleet Ditch, and "afforded easy means of getting rid of the bodies." There was a morass of lanes off Ratcliffe Highway, with names like Hog Yard and Black Dog Alley, Money Bag Alley and Harebrain Court, which were known for "moral degradation." There was also a dwelling near Water Lane, off Fleet Street, known as "Blood Bowl house" named "from the various scenes of blood that were almost daily exhibited, and where there seldom passed a month without the commission of a murder."

In perhaps less sensational a context, a city recorder of the seventeenth century gave evidence of a raid upon Watton's alehouse at Smart's Key beside Billingsgate. The tavern was in reality a school "set upp to learne younge boys to cutt purses." Pockets and purses were hung upon a line with "hawkes bells" or "sacring bells" attached to them; if a child could remove a coin or counter without setting off the bell "he was adjudged a judiciall Nypper." During the following century there was another such school in Smithfield, where a tavern-keeper taught children how to pick pockets, to pilfer from shops by crawling through their wooden hatches, and to break into buildings by a simple expedient: they pretended to be asleep against the wall while all the time they were actively chipping away at the bricks and mortar until a hole had been breached.

It is curious, in this description of crime, that the criminals themselves adopted the terminology of "law." "Cheating law" was the term for playing with false dice, "versing law" the art of passing counterfeit coin and "tigging law" that of cutting purses. It was the alternative law of "low" London.

Yet new crimes could also evolve. In the seventeenth century, for example, highway robbery became known as "high law." The age of coaches meant also the age of coach theft, and in the last days of 1699 John Evelyn wrote: "This week robberies were committed between the many lights which were fixed between London and Kensington on both sides, and while coaches and travellers were passing." Between flaring lights along the high road, there was at night absolute darkness where the robbers could easily strike. We may even hear them talking in the pages of *The London Hanged*. One drover, Edward Smith, suggested to a companion that they "go upon the Ac-compt" (take up highway robbery). "Let us enter into Articles to have no others than ourselves concerned for the future." And if they were caught? There is an account of one thief taken and led back to London—"he was very unruly, pulling the horse about, making Motions with his Hands at every Body that came near him, as if he was firing a Pistol, crying Phoo!" Houn-slow Heath and Turnham Green, Marylebone and Tottenham Court Road, were particular areas of danger for the unwary. These were the places for footpad robberies, known to the criminal fraternity as "low Tobies." It be-came customary in the early eighteenth century for travellers into London to gather in bands for mutual protection, beginning their perilous journey only on the sounding of a bell; at night they would also be accompanied by link-boys carrying lights.

The same flaring torches were necessary for journeys within the city it-self. "A gentleman was stopt in Holborn about twelve at night by two *foot-pads*, who on the gentleman's making resistance shot him dead and then robbed him . . . One Richard Watson, tollman of Marybone turnpike, was found barbarously murdered in his toll-house." A female who served in a public house in Marylebone is quoted in Charles Knight's *London* as having "often wondered why I have escaped without wounds or blows from the gen-tlemen of the pad, who are numerous and frequent in their evening patroles through these fields; and my march extended as far as Long Acre, by which means I was obliged to pass through the thickest of them." A commentator in the same volume has remarked that the citizens of London "looked upon the worshipful company of thieves much in the same way that settlers in a new country regard the wild beasts prowling in the forests around them."

The "judiciall Nyppers" of one period had migrated into another, and it was reported that eighteenth-century London "swarms with pick-pockets, as daring as they are subtile and cunning." They stole under the very gibbet from which they might one day be suspended and "there never is any execution without handkerchiefs and other articles being stolen." If they were caught in the act, by Londoners themselves, they were dragged to the nearest well or fountain "and dipped in the water till nearly drowned." If they were taken up by the authorities, a more severe penalty was imposed. By the middle of the eighteenth century the number of offences, for which men and women could be hanged had risen from 80 to over 350. Yet this may not have been a powerful deterrent. A few years later, in a *Treatise on the Police of the Metropolis*, it was reported that "115,000 persons in London were regularly engaged in criminal pursuits." This would amount to one-seventh of the population. So, in 1774, it was recorded by the *Gentleman's Magazine* that "The papers are filled with robberies and breaking of houses, and with the recital of the cruelties committed by the robbers, greater than ever before." We may surmise, therefore, that in a period of affluence and "conspicuous" wealth, crimes against property were as numerous as crimes against people—and this despite the fact that the larger the sum involved in theft or cheat, the greater the possibility of being hanged.

Peter Linebaugh has scrutinised the statistics for hanging all through the eighteenth century, and has arrived at interesting conclusions. Those born in London tended to hang in their early twenties, an earlier age than that of immigrants to the city. The main trades of those who reached the scaffold were butchers, weavers and shoe-makers. There was a pronounced association between butchers and highway robbers (Dick Turpin himself had been apprentice to a butcher). Cultural and sociological interpretations of this correspondence have been made, but, in general terms, the butchers of the city were always known for their boisterous, individualistic and sometimes violent nature. Certainly they were the most prominent of all London tradesmen, and one foreign visitor to London reported that it was "a marvel to see such quantities of butchers shops in all the parishes, the streets being full of them in every direction." They were often the leaders of their little communities, too; those of Clare Market, for example, worked and dwelled among the patent theatres of the area and were described as "the arbiters of the galleries, the leaders of theatrical rows, the musicians at actresses' marriages, the chief mourners at players' funerals." They were also leaders of the community in times of scarcity and disorder. It was reported of one violent assault, for example, that "The Buttchers have begun the way to all the rest, for within this toe days they all did rise upon the exise man." It is not inconsistent, then, that they or their apprentices should be at the very forefront of adventurous or desperate crime.

In 1751 Henry Fielding published his *Inquiry into the Causes of the Late Increase of Robbers*, and a year later the Murder Act added a further terror to death by declaring that the bodies of the hanged should be publicly dissected by surgeons and anatomists. A measure such as this may have been prompted by a perceived increase in crime, but it was also a direct product of panic fear among the gullible and the anxious.

London has always been the centre of panic, and of rumour. At the end of the twentieth century, for example, an official survey reported that "fear of crime is a social problem in itself" with a significantly higher proportion of Londoners—as opposed to those living elsewhere—feeling unsafe both in their dwellings and in the streets. They might have been echoing the sentiments of a Londoner in 1816 who stated that "from the author's own experience in almost every part of Europe . . . he can mention no place so full of peril as the environs of London." Of course it was then still a relatively compact and enclosed city—the crucial intensity of crime has in fact diminished with London's growth—and indeed its criminals seem to have borrowed their habits and demeanour from its earlier eighteenth-century life.

The "low Toby" or footpad was known in the early nineteenth century, for example, as a "Rampsman" but the violent assault had not changed. The house-breaker of this period was called a "Cracksman," while a "Bug Hunter" was one who picked the pockets of drunks; a "Snoozer" was one who booked into a hotel before robbing its guests, while an "Area Sneak" called at kitchen doors in the hope of finding them open and unattended. These were the crimes typical of the city, and their perpetrators were generally thieves, pickpockets, burglars, and those fraudulent merchants and tricksters who took advantage of the gullibility or credulousness of the passing transient crowd.

Although it would be going too far to say that "the man who knew his London—could recognise each type by his dress and manner," as Thomas

Burke puts it in *The Streets of London*, criminals were still a particular and distinguishable element of city life until the middle of the nineteenth century. Their language, too, like that of the "abraham men" of a previous century, was itself pronounced and peculiar—"Stow that . . . pottering about on the sneak, flimping or smashing a little . . . If I'm nailed it's a lifer." This existence had its own kind of music also. A villain was known as a "sharp" and his victim a "flat."

It was reported, in 1867, that this "criminal class" amounted to 16,000. Yet the streets were by then safer than they had ever been. Five years before there had been an outbreak of "garrotting," the popular name for violent robberies, but that had been effectively suppressed by means of equally violent floggings. It was no longer possible to claim, as the Duke of Wellington had done forty years before, that "the principal streets of London" were "in the nightly possession of drunken women and vagabonds" as well as "organised gangs of thieves." Where in previous periods of the city's history the "vagabonds" and "thieves" were scattered indiscriminately in various "islands" off the main thoroughfares, they had by the middle of the nineteenth century retreated into various quarters on the fringes of the now more civilised metropolis. They were often located in the eastern suburbs or, as it soon became known, the "East End." That area, some sixteen years before "Jack" rendered the region of Whitechapel notorious, was reputed to be a place of thieves' kitchens and ragged public houses "charged with the unmistakable, overpowering damp and mouldy odour" attendant upon street crime. In Bethnal Green, too, there were pubs and houses which acted as "a convenient and secluded exchange and house of call" filled with "dippers" and "broads" and "welshers." These are the words of Arthur Morrison, writing *A Child of the Jago* at the end of the nineteenth century when once more the slang or "patter" had changed in order ever more colourfully to depict the familiar crimes of London. A "house of call," like "exchange," was in fact a word used to describe a dealing room of city business. So, in mockery as well as implicit deference, the terminology of financial and commercial London was parodied by the more secretive, if more notorious, speculators in urban goods.

In Bethnal Green and its environs, Morrison noticed the presence of the most successful late nineteenth-century criminals who belonged to "the High Mobs" or, as one resident put it, " 'Igh mob. 'Oohs. Toffs." Morrison was in fact depicting a traditional London pursuit—that of an organised gang, generally of more than usually skilful or vicious practitioners of the criminal arts, with one or two leaders. The "mob" or gang controlled a certain area of the city or certain specific activities. Dick Turpin led "the Essex Gang" of thieves and smugglers in the 1730s; while a decade earlier such gifted individuals as Jonathan Wild could dominate the general course of London crime. But, as the city expanded, it became divided into separate territories controlled by specific gangs.

In the nineteenth century, rival gangs vied for territory and for influence. In the early twentieth century, east London once again became the scene of murderous conflict. The opposition of the "Harding Gang" and the "Bogard Gang" culminated in a violent confrontation in the Bluecoat Boy public house in Bishopsgate. In the 1920s and 1930s the crime families of the Sabinis and Cortesis fought against each other in the streets of Clerkenwell, over the control of clubs and racetracks, while in the next decade the White family of Islington were challenged by Billy Hill and his "heavy mob" from Seven Dials.

There were other criminal fraternities, known variously as "the Elephant Gang," "the Angel Gang" and "the Titanic Gang." These dealt in organised shoplifting or "smash-and-grab" raids as well as the general business of drugs, prostitution and "protection" racketeering. In the late 1950s and 1960s the Kray brothers of the East End, and the Richardsons from "over the water" in the southern suburbs, controlled their respective areas with notable success. In the Krays' own territory, "the popular admiration for great thieves," to use a phrase of the mid-nineteenth century, had never seriously abated. In 1995, the funeral procession for Ronnie Kray, along Bethnal Green Road and Vallance Road, was a great social event; as Iain Sinclair wrote of the East End in *Lights Out for the Territory*, "no other strata of society has such a sense of tradition." The memories of grand criminality in that neighbourhood go back to Turpin's "Essex Gang" and beyond.

It is hard to say that any aspect of crime or criminal behaviour is altogether new. "Smash and grab" became popular, for example, in the 1940s and 1950s although it did not originate then; there are records of that offence in the seventeenth and eighteenth centuries. The gangs of the Krays and the Richardsons have now been displaced by those with other ethnic origins, the Jamaican "Yardie" and Chinese "Triad" groups, for example, working their own particular areas. In the 1990s, as the trade in drugs such as heroin, khat, crack and ecstasy became ever more lucrative, gang elements from Nigeria, Turkey and Colombia participated in the city's new criminal activity. The "Yardies" are considered to be, in the twenty-first century, responsible for the largest proportion of killings in a city where murder is perpetual. Murder, to paraphrase Thomas de Quincey, is one of London's fine arts.

CHAPTER 28

Horrible Murder

It has come in many different forms. In the eighteenth century it was often remarked that the noses of the victims were bitten off during the act of strangling. Strangulation and stabbing were popular at the end of that century, succeeded in the early nineteenth century by slashed throats and clubbing; at the end of the nineteenth century poison and various forms of mutilation or hacking to death became more favoured.

Yet the element of mystery remains perhaps the most interesting and suggestive aspect of the London murder, as if the city itself might have taken part in the crime. One of the unsolved murders of the seventeenth century, in an age when all were inured to death, concerned a man known variously as Edmund Berry Godfrey or Edmunsbury Godfrey. He was found in 1678 upon what is now known as Primrose Hill, with his own sword thrust through his body but "no blood was on his clothes or about him" and "his shoes were clean." He had also been strangled, and his neck broken; when his clothes were taken off, his breast was found to be "all over marked with bruises." Another curious element lay in the fact that "there were many drops of white wax lights on his breeches." A Catholic plot was suspected and, on concocted evidence, three members of the royal court at Somerset House were arrested and executed; their names were Green, Berry and Hill. The earliest name of Primrose Hill, where the body was found, was Greenberry Hill. The real murderers were never discovered, but it would seem that the topography of London itself played a fortuitous if malign part.

One evening at nine o'clock, in Cannon Street in the spring of 1866, Sarah Millson went downstairs to answer the street-bell. An hour later a neighbour who lived above her discovered her body at the bottom of the stairs. She had been killed by a number of deep wounds to the head but "her shoes had been taken off and were lying on a table in the hall"; there was no blood upon them. The gaslight had been quietly extinguished after the murder, presumably in order to save expense. The neighbour opened the street door to find help, and saw a woman on the doorstep apparently shielding herself against the heavy rain which was then falling. She was asked for assistance but moved away, saying, "Oh! dear no; I can't come in." The murderer was never apprehended, but the characteristics of London mystery are here found in almost emblematic detail—the lodging house in Cannon Street, the heavy rain, the gaslight, the perfectly cleaned shoes. The strange woman shielding herself from the rain only contributes to the air of intimacy and darkness that characterises this crime. Once more it is as if the spirit or atmosphere of the city itself played its part.

That is why the murders committed by "Jack the Ripper" between August and November 1888 are an enduring aspect of London myth, with the areas of Spitalfields and Whitechapel as the dark accomplices of the crimes. The newspaper accounts of "Jack's" murders were directly responsible for parliamentary inquiries into the poverty of these neighbourhoods, and of the "East End" in general; in that sense, charity and social provision followed hard upon the heels of monstrous death. But in a more elusive way the streets and houses of that vicinity became identified with the murders themselves, almost to the extent that they seemed to share the guilt. One scholarly account by Colin Wilson refers to the "secrets" of a room in the Ten Bells public house of the neighbourhood, in Commercial Street, which suggests that the walls and interiors of the then impoverished streets were the killer's confessional. There are contemporary reports of the panic engendered by the Whitechapel killings. M.V. Hughes, author of *A London Girl of the Eighties*, has written that "No one can believe now how terrified and unbalanced we all were by his murders." This is recorded by one who lived in the west of London, many miles from the vicinity, and she adds: "One can only dimly imagine what the terror must have been in those acres of narrow streets where the inhabitants knew the murderer to be lurking."

It is testimony to the power of urban suggestion, and to the peculiar quality of late Victorian London, that popular belief lent "a quality of the supernatural to the work." The essential paganism of London here reasserts itself. Even as the murders were continuing, the books and pamphlets began to appear, among them *The Mysteries of the East End, The Curse Upon Mitre Square, Jack the Ripper: Or the Crimes of London, London's Ghastly Mystery.* The place becomes the central interest, therefore, and soon after the crimes sightseers were flocking through Berners Street and George Yard and Flower and Dean Street; a Whitechapel "peep-show" even provided wax figures of the victims for the delectation of the spectators. Such is the force of the area, and of its crimes, that several daily tours are still organised— mainly for foreign visitors—around the Ten Bells public house and the adjacent streets.

The connection between London and murder is, then, a permanent one. Martin Fido, author of *The Murder Guide to London*, states that more "than half the memorable murders of Britain have happened in London," with the prevalence of certain killings within certain areas. Murder may appear "respectable" in Camberwell, while brutal in Brixton; a litany of cut throats in nineteenth-century London is followed by a list of female poisoners. Yet, as the same narrator has pointed out, "there has been too much murder in London for a comprehensive listing."

There are episodes and incidents, however, which remain emblematic, and it is noticeable that certain streets or areas come to identify the crimes. There were "the Turner Street murders" and the "Ratcliffe Highway murders," for example, the last of which in 1827 prompted de Quincey's memorable essay on "The Fine Art of Murder." He begins his account of a series of killings, "the most superb of the century by many degrees," with an invocation of Ratcliffe Highway itself as "a most chaotic quarter of eastern or nautical London" and an area of "manifold ruffianism." An entire family had been found murdered in a shop beside the highway, in the most gruesome circumstances; less than three weeks later in New Gravel Lane, very close to that highway, a man called out "They are murdering people in the house!" Seven citizens altogether, including two children and one infant, had been dispatched within eight days. One of the killers, John Williams, committed suicide in his cell within Coldbath Fields Prison at Clerkenwell; his dead body, together with the bloody hammer and chisel which had been the means of his crimes, were paraded past the houses where he had assisted in the murders. He was then buried beneath the crossroads of Back Lane and Cannon Street Road or, as de Quincey puts it, "in the centre of a quadrivium or conflux of four roads, with a stake driven through his heart. And over him drives for ever the uproar of unresting London." So Williams became part of London; having marked a track through a specific locality, his own name was buried in the urban mythology surrounding "the Ratcliffe Highway murders." He became instead the city's sacred victim, to be interred in a formalised and ritualistic manner. Some hundred years later workmen, digging up the territory, found his "mouldering remains"; it is appropriate that his bones were then shared out in the area as relics. His skull, for example, was granted to the owner of a public house still to be seen on the corner of the fatal crossroads.

Other roads and streets can prove to be injurious. Dorset Street was the site of Mary Kelly's murder in the winter of 1888, at the hands of "Jack"; it reclaimed its original name of Duval Street after this peculiarly savage crime, as a way of preserving anonymity, only to be the site of a fatal shooting in 1960. In both cases no murderer was ever convicted.

There are many accounts of such anonymous killers, wandering through crowds and crowded thoroughfares, concealing a knife or some other fatal instrument. It is a true image of the city. The remarks of the killers have on occasion been recorded. "Damn her! Dip her again and finish her . . . Yours to a cinder . . . Get the knives out!" The streets themselves then become the object of fascinated enquiry. We read, for example, in *The Murder Guide to London* that the "murder victim in Baroness Orczy's *Lady Molly of Scotland Yard*, had his office in Lombard Street. In Wilkie Collins's *The Moonstone* the gem was pledged to a banker in Lombard Street." An actual police station in Wood Street has been used as an imaginative location by several writers of mysteries, and Edgar Wallace turned All Hallows by the Tower into "St. Agnes on Powder Hill." In a city where spectacle and theatre become an intimate part of ordinary reality, fact and imagination can be strangely mingled.

A complex of streets can also become haunted by crime, so that Martin Fido, himself an eminent criminologist, writes of "the dense murder area of Islington" located "in the back streets behind Upper Street and the City Road"; in this neighbourhood the sister of Charles Lamb killed her mother in the autumn of 1796, only a few yards from the room where Joe Orton was murdered by his lover in 1967. In the early decades of the twentieth century there were killings known generically as the "North London murders," although they were in fact separately conducted by Hawley Harvey Crippen and Frederick Seddon.

The list of London murderers is long indeed. Catherine Hayes, proprietress of a tavern called the Gentleman In Trouble, severed her husband's head in the spring of 1726 and tossed it into the Thames before strewing other parts of the corpse all over London. The head was recovered and placed upon a pole in a city churchyard, where eventually it was recognised. Mrs. Hayes was committed for trial and sentenced to death, earning the further distinction of being one of the last women ever to be burned at Tyburn.

Thomas Henry Hocker, described by an investigating policeman as "a fellow in a long black cloak," was seen springing from behind some trees in Belsize Lane on a February evening in 1845. Singing to himself, he walked past the scene of the murder he had just committed and, still undiscovered, conversed with the policeman who had found the body. "It is a nasty job," he said and then took hold of the dead man's hand. "This site was his own handiwork," as *The Chronicles of Newgate* puts it, "yet he could not overcome the strange fascination it had for him, and remained by the side of the corpse until the stretcher came."

One of the most celebrated of London's mass murderers was John Reginald Christie, whose house at 10 Rillington Place itself became so notorious that the name of the street was changed. Eventually the house was itself torn down, after harbouring a variety of transient lodgers. Extant photographs reveal a characteristic London location. It was a typical example of a Notting Hill tenement in the early 1950s with tattered curtains, cracked and badly stained plaster, bricks dark with soot. Murder, in such a context, can be concealed.

There is another aspect of London killings to be fathomed in the career of Dennis Nilsen who, while living in Muswell Hill and Cricklewood during the late 1970s and early 1980s, murdered and dismembered many young victims. The details of the lives of these murdered men may no longer seem of much significance except that, in the words of one report, "few of them were missed when they disappeared." This is the context for many London murders, where the isolation and anonymity of strangers passing through the city leave them peculiarly defenceless to the depredations of an urban killer. One of Nilsen's victims, for example, was a "down-and-out" whom he had met at the crossroads by the church of St. Giles-in-the-Fields; Nilsen, apparently "horrified by his emaciated condition," killed him and burned him in the garden of his house in Melrose Avenue. Another victim was a young "skinhead" who had inscribed graffiti upon his own body, among them a dotted line around his neck together with the words, "cut here." Here in these brutal and brutalising circumstances the darker face of London seems to emerge.

All that was known of Elizabeth Price, condemned to death for theft in 1712, was that she "had follow'd the Business of picking up Rags and Cinders and at other times that of selling Fruit and Oysters, crying Hot Pudding and Grey Pears in the Streets." We read of "Mary Cut-and-Come-Again" who, when arrested by the watchmen, took out her breasts "and spurted the milk in the fellows' faces, and said, damn your eyes, What do you want to take my life away?" That spirit of contempt against the forces of law and order is characteristic of London life. It is connected, too, with a buoyant paganism, as in the case of a domestic servant charged with murder who was reported to take "a mighty disgust at Things of Religion." In similar spirit Ann Mudd, who was convicted of murdering her husband, was equally defiant. "Why, said she, I stabb'd him in the Back with a Knife for Funn." She spent her last hours singing obscene songs in the condemned cell.

The Whitechapel murders encouraged the earliest use of police photographs recording "the scene of the crime," while a murder in Cecil Court off St. Martin's Lane, in 1961, resulted in the first success of the Identikit picture. The device of placing the head of Catherine Hayes's husband upon a stake, as a means of identification, has had some interesting successors. The essential point remains that crime, and in particular murder, enlivens the urban populace. That is why, in London mythology, the greatest heroes are often the greatest criminals.

CHAPTER 29

London's Opera

*T*he exploits of Jack Sheppard proved how intense could be the excitement aroused in London by the adventures of a criminal. The most notable painter of the day, Sir James Thornhill, visited him in 1724 in order to complete a portrait which was then sold to the public as a mezzotint.

Nine years later, in 1732, Thornhill's son-in-law, William Hogarth, made a similar journey to Newgate; here he sketched another famous malefactor, Sarah Malcolm, herself held in the condemned cell. She had strangled two elderly parties, and then cut the throat of their maid, the recklessness of the crimes lending her notoriety among the London public. She was very young—only twenty-two—and very composed. At her trial she declared the blood on her shift to be the issue of menstruation rather than of murder and, after the sentence of death had been pronounced upon her, confessed that she was a Roman Catholic. Hogarth painted her sitting in her cell, her rosary beads before her, and announced in the public press that his print would be ready within two days. It was an advertisement of his skill as well as a tribute to the notoriety of his subject. In her biography of Hogarth, Jenny Uglow describes how Sarah arrived at her hanging, by the scene of her crimes according to custom, "neatly dressed in a crape mourning hood, holding up her head in the cart with an air, and looking as if she was painted." After she had been cut down, it was reported that there was "among the rest a gentleman in deep mourning, who kissed her, and gave the people half a crown."

Here are all the elements of drama and intrigue which rendered memorable such rituals of crime and punishment in London. Hogarth himself could not resist the lineaments of the condemned. When in 1761 Theodore Gardelle was about to be hanged at the corner of Panton Street and the Haymarket, Hogarth captured his countenance of despair "with a few swift strokes."

It is of some interest, then, that in February 1728 Hogarth attended and enjoyed *The Beggar's Opera* by John Gay. In this drama the "low" criminal life of London is presented in bright theatrical guise. A true London production, part burlesque and part burletta, it was a parody of fashionable Italian opera, as well as a satire upon governmental cabal. With its main characters of Macheath, a highwayman, and Peachum, a receiver of stolen goods, it aspired to be a spirited representation of the London criminal world appropriately completed by the portrait of Lockit, the keeper of Newgate.

The dramatic scenes within Newgate itself confirm two of the city's most permanent images: the world as a stage and the world as a prison. There are other aspects of London life within the drama. Its constant references to commerce and to currency, together with its tendency "to treat people and relationships in commodity terms" according to John Gay's latest and best biographer, David Nokes, mark the powerful and possibly corrupting atmosphere of trade and finance which lingers over all the activities of the city. How else is it possible that the characters from the London streets should reach so casually and easily for "mercantile metaphors"? These people "are invariably valued in trading terms, that is, according to how much may be 'got' by them." Here is the true spirit of city commerce, but it has an interesting and significant ramification. This trading activity is pursued by both "high" and "low," by courtiers as well as highwaymen, so that the gaiety and exuberance of the "opera" are in part based upon its implicit denial of all distinctions of rank and class. It is the egalitarian—one might almost say, antinomian—instinct of the London populace, represented upon the stage in a colourful and spirited form.

In turn, Gay himself was accused of glamorising thieves and receivers of stolen goods, as if in the act of equalising the activities of the beggars and their "betters" he was somehow lending vulgar distinction to the more disreputable elements of London life. It was reported by one contemporary moralist that "several thieves and street robbers confessed in Newgate that they raised their courage at the playhouse by the songs of their hero Macheath, before they sallied forth in their desperate nocturnal exploits." If that was indeed the case, then we see in the fervent and fevered context of London that street life feels no compunction in taking on the lineaments of dramatic art.

That is the significance of Hogarth's admiration for *The Beggar's Opera*. This quintessentially London artist saw the possibility of channelling his own genius through it. He painted the same scene from the play on six separate occasions, in the process, according to Jenny Uglow, "bursting into life as a true painter." It is not hard to understand how this intense depiction of London life invigorated and animated the artist, since in his subsequent work he reveals his own vital engagement with the scenic possibilities of street life. In fact he creates his own tradition of London villains, in the characterisation of "Tom Nero" in *The Four Stages of Cruelty* (1751) and "Thomas Idle" in the *Industry and Idleness* series (1747); both end as murderers, suspended on the gallows, but the course of their fatal careers is given a lurid and sensational aspect by being placed within the context of the streets and "low" haunts of the city.

Everything there conspires to engender dreadful deeds. In *The Four Stages of Cruelty* the life of the city itself is the true engine of that cruelty; as Hogarth put it in his disquisition on these prints, the work was done "in hopes of preventing in some degree that cruel treatment of poor Animals which makes the streets of London more disagreeable to the human mind, than any thing what ever, the very describing of which gives pain." In one scene outside Thavies Inn coffee house in Holborn, along the main route to Smithfield from the rural areas of Islington and Marylebone, the driver of cab number twenty-four is mercilessly belabouring his horse while a sheep is being clubbed to death in the foreground; a child unnoticed falls under the wheel of a brewer's cart while on the wall there is a poster advertising a cock-fight.

At the execution of Thomas Idle, the drunken and violent rabble beneath the gallows act as a mirror of his existence and are an emblem of it. Recognisable figures are also part of the Tyburn crowd—Tiddy Doll, the eccentric seller of gingerbread, Mother Douglas, the fat and drunken procuress, and, on the gallows itself, half-witted "Funny Joe" who amused the populace at executions with his jokes and speeches. A suggestive biblical motto, from Proverbs, at the bottom of the print announces that "then they shall call upon God, but he will not answer." Hogarth is depicting a pagan society from which these criminals have ineluctably emerged.

. . .

If John Gay was intent upon turning thieves or receivers into dramatic heroes or characters, then he was himself following a distinguished London tradition. In the four years before *The Beggar's Opera* had appeared on stage there had been other theatrical representations of *Harlequin Sheppard* and *A Match in Newgate*, the former suggesting a remarkable link between pantomime and crime. More than a century earlier Beaumont and Fletcher, in *The Beggar's Bush*, had given dramatic currency to the tricks and slang of London criminals—again with the powerful insinuation that they were behaving no worse than those "betters" who ruled them. In 1687 Marcellus Laroon similarly depicted in elegant style and form "the Squire of Alsatia," a notorious thief and confidence man, called "Bully" Dawson, who is nevertheless posed in Laroon's print in the manner of a great fop and gentleman. The theatrical manner, and disguise, are emblematic of the contrasts and variety of the streets. All these various works manifest in turn a strange fascination for the life of the vagrant and the outcast, as if the conditions of London might propel anyone into a state of need or outlawry. Why else should the streets of London so haunt Hogarth's own imagination?

The tradition continued in the sensational accounts of the lives of famous criminals, whose exploits were every bit as melodramatic as the characters upon the stage. "You cannot conceive," wrote Horace Walpole in the latter part of the eighteenth century, "the ridiculous rage there is for going to Newgate, the prints that are published of the malefactors, and the memoirs of their lives set forth with as much parade as Marshal Turenne's." Swift satirised that "rage" some decades earlier with his description of "Tom Clinch" being driven to the scaffold:

> The maids to the doors and the balconies ran,
> And said, "Lack-a-day! he's a proper young man."

In the nineteenth century an essay was written on "Popular Admiration for Great Thieves," in which it is noted that in the previous century Englishmen were no less "vain in boasting of the success of their highwaymen than of the bravery of their troops." Hence the widespread popularity of *The Newgate Calendar*, the general title given to a succession of books which began to emerge at the end of the eighteenth century; the first was *The Malefactor's Register or New Newgate and Tyburn Calendar*, and its popularity was such that it can be compared to Foxe's *Book of Martyrs* in the mid-sixteenth century or perhaps the ubiquitous legends about saints of the medieval period. It might even be compared to the vogue for fairy tales emerging in the early nineteenth century. The ambiguity of the genre is further compounded by the school of the "Newgate novel" which emerged in the same period, with such celebrated practitioners as Harrison Ainsworth and Bulwer Lytton. It is perhaps significant that in Newgate itself the inmates were addicted to "light literature . . . novels, flash songs, plays, books." Everyone was copying everyone else.

The content of these various publications was equally ambiguous, hovering somewhere between celebration and condemnation. In similar fashion skill and cunning, disguise and stratagem, were commonly admired as the dramatic expedients of street life. There was the infamous "Little Casey," a nine-year-old pickpocket whose skills made him the wonder of late 1740s London. There was Mary Young, known as Jenny Diver, who practised in the same streets some forty years before; she would dress up as a pregnant woman and, hiding a pair of artificial arms and hands beneath her dress, opened pockets and purses with ease. She, in turn, was celebrated by the London populace for her "skills of timing, disguise, wit and dissimulation."

At a later date there emerged Charles Price or "Old Patch"; he committed sophisticated forgeries, and passed off his bank-notes in a variety of elaborate disguises. He was a "compact middle-aged man" but typically would dress as an infirm and aged Londoner, wearing "a long black camlet cloak, with a broad cape fastened up close to his chin." He had a large "broad-brimmed slouch hat, often green spectacles or a green shade." He dressed up, in other words, as the "old man" of stage comedy.

In the late nineteenth century Charles Peace was also celebrated as a master of disguise and manipulation; the son of a file-maker, he conducted an ordinary life as a suburban householder variously in Lambeth and in Peckham. Yet "by shooting forward his lower jaw he could entirely alter his appearance. He had been a one-armed man, the live limb being concealed beneath his clothes . . . The police declared that he could so change himself, even without material disguises, that he was unrecognisable." He even designed a folding ladder eight feet long which folded down to a sixth of that length, fifteen inches, and could be concealed under the arm. He had once been a street musician and had a great love for fiddles; he even contrived to steal them, although on occasions they furnished an awkward addition to his "swag." After his death on the scaffold, his collection of instruments was put up for auction. Yet in a city of character and spectacle, it was his ability to disguise himself which exerted the most fascination. In the "Black Museum" of Scotland Yard there used to be exhibited the pair of blue goggles "he was accustomed to wear in his favourite character of eccentric old philosopher."

He was also a callous criminal, who murdered anyone who got in his way, and so the celebration of disguise is tempered by disgust at the nature of his crimes. This indeed was a feature of *The Newgate Calendar* itself, as in "A Narrative of the horrid Cruelties of Elizabeth Brownrigg on her Apprentices." She was a midwife chosen by the overseers of the poor of St. Dunstan's parish "to take care of the poor women who were taken in labour in the workhouse." She had several penniless girls working as her servants, at her house in Fleur-de-lis Court off Fleet Street, and she systematically tortured, abused and killed them. As she was led to her death, in the autumn of 1767, the London mob shouted out that "she would go to hell" and that "the devil would fetch her." Her body was anatomised, and her skeleton displayed in a niche of Surgeon's Hall.

After such events came the trade in "Last Dying Confessions." Some were genuinely composed by the felons themselves—who often took great delight in reading their "Last Speeches" in their cells—but customarily it was the "Ordinary" or religious minister of Newgate who wrote what were essentially morbid and moralistic texts. The city then became a stage upon which were presented spectacles for the delight and terror of the urban audience.

There is a short story by Arthur Conan Doyle concerning Sherlock Holmes's exposure of what were then known as "fraudulent mendicants." In "The Man with the Twisted Lip" Neville St. Clair, a prosperous gentleman living in the suburbs of Kent, travelled to his business in the City every morning and returned on the five fourteen from Cannon Street each evening. It transpired, however, that he had secret lodgings in Upper Swandam Lane, a "vile alley" to the east of London Bridge, where he dressed up as a "sinister cripple" called Hugh Boone who was well known as a match-seller in Threadneedle Street with his "shock of orange hair, a pale face disfigured by a horrible scar." This tale was published in 1892, as part of *The Adventures of Sherlock Holmes*. Twelve years later there was a beggar who sold matches in Bishopsgate; he was well known in the vicinity, since he was "paralysed . . . He could be seen dragging himself painfully along the gutter, his head hanging to one side, all his limbs trembled violently, one foot dragged behind him and his right arm limp, withered and useless. To complete the terrible picture his face was most horribly distorted." This account was written by a chief detective inspector of the City police force, Ernest Nicholls, in *Crime within the Square Mile*. In the autumn of 1904 a young detective constable from that force decided to "tail" the match-seller; the policeman discovered that the beggar would drag his paralysed body into Crosby Square and then "make his exit at another corner as a nimble young man." He turned out to be a gentleman, by the name of Cecil Brown Smith, who lived in "the genteel suburbs of Norwood" and who earned a prosperous living from the charity of those who passed him in Bishopsgate. It is a curious coincidence, if no more, and may be accounted as one of the many strange coincidences which life in the city creates.

In the same book of police cases, there is the story of a bloodstained razor being discovered behind the seat of a bus; the young man who found the blade hesitated a few days before giving it to the police, because some years before he himself had slashed the throat of his "sweetheart" with just such a murder weapon. It is as if the city itself brought forth evidence from its own history. The stories of the mendicant beggars may imply that Cecil Brown Smith had read Conan Doyle's story of London vagrancy, and had decided to bring it to life; or it may be that certain writers are able to divine a particular pattern of activity within the city.

In any case that connection of fact and fiction, in the realm of crime, was not wholly lost in the twentieth century. Tommy Steele played Jack Sheppard in *Where's Jack*, Phil Collins was "Buster" Edwards in *Buster*, Roger Daltrey was John McVicar in *McVicar* and two performers from Spandau Ballet enacted the Kray brothers in *The Krays*. The tradition of *The Beggar's Bush* and *The Beggar's Opera* continues.

CHAPTER 30

Raw Lobsters and Others

If villains become heroes, it has been the fate of policemen to become figures of fun. Shakespeare satirised Dogberry, the constable in *Much Ado About Nothing*, in what was already a long tradition of city humour at the expense of its guardians.

At first "the watch," as the police forces were called for many centuries, were literally watchers upon the walls of London. In a document of 1312 it is stipulated that "two men of the watch, well and fittingly armed, be at all hours of the day ready at the gate, within or without, down below, to make answer to such persons as shall come on great horses, or with arms, to enter the City." But what of the enemy within? The "good men" of each ward were by custom responsible for maintaining order, but in 1285 an informal system of mutual protection was supplanted by the establishment of a public "watch" comprising the householders of each precinct under the jurisdiction of a constable. Each householder, when not assuming the offices of beadle, constable or scavenger, had to serve as part of the watch operating under the rules of "hue and cry." So we hear of unruly apprentices being chased, and "night-walkers" arrested. There are constant descriptions of *roreres*—roarers—who drink and gamble and beat people in the streets. These are taken up, locked up, and brought before the city magistrates the following morning.

To act as a member of the watch was considered a public duty, but it became customary for the hard-pressed householder to hire another to take his place. Those who took the job were generally of a low calibre, however; hence the description of the London watch made up of old men "chosen from the dregs of the people; who have no other arms but a lanthorn and a pole; who patrol the streets, crying the hour every time the clock strikes." We also have the watch organised by Constable Dogberry in *Much Ado About Nothing*: "You are thought here to be the most senseless and fit man for the constable of the watch; therefore bear you the lantern." In the 1730s a Watch Act was introduced to regularise the situation; a system of payment out of the rates was supposed to encourage the employment of better watchmen, in some cases by hiring disbanded soldiers or sailors rather than the old pensioners of the parish, but it seems to have made little difference. There is a mid-nineteenth-century photograph of William Anthony, one of the last of the London watch, grasping a pole in his right hand and a lantern in his left. He is wearing the peculiar broad-brimmed hat and greatcoat which marked his profession, and his expression hovers somewhere between sternness and imbecility.

They were known as "Charleys," and were continually mocked. They patrolled certain streets and were supposed to act as guardians of property. "The first time this man goes on his rounds," César de Saussure remarked in 1725, "he pushes the doors of the shops and houses with his stick to ascertain whether they are properly fastened, and if they are not he warns the proprietors." He also awakened early any citizens "who have any journey to perform." But the Charleys were not necessarily reliable. The report of one high constable, who made an unannounced visit to their various lock-ups and boxes, included remarks such as "called out 'Watch!' but could get no assistance . . . No constable on duty, found a watchman there at a great distance from his beat; from thence went to the night-cellar . . . and there found four of St. Clement's watchmen drinking." In the sixteenth century they were well known for "coming very late to the watch, sitting down in some common place of watching, wherein some falleth on sleep by reason of labour or much drinking before, or else nature requireth a rest in the night." Three hundred years later they were still being reviled as old codgers "whose speed will keep pace with a snail, and the strength of whose arm would not be able to arrest an old washerwoman of fourscore returned from a hard day's fag at the wash-tub." The watchmen were in turn the targets of rowdy or drunken "bloods" or "bucks." It was reported that a "watchman found dozing in his box in the intervals of going his rounds to utter his monotonous cry was apt to be over-turned, box and all, and left to kick and struggle helplessly, like a turtle on its back, until assistance arrived." The Charley was often assaulted by roarers, as he made his way through the dark streets.

It is unlikely, therefore, that London was well policed through the fourteenth to eighteenth centuries. The evidence suggests that the medieval concept of co-operation within ward and precinct prevailed for many hundreds of years; the citizens of London themselves ensured that their city was at least relatively safe, and an informal system of local justice prevailed. Pickpockets and prostitutes were ducked, as were fraudulent doctors or merchants. A cuckolded husband was given a "charivari" or scornful music of "tin cans, kettles and marrow bones." It was a system of self-policing which must have been effective, if only because the calls for a city police force were so long re-jected.

But the growth of London demanded more effective measures of control. In the 1750s Henry Fielding almost single-handedly established at Bow Street a police office which acted as a kind of headquarters for the suppression of London crime. His "thief takers" or "runners" were known as "Robin Red-breasts" or "Raw Lobsters" because of their red vests. Their numbers in-creased from six to seventy by the end of the century, while in 1792 seven other "police offices" were set up in various parts of the capital. The old City of London, protecting its medieval identity, had already established its own regular police patrols—the Day Police were formed in 1784, and were im-mediately identified with the blue greatcoat which they wore, according to Donald Rumbelow in *The Triple Tree*, to "lend them an air of distinction when they provided the prisoner's escort on execution day." From such un-happy origins did the conventional police uniform emerge. In 1798 the Thames Police Office was instituted to protect quays and warehouses as well as the newly built docks along the river; it was outside the usual system of ward and precinct. Seven years later a horse patrol was established to deter highwaymen.

There is a painting, dating from 1835, of a watch house. It is a two-storeyed building of early eighteenth-century construction, with shuttered windows on the ground floor. It is situated on the west side of the piazza, just beside the church of St. Paul's, Covent Garden, and shows several blue-coated and black-hatted policemen milling about its iron gateway. There are potted plants on the top window ledge, and the words "Watch House" vividly painted on to the white brick façade. The impression is that of an establishment nicely suited to its surroundings, with the potted plants as a picturesque emblem of Covent Garden. But the appearance is, perhaps, deceptive. There are underground dungeons behind the Queen Anne façade, and the painting was completed some six years after the passing of a Metropolitan Police Act which profoundly altered the face of "law and order" in London.

The problem had been one of corruption. As so often happens in the city, those who were supposed to regulate criminal activity eventually began to condone or even encourage it. The Bow Street Runners were found to be receiving money and goods, while congregating with "villains" in taverns. This is illustrative of the city's demotic as well as commercial spirit. It was with great difficulty, therefore, that Robert Peel was able to enforce proposals to establish an organised and centralised police force for London. It was considered by some to be a direct threat to the city's liberty and, according to *The Times*, "an engine . . . invented by despotism." Yet by excluding the old city police from his ministrations, and by regaling a Select Committee with episodes of street crime and statistics of vagrancy, he ensured the success of his proposals.

In 1829 the office of the "New Police" was established in a small Whitehall courtyard known as Great Scotland Yard, with a force of some three thousand men organised into seventeen divisions. These are the officers to be seen in the painting of the Covent Garden watch house, with their black top hats and blue "swallow-tail" coats. Not popular in the streets of London, they were known as "Blue Devils" or "Real Blue Collarers," the latter an allusion to the depredations of cholera in the 1830s. When in 1832 an unarmed police constable was stabbed to death near Clerkenwell Green, the coroner's jury recorded a verdict of "Justifiable Homicide."

The police came from the same class and neighbourhoods as the policed; they were in that sense considered to be attempting to control and to arrest their own people. Like the "runner" before them they were also open to the charges of drunkenness and immorality. But such offences were punished with summary dismissal, with the result that, according to the *London Encyclopaedia*, "within four years fewer than one sixth of the original 3000 remained." Those who survived were known as "crushers" or "coppers," with the less vivid terms of "peelers" and "bobbies" coming from their association with Robert Peel. Those terms have been transmogrified into the modern "old Bill" which in turn seems to share some of the derogatory tone of the previous "Charleys." There is in fact a continuity in these forms of address. In the middle of the twentieth century a policeman was often known as a "bluebottle" which is precisely the term that Doll Tearsheet hurls at a beadle in the second part of *Henry IV*—"I will have you as soundly swindg'd for this, you blew bottle Rogue." Over more recent years they have also been known as "bogeys" or "rozzers," "slops" or "narks," "fuzz" or "pigs," "creepers" or "flatties." Yet historians of the London police have noted that within two or three decades Robert Peel's force had acquired some degree of authority, and success, in its pursuit of crime.

Allusions to the demeanour and appearance of the individual police officer are often made in this context. "The habitual state of mind towards the police of those who live by crime is not so much dislike as unmitigated slavish terror," one observer wrote. It was a way of suggesting that the darkness of London had been effectively dispelled by the "bull's-eye" lamp of the constables on the beat. In 1853 a foreign traveller, Ventura de la Vega, noted their quasi-military uniform, with their blue coats "closed in the front with a straight collar on which a white number is embroidered" and their hats lined with steel. When necessary, he goes on, "they take from the back pocket of their coat a stick a half a yard long in the shape of a scepter, which has an iron ball on the tip." It is never used, however, since "on hearing a policeman's voice nobody answers and everybody obeys like a lamb." So against the records of the violence and energy of the London crowd, we must place this evidence of almost instinctive obedience. Of course this is not to claim that every costermonger or street trader cowered in fright at the advancing uniform. The statistics of attacks upon the police, then and now, are testimony to that. But the observers are correct in one general respect. There does seem to be a critical point or mass at which the city somehow calms itself down and does not consume itself in general riot or insurrection. A level of instability is reached, only to retreat.

Other shapes emerge to touch upon the very nature of London even in the twenty-first century. It might be suggested, for example, that the "Fenian" explosion at Clerkenwell prison in 1867 was part of a pattern which manifested itself at the Canary Wharf explosion by the IRA in 1996. The Trafalgar Square riots of 1887 occupied the same space as the poll tax riots of March 1990. Complaints about police incompetence and corruption are as old as the police force itself. In 1998 an official investigation into the murder of a black teenager, Stephen Lawrence, revealed many instances of bad judgement and mismanagement; it also suggested implicit racial prejudice within the police force which has indeed been bedevilled by that charge for fifty years. Ever since the first "peeler" put on his blue "swallow-tail" coat, the London police have been the object of derision and suspicion. Yet those officers lingering outside the Covent Garden watch house would no doubt have been surprised to learn that their arm of investigation would be extended to almost eight hundred square miles with the number of offences, according to the latest statistical survey, rising to over 800,000. They would not have been quite so surprised to learn, however, that the "clear-up" rate was only 25 per cent.

CHAPTER 31

Thereby Hangs a Tale

here can be no calculation of the numbers of burnings and stonings, beheadings and drownings, hangings and crucifixions practised in Roman and Saxon times. But by the fourteenth century we have written reports of a condemned man wearing "a striped coat and white shoes, his head covered with a hood" and pinioned to a horse; the hangman rode behind him, the rope in his hand, while his "torturers" rode beside him mocking him all the way from Cheapside to Smithfield. This was a very public, and formalised, ritual of death making its way through the streets of London. Contrition and penance, however, were as important as any severity of punishment. The penalty for one convicted of insulting an alderman was to walk with bare feet, from the Guildhall into Cheapside and through Fleet Street, carrying a three-pound candle in the hands. This carrying of a lighted candle was a common punishment for assaults upon the authority of civic leaders or the Church, and it suggests an atonement to London itself.

The preferred punishment for false trading was the pillory. There the shopkeeper came literally face to face with those whom he had deceived. The convicted man was drawn upon a horse, facing the tail, and wore a fool's cap; he might be preceded by a band of pipers and trumpeters. On arrival at the pillory—there was one in Cheapside and another in Cornhill—

the goods deceitfully sold were burned before his face. If he had committed fraud, false coins or dice were suspended about his neck. If he had been found guilty of lying, a whetstone was hung around him, as if representing a sharpened tongue. The time of the punishment in the pillory was exactly measured. For spreading lying reports that foreign merchants were to be allowed the same rights as freemen—one hour. For selling cups of base metal rather than silver—two hours. For selling stale slices of cooked conger—one hour. Yet the timing was only one measure of pain and humiliation. To be identified and paraded in front of neighbours and fellow tradesmen was, for any citizen of London, the cause of extreme embarrassment and shame. It could also be perilous. Some were plied with rotten fruit, fish and excrement, but the most unpopular or unprincipled offenders were in danger of being pelted to death with sticks and stones. It is a measure of London's conservatism, or strictness, that the pillory was not abolished until the summer of 1837.

Among the other sights of the city were the impaled heads of traitors. Above the main gateway of London Bridge rose iron spikes upon which the remnants of condemned men were fixed; in most illustrations five or six of these mementoes are generally depicted, although it is not clear if demand outstripped supply. In 1661 a German traveller counted nineteen or twenty, which suggests that the civil conflicts of that unhappy period were fruitful in at least one respect.

In the following century the heads migrated to Temple Bar, "where people make a trade of letting spy-glasses at a halfpenny a look"; they were also visible from a telescope set up in Leicester Fields, which suggests that heads were a city attraction. Certainly the citizens seem to have become inured to these solemn spectacles of punishment except, according to "Aleph," "when there had been a recent sufferer; the curious would then stop to ask 'What new head is that?' "

In the late 1760s Oliver Goldsmith was wandering in Poets Corner of Westminster Abbey with Samuel Johnson who, surveying the memorial stones to the great dead, muttered "*Forsitan et nostrum nomen miscebitur istis*" (There may be a chance that our name will be mingled with these). But when they walked up to Temple Bar and observed the heads, Goldsmith stopped Johnson "and slily whispered me '*Forsitan et nostrum nomen miscebitur* istis.' "

During one memorable storm in March 1772, two heads of decapitated Jacobites fell down. Mrs. Black, the wife of the editor of the *Morning Chroni-*

cle, recalled how "Women shrieked as they fell; men, as I have heard, shrieked. One woman near me fainted." Thirty years later the iron spikes were finally removed from the malevolent Bar.

There was no respite in hanging, however. In the fifteenth century eight offences merited that fate, among them arson and "petty treason (the killing of a husband by his wife)." Anyone who could read a passage from the Bible, known as the neck verse, was deemed to be a cleric and therefore given over to the ecclesiastical authorities. Averting death was thus, for two centuries, one of the primary gifts of literacy.

From the twelfth century the favoured site for a hanging was Tyburn, the first (of William Longbeard) being noted in 1196 and the last (of John Austen) in 1783. The actual site of the gallows has been disputed, the notoriety being given variously to Connaught Place or Connaught Square, both on the edge of the desolate Edgware Road slightly to the north of Marble Arch. But antiquarian research has revealed that the site lies on the south-east corner of Connaught Square. A carpenter recalled that his uncle "took up the stones on which the uprights [of the gallows] were placed." When the square itself was being built in the 1820s, a "low house" on the corner was demolished and quantities of human bodies were found. So some of the victims of the gallows were buried *in situ*. Other remains were discovered when the neighbouring streets and squares were laid out in the early decades of the nineteenth century, and a house in Upper Bryanston Street which overlooked the fatal spot "had curious iron balconies to the windows of the first and second floors, where the sheriffs sat to witness the executions." There were also wooden galleries erected around the area, like stands at a race course, where seats were hired by curious spectators. One notorious stallkeeper was known as "Mammy Douglas, the Tyeburn pew-opener."

Yet, of course, and more especially, the executioners themselves became notorious. The first known public hangman was one Bull, who was followed by the more celebrated Derrick. "And Derrick must be his host," Dekker wrote of a horse-thief in his *Bellman of London* (1608), "and Tiburne the land at which he will light." There was a proverb—"If Derrick's cables do but hold"—which referred to an ingenious structure, like a crane, upon which twenty-three condemned could be hanged together. This device was then put in more general use for unloading and hoisting vessels on board ships, and still bears the executioner's name.

Derrick was succeeded by Gregory Brandon upon whose name several puns were elaborated—"Gregorian calendar" and "Gregorian tree" among them—and who was in turn succeeded by his son, Richard, who claimed the public office by inheritance. "Squire" Dun followed, and the post was then given to the notorious Richard Jaquet, alias Jack Ketch, in the 1670s. There were many tracts and ballads directed against Ketch, among them *The Tyburn Ghost: or, Strange Downfal of the Gallows: a most true Relation how the famous Triple Tree, near Paddington, was pluckt up by the roots and demolisht by certain Evil Spirits, with Jack Ketch's Lamentation for the loss of his Shop, 1678*. It was known as the triple tree because the gallows was triangular in shape, with three posts or legs acting as supports. Each of the three beams could accommodate eight people and so, marginally more effective than the derrick, it was possible to hang twenty-four at the same time.

"Execution Day" was a Monday. Those about to be hanged were taken in an open cart from Newgate, generally attended by a huge and enthusiastic crowd. "The English are a people that laughs at the delicacy of other nations," one foreign traveller reported, "who make it such a mighty matter to be hanged. He that is to be takes great care to get himself shaved and handsomely dressed either in mourning or in the dress of a bridegroom . . . Sometimes the girls dress in white with great silk scarves and carry baskets full of flowers and oranges, scattering these favours all the way they go." So the ceremonial way to Tyburn was also the site of celebration. It was customary for famous London criminals to wear white cockades in their hats as a sign of triumph or derision; they were also an emblem, occasionally, of their innocence. The more dashing or notorious criminals were handed a nosegay "from the hand of one of the frail sisterhood"—one of the prostitutes who stood before the Church of Holy Sepulchre opposite the prison.

The procession made its way down Snow Hill and across Holborn Bridge, down Holborn Hill and into Holborn itself, with those about to be hanged greeted with cheers or execrations; they were always surrounded by a group of officers on horseback who restrained the crowds. Ferdinand de Saussure, in *A Foreign View of England*, noted some eighteenth-century criminals "going to their death perfectly unconcerned, others so impenitent that they fill themselves full of liquor and mock at those who are repentant." At the church of St. Giles-in-the-Field the malefactors were ritually handed jugs of ale. After the prisoners had quenched their thirst, the procession moved forward down Broad St. Giles, into Oxford Street, and on to Tyburn itself.

The cart was halted just before the gallows. Those about to die were escorted on to another carriage especially built like a platform for the occasion; it was driven beneath the triple tree. The halters were placed around the necks of the condemned, the horses kicked into action, and there the male-factors would be suspended until death overtook their pains. At this point friends and relatives might be seen "tugging at the hanging men's feet so that they should die quicker, and not suffer."

When the corpses were cut down there was a general rush for them, since the bodies of the hanged were believed to be of curious efficacy in the heal-ing of disease. The *London Encyclopaedia* remarks upon one Frenchman who noted "a young woman, with an appearance of beauty, all pale and trembling, in the arms of the executioner, who submitted to have her bosom uncovered in the presence of thousands of spectators and the dead man's hand placed upon it." There was a disturbing paganism latent beneath the surface of this piece of dramatic theatre. In the mid-seventeenth century such a severed hand could command the price of ten guineas, since "the possession of the hand was thought to be of still greater efficacy in the cure of diseases and pre-vention of misfortunes."

There was also a general struggle over the body, conducted between those who wished to retain it for their own purposes and those hired assistants come to transport it to the surgeons for dissection. In the mêlée "the populace often come to blows as to who will carry the bought corpses to the parents who are waiting in coaches and cabs to receive them." It was all "most di-verting," again according to Ferdinand de Saussure, who was sitting in one of the stands which surrounded the whole event.

One thief and housebreaker, John Haynes, displayed signs of life after being escorted to the house of a famous surgeon. He was asked what he re-membered—"The last thing I recollect was going up Holborn Hill in a cart. I thought then that I was in a beautiful green field; and that is all I remember till I found myself in your honour's dissecting room." So he came to death, and to life, babbling of green fields.

London did indeed become the city of the gallows. In 1776 the *Morning Post* re-ported "that the criminals capitally convicted at the Old Bailey shall in future be executed at the cross road near the 'Mother Red Cap' inn, the half-way house to Hampstead, and that no galleries, scaffolds or other temporary stages be built near the place." This measure was promoted in order to curb rioting among the spectators at a time when a fierce radicalism characterised the politics of London. The site of the executions was, typically, at a cross-roads where the present Camden Town Underground Station now stands. Other crossroads were also used as a natural location for the gallows, sending travellers upon their ambiguous journey—the division between the City Road and Goswell Road in Islington was once in use—but in the seventeenth and eighteenth centuries it was also customary to hang offenders on or near the spot where their crimes had been committed. In 1790, for example, two arsonists were hanged in Aldersgate Street immediately opposite the house which they had fired. The last recorded example of topographical killing occurred in Skinner Street, in 1817, when a thief was despatched in front of the shop of a gunsmith which he had plundered.

At Wapping lay Execution Dock, the place of punishment for all those who had committed high crimes upon the high seas, while the suspended bodies of the hanged could be seen swaying opposite Blackwall and other sites along the Thames such as Bugsby's Hole. The bodies of the condemned could also be seen at Aldgate and Pentonville, St. Giles and Smithfield, Blackheath and Finchley, Kennington Common and Hounslow Heath, so that these mementoes caught the attention of all those travelling into, or out of, London. It was not a pleasant prospect. Murderers, for example, were "first hung on the common gibbet, their bodies are then covered with tallow and fat substances, over this is placed a tarred shirt fastened down with iron bands, and the bodies are hung with chains to the gibbet . . . and there it hangs till it falls to dust." Why this should have been considered an appropriate spectacle for those leaving or entering London is another matter; it is curiously reminiscent of the fact that the principal gates or entrances to the city were also used as prisons, and suggests an attitude both defensive and minatory.

Some forms of punishment, however, were more secret. In Newgate was a "press" reserved for those who refused to plead to their indictments. Here they were stripped "and put in low dark chambers, with as much weight of iron placed upon them as they could bear, *and more*, there to lie until they were dead." There is an eighteenth-century engraving of a felon, one William Spiggot, "under pressure" in Newgate; he lies naked upon a bare floor, his arms and legs stretched and pinioned to hooks against the walls. Upon his naked chest is a wooden board loaded down with great weights. One gaoler, bearing keys, stands over him while another moves forward with a lighted candle to observe his sufferings. This quasi-medieval torture, known as "pressing to death," continued until 1734—an apt indication of the barbarity of city justice.

In that spirit, too, the number of hanged rose in the latter part of the eighteenth century. In one month of 1763, for example, "near one hundred and fifty persons have been committed to New Prison and Clerkenwell for robberies and other criminal offences." It was said in *The Annual Register* that the "reckless wretches seem almost to have crowded in, crying, 'You cannot hang us all.' " But they could try.

Soon enough, however, the venue of slaughter had changed. The gradual spread of gentility to the west meant that the old tribal route from Newgate to Tyburn began to impinge upon the fashionable quarters close to Oxford Street. So in 1783 the authorities removed the gallows to Newgate itself, thus cutting off the procession at its source. The populace at large felt deprived of the spectacle of "the cheat," to use the cant term for the gallows, and the more scholarly Londoners felt that an habitual aspect of the city was being removed in an untimely fashion. "The age is running mad after innovation," Samuel Johnson told Boswell, and "Tyburn is not safe from the fury of innovation . . . No, Sir, it is not an improvement: they object that the old method drew together a number of spectators. Sir, executions are *intended* to draw spectators. If they don't draw spectators, they don't answer their purpose. The old method was most satisfactory to all parties: the public was gratified by a procession: the criminal was supported by it. Why is all this to be swept away?" Boswell might have had his own answer. He himself was addicted to the watching of executions—"I had a sort of horrid eagerness to be there," he once wrote of Tyburn—and through the good offices of Richard Ackerman, the Keeper of Newgate, was able to witness many hangings outside that prison.

The first Newgate hanging was conducted on 9 December 1783, but its revolutionary system of "the new drop" soon claimed more victims. A few days after the sentence of death had been pronounced in the courtroom, the malefactor was "cast" and the "dead warrant" sent down to his cell. The *Newgate Chronicles* themselves detail the hours leading up to his appearance on the "stage." On the first night in the condemned cell "the solemn notification of the impending blow keeps nearly all awake," but soon they slept more easily. "All too have a fairly good appetite," the same chronicler reports, "and eat with relish up to the last moment." The "Italian boy" condemned for murdering a French woman in the Haymarket ate "constantly and voraciously," as if to stuff himself before the final exit. One Jeffreys, who hanged his child in a cellar in Seven Dials, called for roast duck as soon as he entered the condemned cell.

In the hour before execution the condemned man was led from his cell into a "stone-cold room" which was the place where he was pinioned by the "yeoman of the halter" before being taken to "the new drop." The engine of death, which was transportable, was dragged by horses into grooves marked upon Newgate Street itself. It consisted of a stage upon which were constructed three parallel beams. The part of the stage next to the gaol had a covered platform; here were the sheriffs' seats, while around it stood the interested spectators. In the middle of the stage was a trap-door, ten feet long by eight feet wide, above which the beams were placed. The hour of execution was always eight o'clock in the morning and, a few minutes before that time, the sheriffs brought out the prisoners. Upon the dropping of a flag, the bolts holding up the trap were pulled and the convicted men or women fell or "dropped" to their deaths.

There are several contemporaneous prints displaying "The New Gallows in the Old Bailey" with those about to suffer praying or weeping with halters about their necks. Around them, hemmed in by soldiers, are the crowd, who stare up with fascination at the fatal stage. In fact a contributor to *The Chronicles of Newgate* wrote that "the change from Tyburn to the Old Bailey had worked no improvement upon the crowd or its demeanour. As many spectators as ever thronged to see the dreadful show, and they were packed into more limited space, displaying themselves as heretofore by brutal horseplay, coarse jests, and frantic yells."

On one occasion, "A few minutes of most dreadful suspense" took place; "the culprits stood gazing at each other . . . at last the chime struck upon the ear, and the poor fellows seemed startled." In Defoe's account of Moll Flanders's period in Newgate, the sound of the bell of Holy Sepulchre set up "a dismal groaning and crying . . . followed by a confused clamour in the house, among the several prisoners, expressing their awkward sorrows for the poor creatures that were to die . . . Some cried for them, some brutishly huzzaed, and wished them a good journey; some damned and cursed those that had brought them to it."

The night before an execution, outside Newgate, all the paraphernalia of execution—the gallows, the barriers, the platforms—had to be set up. These preparations naturally attracted a crowd of idle or interested observers. The "low taverns and beer-houses about Newgate Street, Smithfield, and the Fleet district, are gorged with company, who sally out at intervals to see how the workmen get on" and "knots of queer-looking fellows form here and there" to discuss the following morning's proceedings. The police moved them on,

but they clustered elsewhere. Just after midnight on Sunday, when most of
the night-revellers had been cleared, the gin shops and coffee houses opened
their doors and hired out their rooms—"Comfortable room!," "Excellent situation!," "Beautiful prospects!," "Splendid view!" Both roofs and windows
in the vicinity were hired out; five pounds were "given for the attic storey of
the Lamb's Coffee House" and a first-floor front could command five times
as much. The crowd began to assemble at four or five in the morning, and the
whole area in front of Newgate was packed by seven o'clock. By the time of
the ceremony itself some of the spectators, pressed up against the barriers for
several hours, had "nearly fainted from exhaustion."

When Governor Wall was marched from the press yard towards the
place of execution, he was greeted with howls of abuse and execration from
the other prisoners of Newgate. While the governor of Goree, in Africa, he
had been responsible for the death of a soldier by excessive flogging—one of
those abuses of authority which Londoners most detest. His appearance on
the scaffold was then accompanied by three harsh and prolonged shouts
from the crowd assembled in Newgate Street. After the hanging was over the
yeoman of the halter offered portions of the rope for sale at one shilling per
inch; a woman known as "Rosy Emma," rumoured to be the yeoman's wife,
"exuberant in talk and hissing hot from Pie Corner, where she had taken her
morning dose of gin-and-bitters," was selling parts of the fatal cord at a
cheaper rate.

Governor Wall met his fate with fortitude and in silence. Arthur Thistlewood, condemned as one of the Cato Street conspirators in 1820, ascended
the scaffold and exclaimed, "I shall soon know the last grand secret!" Mrs.
Manning, convicted in 1849 of a more than usually unpleasant murder—with
the connivance of her husband she had murdered her lover with a ripping
chisel—appeared upon the scaffold in a black satin dress; her "preference
brought the costly stuff into disrepute, and its unpopularity lasted for nearly
thirty years." It is curiously reminiscent of the case of Mrs. Turner, a notorious poisoner in the reign of James I; she was a woman of fashion who had invented yellow-starched ruffs and cuffs. Hence her sentence was to be "hang'd
at Tiburn in her yellow Tinny Ruff and Cuff, she being the first inventor and
wearer of that horrid garb." To emphasise the moral the hangman on that day
"had his hands and cuffs" painted yellow, and from that time the coloured
starch, like Mrs. Manning's black satin, "grew generally to be detested and
disused." It is a measure of the central importance of this ritual of execution
that Newgate, and Tyburn, could affect the fashions of the day. Once more

the idea of the city as spectacle asserts itself. Hanging, then, was essentially a form of street theatre. When five pirates were hanged for mutiny in front of Newgate, the *Chronicles* record that "the upturned faces of the eager spectators resembled those of the "gods" at Drury Lane on Boxing Night . . . The remarks heard amongst the crowd were of course ones of approval. 'S'help me, ain't it fine?' a costermonger was heard to exclaim to his companion." Theatricality and savagery are subtly mingled.

The "unceasing murmur" of the crowd broke into "a loud deep roar" as the condemned man appeared; there were calls of "Hats off!" and "Down in front" as he approached the halter. There followed a moment of silence, abruptly broken by the drop itself. At the moment of descent "every link in that human chain is shaken, along the whole lengthened line has the motion jarred." The silence was replaced, after that sudden "jarring" of the body of the city, by a noise from the crowd "like the dreamy murmur of an ocean shell." And then, more distinctly, the familiar cries of the sellers of "ginger-beer, pies, fried fish, sandwiches and fruit," together with the names of famous criminals whose tracts were still being advertised on the spot where they, too, once fell. With these were soon mingled "oaths, fighting, obscene conduct and still more filthy language," together, perhaps, with the faintest note of disappointment. There was always the hope or expectation that something might go wrong—that the condemned man might fight for his liberty or the engine of death might not function satisfactorily. Charles White, condemned for arson in 1832, sprang forward at the exact moment the trap was opened and balanced on its edge while "the crowd roared their encouragement as he struggled furiously with the executioner and his assistants." He was eventually thrown down the drop with the hangman clinging to his legs. In these instances, the sympathy of the London crowd flooded instinctively to the condemned, as if they were watching their own selves in the act of being despatched by the authorities of the state.

There were occasions when death upon the scaffold was accompanied by death upon the streets. The execution of two murderers, Haggerty and Holloway, took place in February 1807; the anticipation was so great that close to 40,000 people were packed in front of the prison and its vicinity. Even before the murderers appeared upon the scaffold, women and children were trampled to death amid cries of "Murder." At Green Arbour Court, opposite the debtors' door of the prison, a pieman stooped to pick up some of his broken wares and "some of the mob, not seeing what had happened, stumbled over him. No one who fell ever rose again." Elsewhere a cart filled with spectators broke down, "and many of those who were in it were trampled to death." And yet amid these scenes of chaos and death the rite of execution continued. Only after the gallows had been taken down, and the mob partly dispersed, did the officers find the bodies of twenty-eight dead and hundreds injured.

Two great nineteenth-century novelists seemed implicitly to recognise the emblematic significance of these Monday mornings, when the city gathered to acclaim the death of one of its own. William Makepeace Thackeray rose at three on the morning of 6 July 1840, in order to witness the hanging of a manservant, Benjamin Courvoisier, convicted of killing his master. He recorded the scene in an essay, "Going to See a Man Hanged." In a carriage bound for Snow Hill, Thackeray followed the crowd intent upon seeing the execution; by twenty minutes past four, beside Holy Sepulchre, "many hundred people were in the street." Here Thackeray registered his "electric shock" when he first caught sight of the gallows jutting from the door of Newgate. He asked those around them if they had seen many executions? Most assented. And had the sight done them any good? "For the matter of that, no; people did not care about them at all," and, in a transcription of genuine London speech, "nobody ever thought of it after a bit."

The windows of the shops were soon filled with dandies, and with "quiet, fat, family parties," while from a balcony an aristocratic rowdy squirted those assembled with brandy and soda from a siphon. The crowd grew more eager as the hand of the clock came closer to eight. When the bell of Holy Sepulchre tolled the hour, all the men removed their hats "and a great murmur arose, more awful, bizarre and indescribable than any sound I had ever before heard. Women and children began to shriek horribly" and then "a dreadful quick, feverish kind of jangling noise mingled with the noise of the people, and lasted for about two minutes." This was a scene of fever and alarm, as if the whole body of London was starting up from an uneasy sleep. It was the noise, almost inhuman, which Thackeray immediately noticed.

The man about to be hanged emerged from the prison door. His arms were tied in front of him but "he opened his hands in a helpless kind of way, and clasped them once or twice together. He turned his head here and there, and looked about him for an instant with a wild imploring look. His mouth was contracted with a sort of pitiful smile." He walked quickly beneath the beam; the executioner turned him round, and put a black nightcap over "the patient's head and face." Thackeray could look no more.

The episode left him with "an extraordinary feeling of terror and shame." It is interesting that, apparently inadvertently, he uses the word "patient" to describe the condemned; it was the same term applied to the prisoners of Bridewell about to be flogged. It is as if the city were a vast hospital, filled with the diseased or the dying. Yet the city is also a surgeon's hall, where the novelist and the crowd were all the spectators of the doomed and the dead. Thackeray described it as a "hidden lust after blood." He was suggesting that there were permanent and atavistic forces at work.

Charles Dickens had gone down to Newgate early that same morning. "Just once," he told his friends, "I should like to watch a scene like this, and see the end of the Drama." Here a great London novelist instinctively reaches for the appropriate word to mark the fatal occasion. He found an upper room in a house close to the scene, and paid for its hire; from there he eagerly watched the movement of the London crowd, which he was soon to revive in his account of the Gordon Riots in *Barnaby Rudge*. And as he watched the mob, he saw a tall familiar figure—"Why, there stands Thackeray!" Chance encounters in the streets of London suffuse the novels of Dickens and in front of Newgate, amid the great crowd, the actual life of London confirmed his vision.

Nine years later, on a cold November morning, he rose from his bed to watch another execution. The Mannings were to be hanged outside Horsemonger Lane Gaol in Southwark, and immediately after the event Dickens wrote a letter to the *Morning Chronicle*. There, in the mob assembled before the prison, he saw "the image of the Devil." "I believe that a sight so inconceivably awful as the wickedness and levity of the immense crowd . . . could be presented in no heathen land under the sun." Here the evident paganism of London is given express form.

Dickens, like Thackeray, is appalled by the noise of the mob, in particular "the *shrillness* of the cries and howls," like that "feverish kind of jangling noise" which Thackeray heard. There were "screeching and laughing, and yelling in strong chorus of parodies on Negro melodies, with substitutions of "Mrs. Manning" for "Susannah" . . . faintings, whistlings, imitation of Punch, brutal jokes." Another "Mrs. Manning," in the crowd itself, "proclaimed that she had a knife about her and threatened to murder another woman so that she might step up to the gibbet after 'her namesake.' " The fury and excitement of the mob, expressive of "general contamination and corruption," fill Dickens's account of the proceedings. He declared that "there are not many phases of London life that could surprise me." But he was astonished and alarmed by this experience.

The crowd outside Newgate and Horsemonger Lane often jeered and hissed the executioner. That of Courvoisier and the Mannings was one Calcraft, who had previously earned his living by flogging boys in Newgate. The Mannings were his only victims in 1849, and his services were less and less frequently required. Between 1811 and 1832 there were approximately eighty executions a year but from 1847 to 1871 that figure was reduced to 1.48 per annum. William Calcraft was succeeded by William Marwood who perfected the "long drop" method. He once declared that "It would have been better for those I execute if they had preferred industry to idleness," thus in a fatal thread connecting the exercise of his craft with Hogarth's depiction of the hanging of the idle apprentice.

Marwood died of drink. His most recent and celebrated successor within this unique profession was Albert Pierrepoint who boasted that he could kill a man within twenty seconds. Pierrepoint's ministrations, however, were performed in silence and secrecy. The last public hanging outside Newgate was held in 1868, and from that time forward hangings took place in an especially constructed shed or hut behind prison walls. Ruth Ellis was hanged within Holloway Prison in 1955; her execution, and that of eighteen-year-old Derek Bentley two years before, materially assisted the campaign for the abolition of capital punishment. The last execution in London took place in 1964, more than a hundred years after Thackeray prayed for God "to cleanse our land of blood."

Yet here is another mystery of London: according to city superstition, to dream of the gallows is a prophecy of great good fortune. Money and blood still run together.

Voracious London

A detail from an aquatint by Rowlandson entitled "Revellers at Vauxhall";
the gardens of that area had been known for their gentility, but they
eventually degenerated into a place of drunkenness and sexual licence.

CHAPTER 32

Into the Vortex

✤

hen in the early months of 1800 de Quincey travelled towards London in an open carriage he experienced a "suction so powerful, felt along radii so vast, and a consciousness, at the same time, that upon other radii still more vast, both by land and by sea, the same suction is operating." The image here, from his essay "The Nation of London," is of a "vast magnetic range" drawing all the forces of the world towards its centre. When he was within forty miles of London, "the dim presentiment of some vast capital reaches you obscurely, and like a misgiving." An unknown, and unseen, area of energy has found him out and leads him onwards.

One characteristic phrase, "London conquers most who enter it," is perhaps now a truism. There is a famous early nineteenth-century cartoon, which has been embellished and elaborated in a thousand different ways. Two men meet beside a London milestone. One, returning from the city, is bowed and broken down; the other, advancing upon him, full of animation and purposefulness, shakes his hand and asks him, "Is it paved with gold?"

"Long ago," Walter Besant remarked in *East London*, "it was discovered that London devours her own children." It seems as if great city families die out or disappear within a century; the principal names of the fifteenth century, Whittington and Chichele, had vanished by the sixteenth. The families of seventeenth-century London were no longer active in the eighteenth. That is why London must continue to exert a continual attractive energy, and pull in new people and new families to replenish the constant loss. On the road to London de Quincey had noted the "vast droves of cattle," all with their heads directed towards the capital. But the city needs animal spirits as well as animals.

In 1690 records show that "73 per cent of those given the freedom of the City by apprenticeship were born outside London": an astonishing figure. The annual migration to London in the first half of the eighteenth century was approximately ten thousand, and in 1707 it was observed that for any son or daughter of an English family "that exceeds the rest in beauty, or wit, or perhaps courage, or industry, or any other rare quality, London is their North star." The city is the lodestone, or magnet. By 1750 the capital was home to 10 per cent of the population, prompting Defoe's remark that "this whole Kingdom, as well as the people, as the land, and even the sea, in every part of it, are employ'd to furnish something, and I may add the best of every thing, to supply the city of London with provisions." A million people swarmed in the metropolis by the end of the eighteenth century; within fifty years that figure had doubled, and there was no sign of abatement. "Who could wonder," wrote an observer in 1892, "that men are drawn into such a vortex, even were the penalty heavier than this?" Until the middle of the twentieth century the figures bear in one direction only—ever upward, counting by the millions, until in 1939 eight million are recorded to have inhabited Greater London.

Nearer our time these figures have diminished, yet still the power which De Quincey felt exerts its attraction. A recent survey at the Centrepoint night shelter, only a few hundred yards from the old haven of St. Giles-in-the-Fields, discovered that "Four fifths of young people . . . were from outside London and most were recent arrivals."

As Ford Madox Ford has put it, "It never misses, it never can miss anyone. It loves nobody, it needs nobody; it tolerates all the types of mankind." Yet if London needs nobody in particular, it requires everything to sustain its momentum. It draws in commodities, and markets, and goods. The anonymous author of *Letter from Albion* (1810-13) was suitably exultant. "It is impossible not to be astonished in seeing these riches displayed. Here the costly shawls from the East Indies, there brocades and silk tissues from China, now a world of gold and silver plate . . . an ocean of rings, watches, chains, bracelets." Voracity, repeating itself in endless different ways, is one of the most prominent characteristics of London.

It was said of the museum of the Royal College of Surgeons, a somewhat disturbing collection of anatomical specimens, that "the whole earth has been ransacked to enrich its stores." To ransack is to pillage and to destroy—that, too, is the nature of the city. Addison was worked up into a similar enthusiasm by the spectacle of the Royal Exchange, "making this Metropolis a kind of *Emporium* for the whole Earth." *Emporium* in turn excites *Imperium*, since the master of trade is the master of the world. The fruits of Portugal are bartered for the silk of Persia, the pottery of China for the drugs of America; tin is converted into gold, and wool into rubies. "I am wonderfully delighted," Addison wrote in the *Spectator* of 19 May 1711, "to see such a Body of Men thriving in their own private Fortunes, and at the same time promoting the Public Stock . . . by bringing into the Country whatever is wanting, and carrying out of it whatever is superfluous."

Here is an indication that London had become, by the early eighteenth century, the centre of world commerce. It was the age of lotteries and flotations and "bubbles." Everything was for sale—political office, religious preferment, landed heiresses—and, said Swift, "Power, which according to the old Maxim, was used to follow *Land* is now gone over to *Money*." In *The Pilgrim's Progress* (1678) John Bunyan had also derided London's vanity, whereby "houses, lands, trades, places, honours, preferments, titles, kingdoms, lusts, pleasures, and delights of all sorts" all come under the general denomination of "trade."

By 1700, 76 per cent of England's commerce with the world passed through London.

There was trade in money, as well as goods. The centre of commerce was also the centre of credit, with the banker and the jobber taking over the spirit of the merchant adventurer. The bankers emerged out of the Company of Goldsmiths. Goldsmiths knew how to protect their goods, and for a time their offices had been used as informal places of safety for the deposit of money. Yet during the seventeenth century this primary function of hoarding and protecting was subtly supplanted by the issue of banking orders or cheques to facilitate the passage of revenue throughout the capital and beyond. Francis Child and Richard Hoare had both been goldsmiths before establishing their banking houses; with three or four others they were, as Edward, Earl of Clarendon put it in his autobiography of 1759, "men known to be so rich, and of so good reputation, that all the money of the kingdom would be trusted or deposited in their hands." Out of these banking ventures emerged the Bank of England, the single greatest emblem of the City's wealth and confidence; the principal stockholders of this new bank were themselves London merchants, but this essentially speculative venture was soon lent constitutional status when it was guarded by soldiers during the Gordon Riots of June 1780. Its gold was turned into guineas at the Mint of the Tower of London, and its huge reservoir of bullion was the prime agent in maintaining the financial stability of the nation through a succession of bubbles, panics and wars. Yet even as it maintained good governance, it expedited the adventures and trades of London businessmen—from linen and diamond merchants to small-coal men, from the exporters of hats to the importers of sugar.

One of the key figures of the period, derided in verse and drama, was the stockbroker or "jobber." Gay denounced a capital and an age where "In sawcy State the griping Broker sits." They sat, in fact, in the coffee houses of Change Alley. Jobbers were the lineal descendants of the London scriveners who set up documents for the exchange of land or of houses, but now they were concerned with the floating of companies and the transfer of stock or assets. Cibber anatomised the scene in his play *The Refusal*, of 1720. "There (in the Alley) you'll see a duke dangling after a director; here a peer and a 'prentice haggling for an eighth; there a Jew and a parson making up differences; there a young woman of quality buying bears of a Quaker; and there an old one selling refusals to a lieutenant of grenadiers."

Eventually the noise in the coffee houses, such as Jonathan's or Garraway's in Change Alley, grew too loud, and the jobbers removed to New Jonathan's which in the summer of 1773 was renamed "The Stock Exchange." A little more than twenty years later, a new building arose in Capel Court, its voices recorded in *The Bank Mirror* of 1795. "A mail come in— what news? What news? Steady, steady—consols for tomorrow—A great house has stopt—Payment of the Five per Cents commences—Across the Rhine—the Austrians routed!—the French pursuing! Four per cents for the opening!"

The Bank of England and the Stock Exchange still dominate this small compact area of land. The Mansion House stands close by, on the site of the original Stocks Market, where fish and flesh were traded from the thirteenth century. And so this trinity of institutions may mark one of the city's sacred sites. A study of successive maps shows the area being more and more darkly engraved, as the building of the Bank of England gradually grew in size until it took up the entire area between Lothbury and Threadneedle Street. To the south of this site, during the Great Fire of 1666, John Evelyn observed the concurrence of the two great fireballs. It is not necessary to be a psychogeographer to recognise that this area is devoted to energy and to power.

And as the city incorporated more money, and more credit, so steadily it grew. It stretched out to the west and to the east. By 1715 the scheme of building Cavendish Square, as well as certain streets to the north of the Tyburn Road, was first suggested. Then came Henrietta Street and Wigmore Road, the development of which prompted the extraordinary growth of Marylebone. In the 1730s Berkeley Square emerged on the western side. Bethnal Green and Shadwell were built up in the east, Paddington and St. Pancras to the west. The maps grew denser, too, so that one square of the 1799 map covered six squares of the 1676 map. "I have twice been going to stop my coach in Piccadilly, thinking there was a mob," wrote Horace Walpole in 1791, only to realise that it was the usual Londoners "sauntering or trudging" down the thoroughfare. "There will soon be one street from London to Brentford," he complained, "and from London to every village ten miles round." He was announcing a law of life itself. The direct consequence of power and wealth is expansion.

The eighteenth-century "improvements" within the capital were also an aspect of that power and wealth. Lincoln's Inn Fields was enclosed in 1735 and, four years later, the increasingly squalid Stocks Market was removed from the centre of the city. In 1757 the houses upon London Bridge were demolished and, in the same year, the noisome Fleet Ditch was filled and covered and the Fleet River itself embanked. Four years later, the City gates were removed in order to encourage freer access into the centre of London. As the gates went, so did the street-signs, making the thoroughfares "more airy and wholesome" but also divesting London of its old identity. All these measures were designed to encourage the traffic of goods as well as of people, allowing a freer circulation throughout the urban body with a novel emphasis placed upon speed and efficiency.

In this spirit, too, the Westminster Paving Act of 1762 inaugurated legislation for lighting and paving throughout the city, and thus initiated a general cleansing and clearing of the civic thoroughfares. And, in a city which brought in silk and spice, coffee and bullion, why should not light also be imported? In the 1780s a German visitor wrote that "In Oxford Road alone there are more lamps than in all the city of Paris." They represented more illumination for the burgeoning centre of world commerce. These measures had, according to Pugh's *Life of Hanway*, altogether "introduced a degree of elegance and symmetry into the streets of the metropolis, that is the admiration of all Europe and far exceeds anything of the kind in the modern world." "Symmetry" is another expression of uniformity and in the Building Act of 1774 there was a further attempt at standardisation; it categorised the types of London houses in a series of "grades" or "rates" so that the city might become as infinitely reproducible and as uniform as its currency. This was the age of stucco, or white light.

The public monuments were also a credit to commerce, with such homages to trade as the new Custom House, the Excise Office in Old Broad Street, the Corn Exchange in Mark Lane and the Coal Exchange in Lower Thames Street. South Sea House in Threadneedle Street and East India House in Leadenhall Street vied with one another for magnificence, while the Bank of England in 1732 rose to be continually embellished and enlarged. The livery halls of the various trades, too, were constructed in terms of munificent display.

And then there was Westminster Bridge, opened in the winter of 1750 to the accompaniment of trumpets and kettledrums. Its fifteen arches of stone spanned the river to create "a bridge of magnificence." It had a decisive effect upon the appearance of the city in another sense, since its commissioners persuaded Giovanni Canaletto to visit London in order to paint it. It was still in the course of construction when he depicted it in 1746, but already his vision of London was tempered by his Venetian practice. London became subtly stylised, Italianate, stretching out along the Thames in a pure and even light. A city aspiring to fluency and grace had found its perfect delineator.

Yet the diversity and contrast of London are nowhere better exemplified than in the fact that at the same time the city was being celebrated by William Hogarth. In the foreground of a "new improved" street, Hogarth shows a beggar child scoffing pieces of a broken pie.

CHAPTER 33

A Cookery Lesson

*O*ne of the most cheerful origins of "Cockney" is *coquina*, the Latin term for cookery. London was once seen as a vast kitchen and "the place of plenty and good fare." Thus, as has already been observed, it became "Cockaigne" or the fabled land of good living.

In one year, 1725, it consumed "60,000 calves, 70,000 sheep and lambs, 187,000 swine, 52,000 sucking pigs" as well as "14,750,000 mackerel . . . 16,366,000 lb of cheese." The Great Fire began in Pudding Lane and ended at Pie Corner, where the golden figure of the fat boy still occupies a site; he was once accompanied by an inscription noting "This boy is in memory put up of the late fire of London, occasioned by the sin of gluttony, 1666."

Pie Corner itself was known for its cook-shops and, in particular, its dressed pork. Shadwell writes of "meat dressed at Pie Corner by greasy scullions" while Jonson describes a hungry man there "taking his meal" by sniffing the steam from the stalls. The steam of cooked meat drifted just a few yards from Smithfield, where the cooked flesh of the saints once also rose in smoke. A twenty-first century restaurant, beside Smithfield, offers spleen and tripe, pig's head and veal hearts, as part of its menu.

. . .

A kitchen of the second century AD has been reconstructed in the Museum of London; it shows a large stove upon which were cooked portions of beef and pork, duck and goose, chicken and deer. Such was the profusion of wild life in the neighbouring woods and forests that London became a meat-eater's haven. And so it has remained.

In recent years deep excavation of Roman London has also revealed evidence of scattered oyster shells, the stones of cherries and of plums, the remnants of lentils and cucumbers, peas and walnuts. One surviving beaker or *amphora* from Southwark bears the advertisement: "Lucius Tettius Aficanus supplies the finest fish sauce from Antipolis."

The diet of the Saxon Londoner was less exotic. At the times of "noon-meat" and "even-meat," a staple diet of flesh was enlivened by leeks, onions, garlic, turnips and radishes. An ox had a value of six shillings, a pig one shilling, but there is also evidence that at a slightly later date Londoners demanded a plentiful supply of eels. At various spots along the Thames there were eel fisheries which date back at least as far as the eleventh century. From this century, too, excavations beneath St. Pancras have uncovered more plum-stones and cherry-stones.

Bread was the most important commodity throughout London's history. There are many city regulations of the thirteenth century concerning the conduct of bakers, whose profession was divided into those who made "white bread" and those who made "tourte bread." "Pouffe" was French bread; "simnel" or "wastel," white bread, fine as well as common; "bis," brown bread; and "tourte," the inferior bread. The principal bakers were situated to the east, in Stratford, and the loaves were carried by long carts to the various shops and stalls within the city. Bread was indeed the staple of life. Scarce supplies in 1258, for example, had the direct consequence that "fifteen thousand of the poor perished." Shiploads of wheat and grain were imported from Germany, and certain London nobles distributed bread to the crowd, but "innumerable multitudes of poor people died, and their bodies were all lying about swollen from want." The permanent contrast in London, between need and abundance, has taken many different forms. In the more prosperous years of the thirteenth century, however, the diet of the citizen included beef, mutton and pork together with lampreys, porpoise and sturgeon. Vegetables were not greatly in demand but there was a particular delicacy known as "soup of cabbage." Londoners had also invented a kind of mixed meat dish, created by pounding together pork and poultry into one concoction. A household book at the end of the thirteenth century reveals that on fish days there was also a choice of "herrings, eels, lampreys, salmon" and on meat days a similar variety of "pork, mutton, beef, fowls, pigeons and larks" together with "eggs, saffron and spices."

The records of the fourteenth century are less descriptive, but Stow denotes 1392 and 1393 as years of want, when a diet of "apples and nuts" was forced upon the poor. It is an open question whether the poor ever lived well, even in years of prosperity. The average wage of a London labourer was sixpence a day, while a capon pasty cost eightpence and a hen pasty fivepence. A roast goose could be purchased for sevenpence, while ten finches cost one penny. Ten cooked eggs also cost a penny, and a leg of pork threepence. Oysters and other shellfish were cheap, as were thrushes and larks. Here, then, is evidence of a strangely assorted diet, complemented by rich delicacies—"gruel of almondes . . . a potage of whelks . . . Blancmaung of fysshe . . . Gruel of porke . . . Pigges in sawce." In Chaucer's *Canterbury Tales* (*c.* 1387–1400) the Cook is employed "To boil the chicken and the marrow bones . . . maken mortrewes and well bake a pie"—a mortrewe being a soup whose ingredients included fish, pork, chicken, eggs, bread, pepper and ale. One must also imagine the hasty Londoner picking up a roasted lark or thrush from a cook's stall and eating it as he makes his way along the thoroughfare, perhaps picking his teeth with the bones before discarding the remains by the side of the road.

In the fifteenth century the main dish remained that of meat—"swan, roasted capons . . . venison in broth, coney, partridges and roasted cocks"—together with very sweet compound desserts such as Leche Lombarde, which was "a kind of jelly made of cream, isinglass, sugar, almonds, salt, eggs, raisins, dates, pepper and spices." All dishes seem to have been highly spiced, with herbs for meat in particular demand. The author of *London Lickpenny* is assailed by merchants of Newgate—"Comes me one, cryd hot shepes feete/One cryd mackerel"—and as he wanders down into East Cheap "One Crys rybbs of befe, and many a pye." The evidence of fifteenth-century kitchens and monastic gardens, given by an authority known simply as "Mayster Ion Gardener," is of sage, chickweed, borage, rosemary, fennel and thyme as the staple "vegetable" diet. The other favoured vegetables were "garlike, onions and lekes," which does not suggest much taste for green vegetables.

A change in that diet is marked by the Tudor chronicler, Harrison, who notes that "in old days"—by which he means the thirteenth century—herbs and roots were in great demand, but that they became less frequently used in the fourteenth and fifteenth centuries. Yet "in my time their use is not only resumed among the poore comons—I mean of melons, pompines, gourds, cucumbers, radishes . . . carrots, marrowes, turnips, and all kind of salad herbes—but they are also looked upon as deintie dishes at the tables of delicate merchants, gentlemen." At times of commercial success and plenty, however, meat is often required to maintain the animal spirits of Londoners. That is perhaps why there is so much emphasis in the contemporary chronicles on feasting, as a way of exemplifying the power and wealth of the city. Stow writes of one such occasion that "it would be tedious to set down all the preparation of fish, flesh and other victuals spent in this feast" but then goes on to enumerate the twenty-four oxen, the hundred sheep, the fifty-one deer, the thirty-four boars, the ninety-one pigs . . .

There were variations in diet according to the season, with fresh herrings at Michaelmas, pork and sprats at All Saints, veal and bacon at Easter. In the summer of 1562, a Venetian observer noticed that the native population enjoyed raw oysters with barley bread.

Other dietary habits were changed by law. After the partial relaxation of the intricate fast laws, for example, cheap meat was often substituted for fish. Alterations were also fostered by voyages of discovery; yams or sweet potatoes from Virginia and rhubarb from China became sixteenth-century commodities in a city which plucked its fruits from every known country.

In the early seventeenth century we read of the almost emblematic significance of roast beef, as well as fresh oysters, as a token of civic existence. These were invariably followed by a dessert of milk puddings or "apple pippin"; "*To come in pudding time* is as much as to say, to come in the most lucky moment in the world," according to Misson de Valbourg in the early years of the century. In the houses of the more affluent citizens roast beef and pudding were sometimes exchanged for "a Piece of boil'd Beeff, and then they salt it some Days beforehand, and besiege it with five or six Heaps of Cabbage, Carrots, Turnips, or some other Herbs or Roots, well pepper'd and salted and swimming in Butter." For more delicate fare, the London household would sit around a gridiron "roasting slices of buttered bread . . . This is call'd 'toast.' "

From the seventeenth century, too, comes evidence of the food available from the hawkers of London. The illustrator Marcellus Laroon places the costermonger or "regrater" crying out "Buy my fat chicken!" next to the female huckster selling "ripe speragas," because chicken and asparagus together were considered by Londoners to be a dainty dish. Chicken was cheap, too; that, and rabbit, seem to have been the only meats on sale in the streets. The rabbit-seller, shouting "Buy a rabbet a rabbet," was likely to have been an Irishman who came to London in the autumn with his wares. Those sent out to buy from him were advised that "For being new killed, you must judge by the Scent." Milk and water were carried through the streets in vessels, but not wine. Cherries were available in early summer, followed by strawberries later in the season, and apples in the autumn. From autumn to winter the costermonger sold her pears or "wardens" baking hot from a pot she balanced upon her head. The countryman's attitude to these city fruits is perhaps best exemplified by Matthew Bramble in Smollett's *Humphry Clinker* (1771), who declared that "I need not dwell upon the pallid, contaminated mash which they call strawberries, soiled and tossed by greasy paws through twenty baskets crusted with dirt." Here the emphasis is upon dirt, of course, but also the endemic overpopulation of London wherein every item is passed through a selection of anonymous "paws." Eels were a cheap element of the Londoner's diet; sold alive, generally by female vendors, they were skinned on the spot before being used in pies or pastries. They were not the only fish hawked about the main thoroughfare; crabs were cheap, as were mackerel and flounders, while oysters were purchased for "twelve pence a peck" or approximately two gallons.

From the countryside came the young man trading "Lilly white Vinegar, three pence a quart!" Made from cider or white wine, vinegar was employed as a sauce and as a preventive against disease; but its main use was as a preservative. Almost anything could be pickled, including walnuts, cauliflowers, peaches, onions, lemons, oysters and asparagus.

By the eighteenth century roast beef was described as being of "Old England," although in fact it had been only one of many meats burdening the tables of earlier centuries. As a token of national character the myth of roast beef may owe more to the observations of foreign visitors that Londoners were "entirely carnivorous," with the prevailing assumption of voraciousness. In May 1718 a great meat pudding, eighteen feet two inches in length and four feet in diameter, was dragged by six asses to the Swan Tavern in Fish Street Hill but apparently "its smell was too much for the gluttony of the Londoners. The escort was routed, the pudding taken and devoured." "A foreigner," wrote a German pastor visiting London in 1767, "will be surprised to see what flesh-eaters the English are. He will be struck with the sight of an enormous piece of beef such, perhaps, as he never saw in his life, placed before him upon the table." The same observer also noted that "the common people in London" insisted upon "daily beef or mutton" together with white bread and strong beer. The meat may not necessarily have taken the form of rib or haunch, however, since in the 1750s beef sausages became the culinary fashion.

One other aspect of the pastor's account is of interest, in those passages where he remarks upon the fact that Londoners require their food and drink to be vivid in colour. The brandy and wine must be "deeply coloured," the vegetables as bright and as green "as when gathered"; cabbage and peas, for example, are not boiled "for fear they should lose their colour." It is, perhaps, an intimation of the unnaturalness of the London palate; in a city of spectacle, even the food must be completely seen before being understood. But it may also be a symptom of a certain craving after effect which may itself be unhealthy. He observes the whiteness of the veal and mentions that the calves are made to lick chalk in order to procure that colour. He also notices that the poorer Londoners "are much prejudiced in respect of the colour . . . the whiter the bread is, the better they think it to be." One of Smollett's characters considered the white bread to be nothing more than "a deleterious paste, mixed up with chalk, alum and bone-ashes." So Londoners mistake the nature of things by judging upon appearances alone. This, of course, was also the criticism of social moralists who saw villains and parvenus accepted as gentlemen because of their dress and manners.

Yet there are also intimations of a revulsion against so much greedy consumption. "What should they do," as the poet John Lewkenor put it, "with all this greasie Meat?" Another of Smollett's heroes enters a cook-shop filled "with steams of boiled beef" where the sight of "skin-of-beef, tripe, cow-heel or sausages . . . turned my stomach." In this same period the Worshipful Company of Butchers, in debt and pestered by competition in the suburbs, proved wholly incapable of enforcing regulations on the sale of meat. Every kind of shoddy or mouldy flesh could be purchased. Once more the unchecked reign of commerce becomes a symbol of city life.

So it was that in the early part of the nineteenth century "food processing" took its place beside the manufactories along the Thames; essences of meat and meat sauces came from London Bridge, while tinned meat or "patent beef" came from Bermondsey. This was the century of anchovy paste and preserved tongue, of clarified butter and tinned pâté de foie gras. There were also more familiar items. Accounts describe nineteenth-century travellers breakfasting off ham, tongue and "a devil" (kidney), or dining off mutton chop, rump steak and a "weal cutlet," while in less splendid establishments the fare included "hams, and sirloins, the remnants of geese and turkeys, cod-fish reduced to the gills, fins and tail."

But the overwhelming mass of evidence still concerns food provided by the street-sellers of the period. With a restless, large and rapidly moving population the equivalent of fast-food was the most characteristic and appropriate form of sustenance. Whether they bought fried fish sold in oily paper, or boiled puddings in cotton bags, it was the custom of the poorer citizens to eat "upon the stones." New-laid eggs were for sale on Holborn Hill and pork in Broad St. Giles. There was also the ubiquitous baked-potato stall, as well as the shops plying roly poly or plum duff. One trader in Whitechapel informed Henry Mayhew that "he sold 300 pennyworths of pudding in a day. Two thirds of this quantity he sold to juveniles under fifteen years of age . . . The boys are often tiresome: 'Mister,' they'll say, 'can't you give us a plummier bit than this?' or 'Is it just up? I likes it 'ot, all 'ot.' " In competition with these hot delicacies came sandwiches, hailed as "one of our greatest institutions" by Charles Dickens, who saw them, in an image of perpetual activity and perpetual consumption, being engorged by the shelf-load at the Britannia Theatre in Hoxton.

The times of that consumption have changed, both in the commercial and the fashionable areas of the city. An entire history of social manners might be constructed from the essential fact that, over the last five centuries, the time for eating dinner, or the main meal of the day, has advanced by approximately ten hours. In the late fifteenth century, many Londoners dined "at ten o'clock in the forenoon," although others delayed for a further hour; in the sixteenth century, the hour for meat varied between eleven and twelve but no later. In the seventeenth century, the hours of twelve and one became common. But then in the early decades of the eighteenth century there was a rapid acceleration of mealtime. By 1740 two o'clock was the appropriate hour, and by 1770 three was considered the vital moment. In the last decades of the eighteenth, and the first of the nineteenth, the dinner hour slid to five or six. Then Harriet Beecher Stowe, writing about London life in the 1850s, noted that dinner at eight or even nine o'clock in the evening was considered appropriate at "aristocratic" tables.

The reason for this postponement of the main meal was credited by eighteenth-century moralists to the decline of moral fibre and the rise of social decadence, as if it were important to devour food before successfully devouring the day. But a more specific circumstance may have assisted the process, particularly in the early decades of the eighteenth century when, according to Grosley, "the hour of going to Change interfered with dinner time, so that the merchants thought it most advisable, not to dine till their return from Change." Once more commercial imperatives play their part within the intimate texture of London life.

CHAPTER 34

Eat In or Take Away

Eating-houses, or restaurants, have for many centuries been an intricate part of that texture. In the twelfth century one monk describes a great "public place of cookery" by the Thames where ordinary flesh and fish could be purchased—roasted, fried or boiled—while the more dainty could order venison, no doubt with ale or wine for refreshment. It may lay claim to being the first London restaurant, except that one historian of London believes that this place of city refreshment was in fact a survival of a Roman public kitchen. In that case the tradition of London hospitality is ancient indeed. The twelfth-century version included, for example, "a dining room for the rich man, an eating-house for the poor man" with a version of "take-away" in the event of friends calling unexpectedly. Certainly it was a large operation, perhaps equivalent to Terence Conran's vast eateries in Soho and the West End, since according to William Fitz-Stephen "whatsoever multitude of soldiers or other strangers enter into the city at any hour of the day or night, or else are about to depart, they may turn in."

The number of these eating-houses multiplied as the population increased, so that by the fourteenth and fifteenth centuries there were many cook-shops clustered in Bread Street and East Cheap. These thoroughfares were known as the quarters for eating-houses where, under the supervision of the civic authorities, the price of meals was strictly controlled. Sometimes the customers would bring their own food with them, to be cooked in ovens on the spot, with the price varying from a penny to twopence for the cost of fire and labour.

The "ordinaries" were a sixteenth-century variation upon the cook-shop. There were twelve-penny ordinaries as well as three-penny ordinaries, the price varying according to style and comfort as well as the cost of the main meal. Wooden benches and trestle tables stood on a rush-strewn floor and the tapster or his boy wandered among the customers crying out, "What do you lack?" or "What is it that you would have brought?" Meat, poultry, game and pastry were served in succeeding order; "to be at your woodcocks" meant that you had almost finished eating. The citizens arrived about eleven thirty, and wandered about singly or in groups waiting for their meat to be served while some "*published* their clothes, and talked as loud as they could in order to feel at ease." It was indeed an easy environment, and it became the pattern of the London eating-house, continuing well into the succeeding century.

In the late seventeenth century there is a description by François Misson of the butchers' meat on the menu in just such a place—"beef, mutton, veal, pork and lamb; you have what quantity you please cut off, fat, lean, much or little done; with this a little salt and mustard upon the side of a plate, a bottle of beer and a roll." At the end of the meal, when the payment or "reckoning" was made, the server carried a basket to the table and with a knife cleared away the crumbs of bread and morsels of meat. In many such establishments there was a "best room" for those with delicate or expensive appetites, while for the ordinary citizen a sixpenny plate in the "publick room" would suffice.

These eating-houses had by now migrated far beyond the bounds of East Cheap and Bread Street, towards the populous areas of the capital. Bishopsgate Street, Lincoln's Inn Fields, the Old Bailey, Covent Garden, Haymarket and many others besides, all had their local and well-frequented places of call.

In the eighteenth century they became known as "beef-houses" or "chop-houses," together with taverns specialising in more formal or protracted meals. Dolly's Chop-house in Paternoster Row was a particular favourite, serving its meats "hot and hot"—which is to say, delivered up as quickly as they were cooked. There was also a famous resort of cook-shops behind St. Martin-in-the-Fields, known to the natives as "Porridge Island"; it was a somewhat unsavoury haunt, however, where gin and ale provided as much sustenance as the food carried from the cook "under cover of a pewter plate."

. . .

Yet of course the most famous establishments of eighteenth-century London were the coffee houses. In fact, they found their origins in the middle of the previous century when, according to a contemporary note recorded in *The Topography of London*, "theire ware also att this time a Turkish drink to be sould almost in eury street, called Coffee, and another kind of drink called Tee, and also a drink called Chacolate, which was a very harty drink." The first coffee house was set up in St. Michael's Alley, off Cornhill, in 1652; two or three years later a second was established close by, in St. Michael's Churchyard. A third, the Rainbow, located in Fleet Street by the gate of the Inner Temple, was prosecuted in 1657 for being "a great nuisance and prejudice to the neighbourhood"; the principal complaint was of "evil smells" as well as the danger of fire. Yet the popularity of coffee houses among Londoners immediately became apparent, both from "the convenience of being able to make appointments in any part of town," as Macaulay said, and the further convenience "of being able to pass evenings socially at a very small charge." By the turn of the century, there were some two thousand of them in the capital.

An anonymous painting of one, dated approximately 1700, shows several bewigged gentlemen sitting down to "dishes" of coffee; there are candles upon the tables, while the floor is of bare wood. One customer is smoking a long clay pipe, others are reading periodicals. One such periodical, the *Spectator*, opened its first number in the spring of 1711 with an account of the world of coffee houses: "sometimes I am seen thrusting my Head into a Round of Politicians at *Will's*, and listning with great Attention to the Narratives that are made in those little Circular Audiences. Sometimes I smoak a Pipe at *Child's*, and whilst I seem attentive to nothing but the *Post-Man* overhear the Conversation of every Table in the Room. I appear on *Sunday* Nights at *St. James's* Coffee-House, and sometimes join the little Committee of Politicks in the Inner Room, as one who comes there to hear and to improve. My Face is likewise very well known at the *Grecian*, the *Cocoa-Tree* . . ." In all these coffee houses the news and rumours of the day were disseminated.

There were coffee houses for every trade and every profession, and Macaulay noted that "Foreigners remarked that the coffee-house was that which especially distinguished London from all other cities; that the coffee-house was the Londoner's home, and that those who wished to find a gentleman commonly asked, not whether he lived in Fleet Street or Chancery Lane, but whether he frequented the Grecian or the Rainbow." The famous doctor, John Radcliffe, travelled from Bow Street to Garraway's Coffee House, in Change Alley, Cornhill, where at a particular table he was always "to be found, surrounded by surgeons and apothecaries." He timed his visits "at the hour when the Exchange was full," no doubt in the hope of also being attended by rich merchants and brokers.

In other coffee houses, lawyers met clients and brokers met each other, merchants drank coffee with customers and politicians drank tea with journalists. The Virginia and Maryland Coffee House in Threadneedle Street became a recognised meeting-place for those engaged in business with Russia, and so changed its name to the Baltic. The Jerusalem in Cornhill was the haven of West Indies trade, while Batson's in Cornhill was a kind of "consulting room" for doctors waiting to receive their clients in the City. Old Slaughter's Coffee House, in St. Martin's Lane, became the recognised centre for London artists. St. James's of St. James's Street was for Whigs, while down the road the Cocoa-Tree at the corner of Pall Mall was the haunt of Tories and Jacobites. The Grecian in Devereux Court catered for lawyers; Will's on the north side of Russell Street, Covent Garden, was a haven for wits and authors. There was even a floating coffee house, a boat moored off the stairs of Somerset House, which was called the Folley. It was as "bulky as a man-of-war" and was divided into several rooms serving coffee, tea and "spiritous liquours." Like many London establishments on the river it began with fashionable company but, by degrees, attracted drunken or disreputable customers until it seems to have become little more than a floating brothel. At length it decayed, and was sold for firewood. Not being on land, it had no tenacity of purpose.

Coffee houses, on land or on water, were generally somewhat dingy places, reeking of tobacco. The wooden floor was often sanded, with spittoons liberally placed. In some, the tables and chairs were stained and dirty, while in others there were "boxes with upright backs and narrow seats"; the lamps smoked and the candles spluttered. So why were they thronged with ordinary citizens and why did they, like the twentieth-century public house, become a token of city life? There was, as always, a commercial reason. The coffee houses acted as counting-houses and auction rooms, offices and shops, in which merchants and agents, clerks and brokers, could engage in business. Agents who sold estates or property would meet their clients in such places, while the sale of other goods was also encouraged. In 1708, for example, one could read the somewhat chilling notice, "A black boy, twelve years of age, fit to wait on a gentleman, to be disposed of at Denis's coffee-house, in Finch Lane."

The ambience itself could also be used to commercial advantage and sales by auction became a coffee-house speciality. At the "inch-of-candle sales" at Garraway's, coffee, alcohol and muffins were employed to encourage the bidding. Garraway's was opposite the Exchange and therefore a harbour "for people of quality who have business in the City, and for wealthy citizens"; as a result there were sales of books and pictures, tea and furniture, wine and hard wood. Wide and low-roofed, with boxes and seats running down its sides, it had a broad central stairway that led to the sale room upstairs, in such proximity that business and entertainment were curiously mingled. Its genial aspect, complete with sea-coal fire and muffins toasting on forks, is compounded by the description of its customers, by "Aleph" in *London Scenes and London People*, in "admirable humour; sly jokes were circulating from ear to ear; everybody appeared to know everybody." But in London, appearances can be deceptive. Swift, commenting upon the effects of the bursting of the South Sea Bubble, in which fortunes were lost upon the crash of the South Sea Company in 1720, describes the speculators "on Garraway's cliffs" as "A savage race by shipwrecks fed."

"I am quite familiar at the Chapter Coffee-house," wrote Thomas Chatterton to his mother in May 1770, "and know all the geniuses there." The haunt of booksellers and aspiring writers, the Chapter was situated on the corner of Paternoster Row, opposite Ivy Lane, and was characteristic of its class with small-paned windows, wainscoted walls and low ceilings with heavy beams, making it dark even at noon. When Chatterton wrote of the geniuses he may have been referring to a small club of publishers and writers who always sat in the box in the north-east corner of the house and called themselves the "Wet Paper Club." When they chose to recommend "a good book," it was of course one that had sold extensively and rapidly. In this context, and company, it is perhaps worth recalling that Chatterton's apparent suicide was considered to be the direct result of his inability to profit from the commercial practices of the London publishing world.

The Chapter was also known for its custom among the clergy, since according to "Aleph" "it was a house of call for poor parsons who were in hire to perform Sunday duty" and who also wrote sermons on request. The discourses varied in price from 2*s* 6*d* to 10*s* 6*d*—"A buyer had only to name his subject and doctrine" and the appropriate pious lesson would be delivered. If there was "a glut of the commodity" of charity sermons, "a moving appeal," for example, "for a parish school" could be obtained at a very cheap rate.

Prices at the Chapter were on a par with other such establishments. At the turn of the nineteenth century, a cup of coffee was fivepence while four ham sandwiches with a glass of sherry cost twopence; a pot of tea, serving three cups, together with six slices of bread and butter, a muffin and two crumpets, cost tenpence—or, rather, a shilling since twopence extra went to the head waiter, William, one of those London types who seem forever fixed in the establishment where they work, a figure entirely made out of the quintessence of London. Of average height, somewhat stout, William was rumoured to have money "in funds." He was imperturbable, always civil and, as the ever observant "Aleph" put it, "carefully dressed in a better black cloth suit than many of the visitors, wearing knee breeches, black silk hose and a spotless white cravat." Of few words, he was always attentive; "his eyes were in every corner of the room." He expected his "tip" of a penny or twopence but had moments of unexpected generosity; when "he suspected a customer was very needy, he would bring him two muffins and only charge for one." He was on easy terms with regulars, who always called him simply "William," but he inspected strangers "with inquisitive looks." Those whom he deemed not suitable for admission were dismissed by suggesting that they "must have mistaken the house—the Blue Boar was in Warwick Lane."

To this coffee house of hacks or "pen-drivers," seventy years after Chatterton, came Charlotte and Emily Brontë *en route* to Belgium. Charlotte recalled a head waiter, a "grey-haired, elderly man." It is likely to have been William. He led them to a room upstairs which looked out upon Paternoster Row. Here they sat by the window, but "could see nothing of motion, or of change, in the grim dark houses opposite." The street itself was so quiet that every footfall could be distinctly heard. One of Charlotte Brontë's heroines, Lucy Snowe in *Villette* (1853), spends her first night in London in the very same coffee house. She looks out of her window on the following morning and "Above my head, above the house-tops, co-elevate almost with the clouds, I saw a solemn orbed mass, dark-blue and dim—THE DOME. While I looked my inner self moved; my spirit shook its always-fettered wings half loose; I had a sudden feeling as if I, who have never yet truly lived, were at last about to taste life." So, in the shadow of St. Paul's, the London coffee house could produce revelations.

·   ·   ·

The coffee houses lingered well into nineteenth-century London. When some became specialised exchanges, others turned into clubs or private hotels, while others again became dining-houses complete with polished mahogany tables, oil-lamps and boxes with green curtains dividing them. At the beginning of the nineteenth century another kind of coffee house altogether emerged which catered for the breakfasts of labourers or porters on their way to work. It served chops and kidneys, bread and pickles; one familiar order was "tea and an egg." In many of them different "rooms" charged different prices for coffee. At four o'clock in the morning the poor customer would have a cup of coffee, and a thin slice of bread and butter, for one penny halfpenny; at eight o'clock breakfast for the less impoverished would include a penny loaf, a pennyworth of butter and a coffee for threepence. Arthur Morrison in *A Child of the Jago* (1896) describes a coffee house with "shrivelled bloaters . . . doubtful cake . . . pallid scones . . . and stale pickles." Yet it was still a more respectable establishment than the neighbouring cook-shop, filled with steam, and may have given rise to that Cockney expression in the depths of poverty or despair—"I wish I was dead; an' kep' a cawfy shop." In one of his visitations to the East End Charles Booth entered a "rough coffee-house," and found a long counter "on which were piled, in rude plenty, many loaves of bread, flitches of bacon, a quantity of butter, two tea-urns . . . three beer pumps for Kop's ale . . . and a glass jar filled with pickled onions." Note the ubiquity of the pickle; Londoners love sharpness. Thirty years later George Orwell entered a coffee house on Tower Hill, and found himself in a "little stuffy room" with "high-backed pews" that had been fashionable in the 1840s. When he asked for tea and bread and butter—the staple of the working-class breakfast since the beginning of the nineteenth century—he was told "No butter, only marg." There was also a notice upon the wall, to the effect that "Pocketing the sugar is not allowed."

There were other places for a meagre breakfast. "Early breakfast houses" were essentially coffee shops by another name, "stiflingly hot," with the flavour of coffee mingling with the "odours of fried rashers of bacon, and others not by any means so agreeable." Ever since the eighteenth century there had also been "early breakfast stalls," which were essentially kitchen tables set up at the corner of a street or the foot of a bridge, purveying halfpenny slabs of bread and butter together with large pots of tea or coffee heated over charcoal fires. These in turn were succeeded by more elaborate coffee stalls, which were constructed on the pattern of a medieval London shop with a wooden interior and shutters. They were generally painted red, ran on wheels, and were led by a horse to familiar locations at Charing Cross, at the foot of Savoy Street, on Westminster Bridge, below Waterloo Bridge, by Hyde Park Corner, and by West India Dock gates. They sold everything from saveloys to hard-boiled eggs, as well as coffee and "woods" (Woodbine cigarettes).

There is an animated painting, dated 1881, which depicts a variety of Londoners congregating around a "day stall" set up outside the gates of a park or square. The female proprietor is washing up a cup—most of the stalls were indeed run by women on the principle, maintained by many public houses of the present day, that aggressive customers were less likely to cause trouble and offence if a female was present. There is bread on the table, but no sign of the ham sandwiches and "water cresses" which were also part of the daily menu. A boy in a red jacket, bearing the livery of the City of London, sits in a wheelbarrow and blows upon his saucer of liquid; he was one of those employed by the City to run after horses in the street and scoop up their manure. A female crossing-sweeper and a female vendor, both with expressions of sorrow or perplexity, seem to be looking on at the feast. A well-dressed young lady, with umbrella and band-box, sips delicately from her cup on the other side of the stall. It is a suggestive picture of late Victorian London. In competition with such a stall was the baked-potato van, a portable oven wheeled around the streets. There were also oyster stalls where Londoners, as the saying goes, ate "on their thumbs."

The ordinaries and the eating-houses continued well into the nineteenth century as chop-houses or ham-and-beef shops or *à-la-mode* beef-houses. There were also taverns or public houses where it was customary for the client to bring in his own piece of meat which was then dressed and cooked upon a gridiron by a waiter, who charged a penny for the service. The origin of twentieth-century pub food lies in these nineteenth-century establishments where "fine old cheese" and mutton pies and baked potatoes were generally on sale by the counter.

The old chop-houses and beef-houses were not necessarily of good reputation. Nathaniel Hawthorne described one such establishment, in *The English Notebooks* (1853-8), with "a filthy table-cloth, covered with other people's crumbs; iron forks, a leaden salt cellar, the commonest earthen plates; a little dark stall, to sit and eat in." He noticed that the conditions of this place, the Albert Dining-Rooms, were not uncommon. It was a measure of the discomfort and dirtiness to which Londoners, historically, have accommodated themselves. There were gradations in service and comfort, however. In the more formal dining-house a waiter, with napkin over his left arm, would announce to the client what was "just ready"; in a "rapid but monotonous tone" he would go through the list of "Roast beef, boiled beef, roast haunch of mutton, boiled pork, roast veal and ham, salmon and shrimp sauce, pigeon-pie, rump-steak pudding." In the *à-la-mode* beef-houses there was a sixpenny plate and a fourpenny plate—"Two sixes and a four" the waiter would call out to the cook in a nearby kitchen.

Such places of resort, having dominated London in various forms for several centuries, were displaced in the latter half of the nineteenth century by "dining-halls," "restaurants" associated with the new hotels, and "refreshment rooms," connected to the new railway stations. They were not necessarily an improvement on their predecessors. In fact London's reputation as the purveyor of drab and unpalatable food began essentially in the mid-nineteenth century. Henry James, in 1877, was scathing about London's restaurants "whose badness is literally fabulous." And yet they flourished. The St. James's Hotel was reputed to be the one in which "separate tables for dining were first introduced," but it was M. Ritz who capitalised upon the idea; the advent of his hotel restaurant effectively ended the old London fashion "of people dining together at large tables." From the 1860s, the number of restaurants, "dining-rooms" and "luncheon bars" multiplied—the Café Royal opened in 1865 and the Criterion Restaurant (like many, named after an adjacent theatre) in 1874. Spiers and Pond Gaiety Restaurant, next to the Gaiety Theatre in the Strand, opened in 1869. There is a photograph of its "Restaurant & Ballroom"; a hansom is parked outside with men in top hats milling about the entrance. A contemporary description in *Building News* mentions a luncheon bar, a café and two dining-rooms all fitted out with an "ostentation of design" worthy of "the stained glass designer, or even the scene painter." Restaurant and theatre were eventually swept aside for the construction of Aldwych.

Social changes were engineered by the advent of the restaurant. Women, for example, were no longer excluded from dinner. Walter Besant wrote in the early twentieth century that "Ladies can, and do, go to these restaurants without reproach; their presence has made a great alteration; there is always an atmosphere of cheerfulness, if not of exhilaration," a description which by indirection suggests the somewhat mournful or low tone of the old-fashioned, all-male chop-house. The first restaurant to introduce music during meals was Gatti's at Charing Cross, and the fashion spread quickly until by the 1920s only the Café Royal remained defiantly silent. With the new century, too, came the fashion for dancing at dinner and even between the courses. Other alterations were more gradual and subtler. Ralph Nevill, the author of *Night Life* in 1926, noted that the pace of the Victorian restaurant had been much slower with "always a pause between the appearance of the various dishes" as opposed to the speed and hustle of modern restaurants which the author ascribed to the advent of "the motor" on the streets of London. In the city everything connects.

In the new century, too, emerged the great chain of Lyon's Corner Houses; they were instituted in 1909, and sprang from a number of tea shops and restaurants established at the very end of the nineteenth century—including the first entirely underground restaurant, Lyons of Throgmorton Street, with a grill room forty feet below ground level. All types of Londoners mingled within the plainer London coffee houses; similarly the London tea shops were considered to be "democratic . . . in the mixture of classes that you see therein seated together eating and drinking the same things." Theodore Dreiser visited a "Lyons," just above Regent Street, in 1913 and observed "a great chamber, decorated after the fashion of a palace ball-room, with immense chandeliers of prismed glass hanging from the ceiling and a balcony furnished in cream and gold." Yet the dishes were "homely" and the customers "very commonplace." Here, then, the demotic and theatrical characteristics of city living were effortlessly combined.

There is a vivid account of East End food at the beginning of the twentieth century in Walter Besant's *East London*, with descriptions of salt fish for Sunday morning breakfast, of slabs of pastry known as "Nelson," of the evening trade in "faggots, saveloys and pease pudding" and of course of the ubiquitous pie-houses or "eel-pie saloons" where jellied eels, saveloys or hot meat pies with mashed potatoes were the standard fare. These were rivalled only by the fish-and-chip shops.

In the years before the Second World War, a typical "Cockney" menu would comprise saveloy and pease pudding, German sausages and black pudding, fried fish and pickles, pie crust and potatoes, faggot and mustard pickle. Strong tea and lashings of bread and butter were the other staples of life. The situation was more complex in other parts of London, where there was much less emphasis upon a traditional cuisine, but the standard dish was always meat, potatoes and two veg swimming in gravy, thus reinforcing London's reputation as a city with no real culinary skills.

Between the wars, and after the Second World War, London's restau-

rants were considered very much below the standard of other European capitals. Some were restaurants of the middling English sort, serving beef and
mutton and greens, sausage and mash, apricots and custard. But in Soho the
restaurant trade flourished because of the influence of French, Italian, Spanish, Russian and Chinese cooking. In the purlieus of Soho, too, an informality of eating was introduced or, rather, reintroduced. The first sandwich bar,
Sandy's of Oxendon Street, was opened in 1933; very soon sandwich bars and
the new snack bars were springing up all over the capital. This revolution in
taste was complemented, twenty years later, by the opening of the first coffee
bar, also in Soho, the Mika, in Frith Street.

The world of quick eating and quick drinking, a phenomenon previously
noted in the pie-shops of the fourteenth century no less than in the baked-
potato vans of the nineteenth, thus re-established itself. Sandwiches are now
the staple ingredient of the London lunch, from the Pret A Manger chain to
the corner shop on a busy junction. There has been a concomitant increase in
fast food, from burgers of beef to wings of chicken. The staple of the city diet
remains the same, therefore, while the statistics of its voracious appetite also
remain constant. The budget of London households, for "restaurants and
cafés . . . take-aways and snacks" is, according to a survey of national statistics, approximately "a third higher than for the United Kingdom as a whole."

London's reputation as a culinary inferno was gradually dispelled during
the 1980s, when large restaurants catering to every taste in food or ambience
became fashionable. Now the London customer can choose between monk-
fish tempura and chilli breast of chicken with coconut rice, grilled rabbit with
polenta and braised octopus with chickpeas and coriander. Many of these
restaurants soon became flourishing commercial enterprises; their chefs were
recognised and controversial London figures, their owners part of a chic
world of art and society. In the 1990s the connection between food and commerce was rendered all the more distinctive by the "floating" of certain
restaurants on the Stock Exchange; others have been bought by large companies as a profitable form of speculation. Some of the more recently established restaurants are very large indeed, and the fact that few tables remain
unbooked is testimony to the permanent and characteristic voracity of Londoners. That is why it has always been known as a city of markets.

Market Time

he first markets were upon the streets. In fact it is possible to envisage the central axis of twelfth- or thirteenth-century London as one continuous street-market from the Shambles at Newgate to Poultry by Cornhill. At the Shambles, in 1246, "all the stalls of the butchers are to be numbered and it is to be asked who holds them and by what service and of whom." Down the street, in the shadow of St. Michael "le Querne," stood the corn-market. Corn, the staff of life, therefore lies under the aegis of the Church. Just beyond the corn-market were established the markets for fish in Old Fish Street and Friday Street (on Fridays people were to refrain from meat). Bread Street and Milk Street are adjacent, thus setting up a topographical alignment of great significance to the city. The naming of the streets is established upon the food which is purchased there. The city may be defined, then, as that place where people come to buy and sell.

As the citizens of thirteenth-century London walked down West Cheap—now Cheapside—away from the smell of the Shambles and the fish stalls, they passed shops where harnesses and saddles were sold, where cordwainers plied their trade, and where mercers and the drapers laid out their fabrics upon their stalls. Beyond these lay Poultry, of which the meaning is self-explanatory, and Coneyhope Lane where rabbits were sold.

Gracechurch Street was originally "Grass Church" street, named after the herbs which were sold within it.

There are some energetic if idiosyncratic drawings of adjacent street-markets in *A Caveatt for the Citty of London* (1598). Beside St. Nicholas Shambells, flanks of beef, whole pigs and lambs, hang outside a row of butchers' shops. In Gracechurch Street, purveyors of apples, fish and vegetables have set up their stalls beneath pillars and awnings which proclaim their origin in Essex, Kent and "Sorre." Yet not all goods were sold on open stalls, and it has been estimated that there were some four hundred small shops—perhaps like wooden kiosks—along the length of Cheapside. The noise and tumult were intense, and several laws were passed in order to prevent crowds. There were other perils, too, with strict measures against the resale of stolen articles. The clothes-market of Cornhill, for example, was notorious; it was here that the narrator of *London Lickpenny* recognised the hood which had been lifted from him at Westminster. In light of "many perils and great mischiefs . . . many brawls and disorders" during the "Evynchepynge" or evening market at "Cornhulle" it was ordained that "after the bell has been rung that hangs upon the Tun at Cornhulle," no more items were to be taken to the market. One bell rang an hour before sunset, and another thirty minutes later; it is possible to imagine the traders calling out to the slowly diminishing crowds, as the sun begins to decline over the towers and rooftops of the city.

The general confusion of trades was one of the reasons why in 1283 a general "Stocks Market" was established at the eastern end of Poultry, where "fish and flesh" could be sold as well as fruit, roots, flowers and herbs. Its name came not from its "stocks" of provisions but from the stocks set up in that area for the punishment of city offenders. A "privileged market" which remained on the same site for 450 years, before being removed to Farringdon Street in the mid-eighteenth century, it acquired a reputation for having the choicest of all provisions. There is an engraving, limned just before its removal, which shows the statue of Charles II erected in the very heart of the market; two small dogs look up at a stall selling cheeses, while a woman and child sit with their baskets against the steps of the statue. In the background there is an animated scene of trading and bargaining. A pair of lovers meet in the foreground, apparently oblivious to the noise around them, while a Londoner is pointing out directions to a foreign visitor. Here we may remark upon the testimony of a stranger, one of the many hundreds in the three volumes of Xavier Baron's wonderful *London 1066–1914*: "Whatever haste a gentleman may be in, when you happen to meet in the streets; as soon as you speak to him, he stops to answer, and often steps out of his way to direct you, or to consign you to the care of someone who seems to be going the same way." On a balcony above the scene, a young woman is beating out a carpet. In such visions, London may be said to live again.

Billingsgate was perhaps the most ancient of London's markets with its foundation supposedly some four hundred years before the beginning of the Christian era; it is not impossible that fishermen landed their catches of eel and herring here in remote antiquity, but the official records date only from the beginning of the eleventh century. That it was a place apart, from the rest of London, is not in doubt; here, in an atmosphere of reeking fish, with fish-scales underfoot and a "shallow lake of mud" all round, specific types and traditions had sprung up.

There were the "wives" of Billingsgate—perhaps the descendants of the devotees of the god Belin who was once purported to be worshipped here—who dressed in strong "stuff" gowns and quilted petticoats; their hair, caps and bonnets were flattened into one indistinguishable mass, because of the practice of carrying baskets upon their heads. Called "fish fags," they smoked small pipes of tobacco, took snuff, drank gin, and were known for their colourful language. Thus came the phrase to shriek like a fishwife. A dictionary of 1736 defined a "Billingsgate" as "a scolding impudent slut." But gradually throughout the nineteenth century the fish fags were extirpated, to make way for a breed of London porters who wore helmets made of hide with a flap which reached down to their necks so that they could more easily carry their baskets of fish. These fish porters were complemented by the fish salesmen who wore straw hats even in winter. So a definite tradition of dress, and of language, emerges from this small area of London.

The same phenomenon can be witnessed at a variety of sites. Smithfield does not have as long a history as Billingsgate but by the eleventh century the "smothe field" just beyond the City walls was a recognised area for the sale of horses, sheep and cattle, known for drunkenness, rowdiness and such general violence that it had earned the name of "Ruffians' Hall." That violence did not stop with the granting of a royal charter to the cattle-market in 1638.

Market days were held on Tuesday and Friday; the horses were kept in stables in the neighbourhood, but the cattle and other livestock were driven in from the outlying areas causing much distress to the animals and inconvenience to the citizens. It is recorded in *Smithfield Past and Present* by Forshaw and Bergstrom, that "Great cruelty was practised, the poor animals being goaded on the flanks and struck on the head before they could be marshalled in their proper places." In the early part of the nineteenth century a million sheep and a quarter of a million cattle were sold annually; the noise, and the stench, were considerable. The danger, too, was significant. On one day, in 1830, "a gentleman was knocked down by a very powerful bull" in High Holborn and "before he could recover himself he was severely trampled on and gored." In Turnmill Street, another thoroughfare into the market from adjacent fields, a hog "mangled a young child and 'tis judged would have eaten it." The animals were sometimes goaded into stampedes down the narrow and muddy lanes off Clerkenwell and Aldersgate Street, while the general air of chaos and intemperance was exploited by various louche persons who preyed on the drunkenness and unwariness of others.

Dickens had an intuitive sense of place, and fastened upon Smithfield as a centre of "filth and mire." In *Oliver Twist* (1837–9) it is filled with "crowding, pushing, driving, beating" among "unwashed, unshaven, squalid and dirty figures." The protagonist in *Great Expectations* (1860–1) becomes aware that "the shameful place, being all asmear with filth and fat and blood and foam, seemed to stick to me." Eight years before this was written, the market for live animals had been transferred to Copenhagen Fields in Islington, but the atmosphere of death remained; when the Central Meat Market was instituted on the Smithfield site in 1868, it was described as "a perfect forest of slaughtered calves, pigs and sheep, hanging from cast-iron balustrades."

Of vegetable markets, there is no end. Borough Market in Southwark can claim to be the first ever recorded, having its origins at some time before the eleventh century, but Covent Garden remains the most illustrious. Once it was truly a garden, filled with herbs and fruit which seem uncannily to anticipate their later profusion on the same spot; then it was the kitchen garden of Westminster Abbey, contiguous with the garden of Bedford House erected at the end of the sixteenth century. But the market itself sprang from the Earl of Bedford's proposals to build an ornamented and ornamental piazza as part of his grand scheme of Italianate suburban development; the plaza and adjoining houses began to rise in 1630, and very soon afterwards the trade of the populace began to flow towards the area. On the south side of the square, beside the garden wall, sprang up a number of sheds and stalls selling fruit and vegetables; it was a local amenity which had the additional merit of being financially successful, and in 1670 the estate obtained a charter authorising a market "for the buying and selling of all manner of fruits flowers and herbs." Thirty-five years later, permanent single-storey shops were set up in two rows. Gradually, inexorably, the market spread across the piazza.

It became the most famous market in England and, given its unique trading status in the capital of world trade, its image was endlessly reproduced in drawings and in paintings. It was first limned in an etching by Wenceslaus Hollar in 1647, which work, according to the editors of *London in Paint*, has the merit of being "the first close-up depiction of one of London's quarters." Another work, of the early eighteenth century, shows a group of early morning shoppers making their way between lines of wooden shops and open stalls; fresh fruit and vegetables can be seen in wicker baskets, while a horse and cart are driving away from the main scene. Twenty years later, in 1750, the painted image has entirely changed; instead of ramshackle sheds there are now two-storey buildings, and the market activity stretches over the entire square. Everything is in life and motion, from the young boy struggling with a basket of apples to the middle-aged female trader who portions out some herbs. Here are cabbages from Battersea and onions from Deptford, celery from Chelsea and peas from Charlton, asparagus from Mortlake and turnips from Hammersmith; carts and sedan chairs jostle, while the covered wagons from the country make their way through the crowds. This picture depicts the very essence of a trading city, while another painting of slightly later date betrays the evidence of pickpockets and street musicians among the assembly.

The drawings of George Scharf, dated 1818 and 1828, depict in minute and various detail the life of the market. The shop of J.W. Draper "Orange Merchant" has a sign painted "yellow and green," according to Scharf's notes, while there are drawings of the shops of "Potatoe Salesman Whitman" and of "Butler," seller of herbs and seeds. There are wheelbarrows filled with cabbages and turnips and carrots and cocoa nuts, alongside mobile stalls with apples and pears and strawberries and plums. One young costermonger's barrow has a red, white and blue flag flying from it, with the sign that four oranges will cost a penny.

In 1830 a permanent market, with avenues and colonnades and conservatories in three parallel ranges, was completed; it gave the market an institutional aspect, as well as confirming its status as an emporium of world trade. "There is more certainty of purchasing a pineapple here, every day in the year," John Timbs's *Curiosities of London* declares, "than in Jamaica and Calcutta, where pines are indigenous." Steam boats carried articles from Holland, Portugal and the Bermudas.

Order was introduced to the market, also, with vegetables to the south, fruit to the north, and flowers to the north-west. It became customary for Londoners to come and look upon the cut flowers, stealing "a few moments from the busy day to gratify one of the purest tastes." They gazed at the daffodils, roses, pinks, carnations and wallflowers before once again withdrawing into the usual noise and uproar of the city.

The New Market, as it was called, continued for more than a century until in 1974 it was moved to a site in Battersea. The spirit of Covent Garden has of course changed since that removal, but it is still a centre of noise and bustle; the hucksters and hawkers are still there, but the sounds of the basket-sellers have changed into those of travelling musicians and the agile porters have turned into a different kind of street artist.

The great markets—Smithfield, Billingsgate, Covent Garden, the Stocks—were seen as central to London life, and somehow emblematic of it. Charles Booth, in his *Life and Labour of the People in London* (1903), revealed that in Petticoat Lane, on Sunday morning, could be found "cotton sheeting, old clothes, worn-out boots, damaged lamps, chipped china shepherdesses, rusty locks," together with sellers of "Dutch drops" and Sarsaparilla wine, bed knobs, door knobs and basins of boiled peas. Here, in the early twentieth century, Tubby Isaacs set up his stall selling bread and jellied eels: the same small firm remains there at the beginning of the next century. In nearby Wentworth Street there were bakers and fishmongers. In Brick Lane were sold "pigeons, canaries, rabbits, fowls, parrots or guinea pigs." Hungerford Market was known for its vegetables, Spitalfields for its potatoes, and Farringdon for its watercress. In Goodge Street there was a market for fruit and vegetables, while in Leather Lane tools, appliances and peddlers' wares were sold together with "old bed knobs, rusty keys or stray lengths of iron piping." Leadenhall Market, established since the thirteenth century, was first known for its supply of woollen cloths while its main courtyard was used alternately by butchers and tanners. Clare Market, off Lincoln's Inn Fields, was notorious for its butchers. Bermondsey Market was known for hide and skin, Tattersall's for horses. Fish-wives held their own market along the Tottenham Court Road "with paper-lanthorns stuck in their baskets on dark nights." The litany of markets is a litany of London itself—Fleet Market, Newgate

Market, Borough Market, Lisson Grove Market, Portman Market, Newport Market, Chapel Market in Islington.

The metaphor of the market has now spread all over London, and across its trading systems, and yet it springs from places such as Brick Lane, Petticoat Lane, Leather Lane, Hoxton Street and Berwick Street. All these, and almost a hundred others, survive still as street-markets, the majority of them on sites where they first flourished centuries before. Here the poor buy at fifth hand what the rich bought at first hand. Some street-markets, however, have vanished. Rag Fair, by Tower Hill, has gone: a woebegone place, where "raggs and old clothes" were sold beside rotten vegetables, stale bread and old meat, it disappeared beneath its own waste.

CHAPTER 36

Waste Matter

✢

hat the voracious city devours, it must eventually disgorge in rubbish and excrement. Thomas More, who as under-sheriff knew the malodorous and insanitary conditions of London at first hand, decided that in his *Utopia* (1516) anything *sordidum* (dirty) or *morbum* (diseased) should be forbidden within the walls. In the early sixteenth century, this was indeed a utopian state.

The sanitary conditions of London in the centuries of Roman civilisation, when a system of public baths and latrines helped actively to promote urban cleanliness, were as good as anywhere within the empire. Yet it would be unwise to depict a marbled city without stain; refuse heaps, containing the bones of oxen, goats, pigs and horses, were found in the open areas of the city still within the walls, although it is likely that semi-domesticated ravens were always ready to consume offending garbage littered upon the street. The practice of throwing the contents of urine jars out of the window is well known, as is attested by numerous court cases. In the entrance to Roman taverns and workshops, however, have been uncovered large stone vessels which can best be described as urinals. Here is the first physical evidence of London's toilet facilities (in one such site, along Fish Street Hill, was found a bag of cannabis which also testifies to the longevity of the drug culture of the city).

In the period of Saxon and Viking occupation there is evidence of excrement dropped anywhere and everywhere, even within the houses, which suggests a deterioration in healthy practice. In turn we may imagine the medieval town littered with horse dung and cesspools, strewn with the offal of butchers, with wooden chips and kitchen refuse, human excrement and daily rubbish, generally impeding the "channels" which ran down both sides of the street. Regulations of the thirteenth century ordained that "no one shall place dung or other filth in the streets or lanes, but cause the same to be taken by the rakers to the places ordained"; these "places" were an early version of the rubbish tip from which the contents were taken by cart or boat to outlying areas where the dung could be used as manure for the fields. Pigs were allowed to roam through the streets as natural consumers of rubbish, but they proved a considerable nuisance with their custom of blocking narrow lanes and straying into houses; their place after a cull was taken by kites who performed the same function as ravens in first-century London. Indeed there were laws that forbade on pain of death the killing of kites and ravens, which became so tame that they would snatch a piece of bread and butter from a child's hands.

In 1349 Edward III wrote to the mayor, complaining that the thoroughfares were "foul with human faeces, and the air of the city poisoned to the great danger of men passing." As a result the civic authorities issued a proclamation denouncing the "grievous and great abomination" to be found in filth, dung and other nuisances obstructing the streets. From entries in the *Letter Books* and the *Plea and Memoranda Rolls* it is clear that the city leaders, fearing epidemic disease, accepted the need for sanitary legislation. Four scavengers (scawageours) were to be held responsible for rubbish in each ward, and each householder had a duty to ensure that the street outside his door was cleared of noisome waste. There were fines for any citizen found dumping refuse into the Fleet or Walbrook, and a "serjeant of the channels" was appointed to ensure that the rivulets of street and stream remained unimpeded. But old habits persisted. Households overlooking the Walbrook paid a tax or toll in order to build their latrines over the running water of the river, and upon London Bridge itself there were 138 houses as well as a public latrine which showered down upon the Thames.

Public places, in that capacity, were used more often than private spaces. Pissing Lane, later known as Pissing Alley, "leadinge from Paules Church into Pater Noster Rowe," may be mentioned, along with two other alleys of the same name dating variously from the thirteenth to sixteenth centuries. Similarly there were Dunghill Lanes beside Puddle Dock and Whitefriars as well as Queenhithe, while Dunghill Stairs was located to the front of Three Cranes Wharf.

The first public lavatories, since the urns of Roman London, were constructed in the thirteenth century. The new bridge across the river was equipped with one of these modern conveniences, which had two entrances, while the smaller bridges across the Fleet and the Walbrook also made provision for them. Against the streams and tributaries there were "houses of office," too, although many consisted simply of wooden planks with holes carved out of them. More elaborate public privies were constructed, some with four or more holes, culminating in Richard Whittington's fifteenth-century "House of Easement" or "Long House" over the Thames at the end of Friar Lane. It contained two rows of sixty-four seats, one row for men and the other for women, while the refuse dropped into a gully washed with the tides. Public exposure in the city's privies, however, could be dangerous. A quarrel between two men in a privy beside the wall of Ironmonger Lane ended in murder. Death came in other forms from the same source. The privy above the Fleet, near the mouth of the Thames, caused much discomfort to the monks of White Friars who in 1275 declared to Edward I "that the putrid exhalations there from overcame even the frankincense used in their Services and had caused the death of manie Brethren."

Certain other parts of London were renowned, and arraigned, for their dirtiness—Farringdon Without and Portsoken were known for their dung-heaps and rubbish dumps while the inhabitants of Bassinghall Ward and Aldrich Gate [Aldersgate] Ward were fined for "casting out of ordure and urine." One may add to this noisome list the place known as Moorfields which, before being drained in 1527, was said to be "a melancholy region, with raised paths and refuse-heaps, deep black ditches, not unodourous and detestable open sewers." It was a walk, according to one city history, suitable for London suicides and London philosophers.

The London memoranda (court records) of the fourteenth century are filled with complaints and exhortations. A wall "fallith down gobet-mele into the hie strete, and makith the wey foule . . . the commin privey of ludgate is full difectif and perlus, and the ordur thereof rotith the stone wallys." In the parish of St. Sepulchre one Halywell was indicted "for anoyng the feld with donge on both sides horspole," and one Norton for a similar offence "that there may neythir hors ne cart pas for his dong." Fourteen households in Foster Lane were indicted "for castyngh out of ordour & vrine," and in the parish of St. Botolph a nuisance was created by "stuppyng of the water, for by cause that the dunghe and the Robous that is dreuen doune ther-to." All the cooks of Bread Street were arraigned for keeping their "dung and garbage" under their stalls, while a dung-hill in Watergate Street was deemed to create "ordour of Prevees and other orrible sigtis." We can hear the voice of Londoners in these denunciations, and join in their very local vision of the "filth that cometh doun be Trinite Lane and Cordwanerstrete by Garlekhith and goth doun in the lane by twix John Hatherle shop and Rick Whitman shop, of whiche dong moche goth in to Thamise."

The same kind of complaint emerges in every century, and there is a plaintive echo of these London memoranda in Samuel Pepys's words from Seething Lane: "Going down to my cellar, I put my foot in a great heap of turds, by which I find that Mr. Turners house of office is full and comes into my cellar."

Londoners are fascinated by excrement. Sir Thomas More, in the early sixteenth century, uses five names of shit—*cacus*, *merda*, *stercus*, *lutum*, *coenum*—in his polemical work. These are Latin terms but in the English of the same century homage was paid to human excrement with the nickname of "Sir-reverence." In the late twentieth century those quintessentially London artists, "Gilbert and George" of Spitalfields, arranged large exhibitions of their Shit Paintings.

The very houses of London are built upon refuse. Discarded and forgotten objects, left among old foundations, help to support the weight of the modern city, so that beneath our feet are copper brooches and crucibles, leather shoes and lead tokens, belts and buckles, broken pottery and sandals and figurines, tools and gloves, jars and pieces of bone, shoes and oyster shells, knives and toys, locks and candlesticks, coins and combs, plates and pipes, a child's ball and a pilgrim's amulet, all spreading their silent ministry through the earth. But the city is built upon remains and ruins in a more literal sense. In Chick Lane, in 1597, it was discovered that thirty tenements and twelve cottages had been erected upon a great dump of public refuse, while Holywell Street was built upon a site of rubbish and waste which had accumulated for a hundred years after the Great Fire. Even the pavements of the modern city are made, according to *The Stones of London* by Elsden and Howe, "with slabs produced from clinkered household refuse by the municipal authorities."

The streets also bear the marks of waste. Maiden Lane is named after middens, Pudding Lane after the "pudding" sent down it to the dung boats moored on the Thames. Public dumps were also known as laystalls and there

is still a Laystall Street in Clerkenwell. Sherborne Lane was once known as
Shiteburn Lane.

In the period when Pepys was complaining about the substances in his cellar, the privy was being used in most households for kitchen and domestic as
well as human refuse. The streets, despite all the prohibitions and regulations,
were still offensive "with dust and unwholesome stenches in summer and in
wet weather with dirt." This passage occurs in a report of 1654, and eight years
later the city made one of its periodic efforts to cleanse itself with injunctions
that householders on Wednesdays and Saturdays should put their refuse in
"basket tubs or other vessels ready for the Raker or Scavenger"; the approach
of his cart or carriage was meant to be heralded by "a bell, horn, clapper or
otherwise," thus alerting the inhabitants to bring out their rubbish. Excrement
itself was removed from the cesspits by "night-soil men," whose carts were
notoriously leaky; they dropped "near a quarter of their dirt" and the great
eighteenth-century philanthropist Jonas Hanway remarked that they subjected "every coach and every passenger, of what quality whatsoever, to be
overwhelmed with whole cakes of dirt at every accidental jolt of the cart, of
which many have had a most filthy experience." It might be thought the Great
Fire would bring a speedy and fiery end to the city's problems of waste, but the
habits of the citizen were not to be easily changed. The novels of the eighteenth century pay horrified, if somewhat oblique, attention to the malodorous
and generally offensive conditions of the capital.

Yet if the Great Fire did not cleanse London, it is appropriate that commerce should do so instead. Improved methods of agriculture meant that, by
1760, manure had become a valuable commodity. Since household ash and
cinders also began to be employed in brick-making, a whole new market for
refuse emerged. Now there came new dealers, competing upon the exchange
of the streets. In 1772 a city scavenger of St. James, Piccadilly, reported that
he was "greatly injured by a set of Persons called Running Dustmen who go
about the streets and places of this Parish and collect the Coal Ashes." He
begged the parishioners only "to deliver their Coal Ashes but to the Persons
employed by him the said John Horobin who are distinguished by ringing a
Bell." One eighteenth-century advertisement parades the benefits of Joseph
Waller, residing by the Turnpike at Islington, who "keeps Carts and Horses
for emptying Bog-Houses." When rubbish became part of commerce, the
conditions of the city were improved more speedily than by any Paving Acts
or Cleansing Committees.

In the nineteenth century, the history of city refuse became part of the history of city finance. The dust-heap in Dickens's *Our Mutual Friend*, modelled upon a real and ever more offensive pile off the King's Cross Road, was believed to contain buried treasure and had already made a fortune for its owner. "I'm a pretty fair scholar in dust," Mr. Boffin explains, "I can price the Mounds to a fraction, and I know how they can be best disposed of." There were "Mounds" or "Mounts" of refuse in various parts of London. One immediately to the west of the London Hospital was known as "Whitechapel Mount," and from its summit could be seen "the former villages of Limehouse, Shadwell and Ratcliffe." Another was situated at Battle-bridge and was known to the author of *Old and New London* as a mountain with "heaped hillocks of horse-bones" together with cinders, rags and ordure. It became the resort of "innumerable pigs" but its true commercial worth was proved in a remarkable manner when, in the first years of the nineteenth century, the Russians purchased all the ashes from that site to assist in the rebuilding of Moscow after its burning by the French. The area itself, just north of the present King's Cross Station, had become the quarters of "dustmen and cinder-sifters" as well as more general scavengers, or, in other words, all those who lived upon the refuse of the city. In that sense it was a benighted place and, even at the beginning of the twenty-first century, it is characterised by its bleakness and ugliness. The atmosphere of dereliction hangs over it still.

At Letts Wharf, on the southern bank of the Thames near the Shot Tower at Lambeth, another band of Londoners used to sift and pick through the refuse. Most of them were women, who smoked short pipes and wore "strawboard gaiters and torn bonnet boxes for pinafores." Theirs was an old profession, passed from mother to daughter, generation after generation. "The appearance of these women is most deplorable," one medical officer wrote, "standing in the midst of fine dust piled up to their waists, with faces and upper extremities begrimed with black filth, and surrounded by and breathing a foul, moist, hot air, surcharged with the gaseous emanations of disintegrating organic compounds." The dust was sifted into its coarse and fine components, while old pieces of tin were salvaged together with old shoes and bones and oyster shells. The tin often went to make "clamps" for luggage, while the oyster shells were sold to builders; old shoes went to the manufacturers of the famous dye, "Prussian blue." Nothing was wasted.

It was once rumoured that the streets of London were paved with gold and so it is perhaps no surprise that, in the nineteenth century, the refuse "daily swept up and collected from the streets . . . is turned into gold to the tune of some thousands of pounds a year." In photographs of the Victorian city, the gutters are filled with litter and street-sweepings with the added nuisance of multifarious orange peel. The rewards of the city sweepers were based entirely upon locality, but the most obvious product was "street mud" which was sold to farmers or market gardeners. The thoroughfares most highly prized were those where "locomotion never ceases"—Haymarket being "six times in excess of the average streets," followed by Watling Street, Bow Lane, Old Change and Fleet Street. So even movement itself creates profit in a city based upon speed and productivity.

"Street orderlies" swept the streets and crossings. Some were "pauper labourers" set to the task as a convenient method of combining discipline with efficiency, while others were "philanthropic labourers" who were paid by various charitable concerns. By the middle of the century, all were in competition with the new "street-sweeping machines" which had a mechanical power "equal to the industry of five street-sweepers."

The industry was complex, however, and different forms of scavenging were specific. Horse manure was collected by boys in red uniforms, who ran among the traffic shovelling it up and placing it in receptacles by the side of the road; this represented yet more London "gold," at least to farmers in dire need of fertiliser. There were bone-pickers and rag-gatherers, cigar and cigarette pickers, old wood collectors, sweeps and dredgermen, dustmen and "mud larks," all intent upon collecting up "the most abject refuse" of the city in case it might become "the source of great riches."

From one owner of a beer-shop on the Southwark Bridge Road Henry Mayhew, who chronicled the street-finders as a different class of city dwellers, learned how the bone-grubbers took their bags of bones to his establishment. Here they received payment and "sat . . . silently looking at the corners of the floor, for they rarely lifted their eyes up." The rag-finders had their own separate "beats." The "pure" finders took up dog excrement from the street; in the early nineteenth century it had been the profession of women who were known as "bunters" but the increasing demands of the tanning trade, for which the excrement was used as an astringent, meant that male workers were also in demand.

In the hope of "finding fitting associates and companions in their wretchedness . . . or else for the purpose of hiding themselves and their shifts and struggles for existence from the world" the "pure" finders tended to congregate within tenements in the east of the City, just past the Tower of London, between the docks and Rosemary Lane. This was an area, according to Mayhew, "redolent of filth and pregnant with pestilential disease." The inadvertent use of "pregnant" suggests here the general association of dirty people with sexual depravity. Indeed the attempt to take prostitution off the streets of London was itself linked with the removal of excrement for the cleanness of the city. In a similar spirit there were also warnings concerning the revolutionary potential of the poor, with their "fevers and . . . filth." Once more is made the implicit connection between poverty, disease and excrement. It was an association which occurred to the "pure" finders themselves. "There's such a dizziness in my head now," one told Mayhew, "I feel as if it didn't belong to me. No, I have earned no money to-day. I have had a piece of bread that I steeped in water to eat. I could never bear the thought of going into the great house [the workhouse]; I'm so used to the air that I'd sooner die in the street, as many I know have done. I've known several of our people, who have sat down in the street with their basket alongside them, and died."

And thus the dead in turn became rubbish to be removed by the parish and swept away. The cycle of life was completed.

The outlines of age may be seen in the features of the very young. The youthful collectors of river refuse, known as "mud larks," scavenged for pieces of coal or wood which they would then put in kettles, baskets, or even old hats. Many of them were small children, approximately seven or eight years old, and Mayhew questioned one of them. "He had heard of Jesus Christ once . . . but he never heard tell of who or what he was and didn't 'particular care' about knowing . . . London was England and England, he said, was in London but he couldn't tell in what part." For him the condition which made up "London" was everywhere, therefore; and, as Mayhew observed, "there was a painful uniformity in the stories of all the children" of the city.

Another group of scavengers were known as "toshers," hence the pejorative expression "tosh." They were the sewer hunters, burrowing beneath the surface of the city in search of valuable waste. In the early part of the nineteenth century they could enter by the holes along the Thames, braving the crumbling brickwork and rotten stone, in order to creep along the underground labyrinth. But then, in the 1850s and 1860s, everything changed as a result of what was called London's "sanitation revolution."

It is a curious fact of city life that the sanitation of the early nineteenth century did not differ materially from that of the fifteenth century. There had been attempts at superficial improvement, with efforts to maintain the cleanliness of the Kilbourne and the Westbourne, the Ranelagh and the Fleet, the Shoreditch and the Effa, the Falcoln Brook and the Earl, all important rivers and streams. But the central feature of London's sanitation remained its greatest disgrace; there were still cesspools beneath some 200,000 houses. Effluent was forced upwards through the wooden floors of the poorer households.

The solution of the Metropolitan Commission of Sewers in 1847, that all privy refuse was to be discharged directly into the sewers, seemed convincing at the time. But the effect was that the effluent was transported straight into the central reaches of the Thames. As a result the swan and the salmon, together with other fish, vanished in an open sewer. In the words of Disraeli, the river had become "a Stygian pool reeking with ineffable and unbearable horror." Where once rose petals had been papered across the windows of the Westminster Parliament building, now sheets soaked with chlorine were used instead. The problem was compounded by the fact that the water supply for many Londoners was taken directly from the Thames, and from this time forward it was often described as of a "brownish" colour. The prevalence of cholera in the same period, when it was believed that "all smell is disease," only increased the noxious horror of the city where the discharges of three million people were running through its midst. The concentration of people seeking work in the capital, and the rising consumption of the Victorian middle class, had led to a complementary rise in effluence. The pervasive smell may in that sense be regarded as the odour of progress. These were the conditions of London as late as 1858, the year of the "Great Stink."

In 1855, under the pressure of extreme circumstances, a Metropolitan Board of Works had been established to remedy the unhappy situation. Three years later, during a long and hot summer, Joseph Bazalgette began his scheme to divert all sewage from the Thames through different types of sewer (main line and intercepting, storm relief and outfall) to outfalls at Barking and Crossness; it was described by the *Observer* as "the most extensive and wonderful work of modern times," and by the end of this great engineer's ministrations 165 miles of main sewers had been reconstructed in Portland cement with a further 1,100 miles of new local sewers. For all practical purposes, large parts of Bazalgette's system remain in place at the beginning of the twenty-first century. It was a signal example of public health enterprise in the face of a rapidly deteriorating urban environment; characteristic of London administration, however, was that it occurred very quickly and in conditions of near panic. All the great works of the city seem to be in one sense improvised and haphazard.

. . .

By the early twentieth century the dust mounds and open ash-pits were removed from the capital, and most of the rubbish was pulverised, burned or treated with chemicals; the environmental theory of disease, which simply prescribed that waste should be removed to as distant a point as possible, was replaced by the "germ" theory, which meant that waste had effectively to be neutralised. So changes in epidemiological research can affect the topography of the city. The fabric of London is susceptible to theory, therefore, and in the previous century huge areas of sewage purification were complemented by vast incineration plants. The enormous Solid Waste Transfer Station by Smugglers Way in Wandsworth and the great Sewage Works of Beckton are largely unseen; they are monuments to the city's secret industry.

There are still rubbish tips located in various parts of the capital and, although gulls and pigeons have now taken the place of ravens and kites, the vagrant scavenger (once known as a "totter") is still to be seen in the streets of London searching through bins and garbage for cigarette ends, food or drink. The ability—in fact the necessity—of the city to discharge its own rubbish continues in various guises. The quantity of waste in the ever-increasing city has risen higher than any nineteenth-century dust mound, with an average of ten million tonnes produced by the capital each year, among it almost one and a half million tonnes of scrap metal, and half a million tonnes of paper. It is only to be expected, too, that the history of modern effluent is still part of the history of commerce. In the sixteenth century it was discovered that the nitrogen from excreta could be used in the manufacture of gunpowder, but in the twentieth century human faeces yielded a different form of power. Incineration plants, like that at Edmonton, produce hundreds of thousands of megawatts of electricity each year. Gold and platinum are being emitted by the catalytic converters fitted to cars and deposited within exhaust fumes; soon, according to one scientist reported in *The Times* of 1998, "it will make economic sense to pan the deposits" along the city thoroughfares. So London's streets are also now truly paved with gold.

CHAPTER 37

A Little Drink or Two

nd, with the food, arrives the drink. The inhabitants of the London region, some four thousand years ago, imbibed a variety of beer or mead. Londoners have been drinking it ever since. Close to the Old Kent Road a Roman brooch of jasper was recently uncovered. Engraved upon it was the head of Silenus, the drunken satyr who was tutor to Bacchus; no better divinity of London could have been discovered. Thomas Brown noted of London, in 1730, that "to see the Number of Taverns, Alehouses etc. he would imagine Bacchus the only God that is worshipp'd there."

In the thirteenth century London was already notorious for "the immoderate drinking of the foolish." The wines of the Rhineland and of Gascony, of Burgundy and Maderia, the white wine of Spain and the red wine of Portugal, flooded in, but the less affluent drank ale and beer; the hop seems to have been cultivated by the beginning of the fourteenth century, but most ale was spiced with pepper and known as "stingo." This again suggests the partiality of Londoners for highly flavoured comestibles, perhaps as a fitting adjunct to their energetic and competitive lives in the city. In Chaucer's *Canterbury Tales* (c. 1387–1400) the Cook is well aware of the requirements for what the poet elsewhere calls "a draught of moist and corny ale," while his Miller, an ale-drinker, "far-dronken was all pale." In the same period Glutton, in William Langland's *Piers the Plowman* (*c.* 1362), "yglubbed a galon and a gille" of ale. Certainly there were many establishments for that purpose. By the early fourteenth century there were in London "354 taverns and 1,334 breweries," more familiarly known later as boozing kens or tippling offices. Early in the fifteenth century it was recorded that there were some 269 brewers and in 1427 the London Company of Brewers was incorporated with its own coat of arms. Already it had composed rules for its members, such as that in 1423 which ordered that "retailers of ale should sell the same in their houses, in pots of peutre, sealed; and that whoever carried ale to the buyer should hold the pot in one hand and a cup in another, and that all who had pots unsealed should be fined." A similar respect for quality was imposed upon the vintners who by city statute in the early fifteenth century were forbidden to "colaire ne medle" with their wine. One William Harold was, in 1419, sentenced to the pillory for an hour on the charge of "contrefetyng of old and feble spaynissh wyn for good & trewe Romeney, in the parisshe of seynt Martyns in the vyntry."

By the sixteenth century, according to John Stow, the problems of drunkenness had become so acute that two hundred London alehouses were suppressed in 1574. There were some twenty-six brewers in London by that time, and their produce was variously known as Huffe Cup, Mad Dog, Angels' Food, Lift Leg and Stride Wide. The ingredients seem to have varied, with constituents including broom, bay-berries and ivy-berries, together with malt and oats, although only the concoction brewed from hops was given the name of true beer. The Elizabethan chronicler William Harrison noted the drunkards in the streets and remarked that "our malt bugs lie in a row lugging at their dames teats, till they lie still againe, and not be able to wag." Certain alehouses of the period were so identified with London itself, both in ballad and in drama, that they became representative of the city. The Boar's Head in Eastcheap was the vivid setting of Falstaff and Pistol, Doll Tearsheet and Mistress Quickly, and so impressed itself upon the folk memory of Londoners that it was generally agreed that Shakespeare himself must have drunk on the premises. In the eighteenth century members of a literary club assembled there in order to assume Shakespearean roles, and such was the power of its associations that it attracted pilgrims to its site long after its destruction in 1831. There is, however, one specific remembrance. Robert

Preston "late Drawer at the Boar's head Tavern" departed this life at the age
of twenty-seven on 16 March 1730; he "drew good Wine, took care to fill his
Pots" and his headstone lay against the wall of St. Magnus the Martyr.

"The Myter in Cheape," the Mitre of Cheapside, was a haunt of locals
where according to Ben Jonson if "any stranger comes in amongst 'em, they
all stand up and stare at him, as he were some unknown beast brought out of
Africk." The drawer here, George, attained immortality when named in 1599
by Jonson in *Every Man Out of His Humour*—"Where's George? call me
George hither quickly"—and in 1607 by Dekker and Webster in *Westward
Ho!*—"O, you are George the drawer at the Mitre." It is evidence of the way
in which a particular Londoner can become fixed as a type or character in the
eyes of his contemporaries. The peculiar and persistent connection of alehouses with drama was also maintained by the memory of the Mermaid.

> What things have we seen
> Done at the Mermaid; heard words that have been
> So nimble and so full of subtle flame

wrote Beaumont to Jonson. Keats, echoing the sentiment two hundred years
later, knew no

> Happy field or mossy cavern
> Choicer than the Mermaid Tavern

The poet, himself a Londoner who as a child lived on the premises of the
Swan and Hoop in Moorgate, had migrated in imagination to the junction of
Friday Street and Bread Street where the Mitre was consumed in the Great
Fire.

A tavern "is the onlely Rende-vous of boone company," according to the
Guls Horne-Booke of 1609 where it is important to know the bar staff or draw-
ers and "to learn their names such as *Jack*, and *Will*, and *Tom*" to procure
prompt service as well as credit. Then you may say to the waiter, "Boy, fetch
me money from the barre." The bill was known as "the reckoning" or "the
shot." Games of dice were played and travelling fiddlers went from establishment to establishment. We are allowed to peer closely into the rooms of
an early seventeenth-century tavern, by using an inventory from the aptly
named Mouthe in Bishopsgate Street. Here are listed the boarded partitions
separating one room from another in that tavern, each chamber bearing a dif-

ferent name: the Percullis, the Pomgrannatt, the Three Tuns, the Vyne, and
the King's Head. So we have five different "barres" on the same premises,
furnished with tables, benches and stools. In the Percullis, there was "one
longe table of waynscote, with a fforme" as well as "one oyster table," "one
olde wyne-stoole" and "a payre of playinge tables"; in the King's Head
there was also an oyster table, as well as "a child's stoole." In one of the
guests' chambers, on the floor above, were listed down pillows, flaxen sheets
and a tapestried coverlet as well as chests and cupboards.

A poem of 1606 mentions "the Bores head, hard by London stone . . . the
swan at Dowgat . . . The Myter in Cheape . . . the Castel in Fishstreet" and
others "to make Noses red," but it was not only drink and lodging which seventeenth-century tavern-keepers supplied. An advertisement from a landlord, moving from the Swan at Holborn Bridge to the Oxford Arms in
Warwick Lane, mentioned that "He hath also a hearse, and all things convenient to carry a Corps to any part of England." "There are endless inns,"
Thomas Platter wrote in the early 1600s, "beer and wine shops for every
imaginable growth, alicant, canary, muscatels, clarets, Spanish, Rhenish."
Endless, also, are the verses written upon the topic of London alehouses. Ned
Ward's *Vade Mecum for Malt Worms* and John Taylor's *Pilgrimage* are only
two examples of poems that list public houses and their locations as a kind of
topography of the city, in which the nature and shape of London are known
only in terms of intoxicated reverie:

> Hence to Cloak-lane, near Dowgate hill we steer
> And at Three Tuns cast Anchor for good Beer . . .
> Thereafter haste made waste, and sun was set
> Ere to the Shoreditch Flagon I could get.
> At ten I took my leave, and by the moon
> Reached the Bell Inn, and fell into a swoon.

The words of the two poets are conflated here, in order to suggest the precision of their references to the city as a place where one must get drunk in
order to survive.

The excise tax imposed upon beer in 1643 testifies to the increasing popularity of that drink. Pepys noticed during the Great Fire that the women "would
scold for drink and be drunk as devels"; there may of course have been some
excuse for their behaviour during that inferno but a calm observer, Henry
Peacham, writing *The Art of Living in London* in 1642, commands "above all

things beware of beastly drunkenness . . . some are found sometimes so drunk, who, being fallen upon the ground or, which is worse, in the kennel, are not able to stir or move again. Drinking begets challenges and quarrels, and occasioneth the death of many, as is known by almost daily experience . . . Drunken men are apt to lose their hats, cloaks, or rapiers, nor to know what they have spent." Pepys also recorded a lady, dining at the house of a mutual friend, who in one draught knocked back a pint and a half of white wine.

Yet if the seventeenth century might rival any of its predecessors for the amount of alcohol flowing through the veins of London, it was overshadowed by the eighteenth century when drinking reached massive, even crisis, proportions. This was the period when Samuel Johnson, that great London luminary, declared that "a man is never happy in the present unless he is drunk." A vast number of his fellow-citizens seemed to agree.

There was a fashion for "brown ale," a sweet beer, but a further duty upon malt made it important for breweries to introduce more hops into their drink. This became "bitter beer"—"so bitter that I could not drink it," according to Casanova—which, when mixed with regular ale, became known as "half and half." In the same period "pale ale" was produced, and became so popular that pale ale houses were established in the city. In the early 1720s a mellow beer, brewed for four or five months, was introduced; the "labouring people, porters etc found its utility" for drinking at breakfast or at dinner, and thus it became known as "porter." It was a beer brewed only in the city, and led directly to that class of beers known as "stout": brown stout, double stouts, Irish, entire, or heavy wet, or London particular.

It was particular to London, also, that alehouses were directly connected with commerce. For many trades the only employment agency was a specific public house or "house of call." Bakers and tailors, plumbers and bookbinders, congregated in one place where masters arrived "to enquire when they want hands." The landlord himself was often of the same trade, giving credit to those out of employ, chiefly in the medium of drink. The tradesmen paid their employees at pay tables in the same public houses, with obvious and predictable results, compounded by the fact that money was not exchanged until the hours of midnight and one on a Sunday morning.

There were other working practices which demanded the consumption of liquor. "Entry money" for a new apprentice or journeyman was spent in the alehouse, and various fines for late or incomplete work were also paid in the same manner. According to one great historian, M. Dorothy George in *London Life in the Eighteenth Century*, "the consumption of strong drink was connected with every phase of life from apprenticeship"; we may also infer that the spirit of trade, so central to the life of London, thereby remained bright and fiery. Drink and fire go together, and distillers were accused of negligence whereby their stills "gave rise to frequent and terrible fires."

There are some singular vignettes of drunkenness in the city—Oliver Goldsmith putting on his wig back to front to amuse friends in his Temple Lodgings, Charles Lamb staggering home beside the New River where he had once bathed as a schoolboy, Joe Grimaldi being carried home every night on the back of the landlord of the Marquis of Cornwallis. There were, however, less happy episodes. The Restoration dramatist Nathaniel Lee drank himself into Bedlam where he declared: "They said I was mad: and I said they were mad: damn them, they outvoted me." He was eventually released, but on the day of his death "he drank so hard, that he dropped down in the street, and was run over by a coach. His body was laid in a bulk at Trunkits, the perfumer's at Temple Bar, till it was owned." William Hickey, the early nineteenth-century memoirist, was found in a gutter along Parliament Street, "utterly incapable of giving any account of myself, or of even articulating . . . having no more recollection of a single circumstance that had occurred for the preceding twelve hours, than if I had been dead." He awoke the following day "unable to move hand or foot, being most miserably bruised, cut and maimed in every part of my body." Another London particular in the eighteenth century was Richard Porson, the first librarian of the London Institution, who was often seen in the morning staggering "from his old haunt, the Cider Cellars; in Maiden Lane." The editor of Euripides, he was a renowned scholar who "could hiccup Greek like a Helot," but preferred to boast that he could repeat from memory the whole of Smollett's *Roderick Random* (1748). "It was said of Porson," according to Walford's *Old and New London*, "that he drank everything he could lay his hands upon, even to embrocation and spirits of wine intended for the lamp. Samuel Rogers described him returning to the dining room after the people had gone, and drinking all that was left in their glasses." His usual and familiar exclamation, when surprised or perplexed, was "*Whooe!*" and, on the day of his death, he was heard quoting from the Greek *Anthologia*. A friend noticed that on this last occasion "he gave the Greek rapidly, but the English with painful slowness, as if the Greek came more naturally." Revived by wine and jelly dissolved in brandy and water, he was taken to a tavern in St. Michael's Alley, Cornhill, but later died in the London Institution on the stroke of midnight.

. . .

When the phrase "spirituous liquor" is applied to the city's drinking habits, however, the spirit is generally that of gin. It was denounced by the magistrate Sir John Fielding as "this liquid fire by which men drink their hell beforehand." The demon of London for half a century, it was held responsible for the deaths of many thousands of men, women and children. Whatever the truth of mortality rates, and they are open to question, there is no doubting the popularity of gin (concocted from grain, sloe or juniper). It has been estimated that in the 1740s and 1750s there were 17,000 "gin-houses." The slogan, copied by Hogarth for his portrayal of *Gin Lane*, ran "Drunk for 1*d*, dead drunk for 2*d*, clean straw for nothing." These "geneva shops" were located in cellars or in converted ground-floor workshops; they multiplied in poorer quarters, making the more familiar and traditional alehouses of the city seem respectable in contrast. Hogarth himself said of his portrait that "In gin lane every circumstance of its horrid effects are brought to view, in terorem, nothing but Poverty misery and ruin are to be seen Distress even to madnes and death, and not a house in tolerable condition but Pawnbrokers and the Gin shop." In that famous study, an infant is seen falling to its certain death from the emaciated arms of its drunken mother; she is sitting upon wooden stairs, with ulcerated legs, her countenance expressive only of oblivion beyond despair. It may seem melodramatic, but it is a pictorial variant upon a salient truth. One Judith Defour took her two-year-old daughter from a workhouse, for example, and then strangled her in order to strip her of the new clothes with which she had been dressed. She sold the baby's clothes and spent the money, 1*s* 4*d*, on gin.

"A new kind of drunkenness," Henry Fielding wrote in 1751, "unknown to our ancestors, is lately sprung up amongst us, and which if not put a stop to, will infallibly destroy a great part of the inferior people. The drunkenness I here intend is . . . by this Poison called Gin . . . the principal sustenance (if it may be so called) of more than a hundred thousand People in this Metropolis." There had been attempts to put a "stop" to this trade, most notably by the Gin Act of 1736 which was greeted only by "the execrations of the mob." The Act was ridiculed and evaded, with gin being sold as medicinal draughts or under assumed names such as Sangree, Tow Row, the Makeshift, or King Theodore of Corsica. The gin-shops were still filled with men and women "and even sometimes of children" who drank so much that "they find it difficult to walk on going away." The corn distillers of London claimed that they produced "upward of eleven twelfths of the whole distillery of England" and a contemporary, Lord Lansdowne, recognised in 1743 that "the excessive use of gin hath hitherto been pretty much confined to the Cities of London and Westminster." It offered the comfort of forgetfulness to prisoners and vagrants; it provided oblivion to the poor of St. Giles, where one house in four was a gin-shop.

Distilling was highly profitable. The trade was "thrown open" and protected from excessive excise; so the great destroyer of the poor and disadvantaged was actually created by those who wished to make a quick and easy profit. Only belatedly did the authorities respond to crimes of violence against property, fuelled by the demand for gin, and to the number of "weak and sickly" children who were proving a burden upon the parish authorities. Some gin-shops were suppressed in 1751. This measure seemed to work. Improvements in the distilleries, closer inspection of gin-shops and increase in taxes eventually resulted in the observation of 1757 that "We do not see the hundredth part of poor wretches drunk in the street since the said qualifications." The fever passed. The rage for gin subsided as quickly as it had arisen, leading to the surmise that it was some climacteric of the city's history as if London itself had been seized by sudden frenzy and burning thirst.

Yet gin and ale were not considered to be the only addictive and dangerous liquids. There was also tea.

The grocer Daniel Rowlinson was the first man to sell a pound of tea, in the 1650s; fifty years later Congreve described the "auxiliaries to the tea-table" as "orange brandy, aniseed, cinnamon, citron, and Barbadoes water." J. Ilive, author of *A New and Compleat Survey of London* in 1762, also blamed the "excessive drinking of Tea" for enervating "the Stomachs of the Populace, as to render them incapable of performing the offices of Digestion; whereby the Appetite is so much deprav'd." A pamphleteer in 1758 declared tea-drinking to be "very hurtful to those who work hard and live low" and condemned it as "one of the worst of habits, rendering you lost to yourselves, and unfit for the comforts you were first designed for." William Hazlitt was popularly supposed to have died in Frith Street, Soho, in 1830 from the excessive drinking of that plant infusion. The emphasis once again is on the tendency of Londoners—even imported citizens such as Hazlitt—to obsession and excess, so that an apparently harmless cordial can become dangerous. That is also why London tea gardens soon acquired a dubious reputation. Suburban retreats with agreeable names such as White Conduite House, Shepherd and Shepherdess, Cuper's Gardens, Montpelier and Bagnigge Wells, devoted to the drinking of tea and other pleasant pastimes, became associated "with loose women and with boys whose morals are depraved, and their constitutions ruined" and were well known "for the encouragement of luxury, extravagance, idleness and other wicked illegal purposes." It is as if the opportunity for pleasure, or leisure, in London was immediately transformed into excess, viciousness and immorality; the city can never be at peace.

Tea and gin are still with us, but one eighteenth-century drink has utterly disappeared. Saloop was a hot, sweet beverage made from a decoction of sassafras wood, milk and sugar, and sold for three halfpence a bowl; the name is supposed to have been derived from the slopping sound of those drinking it in the street. Coffee and tea were expensive, so stalls selling saloop were found in the poorer areas of London. In summer saloop was sold from an open table on wheels; in winter from a kind of tent made from a screen and an old umbrella. It was considered to be the best possible cure for a hangover, and Charles Lamb recalled the artisan and the chimney-sweep mingling with "the rake" at dawn around the saloopian stalls; "being penniless," the young sweeps "will yet hang their black heads over the ascending steams, to gratify one sense if possible." The spectacle prompted Lamb to reflection upon a city where "extremes meet."

In the same period as Lamb wrote his reflections, designed for the *London Magazine*, the young Charles Dickens entered a public house in Parliament Street and ordered "your very best—the VERY *best*—ale." It was called the Genuine Stunning and the twelve-year-old boy said, "Just draw me a glass of that, if you please, with a good head to it." The spectacle of children drinking in the streets and alehouses was familiar, if not common, in the early years of the nineteenth century. "The girls, I am told," wrote Henry Mayhew as late as the 1850s, "are generally fonder of gin than the boys." They took it "to keep the cold out."

Verlaine (1873) considered Londoners to be "noisy as ducks, eternally drunk," while Dostoevsky (1862) noted that "everyone is in a hurry to drink himself into insensibility." A German journalist, Max Schlesinger (1853), saw the inhabitants of a public house "standing, staggering, crouching, or lying down, groaning, and cursing, drink and forget." An observer closer to home, Charles Booth, noticed that drinking among women in the 1890s had materially increased. "One drunken woman in a street will set all the women in it drinking," he quotes one male inhabitant of the East End as saying. Nearly all women "get drunk of Monday. They say "we have our fling; we like to have a little fuddle on Monday.' " All classes of London women seem to have been drinking, largely because it was no longer considered wrong for a female to enter a public house for a "nip." In the evening, children of the poorer classes were sent around to the local public house to have a jug filled with ale; as Booth reported, "it was constant come and go, one moment to go in and get the jug filled, and out again the next; none of the children waited to talk or play with one another, but at once hurried home."

Gentlemen drank as deeply and freely as the poor. Thackeray noted those "who glory in drinking bouts" with "bottle-noses" and "pimpled faces." "I was *so* cut last night" is one of the phrases he recalled.

In each year of the nineteenth century, approximately 25,000 people were arrested for drunkenness in the streets. Yet the conditions of life often drove poorer Londoners into their condition. One of them, a collector of "pure" (dog excrement) told Mayhew that he had often been drunk "for three months together"—he had "bent his head down to his cup to drink, being utterly incapable of raising it to his lips."

So even though the gin fever had subsided, and its shops closed down, its spirit—we might say—was continued in the "gin palaces" of the nineteenth century. These large establishments, clad in shining plate-glass windows with stucco rosettes and gilt cornices, were resplendent with advertisements lit by gas-lamps announcing "the only real brandy in London" or "the famous cordial, medicated gin, which is so strongly recommended by the faculty." The fine lettering reveals the attractions of "The Out and Out!," "The No Mistake," "The Good for Mixing" and "The real Knock-me-down." Yet the exterior brightness was generally deceptive; the scene within these "palaces" was a dismal one, almost reminiscent of the old gin-shops. There was characteristically a long bar of mahogany, behind which were casks painted green and gold, with the customers standing—or sitting on old barrels—along a narrow and dirty area beside it. It might be noted here, too, that social observers believed drink to be "at the root of all the poverty and distress with which they came into contact." Again the emphasis is upon the unhappy conditions of the city itself, literally driving men and women to drink with its relentless speed, urgency and oppression. Of the skeletons investigated in St. Bride's Lower Churchyard, "just under 10 per cent had at least one fracture." It is also revealed, in the fascinating *London Bodies* compiled by Alex Werner, that "almost half of these were rib fractures, commonly caused by stumbling or brawling."

In the same period the breweries had become one of the wonders of London, one of the sights to which foreign visitors were directed. By the 1830s there were twelve principal brewers, producing, according to Charles Knight's *London*, "two barrels, or 76 gallons, of beer per annum for every inhabitant of the metropolis—man, woman and child." Who would not want to observe all this industry and enterprise? One German visitor was impressed by the "vast establishment" of Whitbread's brewery in Chiswell Street, with its buildings "higher than a church" and its horses "the giants of their breed." In similar fashion, in the summer of 1827, a German prince "turned my 'cab' to Barclay's brewery, in Park Street, Southwark, which the vastness of its dimensions renders almost romantic." He observed that steam engines drove the machinery which manufactured from twelve to fifteen thousand barrels a day; ninety-nine of the larger barrels, each one "as high as a house," are kept in "gigantic sheds"; 150 horses "like elephants" transport the beer. His awareness of the size and immensity of London are here reflected in its capacity for beer and, in a final parallel, he notes that from the roof of the brewery "you have a very fine panoramic view of London."

That emblematic significance was recognised by painters as well as visitors, and by the beginning of the nineteenth century there was established what London art historians have termed "the brewery genre." Ten years after the prince's visit, for example, Barclay's brewery was painted by an anonymous hand; the entrance is depicted, together with the thriving life of London all around it. To the right is the great brewhouse, with a suspension bridge connecting to the other side of the street. In the foreground a butcher's boy, in the blue apron typical of his trade, stands with another customer beside a baked-potato van; barrels of beer on sleds are being drawn by horses into the yard, passing a dray which is just leaving. In the street, to the right, a hansom cab is bringing in more visitors. It is a picture of appetite, with the meat carried on the shoulders of the butcher's boy as an apt token of the London diet, as well as of immense energy and industry.

But there are other ways of conveying the immensity of the city's drinking. Blanchard Jerrold and Gustave Doré visited the same premises for their *London: a Pilgrimage*—"the town of Malt and Hops" as Jerrold called it in 1871—in order to see the brewing of the beer named Entire which assuaged "Thirsty London." Jerrold noted that against the great towers and barrels the working men "look like flies," and indeed in Doré's engravings these dark anonymous shapes tend to their beer-mashing and beer-making duties like votaries; all is in shadow and chiaroscuro, with fitful gleams illuminating the activities of these small figures in vast enclosed spaces. Here again the life of the city is like that within some great decaying prison, with the metal pipes and cylinders as its bars and gates. Jerrold, like the German visitor before him, looked over London "with St. Paul's dominating the view from the north," and apostrophises beer as the city's sacred drink. "We are," he remarked, "upon classic ground."

The gin palace was supplanted by the public house which was the direct descendant of the tavern and the alehouse. Of course taverns survived in the older parts of London, known to their adherents for privacy and quiet, to their detractors for gloom and silence. Public houses continued the tradition of segregation, with saloon, lounge and private bars being distinguished from public bars and jug and bottle departments. Many pubs were not salubrious, with plain and dirty interiors and a long "zinc-topped" counter where men sat solemnly drinking—"You enter by a heavy door that is held ajar by a thick leather strap . . . striking you in the back as you go in and often knocking off your hat." Instead of the gin palace's long bar, the public house bar was characteristically in the shape of a horseshoe with the variously coloured bottles rising up within its interior space. The furniture was plain enough, with chairs and benches, tables and spittoons, upon a sawdusted floor. By 1870 there were some 20,000 public houses and beer-shops in the metropolis, catering to half a million customers each day, reminiscent of "dusty, miry, smoky, beery, brewery London."

A stranger asking directions in 1854, according to *The Little World of London*, was likely to be told "Straight on till you come to the Three Turks, then to turn to the right and cross over at the Dog and Duck, and go on again till you come to the Bear and the Bottle, then to turn the corner at the Jolly Old Cocks, and after passing the Veteran, the Guy Fawkes, the Iron Duke, to take the first turn to the right which will bring you to it." In this period there were seventy King's Heads and ninety King's Arms, fifty Queen's Heads and seventy Crowns, fifty Roses and twenty-five Royal Oaks, thirty Bricklayers Arms and fifteen Watermen's Arms, sixteen Black Bulls and twenty Cocks, thirty Foxes and thirty Swans. A favoured colour in pubs' names was red, no doubt complementing the analogy in London between drink and fire, while London's favourite number seemed to be three: the Three Hats, the Three Herrings, the Three Pigeons, and so on. There were also more mysterious signs such as the Grave Maurice, the Cat and Salutation and the Ham and Windmill.

The variety and plentitude of the nineteenth-century pubs continued well into the twentieth century, with the basic shape and nature changing very little, ranging from the munificent West End establishment to the saw-dusted corner pub in Poplar or in Peckham. Then, in one of those paradoxes of London life, public houses became more mixed and lively places during the Second World War. The beer may have run out before the close of proceedings, and glasses may have been in short supply, but Philip Ziegler suggests in *London at War* that "they were the only places in wartime London where one could entertain and be entertained cheaply, and find the companionship badly needed during the war." There was an odd superstition that pubs were more likely to be hit by bombs, but this did not seem to affect their popularity; in fact, during the forced absence of men, women once again began to use pubs. A report of 1943 recorded that "they were often to be seen there with other women or even on their own." "Never had the London pubs been more stimulating," John Lehmann recalled, "never has one been able to hear more extraordinary revelations, never witness more unlikely encounters."

By the end of that war in 1945 there were still some four thousand pubs in the capital, and peace brought a new resurgence of interest. Novels and films have conveyed the atmosphere of pubs in the late 1940s and early 1950s, from the East End, where the men still wore caps and scarves and the girls danced "holding cigarettes in their fingers," to local saloons where what Orwell described as the "warm fog of smoke and beer" surrounded the "regulars."

That emphasis upon conviviality continued into the twenty-first century, with pianos and juke-boxes being steadily supplanted by video games, fruit machines and eventually wide-screen televisions generally devoted to football. With the gradual take-over of public houses by the larger brewers and the establishment of chains in the 1960s and 1970s, however, there emerged a greater degree of standardisation and modernisation from which many London pubs have never recovered. Certain chains, for example, had the ceilings of their public houses smoked or painted brown to mimic the interior of the ancient alehouses, while various nineteenth-century *objets* and old books were discreetly planted to ensure an air of authenticity. But, of all the cities in the world, artificial history does not work in London.

Among the 1,500 licensed premises now listed within central London the familiar names still exist. Even if there is no real comparison between "London" of 1857 and "Central London" of 2000, it is at least comforting to find a significant number still of Red Lions and Queen's Heads and Green Mans. "Three" is still a favourite number, from the Three Compasses in Rotherhithe Street to the Three Tuns in Portman Mews. There are no more

Spotted Dogs or Jolly Sailors but instead a number of Slug and Lettuces. There are still Saints' and Shakespeare's Heads, but there are now five Finnegans Wakes, a Dean Swift, a George Orwell, an Artful Dodger and a Gilbert and Sullivan. The Running Footman is no more, but there are three Scruffy Murphys.

Despite justified complaints about the standardisation of both beer and the surroundings in which it is drunk, there is at the beginning of the twenty-first century a great deal more variety of public house than at any time in London's history. There are pubs with upstairs theatres and pubs with karaoke nights, pubs with live music and pubs with dancing, pubs with restaurants and pubs with gardens, theatrical pubs in Shaftesbury Avenue and business pubs in Leadenhall Market, ancient pubs such as the Mitre in Ely Passage and the Bishop's Finger in Smithfield, pubs with drag-acts and pubs with striptease, pubs with special beers and theme pubs devoted variously to Jack the Ripper, Sherlock Holmes and other London dignitaries; there are gay pubs for homosexuals and pubs for transvestites. And, in more traditional spirit, bicyclists still meet at the Downs, Clapton, where the Pickwick Bicycle Club first met on 22 June 1870.

There is another continuity. Recent surveys suggest that, despite varying levels of intoxication through the twentieth century, Londoners have returned to their old habits. It is now recorded that the average consumption in the city is higher than elsewhere so that according to a *Survey of Alcohol Needs and Services* published in 1991 "one and a half million Londoners may be exceeding recommended 'sensible' levels" with "a quarter of a million drinking at a dangerous level." So the city manifests, as always, the "immoderate drinking of foolish persons." The names for drunkards and drunkenness in London are many and various—"soaks," "whets," "topers," "piss-heads" and "piss artists" are "boozy," "fluffy," "well-gone," "legless," "crocked," "wrecked," "paralytic," "rat-arsed," "shit-faced" and "arse-holed." They are "up the Monument" or "half seas over"; they are "on a bender," "out of it" or "off their tits."

Today's vagrant drinkers of Spitalfields, Stepney, Camden, Waterloo and parts of Islington, are known as the "death drinkers." They subsist on a diet of methylated spirits (jake or the blue), surgical spirit (surge or the white) and other forms of crude alcohol. It has been estimated that there are between one and two thousand down-and-out alcoholics in the city; they congregate under arches, in small parks, or on open sites where building has yet to begin; these places are known to their inhabitants by various names such as the Caves, Running Water, or the Ramp. These vagrants themselves have names like No-Toes, Ginger, Jumping Joe and Black Sam; they are covered by scars and sores, blackened by the makeshift fires conjured upon bomb-sites. When they die—as they do relatively quickly—they are interred in the City Cemetery at Forest Gate. London buries them because London has killed them.

CHAPTER 38

Clubbing

❧

*O*n the unhappy night of his drunkenness William Hickey was returning from a drinking club at the Red House. "Clubbing" is first used as a term in the seventeenth century; in July 1660, Pepys wrote that "We went to Wood's, our old house, for clubbing." But it was in the succeeding century that a variety of clubs emerged for a variety of members. Addison made the characteristic point that "Man is a sociable animal and we take all occasions and pretences of forming ourselves into those little nocturnal assemblies which are commonly known as *clubs*." A club was not very different from a gang, however, a point which the *Spectator* made on 12 March 1712 in allusion to "a general History of Clubs" then being written. It is suggested that the compendium ought to include a "Set of Men" who have taken "the Title of *The Mohock Club*" and who set out to terrorise the streets of the city where citizens are "knocked down, others stabbed, others cut and carbonadoed." In similar vein the *Spectator* noticed signs of "club" spirit at the opera where the women had placed themselves in opposite boxes with various "Party-signals" to display their loyalty to either Whig or Tory junta.

This is the context, then, for the drinking clubs of the eighteenth century. Characteristically they met weekly, in a tavern, to eat and sing and debate. There was the Kit-Kat Club of notable Whigs, which met in Shire Lane, and there was the Robin Hood Club in Butcher Row, which included "masons, carpenters, smiths, and others." The discussions in Shire Lane continued well into the night, but in Butcher Row "each member has five minutes allowed him to speak." There was the Beefsteak Club, which met in a room in the Covent Garden Theatre, and was devoted to drinking and wit "interspersed with snatches of song and much personal abuse." The atmosphere of such a place is evoked by Ned Ward in *The London Spy*: he entered "an old-fashioned room where a gaudy crowd of odoriferous Town-Essences were walking backwards and forwards with their hats in their hands, not daring to convert them to their intended use, lest it should put the foretops of their wigs into some disorder . . . Bows and crimps of the newest mode were here exchanged . . . They made a humming like so many hornets in a chimney corner." In contrast was the poor man's Twopenny Club where one of the rules declared that "If any neighbour swears or curses, his neighbour may give him a kick upon the shins." A club known as the House of Lords met at the Three Herrings in Bell Yard; it was made up from "the more dissolute sort of barristers, attorneys and tradesmen." There were punch clubs, "cutter" clubs for those with boats upon the Thames, and "spouting" clubs for burgeoning public speakers.

These were centres of argument in the combative London tradition, combining obscene songs and egalitarian speeches in equal measure. They were often known as chair clubs, but there were also card clubs for gamesters and cock and hen clubs for youths and prostitutes. There was a No-Nose Club, and a Farting Club in Cripplegate where the members "meet once a Week to poyson the Neighbourhood, and with their Noisy *Crepitations* attempt to out-fart one another." C.W. Heckethorn, in *London Souvenirs*, intones a litany of other London clubs: a Surly Club at a tavern near Billingsgate, filled with the tradesmen of that quarter who met to sharpen "the practice of contradiction and of foul language"; a Spit-farthing Club, which met weekly at the Queen's Head in Bishopsgate, and was "composed chiefly of misers and skinflints; and the Club of Broken Shopkeepers, which met at Tumble Down Dick in Southwark and comprised bankrupts and others unfortunate in trade. The Mock Heroes Club met in an alehouse in Baldwin's Gardens, where each member would assume the name of a "defunct hero," while the Lying Club congregated at the Bell Tavern in Westminster where "no true word" was to be uttered during its proceedings. A Man-Killing Club which met at a tavern in a back-alley adjoining St. Clement Danes admitted to membership no one "who had not killed his man"; but there was also a Humdrum Club "composed of gentlemen of peaceable dispositions, who were satisfied to meet at a tavern, smoke their pipes and say nothing till midnight" when they went homeward. An Everlasting Club was so called "because its hundred members divided the twenty four hours of day and night among themselves in such a manner that the club was always sitting, no person presuming to rise until he was relieved by his appointed successor."

The club tradition continued into the following century with members of the "free and easy" pub institution subscribing a shilling a week; there were also tavern debating clubs, characteristically to be found among such quarters of artisans as Spitalfields, Soho, Clerkenwell, or Finsbury. They were in part derived from the atheistical societies of the previous century, which had met in Wells Street as well as the Angel and St. Martin's Lane, and were similarly disliked by the civic authorities. Many establishments flourished throughout the early nineteenth century in defiance of official policy, however, among them the Swan in New Street, the Fleece in Windmill Street, the George in East Harding Street and the Mulberry Tree in Moorfields. These taverns became the centre of London radical dissent. In 1817 the Hampden Club met at the Anchor Tavern, for example, from which alehouse issued the first demand for universal male suffrage.

There is a case for arguing that these societies and tavern debating clubs are associated, in London at least, with the informal debates of the early eighteenth-century coffee house. Such was the formative influence of that institution, however, that it can be held responsible for a club quite different from those which met in Windmill Street or Moorfields. It became known as "the gentleman's club" which, according to a nineteenth-century account, arose from the "ill-appointed coffee-house or tavern" to effect "a revolution in the constitution of society." White's Club, the oldest of these establishments (1736), is the direct descendant of White's Chocolate-house; Brooks's and Boodle's are of eighteenth-century date but the others, including the Athenaeum and the Garrick, are all of nineteenth-century foundation. These more recent establishments combined private associations with buildings which were deemed and planned to be on a public scale. They were designed by architects such as Wilkins and Barry and Smirke, and, with their bas-relief sculpture and elaborate modelling, they resembled large country houses or Italian palaces. They remain impressive principally because of the essential vulgarity of their appearance. In that sense they are very much the stage property of London.

The endless contrasts of the city can in fact be exemplified by those other gentlemen's clubs of the nineteenth century, the working men's clubs, generally held on the first floor of the local public house where the atmosphere was one of unrefined entertainment. Lectures were sometimes given, as in George Gissing's *The Nether World*—"What would happen to the landlords of Clerkenwell if they got their due. Ay, what *shall* happen, my boys, and that before so very long"—but adult education or jolly debate often gave way to "the rattle of bones, the strumming of a banjo, and a voice raised at intervals in a kind of whoop." In Arthur Morrison's account (1896) of the Feathers in Bethnal Green, there is a clubroom where "the sing-song began, for at least a score were anxious to 'oblige,' " although the effect is somewhat diminished by Morrison's comment that the countenances of those attending were "as of a man betrayed into mirth in the midst of great sorrow." Here again the importance, indeed the stern necessity, of drink is left unstated.

Such places were known variously, according to their locations, as glee clubs or mughouses. Between songs, there were toasts and speeches. The more formal of these establishments were known as saloons and generally demanded money for entrance in exchange for refreshment varying from "ale, inky-coloured porter, or strong beer" to tea and brandy. Tables with covers of oilcloth or leather were pushed against a wall, while at the end of the room was a table and a piano or harp. "There was no curriculum of entertainment," one customer is reported as saying in Roy Porter's *London: A Social History*, "every now & then one of the young women would say, 'I think I'll sing a song.' " A French visitor reported how, at the sound of an auctioneer's hammer rapped upon the table, "three gentlemen, as serious as Anglican ministers, start singing, sometimes alone, sometimes in chorus, sentimental ballads." He also noticed that in some taverns of the same type the landlords "have unfortunately installed mechanical organs which grind away unceasingly." So complaints about pub entertainment are as old as public houses themselves. These taverns and saloons had their counterparts in "night cellars" such as the Cider Cellars in Maiden Lane and the Coal Hole in Fountain Court, the Strand, where established entertainers appeared as singers or performers among the combined fumes of ale, gas-jets and tobacco . . .

A view of London, c. 1630, from its southern bank. The city is seen
here in all its magnificence, with the great church of Southwark rivalling old St. Paul's.
The multitudinous spires afford a glimpse of the medieval city.

The entrance to the Fleet River, depicted by Samuel Scott in the mid-eighteenth
century. London becomes Italianate in paintings of this nature, its dark and noisome
reality effectively banished by the artist's vision.

A detail from a map of London in 1572. The clean thoroughfares and discrete groups of buildings are in a sense deceptive; the sixteenth century was already spiralling out of control.

By 1730 London had burst through its old boundaries and was moving inexorably to the west and to the east. Here it resembles some living organism endlessly growing.

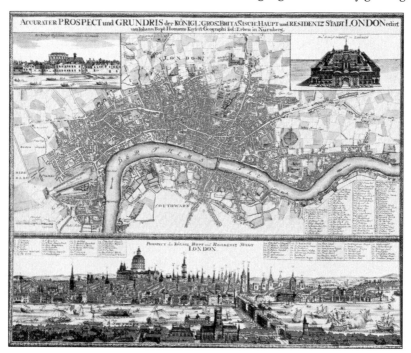

An aquatint of the Great Fire of London of 1666, into which an apocalyptic element has been introduced. Thus London becomes the epitome of all great cities and civilisations upon which punishment and destruction are visited.

Turner's wonderful depiction of the burning of the Houses of Parliament in 1834. This defining moment in the city's history was captured by many different artists.

Thornhill's portrait of Jack Sheppard, the notorious thief who escaped from prison on so many occasions that he became a civic hero. His legend persisted into the nineteenth century when, according to Henry Mayhew, he was better known among children than Queen Victoria.

Cruikshank's cartoon of visiting condemned prisoners in Newgate Prison in the early nineteenth century; those about to hang were part of the theatre of punishment in London.

A strange and disquieting image of mid-eighteenth-century London where the blind street-vendor is surrounded by young chimney sweeps, or "climbing boys." Light and darkness consort together, in a city marked by contrasts.

Meat stalls: in a city of markets and merchants, the role of the shop was fundamental. Butchers, in particular, were known as the leaders of their communities; the melancholy of Londoners was in turn ascribed to the excessive eating of beef.

The greatest market of all was Smithfield. The site of Bartholomew's Fair, it had been the place of burnings, where the martyrs of the Catholic and Protestant faiths met their fate. Thus, farce and mortality came together.

There were certain winters when the Thames was seized with cold and became a thoroughfare of ice. At once the river was turned into a miniature version of London itself, with stalls and shops reflecting the commercial imperatives of the greater whole.

Street entertainment was an integral aspect of London's life; in the early-nineteenth century it was crowded and animated, filled with spectacle and diversion, the city Dickens celebrates in his fiction.

A Rake's Progress.
The rake is about to be
arrested at the top of St. James's
Street. Note the lamplighter spilling
oil upon the unfortunate victim's wig.

The Four Times of Day: Morning.
View of daybreak over Covent
Garden. Here the rake and the rancid
old maid cross each other's path.

Hogarth was the great
caricaturist of London "types,"
inspiring both Fielding and Dickens.

Canaletto's vision of Whitehall was considerably more refined and placid than
the real thing. The sky is important, since London skies are considered — at least by Londoners — to
be unique. COURTESY OF THE TRUSTEES OF THE GOODWOOD COLLECTION

The Adelphi, conceived and executed by the Adam brothers. William Marlow's painting shows the
tower of a waterworks company in the middle distance. Like much else that was beautiful and
memorable in London, the Adelphi was swept away by "improvements."

CHAPTER 39

A Note on Tobacco

All visitors to clubs and pubs saw and smelled "the fume of pipes," and that smoke has hovered over London taverns since Sir Walter Raleigh, according to local legend, first began to smoke in Islington. A few years later an early seventeenth-century German visitor noted that Londoners "are constantly smoking tobacco and in this manner—they have pipes on purpose made of clay, into the farther end of which they put the herb, so dry that may be rubbed into powder, and putting fire to it." Clay pipes are to be found everywhere in archaeological excavations.

Tobacco was at first supposed to have medicinal properties, and could be purchased at the shops of apothecaries, as a "Remedy for phlegmatick people." Children were permitted to smoke it, too, and "in schools substituted a tobacco for breakfast, and were initiated into the trick of expelling the smoke through their nostrils by their masters." One diarist in 1702 recalled an evening with his brother at Garraway's Coffee House where he was "surprised to see his sickly child of three years old fill its pipe of tobacco, after that a second and third pipe without the least concern."

This "strange drug" was everywhere in seventeenth-century London, but it had its detractors who denounced it for creating idleness and stupor.

Even the King, James I, wrote a "Counterblast to Tobacco" in which he describes "an unctuous and oily kind of soot found in some great tobacco-takers that after their death were opened." Yet nothing can dissuade Londoners from taking their amusements, or intoxicants, in a city so reliant upon excess. Although the medicinal properties of tobacco were advertised, its addictive properties soon became evident as a charm against anxiety and isolation—"a Companion in Solitude," as one observer put it, "an Amusement in Company, an innocent Diversion to Melancholy." We hear of early seventeenth-century vagrants, such as the Roaring Boys and the Bonaventoes, smoking pipes. Tobacco became, in that sense, one of the necessary pleasures of the London poor.

Another traveller to seventeenth-century London noted how the citizens smoked their small pipes at a play or in a tavern and how "it makes them riotous and merry, and rather drowsy, just as if they were drunk . . . they use it so abundantly because of the pleasure it gives." It was also a matter of comment that a pipe was "passed round," and that London women smoked "in secret." There was a great trade in tobacco, close to half a million pounds, and so many shops sold pipes and tobacco that in themselves they formed "a large city." So a city of smoke was wreathed within a city of trade. It has been suggested that, in the 1770s, the fashion if not the habit abated; but despite Samuel Johnson's remark, in 1773, that "smoking has gone out," in reality pipe-smoking effortlessly merged with the later use of the cigarette.

Cigarettes entered London soon after the Crimean War: the first manufactory was set up in Walworth in 1857. A second and third were set up in Queen Victoria Street and Leicester Square respectively, under the ownership of Greek immigrants, and the first filter—known as the "Cambridge" cigarette—was manufactured in 1865. "Fag" was the name applied only to the cheaper variety of cigarette. The addiction was always strongly present. In fact the city itself seemed to promote it. "I strive after tobacco," Lamb once wrote, "as other men strive after virtue." The tobacco warehouse in nineteenth-century London Docks contained almost five million pounds' sterling worth of that commodity, and there were very many of the poor who spent time "picking up the ends of cigars thrown away as useless by the smokers in the streets," selling the waste product at a price of 6*d* to 10*d* per pound. Every aspect of London can take part in trade.

CHAPTER 40

A Bad Odour

The smells of London linger. They are "always more pronounced in the heart of the City," according to one late nineteenth-century Canadian writer, Sara Jeanette Duncan, "than in Kensington for instance." She went on to report that "it was no special odour or collection of odours that could be distinguished—it was a rather abstract smell." It has been likened to the smell of rain or of metal. It may be the smell of human activity or human greed. Yet it has been claimed that the smell is not human at all. When rain falls upon the city one of the most characteristic odours is that of "refreshed stone" but that dampness can also produce "the tired physical smell of London." It is the smell of age or, rather, of age restored.

In the fourteenth century the odours were varied and multifarious, from the smell of baking meat to that of boiling glue, from the brewing of beer to the manufacture of vinegar; decayed vegetables competed against tallow and horse-dung, all of which made up "a richly confected cloud of thick and heavy smell which the people had to breathe." This "medieval smell" is at this late date difficult to identify, although perhaps it lingers in stray doorways and passageways where a similar medley of odours confronts the passer-by. There are also parts of the world, as, for example, the *souks* of North Africa, where it is possible to savour something of the atmosphere of medieval London.

Every century, too, has its own smells. In the fifteenth century the dog house at Moorgate sent forth "great noyious and infectyve aiers," while others complained about the reek of the lime kilns situated in the suburbs. The smell of sea coal, in particular, was identified with the smell of the city itself. It was, essentially, the odour of trade which proved unbearable. Thus in the sixteenth century the foundries of Lothbury were a source of much public disquiet. From the north came the smell of burnt bricks, while in the City itself by Paternoster Row emerged "a nauseous smell of tallow." The smell of the Stocks Market, at the eastern end of Cheapside, was so strong that the worshippers in the adjacent church of St. Stephen Walbrook "were overcome by the stench" of rotting vegetables. Those who attended church risked other olfactory perils, however, and the odours emanating from the burial ground of St. Paul's Churchyard alarmed Latimer in the sixteenth century. "I think verily that many a man taketh his death in Paul's Churchyard," he expounded in one of his sermons, "and this I speak of experience, for I myself when I have been there in some mornings to hear the sermons, have felt such an ill favoured unwholesome savour, that I was the worse for it a great while after." This odour of graveyards was in fact one of the most permanent and prolonged smells of the city, with complaints against it from the sixteenth to the nineteenth centuries.

But there is the smell of the living as well as of the dead. References in sixteenth- and seventeenth-century dramatic literature point to the distinctive odour of a London crowd, in particular what Shakespeare described in *Coriolanus* as "their stinking breaths." Julius Caesar is felled by the savour of filthy bodies which belong more to London than to Rome. In the eighteenth century George Cheyne, in *The English Malady*, recoiled from "the clouds of Stinking Breaths and Perspirations . . . more than sufficient to poison and infect the Air for twenty miles." In social reports of the nineteenth century, there are accounts of the noisome scents of "low" tenements and lodging houses which left inspectors faint and sick.

In a city of work and trade one of the principal inconveniences will be that of perspiration, "of greasy cooks at sweating work." London is a kind of forcing house, and within it lies "the mixture of Scents that arose from Mundung as Tobacco, Sweaty Toes, Dirty Shirts, the Shit-Tub, stinking Breaths and uncleanly carcasses." Certainly the more refined Londoner would, on a still day, be aware of the presence of other citizens without necessarily seeing them. The image generally employed is one of close, suffocating contact as if the inhabitants were pressing in on all sides with their rank bodies and dirty breath. This was one of the reasons why strangers and travellers at once felt so anonymous in London: suddenly they became aware of, and part of, the intimate yet cloying smell of human life. When a sixteenth-century report notes that the sick and infirm lie upon the streets of London where "their intolerable miseries and griefs . . . stunk in the eyes and noses of the City," the olfactory sense is linked with the visual to suggest an overpowering sensory horror.

It is also an ageless smell. To walk down a narrow and evil-smelling passage in contemporary London—and there are many such off the main thoroughfares—is to walk again down Fowle Lane or Stinking Alley. To pass too close to an unwashed vagrant is to experience the disagreeable sensation of an eighteenth-century Londoner when confronted with an "Abraham man" or a common beggar. In its smells the city can inhabit many past times.

It should not be assumed, however, that the entire citizenry were unwashed. There was soap as early as the fifteenth century, as well as lozenges to sweeten the breath and unguents to perfume the body. The real problem, as with so many others in the city, concerned the presence and the perceived contamination of the poor. In the seventeenth century the smells of poverty intruded into fashionable areas with "stinking Allies" and "suffocating Yards" beside newly designed squares. The smells of London were a great leveller. The rushes laid upon the floors of poorer households harboured "spittle, vomit, scraps of food, and the leakage of dogs and other animals." In areas such as Bethnal Green and Stepney some of those animals were pigs; in Orchard Street, Marylebone, there were twenty-three houses, which between them contained seven hundred people together with one hundred pigs creating "very nauseous smells." Once more the difference between smell and no smell is decided in London by money. Money is odourless. In the city of finance, poverty stinks. So in the mid-nineteenth century an urban traveller visited the slums of Agar Town by St. Pancras which not even wind and rain could cleanse and where "The stench of a rainy morning is enough to knock down a bullock."

In that century, too, other localities had their own especial odours. The area around Tower Street smelled of wine and tea (in the previous century its aroma was of oil and cheese), while Shadwell's odour was that of the adjacent sugar manufactories. From Bermondsey issued the smells of beer, tanyards,

pickle and "the odour of fruits fomenting for jam" while by the river itself
Thomas Hardy, lodging in Adelphi Terrace, suffered from illness as a result
of the smell of mud at low tide. In nineteenth-century Islington the smell was
of horse-dung and fried fish, while the area around Fleet Street and Temple
Bar was apparently permeated by the "odour of brown stout." Visitors recall
that the "characteristic aroma" of the City itself was of the stables, with an
"anticipatory stench of its cab-stands." The experience of walking from the
Monument to the Thames, however, would unleash a series of identifiable
smells from "damaged oranges" to "herrings."

There were delightful smells as well as disagreeable ones. In the seventeenth century, at midnight, when the bakers of London began to heat their
ovens, and when the kitchens and stoves using sea coal were finally at rest,
then "the air begins to clear and the smoke of the bakeries, which are heated
with wood rather than with coal, spreads a very country-like smell in the
neighbouring air." There were also London streets which had a reputation
for being sweet-smelling; such a place in the sixteenth century was Bucklersbury in "simple" or herb time, and newly built Pall Mall. A Japanese visitor
of 1897 said that the city smelled of food, while at the same time commenting
unfavourably on the breath of London servants. The French poet Mallarmé
suggested that the city had the odour of roast beef as well as the scent of fog
with "a special smell you only find here." At a slightly later date, J.B. Priestley recalled the odour of "greasy little eating houses" as well as that of "a
smoky autumn morning . . . with a railway station smell about it." The smell
of transport, in all its forms, has always been characteristic of the city. In the
spring the omnibus, for example, had the odour of onions and, in winter, of
"paraffin or eucalyptus"; in the summer it was simply "indescribable." Fog
caught the throat "like a whiff of chlorine." Rose Macaulay remembered a
passage off High Street, Kensington, which "smelled of vaseline." Long Acre
smelled of onions, and Southampton Row of antiseptic. Twentieth-century
London has been filled with odours, from the smell of chocolate along the
Hammersmith Road to the smell of the chemical works down Chrisp Street
in the East End and along the locally named "Stinkhouse Bridge."

Old smells have lingered, like the odour of the river and of pubs, while
whole areas have retained their own especial and identifiable atmosphere. An
account of the East End written in the late 1960s notes "an almost overpowering smell of fish" and "boiled cabbage," together with "a musty smell of old
wood and crumbling bricks and stagnant air"; almost a century earlier in 1883
the area was similarly described, in *The Bitter Cry of Outcast London*, as imbued

with "the fragrance of stale fish or vegetables," and the nineteenth-century odour "of drying matchboxes."

The ubiquitous twentieth-century smell, however, has been that of the bus and the motor car. The "air is tainted with their breath," wrote William Dean Howells in 1905, "which is now one of the most characteristic stenches of 'civilisation.' " Other persistent presences include the smell of dog excrement upon the pavements, and the greasy savour emanating from fast-food restaurants. And then, too, there is the dull acrid smell of the underground which is also the smell of London dust and burnt London hair. Worse, however, is the clinging odour of the morning rush hour below the ground with lungfuls of morning breath leaving a metallic quality at the back of the throat. It is both human and inhuman, like the smell of London itself.

CHAPTER 41

You Sexy Thing

Sex, in the city, has commonly been associated with dirt and disease; if not with these, then with trade. The resemblance exists even within the language itself; "hard core" is a term conventionally applied to pornography but its original meaning, in a London context, was that of "hard, rock-like rubbish" used in the building of roads and houses. Where there is rubbish, there is also death. The area around the Haymarket, a notorious haunt of prostitutes, encompasses "a march of the dead. It is a plague-spot—the real plague spot."

From its earliest days London has been the site of sexual activity. A Roman model of a phallus was found in Coleman Street—later, paradoxically, a haven for Lollards and Puritans—as well as an architrave depicting three prostitutes. In the precincts of the Roman temple, where Gracechurch Street and Leadenhall Street now are, there would have been erotic celebrations connected with Saturn or Priapus, and beside the amphitheatre on the present site of the Guildhall we might expect to find a *palaestra* or promenade frequented by male and female prostitutes. There were brothels licensed by the Roman authorities, as well as "fornixes" or arches beneath which were located "mere dirty shacks" employed for the purposes of fornication. E.J. Burford, in his learned *London: the Synfulle Citie*, has remarked that on certain street corners a "herm" was placed, "a short stone pillar of Hermes" with an erect penis and "prepuce painted a brilliant red."

Yet the use of arches and brothels meant that, in this most commercial of cities, sex had itself already been commercialised. In the centuries of Danish and Saxon occupation, young women were bought and sold like any other merchandise. "Gif a man buy a mayden with cattle," according to one Saxon injunction, "let the bargain stand if it be without guile." A thousand years later an eighteenth-century nursery rhyme contained the line, "I had to go to London town and buy me a wife." There are supposed to have been auctions for women in certain secret markets, continuing well into the nineteenth century, and the emphasis upon finance is sustained by the enquiry of the late twentieth-century prostitute, "Do you want any business?" So does the spirit of London imprint itself upon the desires of its inhabitants. London is dedicated to selling. But the poor have nothing to sell, so they sell their bodies. Thus, sexual lust is free to roam down every lane and alley. London has always been the scene of covert debauchery.

Those medieval chroniclers who cited London for its drunkenness and sinfulness also rebuked it for its rapists and its lechers, its harlots and its sodomites. In the twelfth century there is reference to Bordhawe, an area of brothels in the parish of St. Mary Colechurch. In the thirteenth century, and probably much earlier, there was a Gropecuntlane in the two parishes of St. Pancras and St. Mary Colechurch (also known as Groppecountelane, 1276 and Gropecontelane, 1279); the context and meaning here are obvious enough. In the same period there are references to Love Lane "where yonge couples were wont to sport" and Maid Lane "so-called of wantons there."

Beside Smithfields there was also Cock Lane, which in 1241 was "assigned" for sexual congress. It became in a sense the first red-light district, notorious for prostitutes; "at the approach of night they sally forth from their homes . . . low taverns serve them as a retreat to receive their gallants." The description was pertinent at any time from the thirteenth to the nineteenth centuries, and serves to emphasise how one small area can continue the same activity even as the city changes all around it. That lane was inhabited by the very types of London, such as Mrs. Martha King, "a little fat woman, known last winter by her velvet gown and pettecoat," Mrs. Elizabeth Brown, "who has been a dealer in cullies [young girls] ever since she was fifteen; modest and pleasant enough, till after the third bottle," and Mrs. Sarah Farmer, "a great two-handed strapper, having no charms either in person or in humour." In *Piers Plowman* (*c.* 1362) Langland also commemorates "Clarice, of cokkeslane, and the clerke of the cherche."

In the fourteenth century there are records of proceedings against whores, courtesans and bawds as well as whoremongers. In June 1338 William de Dalton was arrested for "keeping a house of ill fame in which married women and their paramours were wont to resort" and in the following month Robert de Stratford was arraigned for harbouring prostitutes.

In the following year Gilbert le Strengmaker, of Fleet Street, was charged with maintaining "a Disorderly House harbouring prostitutes and sodomites" while at the same sessions two courtesans, "Agnes and Juliana of Holborne," were also accused of harbouring sodomites. So there was in medieval London a thriving homosexual community, which aligned itself with the world of brothels and bawds. It would be tempting to describe it as an underworld except that it was well known and ubiquitous.

Charges were laid against brothels in the wards of Aldersgate, the Tower, Billingsgate, Bridge (here one prostitute was known as Clarice la Claterballock), Broad Street, Aldgate, Farringdon and elsewhere. Many of those arrested for sexual offences came from areas far from London itself, however, suggesting that the reports of sexual licence—and profit—had spread throughout the country. London had long ago become the centre of England's sinfulness. A great chronicle of the period, *Brut*, remarks upon "ladies . . . waerynge Foxtayles sewed wythynne to hide their arses," while another reports on the ladies of the town with "breasts and bellies exposed." There were in fact sumptuary laws which proscribed lewd women from wearing the same clothes as "noble Dames and Damsels of the Realm"; they were obliged to wear striped garments as a sign of their profession, which indirectly suggests the level of tolerance exercised in medieval Catholic London: prostitution was neither banned nor excluded.

The level of vice was in late medieval London far higher, or at least more open, than at any period in the nineteenth or twentieth centuries; it reached such an extent that it provoked alarm among the city authorities who in 1483 published a proclamation against "the Stynkynge and Horrible Synne of Lecherie . . . which dayly groweth and is used more than in dayes past by the means of Strumpettes, mysguded and idyll women dayly vagraunt." There were attempts then to remove the "mysguded" from the more respectable thoroughfares of the city, by confining the women to the areas of Smithfield and Southwark beyond the walls. But in Southwark the Bankside brothels south of the river were continually placed in jeopardy by the whims or panics of the authorities, and the women themselves chose to congregate in areas such as St. Giles, Shoreditch (where they still can be seen), and Ave Maria Alley beside St. Paul's Cathedral. They were also to be found in the Harry in Cheapside, the Bell in Gracechurch Street, and a score of other stews within the city. The derivation of the term "stews" comes not from some reference to cloying meat or hot broth, but from the old French for artificially stocked fishponds—*estuier*, to shut up. That sense of closeted heat, stew-boiled, was exacerbated by the incidence of syphilis which in the sixteenth century became the object of outrage from moralists and rage from satirists.

The sexual life of the city continued regardless, in any case, with visitors remarking on the casual intimacy of the relations between the sexes. A Venetian of the sixteenth century commented that "Many of the young women gather outside Moorgate to play with the young lads, even though they do not know them . . . They kiss each other a lot." Married females seem to have taken part in the same pursuit, and in the early seventeenth century a tall flagpole was set up on the shore of the Thames, just past Deptford, "to which horns of all kinds and descriptions are fixed, in honour of all the English cuckolds or horn carriers . . . and the English have much fun and amusement with each other, as they pass by and doff their hats to each other and to all around." It was well known, as the title of one early seventeenth-century London broadside put it, to be *A Marry'd Woman's Case*.

The ubiquity of whores meant that they had a hundred different nicknames—punks, madams, fireships, jilts, doxies, wagtails, drabs, smuts, cracks, mawkes, trulls, trugmoldies, bunters, does, punchable nuns, molls, Mother Midnights, blowzes, buttered buns, squirrels, mackerels, cats, ladybirds, blowzabellas, and others. Madame Cresswell of Clerkenwell was a notorious procuress, who was painted and engraved on several occasions; in her house she kept "Beauties of all Complexions, from the cole-black clyng-fast to the golden lock'd insatiate, from the sleepy ey'd Slug to the lewd Fricatrix" and she corresponded with agents all over England to discover the young and the attractive. She was one of many famous London bawds. In the first of his series *A Harlot's Progress*, Hogarth pictured Mother Needham who owned a notorious brothel in Park Place. But she was pelted to death in the pillory, and Hogarth had to substitute for her Mother Bentley who was equally famous in the streets of London. These "Mothers" were indeed the mothers of a city of lust.

Some of its daughters, and its sons, were young indeed. "Every ten yards," a German traveller wrote, "one is beset, even by children of twelve years old, who by the manner of their address save one the trouble of asking whether they know what they want. They attach themselves to you like limpets . . . Often they seize hold of you after a fashion of which I can give you the best notion by the fact that I say nothing about it."

Boswell's diary of street life in 1762 provides an account of sexual favours currently on offer. On the evening of Thursday 25 November, he picked up a girl in the Strand, and "went into a court with intention to enjoy her in armour [i.e. wearing a condom]. But she had none . . . she wondered at my size, and said if ever I took a girl's maidenhead, I would make her squeak." On the night of 31 March, in the following year, "I strolled into the Park and took the first whore I met, whom I without many words copulated with free from danger, being safely sheathed. She was ugly and lean and her breath smelled of spirits. I never asked her name. When it was done, she slunk off." On 13 April, "I took a little girl into a court; but wanted vigour." Boswell, often a moralist after the event, does not regard the fact that it was a "little girl" as of any significance; this suggests that there were many such thrown upon the streets of London.

When Thomas De Quincey met one of them, Ann, he spent many nights with her walking "up and down Oxford Street" but "she was timid and dejected to a degree which showed how deeply sorrow had taken hold of her young heart." He left her for a while, naming a spot at the corner of Titchfield Street where they should wait for each other. But he never saw her again. He looked for Ann in vain among the thousand faces of young girls in the London crowd and called Oxford Street "stony hearted stepmother, thou that listenest to the sighs of orphans, and drinkest the tears of children." This compassionate attitude to the suffering of young female prostitutes rarely, if ever, emerges in eighteenth-century records, including that of Boswell. The month after taking the "little girl into a court," for example, Boswell picked up a woman and "conducted her to Westminster Bridge, and then in armour complete did I engage her upon this noble edifice." This, in the slang of the time, was probably "a threepenny upright." "The whim of doing it there with the Thames rolling below us aroused me much."

To Boswell she was only a "low wretch" and by definition unclean; therefore, after the event, she became an object of suspicion and threat. Boswell was always terrified of catching venereal disease, like most of his contemporaries. John Gay in a purview of London warned against the pursuit of

the tawdry band
That romp from lamp to lamp—for health expect
Disease, for fleeting pleasure foul remorse
And daily, nightly, agonising pains

Such were the pains suffered by Casanova who, after visiting a prostitute in
the Canon Tavern, was infected with gonorrhoea.

Casanova described how on an earlier occasion he entered another
brothel, the Star Tavern, where he ordered a private room. He engaged in
conversation with "the grave and reverend landlord"—a good aside, touching the assumed character of many London brothel-keepers—before turning
away all the women who came to his room. "Give a shilling for the porters
and send her away," said his host after the first refusal. "We don't trouble
ourselves about ceremonies in London."

There was no ceremony when Samuel Johnson was accosted by a prostitute in the Strand—"No, no, my girl," he murmured, "it won't do." Richard
Steele was approached by another such girl, "newly come upon the Town,"
near the Piazza in Covent Garden. She asked "if I was for a Pint of Wine"
but, under the arches of the Market at twilight, he noticed in her countenance
"Hunger and Cold; Her Eyes were wan and eager, her Dress thin and
tawdry, her Mien genteel and childish. This strange Figure gave me much
Anguish of Heart, and to avoid being seen with her I went away."

The Strand and Covent Garden, as well as all the lanes which crossed
them, were known places of sexual resort. There were public houses in the
vicinity where "posture dancers" performed an eighteenth-century version
of striptease; there were "houses of pleasure" which specialised in flagellation, and there were "Mollie houses" which were frequented by homosexuals. The *London Journal* of May 1726 discovered twenty "Sodomitical
Clubs"—including, it would seem, the "Bog-Houses" of Lincoln's
Inn—"where they make their execrable Bargains, and then withdraw into
some dark Corners to perpetrate their odious Wickedness." Mother Clap's in
Holborn, and the Talbot Inn in the Strand, were favourite meeting-places for
homosexual men, and there was a male brothel by the Old Bailey "where it
was customary for the men to address each other as 'Madam' or 'Ladyship.' "
The Horseshoe in Beech Lane, and the Fountain in the Strand, were the eighteenth-century equivalent of "gay pubs" while the area around the Royal Exchange was known for its "cruising" when, as a contemporary verse put it,
"Sodomites were so impudent to ply on th'Exchange." Pope's Head Alley

and Sweetings Alley were all streets with a similar reputation; the male owner of a tavern or brothel in Camomile Street was known as "the Countess of camomile." At Mother Clap's itself there were beds in every room with "commonly thirty to forty Chaps every Night—and even more—especially on Sunday Nights," while in a Beech Street brothel were found "a company of men fiddling dancing and singing bawdy songs." There was a darker side to these festivities, however. When a certain "Club of Buggerantoes" was raided, several of those arrested committed suicide, among them a mercer, a draper and a chaplain. There were also many cases of blackmail so that there was danger, as well as excitement, in the city. Nevertheless London remained the centre of homosexuality where, under conditions of privacy and anonymity, the elect could pursue their calling. City juries were in any case notoriously reluctant to pronounce the capital sentence for the crime of sodomy; the usual verdict was "attempted" sodomy, for which a fine, short imprisonment, or spell in the pillory, was sufficient. Londoners are characteristically lenient in matters of sexual impropriety. How can they be otherwise in a city where every form of vice and extravagance is continually available?

The sexual ambience of nineteenth-century London, despite the cliché of "the Victorian age" as one of upright family values, was no less lascivious than its eighteenth-century counterpart. In her *London Journal* Flora Tristan wrote in 1840 that "in London all classes are deeply corrupted. Vice comes to them early." She had been shocked by an "orgy" in a tavern where English aristocrats and Members of Parliament disported themselves with drunken women until daybreak. In quite a different sphere Henry Mayhew noted of London street children that "their most remarkable characteristic . . . is their extraordinary licentiousness." As a result of his observations he guessed that the age of puberty came much earlier than most people believed; he declined to give, however, "the details of filthiness and of all uncleanness." Even in the areas where the more respectable working class lived, it was customary for couples as young as thirteen and fourteen to live and procreate without the need for marriage vows; there was a church in Bethnal Green, for example, where these "Cockney marriages" could be performed and where "you might be married for sevenpence if you were fourteen years old." One curate of the East End recalled a Christmas morning when he "stood marrying blaspheming youths and girls to one another . . . ghastly mockery." Here sexual profligacy is associated with a general irreligion or atheism which is another characteristic emblem of London life.

Yet the major concern of nineteenth-century urban observers lay with the extent and nature of prostitution. Surveys—by Mayhew, by Booth, by Acton and others—suggest that it became something of an obsession. There were books entitled *Prostitution in London*, or, more elaborately, *Prostitution, Considered in its Moral, Social & Sanitary Aspects*. There were tables and statistics about where prostitutes were kept, lodged or resorted, with divisions and subdivisions: "Well-dressed living in Brothels," "Well-dressed living in Private Lodgings," "In Low Neighbourhoods," "Introducing Houses" and "Accommodation Houses." There were detailed observations on "Bent and Character of Mind," "Manner of Passing Their Leisure Hours," "Moral Defects" (spiritous liquor) and "Good Qualities" (strong sympathy for one another). Prostitution seems to have been the overwhelming consideration of Victorian social reformers, complementary to the efforts of other workers in matters of sanitation and housing; in that sense all were concerned with the inheritance of a thousand years of unchecked urban living, with a strong effort to cleanse or purify it.

The connection of sexuality and disease was also explicitly made. William Acton, in *Prostitution in London*, revealed that these "rouged and whitewashed creatures, with painted lips and eyebrows, and false hair, accustomed to haunt Langham Place, portions of the New Road, the Quadrant . . . the City Road, and the purlieus of the Lyceum" were on investigation more often than not found to be "a mass of syphilis." The characteristic metaphor of waste or refuse was also adduced. "As a heap of rubbish will ferment, so surely will a number of unvirtuous women." The prostitute then becomes a symbol of contagion, both moral and physical. Of the eighty thousand in London in the 1830s, it was said that eight thousand would die each year. In the London hospitals 2,700 cases of syphilis occurred each year "in children from eleven to sixteen years of age." The actual number of female prostitutes was a subject of endless speculation and invention—seventy thousand, eighty thousand, ninety thousand, or higher, and in the mid-nineteenth century it was computed that "£8,000,000 are expended annually on this vice in London alone." In that sense prostitution itself becomes a token of London's commercial rapacity, as well as of the fears attendant upon the overwhelming growth of both vice and the city itself.

The degradation of civilisation, in the very centre of London, can take

many different forms. Some of them were recorded in Ryan's *Prostitution in
London*, published in 1839. "Maria Scoggins, aged fifteen, held a situation as
a stay-maker. On her way to her father's house in the evening she was decoyed to a brothel kept by Rosetta Davis, alias Abrahams, and turned upon
the streets." Another girl, aged fifteen "was actually sold by her step-mother
to the keeper of one of these houses in the eastern part of London." Unwary
children of both sexes were merchandise. Leah Davis was an elderly female,
the mother of thirteen daughters, "all either prostitutes or brothel-keepers."
The metaphor of youth being sacrificed is redolent of barbaric rituals at the
altars of Troy or Gomorrah, while the image of girls "thrown," "turned," or
"decoyed" upon the streets suggests a vision of a dark and labyrinthine city
where innocence is quickly scented and destroyed. Three girls of fifteen were
despatched to lure many youths together "so as to make their united payments considerable"; "they were admitted to the scene of depravity which the
establishment unfolded . . . These houses were used as lodging houses for
thieves, vagabonds, mendicants, and others of the lowest grade . . . it was well
known that the most diabolical practices were constantly perpetrated within
them . . . in the midst of a dense and ignorant population . . . Men, women and
children, of all ages, were there associated for the vilest and basest purposes . . . spreading a moral miasma around." This is a record of what was
considered to be the shadow of pagan darkness not in the suburbs, or in well-
localised stews, but in the very heart of the city.

But if one image of the London prostitute was of disease and contagion, embodying in striking form all the anxieties and fears which the city itself may
provoke, the other was of isolation and alienation. De Quincey's account of
Ann, daughter of stony-hearted Oxford Street, is one of the first examples of
that urban vision which sees in the plight of the young prostitute the very
condition of living in the city; she had become a prey to all its merciless commercial forces as well as to its underlying indifference and forgetfulness.

Dostoevsky, when wandering down the Haymarket, noticed how
"mothers brought their little daughters to make them ply the same trade." He
observed one girl "not older than six, all in rags, dirty, bare-foot and hollow
cheeked; she had been severely beaten and her body, which showed through
the rags, was covered with bruises . . . Nobody was paying any attention to
her." Here we have an image of suffering in London, amid the endlessly hurrying and passing crowd who would no more pause to consider a bruised
child than a maimed dog. What struck Dostoevsky, who himself was used to

terror and hopelessness in his own country, was "the look of such distress, such hopeless despair on her face . . . She kept on shaking her tousled head as if arguing about something, gesticulated and spread her little hands and then suddenly clasped them together and pressed them to her little bare breast." These are the sights and pictures of London. On another evening a woman dressed all in black passed him and hurriedly thrust a piece of paper in his hand. He looked at it and saw that it contained the Christian message "I am the Resurrection and the Life." But how could anyone believe the precepts of the New Testament, when they had witnessed the pain and loneliness of a six-year-old girl? When the city was described as pagan, it was partly because no one living among such urban suffering could have much faith in a god who allowed cities such as London to flourish.

Yet perhaps the true gods of the city are of a different nature. When the Shaftesbury Memorial Fountain, otherwise known as Eros, was unveiled in 1893 at Piccadilly Circus, it was only a few yards from the infamous Haymarket where mothers had brought their young daughters for sale. Eros was the first statue ever made of aluminium, and in that conflation of ancient passion and new-minted metal, we have an emblem of desire as old and as new as the city itself. Eros has been drawing people ever since. In a twentieth-century novel by Sam Selvon, entitled *The Lonely Londoners*, one of the protagonists, a Trinidadian, notices that the "circus have magnet for him, that circus represent life, that circus is the beginning and ending of the world."

Throughout this century Piccadilly Circus has been the site of nightly sexual encounters, and an area where young people drift in search of adventure. It is a place where all the roads seem to meet, in endless disarray, and it exudes an atmosphere both energetic and impersonal. That is perhaps also why it has been for many decades a centre of prostitution and easy pick-ups, both male and female. It has always been the part of London most identified with casual sex. "There were regular places they haunted," Theodore Dreiser wrote of London prostitutes at the beginning of the twentieth century, "Piccadilly being the best," and that sentiment has been echoed in a thousand novels and documentary reports. The statue of Eros has, after all, commanded a strange power. The city itself is a form of promiscuous desire, with its endless display of other streets and other people affording the opportunity of a thousand encounters and a thousand departures. The very strangeness of London, its multifarious areas remaining unknown even to its inhabitants, includes the possibility of chance and sudden meetings. To be

alone or solitary, a characteristic symptom of city life, is to become an adventurer in search of brief companionship; it also is the mark of the predator.
The anonymity or impersonality of London life is itself the source of sexual
desire, where the appetite can be satisfied without the usual constraints of a
smaller society. So the actual vastness of London encourages fantasy and illimitable desire.

That is why the general sexual condition of London has always remained
the same, in its voraciousness and insatiability. Today, there are strip bars
and clubs where lap dancers perform; a thousand pubs and nightclubs cater
for every kind of sexual perversity; there are streets known for prostitutes
and parks used at night for cruising. Whole areas of London at night assume
a different face, so that the city is like some endlessly fecund source which can
offer alternative realities and different experiences. That is why it is in itself
"sexy," displaying its secret places and tempting the unwary. To turn just one
more corner, or walk down one more path, may bring . . . who knows what?
The telephone booths are littered with advertisements for sadistic or trans-
sexual prostitutes, some of them claiming to be "new in town" or "new to
London." They are reminiscent of the eighteenth-century prostitute in
Covent Garden, "newly come upon the Town." But nothing is ever new in
London, where the young still offer up their bodies for sale.

CHAPTER 42

A Turn of the Dice

Drink, sex and gambling once always consorted together. They were the trinity of London vice and weakness, an unholy threesome which disported happily across the city. They represented recklessness and defiance, in the face of an uncertain life in a city bedevilled by insecurity.

All the commercial and financial institutions of London were established upon a giant gamble, so why not participate in the same perilous but enthralling game? Your encounter with a prostitute might lead to a fatal disease, but a turn of the dice might make you wealthy; then, in the face of all these hazards and difficulties, you might drink to forget. The social historian of eighteenth-century London, M. Dorothy George, noted that the "temptations to drink and gamble were interwoven with the fabric of society to an astonishing extent, and they did undoubtedly combine with the uncertainties of life and trade to produce that sense of instability, of liability to sudden ruin." Many men of business were ruined by dissipation and gambling—*Industry and Idleness*, charting the decline of a London apprentice through drink, dice and women to eventual hanging at Tyburn, was a characteristic London story.

The first evidence of gambling in London can be adduced from the Roman period, with the excavation of dice carved out of bone or jet. The unexpected turns of life, as then experienced, are also revealed in the elaborate equipment of a fortune-teller found beneath Newgate Street. In the early medieval period Hazard was played in taverns and other low houses, together with another dice game known as Tables. In medieval brothels, too, gambling and drinking were part of the service. Quarrels over a game were sometimes fatal and, after one round of Tables, "the loser fatally stabbed the winner on the way home." There was plentiful scope for fraud, also, and there are reports of the gaming boards being marked and the dice loaded. Yet the passion for gaming was everywhere. An excavation in Duke's Place revealed "a piece of medieval roof-tile shaped into a gaming counter," according to a report in *The London Archaeologist,* and as early as the thirteenth century there were rules in Westminster for the punishment of any schoolboy found with dice in his possession. A stroke of the rod was delivered for every "pip" on the dice.

Playing cards were imported into London in the fifteenth century, and their use became so widespread that in 1495 Henry VII "forebad their use to servants and apprentices except during the Christmas holidays." Stow records that "From All hallows Eve to the day following Candlemas-day there was, among other sports, playing at cards, for counters, nails and points, in every house." They were found in every tavern, too: packs of cards had the names of various inns imprinted upon them. Their merits were widely advertised. "Spanish cards lately brought from Vigo. Being pleasant to the eye by their curious colours and quite different from ours may be had at 1/- [one shilling] a pack at Mrs. Baldwin's in Warwick Lane." The business in cards became so brisk that the tax upon their sale is estimated to have furnished in the mid-seventeenth century an annual income of five thousand pounds which meant that "some 4.8 million packs of cards" must have been traded.

Fulham earned a reputation as early as the sixteenth century for its dubious traffic in dice and counters; it is evoked by Shakespeare in *The Merry Wives of Windsor,* where

> For gourd and fullam holds
> And "high" and "low" beguile the rich and poor.

A fullam in this context was a loaded die. Another recognised centre for gambling was Lincoln's Inn Fields. Here boys "gambled for farthings and oranges"; one popular game was the Wheel of Fortune with a movable hand spinning within a circle of figures, "the prize being gingerbread nuts the size of a farthing." These gaming fields of course attracted dissolute Londoners. Lincoln's Inn Fields was the recognised harbour for "idle and vicious vagrants" known collectively as its Mummers. Among them were Dicers and Chetors and Foists who specialised in gambling. Dice were carved out of true so that they seemed "good and square, yet in the forehead longer on the cater and tray than the other."

"What shifts have they to bring this false die in and out?"
"A jolly fine shift that properly is called foisting."

So went a dialogue in a pamphlet entitled *Manifest Detection*, which outlined a score of other tricks used by the fraternity of the Shifters. Another pamphlet, *Look on me, London*, warned against the city's tricks and devices to gull the innocent or the unwary; strangers and visitors were liable to be duped or defrauded by "the Picker-Up, the Kid, the Cap and the Flat," nicknames which seem to span the generations. And, once more, the language used to describe London's principal vices is one of corruption and contagion. Dice and cards "were the Green Pathway to hell, whereby followed a hundred gowtie, dropsy diseases." In a city terrified of sickness and epidemic plague the metaphors for any type of excess, or pleasure, become insistent.

The fever ran unabated. When the floor of the Middle Temple Hall was taken up in 1764 "no less than a hundred pair" of dice were found to have slipped through its boards during the play of previous generations. In the mid-seventeenth century Pepys observed of the players in one gaming house, "how ceremonious they are as to call for new dice, to shift their places, to alter their manner of throwing" and he noticed "how some old gamesters that have no money now to spend as formerly do come and sit and look on as among others." These places became known in London as "hells," and in them Pepys heard the cries of the damned. So "one man being to throw a seven if he could, and failing to do it after a great many throws cried he would be damned if ever he flung seven more while he lived." Another player, who had won, shouted out, "A pox on it, that it should come so early upon me, for this fortune two hours hence would be worth something to me but then, God damn me, I shall have no such luck."

The London gaming houses were often characterised, too, as places where gentlemen and noblemen would sit down with the "meaner" sort, to use Pepys's word. The same observation was made in the late twentieth century, in connection with casinos and gaming clubs where the aristocracy and the underworld consorted. The dissipations of London, like the city itself, act as great levellers. Lord Chesterfield, perhaps struck by the egalitarian mood of the city, once remarked that "he preferred playing with a sharper to playing with a gentleman, for though he might not often win of the former, he was sure when he did win to get paid."

By the early eighteenth century there were approximately forty gaming houses in the city, known as subscription-houses and slaughter-houses as well as hells. There were "more of these infamous places of resort in London," according to Timbs's *Curiosities of London*, "than in any other city in the world." They were recognisable by an ornate gas-lamp in front of the entrance and a green or red baize door at the end of the hallway. Gaming rose in frequency and excessiveness throughout the century, a century which by curious chance was the one most marked by financial uncertainty and sudden ruin. Thus in the age of the Bubble, and other panics, whist was perfected by gentlemen who met at the Crown Coffee House in Bedford Row.

Gaming was declared illegal but, despite nightly raids upon certain selected hells in the city, it continued to flourish. There was always "assembled a mixed crowd of gentlemen, merchants, tradesmen, clerks and sharpers of all degrees and conditions," ready to play at Hazard, Faro, Basset, Roly-poly and a score of other games involving dice and cards. Into these hells came the puffs, the flashers, the squibs, the dunners, the flash captains with a regiment of spies, porters and runners to give notice of approaching constables. At Almacks, a famous gaming club in Pall Mall, the players "turned their coats inside out for luck"; they put on wristbands of leather to protect their lace ruffles and wore straw hats to guard their eyes from the light and to prevent their hair from tumbling. Sometimes, too, they put on "masks to conceal their emotions." At Brooks's, the twenty-first rule stated that there should be "No gaming in the eating room, except tossing up for reckonings, on penalty of paying the whole bill of the members present." There were other less agreeable occasions for a wager, as recorded in *London Souvenirs*. A prospective player once dropped down dead at the door of White's; "the club immediately made bets whether he was dead or only in a fit; and when they were going to bleed him the wagerers for his death interposed, saying it would affect the fairness of the bet."

Londoners, according to one foreign observer, "violent in their desires, and who carry all their passions to excess, are altogether extravagant in the article of gaming." Another visitor offered a similar account. "What will you lay? is the first question frequently asked by high and low, when the smallest disputes arise on subjects of little consequence. Some of the richer class, after dinner over a bottle, feel perhaps an inclination for betting; the one opens a nut with a maggot in it, another does the same, and a third immediately proposes a bet, which of the two worms will crawl first over a given distance."

Betting was of course involved in the games of violence—rat-catching, cockfighting, female wrestling—with which London abounded, but natural phenomena also became the subject of speculation. On the morning after violent tremors in the city, bets were laid at White's "whether it was an earthquake or the blowing up of powder-mills." It was indeed an earthquake, one of the less predictable hazards of London life.

A market-worker in Leadenhall "made a bet that he would walk 202 times around Moorfields in twenty seven hours; and did it." A minister of state, the Earl of Sandwich, "passed four and twenty hours at a public gaming table, so absorbed in play, that, during the whole time, he had no subsistence but a bit of beef, between two slices of toasted bread, which he eat without ever quitting the game. This new dish grew highly in vogue . . . it was called by the name of the minister who invented it."

The traditions of public gaming were continued into the nineteenth century by such places as the Royal Saloon in Piccadilly, the Castle in Holborn, Tom Cribb's Saloon in Panton Street, the Finish in James Street, the White House in Soho Square, Ossington Castle in Orange Street, and Brydges Street Saloon in Covent Garden otherwise known as "The Hall of Infamy" or "Old Mother Damnable's." On the other side of London, in the East End, there were gambling rooms and gambling clubs, to such an extent that one minister working among the poor of the area informed Charles Booth that "gambling presses drink hard as the greatest evil of the day . . . all gamble more than they drink." The street urchins gambled with farthings or buttons, in a card game known as Darbs, and betting on boxing or horse-racing was carried on through the agency of tobacconists, publicans, newsvendors and barbers. "All must bet," according to another informant in Charles Booth's survey of the East End, "Women as well as men . . . men and boys tumble out in their eagerness to read the latest 'speshul' and mark the winner."

And then of course there was the lottery. It was first established in London in 1569. The "passion for lucky numbers" has burned for centuries. "Aleph" in *London Scenes and London People* noted that acquaintances, on a sudden meeting, would talk not about the weather but "the great prize just, or about to be, drawn, and to the fortunate winner, or to the blank you had just drawn, and your confident belief that No. 1,962 would be the £20,000 prize." There were lottery magazines as well as lottery glovers, hat-makers and tea-dealers who offered a small share on their ticket if you used their services. The winning ticket was chosen in the Guildhall by a blindfolded Bluecoat schoolboy (a London version of blindfolded Fortuna), and around the building were "prostitutes, thieves, dirty workmen, or labourers, almost naked—mere children, pale and anxious, awaiting the announcement of the numbers." In *1984*, George Orwell's vision of a future London, there is also "the Lottery": "It was probable that there were some millions of proles for whom the Lottery was the principal if not the only reason for remaining alive. It was their delight, their folly, their anodyne, their intellectual stimulant." Orwell understood London very well, and here he is suggesting some deep connection between the principle of its civilisation and the necessity of the gamble and the cheat. Londoners require the stimulus, and the desperate hope of gain; the chances are infinitesimal but, in so vast and disproportioned a city, that is taken for granted. A wager can be shared with many millions, and still be a wager. The anticipation and anxiety are shared also, so that gambling can be viewed as a sudden spasm of communal attention.

Today the betting shops and casinos are full in Queensway and Russell Square, in Kilburn and Streatham and Marble Arch, and a hundred other locations. Life, in London, can then be construed as a game which few can win.

An etching by James Gillray, which caricatures Sheridan as Punch blowing
theatrical bubbles above the heads of a cheering crowd. London has always
been a theatrical city and its mobs were once part of its *dramatis personae*.

CHAPTER 43

Mobocracy

In a city of rumour and of fluctuating fortune, of excess in every form, the London crowd has over the generations acquired an interesting pathology. The crowd is not a single entity, manifesting itself on particular occasions, but the actual condition of London itself. The city is one vast throng of people. "On looking into the street," one seventeenth-century observer recalled, "we saw a surging mass of people moving in search of some resting place which a fresh mass of sightseers grouped higgledy piggledy rendered impossible. It was a fine medley: there were old men in their dotage, insolent youths and boys . . . painted wenches and women of the lower classes carrying their children." A "medley" suggests a show or spectacle, and in the mid-seventeenth century painters began subtly to examine the London crowd. It was no longer an indistinct mass, seen from a safe distance, but a general group of people whose particular features were differentiated.

There was always the noise, as well as the spectacle. "It was very dark, but we could perceive the street to fill, and the hum of the crowd grew louder and louder . . . about eight at night we heard a din from below, which came up the street continually increasing till we could perceive a motion." The loud indistinct hum, rising to a roar and accompanied by strange general motion, is the true sound of London. "Behind this wave there was a vacancy, but it filled apace, till another like wave came up; and so four or five of these waves passed one after another . . . and throats were opened with hoarse and tremendous noise." There is something crude, and alarming, about this sound; it is as if the voice of the city were primeval, unearthly. The occasion described here, in Burke's *The Streets of London Through the Centuries*, was a late seventeenth-century anti-Catholic procession down Fleet Street, and its air of menace is enlarged by the reference to how "one with a stenterophonic tube sounded 'Abhorrers! Abhorrers!' most infernally." The sound of London can be harsh and discordant. Yet sometimes its collective breath is charged with misery. On the day of the execution of Charles I, 30 January 1649, a great throng was assembled in Whitehall; at the instant of the blow which removed the king's head, "there was such a Grone by the Thousands then present, as I never heard before & desire may never hear again."

Yet, for the royalists of the seventeenth century, the throng of London were "the scum of all the profanest rout, the vilest of all men, the outcast of the people . . . mechanic citizens, and apprentices." The crowd, in other words, became a tangible threat; it was turning into a mob (the word was coined in the seventeenth century) which might become King Mob.

The salient fact was that London had grown immeasurably larger in the sixteenth and seventeenth centuries, and so obviously the size of its crowds was enlarged. In an atmosphere of religious and political controversy, too, there was no model of civic polity to restrain them. Pepys records a crowd "bawling and calling in the street for a free Parliament and money" and, in the summer of 1667, "it is said that they did in open streets yesterday, at Westminster, cry 'A Parliament! a Parliament!,' and do believe it will cost blood." In the following year there were riots in Poplar and in Moorfields, and the new prison at Clerkenwell was broken open by the people to rescue those who had been imprisoned for the old London custom of pulling down brothels. "But here it was said how these idle fellows have had the confidence to say that they did ill in contenting themselves in pulling down the little bawdy-houses and did not go and pull down the great bawdy house at Whitehall." This is the authentic radical and levelling voice of the Londoner, newly become a crowd or throng or mob, in the heart of the city. "And some of them last night had a word among them, and it was 'Reformations and Reducement.' This doth make the courtiers ill at ease to see this spirit among the people."

So London had become dangerous. "When a mob of chairmen or servants, or a gang of thieves or sharpers, are almost too big for the civil authority," wrote Henry Fielding, "what must be the case in a seditious tumult or general riot?" The history of the eighteenth-century crowd displays a gradual change of temper which was disturbing to magistrates such as Fielding. The scorn and insults were no longer primarily levelled at strangers or outsiders but, rather, at those of wealth or authority. "A man in court dress cannot walk the streets of London without being pelted with mud by the mob," Casanova wrote in 1746, ". . . the Londoners hoot the king and the royal family when they appear in public." In this "chaos," as Casanova described it, "the flower of the nobility mingling in confusion with the vilest populace," the "common people affect to show their independence . . . the most wretched Porter will dispute the wall with a Lord." It was similarly reported by Pierre Jean Grosley that "In England no rank or dignity is secure from the insults" and that "no nation is more satirical or quicker at repartee, especially the common people." A Frenchman made the acute point that "This insolence is considered by many only as the humour and pleasantry of porters and Watermen; but this humour and pleasantry was, in the hands of the long parliament, one of their chief weapons against Charles the First." "Repartee" and insult can, in other words, have political consequences. In that context it is perhaps worth noting that the street urchins used the statue of Queen Anne, outside St. Paul's Cathedral, as the target for their practice of throwing stones.

One of the characteristics of the London mob was its irritability and sudden changes of mood, so that when a spark was struck in its depths it flared up very quickly. When an offender did not arrive at a pillory in Seven Dials, as expected, the crowd erupted in a fury which principally fell upon passing hackney coaches; they were pelted with filth and ordure while the coachmen were forced to cry out "Huzza!" as they went along. At one controversial election meeting in Westminster "in a very few minutes the whole scaffolding, benches and chairs and everything else were completely destroyed." The rage of the crowd was random and sporadic, fierce and exhilarating in equal measure. One German visitor, after a visit to Ludgate Hill, noted: "Now I know what an English mob is." He was driving in a coach, at a time of general rejoicing at the release from prison in 1770 of the great London politician, Wilkes, and recalled "half-naked men and women, children, chimney sweeps, tinkers, Moors and men of letters, fish-wives and elegant ladies, each creature intoxicated by his own whims and wild with joy, shouting and laughing."

It is as if the very restriction of the city encouraged the sudden appetite for wildness and licence; the restraints imposed by a mercantile culture, ruinous in its effects upon many who comprised the crowd, encouraged rapid volatility of rage and exhilaration. There were also too many people forced into too small a space, and this massive overcrowding in narrow streets engendered strange fevers and excitements. That is why the instinctive fear of the mob, or crowd, had as much to do with its propensity for disease as its prevalence towards violence. It was the fear of touch, of the unhealthy warmth of London as transmitted by its citizens, which went back to the times of fever and of epidemic plague when, in the words of Defoe, "their hands would infect the things they touched, especially if they were warm and sweaty, and they were generally apt to sweat too."

The mob can also turn upon itself, or upon one of its number. The cry of "a *Pick Pocket!*" in *Moll Flanders* set the crowd alight when "all the loose part of the Crowd ran that way, and the poor Boy was deliver'd up to the Rage of the street, which is a Cruelty I need not describe." There is an element of sudden horror here, as if a whirlpool of rage manifested itself without warning. A record of the last days of a reputed astrologer and magician, John Lambe, in the middle of June 1628, is printed in "The Life and Death of John Lambe," by Leva Goldstein in *Guildhall Studies in London History*. Lambe was recognised by some boys in the Fortune Theatre who waited outside "and followed him when he left." More people joined them, and Lambe hired some passing sailors to form a protective bodyguard; he walked down Red Cross Street, turned left into Fore Street and then left again to the Horseshoe Tavern in Moor Lane, the crowd growing larger and louder all the time. He dined in the inn, while the sailors "kept the crowd at bay" but, when he left and entered the city by Moorgate, the mob once more pursued him with cries of "Witch" and "Devil." The situation was now very serious. He walked quickly down Coleman Street, into Lothbury, where he took refuge in an upstairs room of the Windmill Tavern on the corner of Old Jewry. His bodyguards were assaulted, and both entrances to the tavern watched by the eager citizens. He attempted to leave in disguise but was again marked down; he took refuge in a nearby house, belonging to a lawyer who called out four constables of the ward to guard him. "But the rage of the people so much increased . . . that in the midst of these auxiliaries they struck him down to the ground" and beat him with stones and clubs; he never spoke again, and was carried to the Poultry Compter where he died of his injuries on the following day. This is an accurate report on the actions of a characteristic London crowd.

. . .

If you had any hope of finding "a community life" in London, "all foreigners" agree that it is as if you searched "for flowers in a vale of sand." There was no community in London in the eighteenth century, and no sense of communal life, only a number of distinctive and distinguishable crowds. There were crowds of women attacking bawdy houses or dishonest shops, crowds of citizens alerted by a "hue and cry," crowds of parishioners attacking a local compter, crowds watching a fire, crowds of beggars, and, most ominously, crowds of distressed or unemployed workers. One eminent London historian, Stephen Inwood, has in fact remarked in his *A History of London* that rioters "could be a form of 'collective bargaining' between labourers and masters." In 1710 there was violent rioting by framework-knitters, which presaged decades of unrest and disorder in the poor urban districts such as Whitechapel and Shoreditch.

There were riots by silk-weavers and coal-heavers, hat-makers and glass-grinders, and a host of assorted tradesmen whom creeping industrialisation and increased food prices had rendered ever more desperate. Indian calico was a threat to the weavers of Spitalfields, for example, and one woman was attacked by a crowd who "tore, cut, pulled off her gown and petticoat by violence, threatened her with vile language, and left her naked in the fields." London channelled the energies of its citizens in the crooked shape of its lanes and thoroughfares, rendering them ever more fierce and desperate.

That is why the process of city life itself was seen as a movement within a crowd. Sometimes it is indifferent and banal, an aspect of "the great metropolis" where exists "the vast unhurried audience that will still gather and stare at any new thing." Yet on occasions its speed and confusion were decisive, as in Gray's poem where on the streets of the city the crowd "Tumultuous, bears my Partner from my side." This is a defining image, well expressed in *Moll Flanders*: "I took my leave of her in the very Crowd and said to her, as if in hast, dear Lady *Betty* take care of your little Sister, and so the Crowd did, as it were Thrust me away from her." The impersonal crowd parts friend from friend, and separates loved one from loved one; those dearest to us are no longer near, borne away by the surging tide in unknown directions. Yet for some there is comfort to be found in this anonymity. "I shall therefore retire to the Town," wrote Addison in the *Spectator* of July 1711, ". . . and get into the Crowd again as fast as I can, in order to be alone." The crowd encourages solitude, therefore, as well as secrecy and anxiety.

The nineteenth century inherited all these propensities but, in the enormous Oven or Wen, the crowd became increasingly impersonalised. Engels, the great observer of imperial London, remarked that "the brutal indifference, the unfeeling isolation of each . . . is nowhere so shamelessly barefaced . . . as just here in the crowding of the great city." By which he meant not only the crowding in the thoroughfares, as the indifferent mass of people moved in preordained directions, but the general overpopulation within the capital; it had become dense to blackness with the number of human lives within it. Engels recorded again that "The very turmoil of the streets has something repulsive, something against which human nature rebels. The hundreds and thousands of all classes and ranks crowding past each other . . ." He noticed, too, how "each keeps to his own side of the pavement, so as not to delay the opposing streams of the crowd, while it occurs to no man to honour another with so much as a glance." The nineteenth-century London crowd was a new phenomenon in human history, which is why so many social and political reformers chose to observe it. In Engels's account, for example, it became a mechanism imitating the financial and industrial processes of the city, representing an almost inhuman force. Lenin rode on the top of an omnibus the better to observe the movement and nature of this strange creature; he reported upon "groups of bloated and bedraggled lumpen proletarians, in whose midst might be observed some drunken woman with a black eye and a torn and trailing velvet dress of the same colour . . . The pavements were thronged with crowds of working men and women, who were noisily purchasing all kinds of things and assuaging their hunger on the spot." In his account the London crowd became the fierce embodiment of energy and appetite, with the forces of its dark life intimated by the black eye and black dress of the drunken woman.

When Dostoevsky lost his way, among the crowds, "what I had seen tormented me for three days afterwards . . . those millions of people, abandoned and driven away from the feast of humanity, push and crush each other in the underground darkness . . . The mob has not enough room on the pavements and swamps the whole street . . . A drunken tramp shuffling along in this terrible crowd is jostled by the rich and titled. You hear curses, quarrels, solicitations." He sensed all the chaos of collective experience, in a city which was itself a curse, a quarrel and a solicitation. The whole mass of nameless and undifferentiated citizens, this vast concourse of unknown souls, was a token both of the city's energy and of its meaninglessness. It was also an emblem of the endless forgetfulness involved in urban living. "The children of the poor, while still very young, often go out into the streets, merge with the crowd and in the end fail to return to their parents." They achieved, in other words, the final destiny of city dwellers—to become part of the crowd.

There is a short story by Edgar Allan Poe, set in London in the 1840s, entitled "The Man of the Crowd." The narrator is to be found in a coffee house beside one of the principal thoroughfares, studying the nature and composition of the "two dense and continuous populations" passing the door. Many had "a satisfied business-like demeanour . . . their brows were knit and their eyes rolled quickly; when pushed against by fellow-wayfarers they evinced no impatience." But there also emerged a "numerous class" who "were restless in their movements, had flushed faces, and talked and gesticulated to themselves . . . if jostled, they bowed profusely to the jostlers, and appeared overwhelmed with confusion." Here then are two types of the London crowd. There are the satisfied travellers in the stream of life and time, and the awkward or confused who cannot join its steady progress. They apologise for their confusion, but only by talking to themselves can they manage any communication.

The narrator notices junior clerks, wearing the fashions of last year, and upper clerks or "steady old fellows"; he looks upon pickpockets, dandies, pedlars, gamblers, "feeble and ghastly invalids upon whom death had placed a sure hand," modest young girls, ragged artisans, exhausted labourers, piemen, porters, sweeps, "drunkards innumerable and indescribable—some in shreds and patches, reeling, inarticulate." The London crowd of the mid-nineteenth century is revealed here, "all full of noisy and inordinate vivacity which jarred discordantly upon the ear and gave an aching sensation to the eye."

Then the narrator is arrested by one countenance, that of an old man, which displays caution and malice, triumph and avarice, merriment and "extreme despair." He resolves to learn more about him and, through the night, he follows him. In streets filled with people the old man's pace is quick and restless but in deserted thoroughfares he shows signs of "uneasiness and vacillation." He runs down abandoned streets until he finds a crowd leaving the theatre—here, moving among them, "the intense agony of his countenance abated." He joins a party of gin-drinkers jostling outside the entrance to a public house and "with a half shriek of joy . . . stalked backward and forward, without apparent object, among the throng." In the small hours of the night he walks to an area of poverty and crime, where "the abandoned of London" are "reeling to and fro"; then, at daybreak, he returns "with a mad energy" to a principal thoroughfare where "he walked to and fro, and during the day did not pass from out the turmoil of the street."

Finally the narrator understands who, or what, he has been following. It is the embodiment of the crowd, the no-thing which feeds off the turbulent life of the streets. The old man, with a face expressive "of vast mental power . . . of coolness, of malice," is the spirit of London.

Others came to the city precisely to experience this new and strange life of the crowd. "Whenever I want to get an idea for painting or writing I always throw myself among the thickest crowds such as Earl's Court or Shepherd's Bush," one nineteenth-century Japanese artist wrote. "Let the crowds push me to and fro—I call it a human bath." And Mendelssohn could not disguise his delight at being plunged "in a vortex" where among the endless stream of people he could view "shops with signs as huge as a man and stage coaches piled up with people and a row of vehicles left behind by pedestrians . . . Look at that horse rearing in front of a house where his rider has acquaintances and those men used for carrying advertisements . . . look at the negroes and those stout John Bulls with their slender, beautiful daughters hanging on their arms." A description of Londoners, in 1837, quoted in *London Bodies*, may also be apposite. "The appearance of the people in the streets of London," John Hogg wrote, "is one of the first things that attracts the notice of strangers. The native inhabitants . . . are somewhat under middle size, but their limbs and features are generally well formed. They are of spare habit, but rather muscular; they are characterised by firmness of carriage, and an erect, independent air; they move with a measured step, and generally at a very brisk pace. The features are generally very strongly marked, and pointed; the eye in particular presents an openness and fullness that is remarkable. The tout-ensemble of the countenance bears an air of keenness, animation and intelligence, that distinguish the Londoner from his country neighbour."

The crowd of the nineteenth century was also aware of itself as a new form of human congregation. That great representative of Victorian feeling, W.P. Frith, endlessly depicted crowds in paintings which themselves attracted endless crowds. The London theatres were filled with melodramas in which the transient crowd was the characteristic setting for individual stories of pathos and violence. There is an account by George Gissing of the continuous movement "of millions" on Jubilee Day (1887). "Along the main thoroughfares of mid London where traffic was now suspended; between the

houses moved a double current of humanity . . . a thud of footfalls numberless and the low unvarying sound that suggested some huge beast purring to
itself in stupid contentment." So the crowd becomes a beast, contented and
obedient, wandering through the city which has created it. But then its movements may become suddenly alarming. "These big crossings are like
whirlpools; you might go round and round, and never get anywhere." It is
easy to see "how perilous such a crowd might be."

The crowd, aware of its identity, sends signals to itself. During a bad reverse for British troops during the Crimean War, "we all stood about the
streets—regardless of all appearances, reading the telegrams (in the newspaper) with breathless anxiety . . . There was a perfect sea of newspapers and
curious faces behind, intense gravity prevailed . . . People walked along
speaking in whispers and muttering." The citizens of London then become
one body with a corporate feeling of dismay; the crowd is alive and alert, responding in unison. The cry of "Mafeking is relieved," on 17 May 1900 at
nine thirty in the evening, had an equally instantaneous effect upon this corporate body. "Instantly the cry was taken up on the omnibuses and the people
came clambering down in hot haste to hear the news repeated over and over
again . . . Others rushed off into the byways, carrying the tidings further and
further away, and all the time the streets became thicker with people cheering, shouting and singing." This mass excitement is almost as disturbing as
the "intense gravity" of the crowd recorded four months earlier; both show
symptoms of that excess and over-reaction, close to hysteria, by which city
life is characterised.

There is something childish about the mob in action, as if it had been brutalised, or infantilised, by the condition of living in the city. In the fourteenth
century the London mob greeted one supposed enemy with a "savage yell,"
and five centuries later at a Chartist meeting in Coldbath Fields "a most fearful shout burst from the lips of the crowd." It is the same terrifying and im-
placable voice. In 1810 the crowds during the Burdett riots "stopped all
vehicles and compelled the occupants to signify their adherence to the cause."
In the same period a mob around a pillory "resembled beasts dipped in a stagnant pool." The "vast and tumultuous crowds" which gathered to watch the
battle of Sidney Street in 1911 provoked similar reactions, when a reporter for
the *News Chronicle* noted that "the voices of these many thousands came up to
me in great murderous gusts, like the roar of wild beasts in a jungle."

Yet the city itself is curiously unmoved by its crowds. One of the reasons
for civic peace in London, as opposed to other capitals, lies directly in its size.

Its very scale determines its quietness. It is at once too large and too complex to react to any local outbreaks of passionate feeling, and in the twentieth century the most marked characteristic of riots and demonstrations was their failure to make any real impression upon the stony-hearted and unyielding city. The disappointment of the Chartist uprising in 1848, preceded by a large meeting on Kennington Common, anticipated the inability in 1936 of Oswald Mosley to proceed down Cable Street with thousands of fascist sympathisers. It was as if the city itself rebuked them and held them back. The poll tax riots of the late 1980s, around Whitehall and Trafalgar Square, were another instance of a violent local disturbance which did not affect the relative composure of the rest of the city. No movement could sweep through the entire capital, and no mob could ever control it. The city is so large, too, that it renders the average citizen powerless in its presence. In the early decades of the twentieth century there was something curiously compliant and complacent, not to say conservative, about the Cockneys; unlike the Parisians they did not want to fight the conditions of the city and were happy to live with them unchanged. That happy equilibrium could not last.

One unwelcome novelty of the latter half of the twentieth century, for example, was the race riot, among the most notable being those of Notting Hill in 1958 and of Brixton in 1981. The Notting Hill riots began with individual harassment of black men by gangs of white youths, but an incident on 23 August provoked a full-scale riot. Tom Vague, in the aptly named *London Psychogeography*, describes "a crowd of a thousand white men and some women . . . tooled up with razors, knives, bricks and bottles." In the following week a large mob proceeded down Notting Dale and beat up any West Indian they could find, but the worst rioting took place on Monday 1 September, in the central area of Notting Hill Gate. Mobs congregated in Colville Road, Powis Square and Portobello Road before going on a "smashing rampage, chanting 'Kill the niggers!' . . . women hang out of windows shouting, 'Go on boys, get yourselves some blacks.' " One observer noted that "Notting Hill had become a looking-glass world, for all the most mundane objects which everyone takes for granted had suddenly assumed the most profound importance. Milk bottles were turned into missiles, dustbin lids into primitive shields." So an area of London becomes profoundly charged with the emotions of its inhabitants; everything is irradiated and transformed by their hatred. The accoutrements of a civilised city had suddenly been transformed into primitive weapons.

A youth leader remarked that "Those sort of boys take up any activity to break the boredom," and in the twentieth century boredom had to be considered a component of any crowd behaviour. The sheer daily tedium of living in impoverished and unprepossessing surroundings is enough to break the spirit of many Londoners, who feel themselves trapped in the midst of the city without redress or relief. It creates not apathy but active tedium. Thus the violence starts.

On that Monday evening the West Indians collected together in Blenheim Crescent with "an armoury of weapons including milk bottles, petrol and sand for Molotov cocktails." The white mob entered the area, with shouts of "Let's burn the niggers out!," and were greeted by home-made bombs. The police arrived in force, just before things could develop into out-and-out race war; some rioters were arrested, the others dispersed. Then by curious chance the great heat of these August days was swept away by a thunderstorm, the rain falling among the debris of broken bottles and wooden clubs. At their trial in September certain white rioters were told: "By your conduct you have put the clock back 300 years." But this would only take them back to 1658; they had in fact behaved like their medieval predecessors who "swarmed" upon supposed enemies or aliens with often fatal results.

In the spring of 1981 the young black Londoners of Brixton, enraged by the perceived prejudice and oppression of the local police, erupted in street-rioting. For the first time petrol bombs were used in attacks upon the police, together with the conventional deployment of bottles and bricks, while a general wave of burning and looting left twenty-eight buildings damaged or destroyed. The depth and diversity of the disturbances suggest that they had a cause more fundamental than those of police oppression, however, and we may find it in the propensity among certain Londoners for riot and disorder. It then becomes a way of fighting structural oppression, whereby the very texture and appearance of the streets are oppressive and oppressing.

Poverty and unemployment have also been cited as the causes of sporadic violence, like that in Brixton; certainly they confirm the character of the city as a prison, confining or trapping all those who live within it. What more inevitable consequence, therefore, than rage against its conditions and its custodians? There have been other race riots; there have been riots against the police; there have been riots against the financial institutions in the City of London. Reports produced after the event characteristically refer to "the collapse of law and order" as well as the "fragile basis" of civic peace. But in fact the curious and persistent feature of London life is that "law and order" have never collapsed and that civic peace has been maintained even in the face of grave disorder. It is often wondered how, in its diversity and bewildering complexity, the city manages to function as a single and stable organism. In a similar fashion the fabric of the city, despite a variety of assaults, has always been preserved. Its mobs have never yet dominated it.

CHAPTER 44

What's New?

The crowd lives upon news and upon rumour. Elizabeth I recalled that, as a princess, she had asked her governess, "What news was at London?" On being told that it was rumoured she was about to marry Lord Admiral Seymour, she replied, "It was but a London news." So in the sixteenth century "London news" was considered to be fleeting and inaccurate but, even so, the object of much curiosity. In *King Lear* the "poor rogues / Talk of Court news . . . who loses and who wins; who's in, who's out." Shakespeare also invoked "the newes / Of hurly burly innovation" in *Henry IV, Part One* as well as "the new newes at the new Court" in *As You Like It*. It was often observed that, on entering a coffee house, the first and immediate enquiry was "What news? What news?"

The city is the centre of scandal, slander and speculation; the citizens are rumourmongers and backbiters. In the sixteenth century there were handbills and pamphlets and broadsheets devoted to the more sensational events of the day, and the street-sellers ensured that they were reported from door to door. In 1622 a weekly pamphlet of news was published in London, under the rubric of "Weekly Newes from Italy, Germanie, Hungary, Bohemia, the Palatinate, France and the low Countries etc." Its success was such that it provoked the publication of many other weekly pamphlets which went under the common title of "Corantos." The "news" was treated with great suspicion, however, as if the reports of London were based on faction or fractiousness. It was not an honest city and the editor of the *Perfect Diurnal*, Samuel Peche, was described in the 1640s as being "constant in nothing but wenching, lying and drinking." He was, in other words, a typical Londoner.

There was one other aspect of London "news" which did not escape the attention of Ben Jonson. In his *The Staple of Newes* (1625) he suggests that news ceases to be "news" when it is printed and distributed; its essence is intelligence given in whisper or rumour, the kind of report that in the fifteenth or sixteenth centuries could permeate all London within a very short period. Jonson had his own view, then, of the "stationer" or publisher of news, who

knows Newes well, can sort and ranke 'hem
And for a need can make 'hem.

In 1666 the *London Gazette* emerged as the most authoritative of the public prints. "It inserts no News but what is certain," wrote one contemporary, "and often waits for the Confirmation of it, before it publishes it." It was printed on single sheets each Monday and Thursday, and was sold on the streets by vendors known as "Mercury women" calling out "*London's Gazette here!*" in Cornhill, Cheapside and the Royal Exchange. Macaulay described it as containing "a royal proclamation, two or three Tory addresses, notices of two or three promotions, an account of a skirmish between the imperial troops and the Jannissaries . . . a description of a highwayman, an announcement of a grand cockfight between two persons of honour, and an advertisement offering a reward for a stray dog." It may be considered certain that the highwayman, the cockfight and the dog provoked the most attention.

It is some indication of the appetite for news in London that its first daily newspaper, *Daily Courant*, issued in 1702, predates by some seventy-five years the appearance of a "daily" in Paris. By the end of the eighteenth century there were 278 newspapers, journals and periodicals available in the city. Most of this astonishing number were published within the Strand, Fleet Street and those adjoining streets east of the present Waterloo Bridge and west of Blackfriars.

Fleet Street is an example of the city's topographical imperative, whereby the same activity takes place over hundreds of years in the same small area. In this case, too, it was an activity that dominated the character and behaviour of those who took part in it, so that it can be said that the very earth and stones of London created their own particular inhabitants. In 1500 Wynkyn de Worde set up his printing press opposite Shoe Lane, and in the same year Richard Pynson established himself as a publisher and printer a few yards down the road at the corner of Fleet Street and Chancery Lane. He was succeeded as Printer to Henry VIII by Thomas Berthelet who set up shop by the conduit, again opposite Shoe Lane, and in the early 1530s William Rastell began a printing firm in the churchyard of St. Bride's. William Middleton printed at the George, Richard Tottell at the Hand and Star, John Hodgets at the Flower de Luce—all signs within the narrow and crowded thoroughfare.

"This part of London," wrote Charles Knight, "is a very Temple of Fame. Here rumours and gossip from all regions of the world come pouring in, and from this echoing hall are reverberated back in strangely modified form echoes to all parts of Europe." So it is an echoic as well as ancient place, a part of London from which that strange commodity known as news spreads in all directions.

In the eighteenth century news was disseminated largely by means of the daily and weekly journals provided by coffee houses and taverns. "What attracts enormously in these coffee-houses," wrote Saussure "are the gazettes and other public papers. All Englishmen are great newsmongers. Workmen habitually begin the day by going to coffee-rooms in order to read the latest news. I have often seen shoe blacks and other persons of that class club together to purchase a farthing paper." Another eighteenth-century account, by Count Pecchio, is of "English working men" in taverns for whom "are published a number of Sunday newspapers which contain an abridgement of all the intelligence, anecdotes, and observations, which have appeared in the daily newspapers in the course of the week." "In the coffee-houses, as soon as the newspaper arrived," wrote another commentator, "there was the silence of the grave. Each person sat absorbed in his favourite sheet, as if his whole life depended on the speed with which he could devour the news of the day."

Here we have the image of the Londoner as "devourer" of the news, just as he was a devourer of food and drink. It is one of the first intimations of the "consumer," one who can only experience the world by the act of ingestion or assimilation. A city is perhaps by its nature an artificial arrangement, so it creates artificial demands. Addison characterised as a definite London type "the Newsmonger" that "rose before Day to read the *Postman*" and was avid for the "*Dutch* Mails" and "inquisitive to know what passed in *Poland*." There were those who followed the latest case of rape or divorce in the Sunday newspapers, with the same avidity as their medieval counterparts purchased ballads "o' the newest and truest matter in London." The search for fresh titillation or sensation is strong and enduring and, in a city where the inhabitants are surrounded by a bewildering variety of impressions, only the most recent can be entertained. That is why, in a city of fire, the latest news is "hot," especially at the coffee house "where it is smoking new." "Our News should indeed be published in a very quick Time," commented the *Spectator*, "because it is a Commodity that will not keep cold." It must be shouted out like "Fire!" to arrest the attention of the passers-by.

London itself was like a newspaper, as Walter Bagehot observed, where "everything is there, and everything is disconnected," a series of random impressions and events and spectacles which have no connection other than the context in which they were found. In reading the newspaper, the Londoner was simply continuing with the normal perceptions of urban life; he "read" the public prints and the city itself with the same idle curiosity, as if the newspaper confirmed that vision of the world which London had already imparted to him. The very form of the city was imprinted in the pages of the journals—a man called Everett of Fleet Street sold his wife to one Griffin of Long Lane for a three-shilling bowl of punch (1729), a boar lived off the rubbish of Fleet Ditch for five months (1736), a man found frozen and standing upright in the same ditch had been drunk and fallen into the mud (1763), bread and cheese were thrown to the populace from Paddington steeple according to annual custom (1737), the wife of one Richard Haynes was delivered of a monster with nose and eyes like a lion (1746), a grave-digger was found smothered to death by his own exertions in an open grave (1769), a man stood up in the church of St. Sepulchre and shot at a choir of charity children (1820), a man named James Boyes walked in front of the congregation in a chapel at Long Acre and proclaimed himself Jehova Jesus (1821). And so it goes on, endlessly, the "news" conveying the accidents and disasters of the city in columns of print like thoroughfares. It was well known to the firemen of London, as one of their greatest hazards, that a crowd would spring up immediately around any great conflagration in order to witness the course of its destruction.

That is why, in a period of growth and uproar, the news itself became more strident. The sale of early nineteenth-century newspapers, for example, was a raucous affair. "Bloody News," "Horrible Murder!" and "Extraordinary Gazette" were bellowed out "with stentorian lungs, accompanied by a loud blast of a long tin horn" by porters and costermongers who kept editions of the papers under their hatbands. The advent of the steam-printing press also allowed the newspapers to imitate the "resistless force" of London, with all its energy and expansiveness. Two and a half thousand copies of *The Times* could be printed every hour and the whole process came to the attention of Charles Babbage, the inventor of the prototype computer, who remarked that the great rollers of the steam press devoured sheets of white paper "with unsated appetite." Charles Knight noted that the courts around Fleet Street are "bustling and vivacious" with the production of more news to ever larger readerships—"the fingers of the compositors cease not; the clash and clang of the steam press knows no intermission." Sales of newspapers amounted in 1801 to sixteen million copies; thirty years later it had increased to thirty million, and the figures continued to rise.

Ford Madox Ford in *The Soul of London*, published in the first years of the twentieth century, remarked that in the capital "you must know the news, in order to be a fit companion for your fellow Londoner. Connected thinking has become nearly impossible, because it is nearly impossible to find any general idea that will connect into one train of thought." So the consciousness of the Londoner is composed of a thousand fragments. Ford recalled that, as a child, "the Sunday paper . . . was shunned by all respectable newsagents" and that he had to walk two miles to pick up an *Observer* from "a dirty, obscure and hidden little place." But Sunday sales soon became as large as, if not larger than, daily sales. The hegemony of "news" in London was maintained and increased throughout the century as new techniques of printing and lithography were introduced. Perhaps the most significant transition, however, took place in 1985 when News International moved its production of the *Sun* and *The Times* to Wapping. This sudden and clandestine operation destroyed the restrictive "Spanish practices" of London printers, while the employment of new technology facilitated the expansion of other newspaper organisations which moved from Fleet Street to sites south of the river and to Docklands itself. The echoic force of Fleet Street has gone for ever. But "London news" is still paramount. As one twentieth-century social observer, Lord Dahrendorf, puts it, Britain "is run from London in virtually all respects."

To the history of rumour and of news must be added that of craze and of cheats, again mediated by the collective agency of the crowd. The popularity of fashions and delusions and false prophecies has always been most intense in the capital. The gullibility of the citizens is perpetual. The various bubbles of the eighteenth century encompassed the South Sea financial disaster as well as a fashion for Italian music; "how ill a taste for wit and sense prevails in the world," Swift wrote, "which politicks and South-sea, and party and Operas and Masquerades have introduced." When Mary Tofts was believed to have given birth to a succession of rabbits, in the autumn of 1726, "every creature is in town, both men and women have been to see and feel her . . . all the eminent physicians, surgeons and man-midwives in London are there Day and Night to watch her next production." The seventeenth- and nineteenth-century craze for tulips in the West End was rivalled only by that for the aspidistra in the East End of the early twentieth century. In the early part of that century, too, there was a fashion for china cats "and forthwith no home was complete without a cat." A living cat caught "the news" in 1900: it was the cat that licked a stamp at Charing Cross Post Office, which then attracted crowds wanting it to perform the same feat over and over again. The cat became a "stunt" which, in the words of one journalistic practitioner, represented "the creation of the temporary important." A captured elephant called Jumbo was responsible for songs, stories and a range of sweets known as "Jumbo's chains" before fading out of public memory.

Yet all the fashions of London are transitory. Chateaubriand noticed this in 1850 when he remarked upon "The fashions in words, the affectations of language and pronunciation, changing, as they do, in almost every parliamentary session in high society in London." He remarked how the vilification and celebration of Napoleon Bonaparte succeeded each other with extraordinary swiftness in London, and concluded that "All reputations are quickly made on the banks of the Thames and as quickly lost." "A catch word in every one's mouth one winter," wrote Mrs. Cook in her *Highways and Byways in London*, (1902), "is quite forgotten by next summer." Horace Walpole remarked, on the same subject, that "Ministers, authors, wits, fools, patriots, whores, scarce bear a second edition. Lord Bolingbroke, Sarah Malcolm and old Marlborough, are never mentioned but by elderly folk to their grandchildren, who had never heard of them." To be "out of sight" in London was to be "forgotten." In 1848 Berlioz wrote that in London there were a great many "whom the sight of novelties only makes more stupid." They watch the trajectory of events and careers "with the eye of a postilion at the side of the railway track reflecting on the passing of a locomotive."

And so the history of London is also the history of forgetting. In the city there are so many strivings and impulses which can only momentarily be entertained; news, rumour and gossip collide so quickly that attention to any of them is swift but short-lived. One craze or fashion follows another, as the city talks endlessly to itself. This transitoriness of urban affairs can be traced back to the medieval period. "Certainly by the fourteenth century," G.A. Williams noted in *Medieval London*, "nothing lasted long in London." And forgetfulness itself can become a tradition; on the first Tuesday of June, ever since a benefaction in the late eighteenth century, a sermon is preached at the church of St. Martin within Ludgate upon the theme that "Life is a bubble." It is highly appropriate that London should celebrate its transience in a permanent fashion. It is a city endlessly destroyed and endlessly restored, vandalised and renewed, acquiring its historical texture from the temporary aspirations of passing generations, an enduring myth as well as a fleeting reality, an arena of crowds and rumour and forgetfulness.

A Cockney flower-seller dressed in the traditional accoutrements of her trade. Flower-sellers congregated around Eros in Piccadilly Circus, and were last seen in the early years of the twentieth century. They were generally poor and dishonest.

CHAPTER 45

Give the Lydy a Flower

It may come as a surprise to those who see nothing but narrow streets and acres of rooftops that, according to the latest Land Cover Map taken from the Landsat satellite, "over a third" of London's total land area "is semi-natural or mown grass, tilled land and deciduous woodland." It has always been so. One of the first delineators of London, Wenceslaus Hollar, was surprised by the contiguity of city and country. His *London, Viewed from Milford Stairs, View of Lambeth from Whitehall Stairs* and *Tothill Fields*, all dated 1644, show a city encompassed within trees and meadows and rolling hills. His "river views" also suggest the presence of open countryside just beyond the frame of the engraving.

In the first years of the eighteenth century, pastures and open meadows began by Bloomsbury Square and Queens Square; the buildings of Lincoln's Inn, Leicester Square and Covent Garden were surrounded by fields, while acres of pasture and meadow still survived in the northern and eastern suburbs outside the walls. Wigmore Row and Henrietta Street led directly into fields, while Brick Lane stopped abruptly in meadows. "World's End" beside Stepney Green was a thoroughly rural spot, while Hyde Park was essentially part of the open countryside pressing upon the western areas of the city. Camden Town was well known for its "rural lanes, hedgeside roads and

lovely fields" where Londoners sought "quietude and fresh air." Wordsworth recalled the song of blackbirds and thrushes in the very heart of the
city and De Quincey found some consolation, on moonlit nights, in walking
along Oxford Street and gazing up each street "which pierces northwards
through the heart of Marylebone to the fields and woods."

From the early medieval period onward, almshouses and taverns, schools
and hospitals, had their own gardens and private orchards. The city's first
chronicler, William Fitz-Stephen, noted that "the citizens of London had
large and beautiful gardens to their villas." Stow recorded that the grand
houses along the Strand had "gardens for profit" while within the city and its
liberties there were many "working gardeners" who produced "sufficient to
furnish the town with garden ware." In the sixteenth and seventeenth centuries gardens occupied the area between Cornhill and Bishopsgate Street
while the Minories, Goodman's Fields, Spitalfields and most of East Smithfield were comprised of open meadows. Gardens and open ground were to be
found from Cow Cross to Grays Inn Lane, as well as between Shoe Lane and
Fetter Lane. Milton, born and educated in the very centre of the city, always
professed an affection and admiration for the "garden houses" of London.
His own houses in Aldersgate Street and Petty France were fine examples of
that construction, and it is said that at Petty France the poet planted a cotton-
willow tree in the garden "opening into the Park."

Today there are many "secret gardens" within the City itself, those remnants of
old churchyards resting among the burnished buildings of modern finance.
These City gardens, sometimes comprising only a few square yards of grass
or bush or tree, are unique to the capital; they have their origin in the medieval or Saxon period but, like the city itself, they have survived many centuries of building and rebuilding. Seventy-three of them still exist, gardens of
silence and easefulness. They can be seen as territories where the past may
linger—among them, St. Mary Aldermary, St. Mary Outwich, and St. Peter's
upon Cornhill—or perhaps their lesson can be adduced from the open Bibles
in the hands of sculpted monks in the church of St. Bartholomew in Smithfield. The page to which they attend, as they congregate around the recum-
bent figure of Rahere, reveals the fifty-first chapter of Isaiah. "For the Lord
shall comfort Zion: He will comfort all her waste places; and He will make
her wilderness like Eden, and her desert like the garden of the Lord."

The image of the garden haunts the imaginations of many Londoners.
Among the first painted London gardens is *Chiswick from the River* by Jacob

Knyff. This urban garden is small in scale, and set among other houses. It is dated between 1675 and 1680; a woman walks along a gravelled path, while a gardener bends down towards the earth. They might have appeared in the twentieth century. Albert Camus wrote, in the middle of that century, "I remember London as a city of gardens where the birds woke me in the morning." In the western areas of London of the twenty-first century almost every house either has its own garden or shares a community garden; in northern areas such as Islington and Canonbury, and in the southern suburbs, gardens are an integral feature of the urban landscape. In that sense, perhaps, a Londoner needs a garden in order to maintain a sense of belonging. In a city where speed and uniformity, noise and bustle, are characteristic, and where many houses are produced to a standard design, a garden may afford the only prospect of variety. It is also a place for recreation, contemplation and satisfaction.

The man known as "the father of English botany," William Turner, lived in Crutched Friars and was buried in Pepys's church of St. Olave's, Hart Street, in 1568. It is not at all paradoxical that the first established botanist should be a Londoner, since the extensive fields and marshes beyond the walls were fertile ground. Turner followed the intellectual practice of his time in not giving locations "for the 238 British plants he records for the first time"—this is noted in the indispensable *Natural History of the City* by R.S. Fitter—but it has been revealed that one of them, the field pepperwort, was found in a garden in Coleman Street. Another sixteenth-century botanist, Thomas Penny, lived for twenty years in the parish of St. Andrew Undershaft and collected many of his specimens in the area beside Moorfields. The Tower ditch was also famed for its "aquatic" or water-loving plants such as flote grass and wild celery, while a naturalist of Holborn registered wild celery from "the fields of Holburne, neere unto Graies inn" and vernal whitlow-grass from "the brick wall in Chauncerie Lane, belonging to the Earl of Southampton."

If the suburbs of the west were good hunting-places for naturalists, the unlikely areas of Hoxton and Shoreditch became known for their nursery gardens. A native of Hoxton in the late seventeenth century, Thomas Fairchild, introduced "many new and curious plants"; and wrote a treatise on how best to order "such evergreens, fruit trees, flowering shrubs, flowers, exotick plants etc as will be ornamental and thrive best in the London gardens." He entitled his book the *City Gardener* and by that name he was always afterwards known. Another native of Hoxton, who lived just outside Bishopsgate, George Ricketts, brought into the area trees such as the myrtle, the lime and the cedar of Lebanon. But there were many other gardeners in this strangely fruitful area amid the mud and rubble of the northern suburbs, where grew the buddleia, the anemone and the striped phillyrea.

It has always been said that Londoners love flowers; the craze for "window gardening" in the 1880s represented only the most prominent manifestation of the window boxes or window pots to be seen in almost all prints of the London streets from generation to generation. But the most striking sign of the London passion for flowers comes with the London flower-seller. Scented violets were sold upon the streets, while in early spring primroses were "first cried." To the Cockney, wrote Blanchard Jerrold in *London: a Pilgrimage*, "the wall-flower is a revelation; the ten-week stock a new season; the carnation, a dream of sweet Arabia." They are all part of a busy London trade which began in the 1830s. Before that time the only visible London flowers— or, rather, the only flowers on display—were the myrtle, the geranium and the hyacinth.

Then as the taste for floral decoration extended, particularly among middle-class Londoners, flowers, like everything else in the city, became a commercial proposition, and many of the outlying suburbs began production and distribution on a large scale. The entire north-western corner of Covent Garden Market was given over to the wholesale vendors of roses and geraniums and pinks and lilacs, which were then sold on to shops and other dealers. Very quickly, too, flowers became the object of commercial speculation. The fuchsia arrived in London in the early 1830s, for example, and the traders prospered. The interest in flowers spread ineluctably down to the "humbler classes" with hawkers at street corners selling a bunch of mixed flowers for a penny, while in the market were sold basket-loads of cabbage roses and carnations. Female vendors at the Royal Exchange or the Inns of Court hawked moss-roses; the violet girl was to be seen on every street and the "travelling gardener" sold wares which were notorious for their short lives. The price of commerce, in London, is often death and the city became nature's graveyard. Many millions of flowers were brought into London only to wither and expire. The establishment of large extra-mural public cemeteries, located in the suburbs, in turn led to an enormous increase in the demand for flowers to place upon the newly laid tombs.

The trees of London may also become a token. "We may say," Ford Madox Ford has observed, "that London begins where tree trunks commence to be black." That is why the plane tree is London's own; because of its power to slough off its sooty bark it became a symbol of powerful renewal within the city's "corrupted atmosphere." There was a plane tree growing some forty feet high in the churchyard of St. Dunstan's in the East, but the oldest are those planted in Berkeley Square in 1789. Curiously enough, like many Londoners themselves, the London plane tree is a hybrid: an example of successful inter-marriage between the oriental plane introduced into London in 1562 and the western plane of 1636, it has remained the tree of central London. It is the single most important reason why London has been apostrophised as a "City of Trees" with "solemn shapes" and "glooms Romantic."

That gloom may also descend upon London's parks, from Hyde Park in the west to Victoria Park in the east, from Battersea to St. James's, from Blackheath to Hampstead Heath. No other city in the world seems to possess so many green and open spaces. For those in love with the hardness and bril-liancy of London, they are an irrelevance. But they call to others—to va-grants, to office workers, to children, to all those who seek relief from life "on the stones."

When the horse-drawn omnibuses, going from Notting Hill Gate to Marble Arch, travelled beside Hyde Park "hands on the upper deck would greedily snatch at a twig to take to the City" to be met with "the cries of nuthatch and reed-warbler, cuckoo or nightingale." This observation is taken from Neville Braybrook's *London Green.* Matthew Arnold suggested in "Lines Written in Kensington Gardens," that

> The birds sing sweetly in these trees
> Across the girdling city's hum

immediately setting up a contrast between the quiet presence of pine, elm and chestnut, "amid the city's jar." The paradox is that London contains this peace within itself, that Hyde Park and Kensington Gardens are as much a part of the city as Borough High Street or Brick Lane. The city moves slowly, as well as quickly; it provides a history of silence as well as of noise.

There were also once oases of the countryside to be found in Clerkenwell and Piccadilly, Smithfield and Southwark; here the trades included threshing and milking. The names of the streets bear evidence of London's hitherto rural nature. Cornhill, by obvious derivation, is a token of a "hill where corn was grown," according to Ekwall's *Street Names of the City of London,* and Seething Lane is to be interpreted as "where chaff was plentiful . . . the chaff came from corn threshed and winnowed in the lane." Oat Lane and Milk Street speak of the countryside. Cow Lane was not a place where cows were kept but a "lane along which cows were driven to or from pasture." Addle Street, off Wood Street, and a few yards up from Milk Street, is derived from Old English *adela* or stinking urine and *eddel* or liquid manure; so we derive from it "lane full of cow dung." The Huggin Lanes in Cripplegate and Queenhithe were both known as Hoggenlane in early transcripts. There were no fewer than three Hog Lanes—in East Smithfield, Norton Folgate and Portsoken. Chicken and Chick Lanes occur, together with Duck Lane, Goose Lane and Honey Lane—the latter indicating "that bees were formerly kept in the street." The name of Blanch Appleton, a district of Aldgate, comes from *appeltun*, Old English for orchard.

The natural life of London deserves, then, to be celebrated. There are photographs of horse chestnuts in Watford and of cedars in Highgate, wood-pigeons nesting by the Bank of England and of hay-making in Hyde Park. Insects innumerable and other invertebrates have made their homes in the stones of London while various wild plants such as charlock and mayweed, broad dock and sun spurge, grow luxuriously in the natural habitat of the capital. While the rook and the jackdaw have been slowly driven outside the range of the city, the woodpigeon and the martin have moved in to take their place. The canals intersecting London have preserved territory for aquatic birds as have large water reservoirs. The development of sewage farms in the 1940s, recreated the conditions of the primeval Thames marshes with such inadvertent skill that many thousands of migrating birds descend upon London each year.

There are more than two hundred different species and sub-species of birds in the London area, ranging from the magpie to the greenfinch, but perhaps the most ubiquitous is the pigeon. It has been suggested that the swarms of feral pigeons are all descended from birds which escaped from dovecotes in the early medieval period; they found a natural habitat in the crannies and ledges of buildings as did their ancestors, the rockdoves, amid the sea-girt cliffs. "They nest in small colonies," one observer has written, "usually high up and inaccessible" above the streets of London as if the streets were indeed a sea. A man fell from the belfry of St. Stephen's Walbrook in 1277 while in quest of a pigeons' nest, while the Bishop of London complained in 1385 of "malignant persons" who threw stones at the pigeons resting in the city churches. So pigeons were already a familiar presence, even if they were not treated with the same indulgence as their more recent successors. A modicum of kindness to these creatures seems to have been first shown in the late nineteenth century, when they were fed oats rather than the now customary stale bread.

From the end of the nineteenth century woodpigeons also migrated into the city; they were quickly urbanised, increasing both in numbers and in tameness. "We have frequently seen them on the roofs of houses," wrote the author of *Bird Life in London* in 1893, "apparently as much at home as any dovecote pigeon." Those who look up today may notice their "fly-lines" in the sky, from Lincoln's Inn Fields over Kingsway and Trafalgar Square to Battersea, with other lines to Victoria Park and to Kenwood. The air of London is filled with such "fly-lines," and to trace the paths of the birds would be to envisage the city in an entirely different form; then it would seem linked and unified by thousands of thoroughfares and small paths of energy, each with its own history of use.

The sparrows move quickly in public places, and they are now so much part of London that they have been adopted by the native population as the "sparrer"; a friend was known to Cockneys as a "cock-sparrer" in tribute to a bird which is sweet and yet watchful, blessed with a dusky plumage similar to that of the London dust, a plucky little bird darting in and out of the city's endless uproar. They are small birds which can lose body heat very quickly, so they are perfectly adapted to the "heat island" of London. They will live in any small cranny or cavity, behind drain pipes or ventilation shafts, or in public statues, or holes in buildings; in that sense they are perfectly suited to a London topography. An ornithologist who described the sparrow as "peculiarly attached to man" said it "never now breeds at any distance from an occupied building." This sociability, bred upon the fondness of the Londoner for the sparrow as much as the sparrow for the Londoner, is manifest in many ways. One naturalist, W.H. Hudson, has described how any stranger in a green space or public garden will soon find that "several sparrows are keeping him company . . . watching his every movement, and if he sit down on a chair or a bench several of them will come close to him, and hop this way and that before him, uttering a little plaintive note of interrogation—*Have you got nothing for us?*" They have also been described as the urchins of the streets— "thievish, self-assertive and pugnacious"—a condition which again may merit the attention and admiration of native Londoners. Remarkably attached to their surroundings, they rarely create "fly-lines" across the city; where they are born, like other Londoners, they stay.

And so they become associated with, and characterised by, their surroundings. The "Tower sparrows" were notorious as "feathered murderous ruffians" who kept up continual warfare with the pigeons and starlings of the building even though they had shared quarters with them for many centuries. In the autumn of 1738 a bolt of lightning left the ground covered "with heaps of dead sparrows" at Mile End Turnpike. There is something pitiful and yet splendid about this mass slaughter, as if again they represented the spirit of the city itself. These little creatures embody "sheer invincible fecundity," according to E.M. Nicholson, the author of *Bird-Watching in London*: "they may be massacred perpetually and raise no obstacle, only they never diminish, that is the salvation of the species." So their "incessant and indescribable" noise, when congregated in a roost, is the sound of collective triumph, "all mad and very happy," fluttering and darting in the boughs as if the trees themselves had come alive.

Gulls are now perpetual visitors, although they first arrived in London as late as 1891. They came to enjoy the warmth of the city during a severe winter, and their entry soon excited the attention of Londoners. The citizens thronged upon the bridges and the embankments in order to watch them dive and tumble. In 1892 London magistrates forbade anyone from shooting them, and at that point for the first time the habit of feeding the gulls appeared; clerks and labourers of the 1890s would, during the free hour for lunch, go down to the bridges and offer them various foods. Theodore Dreiser walked upon Blackfriars Bridge one Sunday afternoon, in 1912, and found a line of men feeding "thousands of gulls" with minnows which they purchased at a penny a box. A sense of awe and kindliness, combined, would seem to characterise the native attitude. Yet their success in obtaining food from humans hands led to the continual reappearance of the gulls, until they acquired the reputation of being the principal scavengers of the city, supplanting the services of the raven. So the activity of the city can change the habits, as well as the habitat, of birds.

There are some birds, such as the robin and the chaffinch, which are less approachable and trustful in the city than in the country. Other species, such as the mallard, grow increasingly shyer as they leave London. There has been a severe diminution of the number of sparrows, while blackbirds are more plentiful. Swans and ducks have also increased in number. Some species, however, have all but vanished. The rooks of London are, perhaps, the most notable of the disappeared, their rookeries destroyed by building work or by tree-felling. Areas of London were continuously inhabited by rooks for many hundreds of years. The burial ground of St. Dunstan's in the East and the college garden of the Ecclesiastical Court in Doctors' Commons, the turrets of the Tower of London and the gardens of Grays Inn, were once such localities. There was a rookery in the Inner Temple dating from at least 1666, mentioned by Oliver Goldsmith in 1774. Rooks nested on Bow Church and on St. Olave's. They were venerable London birds, preferring to cluster around ancient churches and ancient buildings as if they were their local guardians. Yet, in the words of the nineteenth-century song, "Now the old rooks have lost their places." There was a grove in Kensington Gardens devoted to the rooks; it contained some seven hundred trees forming a piece of wild nature, a matter of delight and astonishment to those who walked among them and listened to the endless cawing that blotted out the city's noise. But the trees were torn down in 1880. The rooks have never returned.

Yet other birds haunt the city. These are the caged birds, the canaries and the budgerigars, the larks and thrushes, who sing out of their confinement in a manner reminiscent of Londoners themselves. In *Bleak House*, Dickens's novel which is so much a symbolic restatement of London vision, the caged birds belonging to Miss Flite are a central emblem of urban imprisonment. The occupants of Newgate were known as the "nightingales of Newgate" or "Newgate birds." In *Down and Out in Paris and London* (1933) Orwell noted that the inhabitants of doss-houses or low lodging-houses kept caged birds, "tiny, faded things that had lived all their lives underground." He recalled in particular one "old Irishman . . . whistling to a blind bullfinch in a tiny cage," suggesting that there is a strange affinity between the luckless in London and the incarcerated birds. On the stone wall of the Beauchamp Tower, in the Tower of London, was inscribed with a nail "Epitaph on a Goldfinch":

Where Raleigh pin'd within a prison's gloom
I cheerful sung, nor murmur'd at my doom . . .
But death, more gentle than the law's decree,
Hath paid my ransom from captivity.

Beneath it are engraved the words, "Buried, June 23, 1794, by a fellow-prisoner in the Tower of London." The names of Miss Flite's imprisoned birds were "Hope, Joy, Youth, Peace, Rest, Life, Dust, Ashes, Waste, Want, Ruin, Despair, Madness, Death, Cunning, Folly, Words, Wigs, Rags, Sheapskin, Plunder."

There was a trade in caged birds, of course, with street-markets in St. Giles and Spitalfields devoted to selling them. Most in demand was the goldfinch, with a regular supply of trapped and caught birds offered at six-pence to a shilling each; their attraction lay in their longevity, upwards of fifteen years, and in the possibility of cross-breeding. Chaffinches and green-finches were also popular, although the latter bird was described by one street vendor to Henry Mayhew as "only a middling singer." Freshly caught larks were sold at between sixpence and eightpence. Mayhew witnessed "the rest-less throwing up of the head of the caged lark, as if he were longing for a soar in the air"; yet he was trapped in a small and dirty cage in a nineteenth-century slum. The nightingale had also become a favourite of London's bird dealers by the mid-nineteenth century but, again according to Mayhew, "shows symptoms of great uneasiness, dashing himself against the wires of his cage or aviary, and sometimes dying in a few days."

Where there are birds, there are cats. They were ubiquitous throughout London, at least as early as the thirteenth century, and Cateaton Street was named in their honour. Now called Gresham Street, it was in the thirteenth century known variously as Cattestrate and Cattestrete and in the sixteenth as Catlen Strete or Catteten. Cats were considered to be the bearers of good luck, as the fourteenth-century legend of Richard Whittington and his cat at-tests, so there is every reason to believe that they were treated as welcome and perhaps even useful pets. But the London cat is also associated with strange superstitions. There is evidence of ritual cat sacrifice, where the un-fortunate animal has been walled in an alcove and often preserved in mum-mified form. A significant example was discovered, in the autumn of 1946, behind a cornice in the tower of St. Michael Paternoster Royal, which is the church in which Richard Whittington was buried in 1423. Thus the continu-ance of a London legend was deemed worthy of a sacrifice in the rebuilt Wren church of 1694.

No doubt the dead beast was once one of that army of animals known collectively as "the city cats." The night of the capital was their domain, where they sat upon old walls or slunk down dilapidated alleys. They were the guardians of London, patrolling streets and territories down which their distant ancestors once trod on quiet paws. There were other "cat streets" in the metropolis, most notably in the area of Clerkenwell Green and the Obelisk in St. George's Fields as well as the lanes and alleys behind Drury Lane. Here, according to Charles Dickens, the cats took on all the character-istics of the people among whom they lived. "They leave their young fami-lies to stagger about the gutters, unassisted, while they frouzily quarrel and swear and scratch, and spit, at street-corners." It is sometimes observed that pets come to resemble their owners, but it is also possible that a peculiarly London type of animal is produced by urban conditions.

By the close of the nineteenth century it was estimated that there were some three-quarters of a million cats in London, and they were of course variously treated. In late nineteenth-century Whitechapel an ancient prostitute—"a frowzy, debauched, drunken-looking creature," as described by Charles Booth—distributed meat from a basket to every passing stray. Kindness of this nature seems to have emerged in the late nineteenth century. One old resident remarked to Booth: "The day was when no cat could appear in the streets of Bethnal Green without being hunted or maltreated; now such conduct is rare." If there were ever to be written a history of moral emotions, it could do worse than study Londoners' treatment of animals.

Dogs appear in almost every depiction of a London "street-scene," prancing on the road and mingling joyfully with horses and pedestrians alike. There have been dogs at every stage of the city's history, accompanying families in their walks along the fields, barking at passing processions, eager and fierce during riots, growling at and fighting each other in obscure disputes over London territory. In the twelfth century a royal edict declared that "if a greedy ravening dog shall bite" a "Royal beast," then its owner forfeited his life. So we may imagine the inhabitants of early medieval London nervously taking out their dogs for sport, or pastime, or hunting, in any of the fields and meadows beyond the walls of the city. Yet the dogs which were taken to these areas had to be "expeditated"; their claws were cut down to the balls of their feet to stop them from running after deer.

A proclamation was made in 1387 "that dogs shall not wander in the City at large"; yet in the same order a distinction was made between wild or wandering dogs and household dogs. So the concept of the "pet" existed in medieval London. The most prized of London dogs was the mastiff. Many were sent as gifts to prominent persons abroad, and a German traveller of the sixteenth century noted that some of those dogs "are so large and heavy that if they have to be transported long distances, they are provided with shoes so that they do not wear out their feet." They were also used as guard dogs and in the records of London Bridge there are payments made in compensation to those who had been bitten or hurt by the mastiff hounds. The major problem in the city, however, has always been that of strays. A notice at the newly built St. Katherine Docks, by the Tower of London, dated 23 September 1831, warned that "the Gate Keepers will prevent the admission of DOGS, unless the Owners shall have them fastened by a Cord or Handkerchief." The principal complaint against the animals was that they wreaked "Considerable Injury" upon goods, but the age of commerce was also the age of philanthropy. In the mid-nineteenth century a Home for Lost and Starving Dogs was established in London; this is the first instance of canine welfare in the city. "When it first opened there was a disposition to laugh," "Aleph" wrote in 1863, "but subscribers were found, and the asylum flourishes"; removed to Battersea in 1871 after complaints in the neighbourhood about the noise, it flourishes still, as the Battersea Dogs Home.

The flea is as ancient as the dog, but its part in the natural history of London is shrouded in obscurity. The bed bug was first noticed publicly in 1583, while the cockroach was reported by 1634. We may infer, however, that lice and fleas of every kind have infested London from the beginning of its recorded history, to such an extent that its condition has often been taken to resemble them. London, according to Verlaine, was "a flat, black bug."

If animals in London were not used for labour or for food, they were characteristically employed for the purposes of entertainment. Ever since the first lions were placed in the Tower of London in the thirteenth century (to be joined later by a polar bear and an elephant), animals have provided a spectacle for the restless and voracious crowd. The first performing elephant in the London streets was recorded by Robert Hooke in 1679. Londoners could "see the animals" at Exeter Change. A building of three floors at the corner of Wellington Street and the Strand, it was known in the 1780s as "Pidcock's Exhibition of Wild Beasts." The animals were kept on the upper floors "in a small den and cages in rooms of various size, the walls painted with exotic scenery, in order to favour the illusion." The menagerie went through the hands of three separate owners, and an engraving of 1826 shows the old house jutting above the Strand with pictures of elephants, tigers and monkeys daubed upon its front between two grand pillars of Corinthian design. Its popularity was very great, largely because, apart from the Tower zoo, it was the only menagerie of exotic species in London. The less dangerous animals were, on occasions, led through the streets as a living advertisement. Wordsworth mentions a dromedary and monkeys; and J.T. Smith in his *Book for a Rainy Day*, writes of an elephant "being led by its keeper between ropes along the narrow part of the Strand." On 6 February 1826 this elephant, named Chunee, could stand his restraint no longer and, in violent anger, was about to burst out of his cage. A firing squad of soldiers from neighbouring Somerset House could not dispatch him, and a cannon was deployed to no effect. Eventually his keeper killed him with a spear, and he expired with 152 bullets found inside his body. Then the commercial spirit of London pursued him after his death. His carcass was on display to the crowds for some days until it became noisome, at which point it was sold off as 11,000 pounds of meat. The skeleton was displayed thereafter, until it became part of the Hunterian Museum of the Royal College of Surgeons. Chunee was finally obliterated by a bomb in the Second World War. From his promenade along the Strand in 1825 to his destruction by fire in 1941, his story has an authentic London flavour.

The spirit of the city may also explain the passion for performing animals and circuses. In the streets of the capital rats danced on ropes and cats played dulcimers. Performing bears were ubiquitous from the sixteenth to the nineteenth centuries, while performing monkeys and horses were part of the standard repertoire in rings and arenas. In the 1770s, Daniel Wildman specialised in riding upon a horse with a swarm of bees covering his face like a mask. Half a century later the Zoological Society was given a few acres of land in Regent's Park for the erection of various pits and cages in a "zoological garden," which was opened to the public two years later in 1828 and soon became a principal attraction of London; there are many prints showing the citizens enjoying the antics of the imprisoned creatures. In fact serious scientific research was soon overtaken by the demands of entertainment. "It is the very place for quiet easy talk in the open air," Blanchard Jerrold wrote in 1872, "with the animals to point the conversation . . . will pass all London in review in the course of the season." A shop by the bear pit was opened "for the sale of cakes, fruits, nuts and other articles which the visitor may be disposed to give to the different animals," and a long stick was provided for feeding buns to the bears themselves.

Many visitors had their favourites, some preferring the monkey to the lynx or the hippopotamus to the wombat, and would come back each week to mark their condition. But together with pleasurable sympathy, there was always some anxiety that these creatures might break out of their imprisonment and wreak havoc among their captors. That is why both Dickens and Thackeray, joined by interest in public hangings, were also fascinated by the snakes held in confinement. Curiously enough, both of them depicted the same scene at feeding time. This is part of Thackeray's account: "an immense boa constrictor swallowing a live rabbit—swallowing a live rabbit, sir, and looking as if he would have swallowed one of my little children afterwards." So the zoo takes on symbolic importance in the life of a violent and dangerous city; here is violence tamed and danger averted, in the green surroundings of the

Park. Here sits the lion which, in the words of a poem by Stevie Smith, is "Weeping tears of ruby rage."

It would be the merest commonplace to note that the citizens, all dressed alike and walking through the zoo with well proportioned steps, are themselves imprisoned in the city. It was a trite comment even in the nineteenth century, when Gustave Doré depicted the Londoners by the monkey cage or in the parrots' walk as equivalent to the animals—animals which in turn seem to be observing them. Yet there is a resonance between the zoo and the city, in terms of noise and in terms of madness. The confused or shrill sound of the crowd was often compared with the sound of animals, while the deranged at Bedlam were in 1857 said by the *Quarterly Review* to resemble the "fiercer carnivores at the Zoological Gardens." The comparison is obvious enough. The mad were kept in cages where they were visited by curious observers for the sake of entertainment. Said to sound like "ravens, screech-owls, bulls, and bears," the deranged were as "ravenous and unsatiable as wolves" or as "drenched by compulsion as horses." The deranged Londoner, in other words, is an animal; this definition spills over into descriptions of the crowd or mob as a "Beast." The city itself becomes a vast zoo in which all of the cages have been unlocked.

CHAPTER 46

Weather Reports

hen Boswell and Johnson were tasting all the delights of rural life in Greenwich Park, the following conversation ensued.

J.: "Is this not very fine?"
B.: "Yes, Sir; but not equal to Fleet Street."
J.: "You are right, sir."

Robert Herrick celebrated his return to London from Devon in 1640, and declared that

London my home is: though by hard fate sent
Into a long and irksome banishment.

To live in the country is a form of melancholy exile. "If these are comforting for a wife," a sixteenth-century poem suggests, "Defend, defend me from a country life." When a young West Indian boy from Notting Hill of the 1960s was given a week's holiday in a Wiltshire village, he was asked how he had enjoyed the change. "I like it," he replied, "but you can't play in the streets as you can in London." "I love walking in London," Mrs. Dalloway remarks in Virginia Woolf's novel (1925). "Really it's better than walking in the country." To the city dweller the country may not come as a revelation, but as a restriction. It is "dreadful slow," one nineteenth-century Cockney girl is reported as saying, "no swings, no rahndabarts, nor origins [oranges?], no shops, no nothink—jest a great bare field only."

The city is more beautiful than the country because it is rich in human history. Milton, in his blindness, remarked sadly that he was destined never more to look upon the sights "of this fair city." Here he anticipated Wordsworth's famous reflection upon London, from the vantage of Westminster Bridge in 1802: "Earth has not any thing to shew more fair." The great poet of the nineteenth-century natural world wonders upon "the beauty of the morning" as it irradiates "Ships, towers, domes, theatres, and temples":

> Never did sun more beautifully steep
> In his first splendor valley, rock, or hill.

It is a vivid, urban testimony from one whose poetic vision is always associated with landscape. The London suburbs, too, "can be so beautiful," Vincent van Gogh wrote in the 1880s, "When the sun is setting red in the thin evening mist."

The beauty and symmetry of the city are manifest in another sphere, also, as exemplified by Aristotle's remark that "a man that is by nature and not merely by fortune citiless is either low in the scale of humanity or above it," which is to say that humankind belongs to the city as much as fish belong to water. The city is the natural element for all those people who feel a compulsion to look upon the earth for contemporaries and companions. If the city is not "natural" then let us say, with Henry James, that it has recreated nature. "As the great city makes everything," he wrote, "it makes its own system of weather and its own optical laws."

The city is hotter, and dryer, than other parts of the country because the pollution that it creates has the effect of trapping warmth within the streets and buildings while, paradoxically, at the same time obscuring the sun's rays. Many dark buildings retain their heat, and the vertical surfaces of the rising city are also better equipped to catch the low-lying sun; the materials of which London is made also retain the circumambient warmth.

Yet another explanation for the perceptible increase of heat in the capital may be found in the sheer congregation of people within so relatively small an area. The body heat of the citizens pushes up the temperature so that, on modern satellite maps, the city is a pale island among the brown and the green. Two hundred and fifty years ago a seventeenth-century observer made the same point. "The torrent of men, women and children, carts, carriages and horses from the Strand to the Exchange is so strong that it is said that in winter there are two degrees of Fahrenheit difference between this long line of street, and that of the west end."

London's weather shows other variations. Much of Westminster and the adjacent areas are built upon primeval swamps, and in these quarters the exhalation of damp and mist seems more palpable than elsewhere; Cornhill, built upon a summit, seems crisper and drier.

In the sixteenth century the London climate impressed itself upon the scholar and alchemist Giordano Bruno as "more temperate than anywhere else beyond and on this side of the equinoctial, snow and heat being banished from the subjacent earth as well as the excessive heat of the sun, which the perpetually green flowery ground witnesses, and so enjoys a perpetual spring." There is an alchemical, or magical, tendency within his vocabulary which points to the image of London as embodying a mild chemical flame.

But then there was the rain.

> Now in contiguous drops the flood comes down
> Threatening with deluge this devoted Town.

Thus Jonathan Swift celebrates a "city shower" in the autumn of 1710. Annual amounts of rainfall were calculated from 1696, and they demonstrate that London's showers and deluges declined in frequency towards the end of the eighteenth century only to rise again in the period from 1815 to 1844. Even in 1765, however, a French traveller noted the humidity of the city climate, which required fires to be lit "when it might be most easy to do without one"; he noted that as late as May all the apartments of the British Museum had fires within them "to preserve from damps and humidity the books, the manuscripts, the maps."

But there have also been great floods. In 1090 London Bridge was carried away by a tumultuous river, and in 1236 the waters rose so high that boats could be rowed in the middle of Westminster Hall; there, too, in 1579, "a number of fish were left stranded after a flood." The Walbrook became a rushing torrent in the autumn of 1547, sweeping away a young man attempting to cross it, and in 1762 the waters of the Thames were so raised "that the like had never been known in the memory of man." "In less than five hours," the contemporary report goes, "the water rose twelve feet in vertical height" and "people were lost in the high roads." Even at the beginning of the twentieth century Lambeth was so inundated by the waters of the Thames that the houses of the area had to be visited by boats. So the air of London has always been laden with vapours and rains.

Londoners are also more accustomed to the cold than to the heat of summer days. "There's nothing left but London once it's winter," says a character in Elizabeth Bowen's *The Heat of the Day* (1949). London becomes more purely itself in the cold, harder and brighter and far more cruel. In the winter of 1739–40 "Tramps froze to death . . . Birds dropped stiff from the sky, bread hardened into rocks on market stalls." Thirty years later, according to the *Annual Register* of 18 February 1771, "A poor boy who on Tuesday night had crept into a dunghill at a stable yard in London in order to preserve himself from the cold was found dead by the ostler" while "A poor woman also, with a child at her breast, and another about three years old lying by her, was found in Rag Fair."

The cold weather could be so intense that the Thames itself froze regularly over the centuries, some twenty-three times between 1620 and 1814, because the old London Bridge impeded the movement of the water until it became so sluggish that, in the colder conditions, it could not move. In 1281 "men passed over the Thames, between Westminster and Lambeth," and in 1410 "Thys yere was the grete frost and ise and the most sharpest wenter that ever man sawe, and it duryd fourteen wekes so that men might in dyvers places both goo and ryde over the Temse." In 1434, 1506 and 1515 the river was again frozen so that carts and horses and carriages could travel easily from one bank to the other. As early as 1564 such sports as archery and such entertainments as dancing took place at a Frost Fair on the frozen river. Stow and Holinshed record that, on the eve of 1565, "some plaied at the football as boldlie there, as if it had been on the drie land; diverse of the Court being then at Westminster, shot dailie at pricks set upon the Thames; and the people, both men and women, went on the Thames in greater numbers than in anie street of the City of London." So the Thames becomes a newly populous thoroughfare in the greatly expanding city. The emphasis here is upon excitement and recreation but forty-four years later, in 1608, the general atmosphere of trade and commerce in London had exploited even the weather, and many set up booths "standing upon the ice, as fruitsellers, victuallers, that sold beere and wine, shoe makers and a barber's tent." Again in 1684, "The Thames before London was still planted with booths in formal streets, all sorts of trades and shops furnished" so that "another city, as it were, was erected thereon." The city spawns its own replica, with all the characteristics of its own turbulent life—"bull baiting, horse and coach races, puppet plays and interludes, cookes, tipling and other lewd places, so that it seemed to be a bacchanalian triumph or carnival on the water." The perilousness of London life, too, was enacted upon the river, when within hours the ice had melted and swept the whole carnival away; a century later, in 1789, a "sudden breaking up of the ice" occasioned a "fearful scene" of damage and fatality.

The cold winters of London impeded the course of trade as well as that of the river. In the winter of 1813–14, the wax and glue froze in their pots, leaving tailors and shoe-makers without the means of work. Silk deteriorated in freezing conditions, so the silk-makers of Spitalfields and elsewhere were also severely affected. Porters and cab-men, street traders and labourers, were unable to pursue their livelihoods. The price of coal and the price of bread were dramatically increased. The master of a school in St. Giles reported "that of the seventy children in his school sixty had not eaten any food that day until he gave them some at noon." In the severe winters of 1855, 1861, 1869, 1879 and 1886 there were bread riots, and in the latter year mobs of the unemployed looted the shops of central London. In the city there was a direct correlation, then, between weather and social unrest.

There is a connection, too, between outer and inner weather. In the winter "there is a vague smell of alcohol in the streets" since everyone "drinks heavily and incessantly" to combat the aching and intrusive cold. The drink "excites and urges on the rabble to vicious practices." This account, written in 1879, describes the rain falling like liquid mud, the yellow shadows of the fog which render breathing painful and difficult, and the darkness at midday. The description of a physical fact conveys an immense psychological charge. "Vile" weather at Christmas 1876, according to Henry James, "darkness, solitude and sleet in midwinter" within a "murky Babylon." November was the worst month for suicides in London and, during the Blitz of the winter of 1940–1, Londoners were more depressed by the weather than by the air-raids.

The sky in London, like its weather, seems to have different orders of magnitude. In some streets, which are the canyons of the city, it seems infinitely remote; it becomes a distant prospect continually crowded by rooftops and towers. Yet in the large squares of Islington where the houses are low, and in the council "cottage" estates of the western districts, the sky is a vast canopy encompassing all the adjacent areas. In "this low damp city," as V.S. Pritchett

George Scharf's depiction of everyday labour in London; the streets of the city are always being torn up, or demolished, or rebuilt, in a cycle of perpetual change and renewal. London is never still.

Ah! this is what comes of Improvement! this is the happy effects of the March of Intellect. No employment for Scavengers now. When I had the management of the Rubbish concern, I found plenty of employment for all of them.

New Machine for Sweeping Streets Invented by Col Brass

THE SCAVENGER'S LAMENTATION; or, The dreadful Consequences of

One of the consequences of London's "improvement" was the forced retirement of some older trades. The scavenger, like the "tosher" and the "mudlark," was doomed to disappear together with a murkier and more impoverished city.

The Enraged Musician: Hogarth's painting depicts the cacophony of a city which has always been notorious for its noise; in the eighteenth century, it was said, it was impossible to hear yourself speak along the major thoroughfares.

Nineteenth-century London was the first great urban metropolis in the history of the world, and Frith's painting of a railway station celebrates one of its rituals of power.

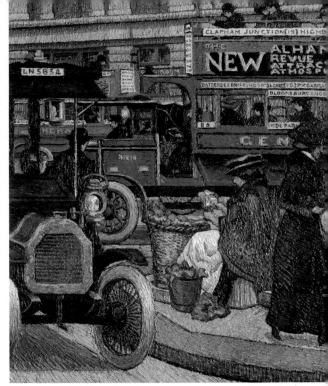

The Crowd by Robert Buss. London has always been a city of crowds and mobs, which gather instinctively before disappearing as mysteriously as they congregate.

Piccadilly Circus by Charles Ginner: a painting of "the Dilly" in 1912. The flower-sellers, at this late date, were about to disappear forever, but the buses to Battersea and Highbury still make their way.

Hammersmith Bridge on Boat Race Day. Walter Greaves's depiction of a good-humoured London crowd in the 1860s, having a "day out."

Walter Sickert's depiction of the audience, or rather spectators, up in "the gods" of the "Old Mo" in Drury Lane. The music-hall represented the great folk art of London, and the Cockney population were its devotees.

The Palais de Danse, Hammersmith, one of those Edwardian venues which took the place of the concert rooms and the pleasure gardens; the social entertainments of London are as old as the city itself.

A coffee-stall in London, c. 1860, with a collection of customers as heterogeneous as London itself. The boy in the red uniform was employed to pick up horse dung from the streets.

A café in London, c. 1914 which, despite its colourful interior, conveys a characteristic melancholy and anonymity.

Allen's Tobacconist Shop painted by the proprietor: a nineteenth-century shop in Hunt Street, off Grosvenor Square. Note the blooms in the flower pots, which have been an integral feature of London streets for many centuries.

Rachel Whiteread's splendid modern sculpture *House*, which gave a new meaning to the concept of "urban spaces." Its brooding presence is also a token of what has been described as London's "burden" and "mystery."

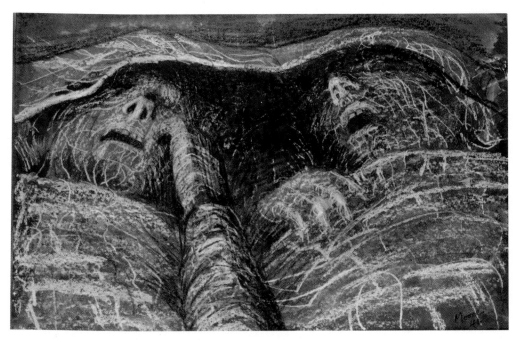

Henry Moore's vision of life underground during the air-raids of the Second World War; there were fears that a subterranean population, as unfamiliar as the two sleepers, would spread through the tunnels and shelters of the city.

Graham Sutherland's haunting evocation of an East End street destroyed by bombing. At certain moments in its history London has become a city of ruins.

Canary Wharf at night, 1991; this great monument of power and commerce has become an integral and inalienable aspect of London topography.

put it, "the sky means a great deal to us." The quality of cloud cover which may or may not bring rain, and the subtle gradations of blue and violet in the evening sky, are sensible reminders of the unique atmospherics of London. A panorama of *London from Southwark* (*c.* 1630), is the first view that grants the city its sky; the westward passage of grey and white clouds gives the painting enormous space and lightness, and in this novel brightness the city itself seems to breathe. It is no longer the tangle of dark buildings beneath a narrow strip of sky but an open city whose towers and spires beckon towards the empyrean.

These are the vertiginous skies when at sunset the west is all on fire, reflected in the shifting mass of cloud; on one January evening, at approximately five o'clock, in the year 2000, the cloud cover was rose-red striated with patches of dark blue sky.

Yet the lights of the sky also reflect the lights of the city, and the very brightness of the modern city obscures the brightness of the stars. That is why the typical London sky seems low, damp and tactile, part of the city itself and its thousand stray lights and gleams. It is the sky which inspired Turner living in Maiden Lane, and Constable in his lodgings in Hampstead. According to G.K. Chesterton, "all the forces which have produced the London sky have made something which all Londoners know, and which no one who has never seen London has ever seen."

The prevailing wind is westerly or south-westerly; the south and west façades of St. Paul's Cathedral show marked deterioration in the face of wind or rain, and the stone itself "is washed clean and exhibits a whitened and weather-beaten aspect." Yet these winds kept the western areas of the city relatively free of the fog or smog which settled over the central and eastern part. Indeed an eastern wind was a token of harm, since all the smoke and stench of the industries situated in the East End filtered over the rest of the capital.

London was, and is, a very windy city. By the eleventh century there were seven windmills erected in Stepney, while the earliest maps show windmills in Moorfields and Finsbury Fields. There was a windmill in the Strand, and one by Leather Lane; there was one in the Whitechapel Road, and one beside Rathbone Place. Great Windmill Street is still at the top of the Haymarket, and there were many windmills along the south side of the river in Waterloo, Bermondsey, Battersea and the Old Kent Road. In February 1761 the wind was so high that, in Deptford, it drove a windmill "with such velocity that it could not be stopped, and took fire, and was entirely consumed, besides a large quantity of flour." John Evelyn recorded that "the Town of

Bowe" had continual winds which mitigated the effects of atmospheric pollution and Charles Dickens wondered why metropolitan gales always blew so hard at Deptford and Peckham. In addition, "I have read of more chimney stacks and house-copings coming down with terrific smashes at Walworth."

Yet in a city established upon extremes, there will also be an extremity of weather. In 1090 six hundred houses, and a score of churches, were overthrown by a mighty wind. The spectacle of Bow Church rafters impaled twenty feet deep within the mud and stone of Cheapside inevitably led to demands for public penance and humiliation to avert the further wrath of God. But the pious citizens of London were not able to turn away the further calamities of their history. In 1439 there came a "grete wynd that dyd a moch harme in many placys"; it tore off the lead roof of the Grey Friars and "it blew almost dovne the ton side of the Old Change" knocking down so many "grete long trees that nether horss ne cart myght pass thorow the streete." In 1626 "a terrible storm of Rain and hail . . . with a very great Thunder and Lightning" knocked down the wall of the churchyard of St. Andrew, and exposed many coffins in the crash. It says something about the attitude of Londoners to death that thereupon "the ruder sort" lifted up the lids of the coffins "to see the posture of the dead Corps lying therein." During this storm a strange mist emerged above the turbulent waters of the Thames "in a round Circle of a good-bigness above the waters" which eventually "ascended higher and higher till it quite vanished away." There was immediately talk of conjuring and black magic.

Pepys described the great storm of January 1666: "The wind being very furious . . . whole chimneys, nay, whole houses in two or three places blowed down." In November 1703 a storm of nine hours descended upon the city— "all the ships in the river were driven ashore" and the barges smashed against the arches of London Bridge; the towers and spires of certain London churches fell to the ground, and in many areas whole houses were lifted up before falling upon the earth. "The lead on the roofs of the highest building, was rolled up like paper," and more than twenty "night-walkers" were killed by falling chimneys or tiles. Daniel Defoe published an account of "the late Dreadful Tempest" in which he revealed that the shriek and frenzy of the wind were such that "nobody durst quit their tottering habitations for it was worst without" and "many thought the end of the world was nigh."

Over the next sixty years London was ravaged by several hurricanes, the last being in 1790 when the copper covering of the new Stone's Buildings, Lincoln's Inn, "was blown off in one sheet and hung over the front like a large carpet or mainsail." On the night of 16 October 1987, "London's Hurricane" hit the capital. It had been preceded by two years of unnaturally cold and windy weather. In January 1987 fifteen inches of snow fell on the higher parts of London, the chimes of Big Ben stopped and the River Thames iced over from Runnymede to Sunbury; in March of that year, sands from the Sahara fell with the rain upon Morden. Then, in that October, the great wind visited the city. The balconies of high-rise flats collapsed, walls were ripped down, roofs stripped of their tiles. Market stalls were thrown through the air, and thousands of trees were destroyed by the effects of the gales.

Extraordinary climatic change is not at all unusual in London; if the city can attract plague and fire, then it also can attract tempest and earthquake. There were three earthquakes during the reign of Elizabeth I (1558–1603), the first of which did not exceed a minute but the shock of which "was so severe that many churches and houses were much shattered and several people killed." One of the incidental features of this catastrophe was the fact that the great bells of the city were so shaken that they began to ring of their own accord—the Westminster clock bell, for example, "spoke of itself against the hammer with shaking"—as if the city itself were heralding its own disaster. There also seems to have been some method in the mayhem; the two further earthquakes of Queen Elizabeth's reign both occurred on Christmas Eve four years apart. The next most notable tremor occurred in February 1750 when two shocks were felt some hours apart, the second being preceded by "a strong but confused lightning darting its flashes in quick succession." People flocked into the street, in panic that their houses were about to fall upon them, and the most powerful forces were visible and audible in the West End near St. James's Park; here "it seemed to move in a south and north direction, with a quick return towards the centre, and was accompanied by a loud noise of a rushing wind." So London has been visited by elemental forces, invading its central areas; the last record of such a visitation, at least notable in its effects, occurred in the spring of 1884. And then there came the fog.

CHAPTER 47

A Foggy Day

☙

Tacitus mentions it in his account of Caesar's invasion, so its spectral presence has haunted London from earliest times. The fog was originally generated by natural means, but soon enough the city was taking over from nature and creating its own atmosphere. As early as 1257 Eleanor of Provence, wife of Henry III, complained about the smoke and pollution of London and, in the sixteenth century, Elizabeth I was reported to have been "herself greatly grieved and annoyed with the taste and smoke of sea-coals." By the sixteenth century a pall of smoke hung over the capital, and the interiors of the more affluent London houses were dark with soot. One of the contributors to Holinshed's *Chronicles* noted that the number of domestic chimneys had greatly increased throughout the latter decades of the sixteenth century, and that interior smoke was considered a preventative against wood decay and a preservative of health. It is as if the city enjoyed its own darkness.

At the beginning of the seventeenth century numerous and various complaints issued from the polluted city. In 1603 Hugh Platt wrote a ballad, "A Fire of Coal-Balles," in which he claimed that the fumes of sea coal damaged plants and buildings; seventeen years later James I was "moved with compassion for the decayed fabric of St. Paul's Cathedral near approaching ruin by the corroding quality of coal-smoke to which it had long been subjected." There was also the prevalent fear of fire; there can be no doubt that the sight and smell of smoke aroused instinctive fears of flame in the thoroughfares of the city.

John Evelyn, in his treatise entitled *Fumifigium, or The inconvenience of the Air and the Smoak of London* (1661), lamented the condition of a city covered by "a Hellish and dismal Cloud of SEA-COAL." Here the invocation of hell is significant, as one of the first manifestations of that connection between the city and the lower depths. The dark and dismal cloak of London comes from "few funnels and Issues, belonging to only *Brewers, Diers, Lime-burners, Salt* and *Sope-boylers* and some other private trades, *One* of whose *Spiracles* alone, does manifestly infect the *Aer*, more than all the chimnies of London put together besides." Here, rising with the sulphurous smoke, is the spectre of infection. The city is literally a deadly place. It is the same image conjured by a contemporary *Character of England* which described London as enveloped in "Such a cloud of sea-coal, as if there be a resemblance of hell upon earth, it is in this volcano in a foggy day: this pestilent smoak, which corrodes the very yron and spoils all the movables, leaving a soot on all things that it lights: and so fatally seizing on the lungs of the inhabitants, that cough and consumption spare no man." It was in this period that in meteorological observations there emerged the incidence of "Great Stinking Fog" as well as that consistent cover of smoke which has become known as the "urban plume." It might be said that the industrial city emerged from this terrible childbed.

Despite written records of great fogs in previous eras, it is commonly believed that nineteenth-century London created the foggy darkness. Certainly Victorian fog is the world's most famous meteorological phenomenon. It was everywhere, in Gothic drama and in private correspondence, in scientific reports and in fiction such as *Bleak House* (1852–53). "I asked him whether there was a great fire anywhere? For the streets were so full of dense brown smoke that scarcely anything was to be seen. 'Oh dear no, miss,' he said. 'This is a London particular.' I had never heard of such a thing. 'A fog, miss,' said the young gentleman. 'O indeed!' said I."

Half a million coal fires mingling with the city's vapour, "partly arising from imperfect drainage," produced this "London particular," rising approximately 200 to 240 feet above street level. Opinions varied concerning the colour of the fogs. There was a black species, "simply darkness complete and intense at mid day"; bottle-green; a variety as yellow as pea-soup, which stopped all the traffic and "seems to choke you"; "a rich lurid brown, like the light of some strange conflagration"; simply grey; "orange-coloured vapour"; a "dark chocolate-coloured pall." Everyone seemed to notice changes in its density, however, when it was sometimes interfused with daylight or when wreaths of one colour would mingle with another. The closer to the heart of the city, the darker these shades would become until it was "misty black" in the dead centre. In 1873 there were seven hundred "extra" deaths, nineteen of them the result of pedestrians walking into the Thames, the docks or the canals. The fogs sometimes came and went rapidly, their smoke and gloom blown across the streets of the city by the prevailing winds, but often they lingered for days with the sun briefly seen through the cold yellow mist. The worst decade for fogs was the 1880s; the worst month was always November.

"The fog was denser than ever," wrote the author Nathaniel Hawthorne on 8 December 1855, "very black indeed, more like a distillation of mud than anything else; the ghost of mud, the spiritualised medium of departed mud, through which the departed citizens of London probably tread in the Hades whither they are translated. So heavy was the gloom, that gas was lighted in all the shop windows; and the little charcoal furnaces of the women and boys, roasting chestnuts threw a ruddy misty glow around them." Again the condition of the city is likened to that of hell itself, but with the additional association that somehow the citizens are privately enjoying—and indeed are rather proud of—their hapless condition.

Fog was called a "London particular" with some measure of satisfaction, since it was a unique emanation from what was then the largest and most powerful city on the earth. Darwin wrote that "there is a grandeur about its smoky fogs." James Russell Lowell, writing in the autumn of 1888, remarked that he was living within a yellow fog—"the cabs are rimmed with a halo" and the people in the street "like fading frescoes"—but at the same time "It flatters one's self-esteem"; he was proud to survive such an extreme condition of the city.

In turn the fog itself conjured up images of immensity. "Everything seems to be checked," wrote a French journalist of the nineteenth century, "to slacken into a phantom-like motion that has all the vagueness of hallucination. The sounds of the street are muffled; the tops of the houses are lost, hardly even guessed . . . The openings of the streets swallow up, like tunnels, a crowd of foot passengers and carriages, which seem, thus, to disappear for ever." The people in this fog "are innumerable, a compact army, these miserable little human creatures; the struggle for life animates them; they are all of one uniform blackness in the fog; they go to their daily task, they all use the same gestures." So the fog renders the citizens indeterminate, part of a vast process which they themselves can hardly understand.

One other aspect of this darkness severely affected the inhabitants of London. Every observer noticed that the gas-lights were turned on throughout the day in order to afford some interior light, and noticed, too, how the street-lamps seemed like points of flame in the swirling miasma. But the ambience of the dark fog settled upon many streets which had no lighting at all, thereby affording cover for theft, violence and rape on an unprecedented scale. In that sense the fog was indeed "particular" to London because it intensified and emphasised all the darker characteristics of the city. Darkness is also at the heart of the notion of this black vapour as an emanation of sickness. If "all smell is disease," as the Victorian social reformer Edwin Chadwick thought, then the acrid smell of the London fog was a sure token of contamination and epidemic fear; it is as if the contents of a million lungs were being disseminated through the streets.

The very texture and colour of the city carried all the marks of its fog. The author of *Letters from Albion*, written as early as 1810, noticed that above the level of the ground "you see nothing but the naked brick fronts of the houses all blackened by the smoke of coal," while an American traveller remarked on the "uniform dinginess" of London buildings. Heinrich Heine was the author of one of the most evocative and instructive remarks upon the city—"this overworked London defies the imagination and breaks the heart" (1828)—and he himself observed that the streets and buildings were "a brown olive-green colour, on account of the damp and coal smoke." So the fog had become part of the physical texture of the city, this most unnatural of natural phenomena leaving its presence upon the stones. Perhaps in part the city defied the imagination, in Heine's phrase, because in that darkness "which seems neither to belong to the day nor to the night" the world itself was suspended; in the fog it became a place of concealment and of secrets, of whispers and fading footsteps.

It can be said that fog is the greatest character in nineteenth-century fiction, and the novelists looked upon fog as might people upon London Bridge, "peering over the parapets into a nether sky of fog, with fog all round them, as if they were up in a balloon and hanging in the misty clouds." When Carlyle called the fog "fluid ink" he was rehearsing the endless possibilities of describing London through the medium of the fog, as if only in the midst of this unnatural darkness could the true characteristics of the city be discerned. In the narratives of Sherlock Holmes, written by Arthur Conan Doyle from 1887 to 1927, the city of crime and of unsolved mysteries is quintessentially the city of fog. On one foggy morning in *A Study in Scarlet*, "a dun-coloured veil hung over the housetops looking like a reflection of the mud-coloured streets beneath." In "the steamy, vaporous air" of a "dense drizzly fog" in *The Sign of Four*, Dr. Watson soon "lost my bearings . . . Sherlock Holmes was never at fault, however, and he muttered the names as the cab rattled through squares and in and out by tortuous by-streets." London becomes a labyrinth. Only if you "soak up the atmosphere," in the cliché of travellers and sightseers, will you not become bewildered and lost.

The greatest novel of London fog is, perhaps, Robert Louis Stevenson's *The Strange Case of Dr. Jekyll and Mr. Hyde* (1886) in which the fable of changing identities and secret lives takes place within the medium of the city's "shifting insubstantial mists." In many respects the city itself is the changeling, its appearance altering when "the fog would be quite broken up, and a haggard shaft of daylight would glance in between the swirling wreaths." Where good and evil live side by side, and thrive together, the strange destiny of Dr. Jekyll does not seem quite so incongruous. Then for a moment the mist melts and the curtain lifts, revealing a gin palace, an eating-house, a "shop for the retail of penny numbers and two penny salads," all this life continuing beneath the canopy of darkness like a low murmur of almost inaudible sound. Then once again "the fog settled down again on that part, as brown as umber, and cut him off from his blackguardly surroundings." This also is the condition of living in London—to be "cut off," isolated, a single mote in the swirl of fog and smoke. To be alone among the confusion is perhaps the single most piercing emotion of any stranger in the city.

Elizabeth Barrett Browning wrote of "the great town's weltering fog" as somehow erasing all the signs and tokens of the city, blurring "Spires, bridges, streets, and squares as if a sponge had wiped out London" (1856). Fear of this invisibility actively assisted the programme of building and decoration that marked the Victorian city. *Building News*, in 1881, discussed the fact that "the smoky atmosphere has done its best to clothe our most costly buildings in a thin drapery of soot . . . they soon become dark and sombre masses . . . all play of light and shade is lost." That is precisely why architects decided to clothe their buildings in bright red brick and shining terracotta so that they would remain visible; the features of nineteenth-century building, which may seem vulgar or gaudy, were attempts to stabilise the identity and legibility of the city.

Of course there were some who extolled the virtues of the fog. Dickens, despite his lugubrious descriptions, once referred to it as London's ivy. For Charles Lamb it was the medium through which his vision, in every sense, was conceived and perfected. Where some saw only the amounts of sulphate deposited in the bowels of the fog, particularly in the City and the East End, others saw the murky atmosphere as clothing the river and its adjacent areas "with poetry, as with a veil, and the poor buildings lose themselves in the dim sky, and the tall chimneys become campanile, and the warehouses are palaces in the night." This devoted invocation is from Whistler, the painter of mist and smoke at twilight, and it contrasts sharply with a comment about the building of the Embankment in the same period as his atmospheric works of art. "Who would think of promenading along the channel of a great hazy, ague-giving river in any case?" But Whistler's opinions were shared by other artists who saw the fog as London's greatest attribute. The late nineteenth-century Japanese artist Yoshio Markino noted that "Perhaps the real colours of some buildings in London might be rather crude. But this crude colour is so fascinating in the mists. For instance that house in front of my window is painted in black and yellow. When I came here last summer I laughed at its ugly colour. But now the winter fogs cover it and the harmony of its colour is most wonderful." It is sometimes observed that the buildings of London look best in the rain, as if they had been built and coloured especially for the sake of showers. A case can be made, then, that even the private houses of Londoners are designed to be pleasing in the fog.

When Monet stayed in London between 1899 and 1901, he had come to paint the fogs. "Then, in London, above all what I love is the fog . . . It is the fog that gives it its magnificent breadth. Those massive, regular blocks become grandiose within that mysterious cloak." Here he is repeating, in more delicate tones, a conversation which Blanchard Jerrold held with that Gothic delineator of fog, Gustave Doré. "I could tell my fellow traveller that he had at last seen one of these famous darknesses which in every stranger's mind are the almost daily mantle of the wonderful and wonder-working Babylon." Here the fog contributes to the city's splendour and awfulness; it creates magnificence, yet, with the suggestion of Babylon, it represents some primeval and primitive force which has lingered over the centuries. For Monet the London fog became a token, or revelation, of mystery; in his depictions of its subtle atmospheres and ever-changing colours, there is also a strong impression that the city is about to dissolve or be hidden for ever. In that sense he is trying to capture the essential spirit of the place beyond particular epochs and phases. His paintings of Charing Cross Bridge, for example, give it the brooding presence of some elemental force; it might be a great bridge constructed by the Romans or a bridge built in the next millennium. This is London at its most shadowy and powerful, powerful precisely because of the shadows which it casts. Ancient shapes loom out of the foggy darkness or the dim violet light, yet these shapes also change quickly in a sudden shaft of light or movement of colour. This again is the mystery which Monet presents; this shrouded immensity is instinct with light. It is prodigious.

In the early years of the twentieth century, there was a marked diminution in the frequency and severity of foggy weather. Some attribute this change to the campaigns of the Coal Smoke Abatement Society, and the various attempts to substitute gas for coal, but the very expansion of the capital might paradoxically have lowered its levels of fog. Industries, and people, were now more widely dispersed and the intense heat-laden centre of smoke and fog was no longer burning so brightly. The whole phenomenon has been ably reported in an essay, "The Mysterious Disappearance of Edwardian London Fog," by H.T. Bernstein, in which it is claimed that coal-burning was not directly related to the incidence of fog. Some of the great London fogs appeared on Sundays, for example, when no factory chimneys were in operation. If fog was in part a meteorological phenomenon, it exhibited local and specific characteristics; it particularly affected parks and riversides, for example, as well as areas with low wind speed. It might swallow up Paddington, where no one could see their way, but leave Kensington less than a mile away to its brightness.

It has been said that "the last real fog was 'presented' on or about December 23, 1904"; it was pure white in colour and "the hansom cabmen were leading their horses, lamps went before the crawling omnibuses and some guests . . . went past one of the biggest London hotels without seeing it." In fact, throughout the 1920s and 1930s "pea-soupers" descended without warning. H.V. Morton, in his *In Search of London* (1951), remembered one such fog "which reduces visibility to a yard, which turns every lamp into a downward V of haze, and gives to every encounter a nightmare quality almost of terror." Here once more there is intimation of fog carrying fear into the heart of the city; it is perhaps no wonder that, when the easterly wind sent the clouds of yellow haze away from the city, the Berkshire farmers called it "blight."

Others, less distant, also suffered from early twentieth-century fogs. The Stoll film studios at Cricklewood had to close during the winter because, according to Colin Sorensen's *London on Film*, "The fog got into the studio for about three months." The element of intrusiveness, or of invasion, also emerges here: many people recall how, upon the opening of a front door, draughts of smoke-laden fog would eddy through a private house and curl up in corners. The "eternal smoke of London" found other pathways, not least through the vent holes of the underground system where Arthur Symons noticed how its "breath rises in clouds and drifts voluminously over the gap of the abyss, catching at times a ghastly colour from the lamplight. Sometimes one of the snakes seems to rise and sway out of the tangle, a column of yellow blackness."

But perhaps the worst of all London fogs were the "smogs" of the early 1950s, when thousands died of asphyxiation and bronchial asthma. In some of the theatres the fog was so thick that the actors could not be seen upon the stage. On the afternoon of 16 January 1955 there was "almost total darkness . . . People who experienced the phenomenon said it seemed as if the world was coming to an end." A Clean Air Act was passed in 1956, as a result of public disquiet, but in the following year another smog caused death and injury. Then again in the winter of 1962 a lethal smog killed sixty people in three days; there was "nil visibility" on the roads, shipping "at a standstill," trains cancelled. A newspaper report put the facts plainly: "The amount of smoke in the London air was 10 times higher than normal for a winter day yesterday. The amount of sulphur dioxide was 14 times higher than normal." Six years later there followed a more extensive Clean Air Act, and this legislation marked the end of London fog in its ancient form. Electricity, oil and gas had largely taken the place of coal, while slum clearance and urban renewal had reduced the level of close-packed housing.

But pollution has by no means disappeared; like London itself, it has simply changed its form. The city may now be in large part a "smokeless zone" but it is filled with carbon monoxide and hydrocarbons which together with "toxic secondary pollutants" such as aerosols can produce what is known as a "photochemical smog." High concentrations of lead in the London air and a general increase of sunshine in the cleaner air have in turn inspired more contamination. There is a problem with ozone at ground level and the effects of "temperature inversion" mean that the emissions from traffic and power stations, for example, cannot be released into the upper atmosphere. So they linger at the level of the streets. The fog that Tacitus described in the first century AD still hovers over London.

Night and Day

A depiction by Gustave Doré of poor vagrants huddled on Westminster Bridge on a starry night in the 1870s; it was said that the number of such vagrants could fully populate an average city.

CHAPTER 48

Let There Be Light

❧

The high death rate in London has been blamed in part upon the lack of natural light. The prevalence of rickets, for example, has been noted in this connection. It is revealed in Werner's *London Bodies* that in St. Bride's Lower Churchyard over 15 per cent of children's skeletons, dating from the nineteenth century, showed signs of that disorder, while those who did not succumb spent their lives upon "badly bowed limbs." So there was a yearning for light, or, rather, an instinctive need for light. If it could not be found naturally, then it must be artificially created to satisfy the appetite of the Londoner.

As early as the fifteenth century lights were established by statutory decree. In 1405 every house beside the main thoroughfare had to display a light at the Christmas watch and, ten years later, the mayor ordered that the same dwellings bear lamps or lights in the dark evenings between October and February, in the hours from dusk until nine o'clock. These lanterns were of transparent horn, rather than of glass. But medieval London remained in relative obscurity except, perhaps, for the light spread by those who carried torches to guide pedestrians or by servants who used the flare of flaming brands to accompany the passage of some great lord or cleric. In the early years of the seventeenth century "link-boys" bearing lights also became a source of brightness.

The great change in the street lighting of the capital did not occur, however, until 1685 when a projector named Edward Heming "obtained letters patent conveying to him, for a term of years, the exclusive right of lighting up London." He stipulated that for a fee he would fit a light in front of every tenth door, from six to twelve, on nights without a moon. Heming's patent was not ultimately satisfactory, however, and nine years later the aldermanic authorities gave permission to the Convex Light Company to illuminate the city; the name of the company itself suggests the development from the horn lantern to more subtle and sophisticated means of lighting with lenses and reflectors. Light had become fashionable. Indeed in the first decades of the eighteenth century, as part of the general "improvements" in the condition of London, the illumination of the streets became of paramount importance. It was still a matter of security—the Kensington Road, a notorious haunt of highwaymen, was the first to introduce oil-lamps with glazed lights, as early as 1694. In 1736 an Act was passed permitting the city authorities to implement a special lighting rate or lamp rate so that all the streets could be properly illuminated each night; as Stephen Inwood has suggested in *A History of London*, "this gave the City around 4,000 hours of lighting a year, compared to 300 or 400 before 1694, and 750 from 1694 to 1736." Suburban parishes also began to levy special rates for lighting; so gradually, and by degrees of illumination, London at night became a different city.

In the early decades of the eighteenth century observers and strangers remarked upon its glare, and upon its "white ways." By 1780 Archenholz reported that "As the English are prodigal of their money and attention in order to give everything that relates to the public an air of grandeur and magnificence, we might naturally expect to find London well lighted, and accordingly nothing can be more superb." It seemed that, as every year passed, the nights of the city became steadily brighter. In 1762 Boswell noted "the glare of shops and signs," while in 1785 another observed that "Not a corner of this prodigious city is unlighted . . . but this innumerable multitude of lamps affords only a small quantity of light, compared to the shops." It is entirely appropriate that in these two accounts of London's brightness the shops, the centre of trade and commerce, shine brightest of all.

Yet if it is an attribute of London that it becomes continually brighter— at first starting at a slow pace but then gradually increasing momentum until

by the late twentieth century it had become almost *over-bright*—the brightness of one generation will also be the dimness of a succeeding one: the light
of eighteenth-century London, the glory of the world, forty years later was
dismissed as little more than a toy. In his *Memoirs*, published in the middle of
the nineteenth century, John Richardson declared that "forty years ago the
lighting of the streets was effected by what were called parish lamps. The
lamp consisted of a small tin vessel, half filled with the worse train oil . . . In
this fluid fish blubber was a piece of cotton twist which formed the wick." In
those days, therefore, the lamp-lighter became a familiar figure in the streets
of London. There is a portrait of one in Hogarth's *A Rake's Progress* lighting
a lamp at the corner of St. James's Street and Piccadilly; his face has an oafish,
if not bestial, cast and he is spilling oil on the wig of the rake beneath. This
must have been a familiar enough mishap upon the streets. Richardson has his
own description of the lamp-lighters. "A set of greasy fellows redolent of
Greenland Dock were employed to trim and light these lamps, which they accomplished by the apparatus of a formidable pair of scissors, a flaming flam-
beau of pitched rope and a rickety ladder, to the annoyance and danger of all
passers-by. The oil vessel and wick were enclosed in a case of semi-opaque
glass . . . which obscured even the little light it encircled." These lamps were
rarely, if ever, cleaned. And so by all accounts the great brightness of eighteenth-century London seemed, at least to later Londoners, to be an illusion.
The streets did not seem ill-lit to their inhabitants at the time, however, because the brightness of London exactly conformed to their sense of the social
milieu. The light is relative to the expectations and preoccupations of the city.

That is why the great change came at the beginning of the era of the imperial city when, in 1807, oil gave way to gas. It was first employed in Beech
Street and Whitecross Street, where now the Barbican stands, but a year
later it was used to light up Pall Mall. There is a cartoon by Rowlandson,
dated 1809 and entitled *A Peep at the Gas Light in Pall Mall*. One gentleman
points a cane towards the new lamp and explains that "the Smoke falling thro
water is deprivd of substance and burns as you see," while a less expert citizen protests: "Aarh honey if this man bring fire thro water we shall soon
have the Thames burn down." In the same print a Quaker declares, "What
is this to the *inward* light," as if the progress of technology were itself a kind
of profanity, while a prostitute tells her client, "If this light is not put a stop
to—we must give up our business. We may as well shut up shop." To which
he replies, "True my dear not a dark corner to be got for love or money."

In 1812 Westminster Bridge was the first to be illuminated by the new fuel. The highly intellectual Hester Thrale declared, in 1817, towards the end of her life, that "such a glare is cast by the gas lights, I knew not where I was after sunset. Old Father Thames, adorned by four beautiful bridges, will hardly remember what a poor figure he made eighty years ago, I suppose, when gay folks went to Vauxhall in barges, an attendant barge carrying a capital band of music playing Handel's 'Water Music'—as it has never been played since." So the river, quite changed by the gas-light, became the object of surprise or bewilderment—"I knew not where I was." Even the music upon the water seemed changed.

There were many illustrations of street-lights in all their variety, modelled in baroque and classical styles, with additional representations of gasometers and elaborate retorts. The old epoch of the lamp-lighter was mocked in the process, but the less advantageous aspects of the new lighting were also depicted. A series of cartoons depicting *A London Nuisance* has one of a lamplighter on the top of his ladder spilling oil over an unfortunate pedestrian, in the old style, while another shows a gas explosion in a chemist's shop. That prospect of combustion was one of the reasons why the domestic use of gas was not fully in place until the 1840s. Yet by 1823 there were four private companies vying for trade, much of which, along the two hundred miles of gas mains laid just beneath the surface of the streets, was once more devoted to the lighting of the principal shops.

The shops of the eighteenth century, with their narrow windows and panes of bulging glass, were lit inside by tallow candles or blinking oil-lamps. With the modern shops of the next century, the encroaching darkness of twilight was suddenly the "herald of such a light such as the sun never darts into the nooks and crannies of traffic; broad streams of gas flash like meteors into every corner of the wealth-crammed mart." The new gas-lighting would not only banish vice and crime from the streets, it would also materially increase the speed and volume of trade: truly London light. "But it is really at night that London must be seen!" wrote Flora Tristan in her *London Journal* of 1840. "London, magically lit by its millions of gas lights, is resplendent! Its broad streets disappearing into the distance; its shops, where floods of light reveal the myriad sparkling colours of all the masterpieces conceived by human industry." A similar enthusiasm is evinced in an account of the Strand where "the shops were all brightness and wonder," and of another thoroughfare where the shops "seem to be made entirely of glass." You might be forgiven for thinking that the great new brightness was the brightness of burgeoning commerce.

Yet there were other attitudes towards the new light. For some it was harsh and unnatural, the lurid emanation of an artificial city. To other Londoners, however, the gas was most glorious for the shadows which it cast. It created a city of softness and mystery, with sudden pools of light fringed by blackness and silence. So in certain areas London's ancient presence stifled its new light; the shadows, and the mystery, returned. This may perhaps account for the speed with which London became accustomed to higher levels of brightness. When they ceased to be dazzled by the illumination of gas, the old presences of London began to reassert themselves. The author of *The Little World of London* noticed down one lane that "the glass of the gas-lamp has been wantonly pelted away to the last fragment. The flame flickers in the night-breeze, and casts its fitful gleams upon every form of poverty and wretchedness and vice, here huddled together as in a common asylum." Gas, instead of being the incandescent banisher of vice and crime, here compounds the misery of the dispossessed. In a poem of the 1890s by Arthur Symons, there is a description of

> The dim wet pavement lit irregularly
> With shimmering streaks of gaslight, faint and frayed

where once again it is the flickering, inconstant and insubstantial nature of the city light that is manifested. It is as if the city has swallowed up the light or, rather, fundamentally changed its nature. In the night paintings of late Victorian London, for example, the dark shapes of the city beneath the moon are only momentarily illuminated by lines of gas-lamps. Paradoxically that which had seemed most new, and revolutionary, in lighting soon became identified with all that was overburdened with age and history. Who has not, in imagination, seen the gas-lamps in the fog? It is the very permanence and longevity of London which transform even the most recent invention into an aspect of its ancient life. The yellow gas in the old square lamps was replaced by green incandescent gases, dancing like so many glow-worms in their glass bottles, but these in turn were replaced by a new force.

The first employment of electric light was upon the Embankment in 1878, followed by the illumination of Billingsgate and the Holborn Viaduct as well as two or three theatres. Since London was then the great centre of world power it is appropriate that the first power station in the world should be at 57 Holborn Viaduct; it was constructed by Thomas Edison in 1883 and less than ten years later, according to that commercial imperative which is by now so familiar, the first electric advertising signs were placed in Piccadilly Circus. The city exploited this new brightness from the beginning, and once more "the golden tint of the electric light" was apostrophised; when "the gold and silver lamps" emerge from the twilight, "The shops shine bright anew." There seems to be no escape from the conjunction of light and trade. Like other forms of light before it, however, electricity was said to render the city unreal and unfamiliar. One Londoner suggested that the novel light lent "a corpse-like quality" to the skin while in the floodlit streets "the crowd looks almost dangerous and garish." This particular light was also more "cruel and clinical" than its predecessors. Those who became accustomed to electricity, however, soon looked back upon gas with the same nostalgic contempt as those living in gas-light regarded the old days of the oil-lamp. Arthur Machen, in the early 1920s, recollected that gas-lit London was "all glorious and glittering" but that now "I should find it sombre and gloomy, an abode of shadows and dark places, ill-lit with flickering and unsteady yellow flames." The electricity moved down Oxford Street and Kensington High Street, Knightsbridge and Notting Hill. It spread from Piccadilly by means of overhead cable to Regent's Park and the Strand. By 1914 there were seventy power stations operating within the metropolis, turning it into a generator of energy and power.

The variety of lighting supplies at first had the effect of turning London into an unevenly lit city; each of its twenty-eight boroughs made their own arrangements with the suppliers of electricity, which means that a car travelling at speed in the 1920s might pass from one street bathed in a very high light intensity to one shrouded in comparative darkness. But this had always been the case, since the city of contrasts had relied upon contrasted light. As Arthur Symons wrote in *London: A Book of Aspects*, "In London we light casually, capriciously, everyone at his own will, and so there are blinding shafts at one step and a pit of darkness at the next." The many accidents in the 1920s, however, created a demand for a level standard of illumination, which in turn led to a standardisation of lamp-posts with columns 25 feet high and 150 feet apart. It is one aspect of London life which even the most knowledgeable citizens scarcely notice, and yet the uniformity of lighting in the major streets is perhaps the most significant aspect of the modern city.

In the autumn of 1931 certain public buildings were illuminated by floodlighting for the first time; so great was the interest and excitement that the streets

were filled with spectators. It is as if London is always revealing itself anew.
Nine years after the floodlighting, however, the night city was plunged into
profound darkness during the black-out, when in certain respects it reverted to
medieval conditions. In the streets themselves, as reported in Philip Ziegler's
London at War, "It seemed . . . sinister to have so many people shuffling
around in the blackness"; familiar roads became "impenetrable mysteries,"
leaving Londoners frightened and confused. One recalled finding her destination but only after becoming "damp with perspiration and quite exhausted."
Storms were welcomed since, in the instantaneous lightning flash, a well-
known corner or crossing could be glimpsed. This sense of bewilderment and
panic could have emerged in the fourteenth and fifteenth centuries no less than
during the Second World War, but this latter-day darkness served only to
confirm how frightening and mysterious London might still become.

When the black-out was lifted in the autumn of 1944 the relief was palpable. "It is no longer inky black, but all softly lit up and shining, and all the
little beams of light are reflected most charmingly in the wet streets." Those
"little beams" in later years gave way to neon, mercury and general fluores-
cence so that, at the beginning of a new century, the city lights up the sky for
many miles around and has become a greater source of brightness than the
moon and stars. For some this is a source of anger, as if the artificial city were
somehow contaminating the cosmos itself. Yet there are still many streets
which are only partly illuminated, and many small passages and byways
which are scarcely lit at all. It is still possible to cross from a brightly lit thoroughfare into a dark street, just as it has been for the last three hundred years,
and to feel afraid.

But does London have its own natural light? Henry James noted "the
way the light comes down leaking and filtering from its cloud ceiling." There
is a sense of damp and misty brightness which other observers have recorded,
as if everything were seen through tears. But James also noticed "the softness
and richness of tone, which objects put on in such an atmosphere as soon as
they begin to recede." Buildings and streets dissolve into the distance, therefore, without the clarity of the light in Paris or New York. It has been said
that nowhere "is there such a play of light and shade, such a struggle of sun
and smoke, such aerial gradations and confusions." Richard Jefferies, who in
his apocalyptic novel *After London* (1885) depicted the city as a miasmic
wasteland, had an eye for just such "aerial gradations"—from a yellow sunset to an "indefinite violet" in the south-west, from the dazzling light of summer to the redness of the winter sun when the streets and buildings are

suffused with a "fiery glow." The faint blue-green mist was known as the light "that London takes the day to be," softening and blending the cityscape while in the parks there hovers "a lovely pearl-grey haze, soft and subdued." Yet there is also a coldness in the light of the streets which may be glimpsed in the grey of winter and the blue mist of spring, the haze of summer and the "orange sunsets of autumn." It is derived from the immensity which the light of London reflects so that, as Hippolyte Taine put it, it becomes the emanation of a "huge conglomeration of human creation" when "the shimmering of river waves, the scattering of the light imprisoned in vapour, the soft whitish or pink tints which cover these vastnesses, diffuse a sort of grace over the prodigious city." That sense of immensity is glimpsed in Virginia Woolf's account of London as "a swarm of lights with a pale yellow canopy drooping above it. There were the lights of the great theatres, the lights of the long streets, lights which indicated huge squares of domestic comfort, lights that hung high in the air. No darkness would ever settle upon these lamps, as no darkness has settled upon them for hundreds of years." The lights of London blaze perpetually. From the air the lights shine for miles like a vast web of brightness. The city will never cool down. It will remain incandescent. Yet where there is light there is also shadow, and the darkness of night.

CHAPTER 49

Night in the City

There have been many accounts of the London night. Books entitled *City Nights* and *Night Life* have been entirely devoted to the subject. James Thomson called it the city of dreadful night (1874). It may be that the city is truly itself, and becomes truly alive, only at night. That is why it exercises a constant fascination. The effect begins at twilight, in that crepuscular hour with "the dusky multitude of chimney pots and the small black houses," of "muddy ways and slatternly passages" when, in the words of Julian Wolfreys's *Writing London*, "the sinister, the threatening, monstrous inhumanity of the limitless city" becomes apparent. These are all accounts from the nineteenth century, but night terrors of earlier centuries are no less substantial. From earliest times the streets of the city have never been safe at night. Curfew was rung at nine and, in theory, the alehouses were closed and citizens were meant to stay indoors. In the later sixteenth and early seventeenth centuries, however, drama, verse, epistles and satires came to emphasise the nature of the city night with lines such as these quoted in Thomas Burke's *The Streets of London*:

Frightening of cullies, and bombastine whores,
Wringing off knockers, and from posts and doors

Rubbing out milk maids' and some other scores,
Scowring the watch, or roaring in the streets,
Lamp-blacking signs with divers other feats . . .

These were the pranks of the "roaring boys," which were juvenile enough compared with the more violent excesses of the gangs, or the thieves, or the rapists, under cover of darkness. Thomas Shadwell, the late seventeenth-century dramatist, remarked how at approximately "two in the morning comes the bell-man, and in a dismal tone repeats worse rhymes than a cast poet of the nursery can make; after him come those rogues that wake people with their barbarous tunes, and upon their tooting instruments make a more hellish noise than they do at a Playhouse when they flourish for the entrance of witches." From the evidence of the drama, and reports such as this, it seems clear that at night the city was almost as noisy as day, with the difference only that the sounds at night were more frantic and desperate, among yells and screams and shouts and whistles punctuating the early hours with their own uneasy refrain. If you were to listen intently you might hear "Who's there?" or "Your purse!" or "Dog, are you dumb? Speak quickly!"

"My ears were so serenaded on every side," wrote Ned Ward at the beginning of the eighteenth century, "with the grave musick of sundry passing bells, the rattling of coaches, and the melancholy ditties of Hot Bak'd wardens and Pippins . . . nothing could I see but light and nothing hear but noise." The unnaturalness of the London night is emphasised here, filled as it is with light and sound rather than the silence and darkness celebrated in the poetry of the evening landscape. When Samuel Pepys accompanied Lady Paulina Montague through the nocturnal streets she was terrified "every step of the way."

The reasons for her fear are outlined in John Gay's poem, "Of Walking the Streets by Night," which is part of his *Trivia*—*trivium* being the point where three streets meet, the word generally used to characterise public thoroughfares of every description. In the "busie Street" at night planks and ladders and low awnings offered continual obstacles to progress. "Now all the Pavement sounds with trampling feet" amid the neighing of horses and the lowing of bullocks; the coachmen hustled each other, and lashed each other with whips; there were fights in the streets also "till down they fall and grappling roll in Mud." Gay noticed one notorious spot for night traffic jams, by St. Clement Danes in the Strand where the church itself acted as a massive impediment; the streets upon either side of it had no posts to distinguish road from pavement, so the result was a confusion of coaches, horses and pedestrians worse compounded by the fact that loaded wagons were brought from the Thames through the narrow side-streets which led on to the main thoroughfare. To be caught in the "mob" or "throng" was dangerous indeed. If the solitary walker was not pushed and jostled and cursed, his wig, or cambric handkerchief, or watch, or snuff-box were likely to be stolen; to the raucous sounds of the night, then, was added the cry of "Stop Thief!" The pedestrian risked being crushed by carriage wheels, or pushed aside by chair-men, but more dangerous were the open cellars from which goods were sold. There was thick mud in the streets and, from above,

> empty Chamber-pots come pouring down
> From Garret Windows; you have cause to bless
> The gentle Stars, if you come off with Piss.

It was wise to pay no attention to the sound of blows being exchanged, or the cries for help.

Yet, at night, even the houses of Londoners were not necessarily havens from the anxiety and unrest of the streets. About two o'clock in the morning on 21 March 1763 Boswell's candle went out at his lodgings in Crown Street, Westminster. He went down to the kitchen in order to find a tinder-box, but he could see nothing of the kind there. "I was now filled with gloomy ideas of the terrors of the night." So the darkness without spread fear within. "I was also apprehensive that my landlord, who always keeps a pair of loaded pistols by him, might fire at me as a thief." The dangers of vandalism and theft were very great, then, if the owner of the house must keep pistols by his bed; it resembles the practice of Samuel Johnson, who always took a stout cudgel with him before he ventured upon the streets. So Boswell "went up to my room, sat quietly till I heard the watchman calling 'Past three o'clock.' I then called to him to knock at the door of the house where I lodged. He did so, and I opened it to him and got my candle relumined without danger." Here is a vignette of London life which, despite its brevity, is arresting—the call of the watchman, the instruction from Boswell, and the hurried lighting of the candle.

The night of nineteenth-century London has a less intimate aspect. The Victorians were fascinated and appalled by it. It is the period when the genre of "night painting" emerged among the artists of London, while in the theatre there were melodramas such as *London By Night* (1845) and *After Dark, a Tale of London Life* (1868). The poetry of the age is filled with intimations and images of the dark city, from Dowson and Lionel Johnson to George Meredith and Tennyson. It is as if the inhabitants of nineteenth-century London were haunted by the night city so that, in the words of Rudyard Kipling recalling his early experience of London in lodgings, "Here, for the first time, it happened that the night got into my head."

In the middle of the nineteenth century there came a vogue for "night walks": sketches or essays in which the solitary pedestrian made his way across the dark city, marking significant moments and scenes in a journey of unknown destination. For Charles Dickens, walking at night was a way of allaying private miseries; as a child he had walked through the city, and even in its nocturnal aspect it offered him a strange comfort and reassurance. It was if, whatever his own personal unhappiness, "it," the thing known as London, would always be there both solid and tangible. It was his true home, after all, and somehow it was incorporated within his own being. So Dickens walked "under the pattering rain . . . walk and walk and walk, seeing nothing but the interminable tangle of streets save at a corner, here and there, two policemen in conversation." This was now a guarded and supervised city, its corners manned by officers of the law; no longer the anarchy and exuberance recorded by John Gay in the 1770s. The silence is the silence of its vastness. Dickens crossed Waterloo Bridge, paying a halfpenny to the toll-keeper wrapped up in his booth, where the Thames had an "awful look" of blackness and reflected light and where "the very shadow of the immensity of London seemed to be oppressively upon the river." This is what is most noticeable about the nineteenth- and twentieth-century city at night: its "immensity," a vast capital stretching outwards into the darkness. Having crossed the bridge Dickens passed the theatres of Wellington Street and the Strand, "with the rows of faces faded out, the lights extinguished and the seats all empty." Here is a representation of London in miniature as one great darkened theatre. It is significant that Charles Dickens next made his way to Newgate Prison in order to touch "its rough stone." London is both theatre and prison. At night its true aspects are outlined clearly, shorn of the vagaries of the day.

He visited the Courts of Law, then at Westminster, before moving on to the abbey where it became for him "a solemn consideration what enormous hosts of dead belong to one old great city and how if they were raised while the living slept, there would not be the space of a pin's point in all the streets and ways for the living to come out into. Not only that, but the vast armies of dead would overflow the hills and valleys beyond the city, and would stretch away all round it, God knows how far." This is perhaps what one inheritor of Dickens's urban vision, George Gissing, meant when he exclaimed "London by night! Rome is poor by comparison." It is the presence of the past, or the presence of the dead, which lends the night images of London their peculiar intensity and power. Of all cities London seems most occupied by its dead, and the one which most resounds to the tread of passing generations. It is not as if the physical fabric of the old city has survived intact. Gissing's comparison with Rome is again appropriate here; the "eternal city" has so many ruins of its greatness that the spirit of the past has had no room in which to flourish. In London the past is a form of occluded but fruitful memory, in which the presence of earlier generations is felt rather than seen. It is an echoic city, filled with shadows, and what better time to manifest itself than at night?

Another night voyager of the mid-nineteenth century, Charles Manby Smith, noticed, in an essay entitled "Twenty Four Hours of London Streets," that the slightest sound reverberated between the great walls of houses and public buildings, with his own footsteps echoing as if "some invisible companion dogged our march." He heard the silence in the old walled City, which is all the more fearful and oppressive after the "humming, booming surge-like sound" of the day.

It represents a great change in the nature of city life which over the years spread wider and wider beyond the old City; that which was most populous during the day is now the least populated at night. Few people lived in the City—and fewer now, at the start of the twenty-first century—and the old centres of habitation have been steadily abandoned for life upon the perimeters. It is the single most important reason for the relative silence and peacefulness of London over the last century.

This mid-nineteenth-century pedestrian anticipated the later environment and atmosphere of London, when he observed "the apparently numberless and interminable rows of streets lying in the voiceless silence, and distinctly mapped out by the long and regular lines of lamps on either side of the way." This is a vision of the city as part of an inhuman, mechanical alignment. "There is no other spectacle, that we know of that intimates so significantly the huge extent of this overgrown metropolis. The dead dumbness that reigns in these long, empty avenues appals the mind, and sends the imagination of the pedestrian wandering for ever onwards and onwards." So at night London becomes a city of the dead, the silence of the nineteenth century continuing through the twentieth into the twenty-first.

In *London Nights*, published in 1925, it is remarked that "the past has a stronger hold on the night than it has on the day"; while walking beneath the Thames in the tunnel which connects the north and south banks, for example, "you might be exploring the tombs of buried London thousands of years hence." In this sense it then becomes an infinite city—"London is every city that ever was and ever will be"—which in its illimitable regions manifests the true nature of the human community. That is why at night the most visible inhabitants of the city are those without a home. In "all manner of holes and corners the homeless may be found sleeping in winter nights; 'mid the ruin of half-demolished houses, on the stairs leading from viaducts, in corners of the Blackwall Tunnel, in recesses in massive buildings, in porches of churches." That reality has not changed in the intervening years. Then, as now, the Embankment remains a central place for the vagrants to gather despite the cold and damp air coming from the Thames. It is almost as if, at night, the river calls them.

There are certain streets which in the present century seem never entirely empty at night—one may name Old Compton Street in Soho, Upper Street in Islington and Queensway in Bayswater as examples—and there are, as there have been over the centuries, all-night restaurants such as those in St. John Street and in the Fulham Road. But the general impression of contemporary London at night is of a dull silence. There is no feeling of real danger, only the awareness that one can walk until dawn, and then a further dawn, without coming to the end of interminable streets with houses on either side. The shopping malls and some of the thoroughfares are monitored by surveillance cameras, so that it is impossible ever to feel completely alone.

The cameras represent one way in which modern London has changed. It has become self-conscious, forever watchful of its own citizens, almost daring them to manifest the energy and violence of their predecessors. There is never complete silence, however; it is punctuated by the humming of neon lamps and by the sirens of police cars or ambulances. That low and remote sound is of the traffic perpetually passing through, while in the east the glow of the lamps becomes paler with the approaching dawn.

CHAPTER 50

A City Morning

God give you good morrow, my master, past five o'clock and a fair morning": that is how the watchman of the seventeenth century heralded the dawn, the time when most of the citizens were waking and preparing for the work of the day.

Then as now the eastern suburbs of the city went to bed earlier, and rose earlier, than their western counterparts. The markets were busy and the produce had already been brought from the surrounding countryside in wagons. One of the complaints of Londoners was that they were perpetually being woken, while it was still dark, by the clatter of the wheels and the neighing of the horses as fruits and vegetables were transported to Leadenhall or Covent Garden. The essayist Richard Steele has a fine description (11 August 1712) of the gardeners who sailed down the river with their produce to the various markets of the city: "I landed with Ten Sail of Apricock Boats at *Strand-Bridge*, after having put in at *Nine-Elms*, and taken in Melons, consigned by Mr. Cuffe of that Place, to Sarah Sewell and Company at their stall in *Covent-Garden*." They unloaded the cargo at Strand-Bridge at six that morning, at the time when the hackney-coachmen of the previous night were just going off duty. Some passing sweeps engaged in "Raillery" with the fruit girls "about the Devil and *Eve*." The details of the wit are not recorded. There are

other descriptions of the cart-horses steaming and stamping in the market as
the dawn breaks, of the carters sleeping upon their sacks, of the lines of
porters carrying fruits and vegetables to their various stalls.

By six o'clock the apprentices were already pulling up the shutters, lighting the fires, or putting out the wares for sale and display. They washed down
the pavement outside, while the maids swept the steps of the more fashionable houses. The street vendors, and sweeps, and other itinerants, were soon
making their way through the thoroughfares which grew more crowded as
the day advanced. And, as the years progressed, the street activity seemed to
increase. In the eighteenth century it was suggested that cheesemongers
"should not set out their butter and cheese so near the edge of their shop-win-
dows, nor put their firkins in the path-ways, by which many a good coat and
silk gown may be spoiled." Here was one indication of the general lack of
room. The sheer crowdedness of the daytime city is always a paramount
feature of its life, and there were remarks that "barbers and chimney sweepers have no right by charter to rub against a person well-dressed, and then offer him satisfaction by single combat." There were other traders whom it was
wise to avoid including the baker with his apron covered in flour and paste,
the small-coal man, the butcher with his bloody leather apron and the chan-
dler from whose basket spots of tallow might fall. There were constant complaints about car-men using the pavement rather than the road to carry their
charges, and about workmen carrying ladders or pieces of timber upon their
shoulders in the middle of crowded thoroughfares.

So there was of necessity an art of walking the streets by day, as well as
by night. There were certain rules which were generally observed. The wall
was "surrendered" to females, so that they would not be jostled on to the
road, while it was considered a duty to direct "the groaping Blind." Never
ask directions from an apprentice, because these young and lively Londoners
were known to delight in sending any stranger in the wrong direction; it was
always best to ask assistance from a shopkeeper or tradesman. If you wished
to urinate go into some court or "secret corner." Avoid Watling Street and
Ludgate Hill because of the crowds that throng there; much better to walk
along the broader pavements of the Strand or Cheapside, but in every main
street, nevertheless,

Full charg'd with News the breathless Hawker runs,
Shops open, Coaches roll, Carts shake the Ground,
And all the Streets with passing Cries resound.

In the early nineteenth century, as occupations and areas began to be differentiated on social lines, various formal urban types appear. At eight o'clock and ten o'clock the postman, in scarlet tunic, made his deliveries in the West End, while the "musicians" and old-clothes-sellers made their way from the East End towards the centre. The commercial clerks walked down the Strand towards the Admiralty and Somerset House, while the government clerks tended to ride down to Whitehall and Downing Street in broughams.

This was the morning tide of the citizens. The nineteenth-century journalist G.A. Sala knew them well. "You may know the cashiers in the private banking houses by their white hats and buff waistcoats; you may know the stock-brokers by their careering up Ludgate Hill in dog-carts, and occasionally tandems ... you may know the Jewish commission agents by their flashy broughams ... you may know the sugar-bakers and soap-boilers by the comfortable double-bodied carriages," and the warehousemen only "by their wearing gaiters."

Between nine and ten the omnibuses arrived at the Bank with thousands of occupants, while on the Thames itself a large number of "swift, grimy little steamboats" had picked up passengers from the piers at Chelsea and Pimlico, Hungerford Bridge and Southwark, Waterloo and Temple, before disgorging them to the piers by London Bridge. Thames Street, both Upper and Lower, was "invaded by an ant-hill swarm of spruce clerks, who mingle strangely with the fish-women and the dock-porters."

The London morning "hungered" for its crowds and, equally voracious, "the insatiable counting houses soon swallow them." Not just the counting-houses were filled, but also all the workshops, warehouses and factories of the metropolis. The bars of the public houses were opened. The baked-potato men and the owners of coffee stalls were engaged in their brisk business. In the West End the shoe-cleaners and commercial travellers were already at their work, while in the adjacent courts and alleys the vast army of the poor swarmed out of doors. There was a nineteenth-century phrase that "you can hardly shut the street door for them" and, even in the poor quarters, the morning brought "a desperate, ferocious levity" as if the opening of each day's misery could elicit only an hysterical response.

There is indeed an insistent rhythm to the routine of London. The Exchange opens and closes its gates, the banks of Lombard Street are filled with and then emptied of customers, the glare of the shops brightens and then fades. In the later decades of the nineteenth century the trains as well as the omnibuses brought in the multitudes from the suburbs. But what the city takes in during the morning it spews forth at evening, so that there is a general pulse of people and power which keeps its heart beating. This is what Charlotte Brontë meant when she recorded that "I have seen the West End, the parks, the fine squares; but I love the City far better. The City seems so much more in earnest; its business, its rush, its roar, are such serious things, sights, sounds . . . At the West End you may be amused; but in the City you are deeply excited." She was "deeply excited" by the process of urban life itself, fulfilling in its own fashion the rhythms of night and day.

By the time the Post Office had barred up its letter boxes on the stroke of six o'clock, the businessmen and their clerks had left the City to its shopkeepers and dwindling number of householders. The full tide of the citizens ebbed and, through a thousand different streets, returned homeward. And, at the close of Dickens's *Little Dorrit*, "as they passed along in sunshine and shade, the noisy and the eager, and the arrogant and the froward and the vain, fretted and chafed, and made their usual uproar," all to return on the following morning.

And if they had woken up fifty, or a hundred, years later no doubt they would still have been able to follow the instinctive movement of the rush hour. Yet there is one distinction. If a nineteenth-century Londoner were to be set down in the City of the twenty-first century, perhaps at twilight in Cheapside when the office workers and computer operators are returning homeward, he would be astonished by the orderliness and uniformity of their progress. He might recognise a type, or an expression of thoughtfulness or anxiety—he might also be familiar with those who mutter to themselves—but the general quietness, together with a lack of human contact and of friendly exchange, might be unnerving.

London's Radicals

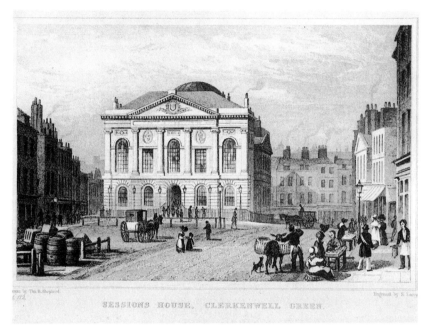

SESSIONS HOUSE, CLERKENWELL GREEN.

The Sessions House on Clerkenwell Green, part of the ritual of riot and punishment which has marked this small area for many hundreds of years.

CHAPTER 51

Where Is the Well of Clerkenwell?

*T*here is a story by *Arthur Machen* in which he describes an area in Stoke Newington where, on occasions, an enchanted landscape can be glimpsed and sometimes even entered; perhaps we may locate it near Abney Park, a somewhat desolate cemetery beside Stoke Newington High Street. This is the street where Defoe lived and where Edgar Allan Poe went unwillingly to school. Few people have seen this visionary place, or even know how to see it; but those who have can speak of nothing else. Machen wrote this story, "N," in the early 1930s, but as the century progressed other enchanted areas of London have emerged into the light. These remain powerful and visible to anyone who cares to look for them. One of these districts finds its centre upon Clerkenwell Green.

It is not "green" at all; it is a small area enclosed by buildings with a disused public lavatory in the middle. On both sides are narrow streets which in turn lead off into alleys or other streets. The green has its restaurants, two public houses, commercial premises and offices for architects or public relations consultants. It is, in epitome, a typical area of central London. But there are other signs and tokens of a different city. Just beyond the green are the relics of the eleventh-century church and hospital of St. John, where the Knights Templar and Knights Hospitaller had their headquarters; the crypt survives intact. A few yards to the south of the crypt, in the early sixteenth century, was erected St. John's Gate; this also still remains. Just on the northern edge of the green itself can be found the original site of the medieval well from which the district derives its name; in the eighteenth and early nineteenth centuries it was simply a broken iron pump let into the front wall of a tenement building but, since that time, it has been restored and preserved behind a thick glass wall. It marked the site of the stage where mystery plays were performed for centuries "beyond the memory of man," and in fact for many hundreds of years Clerkenwell was notorious for its dramatic representations. The yard of the Red Bull Inn, to the east of the green, is reputed to be the first theatrical venue where women appeared on stage. It is one example of the many continuities that charge Clerkenwell and its environs with an essential presence. But perhaps it is best to begin at the beginning.

On Clerkenwell Green the remains of a prehistoric settlement or encampment have been discovered, suggesting that this area of London has been continuously inhabited for many thousands of years. Perhaps the melancholy or ancientness which writers as diverse as George Gissing and Arnold Bennett have intuited, in this location, derives from the weariness of prolonged human settlement with all the cares and woes which it brings.

The area itself is first noticed in the early records of St. Paul's when, in the seventh century, it became part of the property of the bishop and canons of that institution. In the eleventh century William I awarded the land to one of his most successful supporters, Ralph fitz Brian, who in the proper terminology became lord of the fee of Clerkenwell, held of the bishop of London within the manor of Stepney by knight service. It is important to note here that from the beginning Clerkenwell was beyond "the bars" of London, and effectively part of Middlesex.

The heirs of Ralph became lords of the manor of Clerkenwell, and they in turn granted land and property for the maintenance of two religious foundations. The convent of St. Mary in Clerkenwell was established, roughly where the present church of St. James now stands, and the priory of the Knights Templar—known as St. John of Jerusalem—a little to the south-east on the other side of the green. So from the medieval period Clerkenwell became known, and identified, through its sacred or spiritual affiliations. Since the priory was first in the ownership of the Order of St. John of Jerusalem, it was a mustering point for the Crusaders; gradually it grew in size and extent over the adjacent area. The convent of St. Mary was similarly extensive but, as always, the life of the city kept on breaking through.

In 1301 the prioress of Clerkenwell petitioned Edward I "to provide and order a remedy because the people of London lay waste and destroy her corn and grass by their miracle plays and wrestling matches so that she has no profit of them nor can have any unless the king have pity for they are a savage folk and we cannot stand against them and cannot get justice by any law." This is one of the first reports that the Londoners were indeed "savage," and it is intriguing to note that the miracle plays were "their" own; it throws a wholly new light upon the presumed sacredness of early drama. Two generations later an even more "savage" and violent assault was mounted against the priory of St. John when, in 1381, the stone buildings of the Order were put to the torch by Wat Tyler's followers. The priory was badly damaged but not entirely destroyed, while the prior himself was beheaded on the spot because of his role as Richard II's principal tax-collector. Tyler's followers camped upon Clerkenwell Green, watching the hall and dormitory of the Knights go up in flame together with the counting-house, the distillery, the laundry, the slaughterhouse and very many other apartments or stables. It seemed as if the whole of Clerkenwell were on fire.

One of the most notorious lanes in the neighbourhood was Turnmill Street (so named because of its proximity to the many mills which harnessed the current of the Fleet), also known as Turnbull Street (because of the lines of cattle which crossed it in order to reach Smithfield). By the late thirteenth century the salubriousness of the area had been under threat from "filth and ordure and rubbage" thrown into the Fleet and, a century later, Henry IV ordered that it be "cleansed anew." He also obliged the authorities "to repayre a stone brydge over the Flete neare unto Trymyllstreate," the remote ancestor of the bridge over the Underground line which was once more repaired in the late 1990s.

Yet public works could not affect the public reputation of Clerkenwell; since it was "beyond the bars" it became the harbour for the outcast and those who wished to go beyond the law. So, from the beginning, it has been the home of groups who wish to be separate and separated. In Turnmill Street one William the Parchmenter in 1414 harboured the Lollard, Sir John Oldcastle, and was subsequently hanged, drawn and quartered for his hospitality. Clerkenwell also became the home of Jesuits and other recusants, and the district "was notorious as a centre for papists"; three suspected papists were hanged, drawn and quartered on Clerkenwell Green in the late sixteenth century. The Catholics moved out under the threat of persecution, although they returned in another guise 235 years later when Clerkenwell became an Italian quarter; in the interim other proscribed religious groups such as the libertarian Quakers, the Brownists, the Familists and the Schismatics congregated in the area of the green. Here is further evidence, then, of continuity in persecutions and outlawry. In more recent years the Freemasons have entered the area, with their headquarters in the Sessions House upon the green.

But if Turnmill Street began life as a haven for heretical Lollards and other radical proselytisers, it soon acquired a more dissolute reputation. It was marked down for condemnation in an ordinance of 1422 for "the abolition of Stewes within the City" but, since it was literally "without" the walls, few public measures touched it. In 1519 Cardinal Wolsey raided houses in Turnmill Street and the aptly named Cock Alley. "Now Farewel to Turnbull Street," writes the anonymous author of *The Merrie Mans Resolution* in 1600, "For that no comfort yields." E.J. Burford in *London: the Synfulle Citie* has reconstructed the topography of the street itself, with no less than nineteen "rents"—alleys, yards or courts—issuing off it. Their conditions were generally described as "noysome" which, in the context of sixteenth-century London, suggests a degree of nastiness which is perhaps not now imaginable. One of them was only twenty feet long and two feet six inches wide, so that "there was not room to get a coffin out without turning it on edge." Turnmill Street appears very often in city records as the haunt of crime as well as prostitution. In 1585 "Bakers hause, Turnmyll Street" was known as a harbouring house "for masterless men, and for such as lyve by thiefte and other such lyke sheefts," while, seven years later, a pamphlet entitled *Kinde Hartes Dreame* cited Turnmill Street as a place in which the owners charged "forty shillings yearly for a little Room with a smoky chimney . . . where several of these venereal virgins are resident." The association of Clerkenwell, and Turnmill Street in particular, with prostitution did not end in the sixteenth century. In 1613 Joan Cole and three more "Turnbull Street Whoares" were sentenced to be carted and whipped through the streets; one of them, Helen Browne, had been arrested while concealed "in a lewd house in Turnbull Street in a dark cellar."

If you come out of Farringdon Road Underground Station and walk a few feet to the left, you will find yourself in the very same Turnmill Street. Its left-hand side makes up the dead wall of the railway tracks, laid where the

Fleet River once flowed, while on the other side are office premises and warehouses of a generally unprepossessing nature. There are one or two alleys which act as a reminder of its interesting past; Turks Head Yard, formerly known as Bull Alley, Broad Yard on the site of Frying Pan Yard, and Benjamin Street, first laid down in 1740, are still to be seen. Yet echoes of a more distant past also survive. At the very top of Turnmill Street was, until recent years, a twenty-four-hour night-club of equivocal reputation known as Turnmills. *Mad Frank*, the memoirs of Frankie Fraser, a member of a notorious London gang, begins: "The *Independent* had it wrong when their reporter said I'd been shot dead outside Turnmills Night Club in 1991. I was only in hospital for two days that time." Streets such as this are reminiscent of Henry James's description of Craven Street, which runs down from the Strand, as "packed to blackness with accumulations of suffered experience." And, if there is a continuity of life, or experience, is it connected with the actual terrain and topography of the area? Is it too much to suggest that there are certain kinds of activity, or patterns of inheritance, arising from the streets and alleys themselves?

Clerkenwell Green is notable in other respects. The invasion of Clerkenwell by Wat Tyler and his followers is an example of its continuing radicalism, while the popular obloquy directed against the wealthy nuns of the priory beside the green speaks for the individual and the dispossessed. But the ramifications of these actions are rich and complex indeed. That great populist and demagogue John Wilkes, commemorated in the phrase "Wilkes and Liberty," was born just off the green in St. James's Close in 1727. One of the first meeting-places of the egalitarian London Corresponding Society was established at the Bull's Head in Jerusalem Passage just east of the green, and in 1794 "Clerkenwell crowds attacked recruiting offices at Battle Bridge and at Mutton Lane at the foot of the Green" with no doubt the same intensity as early fourteenth-century Londoners showed in attacking the Clerkenwell Priory. A group of radical plotters, the United Englishmen, were seized "at a low public house at Clerkenwell" in the spring of 1798 and then, a year later, a number of United Irishmen were arrested in the Nag's Head, St. John's Street, which leads away from the green towards Smithfield. Here undoubtedly is a catchment area of dissent and possible radical disruption.

In 1816 Henry Hunt, one of the leaders of the Chartist movement which called for universal suffrage, spoke to a crowd of 20,000 above the Merlin's Cave Tavern just north of Clerkenwell Green. Ten years later William Cobbett addressed a meeting on the green itself in opposition to the Corn Laws;

then, in 1832, the National Union of the Working Classes advertised a meeting in Coldbath Fields north of the green preparatory to a "National Convention, The only Means of Obtaining and Securing The Rights of The People." On the day itself "a man wearing a new white hat excited passers-by by reciting passages from a publication called *The Reformer* and loudly proclaiming that people in such an emergency ought to carry arms openly," a sentiment which had already been heard many times, over many centuries, in this neighbourhood.

The mass meeting was held and an affray took place in which a policeman was killed, all this in the immediate vicinity of Coldbath Prison, one of a number of penal institutions in the area. On Roque's map of London, delineated in the 1730s and 1740s, the area of Clerkenwell is seen to be exceedingly well regulated indeed and, as the editor of *The History of London in Maps* noticed, "Clerkenwell Green has a watch-house for policing; a pound for felons; a pillory to put them in; and a turnstile to provide a check on people passing through." As a known centre of radical activity, there was a strong emphasis on official surveillance. On Roque's map, too, can be seen the outline of Clerkenwell Gaol just to the east of the green.

It was a notorious prison, built in 1775, part of which comprised a number of underground tunnels lined with cells. Many radicals and schismatics were incarcerated there, and it became known as "a jail for hereticks." Of the inmates it was observed in W.J. Pinks's *History of Clerkenwell* that "they were lamentably ignorant and superstitious, and took great delight in sitting in a ring and telling their adventures and relating their dreams; they tell stories of spirits." We find in the "New Prison" of Clerkenwell one John Robins who "said that he was God Almighty . . . Richard King said his wife was with child of him that should be the saviour of all those that shall be saved . . . Joan Robins said she was with child, and the child in her womb was the Lord Jesus Christ." Richard Brothers, the self-styled "Prophet of the Lost Tribe" and "Slain Lamb of Revelation," was imprisoned a few yards up the road in the madhouse of Ashby Street. The Quakers, who in the mid-eighteenth century "went naked for a sign," met in Peel Court off St. John Street, while in 1830 was instituted a Free-Thinking Christian Meeting House in St. John Square in the centre of the old Templar priory. There is evidence once more of a continuity.

The radical history of Clerkenwell did not end with the riot of 1832. Five years later the Tolpuddle Martyrs, on their return from Botany Bay, were first greeted on the green, and a year later there was a great Chartist meeting on the same spot. In 1842 Prime Minister Peel "banned meetings on Clerkenwell Green," but, in the same period, the Chartists met each week in Lunt's Coffee House at 34 Clerkenwell Green; there were other radical meeting-places close by, such as the Northumberland Arms at 37 Clerkenwell Green. The unions, too, met in public houses in precisely the same area: the Silver Spoon-makers at the Crown and Can, St. John Street; the Carpenters at the Adam and Eve, St. John Street Row; and the Silversmiths at St. John of Jerusalem; altogether the *Trade Union Directory* lists nine separate unions meeting regularly in Clerkenwell. The disturbances and meetings in that area continued throughout the 1850s and 1860s, with marches leaving from the green, while an additional strength was lent to the area by the pro-Fenian Irish radicals of the Patriotic Society who used regularly to meet at the King's Head in Bowling Green Lane a few yards north of Clerkenwell Green itself. At the time of the Paris Commune in 1871, "a red flag, surmounted by a 'cap of liberty,' crowned a lamp-post in the Green." These events may provide an explanation why, in the press and on the music-hall stage, the area became a synonym for radical change.

Yet not all the forces at work there were violently libertarian. John Stuart Mill was one of a number of subscribers who set up a fund to endow "a place for political lectures and discussions independent of coerced tavern keepers and licensing magistrates"; a location was chosen, "in a neighbourhood well known to the democracy of London," and the hall was established at 37a Clerkenwell Green which had once been a school for the children of Welsh Dissenters. It became known as the London Patriotic Club and its history of twenty years "is a history of radical issues"; Eleanor Marx Aveling, Bradlaugh and Kropotkin all used it as a centre for demonstrations and mass meetings. But perhaps the most interesting occupant was one of the last. A socialist press had been founded at the premises in the 1880s, and in 1902 Vladimir Ilyich Lenin walked every day from his lodgings in Percy Circus to Clerkenwell Green in order to edit an underground revolutionary journal entitled *Iskra*, "The Spark," which was meant to ignite Russia. It might be mentioned here that in the seventeenth century the printers of Clerkenwell were denounced for issuing "Blasphemous and seditious" literature. That prolonged pattern or alignment of activities continued well into the twentieth century when the Communist newspaper, the *Morning Star*, had its offices just west of the green in Farringdon Road. In the 1990s the magazine for the homeless and the unemployed, the *Big Issue*, took up residence a few yards south of the green in the same area where Wat Tyler had led his army of radical protesters more than six hundred years before.

So over a period of time, in one tiny part of the city, at first outside "the bars" and then within the ever expanding capital, the same forms of activity have taken place. It may simply be coincidence that Lenin followed in the path of the seventeenth-century printers. It may have been in conformity to habit, custom, or some kind of communal radical memory that the Chartists, the London Corresponding Society and the unions chose the same area for their meetings and demonstrations. It may be chance that the nineteenth-century affrays took place in the same vicinity as those of the fourteenth century. The editor of the *Big Issue* has assured the present author that he had no notion of Clerkenwell's radical history when he decided to situate the office of his magazine in the area.

But other territorial clusters abound. The emergence of Clerkenwell as an instigator or abettor of radical activity is paralleled, for example, by the gradual identification of Bloomsbury with occultism and marginal spiritualism. When the great London mythographer William Blake was completing his apprenticeship in Great Queen Street, an elaborate Masonic lodge was being constructed opposite his employer's workshop. It was the first city headquarters for what was then a controversial occult order of adepts who believed that they had inherited a body of secret knowledge from before the Flood. Before the erection of their great hall they had congregated at the Queen's Head in Great Queen Street, and, in the same street less than a century later, the occult Order of the Golden Dawn held their meetings. The Theosophical Society met in Great Russell Street while around the corner, opposite Bloomsbury Square, exists the Swedenborg Society. Two occult bookshops can be found in the vicinity, while the Seven Dials close by marks the convergence of astrologers in the seventeenth century. So here again there seems to be a congregation of aligned forces, by coincidence or design, remaining active within the neighbourhood of a very few streets.

One street, and a particular church, also throw a suggestive light upon London itself. According to Stephen Inwood in *A History of London*, St. Stephen's, Coleman Street, was "an old Lollard stronghold"; in the early sixteenth century it became a centre of incipient Lutheranism where heretical texts were placed on sale. In 1642 the five Members of Parliament whom Charles I rashly tried to arrest on charges of treason took refuge in Coleman

Street—"a loyal street to the Puritan party"—which was "their stronghold." Six years later Oliver Cromwell met with his supporters in the same street, as can be gathered in the trial of Hugh Peters after the Restoration.

> COUNSEL: Mr. Gunter, what can you say concerning meeting and
>   consultation at the "Star" in Coleman Street?
> GUNTER: My lord, I was a servant at the "Star" in Coleman Street . . .
>   that house was a house where Oliver Cromwell, and several
>   of that party, did use to meet in consultation.

During this period, too, the parish and local congregation were also of strongly Puritan sympathies. Then in 1645 there were weekly public lectures "near Coleman Street," established by women proselytisers and characterised by "confusion and disorder" during discussions subsequent to the lectures. A few years later, in a "conventicle" in an alley off Coleman Street, "that dangerous fanatic Venner, a wine-cooper and Millenarian, preached to 'the soldiers of King Jesus' and urged them to commence the Fifth Monarchy." During the rising of the Anabaptists we read that "these monsters assembled at their meeting house, in Coleman Street, where they armed themselves and sallying thence, came to St. Paul's in the dusk." Even after the Restoration Coleman Street maintained its Puritan allegiances: the old Dissenting preacher, who had been presented with the living of St. Stephen's in 1633, "opened a private conventicle" after the destruction of the Commonwealth from which he ministered to the "too-too credulous soul-murdered proselytes of Coleman Street and elsewhere." We read of "Radical independents inhabiting the same quarter," among them "Mark Holdesby of St. Stephen Coleman Street."

So there is evidence here of a broad continuity over several centuries, from the Lollards to the Anabaptists, suggesting once again a certain destiny or pattern of purpose among the streets of the capital. Arthur Machen was only one commentator who recognised that "the stones and regions of the great wilderness have their destinies and that these destinies are fulfilled." Thus there are certain "quarters which are appointed as sanctuaries."

So the secret life of Clerkenwell, like its well, goes very deep. Many of its inhabitants seem to have imbibed the quixotic and fevered atmosphere of the area; somehow by being beyond the bars of the city, strange existences are allowed to flourish. Mrs. Lewson lived in Coldbath Square until her death at the age of 116; in the early nineteenth century she still wore the dress of the 1720s, thus earning herself the nickname of "Lady Lewson." She lived in one room of a large house which for thirty years was "only occasionally swept out, but never washed." In addition it is revealed in W.J. Pinks's *The History of Clerkenwell* that "She never washed herself, because she thought those people who did so were always taking cold, or laying the foundation of some dreadful disorder; her method was to besmear her face and neck all over with hog's lard, because that was soft and lubricating, and then, because she wanted a little colour on her cheeks, she bedaubed them with rose pink." Her house was lined with bolts and boards and iron bars so that no one might enter, and she never threw anything away; even "the cinder ashes had not been removed for many years; they were very neatly piled up, as if formed into beds for some particular purpose." The case of "Lady" Lewson has other parallels in London history; there are many instances of old women for whom time has suddenly come to a halt, and who characteristically wear white as some emblem of death or virginity. It may be that, for those whose lives have been damaged by the turbulence and inhumanity of the city, it is the only way of withstanding chance, change and fatality.

Another lady of Clerkenwell, living outside London time, was the Duchess of Newcastle, known as "Mad Madge." She rode in a black and silver coach with her footmen all in black; in addition "she had many black patches because of pimples about her mouth," wrote Samuel Pepys (1 May 1667), ". . . and a black juste-au-corps." This lady in black wrote books of experimental philosophy, the most famous being *The Description of A New World, called The Blazing World.* "You will find my works," she told a friend, "like infinite Nature, that hath neither beginning nor end; and as confused as the chaos, wherein is neither method nor order, but all mixed together, without separation, like light and darkness." Pepys, having read some of them, called her "a mad, conceited, ridiculous woman."

But if an area such as Clerkenwell can engender activity of a certain kind, perhaps a single street or house might exert its own influences. In the same house, where the Duchess of Newcastle once resided, lived another crazed duchess just fifteen years later. The Duchess of Albemarle on the death of her husband "was so immensely wealthy that pride crazed her, and she vowed never to marry anyone but a sovereign prince. In 1692 the Earl of Montague, disguising himself as the Emperor of China, won the mad woman, whom he then kept in constant confinement." But she outlived him by thirty years, and to the end remained insane with pride; she insisted, for example, that all her servants knelt while ministering to her and then walked backwards in her presence. It is suggestive, perhaps, that the house which contained these two mad women was located on the same site as the cloister of the black nuns of the medieval period.

In Pentonville Road, in the parish of Clerkenwell, lived that most notorious miser Thomas Cooke, who did not care to pay for his food and drink but "when walking the streets he fell down in a pretended fit opposite to the house of one whose bounty he sought." With his powdered wig and long ruffles, he seemed a respectable citizen; so he was promptly taken in, given some wine and nourishing victuals. "A few days after he would call at the house of his kind entertainer just at dinner time, professedly to thank him for having saved his life . . ." He begged his ink from the various counting-houses he visited and, according to Pinks, "his writing paper was obtained by purloining pieces which he saw upon the counter of the bank, on his daily visits." Here is a true London original, taking advantage of the urban world to float himself. He turned his flower garden into a cabbage patch, which, in order to waste nothing, he enriched with his own and his wife's excrement. On his death-bed, in the summer of 1811, he refused to pay for too much medicine since he was convinced that he would live only six days. He was buried at St. Mary's, Islington, and "some of the mob who attended the funeral threw cabbage stalks on his coffin when it was lowered into the grave." Yet it was a life consistent to the point of perfection, that of a native of Clerkenwell who rarely strayed beyond its bounds.

Yet perhaps the most curious and notable resident of Clerkenwell was Thomas Britton, known everywhere as "the musical small-coal man." He was an itinerant vendor of coals who lived above his coal-shed in Jerusalem Passage, between Clerkenwell Green and St. John's Square; despite his humble trade, in the words of Walford's *Old and New London*, he "cultivated the highest branches of music, and drew round him for years all the great musicians of the day, including even the giant Handel." The musicians met every Thursday evening, in his room above the coal-shed; to reach this temporary concert hall, they had to climb a ladder or, as Britton put it in his invitations:

Vpon *Thursdays* repair
To my palace, and there
Hobble up stair by stair.

Ned Ward described Britton's house as "not much higher than a canary-pipe, and the window of his State-Room but very little bigger than the Bung-hole of a Cask." He himself played the viol di gamba, in the company of his excellent musicians, and afterwards served coffee to his distinguished visitors at a penny a cup. Then in the mornings he would take up his sack of coal, and tread the familiar streets calling out his trade. Britton's death was no less fanciful than his life. A ventriloquist named Honeyman or "Talking Smith" "threw" his voice and announced that, unless Britton recited the Lord's Prayer immediately, he would expire within hours. Britton fell on his knees and prayed "but the chord of his life was unstrung by this sudden shock"; he died a few days later in the autumn of 1714. It was rumoured that he was a Rosicrucian, one of the sects which haunted Clerkenwell, and naturally believed in the efficacy of invisible spirits. So the trick of the ventriloquist, or the atmosphere of the area, deeply affected a credulous mind.

Another native of Clerkenwell, Christopher Pinchbeck, may also throw a curious light upon the neighbourhood. He proclaimed himself, in the summer of 1721, as the "Inventor and Maker of the famous Astronomical-Musical Clocks . . . for showing the various motions and Phenomena of planets and fixed stars, solving at sight several astronomical problems." He has been denominated "The Near-Alchemist," yet his was the alchemy of time which bore strange fruit in the vicinity.

By the end of the eighteenth century some seven thousand artisans—almost half the parish—were dependent upon watch-making. Clerkenwell itself produced some 120,000 watches each year. In almost every street there were private houses which had as door-plates the sign of escapement-maker, engine-turner, springer, finisher, and so on. These were modest but solid properties, with the workshop generally constructed at the back. But not all the tradesmen were so fortunately placed, and a nineteenth-century essay upon clocks in Charles Knight's *Cyclopaedia of London* remarks that "if we wish to be introduced to the workman who has had the greatest share in the construction of our best clocks, we must often submit to be conducted up some narrow passage of our metropolis, and to mount into some dirty attic where we find illiterate ingenuity closely employed in earning a mere pittance." The passages, closets and attics may be compared with the wheels and dials of the clocks themselves, so that Clerkenwell itself becomes a vast mechanism emblematic of time and the divisions of time. The census of 1861 listed 877 manufacturers of clocks and watches in this small parish. But why

here? The historians of horology have pondered the question and arrived at
no satisfactory conclusion; "the commencement of that remarkable localisa-
tion" is not certain, according to one authority cited by Charles Knight, except that "it appears to have made a noiseless progress." Another remarks:
"nor have we heard any plausible reason assigned by those who, residing on
the spot, and carrying on these branches of manufacture, might be supposed
to be best informed on the matter." So, we may say, it just happened. It is one
of those indecipherable and unknowable aspects of London existence. A certain trade emerges in a certain area. And that is all.

But in Clerkenwell we have learned, perhaps, to find larger patterns of
activity. Did the presence of skilled artisans in the eighteenth and nineteenth
centuries actively promote the cause of radicalism? By 1701 the manufacture
of the watch was being used as the best example of the division of labour, so
that one might say that the creation of time-pieces formed the paradigm of industrial capitalism. "Here every alley is thronged with small industries,"
George Gissing wrote of Clerkenwell in *The Nether World* (1889), "here you
may see how men have multiplied toil for toil's sake . . . have worn their lives
away imagining new forms of weariness." Lenin and Eleanor Marx had found
fertile ground. Or was it that the creation of the division and subdivision of
time was an obvious neighbourhood idol, to be smashed by those patriotic
radicals who wished to return to an earlier polity and a more innocent state of
society? Nevertheless the clock- and watch-makers are there still. The
mystery of the place remains.

The Marx Memorial Library is still to be found on Clerkenwell Green, within
which is preserved the small office where Lenin once edited *Iskra*. Beside it
are a snack bar and a restaurant, which have been owned by the same Italian
family for many years. Until recent days Clerkenwell Green and its vicinity
retained that dusty, faded look which was a direct inheritance of its past. It
was secluded, out of the way of the busy areas to the south and west, something of a backwater which few Londoners visited except those whose business it was to be there. The green harboured printers, and jewellers, and
precision-instrument makers, as it had done for many generations. St. John's
Street was dark and cavernous, lined with empty or dilapidated warehouses.

Then, in the 1990s, all was changed. Clerkenwell became part of a social
revolution, in the process of which London seemed once more able to renew
itself. The great transition occurred when Londoners decided that they
would rather live in lofts or "shell" spaces than in terraced houses; these were

not the same as Parisian apartments, since the loft offered inviolable privacy as well as proximity. Since Clerkenwell itself was noticeable for its warehouses and commercial properties, it became part of that movement of refurbishment and modernisation which had begun in the warehouses of Docklands before reaching other parts of inner London. St. John's Street, and the lanes around it, have now been extensively redeveloped with floors of glass attached to old structures and new buildings rising so fast that parts of the area are now almost unrecognisable. As one character says in Arnold Bennett's *Riceyman Steps*, a novel set in early twentieth-century Clerkenwell, "You'd scarcely think it . . . but this district was very fashionable once." It was indeed "fashionable" in the sixteenth and seventeenth centuries, as even the presence of the mad duchesses testifies, and now perhaps that period has returned. Yet that same speaker when alone had another realisation, of "the ruthless, stoney, total inhospitality of the district." Even in the middle of its restoration and rebuilding, St. John's Street is curiously empty; from dusk to dawn it affords echoic effects rather than the energy of any real movement or business. One is reminded of the fact that in the eighteenth century travellers felt obliged to walk together down this road, guarded by link-boys bearing lights, in case they were harassed or attacked. Whether it was wise of property speculators and developers to choose the street as a great site of renovation is an interesting question, therefore, since it may not be easy to impose a new method of living upon a thoroughfare with so ancient and violent a past.

Clerkenwell persists in London's history as a kind of shadowland, therefore, complete with its own recognisable if ambiguous identity. But it is also important to realise that the same effects may be found almost anywhere within the city. Of violence, for example, there is no end.

Violent London

The Burning & Plundering of Newgate & Setting the Felons at Liberty by the Mob.

An anonymous engraving of the Gordon Riots in London in 1780; here
the mob attacks and fires Newgate Prison, one of the most hated symbols of
the city's oppressive authority.

CHAPTER 52

A Ring! A Ring!

ondon has always possessed a reputation for violence; it stretches
back as far as the written records. In a signal instance of city savagery the coronation of Richard I in 1189, for example, was marked
by the wholesale murder of the Jews in London; men, women and children
were burned and cut to pieces in one of the first but not the last pogroms
against resident foreigners. Under cover of the general savagery of the Peas-
ants Revolt, which was also a London revolt, apprentices and others fell upon
the Flemings and butchered many hundreds while "the cries of the slayers
and slain went on long after sunset, making night hideous."

But the violence was not directed at aliens alone. The record of bloody
attacks upon tax-raisers like William de Aldgate (stabbed to death) and John
Fuatara (finger bitten off by a woman) emphasises what one historian, G.A.
Williams in *Medieval London*, has called the Londoner's reputation for "reckless violence." In the Latin records of London's courts in the early thirteenth
century, that violence is vividly depicted. "Roger struck Maud, Gilbert's
wife, with a hammer between the shoulders, and Moses struck her in the
face with the hilt of his sword, breaking many of her teeth. She lingered until Wednesday before the feast of St. Mary Magdalen and then died . . . while
he was conducting him to the sheriffs the thief killed him . . . They dragged

him by the feet on to the stairs of the solar, beating him severely about the body and under the feet, and wounding him in the head."

Violence was everywhere—"endemic" is the word used by one scholar. Robberies, assaults and manslaughters are recorded with predictable frequency; quarrels degenerated quickly into fatal affrays, while street fights often turned into mass riots. Random brutality was common, and at times of political crisis the crowd to the well-known cry of "Kill, kill!" would set upon perceived enemies with unmatched ferocity. Many of the trades—notoriously those of saddler, goldsmith and fishmonger—were prone to "periodical gusts of homicidal rage," while the guilds fought one another in the most pugnacious way. The religious orders were not immune from violence. The prioress of Clerkenwell took barley from disputed land belonging to the prior of St. Bartholomew's "with force and arms to wit with swords, bows and arrows." The memoirs of every century are filled with blood lust.

There was also violence against animals. When a horse being baited by dogs seemed likely to be spared, a seventeenth-century London crowd "cryed out it was a cheat, and thereupon began to untyle the house, and threatened to pull it quite down, if the Horse were not brought again and baited to death. Whereupon the Horse was again brought to the place, and the dogs once more set upon him; but they not being able to overcome him he was run through with a sword and dyed." Cock-fighting was the Shrove Tuesday sport of schoolboys, so that the young Londoner could acquire an early taste for blood and death. Bears and bulls were often baited together, and "at such times you can see the breed and mettle of the dogs, for although they receive serious injuries from the bears, are caught by the horns of the bull, and tossed into the air so frequently to fall down again upon the horns . . . one is obliged to pull them back by the tails and force open their jaws." Evelyn, a more fastidious citizen than most, complained about the "barbarous cruelties" as well as the "rude and dirty" pastimes of the people. He remarked, on visiting the famous bear garden by the Bankside, that "One of the bulls tossed a dog full into a lady's lap, as she sate in one of the boxes at a considerable height from the arena. Two poor dogs were killed: and so all ended with an ape on horseback." It might be remarked that blood sports are common to every culture and to every city; nevertheless this form of London violence is described as something intrinsic and particular. As Dryden put it in the seventeenth century:

> Bold Britons, at a brave Bear-garden fray,
> Are rouz'd: and, chatt'ring Sticks, cry Play, Play, Play.

Mean time, your filthy Foreigner will stare,
And utter to himself, Ha! gens barbare!

This was indeed how Europeans considered Londoners—as barbarous
people—although, as Dryden's couplets intimate, that ferocity was perhaps a
matter of civic pride. "If two little boys quarrel in the street," one seventeenth-
century French traveller observed, "the passengers stop, make a ring round
them in a moment, and set them against one another, that they may come to
fisticuffs . . . During the fight the ring of bystanders encourages the combatants with great delight of heart . . . The fathers and mothers of the boys let
them fight on as well as the rest."

"A ring! A ring!" was one of the perennial cries of the London street.
"The lower populace is of a brutal and insolent nature," another traveller remarked, "and is very quarrelsome. Should two men of this class have a dis-
agreement which they cannot end up amicably, they retire into some quiet
place and strip from their waists upwards. Everyone who sees them preparing for a fight surrounds them, not in order to separate them, but on the contrary to enjoy the fight, for it is a great sport to the lookers-on . . . the
spectators sometimes get so interested that they lay bets on the combatants
and form a big circle around them." This is "congenital to the character" of
Londoners, according to yet another foreign reporter, which suggests how
unfamiliar and alarming these street fights in fact were to non-Londoners.

Combats between men and women were also frequent—"I saw in Hol-
bourn a woman engaged with a man . . . having struck her with the utmost
force, he retreated back . . . the woman seized these intervals to fall upon his
face and eyes with her hands . . . The Police take no cognizance of these combats of individuals." By "the Police" is meant the watch in each ward, which
took no notice of these fights because they were common and familiar. Yet it
did not end there. "If a coachman has a dispute about his fare with a gentleman that has hired him, and the gentleman offers to fight him to decide the
quarrel, the coachman consents with all his heart." This pugnacity could, and
often did, have fatal consequences. Two brothers fought, and one killed the
other outside the Three Tuns Tavern—"His brother intending, it seems, to
kill the coachman, who did not please him, this fellow stepped in and took
away his sword, who thereupon took out his knife . . . and with that stabbed
him."

A "diversion" of the English, according to many reports, was female
combat in places of resort and amusement such as Hockley-in-the-Hole. It

was recorded that the "women fought almost naked with two handled swords which, at the points, were sharp as razors." Both combatants were frequently cut with these weapons, and retired briefly to have their wounds "sown up" without the benefit of any anaesthetic other than their own animosity. The fight continued until one of the participants swooned, or was so badly wounded that she could fight no more. On one occasion, one combatant was twenty-one and the other sixty. It became a highly ritualised, if bloody, affair. The two female warriors would bow to the spectators and salute each other. One was decked in blue ribbons, the other in red; each carried a sword, about three and a half feet in length with a blade approximately three inches wide. With these fierce weapons, and only a wicker shield for defence, they attacked each other. In one fight a swordswoman "received a long and deep wound all across her neck and throat"; some coins were thrown to her from the crowd, but "she was too badly hurt to fight any more."

The introductory "chaff" between the two women (one declaring, for instance, that she beat her husband every morning to keep her hand in) was also echoed in the advertisements or "notices" which preceded each fight. "I Elizabeth Wilson, of Clerkenwell, having had some words with Hannah Highfeld and requiring satisfaction, do invite her to meet me on the stage and box with me for three guineas, each woman holding half a crown in each hand, and the first woman that drops her money to lose the battle." The coin was held to prevent the participants scratching each other. To which a reply was printed: "I Hannah Hyfeld, of Newgate Market, hearing of the resolution of Elizabeth, will not fail to give her more blows than words, desiring home blows and from her no favour." The *London Journal* reported in June 1722 that "They maintained the battle with great valour for a long time, to the no small satisfaction of the spectators."

Men also fought one another with swords, each with a "second" bearing a large wooden club to ensure fair play, and again the struggle ended only when the participants' wounds were too disabling for them to continue. On many occasions the audiences joined in the battle. "But Lord!" Pepys wrote, "to see in a minute the whole stage was full of watermen to revenge the foul play, and the butchers to defend their fellow, though most blamed him; and there they all fell to it, to knocking down and cutting many on each side. It was pleasant to see, but that I stood in the pit, and feared that in the tumult I might get some hurt." This account emphasises the almost tribal loyalties engaged in civic violence, the effect of which could be witnessed in even the most "polite" circles. When the speculator Barebone engaged some workmen to build upon Red Lion Fields, the lawyers of the adjacent Gray's Inn "took notice of it, and thinking it an injury upon them, went with a considerable body of one hundred persons; upon which the workmen assaulted the gentlemen, and flung bricks at them, and the gentlemen at them again; so a sharp engagement ensued."

The tribalism of the city was manifested, in a no less unhappy way, with the exploits of a group of young people known as the Mohocks, named after "a sort of cannibals in India," according to the *Spectator*, "who subsist by plundering and devouring all the nations about them." These young Londoners would rush down the streets with linked arms for the pleasure "of fighting and sometimes maiming harmless foot passengers and even defenceless women." Street-brawling has an ancient history within the city, and similar gangs of youths were known in previous generations as Muns and Tityre-Tus, then Hectors and Scourers, and then Nickers and Hawkubites. The Mohocks themselves began the evening by drinking too much, before tumbling on to the streets with their swords ready. The consequences are revealed in Walford's *Old and New London*. As "soon as the savage pack had run down their victim, they surrounded him, and formed a circle with the points of their swords. One gave him a puncture in the rear, which very naturally made him wheel about; then came a prick from another; and so they kept him spinning like a top." That is why they became known as Sweaters, and also as Slashers since in more ferocious mood they took pleasure "in tattooing, or slashing people's faces with, as Gay wrote, 'new invented wounds.' " Another poet of London has memorialised their exploits in more expressive verse:

> And in luxurious cities, where the noise
> Of riot ascends above their loftiest towers,
> And injury and outrage, and when night
> Darkens the streets, then wander forth the sons
> Of Belial, flown with insolence and wine.

So did John Milton place the violence of London within the context of myth and eternity.

Within the context of the streets, the Mohocks were not alone in their depredations. In the 1750s William Shenstone wrote that "London is really dangerous at this time; the pickpockets, formerly content with mere filching, make no scruple to knock people down with bludgeons in Fleet Street and the

Strand, and that at no later hour than eight o'clock at night; but in the Piazzas, Covent Garden, they come in large bodies, armed with couteaus, and attack whole parties." Here is a graphic illustration of how at night the city,
without an adequate police force, could become terrifying. Sir John Coventry had his nose slit by a street gang. A courtesan named Sally Salisbury, dis-
pleased by an admirer's speeches, "seized a knife and plunged it into his
body"; she was conveyed to Newgate, surrounded by plaudits. "Now it is the
general complaint of the taverns, the coffee-houses, the shop-keepers and
others," wrote the City Marshal in 1718, "that their customers are afraid
when it is dark to come to their houses and shops for fear that their hats and
wigs should be snitched from their heads or their swords taken from their
sides, or that they may be blinded, knocked down, or stabbed; nay, the
coaches cannot secure them, but they are likewise cut and robbed in the public streets etc. By which means the traffic of the City is much interrupted."

"Traffic" is as much in goods as in vehicles, and this is one of the indica-
tions that the prosperity of the city was being threatened by the violent
propensities of some of its citizens. In this period, too, the apprentices would
"go to Temple Bar in the evening, set up a shouting and clear the pavement
between that and Fleet Market of all the persons there. The boys all knew
boxing, and if anyone resisted one or two would fall upon him and thrash him
on the spot, nobody interfered."

James Boswell was very observant of the streets in the decade after Fielding's death (1754). "The rudeness of the English vulgar is terrible," he confided to his diary in December 1762. "This indeed is the liberty which they
have: the liberty of bullying and being abusive with their blackguard
tongues." On many occasions he would have heard the familiar shouts of
"Marry, come up!" and "Damn your eyes!" A month later he was reporting
that "I was really uneasy going home. Robberies in the street are now very
frequent" and then, in the summer of 1763, he recorded that "There was a
quarrell between a gentleman and a waiter. A great crowd gathered round,
and roared out '*A ring—a ring*.'" It may also be that in that cry there is a folk
memory of the chant "A ring-a ring of roses" which commemorated the
period of the Plague when scarlet tokens upon the flesh were harbingers of
death. In the streets of London, fear and violence are fatally mingled.

In the eighteenth century there are accounts of mobs with lighted torches
and sticks or clubs; their leaders would read out the names of people, or of
specific streets, in order to direct the violence against local targets. Houses
and factories and mills could be literally pulled down; looms were cut apart.

Sometimes we can hear them shouting—"Green you bugger, why don't you fire? We will have your heart and liver!" There is also a remarkable collection of threatening letters, which testifies to the spirited and violent language of Londoners when addressing one another, "Sir, Damn Your Blood if You do not Ryes Your Works Too 2 pence a Pair moor We Well Blow your Braines out For We will Bllow your Brans out if You Doo not Do itt You slim Dog We shall sett You Houes on fier . . . if you do not Lay the Money at the place that we shall mention we will set your House and all that belongs to you on fire for it is in my power for to do it . . . Mr. Obey, we gave you now an Egg Shell of Honey, but if you refuse to comply with the demands of yesterday, we'll give you a Gallon of Thorns to your final Life's End."

It is perhaps significant, in the context of the violent language of London, that much Cockney dialect springs immediately from pugilism: "breadbasket" for stomach, "kisser" for mouth, "conk" for nose, "pins" for legs and "knock-aht" for a sensation. Many of the words for beating, such as "hammer," "lick," "paste," "whack" and "scrap," also derive from the ring, suggesting that the vernacular of confrontation and pugnacity remains very much to the taste of the Londoner.

Fights took place off the streets as often as upon them, and the printed records testify to the fact that the "lower" drinking clubs and alehouses were characterised by violence as well as liquor. William Hickey reported upon his visit to a den called Wetherby's in Little Russell Street off Drury Lane where "the whole room was in an uproar, men and women promiscuously mounted upon chairs, tables, and benches, in order to see a sort of general conflict carrying on upon the floor. Two she-devils, for they scarce had a human appearance, were engaged in a scratching and boxing match, their faces entirely covered with blood, bosoms bare, and the clothes nearly torn from their bodies. For several minutes not a creature interfered between them, or seemed to care a straw what mischief they might do each other, and the contest went on with unabated fury." Here it is the indifference and callousness of the crowd that are most evident, an indifference which, it can be presumed, was carried over into their general demeanour at work or upon the streets. The phrase "Never mind it" was a frequent one. Another phrase in Hickey's account, "promiscuously mounted," also, if no doubt inadvertently, introduces the element of sexual excitement and sexual congress into this account of bloody combat; sex and violence are, in the city, indissolubly connected.

Hickey watched another beating in a corner of Wetherby's where "an uncommonly athletic young man of about twenty five seemed to be the object of universal attack." Hickey then experienced, naturally enough, "an eager wish to get away" but was stopped at the door. "No, no, youngster," he was told, "no tricks upon travellers. No exit here until you have passed muster, my chick"; not until he had paid his "reckoning," in other words, or had his purse stolen. He was then called a "sucker," a word which lingered for more than two hundred years. Hickey was literally imprisoned within "this absolute hell upon earth" which then itself became a very emblem of the city as a prison.

No biography of London would be complete without reference to the most violent and widespread riot of its last thousand years. It started as a demonstration against legislation in favour of Roman Catholics, but quickly turned into a general assault upon the institutions of the state and the city.

On 2 June 1780, Lord George Gordon assembled four columns of his supporters in St. George's Fields, in Lambeth, and led them to Parliament Square in order to protest against the Catholic Relief Act; Gordon himself was a quixotic figure of strange and marginal beliefs, but one who managed to inspire the vengeful imagination of the city for five days. He always protested, in later confinement, that he had never meant to uncork the fury of the mob, but he never properly understood the moods and sudden fevers of the city. His supporters were described as "the better sort of tradesmen," and Gordon himself had declared that for the march against Parliament they should be decent and "dressed in their sabbath days cloaths." But no crowd in London remains unmixed for long; soon more violent anti-papist elements, such as the weavers of Spitalfields bred from Huguenot stock, merged with the general crowd.

Charles Dickens, in *Barnaby Rudge*, has given an account of the riots; the novel is fired by his interest in violence and by his fascination with crowds but it is also conceived after much reading and research. From the *Annual Register* of 1781, for example, he could have learned that the day was "intensely hot, and the sun striking down his fiercest rays upon the field those who carried heavy banners began to grow faint and weary." Yet they marched in the heat three abreast, the main column some four miles in length, and when they converged outside Westminster they raised a great yell. The heat now inflamed them, as they invaded the lobbies and passages of Parliament. So great was the crowd that "a boy who had by some means got among the concourse, and was in imminent danger of suffocation, climbed to the shoulders of a man beside him and walked upon the people's hats and heads into the open street."

Now this great multitude threatened the government itself; their petition was carried into the chamber of the House of Commons while, outside, the crowd screamed and yelled in triumph. They even threatened to invade the chamber but, even as they threw themselves against the doors, a rumour spread that armed soldiers were advancing in readiness to confront them. "Fearful of sustaining a charge in the narrow passages in which they were so closely wedged together, the throng poured out as impetuously as they had flocked in." In the ensuing flight a body of Horse Guards surrounded some of the rioters and escorted them as prisoners to Newgate; this removal was, as events demonstrated, an unfortunate one.

The mob dispersed, among a hundred rumours which resounded through the city, only to gather itself again as evening approached. Doors and windows were barred as the nervous citizenry prepared itself for further violence. The crowd had diverted its energies from Westminster to Lincoln's Inn Fields where a notorious "mass house" was situated; it was in fact the private chapel of the Sardinian ambassador, but no diplomatic nicety could assuage the temper of the mob which burned it down and demolished its interior. According to a contemporary report "the Sardinian Ambassador offered five hundred guineas to the rabble to save the painting of our Saviour from the flames, and 1,000 guineas not to destroy an exceeding fine organ. The gentry told him they would burn him if they could get at him, and destroyed the picture and organ directly." So opened a path of destruction which would burn its way across London.

The next day, Saturday, was relatively quiet. On the following morning, however, a mob met in the fields near Welbeck Street and descended upon the Catholic families of Moorfields. There they burned out houses and looted a local Catholic chapel. On Monday the violence and looting continued, but now it was also directed against the magistrates involved in confining some of the anti-Catholic rioters to Newgate as well as against the politicians who had inaugurated the pro-Catholic legislation. Wapping and Spitalfields were in flames. It was not a "No Popery" protest now but a concerted assault upon the established authorities.

Yet in promoting disorder they had themselves fallen out of all order or preconcerted arrangement. When "they divided into parties and ran to different quarters of the town, it was on the spontaneous suggestion of the moment. Each party swelled as it went along, like rivers as they roll towards the sea . . . each tumult took shape and form from the circumstances of the moment." Workmen, putting down their tools, apprentices, rising from their benches, boys running errands, all joined different bands of rioters. They believed that, because they were so many, they could not be caught. Many of the participants were in turn motivated "by poverty, by ignorance, by the love of mischief, and the hope of plunder." This is again according to Dickens, but he was one who knew the temper and atmosphere of London. He understood that, once one breach had been made in the security and safety of the city, others would follow. The city enjoyed a very fragile equilibrium, and could be rendered unsteady in a moment. "The contagion spread like a dread fever: an infectious madness, as yet not near its height, seized on new victims every hour, and society began to tremble at their ravings." The image of distemper runs through London's history; when it is combined with the imagery of the theatre, where each incendiary incident becomes a "scene," we are able to glimpse the complicated life of the city.

On Tuesday, the day of Parliament's reassembly, the crowds once more gathered at Westminster. It is recorded in "Lord George Gordon's Narrative" that when the members of the Commons were informed that "people from Wapping were just then arriving with large beams in their hands and seemed determined to make an attack upon the soldiers" it was decided that the session should be adjourned. There were now mobs all over the city; most citizens wore a blue cockade to signal their allegiance to the rioters, and houses displayed a blue flag with the legend "No Popery" inscribed upon their doors and walls. Most of the shops were closed, and throughout London there was fear of violence "the like of which had never been beheld, even in its ancient and rebellious times." Troops had been stationed at all the major vantage points, but they also seemed to be sympathetic to the cries and demands of the mob. The Lord Mayor felt unable, or was unwilling, to issue direct orders to arrest or shoot the rioters. So fires and destruction started up in various areas.

A contemporary account, in a letter by Ignatius Sancho written from Charles Street dated this Tuesday, 6 June and reprinted in Xavier Baron's exhaustive *London 1066–1914*, complains that "in the midst of the most cruel and ridiculous confusion, I am now set down to give you a very imperfect sketch of the maddest people that the maddest times were ever plagued with . . . There is at this present moment at least a hundred thousand poor, miserable, ragged rabble, from twelve to sixty years of age, with blue cockades in their hats, besides half as many women and children, all parading the streets, the Bridge, the Park, ready for any and every mischief. Gracious God, what's the matter now? I was obliged to leave off, the shouts of the mob, the horrid clashing of swords, and the clutter of a multitude in swiftest motion drew me to the door where every one in the street was employed in shutting up shop. It is now just five o'clock, the ballad mongers are exhausting their musical talents with the downfall of Popery, Sandwich and North . . . This instant about two thousand liberty boys are swearing and swaggering by with large sticks, thus armed in hopes of meeting with the Irish chairmen and labourers. All the Guards are out and all the horse, the poor fellows are just worn out for want of rest, having been on duty ever since Friday. Thank heavens, it rains."

The letter is interesting because of its rush and immediacy, and it is worth noting, for example, that the correspondent writes of the demonstrators being "poor, miserable, ragged"; in more scathing terms Dickens describes them as "the Scum and refuse" of the city. So here we have a vast army of the disadvantaged and the dispossessed turning upon the city with fire and vengeance. If ever London came close to a general conflagration, this was the occasion. It was the most significant rebellion of the poor in its entire history.

A postscript to the letter from Charles Street has equally interesting news. "There is about a thousand mad men armed with clubs, bludgeons and crows, just now set off for Newgate, to liberate, they say, their honest comrades." The firing of Newgate, and the release of its prisoners, remains the single most astonishing and significant act of violence in the history of London. The houses of certain judges and law-makers had already been burned down, but as the various columns of rioters descended upon the prison to the cry of "Now Newgate!," something more fundamental was taking place. One of these leading the riot described it as "the Cause"; on being asked what this cause was, he replied: "*There should not be a prison standing on the morrow in London.*" Clearly this was not simply an attempt to release the "No Popery" rioters incarcerated a few days before. This was a blow against the oppressive penal institutions of the city, and those who watched the spectacle of the fire received the impression that "not only the whole metropolis was burning, but all nations yielding to the final consummation of all things."

The columns marched on the prison from all directions, from Clerkenwell and Long Acre, from Snow Hill and Holborn, and they assembled in front of its walls at a little before eight o'clock that Tuesday evening. They surrounded the house of the Keeper, Richard Akerman, which fronted the street beside the prison. A man appeared on the rooftop, asking what it was that they wanted. "You have got some friends of ours in your custody, master." "I have a good many people in my custody." One of the mob leaders, a black servant called John Glover, was heard to cry out: "Damn you, Open the Gate or we will Burn you down and have Everybody out." No satisfactory answer was given, and so the mob fell upon Akerman's house. "What contributed more than any thing to the spread of the flames," one eyewitness, Thomas Holcroft, reported, "was the great quantity of household furniture, which they threw out of the windows, piled up against the doors, and set fire to; the force of which presently communicated to the house, from the house to the Chapel and from thence, by the assistance of the mob, all through the prison." It seems to have been the actual sight of the prison, with its great walls and barred windows, which roused the mob to fury and instilled in them a determination as fiery as the brands which they flung against the gate.

That great door was the focus of their early efforts; all the furniture of the Keeper's house was piled against it and, smeared with pitch and tar, was soon ablaze. The prison door became a sheet of flame, burning so brightly that the clock of the church of the Holy Sepulchre could clearly be seen. Some scaled the walls and threw down blazing torches upon the roof. Holcroft went on to report that "A party of constables, to the amount of a hundred, came to the assistance of the keeper; these the mob made a lane for, and suffered to pass until they were entirely encircled, when they attacked them with great fury, broke their staffs and converted them into brands, which they hurled wherever the fire, which was spreading very fast, had not caught."

The poet George Crabbe watched the violence and recalled that "They broke the roof, tore away the rafters, and having got ladders they descended. Not Orpheus himself had more courage or better luck; flames all around them, and a body of soldiers expected, they defied and laughed at all opposition." Crabbe was one of four poets who observed these events, Johnson, Cowper and Blake comprising the others. It has been suggested that all the defiance and laughter of the incendiary mob are represented in one of Blake's drawings of this year, *Albion Rose*, which shows a young man stretching out his arms in glorious liberation. Yet the association is unlikely; the horror and pathos of the night's events instilled terror, not exultation, in all those who observed them.

When the fire had taken hold of the prison, for example, the prisoners themselves were in peril of being burned alive. Another witness, Frederick Reynolds, recalled that "The wild gestures of the mob without and the shrieks of the prisoners within, expecting instantaneous death from the flames, the thundering descent of huge pieces of building, the deafening clan-

gour of red-hot iron bars striking in terrible concussion on the pavement below, and the loud, triumphant yells and shouts of the demoniac assailants on
each new success, formed an awful and terrific scene." Eventually the gate,
charred and still in flames, began to give way; the crowd forced a path
through the burning timbers and entered the gaol itself.

Holcroft noted that "The activity of the mob was amazing. They
dragged out the prisoners by the hair of the head, by arms or legs, or whatever part they could lay hold of. They broke the doors of the different entrances as easily as if they had all their lives been acquainted with the
intricacies of the place, to let the confined escape." They ran down the stone
passages, screaming exultantly, their cries mixing with the yells of the inmates seeking release and relief from the burning fragments of wood and the
encroaching fire. Bolts and locks and bars were wrenched apart as if the
strength of the mob had some unearthly vigour.

Some were carried out exhausted and bleeding; some came out shuffling
in chains and were immediately taken in triumph to a local blacksmith to the
shrieks of "A clear way! A clear way!" from the multitude who surrounded
with joy those who had been released. More than three hundred prisoners
were liberated. Some had escaped from imminent execution, and were like
men resurrected; others were hurried away by friends; others, habituated to
the prison, wandered in astonishment and bewilderment through the wreckage of Newgate. Other prisons were fired and opened that night, and it was—
for that night, at least—as if the whole world of law and punishment had been
utterly demolished. In subsequent years the Londoners of the area recalled
the unearthly light which seemed to shine from the very stones and streets of
the city. The city was momentarily transformed.

It was appropriate, therefore, that the crowd should then make its way
from the burning ruins of the prison to the home of the Lord Chief Justice,
Lord Mansfield, in Bloomsbury Square. It is one of the aspects of eighteenth-
century London that the house of every notable or notorious citizen was well
known. The serried spearpoint railings were torn down and hurled within;
the windows were broken; the mob entered the house, went through all of its
rooms, broke or set fire to its furniture. Mansfield's paintings and manuscripts
were consigned to the fire, together with the contents of his law library; this,
in vivid form, was the burning of the Law. A curious episode might be mentioned here, as all the power and oppression of the city are despatched to the
flames. From the window of the burning house one demonstrator exhibited
to the roaring mob "a child's doll—a poor toy . . . as the image of some un-

holy saint." On reading this account Dickens immediately assumed that it was a token of that which the late occupants had worshipped but in fact this strangely anonymous, almost barbaric, object can be seen as the deity of the crowd.

On the following morning Samuel Johnson toured the scene of that night's riots. "On Wednesday I walked with Dr. Scot to look at Newgate, and found it in ruins with the fire yet glowing. As I went by the Protestants were plundering the Sessions-house at the Old Bailey. There were not, I believe, a hundred; but they did their work at leisure, in full security, without sentinels, without trepidation, as men lawfully employed, in full day." He added a curious statement: "Such is the cowardice of a commercial place." By this he meant, no doubt, that there was no communal spirit or civic pride abroad to avert or prohibit these outrages; London, as a commercial city, had no defences except those of fear and oppression. When those twin guarantors of security were lifted, then theft and violence naturally and inevitably emerged in their stead. A "commercial place" is an arena of rapine and anxiety under another name. Samuel Johnson, who understood the pleasures and virtues of the city, also understood its debilitating faults better than any of his contemporaries.

But that day witnessed more than the smoking ruins of the Law. Horace Walpole termed it, in a phrase that was not then a cliché, "Black Wednesday." It might almost have been termed Red Wednesday. That morning the "cowardice" of London was manifest in the closed shops and shuttered windows. Many of the citizens were so dismayed and astounded by the destruction of Newgate, and the complete failure of the city authorities to punish or apprehend those who were responsible, that it seemed to them that the whole fabric of reality was being torn apart before their eyes. And "round the smoking ruins people stood apart from one another and in silence, not venturing to condemn the rioters, or to be supposed to do so, even in whispers." There was another curious aspect of this lawlessness. Some prisoners lately released sought out their gaolers, "preferring imprisonment and punishment to the horrors of such another night as the last," while others actually returned to Newgate in order to wander among the smoking ruins of their erstwhile place of confinement. They were brought there by some "indescribable attraction," according to Dickens, and they were found talking, eating and even sleeping in the places where their cells had once stood. It is a curious story but somehow all of a piece with the greater story of London, where many will dwell upon the same stones for the whole of their lives.

Troops had been stationed throughout the city, but the energy and purpose of the rioters were not significantly diminished; in fact the burning of the night before seemed only to have increased their rage and resentment. Threatening letters were posted up outside those prisons which had remained secure, including the Fleet and the King's Bench, assuring their keepers and gaolers that they would be fired that night; the houses of prominent legislators were similarly picked out. The leaders of the riot declared that they would take and fire the Bank, the Mint and the Royal Arsenal—and that they would occupy the royal palaces. A rumour spread that the demonstrators would also throw open the gates of Bedlam, thus contributing a curious terror to the general fear of the citizens. Truly then the city would become a hell with the desperate, the doomed and the distracted wandering its streets against buildings collapsing and houses on fire.

That night it seemed that the fire of 1666 had come again. The rioters emerged upon the streets "like a great sea," and it seemed their purpose "to wrap the city in a circle of flame." Thirty-six major fires were started—the prisons of the Fleet, the King's Bench and the Clink were all alight—while the soldiers fired upon the crowds with sometimes fatal effect. Some of the greatest conflagrations were in the vicinity of Newgate itself, beside Holborn Bridge and Holborn Hill, as if the destruction of the previous night had somehow magnetised the area so that it drew more vengeance upon itself. The image of the blank-faced doll, as some anonymous and infernal deity of the riotous city, seems appropriate.

Samuel Johnson wrote to Mrs. Thrale that "one might see the glare of conflagration fill the sky from many parts. The sight was dreadful." And, from Horace Walpole: "I never till last night saw London and Southwark in flames." This spectacle of the burning city, again according to Johnson, created a "universal panick." There were sporadic riots on the next day, Thursday, but the incandescent scenes of the day before seem to have exhausted that lust for violence which had so suddenly visited the streets of London. The military had been posted at all the appropriate sites, while bands of soldiers were actively seeking out and arresting rioters, so that by Friday the city was quiet. Many of those who had left London in fear of their lives still remained apart, and the majority of shops were closed, but the insurrection had passed as quickly and as generally as it had gathered just a week before. Two hundred were dead, more lying badly and often fatally injured, while no one was able to compute the numbers of those who had burned to death in cellars or hiding-places. Lord George Gordon was arrested and taken to the Tower of London, and hundreds of rioters were confined in the prisons that had not already been destroyed by fire. Twenty-five were hanged on the spots where their crimes had been committed; two or three boys were suspended before Lord Mansfield's house in Bloomsbury Square.

So ended the most violent internecine episode in the city's history. Like all London violence it burned brightly but quickly, the stability and reality of the city being distorted by the heat of its flames before once more settling down.

The violence upon the Broadwater Farm Estate, in north London, in 1985, suggests a prevalent instinct towards riot which has never been suppressed. It is necessary only to look into the inner courtyards of a council-house estate, with graffiti on every wall, the windows covered with metal grilles and the doors padlocked, to understand that state of siege in which part of London still lives. The anxiety is still palpable in certain districts, and along certain roads, where the forces of repressed anger and fear are overwhelmingly present. An additional and unpredictable element in the general level of city violence is added in those parts of London that are infected with drug gangs.

The Broadwater Farm disruption began in the autumn of 1985, upon a predominantly black council estate, where for several months there had been "rumours of riots." A series of separate incidents in the early autumn had exacerbated already emerging tensions. But the death of Mrs. Cynthia Jarrett on the night of 5 October, allegedly while the police were searching her flat, precipitated the disturbances upon the estate. The official report, *Broadwater Farm Enquiry* (1986), includes the statements of witnesses as well as descriptive analysis of the violence itself. "So I thought: 'Oh my God they down there and those children are there.' " The actions of the police were reported in similar fashion. "There was cries of 'wait until we get in there and get you . . . get back in there, you bastards, get back in there' . . . The only people who may not have been pushed back were a few of the older ones . . . A lot of people said 'No. Don't go back. Why should we go back?' . . . It was a general state of confusion. There were young girls there with young children and then a lot of screaming, a lot of shouting." These could be the voices of any angry crowd, scattered across London over the past centuries, but it is incarnated here within a group of black youths confronted by lines of police in riot gear attempting to force them back upon the council estate as if they were prisoners being driven back into their cells.

"Some of the youths then began to turn over cars, and missiles were thrown at a line of police. Two cars were turned over and burned close to the junction. They attempted to turn over another car but were stopped . . . Soon after a wall at the corner of Willan Road and The Avenue was knocked down and dismantled for ammunition to throw at the police line. The fighting had started." It spread rapidly, in characteristic fashion, and from the estate came "constant volleys of dangerous missiles. Slabs of pavement were broken up and thrown. When the available slabs from nearby were used up, young people were seen rushing through the estate carrying missiles in various containers. A shopping trolley, a milk crate and a large communal rubbish bin were all mentioned to us as being used. At a later stage, tins stolen from the supermarket became a common form of ammunition." Once more the common "reality" of the city was being disrupted and changed. Crude and often ineffective petrol bombs were hurled at the encroaching police. "Two people, both black, started shouting orders at the others: 'we need more ammunition.' Immediately five or six responded by running round the houses gathering up empty milk bottles, while four others turned over a car for petrol. In less than five minutes I counted more than 50 petrol bombs completed." Curiously and perhaps significantly this testimony came from "Michael Keith, a research assistant at St. Katherine's College, Oxford" who "had been preparing a history of rioting." So the historical dimension or historical resonance is confirmed by one who, witnessing the events of 1985, had other riots in his head. Perhaps the Gordon Riots provided an echo or parallel.

Many of the demonstrators wore masks or scarves in order to conceal their identity, but, as in previous incidents over the centuries, some emerged who took command of the riots. "It was like when you look at ants," one witness on Broadwater Farm explained, "you see how ants move and you identify which ones are the workers. Because you see them from high. Now what I saw, was three or four people moving and giving signs to each other with their hands . . . and they were moving like a group. You could see they were white by the hands." One of the characteristics of accounts of the Gordon Riots was the allegation that secret managers exploited the violence and mayhem for their own ends. On Broadwater Farm the same phenomenon emerged. "They were outsiders doing it to our Estate," a witness explained, suggesting in turn that there are some people who relish urban conflagration for its own sake or as a means of affecting the entire social and political system. The fact that these strange organisers were apparently white, as witnessed by others, may suggest that sixth columnists wanted to inflame hatred against the black Londoners who lived upon the estate.

Yet the general movement of the crowd was as ever one of controlled confusion. The historian of rioting noted that "Most of the people were united by a sense of anger which regularly escalated to fury. In this situation a dramatic cast, representative of any cross-section of society, was clearly evident." Here his understanding of the patterns of riot comes into play, with his reference to "a dramatic cast" as if it were part of London's theatre. He mentioned those, too, who attempted to compete in their bravery and aggression against the ranks of the police. "Many more spent most of their time giving moral support, joking with each other, but no less committed in occasional forays." He noticed some who tried to establish a plan of concerted action and impose order upon incipient chaos. But they were not wholly successful. "In this sense," he concluded, "organisation was extemporised." These are precisely the sentiments expressed by those who watched the unfolding of the Gordon Riots, and they suggest a great truth about violence in the city.

Another witness observed that "When people thought that their lines were a bit thin, then they went to reinforce the lines running from one point to another. There were no generals." This suggests another aspect of London riots; they are rarely orchestrated but patterns emerge from within the crowd itself. It might also be construed as part of that egalitarian spirit of the city that there can be no "generals" or leaders. One observer on the Broadwater Farm, speaking of the rioters, was "struck by how young they were. She saw 'kids of 12 and 13.' " It may be recalled here that children were hanged in the aftermath of the Gordon Riots.

After the first confrontation there was no sustained attack but intermittent forays. Cars were overturned and shops looted. "I discovered he was an Irish boy and he said that it's the first time he has had so much food in six months because he's unemployed." Yet the most violent incident took place in the Tangmere precinct of the estate. One of the policemen despatched to guard the fire-fighters putting out a blaze in a newsagent's shop, PC Keith Blakelock, slipped and fell in the face of a pursuing mob. D. Rose, in *A Climate of Fear*, takes up the narrative. "The rioters came at Blakelock from all sides . . . he was kicked on the ground and stabbed again and again." Here we have an example of the sudden viciousness of a London mob. "In the words of PC Richard Coombes, the mob were like vultures, pecking at his body as his arms rose and fell to death with their blows." Another observer described them as "a pack of dogs," inadvertently using a simile which has become customary in dealing with the threatening crowd. Older than Shakespeare's line in *Coriolanus*, "What would you have, you curs?," it suggests the wildness and the untamed savagery latent within the civic order. "The instruments were going up and down being flayed at him. The last I saw of PC Blakelock was he had his hand up to protect himself . . . Blakelock's hands and arms were cut to ribbons . . . His head seems to have turned to one side, exposing his neck. There he took a savage cut from a machete." And there he died.

It was another terrible episode in the history of London violence, where all the rituals of blood and vengeance have their place. The Tangmere precinct itself "is a big, squat building, shaped in conscious imitation of a Babylonian ziggurat." Babylon is ever associated with paganism and savagery.

There were gunshots, and sporadic fires started upon the estate, but by midnight the rioters had begun to disperse. It started to rain. The violence ended as quickly and as suddenly as it had begun except, that is, for examples of brutality among the police towards various unnamed and still unknown suspects. That same pattern of vengeance was no doubt also part of the aftermath of the Gordon Riots.

It would be absurd to declare that these two events, separated by two hundred years, are identical in character and in motive. The fact that one was on a general and the other on a local scale, for example, is a comment on London's huge expansion over that period. One travelled along the streets, and the other was confined to the precincts of a council estate; this also testifies to changes within the society of London. Yet both sets of riots were against the power of the law, symbolised by the walls of Newgate Prison in the one case and by the ranks of police officers in riot gear in the other. It might be said that both therefore reflect a deep unease about the nature and presence of authority. The Gordon rioters were generally poor, part of the forgotten citizenry of London, and the inhabitants of the Broadwater Farm Estate were, according to Stephen Inwood, predominantly "homeless, unemployed or desperate." There may, again, be a connection. In both cases, however, the riots burned themselves out fierily and quickly. They had no real leaders. They had no real purpose except that of destruction. Such is the sudden fury of London.

Black Magic, White Magic

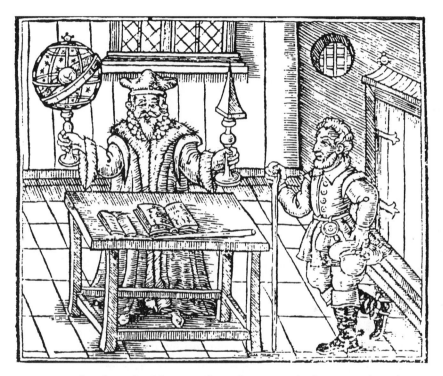

A woodcut from the title page of *Astrologaster or the figure caster* by John Melton; Londoners were notoriously fearful and superstitious so astrologers and seers of every variety were readily available. Many astrologers congregated in lodgings around Seven Dials.

CHAPTER 53

I Met a Man Who Wasn't There

And in this dark city, whom or what would we expect to see? In 1189 Richard of Devizes records that "a sacrifice of the Jews to their father the devil was commenced in the city of London, and so long was the duration of this famous mystery, that the holocaust could scarcely be accomplished the ensuing day." But then it truly became a city of devils as the citizens fell upon, and slaughtered, the innocent inhabitants of old Jewry.

In London, the home of pride and wealth, the devil was always greatly feared. In 1221, according to the *Chronicles of London*, "that ys to say vpon seynt Lukys Day, ther Blewe a grete Wynde out off the North Est, that ouerthrewe many an house and also Turrettes and Chirches, and fferde ffoule with the Woddes and Mennys orcherdes. And also fyrye Dragons Wykked Spyrites weren many seyn, merveyllously ffleynge in the eyre." A similar vision of flying fiends was vouchsafed at a much later date in London's history in Stopford Brooke's *Diary*: "Oct. 19, 1904. England was in sunshine till we came to the skirts of London, and there the smoke lay thick. I looked down to the streets below, filled with the restless crowd of men and cars. It was like looking into the alleys of Pandemonium, and I thought I saw thousands of winged devils rushing to and fro among the mad movement of the host. I grew sick as I looked upon it."

In medieval London many noble personages were buried within the precincts of Blackfriars, suitably robed, because it was believed that to be interred in the habit of a Dominican monk was a certain means of warding off the devil. Yet there were some who were so far beaten down by the city that they identified with the fiend. When one London thief and beggar was taunted for his infamy on his way to the Tyburn gallows he replied: "What would the Devil do for company, if it was not for such as I?" "A Straunge Sighted Traueller," of 1608, coming to London in a poem by Samuel Rowlands, visited the whores of Shoreditch and the statue of King Lud, "and swore in London he had seene the Deuill." A real devil was supposed to have appeared at a performance of Marlowe's *Doctor Faustus* in the Belle Sauvage Inn on Ludgate Hill.

Yet when the devil does emerge in London he is often, according to folklore, gulled and outwitted by the cheating citizens who are more than his match in dishonesty and double-dealing. In Jonson's *The Devil Is an Ass*, the foul fiend is first shown the city as a kind of inferno:

> Child of hell, this is nothing! I will fetch thee a leap
> From the top of Paul's steeple, to the Standard in Cheap.

But within twenty-four hours "he has been cheated, robbed, cudgelled, thrown into prison and condemned to be hanged."

The devil can be found everywhere and anywhere in London, ranging far and wide from his own street, Devil's Lane in Lower Holloway which has since been renamed. Richard Brothers, the self-styled prophet, claimed to have met him "walking leisurely up Tottenham Court Road." Some claim to have seen him near the stake of the martyrs—"Thou art the seat of the Beast, O Smithfield"—and, at midnight in the streets of Victorian London, where "The devil puts a diamond ring on his taloned finger, sticks a pin in his shirt, and takes his walks abroad." In ancient fashion Punch tells Old Nick that "I know you have a deal of business when you come to London." One of the devil's duties is to wander through the prisons. Coleridge and Southey envisaged him touring the notorious Coldbath Prison, and admiring the interior of the cell set aside for solitary confinement. Byron called London the "Devil's drawing-room."

He has his guests, and his familiars. There is a tradition of witches in London, with the names of Old Mother Red Cap and Old Mother Black Cap still used upon shops and signs. Perhaps the most notorious was Mother Damnable of Camden Town, whose cottage lay at a fork in the road where the Underground station is now to be found. In the mid-seventeenth century she was known as a healer and fortune-teller with "her forehead wrinkled, her mouth wide, and her looks sullen and unmoved." Her story is told in *The Ghosts of London* by J.A. Brooks. On the day of her death "Hundreds of men, women and children were witnesses of the devil entering her house in his very appearance and state, and . . . although his return was narrowly watched for, he was not seen again . . . Mother Damnable was found dead on the following morning, sitting before the fire place, holding a crutch over it, with a tea-pot full of herbs, drugs, liquid." And what a sight that must have been, the devil making his way through Camden Town.

Stranger still is the case of "Spring-Heeled Jack." He appeared in the streets during the 1830s and was soon known as "the terror of London." One statement, given by Jane Alsop at Lambeth Street Police Office, describes how the unfortunate girl encountered him on her doorstep. "She returned into the house and brought a candle and handed it to the person, who appeared enveloped in a large cloak, and whom she at first believed to be a policeman. The instant she had done so, however, he threw off his outer garment, and applying the lighted candle to his breast, presented a most hideous and frightful appearance, and vomited forth a quantity of blue and white flame from his mouth and his eyes resembled red balls of fire." This may seem the merest fantasy, and yet the particulars are confirmed in an account of another attack by "a tall thin man, enveloped in a long black cloak. In front of him he was carrying what looked like a bull's eye lantern. With one bound he was in front of her, and before she had a chance to move, he belched blue flames from his mouth into her face." The entire grotesque history is narrated by Peter Haining in *The Legend and Bizarre Crimes of Spring Heeled Jack*.

Jane Alsop's testimony had other, equally disturbing elements. From "the hasty glance which her fright enabled her to get at the person, she observed that he wore a large helmet; and his dress, which appeared to fit him very tight, seemed to her to resemble white oilskin. Without uttering a sentence he darted at her, and catching her part by the dress and the back part of her neck, placed her head under one of his arms, and commenced tearing her gown with his claws, which she was certain were of some metallic substance."

She screamed aloud, and her sister came to the door. But in her police state-ment that sister, Mary Alsop, admitted that although she "saw a figure as al-ready described . . . She was so alarmed at his appearance, that she was afraid to approach or render any assistance." A third sister then ran down and dragged Jane away from the terrible assailant, yet his grip was so strong that "a quantity of her hair was torn away." She slammed shut the door but "notwithstanding the outrage he had committed, he knocked loudly two or three times at the door." This knocking at the door, so strange that it could scarcely have been invented, is perhaps the most alarming moment in an en-tire alarming episode. It is as if to say—Let me in, I have not finished with you yet.

It is not at all surprising that in the popular urban imagination "Spring-Heeled Jack" was identified as the offspring of the devil, and described by witnesses as possessing horns and cloven feet. In February 1838 he was re-ported to have been seen in Limehouse with blue flames issuing from his mouth, and in the same year was said to have thrown a prostitute into the wa-ter at Jacob's Island in Bermondsey. Peter Haining has suggested that the perpetrator was a fire-eater who wore a helmet or mask to protect his face. The great leaps and bounds that were also ascribed to him were perhaps the effect of springs concealed in the heels of his shoes. The metallic "claws" have yet to be fully explained. Yet the point is that "Spring-Heeled Jack" be-came a true London myth because he was so fantastic and artificial a monster. With his helmet and "white oilskin suit," breathing fire like a circus per-former, he is a London devil curiously resembling the fiends portrayed in the Clerkenwell mystery plays. Accounts of his appearance and behaviour spread very rapidly all over the city; he was seen, or was reported to have been seen, in various locations. It is almost as if this bizarre figure emerged from the streets themselves, like a "golem" which is supposed to be made from the mud and dust of a certain vicinity. The fact that "Jack," like a later and more notorious "Jack," was never apprehended serves only to deepen that sense of anonymity which suggests the monstrous figure to be some token or representation of London itself.

For the city is seen, by many, to be a kind of hell. It became a cliché in the poetry of the nineteenth century; its citizens resembled a "Satanic throng" while the atmosphere was that of a "brown Plutonian gloom." The sul-phurous smell of coal dust and smoke provoked images of Satan, while the manifold and manifest vices of the city represented all the works of the devil incarnate.

Images of Babel and Sodom abound, therefore, yet there is a more profound sense in which the city represents hell. It is the ultimate place of degradation and despair, where solitude is sought as an escape from the exactions of pity or compassion and where the only fellowship found is the fellowship of misery. Of all writers perhaps George Orwell possessed that sense of the city most strongly and, in *Keep the Aspidistra Flying*, Gordon Comstock, surveying the brightness of Piccadilly Circus in 1936, remarks that "The lights down in hell will look just like that." Often "The fantasy returned to him that he was a damned soul in hell . . . Ravines of cold evil-coloured fire, with darkness all above. But in hell there would be torment. Was this torment?"

There are still, in this city, places where suffering seems to linger. On a small garden or patch of waste ground, near the intersection of Tottenham Court Road and Howland Street, solitary people sit in postures of despair. It was close by, at 36 Howland Street, that Verlaine composed his wonderful poem "*Il pleure dans mon coeur / Comme il pleut sur la ville.*" "It weeps in my heart just as it rains upon the city," all the loneliness and sorrow of London are caught in this image of the grey and falling rain. The cemetery garden behind the Hawksmoor church of St. George's-in-the-East, beside Wapping, attracts the lonely and the unhappy. The garden of another church, Christ Church, Spitalfields, by chance by the same architect, was for many years a resting place for the vagrant and the deranged; it was known as "Itchy Park." There was a famous area known as "Poverty Corner" along the Waterloo Road, by the corner of York Road; here out-of-work actors, artistes and music-hall "turns" used to wait in the generally forlorn hope of being seen or chosen by the music-hall agents. That corner has remained an anonymous and transient locale, between the bridge and the station, with its own peculiar sense of desolation.

Whole areas can in their turn seem woeful or haunted. Arthur Machen had a strange fascination with the streets north of Grays Inn Road—Frederick Street, Percy Street, Lloyd Baker Square—and those in which Camden Town melts into Holloway. They are not grand or imposing; nor are they squalid or desolate. Instead they seem to contain the grey soul of London, that slightly smoky and dingy quality which has hovered over the city for many hundreds of years. He observed "those worn and hallowed doorsteps," even more worn and hallowed now, and "I see them signed with tears and desires, agony and lamentations." London has always been the abode of strange and solitary people who close their doors upon their own secrets in the middle of the populous city; it has always been the home of "lodgings,"

where the shabby and the transient can find a small room with a stained table
and a narrow bed.

A true Londoner will tell you that there is no need to travel when you have the
unexplored mysteries of the city all about you; a walk down Farringdon
Road, or Leather Lane, will give you as much cause for wonder and surprise
as any street in Paris or Rome. "I do not understand my own city," you might
say, "so why travel elsewhere in search of novelty?" There is always a sense
of strangeness in London, to be experienced around unexpected corners and
in unknown streets. As Arthur Machen said, "it is utterly true that he who
cannot find wonder, mystery, awe, the sense of a new world and an undiscovered realm in the places by the Grays Inn Road will never find those secrets elsewhere, not in the heart of Africa."

It has often been observed that certain streets or neighbourhoods carry
with them a particular atmosphere over many generations. An air of emptiness
or ennui, for example, can be sensed along those thoroughfares that have been
created by municipal edict and have taken away much of older London in their
construction—Victoria Street and New Oxford Street, artificial creations of
the nineteenth century, remain anonymous unhappy places. Kingsway, cut
through ancient dwellings in the early twentieth century, is merely dull. The
Essex Road and the unluckily named Balls Pond Road are areas of manifest
greyness and misery. Another cold spot, over many years, has been Shepherd's Bush Green; it was described as "bald, arid, detestable" at the beginning
of the twentieth century and has remained thus ever since.

There were nineteenth-century alleys and courts which gave an immediate sensation of penury and wickedness. The air was "poisonous with miasma
and nauseous with dank and dismal stenches," remarked Charles Manby
Smith in *The Little World of London*. "Rags and brown paper substitute half
the glass of the windows, and what is left is so crusted with dirt that it shuts
out the light it was intended to admit." Andrew Mearns, in his *Bitter Cry of
Outcast London*, records that "You have to ascend rotten staircases, which
threaten to give way beneath every step . . . You have to grope your way
along dark and filthy passages swarming with vermin." Who can say what
mark such places leave upon the city? "In that close corner where the roofs
shrink down and cower together as if to hide their secrets from the handsome
street hard by, there are such dark crimes, such miseries and horrors, as could
hardly be told in whispers."

The area in the vicinity of prisons has a strangely oppressive and clandestine atmosphere. This is perhaps why the entire area of Southwark and the Borough has for centuries conveyed an impression of meanness and mournfulness. There have been many prisons in the vicinity, the Marshalsea and the King's Bench among them, and "there is no place like this in the suburbs of London," according to Walford's *Old and New London*, "a spot that looks so murderous, so melancholy and so miserable . . . There is a smell of past ages about these ancient courts, like that which arises from decay—a murky closeness . . . and all old things had fallen and died just as they were blown together and left to perish." And so it remains today, with an atmosphere quite unlike that of any other part of London. The area of East Acton, beside the prison of Wormwood Scrubs, is an example of a modern neighbourhood that is enveloped by the shadow of the gaol.

Death can cast its own shadow over a specific locale. Viaducts and crossroads can also be objects of inexplicable gloom. One young Londoner of the early twentieth century, Richard Church, recalled a crossroads south of the river near the Battersea Road, "a crossroads called The Latchmere, a sinister junction that always filled me with dread."

There are other streets and areas that seem to emanate misery. Along the Embankment there have always been iron seats at regular intervals, and here in the evening or at night you will find solitary figures sitting and looking down at the river or up at the sky. In 1908 H.G. Wells walked beside them and noticed "a poor old woman with a shameful battered straw hat awry over her drowsing face, now a young clerk staring before him at despair; now a filthy tramp, and now a bearded frock-coated collarless respectability; I remember particularly one ghastly long white neck and white face that lopped backward, choked in some nightmare." The tramps are still there but more disquieting are the young who often sit in some daze of *not belonging anywhere*. There are middle-aged men in respectable clothes so worn down that their compulsion to wear them provokes pity; and there are old women with their worldly possessions in plastic carrier bags. The Embankment is a haven for them all, and will no doubt continue to be so for many centuries.

The small streets beside Drury Lane were renowned for their misery. Summer Gardens, in winter, was a picture of urban desolation with its gutters filled with frozen dirt. It was the abode of costers, and the narrow road was littered with paper wrappings from the oranges upon their barrows. Charles Booth noted that "In one street is the body of a dead dog and near by two dead cats which lie as though they had slain each other. All three had been crushed flat by the traffic which has gone over them and they, like everything else, are frozen and harmless." There was also a great quantity of scraps and bread crumbs strewn over the road which, according to Booth, is "the surest sign of extreme poverty all over London."

There was also the notorious Whitecross Street, once Whitecross Place, with its gaol blighting the vicinity. "It is said, God made everything. I don't believe it; He never made Whitecross Place." And if God did not, who did? Who is the "author of filthy lanes and death-breeding alleys?" Of Clifford's Inn, in Chancery Lane, long known for its legal obfuscation and delay, Walford states: "I should say that more misery has emanated from this small spot than from any one of the most populous counties in England." Only a gate and passage now remain; some flats were built over the ancient quadrangle which, in 1913, Virginia and Leonard Woolf found to be "incredibly draughty and dirty . . . and all night long there fell a slow gentle rain of smuts so that, if you sat writing by an open window, a thin veil of smuts covered the paper before you had finished a page."

The vicinity of Old St. Pancras, with the graveyard as its centre, has been an area of dereliction for many centuries. Norden, in the sixteenth century, cautioned "Not to walk there late"; in the early years of the twenty-first century it is encompassed by railway arches within which small garages and car repairers have set up their trades. Much of it remains waste ground. Swain's Lane, leading down to the great mound known as "Parliament Hill" on Hampstead Heath from the walls of Highgate Cemetery, is considered to be unfortunate. The local press and local historians have investigated the condition of the place without notable success, except for certain inexplicable or at least unexplained "sightings": "I have seen what appeared to be a ghost like figure inside the gates at the top of Swains Lane." In the weeks after this report appeared in the *Hampstead and Highgate Express*, in February 1970, other local correspondents conveyed their apprehension: "My fiancee and I spotted a most unusual form about a year ago. It just seemed to glide across the path. I am glad somebody also has spotted it . . . To my knowledge the ghost always takes the form of a pale figure and has been appearing for several years . . . a tall man in a hat who walks across Swains Lane . . . Suddenly from the corner of my eye I saw something move . . . which seemed to be walking towards us from the gates, sent us running up Swains Lane as fast as we could . . . I have also had a strange happening at the lower end of Swains Lane . . . My advice is to avoid Swains Lane during dark evenings, if at all possible."

. . .

Yet there are also areas of peacefulness and care. The old Foundling Hospital in Coram Fields has long been demolished, but on the perimeter of its site is now the Great Ormond Street Hospital for Sick Children. Wakley Street, a short and narrow thoroughfare between Goswell Road and the City Road, has on one side the headquarters of the National Children's Bureau and on the other the National Canine Defence League.

In another context it is perhaps encouraging to note that the pitches of puppet-shows were set upon a fixed local abode for decades, and that together they form a kind of charmed circle around the centre of London—Holborn Bridge, Lincoln's Inn Fields, Covent Garden, Charing Cross, Salisbury Change and the Fleet Bridge.

On the perimeter of this circle lies Fountain Court, amid the buildings of the Temple; there has been a small fountain there for three hundred years, commemorated by writers as diverse as Dickens and Verlaine, while the softness and serenity of this small spot have been experienced by many generations. The fountain and its pool were once square-fenced with palisades, then encircled by iron railings, but now stand unbarred; whether in a square, or a round, or open on all sides, the fountain plays on, and its atmosphere has remained constantly evocative. One Londoner came here as a schoolboy, with no knowledge of its history or its associations, and immediately fell under the spell of its enchantment; it was as if innumerable good acts or kind words had emerged here as calmly and as quietly as the little fountain itself. At last, in these pages, he has the chance of recording his debt.

If persistence through time can create harmony and charity, then the church of St. Bride's—only a few yards from Fountain Court—has some claim to good fortune. A prehistoric ritual site, as well as evidence of a Roman temple and wooden Saxon church, have been found within its grounds. So the various forms of divinity have been venerated on one spot for many thousands of years. London is blessed as well as cursed.

CHAPTER 54

Knowledge Is Power

*T*here was, *in the city,* another way of opening the gate of heaven. The pursuit of knowledge has always been one of the city's defining characteristics, even though it may take unfamiliar forms.

In the reign of Edward III a man was taken "practising with a dead man's head, and brought to the bar at the King's Bench, where, after abjuration of his art, his trinkets were taken from him, carried to Tothill, and burned before his face." During the reign of Richard I one Raulf Wigtoft, chaplain to the archbishop of York, "had provided a girdle and ring, cunningly intoxicated, wherewith he meant to have destroyed Simon [the dean of York] and others, but his messenger was intercepted, and his girdle and ring burned at this place before the people." "This place" was again Tothill which is supposed to have been the site of druid worship; the tools of conjurors and alchemists were no doubt traditionally destroyed here because it was considered an area of more powerful magic.

But in London it is impossible to distinguish magic from other versions of intellectual and mechanical aptitude. Dr. Dee, the great Elizabeth magus of Mortlake, for example, was an engineer and a geographer as well as an alchemist. In 1312, Raymond Lully, attracted by its scientific reputation, came to London, where he practised alchemy both in Westminster Abbey and the

Tower. The magician Cornelius Agrippa arrived in the city at the end of the fifteenth century, in order to associate with the great divines and philosophers of the period; he struck up a particular friendship with John Colet, dean of St. Paul's and founder of St. Paul's school, who had become interested in magic during his Italian travels. An alchemist named Hugh Draper was imprisoned within the Salt Tower of the Tower of London for sorcery and magic; he inscribed upon his cell wall a great horoscope, which he dated on 30 May 1561, and then added that he had "MADE THIS SPHEER" with his own hands.

By chance, or coincidence, many astrologers came to inhabit Lambeth. The name itself, however, may have drawn them. Beth-el was in Hebrew the name for a sacred place, here fortuitously connected with the Lamb of God. At Tradescant's house in south Lambeth dwelled Elias Ashmole, who convinced John Aubrey of the powers of astrology. The interment of Simon Forman, the great Elizabethan magus, is entered within the Lambeth parish registers. Lully stated that Forman wrote in a book, found among his possessions, "this I made the devil write with his own hand in Lambeth Fields, 1569, in June or July, as I now remember." Captain Bubb, who was a contemporary of Forman, dwelled in Lambeth Marsh where he "resolved horary questions astrologically," a pursuit which led him eventually to the pillory. At the north-east corner of Calcott Alley, in Lambeth, lived Francis Moore, an astrologer and physician, who has now entered the realm of the immortals as the author of the almanac which bears his name. In Lambeth there were many rare devices. In the collection of Tradescant, later to become a museum in the area, were gathered salamanders and "Easter egges of the Patriarchs of Jerusalem," dragons two inches long and two feathers from a phoenix, a piece of stone from the tomb of John the Baptist and "Blood that rained in the Isle of Wight, attested by Sir Jo. Oglander," a white blackbird and "halfe a haslenut with seventy pieces of household stuffe in it." Those were once the sights of Lambeth.

The close associations between alchemy and the beginnings of science were also present in the very heart of London. When Newton came up to the city in order to purchase the material for his researches, he took the coach to the Swan Tavern in Grays Inn Lane before walking or riding to Little Britain. Here, through a bookseller called William Cooper, he bought such texts of alchemical knowledge as Zetner's *Theatrum Chemicum*, and *Ripley Reviv'd* by the London alchemist George Starkey. In the process, Newton became acquainted with a secret group of London magicians and astrologers. Many of the original founders of the Royal Society, which in later days was explicitly associated with "modern" scientific research and knowledge, were in fact part of the "Invisible College" of adepts who practised alchemy as well as mechanical philosophy. They were part of that tradition adumbrated by John Dee which saw no necessary disparity between the various forms of occult and experimental understanding. Samuel Hartlib was the prime mover among a group of London experimenters who wished to marry rationality and system with alchemy in order to create a practical magic; among his friends and supporters were Robert Boyle, Kenelm Digby and Isaac Newton himself. They corresponded by means of code-names, and used pseudonyms in the publication of their work; that of Newton was "Jeova Sanctus Unus."

Yet there emerged out of this a society which was, in the words of Macaulay, "destined to be a chief agent in a long series of glorious and salutary reforms." The Royal Society held its first meetings in Gresham House in Bishopsgate before removing to Crane Court off Fleet Street and beside Fetter Lane; on the nights upon which the members met, a lamp was hung out over the entrance to the court from Fleet Street. The pragmatism and energy of their consultations are evident in some of their earliest labours—"to promote inoculation . . . electrical experiments on fourteen miles of wire near Shooters Hill . . . ventilation *apropos* of gaol feaver . . . discussion on Cavendish's improved thermometers." Not all the experimenters were of London, and not all of them lived in London, but the city became the chief centre of that empirical philosophy and practical experiment which developed out of alchemical research. The pragmatic spirit of London science must be emphasised in all these varied and various areas; it is the spirit that has pervaded its learning ever since.

There were experiments in agriculture and in horticulture; medicine "became an experimental and progressive science," and the example of the pestilence of 1665 led the members of the society to examine "the defective architecture, draining and ventilation of the capital." Sir William Petty created the science of political arithmetic, so that we might plausibly suggest London as the nurse of statistical enquiry. It was another form of understanding, and controlling, the population. Yet in a city of commerce the introduction of statistics also had a financial advantage; the Board of Customs in 1696 represented to the Treasury "the need they felt to collect certain basic material if they were able 'to make a balance of the trade between this Kingdom and any part of the world.' " Newton himself spent many of his latter years as Warden of the Mint, in which capacity he refined and ordered the currency of the kingdom. He brought to the manufacture of coin all the precision and thoroughness of his experimental work, thus creating the scientific economy which exists still. In turn he became the prosecutor of anyone who defied his inexorable laws, despatching to the gallows all who clipped the coins or counterfeited the currency. Science, in London, truly was power.

In the fields of induction and mathematical demonstration, both relying upon a close observation of particulars, the London genius was most successful. John Wallis "placed the whole system of statics on a new foundation," again according to Macaulay, while Edmond Halley investigated the principles of magnetism and the flow of the sea. So from Crane Court in the city issued lines of thought which connected the earth to the sea and the sky. It may seem fanciful to suggest that any one city can affect the cast of thought, or the science, of its inhabitants but Voltaire himself announced that "A Frenchman arriving in London finds things very different, in natural science as in everything else . . . In Paris they see the universe as composed of vortices of subtle matter, in London they see nothing of the kind . . . For a Cartesian light exists in the air, for a Newtonian it comes from the sun in six and a half minutes. Your chemist performs all its operations with acids, alkalis and subtle matters." Once more the theoretical spirit of Parisian enquiry is implicitly opposed to the practical bent of London science. "Where finds philosophy her eagle eye?" Cowper wrote, and then answered his own question:

> In London: where her implements exact,
> With which she calculates, computes, and scans,
> All distance, motion, magnitude, and now
> Measures an atom and now girds a world.

It is sometimes suggested that, by the end of the eighteenth century, the climate and pace of industrial development had shifted away from London to the manufacturing towns of the north. But this is to misunderstand, and certainly to underestimate, the force of practical intelligence within the capital. One of the founders of the Royal Society, Robert Hooke, was the direct inspiration behind advances in the technology of time, while Henry Maudslay's exceedingly accurate machine tools were produced in Lambeth. In 1730 John Harrison came to London in order to develop his marine chronometer which for the first time fixed degrees of longitude. That spirit was maintained by the mechanical engineers of the nineteenth century who in the workshops of

Lambeth produced the steam-hammer and the automatic spinning mule. Lambeth was, then, still a centre of transformation.

Yet in London the pursuit of knowledge was not confined to the search for technical proficiency. From his lodgings in Great Marlborough Street, after his famous voyage, Charles Darwin wrote that "It is a sorrowful but I fear too certain truth that no place is at all equal, for aiding one in Natural History pursuits, to this dirty smokey town." After travelling around the world Darwin considered London to be the most appropriate place for his research, as if the whole of evolutionary nature could be viewed and studied there. He wrote this in 1837 and his insight was confirmed, forty-seven years later, when the prime meridian of zero degrees longitude was established upon a brass rail in Greenwich.

In true London tradition, science also was turned into theatre, with lectures and demonstrations all over the capital. The early nineteenth century in particular witnessed a great public demand for scientific knowledge; the London Institution of Moorfields, the Surrey Institution of Blackfriars Bridge, the Russell Institution in Bloomsbury and the City Philosophical Society in Dorset Street were only some of the many clubs and societies devoted to disseminating the new understanding. There were societies all over the city, founded in the 1820s and 1830s, among them Geological, Astronomical, Zoological, Medico-Botanical, Statistical, Meteorological and British Medical. In the capital there were also many inventors and theorists who were able to meet and to work together. The contributors to "Scientific London" in *London World City* remark that "London was a crucial instrument for forging new specialist disciplines." It was as if new commodities were being produced and traded in this intensely heated atmosphere. Bessemer developed his steel-making process in St. Pancras, while Hiram Maxim invented the machine-gun in his Clerkenwell workshop.

The pragmatism and practicality of London science were then disseminated into its teaching. In 1826 the first university college in London was established in Bloomsbury with specifically utilitarian aims; its purpose was not to educate scholars and divines, on the model of Oxford and Cambridge, but to train engineers and doctors. It was a true London institution, its founders comprising radicals, Dissenters, Jews and utilitarians. It is not at all surprising, therefore, that it should be infused with a radical egalitarian spirit which began with the inclusion of non-Anglican students. It became a university in 1836, opening its gates to women twelve years later and from the 1850s creating evening classes for working Londoners.

The university also began to teach science as a separate discipline, and created the first Faculty of Science in 1858; there was also established a school of medicine which reached into practical areas as diverse as mathematics and comparative anatomy. It was a progressive, enquiring energy which animated all of these concerns. It has been termed the energy of empire since the vast power and resourcefulness of nineteenth-century London, at the centre of the imperial world, had somehow managed to infiltrate all aspects of its life. In the early nineteenth century statisticians, mathematicians and engineers, again according to *London World City*, "saw the city as a potentially universal centre of calculation whence trade and machinery would link world-wide networks of British power." Charles Babbage, together with colleagues such as Herschel, established the Astronomical Society in 1820 during a meeting at the Freemasons' Tavern in Great Queen Street. In his workshop Babbage created the "Difference Engine" which is the harbinger of the modern computer, and so it may be suggested that information technology itself was created in London. In the process of invention he had employed precision engineers and of course skilled workmen, so that once again the capital became the home of major technical innovation and technological progress.

London has often been apostrophised as the city of gold. It is a home of golden dragons and golden cocks, while the golden cross and golden ball on the dome of St. Paul's have become a symbol of London's energy. On a summer morning, when the shimmering brightness envelops the city in a haze, and all is quiet, then it might be transformed: " 'Tis El Dorado—El Dorado plain, The Golden City!" It is all before you, its vistas unexplored, and becomes in the words of Wordsworth,

> The great city, an emporium then
> Of golden expectations.

The golden city has been built out of the will and desire of a human community, and that is why in the verse of W.E. Henley it burns so brightly and why

> Trafalgar Square
> (The fountains' volleying golden glaze)
> Shines like an angel-market.

And as the sun descends in *The Secret Agent* "the very pavement under Mr. Verloc's feet had an old-gold tinge in that diffused light . . . Mr. Verloc was going westward through a town without shadows in an atmosphere of powdered gold." This is a gleam of brightness in an otherwise dark novel, and the effect is that of the alchemist creating gold out of base materials. Alchemy and science provide the seeds of light and knowledge in a dark city so that, as it seemed to Don Juan looking at London from the heights of Highgate:

> each wreath of smoke
> Appear'd to him but as the magic vapour
> Of some alchymic furnace.

Dryden, too, had the same vision:

> Methinks, already, from this chymic flame
> I see a City of more precious mould . . .
> Now deified, she from her fires does rise.

It is the magical energy of London, visible in every one of its giant transformations, like that after the Great Fire when empirical knowledge and practical genius helped to rebuild the city. This magical energy survives still.

A Fever of Building

A drawing by George Scharf which illustrates the building of Carlton House Terrace in the early 1830s, part of Nash's original grand design to embellish London. Note that the workmen are wearing hats.

CHAPTER 55

London Will Soon Be Next Door to Us

rom the middle of the eighteenth century London expanded in a fitful
and almost feverish manner according to a cycle of profit and prof-
iteering. The metaphor of fever was taken up by Henry Kett who,
in 1787, suggested that "The contagion of the building influenza . . . has extended its virulence to the country where it rages with unabating violence . . .
The metropolis is manifestly the centre of the disease . . . Mansions daily arise
upon the marshes of Lambeth, the roads of Kensington, and the hills of
Hampstead . . . The chain of buildings so closely unites the country with the
town that the distinction is lost between Cheapside and St. George's Fields.
This idea struck the mind of a child, who lived at Clapham, with so much
force, that he observed, 'If they go on building at such a rate, London will
soon be next door to us.' " By the time he grew to be a man, his words had
come to pass.

The "hills of Hampstead" were in part threatened by the "New Road"
from Paddington to Islington, upon which work began in 1756; it acted as a
bypass, avoiding the congerie of narrow and unpaved roads which led to the
centre of the city, and for a while was considered to be a northern perimeter
road, acting as a barrier between the city and the country—or, rather, between the city and the assortment of brick-fields, tea gardens, orchard gar-

dens, cow-yards, tenter-grounds, allotments and sodden marsh-like fields which were always a feature of the land immediately surrounding the capital. But then the city, almost in a bound, travelled to its other side with the erection of Somers Town and Pentonville, Camden Town and Kentish Town. The new road became a road within, rather than outside, the city; and as such it remains.

The "marshes of Lambeth" were invaded by a more deliberate act of policy, designed to increase the speed of business within the city and to open up the capital to its outer regions. Until 1750 only London Bridge acted as a conduit between the northern and southern areas of the Thames; the river itself was at the centre of all traffic. But the construction of Westminster Bridge over a period of twelve years entirely changed the relationship between the northern and southern sections; instead of being isolated and apart, almost like different countries sharing the same border, they became interrelated. A new road was built from the bridge into Lambeth for some half a mile, where it then touched existing roads which were in turn extended and widened in order to create a free-flowing route "for promoting the intercourse and commerce" between both parts of the city. In the process both Kent and Surrey became so accessible that much open country disappeared beneath streets and squares.

The experiment was so profitable that four other bridges followed at Blackfriars, Vauxhall, Waterloo and Southwark. London Bridge itself was stripped of its houses and shops in order to render it suitable for the faster movement of a new age. Everyone was going faster. Everything was going faster. The city was growing faster, too, and the traffic within its bounds was moving ever more rapidly, starting a momentum which has never stopped. By the latter half of the eighteenth century the evidence of London's commercial power, and future imperial status, was already present. It was about to burst its bounds completely, and become the first metropolis of the world. So almost by instinct the old boundaries and gateways were destroyed; in a symbolic act of relinquishment, London prepared for its future.

The "roads of Kensington" then found the city to be advancing upon them. In the early eighteenth century the area of Mayfair, south of Oxford Street and east of Hyde Park, was established in a series of streets and squares; in its immediate vicinity the Portland estate laid out the territory north of Oxford Street. Cavendish Square, Fitzroy Square and Portman Square arose. Grosvenor Square was completed in 1737 and, at a size of six acres, remains London's largest residential square. It was followed by the building of Berkeley Square only three streets away, so that the entire area was given a uniform discipline and appearance. The idea of the square and its surrounding streets took possession of London. The Bedford estate in Bloomsbury moved beyond its origin in Covent Garden to establish Bedford Square in 1774, and twenty-five years later this was succeeded by Russell Square, Tavistock Square, Gordon Square, Woburn Square and their network of interconnecting terraced streets. In its turn the Portman estate established Dorset Square, Portman Square and Bryanston Square. Square upon square, giving London its now familiar appearance.

But the city did not stop there. The districts of Shoreditch, Whitechapel and Bethnal Green in the east continued their steady growth, while south of the river areas such as Southwark, Walworth, Kennington and St. George's Fields grew up beside the new thoroughfares. Fields were filled with terraced streets rather than corn. The population itself expanded to meet London's demands, so that a figure of 650,000 in 1750 had reached over a million fifty years later. It was not until 1790 that baptisms exceeded burials, but from that time forward the momentum could not be stopped. In each of the five succeeding decades, after 1800, the population would rise by 20 per cent.

By the end of the eighteenth century "the City of London" was only part of the city; instead of being essentially London it had turned into an enclave within London. This led to no diminution in its power: the dispersal of its population, and the attendant removal of various trades and occupations, allowed it to focus its energies even more fiercely upon commercial speculations. The City became purely a place of business. It remained the financial capital of the world, even if it was not in itself the capital of England; for that purpose, it was continually recreating itself in each generation. Many of the great livery halls were rebuilt or refaced; the largest commercial enterprises, private banks and insurance companies established their premises on a grand scale, imitating or in some cases anticipating the construction of the Bank of England and the Stock Exchange. It truly became a city of Mammon, with precincts and labyrinths and temples devoted to that deity. There was a new Custom House, a new Excise Office, a new Stocks Market, while Sir John Soane and George Dance exercised all their gifts for a "neo-classicism" not untouched by an acquaintance with the mysteries of Piranesi and of Egyptian form. The destruction of the old walls allowed more development upon the northern perimeters of the city, where Moorfields and Finsbury Circus were laid out. The hospitals and prisons were rebuilt or refurbished, although it is not clear which of the two institutions imitated the other. We might speak of religious architecture, such as Hawksmoor's wonderful if barbaric St. Mary Woolnoth, except that by this date Christianity itself had little impact upon the momentum or atmosphere of the newly resurgent City.

But even as London grew, it maintained and deepened its coherence. There were Road Acts, Lighting Acts and Pavement Acts. The Building Act of 1774 had a greater effect upon London than any other legislative measure. It standardised and simplified houses into four categories, thereby recreating large areas in a uniform image. It may not be too fanciful to suggest that this method of identifying and controlling London in the course of its immense expansion represented a means of purging all the excess and theatricality of the city in order to make it fit for its imperial destiny.

Such an exercise in architectural uniformity, however, could never succeed. London was too large to be dominated by any one style or standard. Of all cities it became the most parodic and the most eclectic, borrowing architectural motifs from a score of civilisations in order to emphasise its own position as the grandest and most formidable of them all. Indian, Persian, Gothic, Greek and Roman motifs vied for position along the same thoroughfare. It says much for the heterogeneity of its development in this period, for example, that architects as unalike as Robert Adam and William Chambers were working within a few hundred yards of each other on strikingly different projects which leave their mark upon London still; Chambers was presiding over Somerset House, while Adam was working upon Adelphi. Where Adelphi had a light and extravagant aspect, Somerset House was solid and conservative in feeling; one is the work of innovative genius, the other of academic solemnity. Both architects found a place within the city.

The only successful and permanent attempt to bring uniformity and order to London's chaos was the grand scheme to link St. James's Park in the south with Regent's Park in the north. With the creation of Regent Street and Waterloo Place, it remains the single most important exercise in city planning within the metropolis. That it worked is not in doubt; the combination of the genius of John Nash with shrewd speculation was perhaps unstoppable in such an opportunistic age and city. Nash formulated the plans for Trafalgar Square; he created the conditions for Piccadilly Circus; he designed the reconstruction of Buckingham Palace; he laid out the terraces on the perimeter of Regent's Park; he created Oxford Circus. "London," wrote Prince Pückler-Muskau in 1826, is "extremely improved . . . Now for the first time, it has the air of a seat of Government, and not of an immeasurable metropolis of 'shopkeepers' to use Napoleon's expression."

But this "air" of government was only achieved by demarcating poorer and richer areas, in effect cutting off the rich from the sight and odours of the poor. Nash himself declared that he wished to create a line or barrier "between the Streets and Squares occupied by the Nobility and Gentry" and "the narrow Streets and meaner houses occupied by mechanics and the trading part of the community."

It has been suggested that Nash's achievement was out of keeping with the history and atmosphere of the city, but he was a Londoner by birth, probably homosexual, who became prosperous through a legacy from a merchant uncle; here was a man who understood in every sense the workings of the city. From these roots sprang his genius for theatricality, for example, and it has been observed that the curve of Regent Street resembles that of an amphitheatre. The great designs of Trafalgar Square, Buckingham Palace and Oxford Circus have been in turn seen as a form of popular stage-set combining all the energy and spectacle of London in a great work of cunning artifice. When Nash took advantage of the reversion of Marylebone Park to the Crown in 1811, and fashioned Regent's Park out of an undistinguished patch of land, all his skills as a theatre designer were used to project a grand double circus with what was described as a "National Valhalla" rising in the centre. Financial restrictions, however, made such a scheme implausible and impossible; what emerged from the wreckage of Nash's ambition were eight villas and the ring of terraces which still possess what Sir John Summerson has described as "an extravagant scenic character . . . dream palaces, full of grandiose, romantic ideals" but, behind the scenes, comprising "identical houses, identical in their narrowness, their thin pretentiousness, their poverty of design." He concludes that the terraces of the park are "architectural jokes . . . an odd combination of fantasy and bathos." Yet in that sense they convey the sheer vulgar theatricality and opportunism of the city, and of Nash himself; that is why the great tourist attractions of Buckingham Palace and Trafalgar Square seem in a sense to be a joke upon their visitors themselves.

In other respects the pressures of commerce and property speculation have damaged Nash's dream city beyond repair. Regent Street had been first constructed on a purely commercial basis, with the selling of prime sites along the road, but what is born in commerce dies in commerce; the famous colonnade lasted for thirty years before being removed on the grounds that business was being lost in its obscurity, while the street itself was extensively remodelled in the 1920s and 1930s. The dereliction or damage also suggests a more general truth about London, where grand and large-scale developments have rarely been successful. The finest of London's public buildings, like the Bank of England, are somehow secret and withdrawn, as if not wishing to overstate their case. In the same way grandiose projects failed because, as Andrew Saint has observed in *London World City*, "any but the most pragmatic approach to planning was doomed to failure." Once again that note of pragmatism, so intrinsic to the intellectual and social life of the capital, is struck.

The "improved" London of the early nineteenth century had acquired a momentum of its own. The National Gallery, the British Museum, the Marble Arch, Westminster Palace, the Royal College of Surgeons, the Law Courts, the screen and arch at Hyde Park Corner, the General Post Office at St. Martin's le Grand, London University, the Inner and Middle Temples, as well as various theatres, hospitals, prisons and gentlemen's clubs, completely changed the external aspect of London. For the first time it became a public city. The detailed drawings of George Scharf, throughout this period, provide a significant account of the work itself. A great mobile crane stands before a half-completed Marble Arch, while a man in a top hat is perched upon a wooden scaffolding making notes; a new portico is being constructed, and Scharf notes the iron rod which is being cased within brick to form a pillar; plasterers are at work, standing upon wooden stalls, while two workmen strain upon a rope to raise a beam. These are views of building sites which could have been taken in London in any period over the last six hundred years. There is always building and rebuilding. Yet Scharf emphasises the human scale of this new London, before the advent of the Victorian megalopolis. He shows citizens in small groups, or as couples, rather than crowds; people are seen talking from upstairs windows, and Scharf is very interested in particular trades and in the names of individual shops or shopkeepers. Yet he still manages, in this compendium of local and specific detail, to capture a sense of progress and renewal; there is something distinctly and distinctively inspiriting in the air of these drawings. The city had lost something of its old packed intensity but it had recaptured its sense of the marvellous. Talleyrand, arriving in London in 1830 after an interval of thirty-six years, described it as "much more beautiful," while an American visitor believed it to be "a thousand times more beautiful." A visiting Italian general wrote in 1834 that London "has become an exceedingly beautiful and magnificent city; it is, in short, the leading capital of the world."

But had there been any concomitant improvement in the lives of its citizens? Some contemporaries believed that there was a true connection. Francis Place, the London radical and democratic reformer, declared that "the progress made in refinement of manners and morals seems to have gone on simultaneously with the improvement in arts, manufactures and commerce. It moved slowly at first, but has been constantly increasing in velocity . . . we are much better people than we were then [in the 1780s], better instructed, more sincere and kind-hearted, less gross and brutal." This enthusiastic report may seem surprising, in the light of subsequent denunciations of the Victorian city by writers as diverse as Engels and Booth, but it cannot be dismissed. Place was very close all his life to the actual conditions of the city, and he had seen a clear diminution in mob violence, open licentiousness and the intermittent savagery of ordinary life. He was a moral as well as a social reformer, and noticed with satisfaction an abatement of observable vice and squalor.

In fact the "improvements," with the new roads as well as the changes in transportation, had a general and profound effect upon the nature of the city. As one historian of London, Donald Olsen, has put it, in *The Growth of Victorian London*, "The nineteenth century saw the systematic sorting out of London into single-purpose, homogenous, specialised neighbourhoods . . . Strict social segregation became a prerequisite for success in any new development." In addition, "the shift from multi-purpose to single-purpose neighbourhoods reflected the pervasive move towards professionalisation and specialisation in all aspects of nineteenth century thought and activity." The generalisation is perhaps too broad, since there continued to be areas where rich and poor were obliged to mingle, but it hits upon an important truth. It is the truth which Francis Place in part expressed, albeit unwittingly. The vices of the poor could no longer be seen, and therefore there must have been an improvement. In fact they had departed into areas of misery created by the slum clearances of the new city. They had moved "behind the scenes" of the newly dramatised London.

CHAPTER 56

Nothing Quite Like It

❦

Of London areas, there is no end. The vibrancy of Walthamstow, the mournful decay of Pimlico and Mornington Crescent, the confusion of Stoke Newington, the intense and energetic air of Brixton, the watery gloom of Wapping, the bracing gentility of Muswell Hill, the excitement of Canary Wharf, the eccentricity of Camden Town, the fearfulness of Stepney, the lassitude of Limehouse, can all be mentioned in the vast oration of London. Every Londoner has his or her own favourite location, whether it be Victoria Park in Hackney or rolling Long Lane in Southwark, although it must also be admitted that most inhabitants of the city rarely know or visit anywhere beyond their own neighbourhood. Most citizens identify themselves in terms of their immediate locale.

There is a passage in G.K. Chesterton's *The Napoleon of Notting Hill* where he envisaged a city with its own assertive districts as, for example, "Clapham with a city guard. Wimbledon with a city wall. Surbiton tolling a bell to raise its citizens. West Hampstead going into battle with its own banner." Of the eponymous region of the book, he writes, "There has never been anything in the world absolutely like Notting Hill. There will never be anything quite like it to the crack of doom." In this, at least, he will be proved correct.

Where Notting Hill Gate now stands, a beacon was situated in the Roman period; part of a Roman sarcophagus was found in St. John's Vicarage
off Ladbroke Grove. The district's name comes from a band of Saxons, "sons
of Cnotta." For 1,700 years it remained in open countryside, with a reputation for springs and healthy air; there were in the eighteenth century, however, colonies of brick-makers and Irish pig-keepers apparently marring the
sylvan peace of the neighbourhood. Complaints were lodged but nothing
ever done. One of the peculiar characteristics of Notting Hill is that it was attached to the city, but not of it, and so was characterised by a "mixed" atmosphere at once urban and suburban. Hence its ambivalent air.

In the 1850s, for example, the east end of Notting Hill High Street was
inhabited by "private people, foreigners, adventurers, or respectable confi-
dential *employés* of west-end commercial houses," while almost fifty years
later Percy Fitzgerald complained that the grand terraces and houses were
"mixed up" with "flashy shops and all the vulgar incidents of traffic." A race-
course was opened in 1837 where Kensington Park Gardens and Ladbroke
Grove now meet; it was known as the Hippodrome, and was advertised as "a
racing emporium more extensive and attractive than Ascot or Epsom." It was
not a success and, from the 1840s onward, houses and villas were being constructed over the entire area.

So by degrees it assumed its present shape, but not before a cycle of
speculations and bankruptcies lent the neighbourhood another of its characteristic tones. In the 1820s James Ladbroke tried but failed to develop the
area; in the boom of the 1840s great developments were undertaken before
the speculators went bankrupt in the bust of the 1850s. In the 1860s Notting
Hill was described in *Building News* as "a graveyard of buried hopes . . .
naked carcasses, crumbling decorations, fractured walls, slimy cement. All
who touch them lose heart and money by the venture." Ever since that
period, there has been a persistent pattern of decay and recovery. In the
1870s, for example, there was a resurgence of activity and habitation but by
the next decade some of the imposing novelty of the site had diminished. As
urban development began to hesitate and falter at Earl's Court, always a
wilderness, there was a resurgent tide in favour of Notting Hill which
gathered strength in the 1890s. By the early decades of the twentieth
century, however, the stucco mansions of Kensington Park Gardens and its
environs once more began to fade and peel. The great houses were turned
into flats by the 1930s, less than a century after they had been erected, and in
the place of what was once termed "the upper middle class" came "Viennese

professors and Indian students and bed-sitter business girls." This description is by Osbert Lancaster, who lived in the area during the slow decline of its "Edwardian propriety."

In the late 1940s and the 1950s, however, Notting Hill declined into "slumdom" with broken windows and racketeering landlords. During the 1950s immigrants from the West Indies congregated in the area, like the Irish before them, which in turn led to riots; in the 1960s and early 1970s, precisely because of this mixed and heterogeneous past, it became a haven for those who, like the hippies of the period, required a kind of louche informality in which to pursue their lives. The peeling streets, the grimy balconies, were combined with the street-market along the Portobello Road to produce an atmosphere of happy dereliction. In the 1980s there were festivals. Here, in miniature, we see the passage of many different London cultures.

Then again, in one of the strange and instinctive processes of urban life, the conditions of the area seemed slowly to change. The harbinger of that change might be found in 1967 when large areas of Notting Hill were protected by a Conservation Act, so that the original streets of the 1840s and 1850s became privileged territories beyond the reach of speculators and developers. By the late 1970s this special status began to attract back the wealthy Londoners who had deserted the neighbourhood fifty years before. The area was itself gradually restored to its former state of lambent stucco; to walk down Kensington Park Gardens in 2000 is to experience that wide thoroughfare as it had emerged 150 years before.

The area in recent years has acquired a certain solidity and strength of purpose; it is no longer as fluid and as heterogeneous as once it was. Situated between the bewildering cosmopolitanism of Queensway, where the Tower of Babel might once more be constructed, and the mournful region of Shepherd's Bush, it is an enclave of quiet urban solidity. Accepting its past, Notting Hill has incorporated it within its being, so that now the summer Notting Hill Carnival is a truly mixed urban celebration. Of course there are still areas of relative poverty and deprivation within its bounds—Trellick Tower of the Kensal Estate, for example, dominates the northern skyline and lends an atmosphere of old and poor communal living to the market of Golborne Road within its shadow. Here, too, are the first intimations of the maze of West Kilburn to the north of the Harrow Road. But Notting Hill itself has retrieved its charm and good humour, principally because it has come to terms with its destiny.

. . .

Go to the north-east, and discover mournful Paddington which has always been blasted as a place of transit and of transience. In that it resembles the other gateways into the city. The area around the railway terminus at King's Cross, for example, has acquired a wandering population which takes advantage of travellers and tourists who venture into the immediate streets. The area around Victoria Station is anonymous and unhappy. But Paddington has a desolation all of its own. It is a place of transit in more than one sense, since one of its main sites was once the gallows of Tyburn. Lord Craven also donated some land, now covered by Craven Gardens, which, if London should once more be touched by pestilence, will be made available as a burial pit. Presumably the current inhabitants of Craven Gardens are not aware of this noble intention. The hospital is beside the station, and the gloomy brown brick exterior of the original institution still exudes in its own way the recognition of transit and mortality. The message of Paddington, in the words of William Blake, which predate the railway and the hospital, "mournful ever-weeping," seems to be that we are all travellers passing through.

If we travel further north-east, over Cato Street where the conspirators met in 1820, over the then New Road, which is now the Marylebone Road, and the Euston Road, past the broken columns of the old Euston Arch in front of the modern station, past bleak and windy King's Cross, past Penton Hill where the Druids may once have met, past the tribal trackway which exists beneath the modern layout of the Angel, we will arrive at Islington.

The Romans fought their battles there against Boudicca; there is evidence of a Roman encampment at Barnsbury, and the area of King's Cross was once known as Battle Bridge. A now forgotten track, Hagbush Lane, exists beneath the Liverpool Road. An ancient British settlement lies to the immediate south-east of Islington Green. The Saxon King Aethelbert granted Islington to the canons of St. Paul's (hence the name Canonbury), and it appears in the Domesday Book that the ecclesiastical authorities owned approximately five hundred acres of territory. Fitz-Stephen depicts the area as "fields for pasture and open meadows, very pleasant, into which the river waters do flow, and mills are turned about with a delightful noise . . . beyond them an immense forest extends itself, beautified with woods and groves, and full of the lairs and coverts of wild beasts . . . and game, stags, bucks, bears and wild bulls." The theme of the waters here is significant, since it dominated Islington's subsequent history as a source of health and refreshment. The pursuit of sport and hunting in the area, outside the confines of the city, is again a persistent one so that for some thousand years it was a haven of relaxation and entertainment for those ordinarily trapped within the city. In the time of Henry II (reigned 1154-89) "citizens played ball, exercised on horseback and took delight in birds, such as sparrow hawks, goss hawks, and in dogs for following the sports of the fields of Iseldon." In the sixteenth century Stow described Islington as a place of "fields commodius for the citizens therein to walke, shoote and otherwise to recreate and refresh their dulled spirits in the sweete and wholesome ayre." Immediately south of the Angel, fields were set aside for target practice; on eighteenth-century maps almost two hundred "marks" can be discerned, with the most proficient archers being awarded titles such as the "Marquis of Islington," the "Marquess of Clerkenwell" and the "Earl of Pancridge."

It was in Islington that Sir Walter Raleigh first smoked tobacco; the site of his house later became an inn for the citizens seeking refreshment of another kind. Islington was famous for its hostelries, among them the Three Hats, Copenhagen House, White Conduit House and the Angel itself, which gave its salubrious name to an entire district. Here also were Sadler's Wells, Islington Spa, the New Wells, the Pantheon in Spa Fields, the English Grotto in Rosoman Street, the London Spa, Merlin's Cave, Hockley-in-the-Hole, Bagnigge Wells, St. Chad's Well in Gray's Inn Road and Penny's Folly on the Pentonville Road; the entire area was covered by tea gardens, walks and entertainments. Charles Lamb, the great romantic antiquary of London, settled here in 1823 and according to William Hazlitt "took much interest in the antiquity of 'Merrie Islington' . . . the ancient hostelries were also visited, and he smoked his pipe and quaffed his nut brown ale at the Old Queen's Head." The air of liberation which Islington induced was still with Lamb two years later, when he remarked that "It was like passing from life into eternity . . . Now when all is holyday there are no holydays . . . Pleasuring was for fugitive play days; mine are fugitive only in the sense that life is fugitive. Freedom and life co-existent!" That is why there are so many ballads about Islington, "The Bailiff's Daughter of Islington" and "Tom, Tom of Islington" among them; for many centuries it remained a haven of carelessness.

But Charles Lamb's residence, Colebrook Cottage, became attached to other houses; then they became a terrace; then became part of a row of terraces as London crept northward. In the early 1800s houses "of a very small and slight character" were built in the environs of Colebrook Cottage, only to become slums. In the 1830s, the Northampton estate built cheap tenements on its vacant ground, while sixteen years later the Packington Estate constructed a network of wide streets in the area which still bears its name. Soon the entire region was covered with terraces, villas and the general ribbon development which characterised the tentacular stretch of London. An issue of *Building News* in 1863 named Islington as an area of "trumpery allotments which have been dealt out to builders, and the closely packed streets and terraces which have arisen." And all those who lived in these new terraces moved daily to the centre of their being. Dickens noticed them in one of his early sketches. "The early clerk population of Somers and Camden Towns, Islington and Pentonville, are fast pouring into the city, or directing their steps towards Chancery Lane and the Inns of Court. Middle-aged men, whose salaries have by no means increased in the same proportion as their families, plod steadily along, apparently with no object in view but the counting-house; knowing by sight almost everybody they meet and overtake, for they have seen them every morning (Sundays excepted) during the last twenty years, but speaking to no one . . . Small office lads in large hats . . . milliners' and staymakers' apprentices." All of them can be imagined walking into the city, acquiring a settled anonymity as they steadily approach it. Dickens was very interested in Islington; he placed several of his characters in that vicinity, denominating most of them as clerks. Potters and Smithers and Guppy are all clerks of Islington and Pentonville, for example, as if those areas adjacent to the centres of finance and power had themselves a subsidiary clerkly function.

The more affluent Londoners moved further out to Sydenham or Penge, even as the poor travelled north. So by stages Islington itself became poor. Rows of terraced houses, of two or three or four storeys, can be seen in early photographs; their grimy stucco is matched by the darkness of their brick, and they seem to stretch on interminably. In 1945 Orwell depicted the area as having become one of "vague, brown-coloured slums . . . He was walking up a cobbled street of little two-storey houses with battered doorways which gave straight on the pavement and which were somehow curiously suggestive of rat-holes. There were puddles of filthy water here and there among the cobbles. In and out of the dark doorways, and down narrow alley-ways that branched off on either side, people swarmed in astonishing numbers . . . Perhaps a quarter of the windows in the street were broken and boarded up." This is taken from *1984*, a novel of the future, but the details are based directly on Orwell's observation of the streets beside Essex Road. It is as if the dereliction had entered his soul and he had come to believe that London, somehow, will always be sordid, and grimy, and squalid. Islington will always be Islington.

Certainly it entered the postwar era in an impoverished state. It has been recorded that "three quarters of its households did not even have running water, an inside lavatory nor a bath." One resident recalled that "We had sixteen people using one toilet." Islington, once a village in the environs of London, had been transformed into a central core of slum conditions. A familiar pattern then reasserted itself. Swathes of Victorian and Georgian terraces were razed in order to accommodate council-house estates and tower blocks; the urge to destroy, however, was quickly succeeded by the need to conserve. Islington may stand as representative of London in this respect, where the fashion for wholesale redevelopment was displaced by a no less urgent desire for preservation and improvement. It is as if an amnesiac had suddenly recovered his memory. A process of gentrification then ensued whereby generally middle-class couples, attracted by the prospect of "improvement grants" from the civic authorities of Islington, settled in the neighbourhood and began to restore or rejuvenate their properties. They were the direct successors of those who had arrived in the 1830s and 1840s, and in fact the newly refurbished streets acquired their original characteristics. There were of course disadvantages. The poorer "locals" were now congregated upon the housing estates of Islington, or had dispersed. What has been lost in the process? Certainly that sense of belonging to a small patch of local territory, however squalid, disappeared. Or perhaps it is better to say that it had changed hands. The poor colonised the area for a hundred years: they had driven out the more affluent residents of Islington in the 1880s and 1890s, but now in turn they were being driven away.

But a larger pattern has also been introduced. Where there was once a rooted and identifiable community in Islington, there is now a greater sense of transience. Like the rest of London it has grown more mobile but also more impersonal. Another paradox has emerged in the process, however, emphasising the unique conditions of each urban area. In the course of its present changes, Islington has reacquired its principal or original identity. Where once it was known for its inns and tea gardens, it is now celebrated for its bars and restaurants. Along the central highway of Upper Street there are now proportionally more restaurants than in any other part of London, with the possible exception of Soho, and so the area has regained its reputation for hospitality and conviviality which it possessed long before it ever became part of London. The old presence lingers beneath every change of appearance.

The City Road, emanating from Islington, directly approaches the site of London's old wall. Before its arrival there it crosses Old Street, where to the east Shoreditch and Spitalfields beckon. These once forlorn areas still bear the marks of their past. In the mid-seventeenth century Shoreditch "was a disreputable place, frequented by courtesans." The female prostitutes still ply their trade at the upper end of Commercial Street, a dismal thoroughfare between the two areas, while Shoreditch High Street is notorious for its strip pubs catering for local residents as well as gentlemen from the City who symbolically pass beyond the old walls of London, through Bishopsgate, in order to indulge themselves. In the late nineteenth century violent street gangs issued out of the slums of "Old Nichol," a congerie of streets around Old Nichol Street which might have been named after Old Nick himself. Violence flares still; a murder, or a suicide, awakens memories of the not so recent past.

The name itself derives from Soerditch, a ditch issuing into the Thames, but the idea of a sour ditch is suggestive. The later addition of Shore suggests something stranded or laid up. In turn the name Spitalfields, detached from its origin in "spital," a house for the sick, suggests spittle—something spat out, violently ejected. Thus it became a haven for refugees. The wrong etymology is often accurate about the nature of an area.

So we may move on to the hunting grounds of Soho, "So-ho" or "So-hoe" being the call of the huntsmen who originally rode across its fields. Now, with its sex shops and strip clubs, the hunt is on for another kind of game. Of all the regions of London, this is the one that has most fully preserved its appearance. Gerrard Street may have been transformed into the centre of Chinatown, but the house in which John Dryden lived is still recognisable. In Soho every street is a memorial; here is where Marx lived, here Casanova, here Canaletto, and here De Quincey.

There are deeper continuities, too, since the area had a reputation for its cuisine long before it was ever populated. In 1598 Stow wrote of the conduit in Soho Fields that "The Lord Mayor, aldermen, and many worshipful persons rode to the conduit . . . according to custom, and then they went and hunted a hare before dinner and killed her; and thence went to dinner at the banqueting house at the head of the conduit, where a great number were handsomely entertained by the chamberlain." So the air of dining and conviviality has always been part of the neighbourhood. On the same patch of ground where sixteenth-century dignitaries ate, the modern traveller can still dine at the Gay Hussar, Quo Vadis or L'Escargot.

There was a parish located here by 1623, and in 1636 certain people were described as living at "the brick kilns near Soho," but the area first began to flourish in the 1670s when Gerrard Street, Old Compton Street, Greek Street and Frith Street emerged as part of a development north of Leicester Fields. A proclamation from the Court, dated as early as April 1671, forbade the erection of "small cottages and other tenements" in "the windmill Fields, Dog Fields and the fields adjoining So-Hoe" but, as usual, the social and commercial imperatives of the city over-ruled royal proclamations.

How Soho itself acquired its "raffish" flavour is obscure. The area just to its east, beside St. Martin's Lane, was already inhabited by artists or artisans who catered to the rich or the fashionable. Art studios and art schools also began to cluster there, alongside the inevitable taverns and coffee houses. But they did not directly affect Soho itself. A sudden influx of French residents was of more consequence. In the area of Newport Market and Old Compton Street it was remarked by Maitland that "many parts of the parish abound with French, so that it is an easy matter for a stranger to fancy himself in France." By 1688 over eight hundred of the empty and newly built houses had been filled with Huguenots, who characteristically transformed the ground floors into "genuine French shops," cheap cafés and restaurants "like those near 'the barrier' in Paris." So by degrees this emerging region of London came to be compared with the French city. It maintained that ambience for more than 150 years, and as late as 1844 Soho was still being described as "a sort of petty France." It was recorded that "Most of the shops are thoroughly French, and they evidently have been established solely for the supply of the foreign colony. Here are French schools for the education of the young, and wine-shops and restaurants where an Englishman who entered would be looked on with surprise." Perhaps the most notable institution, in the early days of twenty-first-century Soho, is the York Minster or French Pub known colloquially as "the French"; it is said to have been the meeting-place of the French Resistance during the Second World War. Again a small area of London, no more than a few streets and a market, has retained its traditional culture for more than three hundred years.

But the presence of the French immigrants in a place where the arrival of an Englishman would be a "surprise," in turn created an odd air of strangeness or unfamiliarity which encouraged natives of other countries to feel more secure in its environs. In certain respects it was *not English*. "Of all quarters in the queer adventurous amalgam called London," Galsworthy wrote in *The Forsyte Saga*, "Soho is perhaps least suited to the Forsyte spirit . . . Untidy, full of Greeks, Ishmaelites, cats, Italians, tomatoes, restaurants, organs, coloured stuffs, queer names, people looking out of upper windows, it dwells remote from the British Body Politic." From the start it was a mixed area, both in terms of demography and of trade. "This district," according to one *Handbook*, "is also a principal rendezvous for foreigners in London, many of whom here ply their avocations as artists and mechanics." There were emporia of furniture acquired from various eras and various cultures, curiosity shops filled with multifarious relics of the Romans or the Habsburgs, musical-instrument makers and print-sellers, china manufacturers, booksellers and taverns where artists and literary gentlemen gathered. Modern institutions, such as the French Pub and the Colony Room Club, still attract poets and painters.

The phenomenon of transference from age to age is in certain respects inexplicable. It may be that the previous reputation of an area attracts its new residents, so that there is a kind of advertised continuity; but this does not apply to other districts which simply flare and fade away. Or is it that an atmosphere of freedom and unfamiliarity, first created by the Huguenots liberated from the cruelty of their compatriots, has continued to linger? Certainly immigrants arrived in their wake, from Russia and from Hungary, Italy and Greece. In the churchyard of St. Anne's, Soho, there was a tablet with the following inscription: "Near this place is interred Theodore, King of Corsica, who died in this parish, December 11, 1756, immediately after leaving the King's Bench Prison by the benefit of the Act of Insolvency; in consequence of which he registered his kingdom of Corsica for the benefit of his creditors." He had accepted his crown in March 1736, but could not raise enough money to pay for his army; so he travelled to London where, finding himself in debt, he was soon arrested and consigned to prison. On his release on 10 December 1756, he took a sedan chair to the house of a tailor and acquaintance in Little Chapel Street Soho. But he died the next day, and his funeral expenses were paid by an oil-man in Old Compton Street. So a foreign king is buried in the middle of Soho, thus emphasising its reputation as a foreign land in the heart of London. This penniless exile might almost be considered the true monarch of the area.

Its reputation for heterogeneity and freedom was also associated with liberties of another sort, and by the end of the eighteenth century it was notorious for courtesans. A celebrated member of that order, Mrs. Cornelys, arranged weekly assemblies in Carlisle House on the south side of Soho Square. There was a notice outside in which she "begs the chairmen and hackney-coach drivers not to quarrel, or to run their poles through each other's windows," which suggests that the spirit of disorder affected anyone who came within the parish. In Carlisle House were held masquerades and promenades which featured scantily dressed ladies "in violation," according to one observer, "of the laws, and to the destruction of all sober principles." Mrs. Cornelys was one of those redoubtable London characters holding court to thieves and nobility alike, who dominated all company with a quick wit and a loud if vulgar manner. She was enterprising, irrepressible, charming and scathing in equal measure; she created a great stir in the 1760s and 1770s until after the failure of one of her fashionable schemes she "retired into private life." She started selling asses' milk in Knightsbridge, and in 1797 died in the Fleet Prison.

She was the very type of the London club hostess, a figure so much larger than life that no one—not even the most drunken or aristocratic customer— would dare to cross her. Kate Hamilton and Sally Sutherland both managed dubious "night-houses" of the 1860s, and Kate was described as "presiding as a sort of Paphian queen" over her scantily clad dancers. There is a wonderful description of her "weighing some twenty stone, with a countenance that had weathered countless convivial nights. Mrs. Hamilton presented a stupendous appearance in the low cut evening dresses which she always wore. From midnight to dawn she sipped champagne [and] with her foghorn voice, knew how to keep her clients of both sexes in order." Her establishment was in Leicester Square, which by the mid-nineteenth century had become associated with the delinquencies of neighbouring Soho, and her twentieth-century successor was Muriel Belcher who ran the Colony Room Club, a drinking room in Dean Street. She also kept her clients in order with a voice as piercing, if not as loud, as a foghorn, and specialised in a form of obscene badinage which only the vulgar mistook for wit.

From its beginning, in fact, Soho has been associated with demonstrative and sometimes difficult women. In 1641 "a lewd woman," Anna Clerke, was bound over for "threteninge to burne the houses at Soho" for reasons unknown. A once famous inn known as the Mischief, in Charles Street, had as its sign a drunken courtesan straddling a man's back while holding a glass of gin with the legend "She's as Drunk as a Sow" inscribed beside her. The female, and male, prostitutes of the area were well known by the middle of the

nineteenth century; once more the relative "foreignness" of the neighbourhood ensured that it would be the context for more relaxed sexual behaviour
than in Lombard Street, for example, or in Pimlico. The proximity of the
rookeries, in St. Giles and elsewhere, also meant that there was no shortage
of fresh bodies for the clients. Only the recommendations of the Wolfenden
Report, in 1957, managed to keep "the girls" off the streets; but they migrated
instead to small rooms and attic spaces in the same area.

There were the "Argyll Rooms," Laurent's Dancing Academy, the Portland Rooms, and a score of other venues. The night-houses and flash-houses
changed into nightclubs, the penny gaffs and cheap theatres into striptease
joints, the gaming clubs into bars, but despite the external alterations governed by time and fashion the essential atmosphere and purpose of Soho have
remained the same. It was estimated that in 1982 there were some 185
premises used as part of the sex industry; more recent legislation has attempted to mitigate the business but, at the beginning of a new century, Soho
remains the centre of a flourishing trade in prostitution. The spirit of the area
has also asserted itself in another guise, with Old Compton Street becoming
in the 1980s and 1990s a centre of "gay" pubs and clubs. The narrow thoroughfares of Soho are always crowded now, with people in search of sex,
spectacle or excitement; it has retained its "queer adventurous" spirit and
seems a world away from the clubs of Pall Mall or the shops of Oxford Street
which lie respectively to its south and north.

This is only to be expected, however. Each area of London has its own
unmistakable character, nurtured through time and history; together they resemble a thousand vortices within the general movement of the city. It is impossible to look at them all steadily, or envisage them as a whole, because the
impression can only be one of opposition and contrast. Yet out of these op-
positions and contrasts London itself emerges, as if it sprang into being out of
collision and paradox. In that sense its origins are as mysterious as the beginning of the universe itself.

Plate XIX.   Vol. V. To face the Title.

F. Hayman inv. et del.   C. Grignion sculp.

Here strip my Children! here at once leap in,
Here prove who best can dash thro' thick and thin.

Dunciad. Book II

An engraving by Charles Grignion, after Francis Hayman,
of the insalubrious Fleet River; since it was the last resting place of
dead dogs, corpses, human waste and noxious refuse, it is hard to
believe that anyone actually swam in it.

CHAPTER 57

You Cannot Take the Thames with You

※

It has always been the river of commerce. The watercress-growers of Gravesend, the biscuit-bakers and store-shippers of Tooley Street, the ship-chandlers of Wapping, the block-makers and rope-makers of Limehouse, all owe their trades to the Thames. The great paintings of its business, with its warehouses, refiners, breweries and builders' yards, all bear testimony to its power and authority. Its predominance within the city was understood long before the Romans came. Copper and tin were transported along it as early as the third millennium BC; as a result of commerce upon the river the area comprising London acquired, by 1500 BC, supremacy over the region of Wessex. That is perhaps why ceremonial objects were thrown into its waters, where they lay hidden until recent archaeological discoveries.

The city itself owes its character and appearance to the Thames. It was a place of "crowded wharfs and people-pestered shores," the water continually in motion with "shoals of labouring oars." The movement and energy of London were the movement of horses and the energy of the river. The Thames brought in a thousand argosies. Venetian galleys and three-masted ships from the Low Countries vied for position by the riverside, while the water itself was crowded with wherries and ferries transporting the citizens from one shore to the other.

The other great commercial value of the Thames lay in its fish, and in the fifteenth century we read of "barbille, fflounders. Roaches. dace. pykes. Tenches," all caught in nets with baits of cheese and tallow; there were eels and kipper salmon, mullet, lamprey, prawn, smelt, sturgeon and "white bayte." A vast range of vessels also plied their trades upon the water. Barges and barks sailed beside chalk-boats; they were joined by cocks, or small work boats, by pikers, rush-boats, oyster-boats and ferry-boats, by whelk-boats and tide-boats.

Most Londoners earned their living directly off the river, or by means of the goods which were transported along it. Documents of the fourteenth and fifteenth centuries reveal a host of Thames employees, from the "conservators" who were in charge of river safety to the "tidemen" whose work on embanking or building upon the river depended upon the state of the tide. There were boatmen and chalkmen, eelmen and baillies, gallymen or garthmen, ferriers and lightermen, hookers and mariners, petermen and palingmen, searchers and shipwrights, shoutmen and piledrivers, trinkers and water-bailiffs and watermen. There are recorded no fewer than forty-nine ways of trapping or catching fish, from nets and weirs to enclosures and wicker-baskets. But there were many other activities such as the erection of dams and barriers, the construction of landing-stages and jetties, the repairing of watergates and causeways, quays and stairs. We may call this the early stage of the Thames when it remained the living centre of the city's development and trade.

But then it first touched the imagination of poets and chroniclers. It became the river of magnificence, used as a golden highway by princes and diplomats. Barges were "freshly furnished with banners and streamers of silk" while other boats were "richly beaten with the arms or badges of their craft"; there were many covered with awnings of silk and silken tapestry, while around them the wherries took their course heavily weighted with merchants or priests or courtiers. This was a time when, in the early years of the sixteenth century, the oars of the London watermen might become entangled in water lilies while they kept stroke "to the tune of flutes" which made "the water which they beat to follow faster." The Thames has always been associated with song and music, beginning with the watermen's chant of "Heare and how, rumblelow" or "Row, the boat, Norman, row to thy lemen" dated respectively to the fourteenth and fifteenth centuries.

More formal music, beating not to the ebb and flow of the current but rather to its history, could be heard on diplomatic or nuptial occasions. When

in 1540 Henry VIII and Anne of Cleves, his fourth wife, removed to Westminster by water on their bridal day they were accompanied by "instruments
sweetly sounding" in barges "gorgeously garnished with banners, pennons
and targets richly covered." On the previous ceremonial entrance of Henry's
second wife Anne Boleyn from Greenwich into London in 1533, "there were
trumpets, shawms, and other divers instruments, all the way playing and
making great melody." Her welcome provided one of the richest pageants
upon the Thames ever recorded, with the state barge of the mayor leading the
procession "adorned by flags and pennons hung with rich tapestries and ornamented on the outside with scutcheons of metal, suspended on cloth of
gold and silver." It was preceded by a flat vessel, rather like a floating stage,
upon which "a dragon pranced about furiously, twisting his tail and belching
out wildfire." Here the freedom of the river inspires extravagance as well as
music. The barge of the mayor was followed by fifty other barges belonging
to the trades and guilds, "all sumptuously decked with silk and arras, and
having bands of music on board." Here commerce makes its own music upon
the water, which was itself the conduit of its wealth.

It is clear, however, that the Thames can harbour and accommodate supernatural forces as well as more conventional goods. It was typically described as the colour of silver, the great alchemical agent; the "silver
streaming Thames" in Spenser is followed by "the silver-footed Thamesis"
in Herrick and the "silver Thames" in Pope. Herrick introduces nymphs and
naiads, but his central tone is one of mournful regret upon being forced to
abandon the river in leaving London for the country—no more sweet
evenings of summer bathing, no more journeys to Richmond, Kingston or
Hampton Court, no more departures "and landing here, or safely landing
there." Drayton invokes the "silver Thames" also, and uses the familiar
metaphor of a "clearest crystal flood," where Pope describes "Old Father
Thames" whose "shining horns diffused a golden gleam." It has often been
suggested that rivers represent the feminine principle within the general masculine environment of the city, but with the Thames this is emphatically not
the case. It is the "Old Father," perhaps in a somewhat menacing or primeval
way equivalent to William Blake's vision of "Nobodaddy."

It looked, from a distance, as if it were a forest of masts; there were approximately two thousand ships and boats each day upon the water, as well
as three thousand of the then notorious watermen who transported goods and
people in every direction. "The Pool of London," the area between London
Bridge and the Tower, was filled to capacity with barges and barks and

galleons, while a map of the middle sixteenth century shows boats moored beside the various stairs which were the transportation stops of the capital. Upon this map the streets are depicted as almost devoid of activity while the river is a hive of business; it was a pardonable exaggeration, designed to emphasise the paramount importance of the Thames. There is a London story which is appropriate. One sovereign, more than usually irate about the reluctance of London to subsidise his adventures, threatened to move his court to Winchester or Oxford; the mayor of London replied, "Your Majesty may with ease move yourself, your Court and your Parliament, wheresoever you wish, but the merchants of London have one great consolation—you cannot take the Thames with you."

When Wenceslaus Hollar arrived in England in December 1636, he travelled to London by barge from Gravesend. He was given lodgings in Arundel House, beside the Thames, so that his first and earliest views were of the river. His sketches and etchings are filled with its breadth and light, while its continual activity spills over upon its banks and embarkation points; the wherries and barges are crowded, seeming to skim the water before the small quiet buildings which line its shores. It is the river which breathes life within his great panorama of the city; the streets and houses seem deserted, as if all London were gathered by the riverside. The names of each wharf are prominently displayed—"Paulus wharfe . . . Queen hythe . . . The 3 Cranes . . . Stiliard . . . Cole harbour . . . The Old Swan"—while their stairs and landing-stages are busy with the activity of tiny human figures. The great sheet of bright water is lent depth and interest by the numerous craft, some of which are named; "the Eel Ships" lie among barges carrying vegetable produce, while small boats with two or three passengers voyage from shore to shore. Below London Bridge many great ships are moored while around them teems the marine business of the port. In the right-hand corner of this engraving the figure of a water god, Father Thames, holding an urn from which pour a multitude of fish, completes an image of the river as the source of power and life. Just as its swans were in the pre-Christian era under the protection of Apollo and of Venus, so the river itself lies under divine tutelage. It is of some significance, too, that the classical deity, depicted by Hollar as pointing to the cartouche of "LONDON," is Mercury who is the god of commerce.

Hollar's prospect is taken from a high point south of the river and just west of London Bridge; it was a real location, on top of St. Mary Overy (now Southwark cathedral), but it also became a conventional or idealised vantage point. An earlier etching by Claes Jansz Visscher takes approximately the same position but from a theoretical high locality further westward; this allowed him to suggest a great central sketch of the busy river, and he emphasised the point with the Latin inscription of London "emporium que toto orbe celeberrimum" (the most famous market in the entire world). The power and persuasiveness of this slightly fictionalised topography affected many later artists and engravers, who kept on borrowing each other's mistakes and false perspectives in their continuing effort to celebrate the Thames as representing the commercial destiny of the city. Just as the river had been the great subject of sixteenth- and seventeenth-century London poetry, so it became the central theme of London painting.

As trade and commerce increased, so did the significance of the river. It has been estimated that the volume of business grew three times between 1700 and 1800; there were thirty-eight wharves on both sides of the river, from the bridge to the Tower, and nineteen further below. It has been estimated that, even by 1700, the London quays were handling 80 per cent of the entire country's imports and 69 per cent of its exports. Within the river's banks sailed tea and china, as well as cotton and pepper, from the East Indies; from the West Indies came rum and coffee, sugar and cocoa; North America brought to the Thames tobacco and corn, rice and oil, while the Baltic states offered hemp and tallow, iron and linen. When Daniel Defoe wrote of trade "flowing" in and out of London, he was using the river as a metaphor for London's life.

It is rare to find a picture of London that does not contain a glimpse of the river; there are views from Westminster Pier and from Lambeth as well as from Southwark. Three very popular collections of river prints were published in the latter part of the eighteenth century—Boydell's *Collection of Views* (1770), Ireland's *Picturesque Views of the Thames* (1792) and Boydell's *History of the Thames* (1794–6)—in which the most usual "views" were those west of London Bridge where the newly renovated city was matched by images of a dignified and elegant river.

Of course Canaletto is the master of these riverscapes in which he creates a city aspiring towards magnificence. Two companion portraits, in particular, *The Thames from the terrace of Somerset House, Westminster in the distance* and *The Thames from the terrace of Somerset House, the city in the distance*, take the measure of London as essentially a noble European city. It seems likely that Canaletto came to London in the 1740s specifically to paint the recently constructed Westminster Bridge and to give an aesthetic imprimatur to the city's latest public building, but his is an idealised city and an idealised river. The sky is free of fog and soot, so that the buildings shine with expressive clarity; the river itself is luminous, its surface iridescent, while the activity upon it is so calm and bright that it is no longer a picture of commerce but of contentment.

A more direct and intimate depiction of the eighteenth-century Thames is found in what is generally classified as the British School, but might as well be termed the London School. William Marlow's *Fresh Wharf, London Bridge* and *The London Riverfront between Westminster and the Adelphi*, for example, acquire much of their strength from their detail. The view of Fresh Wharf shows the work of the wharf with its wooden barrels and olive jars and bales of merchandise being inspected or unloaded; scaffolding and fencing on the north side of London Bridge are an indication that the shops and houses which were once located there have been only just removed. The painting of the London riverfront also acquires its power from its specificity. Here can be seen Buckingham Street and Adam Street, together with the tower and chimneys of the York Buildings Waterworks Company. In the foreground are displayed all the multifarious activities of a messy and grubby river. A coal barge is being unloaded by men in dirty smocks while a woman, surrounded by a pile of baskets, is being ferried towards the shore.

It was in just such a place, and among just such activity, that the youthful imagination of Turner, born in 1775 in Maiden Lane, first moved towards the Thames. In *Modern Painters* (1843) John Ruskin describes the painter's early life as involved intimately with "the working of city-commerce, from endless warehouses, towering over Thames, to the back shop in the lane, with its stale herrings." Here he ventured into the world of barges and ships, "that mysterious forest below London Bridge—better for the boy than wood or pine or grove of myrtle." Turner was, in other words, a child who derived his inspiration from the city and its river rather than from more conventional and pastoral settings. "How he must have tormented the watermen," Ruskin goes on to suggest, "beseeching them to let him crouch anywhere in their bows, quiet as a log, so that only he might get floated down there among the ships, and by the ships, and under the ships, staring and clambering;—these the only quite beautiful things in the world." The great world itself was for Turner contained within the city and its river.

The Thames flowed through him, giving him light and movement. As a child he walked down from his birthplace in Maiden Lane and crossed the Strand to wander among the myriad small streets which led to the river; as an old man he died looking over the Thames in Cheyne Walk. For most of the intervening years he lived "on or within easy reach of its banks." So we must consider Turner, more than Canaletto or Whistler, as the true child of the river—or, rather, one through whom the spirit of the river emerged most clearly and abundantly. On certain occasions he clothed it with classical beauty, invoking the gods and nymphs which once haunted its banks, while in other paintings he depicted all the immediate and instinctive life of its waters. One of his early sketches was of *Old Blackfriars Bridge* where he emphasised the tide of the river by painting the piers of the bridge as if they were still dark and wet. An early watercolour of *Old London Bridge* exhibited the same intense and absorbed observation: here the water wheel of the London Waterworks Company is the central focus, with the force of the water rushing upstream at precisely twenty-five to eleven according to the clock of St. Magnus the Martyr just beyond the bridge.

Vessels were moored side by side, with each ship being assigned its place on its arrival. Barges or smaller boats came alongside in order to receive the goods, which were then rowed upstream to the various official quays and wharves. It was a cumbersome procedure, given the general overcrowding of the Pool, and one which obviously led to theft and dishonest dealing on a large scale. As a result of various parliamentary inquiries, however, a decision was eventually taken to build proper docks, where cargo could be more expeditiously handled and enclosed. So began the great scheme of the "wet docks." In 1799 the West India Dock Company Act was passed, and the whole Isle of Dogs began its transformation into its home. It was followed by the London Dock at Wapping, the East India Dock at Blackwall and the Surrey Dock at Rotherhithe. It was the largest single, privately funded enterprise in the history of London. Great fortress-like structures with gates and high walls were built, beside what were essentially artificial lakes covering some three hundred acres of water. The Isle of Dogs, formerly a wasteland of marsh, was turned into something like an elegant prison island; the sketches and aquatints of a contemporary artist, William Daniell, show grand avenues of brick warehouses. A new road was built connecting the docks to the City of London, from Aldgate to Limehouse; hundreds of houses were demolished in its path, and it entirely changed the aspect of east London. The Commercial Road was in that sense aptly named since this transformation of the city was done solely in the name of profit. The foundation stone of the West India

Dock was inscribed with the motto: "An Undertaking which, under the Favour of God, shall contribute Stability, Increase and Ornament, to British Commerce." Further changes followed with the building of the Regent's Canal to connect the docks with the greater world, by means of a waterway going westward until it met the Grand Union Canal at Paddington Basin. Once again the city was opened up to more transport and traffic.

The whole enterprise was considered at the time to be an almost visionary undertaking, and the apotheosis of successful commercialism. The tobacco warehouse at Wapping was celebrated for "covering more ground, under one roof, than any public building, or undertaking, except the pyramids of Egypt." Many of these Wapping warehouses were the work of Daniel Asher Alexander, who also built the huge prisons of Dartmoor and Maidstone; we may see here the association between money and the nature of power. One architectural historian has compared the edifices of Alexander with the architectural engravings of Piranesi. "While Coleridge turned the plates of the *Opere Varie* and young De Quincey drugged himself into Piranesian frenzy," Sir John Summerson wrote in *Georgian London*, "Alexander built these reminiscences of the Carceri into gaols and warehouses." Here money and power are given visionary, or mythic, potential.

The drawings and engravings which display the dock works in progress also command grand vistas and vast numbers of workmen to emphasise the scope of the enterprise. There were crowds when the work was completed, crowds when the waters of the Thames were allowed to flow into the basins, crowds when the first vessels were admitted. These were schemes of immensity, and resembled "the hydraulic works of ancient river civilisations," suggesting that London's great riverine adventure revived memories of ancient empires. "The docks are impossible to describe," Verlaine wrote in 1872. "They are unbelievable! Tyre and Carthage all rolled into one!" He and his companion, Rimbaud, spent hours in the vast region noting the myriad goods and the myriad types of humanity jostling together; "they heard strange languages spoken," Enid Starkie wrote in her biography of Rimbaud, "and saw printed on the bales of goods mysterious signs that they could not read." James McNeill Whistler is generally considered to be the painter who evokes the poetry of the Thames when it is subdued by mist and occluded light, but that opinion neglects half of his achievement as a painter of the river. In his early sketches of the Thames between Tower Bridge and Wapping, the central images are of wharves and warehouses where work and trade are the persistent, essential London element. These etchings in fact elicited a remark from Baudelaire that they manifested "the profound and complex poetry of a vast capital."

Here the experience of confusion is compounded by the sense of mystery—of something living and alien—that lies at the heart of the city's life. This is also the effect manifested in Gustave Doré's engravings of the docks where the carters and the porters, the sailors and labourers, become darkly anonymous figures tending to the trade of London like ancient votaries; the warehouses and custom houses are generally enmeshed in shadow and chiaroscuro, like the thick netting of sails and masts which dominates the foreground. Fitful gleams can be seen upon the dark water "black with coal, blue with indigo, brown with tides, white with flour, stained with purple wine, or brown with tobacco." These are the ranges of colours which Doré knew, at first sight, to be "one of the grand aspects of your London." Again his scenes conjure up images of Piranesi, with the rigging and the spars and the ropes and the land bridges and planks blending together to form a picture of endless turmoil. "A whole people toil at the unloading of the enormous ships," another French observer, Gabriel Mourey, wrote, "swarming on the barges, dark figures, dimly outlined, moving rhythmically, fill in and give life to the picture. In the far distance, behind the interminable lines of sheds and warehouses, masts bound the horizon, masts like a bare forest in winter, finely branched, exaggerated, aerial trees grown in all the climates of the globe."

Since the docks had become one of the wonders of creation, many travellers felt obliged to visit them. It was necessary to obtain a letter of introduction for the captain of each dock, and then hire a boat from one of the stairs to take advantage of the ebbing tide. "You see shipping at anchor on both sides, many Dutch, Danes, Swedes, with licences I suppose, and many Americans": this is from the 1810 diary of a French visitor. A German had pronounced upon the same subject in 1787: "It is an area of restless activity," he wrote, "of constant noise, and of the hubbub of people . . . broad quays, large splendid warehouses like palaces." This visitor also commented that "nearby rural pleasures seem to be very far away." Since those pleasures, at Greenwich and Gravesend, were themselves upon the Thames the sheer imposition of the city's trading machinery seemed to have obliterated their presence. When Prince Herman Pückler-Muskau visited the docks in 1826 he conceded "astonishment, and a sort of awe at the greatness and might of England . . . Everything is on a colossal scale" with "sugar enough to sweeten the whole adjoining basin, and rum enough to make half England drunk." He might have commented, too, that nine million oranges arrived each year, together with twelve thousand tons of raisins. The peripatetic prince had just visited the great breweries of the city and, after his journey to the docks, he went to a freak-show. So the spectacles of London merge into an unnatural phantasmagoria.

The history of the docks is in fact the central story of the commercial Thames in the nineteenth and twentieth centuries. It is the story of a riverside thoroughfare busy for 150 years. In Commercial Road, and Thames Street, and a score of narrow streets between them descending to the riverside, there were wagons and vans; Mile's Lane, Duck's Foot Lane and Pickle-Herring Street were filled with the sound of carts, horses, cranes and human voices mingling with the whistles of the railway. On the banks themselves there was a profusion of commercial activity, with factories and warehouses approaching as close to the water as they dared, while its wharves and mills and landing-stages pulsated with the energies of human life and activity. Further upriver, between Southwark Bridge and Blackfriars Bridge, the riverside scene subtly changed; the warehouses and houses here were older and more dilapidated. They leaned towards the river, narrow and lopsided, while between them were the openings of little alleys, through which sacks and barrels were taken from the river into the city. By Ludgate a huge steam flour-mill could be seen, while on the other bank lay a whole range of factory chimneys. This was a true avenue of commerce, with its institutions on both sides.

But there was also less serious business upon the Thames. There were halfpenny steamers, penny steamers and twopenny steamers going to Greenwich or Gravesend, Ramsgate and Margate. There was a Dover boat and a Boulogne boat, an Ostend boat and a Rhine boat; there were coasters to Ipswich, Yarmouth and Hull, and steamboats to Southampton, Plymouth and Land's End. There were slower boats which made the journey to Kew, Richmond and Hampton Court complete with musical bands.

Then beyond the shoreline itself lay a whole host of commercial properties dependent upon the river and its tides—ship yards, sailors' lodgings and public houses, marine stores, the hovels of porters, apple stalls and oyster shops waiting for custom. The whole panoply of street life attended the river, then, with a group of sailors getting out of hansom cabs to descend upon a public house, a breakdown of a wagon in the streets attracting a crowd of spectators, the endless chaff of speech resounding against the walls and bridge. "Go it!" "I can come it *slap*." "She can be very *choice*!"

By 1930 the port and docks of London gave employment to a hundred thousand people and carried thirty-five million tons of cargo within their seven hundred acres; there were in addition almost two thousand riverside wharves. In this period, too, heavy industries such as gas production and food processing clustered around the river as if in homage to its ancient mercantile past; other industries such as timber and chemicals made use of the Regent's Canal and the River Lea as avenues to and from the Thames.

In the following decade the business of the river was amplified by "rapid handling" methods which lifted cargo by fork-lift trucks and fast-moving cranes, but by the 1960s the equally rapid changes in the industrial process left the docks almost literally high and dry. The new phenomenon of containerisation, whereby goods were transported in vast boxes from ship to truck, precluded the system of warehousing; the vessels were too large for the original early nineteenth-century docks to handle.

The docks are silent now, and, within memory, the great buildings of the early nineteenth century have become a wasteland. The East India Dock closed in 1967, while the London Dock and St. Katherine's Dock followed just two years later. The West India Dock survived until 1980, but by then the active and busy life of the region seemed to have gone for ever. The economy of the East End was severely depleted, and unemployment among the population reached very high levels. Yet out of this dereliction, ten years later, rose the shining edifices and refurbished warehouses known as Docklands, confirming that pattern of deliquescence and renewal which is at the heart of London's life. As Mrs. Cook said of the Thames in *Highways and Byways of London* (1902), "nothing destroys antiquity like energy; nothing blots out the old like the new."

In place of a derelict St. Katherine's Wharf a new hotel and a world trade centre were constructed, the latter at least an appropriate edifice beside the ancient river which had for two thousand years carried the trade of the world. The restoration of other dock areas continued in a similar manner, although the greatest scheme of all was the regeneration of what became known as the East Thames Corridor between Tower Bridge and Sheerness. There will be no diminution in the mysterious ability of the commercial Thames to attract money and enterprise in the twenty-first century. The building of great offices upon the Isle of Dogs can be compared only with the original development of the West India Dock upon the same site; in both cases, that of 1806 and that of 1986, the enormous scale of the enterprise was noted. In typical London fashion both giant works were funded by the private money of speculators and businesses, with discreet public help in the nature of tax-incentives, and on both occasions new forms of transport had to be provided. The Docklands Light Railway, in its size and character, is the late twentieth-century equivalent of the Commercial Road. On the western quay of the Brunswick Dock, built in the late eighteenth century, stood a great mast-house of some 120 feet which for many years dominated and symbolised the area as one of marine commerce and London's maritime power; now, only a little distant, the Canary Wharf Tower fulfils a similar function in the celebration of power and commerce. The Thames runs, softly or powerfully according to the tidal currents, and its dark magniloquent song is not over.

CHAPTER 58

Dark Thames

❧

From early times it was a river of the dead, to which the bodies of the local population were consigned. The number of human skulls found in Chelsea has given it the name of "our Celtic Golgotha." As Joseph Conrad said, of another stretch of the Thames, "And this also has been one of the dark places of the earth." The derivation of its very name, pre-Celtic in origin, is *tamasa*, "dark river." How can so many influences and associations be denied when, in modern times, lonely and unhappy people are often to be seen staring down into its turbulent depths? The German poet Heinrich Heine in 1827 described "the black mood which once came over me as toward evening I stood on Waterloo Bridge, and looked down on the water of the Thames . . . At the same time the most sorrowful tales came into my memory."

The river has embraced many such tales, as the old "dead houses" along its banks might testify. Here were brought the bodies of those who in the words of the ubiquitous posters were "found drowned." Three or four suicides, or accidents, every week were laid upon a shelf, or within a wooden "shell," to await the attentions of beadle and coroner. Heine went on to declare that "I was so sick in spirit that the hot drops sprang forcibly out of my eyes. They fell down into the Thames and swam forth into the mighty sea, which has already swallowed up such floods of human tears without giving them a thought." It might be said that the river had swallowed them already. The toll-keepers upon the bridges were well known for their willingness to discuss the suicides—how many they were, how difficult to stop them, how difficult, indeed, to find them once they jumped. The river can in that sense become a true emblem of London's oppression. It can carry away all of life's hopes and ambitions, or deliver them up quite changed.

The river banks mark that point where the stone of the city and the water meet in perpetual embrace, with the scattered debris of ships and urban waste mingling together; here are found sheets of metal, planks of rotten wood, bottles, cans, ash, bits of rope, pieces of board of no identifiable purpose or origin. The river also affects the fabric of the city with what Dickens described in *Our Mutual Friend* as "the spoiling influences of water—discoloured copper, rotten wood, honeycombed stone, green dank deposit."

There were small communities beside it which became a picture of urban dereliction. The area of Deptford was described in the nineteenth century as quite "the worst part of the great City's story." It is a record of that city's decay when its commercial life has departed, with "the muddy, melancholy banks . . . the desolation of empty silent yards." This, in the words of Blanchard Jerrold, was the "dead shore"; yet not so dead that there were not inhabitants of the area, living off the detritus which the Thames offered. These were the people of the river. They lived, too, in Shadwell ("the well of shadows"). Here, in the early twentieth century, "the houses of the people are square and black and low. The walls of storages are sheer and blind upon the narrow streets." The darkness of the river against the darkness of the surrounding buildings renders it "invisible." On the other bank, close to Rotherhithe, can be found Jacob's Island which was also black with the "dust of colliers and the smoke of close-built low-roofed houses"; where once the bright water reflected and illuminated the brightness of the buildings along its banks, in the nineteenth century darkness called to darkness. Jacob's Island, too, was "the filthiest, the strangest, the most extraordinary of the many locations that are hidden in London, wholly unknown, even by name, to the great mass of its inhabitants."

It is those elements of anonymity, and of secrecy, which the river accommodates within itself. Conrad compared the buildings that lined the shores to "the matted growths of bushes and creepers veiling the silent depths of an unexplored wilderness, they hide the depths of London's infinitely varied, vigorous seething life . . . Dark and impenetrable at night, like the face of a forest, in the London waterside." Sometimes it becomes almost too black and sad to bear examination. The author of *London Nights*, Stephen Graham, describes his pilgrimages within the "long, strange passages under the Thames in East London" where "one is descending, one is going back, one is bearing all London." Just as Heine spoke of his instinctive and intuitive sorrow at the sight of the dark river, so in Stephen Graham's book the Thames itself and all its submerged secrets "told of an enigma which would never be solved; the enigma of London's sorrow, her burden, her slavery." The river has brought London money and power, but at the cost of the city's being enslaved to those insidious principles. One late twentieth-century writer, Iain Sinclair, has described the Thames in his novel *Downriver* as "breathless, cyclic, unstoppable. It offers immersion, blindness: a poultice of dark clay to seal our eyes for ever from the fear and agony of life . . . passions reduced to silt."

No wonder the watermen of the Thames, from the thirteenth century to the nineteenth, were known for their insulting and foul language. The violent and blasphemous abuse they used was known as water-language, to which anyone could be subject. Monarchs were often reviled in this manner when they took to the water and H.V. Morton, in *In Search of London* (1951), notes that "remarks which on land would have been treasonable were regarded as a joke upon the Thames." It has even been suggested that Handel's *Water-Music* was composed in order to "drown the torrent of abuse that would have greeted the new king, George I, during his first river-progress" (1714). It may be that the antiquity of the Thames has given its watermen licence to speak without fear; in that sense the river can be considered the essence of that radical and egalitarian temper so often associated with London.

But that sense of darkness, continually moving upon the face of the water, also acts as a toughening and coarsening presence for all those who work there. Nathaniel Hawthorne wrote of "the muddy tide of the Thames, reflecting nothing, and hiding a million of unclean secrets within its breast—a sort of guilty conscience as it were, unwholesome with the rivulets of sin that constantly flow into it."

When Samuel Johnson gave the injunction to Boswell "to *explore Wapping*" as one way of understanding "the wonderful extent and variety of London" he could not have guessed the curious construction that might have been applied to his words in the nineteenth and twentieth centuries. By the early decades of the twentieth century Wapping was as much blasted by decay as Shadwell or Jacob's Island. Where the banks of the Seine are open and approachable, there are stretches of the Thames which actively deter visitors. The area of Wapping was itself hard to find, with its high street running beneath the great walls of the old warehouses, while the adjacent streets seemed to wish to conceal themselves behind gasworks and tenements. It had always been a lawless area, beyond the jurisdiction of the city, but its dereliction at the beginning of the century was also an echo of the shame and waste of the short-time labouring system at the docks; crowds of men seeking work would gather outside the gates, while only a few were ever selected by the foremen. The rest slunk back to that life of poverty, drink and oblivion so well documented by Charles Booth as well as Sidney and Beatrice Webb. "Indeed it is a sight to sadden the most callous," according to Henry Mayhew, "to see thousands of men struggling for one day's hire . . . To look in the faces of that hungry crowd is to see a sight that must be ever remembered . . . For weeks many have gone there, and gone through the same struggle—the same cries; and have gone away, after all, without the work they had screamed for." So the Thames, the begetter of commerce, is also the most visible harbour for the misery which commercial principles can impose.

In the forlorn graveyard of St. George's in the East, one of the unhappy and ill-favoured places of London over many generations, lay "the sailors' women, inured to immorality from childhood, rotten with disease." Wapping was also a place of death at Execution Dock, where those accused of crimes upon the "high seas" were summarily despatched into eternity. In the police station at Wapping was kept what has been described as "one of the saddest books in the world"; it is a journal of the narratives of attempted suicides, with the events and circumstances which led each towards the river. The author of *Unknown London*, Walter George Bell, wandering through the area in 1910, observed the "reeking drink shops; inexpressible in their squalor and dirt, the natural home for every kind of abomination" with "the inner recesses of the hive" being a "gloomy slum area." So we may take to heart Samuel Johnson's injunction to "*explore Wapping*" in order to understand London.

CHAPTER 59

They Are Lost

☙

There are other rivers of London which lie concealed, encased in tunnels or in pipes, occasionally to be heard but generally running silently and invisibly beneath the surface of the city. To name them in order, west to east—Stamford Brook, the Wandle, Counter's Creek, the Falcoln, the Westbourne, the Tyburn, the Effra, the Fleet, the Walbrook, Neckinger and the Earl's Sluice, the Peck and the Ravensbourne.

It has always been said that enchantment is bought in the burying alive of great waters, yet the purchase may be a perilous one. The "lost rivers" can still create stench and dampness. The Fleet River, at times of storm, can still reach beyond its artificial containment and flood basements along its route; at its source in Hampstead it was the expediter of agues and fevers. The valleys of these rivers, many now converted into roads or train-lines, were subject to fog as well as damp. According to the author of *The Lost Rivers of London*, Nicholas Barton, rheumatism "was unusually common both sides of Counter's Creek from Shepherd's Bush to Chelsea," while the London "ague" of the seventeenth century has been suggestively associated with streams and rivulets now sunk beneath the earth.

The lost rivers may provoke allergies also. One recent investigation of patients in London hospitals revealed that "38 out of the 49 allergic patients (i.e. 77.5 per cent) lived within 180 yards of a known watercourse" while among asthmatics "17 out of the 19 [were] living within 180 yards of a watercourse," in most cases the "buried tributaries of the Thames." The reasons for this strange correlation are still unknown, although those who understand the various powers of London places may have their own theories. But the enchantment, white or black, does not end there. A study published in 1960, *The Geography of London Ghosts* by G.W. Lambert, has found that approximately 75 per cent of these disturbances occurred "in houses significantly close to watercourses," where perhaps the spirit as well as the sound of buried waters may be asserting themselves.

We may take the fate of the Fleet River as characteristic. As befits an ancient river, it has gone by many names. It was christened the Fleet in its lower reaches, from the Anglo-Saxon term for a tidal inlet; in its upper reaches it was known as the Holebourne, and in its middle section as Turnmill Brook. It has in a sense been the guardian of London, marking the boundary between Westminster and the City from ancient times. It has always been used as part of London's defences; during the Civil War, for example, great earthworks were built on either bank. Of all the city's lost rivers, therefore, it is the one which is best documented and most often depicted. It has shared in the defilement of London, as a repository of its discarded and forgotten objects. An anchor was discovered as far north as Kentish Town, which may provide some indication of its width and depth at this far point, but more generally it has been the last resting place for the more local and immediate items of urban existence—keys, daggers, coins, medals, pins, brooches and the detritus of such riverine industries as tanning. It needed continually to be cleansed of its mud and general filth, so the scouring of the river took place every twenty or thirty years. Those who wished to rail against London, and all its squalor, inevitably chose the Fleet River as their example; it epitomised the way in which the city fouled water once sweet and clear. It carried the savour of each street, readily identifiable; it was full of dung and dead things. It *was* London in essence. "The greatest good that I ever heard it did was to the undertaker," Ned Ward wrote, "who is bound to acknowledge he has found better fishing in that muddy stream than ever he did in clear water." The Fleet, like the Thames its father, was a river of death.

It has always been an unlucky river. Once it moved through the regions of Kentish Town and St. Pancras, melancholy still with the touch of the water; then at Battle Bridge it entered "the pleasure grounds of Giant Despair," according to William Hone, where "trees stand as if not made to vegetate;

clipped hedges seem willing to decline, and weeds struggle weakly upon un-
limited borders." It then moved around Clerkenwell Hill and touched the
stones of the Coldbath Prison; passed Saffron Hill, whose fragrant name concealed some of the worst rookeries in London; and entered the path of Turnmill Street, the vicious reputation of which has already been chronicled. Then
it flowed down into Chick Lane, later known as West Street, which was for
many centuries the haven of felons and murderers; the river here became the
dumping ground of bodies slain or robbed when dead drunk. Once more it
became the river of death before flowing in front of the noxious Fleet Prison.

Prisoners died of its stench, and of the diseases which it carried with it.
In the valley of the Fleet, wrote a doctor in 1560, and "in its stinking lanes,
there died most in London and were soonest inflicted, and were longest continued, as twice since I have known London I have marked it to be true." In
later testimony quoted in *The Lost Rivers of London*, it was revealed that "In
every parish along the Fleet, the Plague stayed and destroyed." It might be
asked why the area was always so fully populated, therefore, were it not for
the fact that the river seemed to draw certain people towards its banks by
some form of silent contagion. It attracted those who were already dirty, and
silent, and evil-smelling, as if it were their natural habitat. It was treacherous,
too, in its natural state. In stormy weather it was liable to sudden increase of
volume, causing inundation of its surrounding areas. At times of thaw, or in
periods of heavy rain, it became a dangerous torrent tearing down streets and
buildings. The deluge of 1317 carried away many citizens as well as their
houses and sheds; in the fifteenth century the parishioners of St. Pancras were
moved to plead that they could not reach their church "when foul ways is and
great water."

Every attempt to render it clean or noble failed. After the Great Fire,
when the wharves along the Thames were utterly destroyed with all their
merchandise within them, its banks were raised upon brick and stone while
four new bridges were constructed to maintain its formal harmony. But the
refurbishment of the New Canal, as it was then called, was not successful;
the waters once more became sluggish and noxious, while the neighbouring
streets and banks continued their notorious lives as harbours for thieves,
pimps and malingerers. So, within fifty years of the grand development, the
river itself was bricked over. It is almost as if it represented a flow of guilt
which had to be concealed from public view; the city literally buried it. In
1732 it was bricked in from Fleet Street to Holborn Bridge and then, thirty-
three years later, it was bricked in from Fleet Street to the Thames. At the be-

ginning of the next century its northern reaches were buried underground so
that no trace of this once great guardian of London remained.

Yet its spirit did not die. In 1846 it blew up, "its rancid and foetid gas,"
trapped within brick tunnels, "bursting out into the streets above"; three
posthouses were swept away by "a tidal wave of sewage" and a steamboat
was crushed against Blackfriars Bridge. The waters of the Fleet Ditch then
actively hampered the efforts to construct an underground railway beneath it:
its waters filled the tunnels with dark and fetid liquid, and for a while all work
was abandoned. It is now employed only as a storm sewer, with its outfall
into the Thames by Blackfriars Bridge, but it still manifests its presence. In
storms it may still flood the roadway, while building works upon its old
course have regularly to be pumped out. So the waters from ancient streams
and wells collect themselves in their old courses and run along the familiar
beds of the now enclosed main rivers.

The rivers themselves are not wholly dead, then, and occasionally
emerge into the light. The course of the Westbourne River can be observed
rushing through a great iron pipe above the platform of Sloane Square
Underground Station; the Tyburn is also carried in great pipes at the tube stations of Baker Street and Victoria. In February 1941 the Tyburn was observed flowing at the bottom of a bomb crater. The Westbourne was not
covered until 1856. *The Lost Rivers of London* reveals that in Meard Street,
Soho, is "a grate in the basement beneath which waters can be seen running
in a southward direction"; the phenomenon is mysterious but it has been suggested that this water is pursuing the course of a seventeenth-century sewer
and has created an unknown stream. As Nicholas Barton has put it, "once a
channel has been made they cling to it with great persistence." It raises the
possibility of other streams and tributaries, still flowing beneath the streets of
the city, replete with their own underground ghosts and nymphs.

THE SEWER-HUNTER.

[*From a Daguerreotype by* BEARD.]

A portrait of a sewer-hunter, taken from Henry Mayhew's *London Labour
and the London Poor*; theirs was a dangerous and despised occupation, but the
city has always been characterised by the search for profit of any kind.

CHAPTER 60

What Lies Beneath

✦

There are always rumours of a world under the ground. Underground chambers and tunnels have been reported, one linking the crypt of St. Bartholomew the Great with Canonbury, another running a shorter distance between the priory and nunnery of Clerkenwell. There are extensive catacombs in Camden Town, beneath the Camden goods yard. Roman temples have been discovered within "hidden" London. Statues of ancient deities have been found in a condition which suggests that, for reasons unknown, they were deliberately buried. At All Hallows, Barking, a buried undercroft and arch of a Christian church were constructed with Roman materials; a cross of sandstone was also found, with the inscription WERHERE of Saxon date; it is somehow strangely evocative of WE ARE HERE. Lost beneath Cheapside, and found only after the bombing of London, was the figure of the "Dead Christ" laid horizontally in a stratum of London soil. Evidence of the passage of generations, themselves buried in the clay and gravel, was found on the corner of Ray Street and Little Saffron Hill; thirteen feet below the surface, in 1855, "the workmen came upon the pavement of an old street, consisting of very large blocks of ragstone of irregular shape. An examination of the paving-stones showed that the street had been well used. They are worn quite smooth by the footsteps and traffic of a past generation." Beneath these ancient stones were found piles of oak—thick, hard and covered with slime—interpreted as fragments of a great mill. Beneath the oak, in turn, were crude wooden water pipes. The great weight of the past had pressed all this material of London "into a hard and almost solid mass, and it is curious to observe that near the old surface were great numbers of pins." The mystery of the pins remains.

The author of *Unknown London* has remarked: "I have climbed down more ladders to explore the buried town than I have toiled up City staircases," which may lead to the impression that there is more beneath than above. One of the characteristic drawings of the city is that of its horizontal levels, from the rooftops of its houses to the caverns of its sewers, bearing down upon and almost crushing one another with their weight. It was well said, in one guide to the city's history, that "certain it is that none who know London would deny that its treasures must be sought in its depths"; it is an ambiguous sentence, perhaps, with a social as well as a topographical mystery associated with it.

Another great London historian, Charles Knight, suggested that if we were to "imagine that this great capital of capitals should ever be what Babylon is—its very site forgotten—one could not but almost envy the delight with which the antiquaries of that future time would hear of some discovery of a *London below the soil* still remaining. We can fancy we see the progress of the excavators from one part to another of the mighty but, for a while, inexplicable labyrinth till the whole was cleared open to the daylight, and the vast systems laid before them." It is a stupendous conception, but no more stupendous than the reality.

There is indeed a London under the ground, comprising great vaults and passageways, sewers and tunnels, pipes and corridors, issuing into one another. There are great networks of gas and water pipes, many long since disused but others being transformed into conduits for the thousands of miles of coaxial cables which now help to organise and control the city. Walter George Bell, the author of *London Rediscoveries*, noticed how in the early 1920s Post Office workmen were laying earthenware conduits for their telephone cables within a trough created by the wall of a Roman villa lying in Gracechurch Street, so that, as he said, "our messages go whispering" through rooms where once the citizens of a lost London spoke in an alien tongue. There are deep-level tunnels for British Telecom and for the London Electricity Board, with National Grid cables carried in conduits and trenches. A great system of Post Office tunnels was inaugurated after 1945, complicat-

ing the topography of this subterranean region. There are more tunnels under the Thames than under the river of any other capital city—tunnels for
trains, for cars, for foot passengers as well as for the supplies of public utilities. The whole area under the river, and indeed under the whole of the city,
is a catacomb of avenues and highways mimicking their counterparts above
ground.

Yet something happens when you travel beneath the surface of London;
the very air itself seems to become old and sorrowful, with its inheritance of
grief. The Thames Tunnel, built between 1825 and 1841, was, for example,
established only at the cost of much labour and suffering. Its history is
recorded in *London Under London* by Richard Trench and Ellis Hillman. Marc
Brunel began the tunnel at a depth of sixty-three feet, using a great "shield"
to take out the earth, while the bricklayers continually formed the walls of the
tunnel itself. There were often eruptions of earth and deluges of water; the
workmen were "like labourers in a dangerous coal-mine, in constant terror
from either fire or water." One labourer fell down the great shaft, while
drunk, and died; some drowned in floods, others died of "ague" or dysentery,
and one or two suffocated in the "thick and impure air." Marc Brunel himself
suffered a paralytic stroke, yet insisted upon continuing his work. He left a
diary which is sufficiently compelling to need no description—"16 May,
1828, Inflammable gas. Men complain v. much. 26 May. Heywood died this
morning. Two more on the sick list. Page is evidently sinking very fast . . . I
feel much debility after having been some time below. 28 May. Bowyer died
today or yesterday. A good man." The metaphor of "sinking" is instructive
in this context, as if the whole weight of the underground world were fatal.
The air of dream, of hopelessness and dreariness, seems to have haunted this
tunnel. "The very walls were in a cold sweat," *The Times* reported upon its
opening in 1843.

It is suggestive that Marc Brunel discovered his unique way of tunnelling
underground while incarcerated in a debtors' prison in London; here he noticed the activities of a worm, *teredo navalis*, which itself is a "natural tun-
neler." The atmosphere of prison, too, is incorporated within the very
structure of these tunnels. Nathaniel Hawthorne descended into the depths of
the Thames Tunnel after its completion, down "a wearisome succession of
staircases" until "we behold the vista of an arched corridor that extends into
everlasting midnight." Here is a depiction of melancholy anxiety transformed
into brick and stone, "gloomier than a street of upper London." Yet there
were some Londoners who soon became acclimatised to the depth and the

dankness. Hawthorne observed in the dusk "stalls or shops, in little alcoves, kept principally by women . . . they assail you with hungry entreaties to buy their merchandise." It was his belief that these subterranean women "spend their lives there, seldom or never, I presume seeing any daylight." He describes the Thames Tunnel, therefore, as "an admirable prison." It was for this reason, precisely, that it never succeeded as a pathway for vehicles or pedestrians; the gloomy associations and connotations were just too strong. So it was little used after its inception, and in 1869 it was taken over by the East London Railway. In that capacity it has existed ever since, and now forms the underground connection between Wapping and Rotherhithe.

The other tunnels under the Thames have not lost their overpowering sense of gloom. Of the Rotherhithe Road Tunnel, built between Stepney and Rotherhithe, Iain Sinclair has written in *Downriver*, "If you want to sample the worst London can offer, follow me down that slow incline. The tunnel drips with warnings: DO NOT STOP" and he goes on to suggest that "The tunnel can achieve meaning only if it remains unused and silent." That silence can be forbidding: the Greenwich Foot Tunnel, opened in 1902, can seem more lonely and desolate than any other part of London. Yet there are some, like the female shopkeepers pleading in the dusk of the Thames Tunnel, who seem to belong to this subterranean world.

An eighteenth-century German traveller observed that "one third of the inhabitants of London live under ground." We may date this inclination to the Bronze Age, when underground tunnels were built a little to the west of where the Greenwich Observatory is now situated. (It has been suggested that the wells or pits which ventilate them were themselves early forms of stellar observation, which may once more suggest that continuity for which London is notable.) The German traveller was in fact remarking upon the curious basements or "cellar dwellings" of eighteenth-century London, which had already been a feature of the city for two hundred years. They were let to the very poor who "entered by steps from the street down a well which was supposed to be closed at nightfall by a flap." In the transcripts of the poor we have some brief glimpses of this subterranean life—"I am a cobbler. I live in a cellar . . . I am a shoemaker. I keep a kitchen [basement dwelling] in Monmouth Street . . . I do not know the landlady's name, I pay my money every Monday." But these traps of dampness and darkness also had more nefarious uses. "I keep a public cellar" seems to have meant that vagrants or drunks or debauchees had access to a buried life.

This tendency to seek refuge beneath the city became most noticeable in the twentieth century. It has been estimated that during the First World War, one-third of a million Londoners went underground in February 1918, to shelter in the tube stations which extended below the capital. They became accustomed to their buried life, and even began to savour it. Indeed, according to Philip Ziegler in *London at War*, one of the principal fears of the authorities was that a " 'deep shelter' mentality might grow up and result in paralysis of will among those who succumbed to it." It was also suggested that the underground Londoners "would grow hysterical with fear and would never surface to perform their duties."

In the autumn of 1940 Londoners were once more buried. They flocked to underground shelters or the crypts of churches, and certain people "lived underground, and saw less of the sky than any miner." In each of the deep shelters more than a thousand people might congregate "lying closer together than the dead in any graveyard" while those in the crypts "sought shelter amongst the dead." This is a constant image in descriptions of the subterranean life. It is *like being dead*, buried alive beneath the great city. The most famous of these caverns under the ground was the "Tilbury" beneath Commercial Road and Cable Street where thousands of East Enders sheltered from the bombs.

The tube stations were the most obvious locations of safety. Henry Moore wandered among their new inhabitants, and made preliminary notes for his drawings. "Dramatic, dismal lit, masses of reclining figures fading foreground. Chains hanging from old cranes . . . Mud and rubbish and chaotic untidiness everywhere." The stench of urine was noticeable, as well as fetid human smells: this is a picture of London in almost primeval state, as if in the journey under ground the citizens had gone back centuries. "I had never seen so many reclining figures and even the train tunnels seemed to be like the holes in my sculpture. And amid the grim tension, I noticed groups of strangers forming together in intimate groups and children asleep within feet of the passing trains." He compared it to "the hold of a slave ship" except that its passengers were sailing nowhere. Once again, as in the previous episodes of wartime bombing in London, the vision of a subterranean population alarmed the authorities. In Michael Moorcock's *Mother London*, a late twentieth-century hymn to the city, the narrator had once "sought the safety of the tubes" during the Blitz, and had since that time become obsessed with "lost tube lines" and the whole world under the surface of the city. "I discovered evidence that London was interlaced with connecting tunnels, home of a troglodytic race that had gone underground at the time of the Great

Fire . . . Others had hinted of a London under London in a variety of texts as far back as Chaucer." It is a wonderful fantasy, but in the early 1940s there was a genuine fear that these "subterraneans" would become a reality.

"We ought not to encourage a permanent day and night population underground," Herbert Morrison stated in the autumn of 1944. "If that spirit gets abroad we are defeated." The prospect of defeatism was not the only concern. It was also noticed that the experience of living underground encouraged an anti-authoritarian and egalitarian spirit, as if the conditions above the ground could be reversed. Here, out of sight, radicalism might flourish; one newsletter which circulated among the subterraneans denounced the wartime authorities for "indifference amounting almost to callousness, neglect, soulless contempt for elementary human decencies." So those under the ground instilled an element of fear in those who remained above it; it resembles the ancient superstitious fear of the miner, as an emblem of the dark world in which he works. It is the fear of the depths.

That is why the figure of the underground man is so potent, known over the centuries as the fermor, the raker and the flusher, whose employment it was to clean out the sewers and clear them of obstruction. There were sewer-hunters as well, also known as toshers, who wandered through the sewers looking for articles which they could sell. "Many wondrous tales are still told among the people," Henry Mayhew wrote, "of men having lost their way in the sewers, and of having wandered among the filthy passages—their lights extinguished by the noisome vapours—till, faint and overpowered, they dropped down and died on the spot. Other stories are told of sewer-hunters beset by myriads of enormous rats . . . in a few days afterwards their skeletons were discovered picked to the very bones." These alarming stories testify to the fear associated with the underground passages of London, and there were indeed real dangers in this enterprise of converting rubbish—iron, copper, rope, bone—into money. The brickwork was often rotten and liable to crumble or to fall, the air was noxious, and the tides of the nineteenth-century Thames swept through the sewers leaving some victims "quite dead, battered and disfigured in a dreadful manner." They worked silently and stealthily, closing off their bull's-eye lanterns whenever they passed beneath a street-grating "for otherwise a crowd might collect overhead." They wore greasy velveteen coats with capacious pockets, and trousers of dirty canvas. They were, in the words of one Londoner not meaning to make a pun, "the lowest of the low."

There are more recent accounts of the honest flushers and gangers who are gainfully employed to clear the sewers of soft mud and grit. A newspaper account of 1960 reports, of a Piccadilly sewer which drained into the Tyburn, that "it was like crossing the Styx. The fog had followed us down from the streets and swirled above the discoloured and strong-smelling river like the stream of Hades." So the descent conjures up mythological imagery. Eric Newby descended into the sewer of the Fleet and "seen fitfully by the light of miners' lanterns and special lamps, it was like one of the prisons designed by Piranesi." Again the imagery of the prison emerges. One sewerman told an interested guest below: "You should see some of 'em under the City. They're medieval. They don't show 'em to visitors." In that medieval spirit we read then of a "cavernous chamber . . . with pillars, arches, and buttresses, like a cathedral undercroft." It is a strange city beneath the ground, perhaps best exemplified by worn manhole covers which, instead of reading SELF LOCKING, spell out ELF KING.

No account of underground London, however, could be complete without the Underground itself. It is a great subterranean metropolis covering an area of 620 square miles, 254 miles of railway connecting this extraordinary profusion of tunnels and stations with their mysterious names such as Gospel Oak, White City, Angel and Seven Sisters.

The scheme for transport under London had been broached in the 1840s and 1850s, but had met with serious objections. It was feared that the weight of traffic overhead (which an underground system was meant to relieve) would crush any tunnels beneath, and that the houses above the proposed routes would shiver and fall from the vibrations. Eventually in 1860 one scheme was accepted. The Metropolitan Railway was constructed from Paddington to Farringdon Street within three years, by means of the "cut and cover" method, and immediately proved a great success. The enterprise represented a triumph of mid-Victorian energy and ingenuity; there is an engraving of the "Trial Trip on the Underground Railway, 1863" in which the open carriages are filled with men waving their stove-pipe hats in the air as they pass beneath a tunnel. On opening day "the crowd at the Farringdon Street station was as great as at the doors of a theatre on the first night of some popular performer," and in fact the sheer vivacity and theatricality of the undertaking were a large part of its popularity; the spectacle of steam trains disappearing under the ground, like demons in a pantomime, satisfied the London appetite for sensation.

By the early twentieth century the shape of the contemporary underground "network" was beginning to emerge. The City and South London Railway opened in 1890, for example; because the route from King William Street to Stockwell was created by means of tunnelling rather than the older "cut and cover" method, it has the distinction of being the first named "the tube." It had the further distinction of being the first electrically operated underground system in the world, after years of steam; the carriages had no windows, on the understandable principle that there was nothing particular to see, and the luxurious furnishings gave them the nickname of "padded cells."

The tube was followed by the Central Line in 1900, the Bakerloo and the Piccadilly in 1906, and the Hampstead (or Northern) line in 1907. It had ceased to be a spectacular or even surprising innovation, and had become an inalienable part of London's quotidian life. By slow degrees, too, it acquired the familiar characteristics and aspects of the city. Or perhaps it is the case that the city above ground has made a replica of itself below. The Underground has its streets and avenues which the pedestrians quickly recognise and follow. It has its short cuts, its crossroads, its particular features (no escalators at Queensway, deep lifts in Hampstead, long escalators at the Angel) and, just like the city itself, areas of bright lights and bustle are surrounded by areas of darkness and disuse. The rhythms of the city are endlessly mimicked beneath the city, as well as its patterns of activity and habitation.

Like the great city, too, the thoroughfares of the Underground have their own particular associations and connections. The Northern Line is intense and somehow desperate; the Central Line is energetic, while the Circle is adventurous and breezy. The Bakerloo Line, however, is flat and despairing. The gloom of Lancaster Gate sits between the bustle of Bond Street and the brightness of Notting Hill Gate. Where disasters have occurred, such as Moorgate and Bethnal Green, the air is still desolate. But there are stations, like Baker Street and Gloucester Road, which lift the spirit. The air itself becomes quite different as the passengers travel towards the oldest sections of London in the City. As the Circle Line moves from Edgware Road and Great Portland Street towards the ancient centre, it travels through ever deeper levels of anonymity and oblivion. On one stretch of that line G.K. Chesterton noticed that the names of St. James's Park, Westminster, Charing Cross, Temple, Blackfriars "are really the foundation stones of London: and it is right that they should (as it were) be underground" since "all bear witness to an ancient religion."

These images are entirely appropriate for an enterprise which, in its operations, has descended so deeply that it has reached the levels of the old primeval swamp which once was London; beneath Victoria Underground Station some fossils, fifty million years old, were uncovered. These ancient depths may indeed account for the peculiar sensation and atmosphere which the Underground evokes. There are accounts of ghosts, or presences, in the subterranean depths. Certainly there are "ghost stations" with long-forgotten platforms, some of them still retaining their faded hoardings and posters. There are some forty of them remaining—British Museum, City Road, South Kentish Town, York Road, Marlborough Road and King William Street among them—silent and generally invisible.

The Underground is also a place of chance meeting and coincidence, but it generates greater fear and anxiety—of strangers, of thieves, and of the mad who haunt its endlessly running trains. Yet it has become familiar. Ford Madox Ford, in *The Soul of London*, wrote that "I have known a man, dying a long way from London, sigh queerly for a sight of the gush of smoke that, on a platform of the Underground, one may see, escaping in great woolly clots up a circular opening, by a grimy, rusted, iron shield, into the dim upper light." Here is a true Londoner, wishing on his death-bed once more to see and savour the smoke of the Underground, like a prisoner dreaming once more of his confinement. And still the work goes on. As London expands, so does its buried counterpart grow and stretch beneath it.

If in the last days of the twentieth century you sat in the shadow of the great tower of Canary Wharf, you would have seen hundreds of workmen hurrying around the track of the Jubilee Line extension; the work was endless and noisy, with great arcs of light and gleams of silver fire charging the night air with power in alliance with some unknown future city.

Victorian London, as it might be seen from the window of a passing train; in certain areas the view has hardly changed, testimony to the conservatism of Londoners in their love for a house and back garden.

CHAPTER 61

How Many Miles
to Babylon?

y the mid-1840s London had become known as the greatest city
on the earth, the capital of empire, the centre of international
trade and finance, a vast world market into which the world
poured. At the beginning of the twentieth century the sanitary historian,
Henry Jephson, considered this megalopolis in other terms. "Of that period,"
he wrote, "it is to be said that there is none in the history of London in which
less regard was shown for the conditions of the great mass of the inhabitants
of the metropolis." Charles Dickens, Henry Mayhew and Friedrich Engels
are three of the Victorian city-dwellers who cried "havoc" over the exhaustive and exhausting city. In contemporary photographs and drawings the
most striking images are those of labour and suffering. Women sit with their
arms folded, hunched over; a beggar family sleep upon stone benches in a re-
cess of a bridge, with the dark shape of St. Paul's looming behind them. As
Blanchard Jerrold put it, "The aged, the orphan, the halt, the blind, of
London would fill an ordinary city." This is a strange conception, a city entirely composed of the maimed and injured. But that is, in part, what London
was. The number of children and tramps, too, sitting resignedly in the street,
is infinite; infinite also are the street-sellers, generally depicted against a dull
background of brick or stone.

The poor interiors of the Victorian city are generally crepuscular and filthy, with rags hanging among reeking tallow lamps; many of the inhabitants seem to have no faces, since they are turned towards the shadows, around them dilapidated wooden beams and staircases in crazed confusion. Many, outdoors and indoors, seem hunched up and small as if the very weight of the city had crushed them down. Yet there is another aspect of the Victorian city that photographs and images evoke: of vast throngs innumerable, the streets filled with teeming and struggling life, the great inspiration for the work of nineteenth-century mythographers such as Marx and Darwin. There are also flashes of feeling—of pity, anger, and tenderness—to be observed upon passing faces. And all around them can be imagined a hard unyielding noise, like an unending shout. This is Victorian London.

"Victorian London" is of course a general term for a sequence of shifting patterns of urban life. In the early decades of the nineteenth century, for example, it still retained many of the characteristics of the last years of the previous century. It was still a compact city. "Draw but a little circle above the clustering housetops," the narrator of Dickens's *Master Humphrey's Clock* suggests (1840–1), "and you shall have within its space everything, with its opposite extreme and contradiction close by." It was still only partially illuminated by gas and most of the streets were lit by infrequent oil-lamps with link-boys bearing lights to escort late pedestrians home; there were "Charleys" rather than policemen walking their beats. It was still hazardous. The outskirts retained a rural aspect; there were strawberry fields at Hammersmith and at Hackney, and the wagons still plied their way among the other horse-drawn traffic to the Haymarket. The great public buildings, with which the seat of empire was soon to be decorated, had not yet arisen. The characteristic entertainments were those of the late eighteenth century, too, with the dogfights, the cockfights, the pillory and the public executions. The streets and houses all contained plastered and painted windows, as if they were part of a pantomime. There were still strolling pedlars hawking penny dreadfuls, and ballad-singers with the latest "air"; there were cheap theatres and print-shops displaying in their windows caricatures which could always catch a crowd; there were pleasure gardens and caves of harmony, mug-halls and free-and-easies and dancing saloons. It was a more eccentric city. The inhabitants had had no settled education and no social "system" (a word which itself did not spring into full life until the 1850s and 1860s) had yet been introduced. So it was a more varied, more unusual, and sometimes

more alarming city than any of its successors. It had not yet been standardised, or come under the twin mid-Victorian agencies of uniformity and propriety.

It is impossible to gauge when this transformation occurred. Certainly London took on quite another aspect when it continued to grow and stretch itself through Islington and St. John's Wood in the north; then through Paddington, Bayswater, South Kensington, Lambeth, Clerkenwell, Peckham and all points of the compass. It became the largest city in the world, just at the time when England itself became the first urbanised society in the world.

It became the city of clock-time, and of speed for its own sake. It became the home of engines and steam-driven industry; it became the city where electromagnetic forces were discovered and publicised. It also became the centre of mass production, with the impersonal forces of demand and supply, profit and loss, intervening between vendor and customer. In the same period business and government were supervised by a vast army of clerks and book-keepers who customarily wore uniform dark costumes.

It was the city of fog and darkness but in another sense, too, it was packed to blackness. A population of one million at the beginning of the century increased to approximately five million by its close. By 1911, it had risen to seven million. Everything was becoming darker. The costumes of the male Londoner, like those of the clerks, switched from variegated and bright colours to the solemn black of the frock-coat and the stove-pipe hat. Gone, too, was the particular gracefulness and colour of the early nineteenth-century city; the decorous symmetry of its Georgian architecture was replaced by the imperialist neo-Gothic or neo-classical shape of Victorian public buildings. They embodied the mastery of time as well as that of space. In this context, too, there emerged a London which was more massive, more closely controlled and more carefully organised. The metropolis was much larger, but it had also become much more anonymous; it was a more public and splendid city, but it was also a less human one.

Thus it became the climax, or the epitome, of all previous imperialist cities. It became Babylon. There was in the twelfth century a part of London Wall called "Babeylone," but the reasons for that name are unclear; it may be that in the medieval city the inhabitants recognised a pagan or mystical significance within that part of the stone fabric. It was unwittingly echoed by a piece of late twentieth-century graffiti, by Hackney Marsh, with the simple scrawl "Babylondon." There was of course the mysterious song

How many miles to Babylon?
Three scores miles and ten.
Can I get there by candle light?
Yes, and back again.
If your heels are nimble and light,
You may get there by candle light.

Although the derivation and meaning of the verse are unclear, the image of the city seems to assert itself as a potent beckoning force; in a variant of this song "Bethlehem" takes the place of Babylon, and may point to the madhouse in Moorfields rather than any more remote destination.

In the eighteenth century, too, London was considered "*cette Babilone, le seul refuge des infortunés*" in which the association of size and power is coloured by the invocation of the "infortunés" or refugees; this indeed is the other connotation of London as Babylon, a city loud with many disparate and unintelligible voices. To name London as Babylon, then, was to allude to its essential multiplicity. So William Cowper, the eighteenth-century poet, spoke of this "increasing London" as more diverse than "Babylon of old."

Yet the association or resemblance became pressing only in the nineteenth century when London was continually described as "modern Babylon." Henry James referred to it as "this murky Babylon" and, for Arthur Machen, "London loomed up before me, wonderful, mystical as Assyrian Babylon, as full of unheard-of things and great unveilings." So Babylon has many associations; it conjures up images of magnitude and darkness, but also intimations of mystery and revelation. In this great conflation, even the gardens of Park Lane became known as the "hanging gardens," although some echo may be found here of the Tyburn tree which was once located beside them.

By 1870 the sheer quantity of life in the city was overwhelming. Every eight minutes, of every day of every year, someone died in London; every five minutes, someone was born. There were forty thousand costermongers and 100,000 "winter tramps"; there were more Irish living in London than in Dublin, and more Catholics than in Rome. There were 20,000 public houses visited by 500,000 customers. Eight years later there were more than half a million dwellings, "more than sufficient to form one continuous row of buildings round the island of Great Britain." It is perhaps not surprising that mid-nineteenth-century Londoners were themselves struck with awe, admiration or anxiety at the city which seemed without any apparent warning to have grown to such magnitude and complexity. How could it have happened? Nobody seemed quite sure. Frederick Engels, in his *The Condition of the Working Classes in England in 1844* (1845), found his own considerable intellectual faculties to be strained beyond use. "A town such as London," he wrote, "where a man may wander for hours together without reaching the beginning of the end . . . is a strange thing." The strange city is indescribable, and so Engels could only resort to continual images of immensity. He writes of "countless ships," "endless lines of vehicles," "hundreds of steamers," "hundreds of thousands of all classes," "the immense tangle of streets," "hundreds and thousands of alleys and courts" together with "nameless misery." The sheer incalculability of the mass seems to render it also unintelligible, and therefore induces fear.

So great was London that it seemed to contain within itself all previous civilisations. Babylon was then joined with other empires. The naves and transepts of Westminster Abbey were compared to the City of the Dead beyond Cairo, while the railway terminus at Paddington invoked images of the pyramid of Cheops. Nineteenth-century architects, in their fantastic images of London, created pyramids for Trafalgar Square and Shooters Hill while also designing great pyramidal cemeteries beside Primrose Hill. Here we see the power of imperial London creating a cult of death as well as of magnificence.

In Ree's *Cyclopaedia* of 1819, the docks once more arouse primitive imagery. The climate and atmosphere of London in turn create "startling hieroglyphics that are written by soot and smoke upon its surface." So the stones of London became ancient by association. Somehow the spectacle of the metropolis encourages intimations of unfathomable age—"petrified," to have been turned into stone, may also be covertly introduced into this vision in its contemporary sense of great fear.

And beyond Egypt there was Rome. The subterranean vaults beneath the Adelphi reminded one architectural historian of "old Roman works" while the sewer system of Joseph Bazalgette was often compared with the Roman aqueducts. It was the sense of magnificence, combined with the triumphalism of empire, which most notably impressed these observers of the nineteenth-century city. When Hippolyte Taine ventured into the Thames Tunnel, itself compared with the greatest feats of Roman engineering, he described it "as enormous and dismal as the gut of some Babel." Then the association of ideas and civilisations became too strong for him. "I am always discovering that London resembles ancient Rome . . . How heavy this modern Rome, as did the ancient one, bear down upon the backs of the working classes. For every monstrous agglomeration of building, Babylon, Egypt, the Rome of the Caesars, represents an accumulation of effort, an excess of fatigue." Then he described "the Roman machine" which made slaves of those who toiled for it. This was another truth, then, about London as Rome: it turned its citizens into the slaves of the machine.

As a model for the archway leading to the Bullion Yard of the Bank of England, Sir John Soane chose the Roman triumphal arch; the walls of Lothbury Court beside it were inscribed with allegorical figures taken from Roman mythology. The massive corner of the Bank, between Lothbury and Princes Street, was based upon the Temple of Vesta at Tivoli. The interiors, as well as the exterior, of the Bank had Roman antecedents. Many halls and offices constructed within, like the Dividend Office and the Bank Stock Office, were designed from models of the Roman baths; in addition the chief cashier's office, forty-five feet by thirty, was built in homage to the Temple of the Sun and Moon at Rome. Here then, in direct form, is the worship of money based upon Roman originals; when the association is made with that ancient city, it is essentially one of barbaric triumphalism.

But there were other associations. Verlaine suggested that it was "a Biblical city" ready for the "fire of heaven" to strike it. Carlyle described it in 1824 as an "enormous Babel . . . and the flood of human effort rolls out of it and into it with a violence that almost appals one's very sense." So in one context it is compared with the greatest civilisations of the past, with Rome or Egypt, and yet in another it is quickly broken down into a violent wilderness, a savage place, without pity or restraint of any kind. When Carlyle adds that London is also "like the heart of all the universe," there is a suggestion that London is an emblem of all that is darkest, and most extreme, within existence itself. Is it the heart of empire, or the heart of darkness? Or is one so inseparable from the other that human effort and labour become no more than the expression of rage and the appetite for power?

In one sense London has always been known as a wilderness or jungle, a desert or primeval forest. "Whoever considers the Cities of London and Westminster, with the late vast increases of their suburbs," Henry Fielding wrote in 1751, "the great irregularity of their buildings, the immense number of lanes, alleys, courts and bye-places, must think that had they been intended for the very purpose of concealment, they could not have been better contrived. Upon such a view the whole appears as a vast wood or forest in which the thief may harbour with as great security as wild beasts do in the deserts of Arabia and Africa." He described another aspect of this wilderness in *Tom Jones*, where he dwelled upon the difficulties of London life, "for as you are not put out of countenance, so neither are you cloathed or fed by those who do not know you. And a man may be as easily starved in Leadenhall Market as in the deserts of Arabia."

Fielding's contemporary Tobias Smollett had the same vision. London "being an immense wilderness, in which there is neither watch nor ward of any signification, nor any order or police" affords thieves and other criminals "lurking places as well as prey." The images of jungle and desert are used as if they were alike precisely because they both suggest the "wilderness" of untamed and uncharted human nature; London represents some primeval force or habitat in which the natural instincts of humankind are allowed free expression.

In the nineteenth century the connotations of wilderness changed from unconstrained and uncurtailed life to one of barren desolation. The city is what Mayhew called "a bricken wilderness," and the image of dense cover is replaced by one of hard stone with "its profuse rank undergrowth of low, mean houses spreading in all directions." This is the nineteenth-century desert, far larger and far more desolate than that of the eighteenth century. It is what James Thomson, in "The Doom of a City" published in 1857, described as the "desert streets" within "a buried City's maze of stone." The endlessness of the city streets, so well evoked by Engels, is here associated with the coldness and hardness of stone itself; it represents not the wilderness of burgeoning life but the wilderness of death without sorrow or pity. "Wilderness! Yes, it is, it is," a character says in *Nicholas Nickleby*. "It *is* a wilderness," says the old man with such animation. "It was a wilderness to me once. I came here barefoot—I have never forgotten it." And Little Dorrit cries out, "And London looks so large, so barren and so wild."

So in turn London has recalled Pompeii, another wilderness of stone. After the bombardments of the Second World War, for example, it was remarked that London already looked "as ancient as Herculaneum." But London has not been buried or overwhelmed by the lava-flow of time. All the constituents of its life return. An Italian visitor, perhaps more astute than those who preferred the conventional analogies, described London as "the Land of the Cyclops." In a survey of late twentieth-century Docklands we find a great "Cyclops Wharf." There is a photograph of South Quay in the same vicinity, where the tower of South Quay Waterside is surmounted by a pyramid. The great tower of Canary Wharf is adorned with a pyramid in similar fashion, suggesting that the associations with that empire have never really faded. Even the pumping station for storm water in the Docklands has been constructed, like some guardian of the waters, in the image of an Egyptian monument.

Yet there is one more salient aspect to this continual analogy of London with ancient civilisations: it is the fear, or hope, or expectation that this great imperial capital will in its turn fall into ruin. That is precisely the reason for London's association with pre-Christian cities; it, too, will revert to chaos and old night so that the condition of the "primeval" past will also be that of the remote future. It represents the longing for oblivion. In Doré's vivid depiction of nineteenth-century London—London, essentially, as Rome or Babylon— there is an endpiece. It shows a cloaked and meditative figure sitting upon a rock beside the Thames. He looks out upon a city in awful ruin, the wharves derelict, the dome of St. Paul's gone, the great offices simply piles of jagged stone. It is entitled "the New Zealander" and derives its inspiration from Macaulay's vision of a "colonial" returning to the imperial city after its destiny and destruction were complete; he wrote of the distant traveller as one "who shall take his stand on the broken arch of London Bridge to sketch the ruins of St. Paul's." It is a vision which, paradoxically, emerged during the period of London's pride and greatness.

Towards the end of the eighteenth century Horace Walpole described a traveller from Lima marvelling at the ruins of St. Paul's. Shelley looked towards that far-off time when "St. Paul's and Westminster Abbey shall stand, shapeless and nameless ruins in the midst of an unpeopled marsh." In his imagination Rossetti destroyed the British Museum and left it open for the archaeologists of a future race. Ruskin envisaged the stones of London crumbling "through prouder eminence to less pitied destruction." The vision is of a city unpeopled, and therefore free to be itself; stone endures, and, in this imagined future, stone becomes a kind of god. Essentially it is a vision of the city as death. But it also represents the horror of London, and of its teeming life; it is a cry against its supposed unnaturalness, which can only be repudiated by a giant act of nature such as a deluge. There may then come a time when London is recognisable only by "grey ruin and . . . mouldering stone," sunk deep into "Night, Gothic night."

. . .

Yet the term "Gothic" has associations of its own which are no less powerful than those of Rome or Babylon, Nineveh or Tyre. The author of *The London Perambulator*, James Bone, has suggested that the shapes and textures of London stones might reveal "a Gothic *genius loci* of London fighting against the spirit of the classic." But what, then, is this spirit of London place? It brings with it suggestions of excess and overpowering amplitude, of religious yearning and monumentality; it suggests ancient piety and vertiginous stone. In the eighteenth century Gothic acquired connotations of horror, then horror combined with hysterical comedy. All this the city can encompass.

Nicholas Hawksmoor, the great builder of London churches, defined a style which he termed "English Gothick": it was marked by dramatic symmetries and sublime disproportion. When George Dance designed the Guildhall in the late 1780s with an elegant amalgam of Indian and Gothic elements, he was restoring a form of extravagance and vitality in homage to the great age of the city. But if Gothic was an intimation of antiquity, it was also an aspect of veneration. That is why the churches of Hawksmoor provide such a powerful statement in the places where they are located, among them the City, Spitalfields, Limehouse and Greenwich. As one eighteenth-century artist, Flaxman, remarked of the tombs within Westminster Abbey, they are "specimens of magnificence . . . which forcibly direct the attention and turn the thoughts not only to other ages but to other states of existence." There is that within London which compels recognition as *not of this earth*.

Its most extravagant and notable manifestations were in the nineteenth century, however, when the spirit of neo-Gothic infused London. It found its first significant incarnation in the rebuilding of the Houses of Parliament after the great fire of 1834, but by 1860 "Gothic was the recognised language of all leading architects." It has been suggested that the Gothic style embodied "the influence of London's past." That is why the Law Courts were constructed in Gothic style as a way of instilling the authority of time upon the judicial deliberations of the present; it is also the reason why London churches of the mid-nineteenth century were invariably in the Gothic style. Ironwork was fashioned in the same manner, and suburban villas were rendered in what was known as "Wimbledon Gothic"; the area of St. John's Wood, in particular, is known for its toy or ornamental Gothic. Anything which might be considered too recent, or too newly made, was covered with a patina of false age.

So, in the nineteenth-century city, Gothic possessed the consolation of supposed antiquity; in a city which seemed to be careering beyond all familiar or predictable bounds, it offered the reassurance of some theoretical or presumed permanence. But sacred images have the strangest way of showing another face. The power of Gothic originals can also be associated with the presence of the pagan or the barbaric. That is why the city of empire was also known as a city of savages.

CHAPTER 62

Wild Things

✢

As there is a darkest Africa, is there not also a darkest England . . . May we not find a parallel at our own doors, and discover within a stone's throw of our cathedrals and palaces similar horrors to those which Stanley has found existing in the great Equatorial forest?" These are the words of William Booth in the 1890s. He notes in particular "dwarfish dehumanised inhabitants, the slavery to which they are subjected, their privation and their misery." In this sense the city has created and nurtured a wild population. The poor of the slums and tenements were characteristically described by other observers as "savages" and even at the time of great national religious revival among the middle classes, when England was supposed to be the quintessentially Christian nation, the working class of London remained outside the Church. A report of 1854 concluded that the poor of London were "as utter strangers to religious ordinances as the people of a heathen country" or, as Mayhew put it, "religion is a regular puzzle to costers." How could there be devotion, or piety, in such an oppressive commercial city where there was little chance of beauty or dignity, let alone worship?

The city of empire and commerce contained dens and lodging-houses "in the midst of a dense and ignorant population" where "the most diabolical practices were constantly perpetrated." "I have seen the Polynesian savage in his primitive condition," Thomas Huxley wrote, "before the missionary or the blackbirder or the beachcomber got at him. With all his savagery he was not half so savage, so unclean, so irreclaimable, as the tenant of a tenement in an East London slum." The paradox here is that the imperial city, the city which maintained and financed a world empire, contained within its heart a population more brutish and filthy than any of the races it believed itself destined to conquer. "He thought he was a Christian," Mayhew wrote of a young "mudlark" or river scavenger, "but he didn't know what a Christian was."

The poorest Irish immigrants sensed the atmosphere. "The Irish coming to London seem to regard it as a heathen city," according to Thomas Beames in *The Rookeries of London*, "and to give themselves up at once to a course of recklessness and crime." So the savagery was endemic, and also contagious; the inhabitants of the city were brutalised by its conditions.

Verlaine believed that, after Paris, in London he was living "among the barbarians," but his commentary is on a wider scale; he is referring to the fact that in the alien city the only worship was that of money and power. Again the name of Babylon emerges to encompass this great pagan host. As Dostoevsky expressed it in 1863, on his journey to London, "It is a biblical sight, something to do with Babylon, some prophecy out of the Apocalypse being fulfilled before your very eyes. You feel that a rich and ancient tradition of denial and protest is needed in order not to yield . . . and not to idolise Baal." He concluded that "Baal reigns and does not even demand obedience, because he is certain of it . . . The poverty, suffering, complaints and torpor of the masses do not worry him in the slightest." His heathen slaves and worshippers are in that sense powerless as, with the break of each day, "the same proud and gloomy spirit once again spreads its lordly wings over the gigantic city."

If mid-Victorian London was indeed a city of heathenism and pagan apocalypse, as Dostoevsky suggests, then what more appropriate monument for it than the one erected in 1878? An obelisk, dating from the Egyptian pharaohs of the eighteenth dynasty, was brought in a sealed ship to London; it had previously stood before the Temple of the Sun in On, or Heliopolis, where it had remained for 1,600 years. "It looked down upon the meeting of Joseph and Jacob, and saw the boyhood of Moses." In 12 BC it had been moved to Alexandria but was never erected there, lying prone in the sand until its removal to London. The monolith of rose-coloured granite, hewn in the quarries of southern Egypt by bands of slaves, now stands beside the Thames guarded by two bronze sphinxes; on its side are hieroglyphics naming Thothmes III and Rameses the Great. This stone, known as Cleopatra's Needle, has become a tutelary presence. As one French traveller noted of the Thames at this point, "the atmosphere is heavy; there is a conscious weight around, above, a weight that presses down, penetrates into ears and mouth, seems even to hang about the air." Tennyson, on contemplating the pagan monument of a pagan London, gave it a voice. "I have seen the four great empires disappear! I was when London was not! I am here!" The granite has slowly disintegrated through the perpetual influence of fog and smoke, and the hieroglyphics have begun to fade; there are "chips and gashes" where a bomb fell in the autumn of 1917. Yet it has survived. Still buried beneath it, in jars sealed in 1878, are a man's suit and a woman's costume, illustrated newspapers and children's toys, cigars and a razor; most significant, however, for the imperial obelisk, is a complete set of Victorian coinage embedded in its base.

Other pagan associations are intimately linked with the nineteenth-century city. Here the Minotaur made its appearance. In pagan myth the monster in the labyrinth was each year given seven youths and seven maidens, both as food and tribute. So Victorian crusaders against poverty and prostitution were, in the public prints, given the name of Theseus who killed the monster. Yet it did not wholly die. One journalist in the *Pall Mall Gazette* of July 1885 compared "the nightly sacrifice of virgins in London to the victims of the Athenian tribute to the Minotaur," and it seemed that the "appetite of the minotaur of London is insatiable." It was also described as the "London Minotaur . . . moving about clad as respectably in broad cloth and fine linen as any bishop." This indeed is a vision of horror, worthy of Poe or De Quincey, but the suggestion of a pagan beast alive and rampant is one curiously aligned to the nineteenth-century perception that the city had indeed become a labyrinth to rival anything upon the Cretan island. In response to these articles on child prostitution in London George Frederic Watts depicted the horned beast, half man and half bull, gazing over a parapet of stone across the city.

In his *Remaines* of 1686 John Aubrey wrote that "on the south side of Tooley Street, a little westward from Barnaby Street, is a street called the Maes or Maze, eastward from the Borough (another name for labyrinth). I believe we received these mazes from our Danish ancestors." Less than two hundred years later, however, new labyrinths emerged. Arthur Machen, reaching what he believed to be the outskirts of the city, "would say 'I am free at last from this mighty and stony wilderness!' And then suddenly, as I turned a corner the raw red rows of houses would confront me, and I knew that I was still in the labyrinth." Of the labyrinth as a device the architectural theorist Bernard Tschumi has stated: "One can never see it in totality, nor can one express it. One is condemned to it and cannot go outside and see the whole." This is London. When De Quincey wrote of searching for the young prostitute Ann whom he had befriended, he described their passing "through the mighty labyrinths of London; perhaps, even within a few feet of each other— a barrier no wider than a London street, often amounting in the end to a separation for eternity!" This is the horror of the city. It is blind to human need and human affection, its topography cruel and almost mindless in its brutality. The fact that the young girl will almost certainly be betrayed into prostitution once more conjures up the beast at its centre.

For De Quincey Oxford Street was made up from "never-ending terraces" and "innumerable groans." Here the streets tease and bewilder. Of the City it has been written that a "stranger would soon lose his way in such a maze" and in fact the old centre is characterised by its curious serpentine passages, its secluded alleys and its hidden courts. H.G. Wells noted that if it were not for the cabs "in a little while the whole population, so vast and incomprehensible is the intricate complexity of this great city, would be hopelessly lost for ever." This is curiously suggestive—a population lost in its own city, as if it had been swallowed up by the streets and the stone. A writer at the beginning of the nineteenth century, Robert Southey, had a similar vision with his realisation that "It is impossible ever to become thoroughly acquainted with such an endless labyrinth of streets; and, as you may well suppose, they who live at one end know little or nothing of the other." The image is of a labyrinth which is constantly expanding, reaching outwards towards infinity. On the maps of England it is seen as a dark patch, or stain, spreading slowly but inexorably outwards.

CHAPTER 63

If It Wasn't for
the 'ouses in Between

In many works of *nineteenth-century fiction,* characters stand upon an eminence, such as Primrose Hill or Fish Street Hill, and are struck into silence by the vision of the city's immensity. Macaulay acquired the reputation of having walked through every street in London but by the year of his death, in 1859, it was unlikely that anyone would have been able to reproduce that feat of pedestrianism. Here was a source of anxiety for an indigenous Londoner. He or she would never know all of the city thoroughly; there would always be a secret London in the very act of its growth. It can be mapped, but it can never be fully imagined. It must be taken on faith, not on reason.

It grew so large in the nineteenth century that Donald Olsen has remarked in *The Growth of Victorian London* that "Most of the London we enjoy is Victorian either in its fabric or its layout, or at least its inspiration." And what is that inspiration? A passage in *Building News* of 1858 put the case that "It is the duty of our architecture to translate our character into stone." The great rebuilding and extension heralded an equally great destruction of the past; that, too, was part of the Victorian "character." Its improvements destroyed "the old gabled shops and tenements, the quaint inns and galleried court-yards, the churches and the curious streets that were the existing records of the life of another century." Yet just as the Church yielded to commerce so the narrow streets gave way to wide and ever wider thoroughfares lined by new dwellings; great hotels, office buildings and blocks of flats, in brilliant limestone or burnished brick or terracotta, rose above the city. Shaftesbury Avenue, Northumberland Avenue, Holborn Viaduct, Queen Victoria Street, Charing Cross Road, all were driven through the capital so that a reporter in 1873 could observe that "old London . . . the London of our youth . . . is becoming obliterated by another city which seems rising up through it." There was a disconcerting sensation, much remarked upon, that a strange city was emerging ineluctably like a phantom in a mist. And it was changing everything that it touched. The concerted impulse to create a gigantic London—to widen streets, to put up great monuments, to create museums and law courts, to drive huge new thoroughfares from one part of the capital to another—meant a chaos of demolition and reconstruction, with entire areas becoming building sites complete with hoardings and heavy machinery. The Holborn Viaduct was built to span the valley of the Fleet, linking Holborn Circus with Newgate Street; the great enterprise of the Victoria Embankment transformed the northern bank of the river and was extended into the heart of the city by Queen Victoria Street; Victoria Street transformed all of Westminster, while Shaftesbury Avenue and Charing Cross Road created the "West End" as it is commonly understood. The City itself was steadily being depopulated, as bankers and merchants moved out to Kensington or Belgravia, until it became nothing but a counting-house. "This monster London is really a new city," Charles Eliot Pascoe wrote in 1888, "new as to its life, its streets and the social conditions of the millions who dwell in them, whose very manners, habits, occupations and even amusements have undergone as complete change within the past half-century as the great city itself." This is one aspect of London which the nineteenth century thoroughly revealed; the city itself changes its inhabitants, for better or worse, and actively intervenes in their lives. From that, of course, may spring a sense of oppression or imprisonment.

Yet there was a genuine feeling of awe concerning the vast extent of the city, as if a quite new thing had been created in the world. Where some saw only poverty and deprivation, others saw intelligence and industry; where some recognised only shabbiness and ugliness, others noted the blessings of trade and commerce. In effect London was now so large that practically any opinion could be held of it, and still be true. It was the harbinger of a consumer society. It represented energy, and zeal, and inventiveness. But it was also the "Great Wen," a monstrous growth filled with "the bitter tears of outcast London."

Another aspect of its size, therefore, was the fact that it contained everything. When Henry Mayhew ascended above London in a balloon he observed "that vast bricken mass of churches and hospitals, banks and prisons, palaces and workhouses, docks and refuges for the destitute" all "blent into one immense black spot . . . a mere rubbish heap" containing "vice and avarice and low cunning" as well as "noble aspirations and human heroism." But in such a vast metropolis, forever growing, "vice" and "heroism" become themselves unimportant; the sheer size of London creates indifference. This, in a sensitive mind such as that of Henry James, can lead to acute depression or feelings of estrangement. "Up to this time," he wrote to his sister in 1869, "I have been crushed under a sense of the sheer magnitude of London—its inconceivable immensity—in such a way as to paralyse my mind . . . The place sits on you, broods on you, stamps on you." That is another aspect of its unimaginable size; it acts as a giant weight or burden upon each individual life and consciousness. It is not simply that the citizens were literally dwarfed by the huge blocks and intricate machinery of the Victorian city, but rather that the sheer scale of London haunted its inhabitants. No one could ever memorise a map of Victorian London with its streets packed so tightly together that they could hardly be made out; it was beyond human capacity. But a place of such vastness, without limit, is also horrifying. It weighs upon the mind. It may lead to desperation, or release energy.

Disraeli remarked upon this "illimitable feature" as the "special character" of London but in turn it resulted in the city's becoming "very monotonous." That is another paradox of this paradoxical city. Sheer size may arouse not sensations of awe and admiration but rather those of dullness and ennui. Disraeli was possessed by a vision of "flat, dull, spiritless streets" stretching in all directions so that "London overpowers with its vastness" and its sameness. If it was the largest city in the world it was also the most impersonal, spreading its dull life everywhere.

One of the characteristics of London faces was the appearance of tiredness. To journey through the city was itself fatiguing enough; it had grown too large to be manageable. The Londoner returned home exhausted, spiritless, dead to the world. So London wears out its citizens; it drains them of their energies, like a succubus. Yet for some "this senseless bigness," as Henry James described it, was a source of fascination. Disraeli's vision of a vast uniformity was reversed in that context, because the absence of limits could also mean that everything is there; there were myriad shapes to be discerned, an endless profusion and prodigality of scenes and characters.

"When I came to this great city," an African traveller wrote, "I looked this way and that way; there is no beginning and no end." He could have walked through Kennington and Camberwell, Hackney and Bethnal Green, Stoke Newington and Highbury, Chelsea and Knightsbridge and Kensington without ceasing to marvel. Between 1760 and 1835 the development rivalled that of the preceding two hundred years. By the latter date streets and terraces had reached Victoria, Edgware, the City Road, Limehouse, Rotherhithe and Lambeth. In the next sixteen years alone the city conquered Belgravia, Hoxton, Poplar, Deptford, Walworth, Bethnal Green, Bow Road and St. Pancras. By 1872 it had expanded exponentially again to encompass Waltham Green, Kensal Green, Hammersmith, Highgate, Finsbury Park, Clapton, Hackney, New Cross, Old Ford, Blackheath, Peckham, Norwood, Streatham and Tooting, all of it growing and coming together beyond any civic or administrative control. The roads and thoroughfares were not planned by any Parliament or central authority; that is why the city's development was often compared to some remorseless instinctive process or natural growth. London colonised each village or town as it encompassed them, making them a part of itself, but not necessarily changing their fundamental topography. They were now London, but they retained streets and buildings of an earlier date. Their old structure can just be recognised in the remains of churches, marketplaces and village greens, while their names survive as the titles of Underground stations.

It was often said that all England had become London, but some considered London to be an altogether separate nation with its own language and customs. For others London corresponded to the great globe itself or "the epitome of the round world," as one nineteenth-century novelist put it. It is an indication of its prodigiousness, when such a great mass exerts its own form of gravity and attraction—"lines of force," Thomas De Quincey called them in an essay entitled "The Nation of London."

Ordinary human existence seems uninteresting or unimportant in this place where everything is colossal. "No man ever was left to himself for the first time in the streets, as yet unknown, of London," De Quincey continued, "but he must have been saddened and mortified, perhaps terrified, by the sense of desertion and utter loneliness which belongs to his situation." Nobody regarded De Quincey; nobody saw or heard him. The people rushing past, bent upon their own secret destinations and contemplating their own hurried business, seemed "like a mask of maniacs" or "a pageant of phantoms." Against the magnitude of stone, the city dwellers are like wraiths, replacing others and in turn to be replaced. It is a function of London's size, and of its age, that all of its citizens seem merely its temporary inhabitants. Within the immensity of London any individual becomes insignificant and unnoticed; this is a tiring condition, too, and may also help to explain the weariness and lassitude which mark many London faces. To be perpetually reminded that the single human life is worth very little, that it is reckoned merely as part of the aggregate sum, may induce a sense of futility.

To live in the city is to know the limits of human existence. In many Victorian street-scenes the city dwellers seem lonely and unregarded, trudging along the crowded avenues with their heads lowered, carrying their burdens patiently enough but isolated none the less. This is another paradox of Victorian London. There is an appearance of energy and vitality in the mass, but the characteristic individual mood is one of anxiety or despondency.

"What is the centre of London for any purpose whatever?" De Quincey asked, and of course the city has no centre at all. Or rather, the centre is everywhere. Wherever the houses are built, that is London—Streatham, Highgate, New Cross, all as characteristically and indefinably London as Cheapside or the Strand. They were part of the malodorous, coruscating city, awakened from its grandeur and rising into shabby daylight as a wilderness of roofs and tenements. Not all were stable; not all were noble. This was another aspect of the ever expanding city; there were areas which were only of fragile growth. The various classes, and subdivisions of classes, were broadly segregated in distinct neighbourhoods; the difference between working-class Lambeth and genteel Camberwell, both south of the river, for example, was immense. But there were areas of more uncertain nature, where the chances of going up or down were precariously balanced. Pimlico was one such neighbourhood; it could have become grand or respectable, but was constantly on the verge of shabbiness. This in turn reflected a general anxiety among middle-class city dwellers; it was easy to go under, through drink or unemployment, and the tense respectability of one year might be succeeded by wretchedness in the next. Will this newly built terrace along the Walford Road become the dwellings of ambitious city workers, or will it degenerate into a set of tenements? This was the unspoken question about much of London's development.

And then there was the immensity registered by its endless crowds. That is why the urban fiction of the nineteenth century is filled with chance encounters and coincidental meetings, with sudden looks and brief asides, with what H.G. Wells called "a great mysterious movement of unaccountable beings." Travellers were frightened at street-crossings where the sheer number and speed of pedestrians created the effect of a whirlpool. "A Londoner jostles you in the street," a German journalist observed, "without ever dreaming of asking your pardon; he will run against you, and make you revolve on your own axis, without so much as looking round to see how you feel after the shock." Workers walked to the City from Islington and Pentonville, but now they came in from Deptford and Bermondsey, Hoxton and Hackney, as well. It has been estimated that, in the 1850s, 200,000 people walked into the City each day. As Roy Porter has put it in *London: a Social History*, "dislocation and relocation were always occurring—nothing ever stood still, nothing was constant except mobility itself." To be engaged in a process of perpetual growth and change for their own sake, and to be sure of nothing but uncertainty, may be discomfiting.

Yet as the city expanded so continuously and so rapidly, there was no possibility of walking over its vast extent; as it grew, so did other forms of traffic emerge to steer a way through its immensity. The most extraordinary agent of innovation came with the advent of the railway; nineteenth-century London, in the process of its great transformation, was further changed by the building of Euston in 1837 followed by Waterloo, King's Cross, Paddington, Victoria, Blackfriars, Charing Cross, St. Pancras and Liverpool Street. The entire railway network, which is still in use almost 150 years later, was imposed upon the capital within a space of some twenty-five years between 1852 and 1877. The termini themselves became palaces of Victorian invention and inventiveness, erected by a society obsessed by speed and motion. One consequence was that the city became truly the centre of the nation, with all the lines of energy leading directly to it. Together with the electric telegraph, the railways defined and maintained the supremacy of London. It became the great conduit of communication and of commerce in a world in which "railway time" set the standard of the general hurry.

The influence was also felt much closer to the capital itself, with the proliferation of branch or suburban lines in the northern and southern suburbs. By the 1890s there were connections between Willesden and Walthamstow, Dalston Junction and Broad Street, Richmond and Clapham Junction, New Cross and London Bridge, the whole perimeter of the city being ineluctably drawn into its centre with characteristic stone arches on both sides of the river.

When William Powell Frith exhibited his painting of Paddington Station, *The Railway Station*, in 1838, the "work had to be protected by railings from enthusiastic crowds"; they were fascinated by the crowds depicted upon the canvas itself, conveying all the magnitude and immensity of the great railway enterprise. Nineteenth-century Londoners were drawn to the spectacle of themselves, and of the achievements wrought in their name; it was indeed a new city, or, at least, the quality of experience within it had suffered a change. Somehow the great heavy urban mass had been controlled; the new lines of transport which crossed it also managed to hold it down, to elucidate it in terms of time and distance, to direct its palpitating life. "The journey between Vauxhall or Charing Cross, and Cannon Street," wrote Blanchard Jerrold, "presents to the contemplative man scenes of London life of the most striking description. He is admitted behind the scenes of the poorest neighbourhoods; surveys interminable terraces of back gardens alive with women and children." London had become viewable, and therefore legible. There was the phenomenon of railway-mania, too, when the stocks and shares of the variously competing companies traded high in the City; by 1849 Parliament had agreed the building of 1,071 railway tracks, nineteen in London itself, and it could be said that the whole country was transfixed by the idea of rail travel. The railway even managed to recreate London in its own image; thousands of houses were demolished to make way for its new tracks, and it has been estimated that 100,000 people were displaced in the process.

The opening of a new railway station provided mixed benefits. Older suburban retreats such as Fulham and Brixton came within range of the new commuters, previously unable to live at such a distance from their place of work. City dwellers poured in, and small or cheap houses were constructed for them. The growth of the railway system actually created new suburbs, with the Cheap Trains Act of 1883 materially assisting the exodus of the poorer people from the old tenements to new "railway suburbs" such as Walthamstow and West Ham. Areas such as Kilburn and Willesden became flooded with new population, creating the vague monotony of terraced housing which still survives; in these latter two districts lived the colonies of navvies who were themselves involved in the building of more railways.

But railways were by no means the only form of transportation within the capital; it has been estimated that in 1897 the junction of Cheapside and New-

A photograph of Regent Street in the nineteenth century, with its relatively new phenomenon of the "sandwich man" as well as the horse-drawn omnibuses.

The porters at Billingsgate were well known for their characteristic attire.
In a city of appearances, and street theatre, it was important to be dressed for the part.
No man, whatever his trade, was seen without a hat.

Old houses in Bermondsey, at the end of the nineteenth century; they were swept away, or bombed, while in their place arose one of the great council estates of south London.

Clerkenwell Green: this inoffensive and often overlooked "green," in the middle of Clerkenwell, has been the site of more riots and more radical activity than any other part of London. What is its secret?

River scavengers: these were the real tradesmen of the city, earning a meagre living by combing the banks of the tidal river.

Women sifting dust mounds: in a city where everything had its price, there was money to be made out of refuse of every kind. These women, sometimes known as "bunters," inherited their noxious trade.

A wheel at the exhibition in the 1890s (and a similar wheel at Bartholomew's Fair in the seventeenth century) anticipated the modern wheel of the "London Eye" in the year 2000. In a similar echoic spirit, the modern Lloyd's building was erected on the site of the old London maypole.

William Whiffin's marvellous photograph of children following a water cart.
Many London children went barefoot in all weathers, however.

The stance and attitude of this
ragged boy epitomise the defiance and
independence of London children who were
often brought up "on the stones." The miracle is
that they survived at all.

A photograph of a Millwall street, taken in 1938.
Street games have been characteristic of London
children ever since London was established, and
somehow the most barren districts have become
areas of play. Not all streets, however, are
shadowed by great ships.

The "London particular" was the name given to the characteristic fogs of the city which descended without warning and created darkness at noon. This gaily dressed citizen is attempting to protect himself against what was considered to be a bearer of disease.

The "smog" of the Fifties and Sixties was a miasma of fog and smoke.

A Paraleytic Woman:
Géricault visited London in the
1820s and was at once intrigued and
horrified by the predicament
of the poor. In a city based
upon money, the indigent and the
vagrant are the sacrificial victims.

Stanley Green, "Protein Man,"
walked up and down Oxford Street
for many years, parading the same
dietary message. He was commonly
ignored by the great tide of people
who washed around him, and thus
became a poignant symbol of the
city's incuriosity and forgetfulness.

The ruins of Paternoster Row, beside St. Paul's, photographed during the air-raids of the Second World War by Cecil Beaton. It had been a street of stationers and publishers for three hundred years, but is now only a name.

Don McCullin's photograph, taken near Spitalfields in 1969, provides an image of anger and helplessness. The poor and the desperate have always been a part of London's history, and it might be said that the city is most recognisable by the shadow they cast.

gate "was passed by an average of twenty three vehicles a minute during working hours." This was the great roar, like that of Niagara, by which the city dwellers were surrounded. This vast crowd of moving vehicles comprised omnibuses and hansoms, carts and trams, horses and early cars, broughams and motor buses, taxis and victorias, all somehow managing to manoeuvre through the crowded granite streets. A wagon might break down, and bring a long line of carriages to a halt; a cart, a carriage, a dray and an omnibus might follow each other in slow procession, while the quicker cabs darted between them. In early moving pictures of London's traffic you see the boys running among the vehicles to clear up horse-dung, while pedestrians make sorties into the road with the same courage and defiance as they do still. In photograph, or on film, it is a scene of indescribable energy as well as confusion; it might be a bacterium, or an entire cosmos, so instinctive its movement seems.

The omnibus first emerged upon the streets of London in 1829 and, twenty-five years later, there were some three thousand of them, each one carrying approximately three hundred passengers a day. There is a painting of 1845 by James Pollard, entitled *A Street Scene with Two Omnibuses*, which vividly recalls the transport of that period. Each of the two buses is being pulled by two horses; in the first bus eight gentlemen in stove-pipe hats are sitting on the open roof behind the driver, while other passengers can be glimpsed sitting within. The bus is painted green and in large letters along the side it is advertised as part of the "FAVORITE" group; a board on a post attached to the back proclaims that it drives between Euston and Chelsea, while on the side are painted its other destinations. The original fares were sixpence rising to a shilling, so this form of transport was not favoured by the labouring classes of London, yet steady competition reduced the prices of tickets to twopence or a penny. The first journey of the day was filled with office clerks, and a second with their employers, the merchants and the bankers; towards midday "the ladies" entered the bus for shopping expeditions, together with mothers taking their children "for a ride." In the evening the vehicles were filled with all those returning to the suburbs from the City while, in the other direction, travelled those who were "out for the night" at the theatres or supper-clubs.

A traveller in 1853 noted that "the omnibus is a necessity and the Londoner cannot get on without it," and added that "the word 'bus' is rapidly working its way into general acceptation"; he remarked upon the prepossessing appearance of these carriages, brightly painted red or green or blue, as well as the high spirits of conductors and drivers alike. The former shouted out "All right!" and banged the roof of the vehicle to signal that it was time to move on, and all through the journey he was "never silent" but calling out destinations continually—"Ba-nk! Ba-nk!"

The London horses deserve attention and celebration, also, because their training in the streets and their "natural sagacity" meant that they could proceed through the crowded thoroughfares at a good pace without causing accidents. One late Victorian recalled that, at one of those moments when traffic came to a halt, he could see "hundreds of horses" which "tossed their heads and blew air from their nostrils" while their drivers "shouted and bellowed" greetings and pleasantries to one another.

Of all vehicles, however, the hansom-cab became most closely associated with Victorian London. Introduced in 1834 it was a four-wheeled vehicle with an interior more comfortable than that of the previous two-wheeled cab, and with the driver at a more impersonal distance behind the carriage. Once again the changing appearances of transport reflected the changing culture of London. But if the form of the cabs was altered, the appearance and manner of their drivers remained constant; they were well known for their "chaff" or insolence, and their dishonesty. "Whenever a stranger is bold enough to hail a cab, not one, but half a dozen come at once"; this German traveller's observation is supported by other accounts of the violent competitiveness of cab-drivers all over the capital. They became the tutelary spirits, or imps, of the road. Although there were statutory fees they would attempt to bargain, with the customary phrase "What will you give?" They were also notorious for their drunkenness and, in turn, for their argumentativeness. "An old Londoner only may venture to engage in a topographical or geometrical disputation with a cabman, for gentlemen of this class are not generally flattering in their expressions or conciliating in their arguments; and the cheapest way of terminating the dispute is to pay and have done with the man." The drivers of the hansom cabs were "as full as exacting and impertinent as their humbler brethren," the drivers of the growlers or four-wheeled cabs, but they had more spirit, "most skilful in winding and edging their light vehicles through the most formidable knot of wagons and carriages." London's cab-drivers epitomise the spirit of the city—fast, restless, audacious, with a propensity for violence and drunkenness. They are closely related to the butchers and the street-criers, whose trades are also intimately attached to the life of the city: all part of London's family.

By the end of the nineteenth century there were more than ten thousand cabs of various kinds, and even the new thoroughfares could scarcely accommodate the onrushing flood of vehicles of every description. Sometimes the crush grew too great, and there was a "stop" or "lock" (in the twentieth century, a "jam"). Nevertheless it is a matter for astonishment that through the centuries the city has managed to keep its avenues and thoroughfares open to the ever increasing demands of its traffic. At the beginning of the twenty-first century, the endless stream of cars and buses and taxis and lorries is coursing along roads which were built in the eighteenth and nineteenth centuries for quite different forms of transport. The city has the ability to recreate itself silently and invisibly, as if it were truly a living thing.

London's Outcasts

Géricault's engraving entitled "Pity the Sorrows of
a Poor Old Man" emphasises the isolation and misery of the
London outcasts; the companionship of a dog continues to be
a token of the wandering life in the city.

CHAPTER 64

They Are Always with Us

✥

"Mrs. *Ambrose understood that* after all it is the ordinary thing to be poor, and that London is the city of innumerable poor people": this sentence from Virginia Woolf's *The Voyage Out* expresses a great truth about the nineteenth century in which she was born.

The poor have always been part of the texture of the city. They are like the stones or the bricks, because London has risen from them; their mute suffering has no limits. In the medieval city the old, the crippled, the deformed and the mad were the first poor; those who could not work, and thus had no real or secure place in the social fabric, became the outcast. By the sixteenth century there were poor sections of the city such as East Smithfield, St. Katherine by the Tower and the Mint in Southwark; it could be said that by some instinctive process the poor clustered together, or it might be concluded that parts of the city harboured them. They were hawkers or pedlars or criers or chimney-sweeps, but they belong to that underclass which Defoe described as "The Miserable, that really pinch and suffer want."

In eighteenth-century accounts we read of squalid courts and miserable houses, of "dirty neglected children" and "slipshod women," of "dirty, naked, unfurnished" rooms and of men who stayed within them because their "clothes had become too ragged to submit to daylight scrutiny." Those who lacked even this primitive accommodation slept in empty or abandoned houses; they sheltered in "bulks" or in doorways. In *London Life in the Eighteenth Century* M. Dorothy George estimated that by that century's end there were in London "above twenty thousand miserable individuals of various classes, who rise up every morning without knowing how . . . they are to be supported during the passing day, or where in many instances they are to lodge on the succeeding night." This has been plausibly related to "the general uncertainty of life and trade characteristic of the period." So we may say that the underlying nature of London is most visible, or most sharply manifested, in the lives and appearance of its poorest inhabitants. Other city dwellers, rendered fearful, shunned the poor. The very presence of the poor increased the morbid nervousness and restlessness of all Londoners. We see the shape of the city from the shadow that it casts.

That shadow can be traced within the contours of Charles Booth's "poverty map" of 1889 where blocks of black and dark blue, denoting the "Lowest class. Vicious, semi-criminal" and the "Very poor, casual. Chronic want," creep among the red and gold bars of the affluent. A larger-scale map outlining the districts of the poor identified poverty in 134 areas "each of about 30,000 inhabitants"; here the dark blue areas cluster around the banks of the Thames but elsewhere there is a pattern of concentric rings "with the most uniform poverty at the centre." They were London-born and London-bred, in Paddington and in Pimlico, in Whitechapel and in Wapping, in Battersea and Bermondsey.

Travellers noticed impoverishment everywhere and commented how degrading and degraded were the London poor, quite different from their counterparts in Rome or Berlin or Paris. In 1872 Hippolyte Taine remarked that he recalled "the lanes which open off Oxford Street, stifling alleys thick with human effluvia, troops of pale children crouching on filthy staircases; the street benches at London Bridge where all night whole families huddle close, heads hanging, shaking with cold . . . abject, miserable poverty." In a city based upon money and power, those who are moneyless and powerless are peculiarly oppressed. In London, of all cities, they are literally degraded, stripped of all human decency by the operations of a city that has no other purpose except greed. That is why the poor were "abject" in the streets of nineteenth-century London and, as the city increased in power and magnitude, so did the numbers of the poor increase.

They represented almost a city within the city, and such a large aggregate of human misery could not be ignored. John Hollingshead's *Ragged London*, published in 1861, suggested that one-third of the urban population lived "in unwholesome layers, one over the other, in old houses and confined rooms" which themselves were to be found in "filthy, ill constructed, courts and alleys." The atmosphere of disgust and menace here is only barely suppressed. In London, Mrs. Cook concluded in *Highways and Byways of London* (1902) "misery is strangely prolific," which suggests that the fear of the poor derived from the fact that they were likely to multiply indefinitely. She was speaking of the Borough: there poverty and misery seemed to have grown to such an extent that Southwark was overcome by it, but she could have been referring to a hundred other parts of the city. The places of the poor were "pestilential," according to the author of *The Bitter Cry of Outcast London* in 1883, thus confirming the fear that this kind of abject poverty and degradation was, in the conditions of London, somehow contagious; the futility and the despair might spread throughout the rookeries, where "tens of thousands are crowded together amidst horrors."

It is as if the streets themselves engendered these huddled masses. A newspaper report of 1862 named "Nichols Street, New Nichols Street, Half Nichols Street, Turville Street, comprising within the same area numerous blind courts and alleys." Here the litany of street names itself is meant to conjure up degeneration, where the "outward moral degradation is at once apparent to any one who passes that way." So the houses and lanes themselves are guilty of "moral degradation." Does the city reflect its inhabitants, or do its inhabitants mimic the conditions of the city? Dwellers and dwelling places become inexact metaphors for one another, as in this passage from Jack London's *The People of the Abyss* (1903): "Everything is helpless, hopeless, unrelieved and dirty . . . The people themselves are dirty, while any attempt at cleanliness becomes howling farce, when it is not pitiful and tragic . . . The father returning from work asks his child in the street where her mother is: and back the answer comes, 'In the buildings.' " Observers were generally agreed that the life of the poor had reached such a level of hopelessness and squalor that "a new race has sprung up" and, further, that "it is now hereditary to a very considerable extent." If Victorian London was itself so changed as to have become a new city, here was the new population with which it was filled.

This was the urban phenomenon which Engels diagnosed, and which he watched closely. In St. Giles, "the extent to which these filthy passages are fallen into decay beggars all description . . . the walls are crumbling, the door posts and window frames are loose and rotten." Marx lived a few yards away in Soho. So the condition of the mid-nineteenth-century city directly inspired the founders of communism; it might be said that their creed issued out of the slums of London, and those Victorian observers who believed that some great or alarming new reality would emerge from the pervasive presence of the poor were not wholly wrong. The London poor did indeed generate a new race or class, but in countries and civilisations far distant.

In Long Acre, Engels noticed, the children are "sickly" and "half-starved." He conceded that the worst forms of poverty were not visited upon all "London workers," but "every working man without exception may well suffer a similar fate through no fault of his own." This was one of the most tenacious visions of poverty as a palpable threat, this the despair that the city could breed, precisely because the conditions of London itself were enough to drive people into the slums. The uncertainty of employment, for example, was one of the most pressing reasons why people "broke" (to use an early nineteenth-century word) and were reduced to beggary. A cold winter meant that dockers and building workers were thrown out of work or, in the phrase of the period, "turned off." To turn someone off—in an age when all the talk was of energy and of electricity, this was the ultimate dehumanising and degrading force.

Areas where the poor lived were also "turned off." The city had grown so large that they could be concealed in its depths. Engels quotes one clergyman who declared that "I never witnessed such thorough prostration of the poor as I have seen since I have been in Bethnal Green," but who reiterated that this area was quite unknown to, and unvisited by, other Londoners. In other quarters of the city "about as little was known . . . of this destitute parish as the wilds of Australia or the islands of the South Seas." The image of the wilderness once more emerges, but now with connotations of darkness and impenetrability.

Here again was another monstrous feature of the great metropolis, where rich and poor could live side by side without noticing each other's existence. Engels quotes from an editorial in *The Times* of 12 October 1843, which suggested that "within the most courtly precincts of the richest city of GOD's earth, there may be found, night after night, winter after winter . . . FAMINE, FILTH AND DISEASE." From this vantage Engels looked at the whole society of London, and concluded that it was not sane or whole. "The more that Londoners are packed into a tiny space, the more repulsive and disgraceful becomes the brutal indifference with which they ignore their neighbours and selfishly concentrate upon their private affairs."

So London has created a new phase in human existence itself; its poverty has in a real sense impoverished all who, in the mad pursuit of getting and spending, have created a human society of "component atoms." A new race was therefore being created not only in the tenements of St. Giles but over the whole face of London where "the vast majority . . . have had to let so many of their potential creative faculties lie dormant, stunted and unused." Engels suggests that this is the real poverty within the city, which only a revolution could extirpate.

Nineteenth-century London, then, created the first characteristically urban society on the face of the earth. What now we take for granted—"they rush past each other as if they had nothing in common"—was then greeted with distaste. For anyone who marvelled at the greatness and vastness of the Victorian city, there were others who were disturbed and horrified. Here, in the streets of London, real "social conflict, the war of all against all," actually existed. It was a harbinger of the future world, a cancer that would not only spread throughout England but eventually cover the great globe itself.

One of the great studies of poverty in late nineteenth-century London was, and remains, Charles Booth's *Life and Labour of the People in London* (1903); it ran to seventeen volumes, and went through three editions. Like the city that it was examining, it was on the largest possible scale. A monumental work, it is filled with suggestive details and suffused by a curious pity. It is in fact the vision of London lives which renders Booth's work so significant. "The last occupant of the back room was a widower, scavenger to Board of Works, a man who would not believe in hell or heaven . . . At No. 7 lives a car-man in broken-down health. He fell off his cart and being run over broke his leg. On the floor above is a very poor old lady living on charity, but a happy soul expectant of heaven." In the neighbourhood lived a man who was "a notorious Atheist, one who holds forth on behalf of his creed under railway arches, saying that if there be a God he must be a monster to permit such misery as exists. This man suffers from heart disease, and the doctor tells him that some day in his excitement he will drop down dead." These are the permanent inhabitants of London. "On the ground floor live Mr. and Mrs. Meek. Meek is a hatter and was engaged in dyeing children's hats in a portable boiler. A cheery little man . . . At the back lives Mrs. Helmot, whose husband, formerly an optician, is now at Hanwell suffering from suicidal melancholia." All the variety of human experience is revealed here; the cheerful hat-maker and the suicidal optician are more suggestive than any characters in nineteenth-century urban fiction.

It is as if the city had become a sort of desert island, upon which its occupants picked their way. But there was another life which, against all the odds, kept on breaking through. "How the poor live," a nurse told Booth, "when they are helpless remains a mystery, save for their great kindness to each other, even to those who are strangers. This is the great explanation." A Nonconformist preacher also told him that "It is only the poor that really give. They know exactly the wants of one another and give when needed." A Roman Catholic priest informed him, "To each other their goodness is wonderful." Here is another reality lying concealed beneath all the descriptions of filth and squalor. The intimate experience of shared suffering did not necessarily injure the spirits of the very poor. The conditions of urban life could lead to despair, and drunkenness, and death, but there was at least the possibility of another form of human expression in kindness and generosity to those trapped within the same harsh and noisome reality.

Booth ends his account with a memorable paragraph: "The dry bones that lie scattered over the long valley that we have traversed together lie before my reader. May some great soul, master of a subtler and nobler alchemy than mine, disentangle the confused issues, reconcile the apparent contradictions in aim, melt and commingle the various influences for good into one divine uniformity of effort and make these dry bones live, so that the streets of our Jerusalem may sing with joy." It is an astonishing revelation. Charles Booth more than any other man understood the horror and the misery of nineteenth-century London, yet he invoked the image of a joyful Jerusalem to conclude his discourse.

By the time he had completed his labours, which took eighteen years, Booth recognised that the very worst conditions had been alleviated, but only the very worst. Many of the slums had been removed, some of their erstwhile inhabitants moving to "model dwellings" or to the newly established council houses on council estates. Improved sanitation, and a more general concern with urban hygiene, also affected the lot of the poor in marginal ways. But where would the city be without its poor?

A survey conducted in the late 1920s, the *New Survey of London Life and Labour*, calculated that 8.7 per cent of Londoners were still living in poverty; the same figure, however, has been re-estimated in other contexts as 5 per cent and 21 per cent. This illustrates the problems in any discussion of poverty—levels of deprivation are relative, but relative to what? The depression of the 1930s, for example, led to the creation of what were then known as "the new poor," and another survey in 1934 reported that 10 per cent of London families lived beneath the "poverty line." There was no famine, but there was malnutrition; there were fewer rags, but still a plethora of ragged clothes. The first decades of the twentieth century were marked by hunger marches and marches of the unemployed, the effects of which were mitigated by the introduction of unemployment benefit and more enlightened use of the Poor Laws.

Yet poverty never leaves London. It merely changes its form and appearance. In a recent survey into "measures of deprivation," the highest counts were in Southwark, Lambeth, Hackney and Tower Hamlets (formerly Bethnal Green and Stepney); these are precisely the areas where the poor of the eighteenth and nineteenth centuries congregated. So there is a continuity of need or distress, clustering around significant localities. Asian children now play in Old Nichol Street and Turville Street, and the area is curiously silent after its raucous and terrible life as the "Jago," the area of Shoreditch immortalised in Arthur Morrison's *A Child of the Jago* (1896). Poverty has now become less noisy, and noisome, than in any of its previous incarnations but it is present nonetheless, an intrinsic and instinctive part of the city. Were there no poor, then there would be no rich. Like the women who accompanied eighteenth-century armies, dependent and defenceless, so do the poor accompany London on its progress. It created the poor; it needed the poor, not least for the purpose of cheap or casual labour; now they have become the shadows which follow it everywhere.

CHAPTER 65

Can You Spare a Little Something?

The most visible manifestations of poverty came to London in the form of mendicants and beggars. They were arguing with each other at the end of the fourteenth century. "John Dray in his own person denied the charge, and said that on the day and in the place mentioned he and the said Ralph were sitting together and begging, when John Stowe, a monk of Westminster came by and gave them a penny in common. Ralph received the penny, but would not give Dray his share. A quarrel arose and Ralph assaulted him with a stick." Such a scene could have occurred centuries before, or centuries after. Where else could a beggar find a better plot than London itself, filled with people and according to legend replete with money?

There were religious mendicants, or hermits, mumbling in stone alcoves beside the principal gates of the city; there were lame beggars on street corners; there were prison beggars, calling out for alms from the gratings which held them; there were old women begging outside churches; there were children begging in the street. In the early twenty-first century some of the principal thoroughfares are lined with beggars, young and old; some lie huddled in doorways, wrapped in blankets, and stare up with imploring faces with the customary cry, "Spare any change?" The older of them tend to be drunken vagrants, existing altogether out of time; which is as much to say that they uncannily resemble their counterparts in previous ages of London's history.

Sir Thomas More recalled the crowds of beggars who swarmed around the gates of the monasteries of London, and in the late medieval city it was common practice for servants of great houses and institutions to gather up the broken bread and meat of a public feast in order to distribute them to the sup-plicants begging for dole outside the doors. In one of his English works More wrote: "I se somtyme my selfe so many poore folke at Westmynster at the dolys . . . that my self for the preace of them haue ben fayn to ryde another waye." But though he would have preferred to ride in another direction, avoiding the press and the smell of them, he alighted and spoke to one of them. When More praised the generosity of the Westminster monks, he drew the retort that it was no thanks to them, since their lands had been given to them by good princes. The beggars were desperate, but not destitute of re-sentment or a certain type of moral clarity; the position of a beggar in London is that of a supplicant but through the ages it has always been compounded by bitterness or anger at the condition to which he or she has been reduced. Cit-izens gave them money out of embarrassment as much as pity.

There were already "shamming" beggars, who counterfeited deformity or sickness, but it was not yet a trade of shame. Some of their names have come down to us from the twelfth century, among them George a Greene, Robert the Devil and William Longbeard. Reputed to be the king of London beggars, in the reign of Henry II William Longbeard sought sanctuary in St. Mary le Bow after causing disturbances in Cheapside. Eventually he was smoked out by the officers of the court, but he was one of those early outcasts whose dispossession was a mark of pride. They were people wedded to poverty and isolation, who therefore became symbols of unaccommodated humankind. "Doe we not all come into the Worlde like arrant Beggars with-out a rag upon us?" Thomas Dekker wrote in the early seventeenth century. "Doe we not all go out of the Worlde like Beggars, saving an old sheete to cover us? And shall we not all walke up and downe in the Worlde like Beg-gars, with an old Blankett pinned about?" If God made humankind in His own image, then what curious broken-down divinity did these men and women display? This was the superstitious awe which the beggars provoked in those who passed them.

In the sixteenth century first emerged "brotherhoods" of beggars, who went by such names as the Roaring Boys, the Bonaventoes, the Quarters and the Bravadoes. They collected in Whitefriars and Moorditch and Hoxton, the field of Lincoln's Inn and the porch of St. Bartholomew the Great; the last two locations are still used by vagrants today. All of them smoked pipes, as an emblem of their status, and were well known for their violence and their drunkenness. In Coplande's *Hye Way to the Spitel Hous* (1531), he depicts beggars dolefully singing along the approach to St. Paul's from the east, and reports one beggar asking him to "make this farthyng worth a half-penny, for the fyve joyes of our blessed lady." Thomas Harman published accounts of London beggars in pamphlet form, emphasising their more sensational attributes and exploits. Of one Richard Horwood, a Londoner, he writes: "Well nigh eighty years old, he will bite a sixpenny nail assunder with his teeth, and a bawdy drunkard to boot." In the spring of 1545 Henry VIII issued a proclamation against vagrants and beggars who haunted "the Bancke, and such like naughtie places"; they were to be whipped, or burned, or imprisoned upon a diet of bread and water. But nothing could stop their coming. The pace of enclosures in the countryside left many unemployed and homeless, and the return of soldiers from foreign wars increased that turbulent element. To these were added the native unemployed or unemployable, "maisterless men" as they were called, to denote very firmly the fact that they were not part of the social fabric established upon hierarchy. In 1569 some thousands of "maisterless men" were imprisoned, and in the same year the citizens manned their gates in order to prevent the entry of any groups of beggars; all the barges from Gravesend, and other likely points of departure, were searched. From this period may date the doggerel

Hark hark the dogges do bark
The Beggars are coming to Town!

In a city of wealth, the insurrection of the poor is that which is most feared. In 1581 Elizabeth I was riding by Aldersgate Bars towards the fields of Islington when she was surrounded by a group of sturdy beggars "which gave the queen much disturbance." That evening the Recorder, Fleetwood, scoured the fields and arrested seventy-four of them. Eight years later a band of five hundred beggars threatened to sack Bartholomew Fair; at the same time they held their own fair, Durrest Fair, where stolen goods were sold.

By 1600, it was estimated that there were 12,000 beggars inhabiting the city: a large group of disaffected people who alternately cajoled or threatened the other citizens. One method of assault was the "whining chorus," complete with wooden clappers and doleful songs such as

One small piece of money—
Among us all poor wretches—
Blind and lame!
For His sake that gave all!
Pitiful Worship!
One little doit!

Their technique depended upon their terrible appearance and their whining words.

Yet the city can harbour many forms and many disguises. In the middle of the seventeenth century Thomas Harman observed one vagrant, Genings, who begged about the Temple. He described how "his body lay out bare, a filthy foul cloth he wear on his head, being cut for the purpose, having but a narrow place to put out his face . . . having his face from the eyes downward, all smeared with blood, as though he had new fallen, and had been tormented with his painful pangs, his jerkin being all bewrayed with dirt and mire . . . surely the sight was monstrous and terrible." Harman, suspicious of his manner, hired two boys to watch and follow him; they discovered that after his day's work at the Temple he would return to the fields behind Clement's Inn where he "renewed his stains from a bladder of sheep's blood and daubed fresh mud over his legs and arms." Apprehended by the parish watch, he was found to have a large sum of money on his person; he was forcibly washed and "seen to be a handsome stalwart with a yellow beard and astonishingly fair skin." His genius for disguise served him well, in a city enthralled to spectacle and enamoured by appearances; how else could he make his mark upon the swiftly passing scene without being theatrical to the highest degree?

There emerged beggars who posed as madmen, otherwise known as "lurkers on the Abram sham." They would stand on street corners, showing the mark of Bedlam—ER—upon their arms. "Master, good worship, bestow your reward on a poore man that hath lyen in Bedlam without Bishopsgate three years, four moneths, and nine days. Bestow one piece of your small silver towards his fees, which he is indebted there." They would stick pins and nails into their flesh as a symbol of their lunacy; they would roar imprecations, or speak madly of themselves as "poor Tom." Characteristically they wore the same garment—a jerkin with hanging sleeves—with their hair tangled in knots; they carried with them a stick of ash-wood, with a piece of bacon tied to the end of it. This in turn suggests that their mad medley became something of a theatrical routine, and that their presence on the London streets became an integral part of its scenery of suffering. Yet mingled with them also were the genuinely mad.

It has been supposed that the beggars' brotherhoods of the sixteenth and early seventeenth centuries were quite formal affairs with their own rites of initiation, ceremonies and rules of procedure. Each beggar was given a nickname on joining their fellowship—Great Bull, Madam Wapapace, Hye Shreve and so on—and recited a list of beggar commandments. These included such admonitions as "Thou shalt share all winnings" and "Thou shalt not divulge the secret of the canting tongue." This tongue was not in fact unknown to Londoners, who incorporated some of its terms into Cockney, but it was unique nevertheless. It was composed of various tags and terms from other languages—Welsh, Irish, Dutch, Cockney and Latin among them—so it was in one sense an international argot. In "canting speech" "pannass" was bread and "patrico" a priest, "solomon" an altar and "prat" a buttock. "Chete" was variously applied to different things, so "crashing chetes" were teeth, "grunting chetes" were pigs and "lullaby chetes" were children. Life itself, it might be said, was a chete. The canting tongue was "said to have been invented somewhere about 1530 and its originator to have been hanged."

In all the pamphlets and books of beggars, certain key individuals emerge as types or emblems of beggary. There was London Meg of Westminster who in the early seventeenth century became barmaid of the Eagle Inn, and was very soon notorious as a receiver of stolen goods and "protector of stray vagabonds." She was the first of the "Roaring Girls," one of a number of roistering and redoubtable females who walked a fine line between vagabondage, thievery and thuggery. She was "of quick capacitie, and pleasant disposition, of a liberall heart, and such a one as would be sodainely angry, and soone pleased." She liked nothing better than at night to dress as a man, and wander through the streets of London in search of adventure; she became one of those pure urban types who are filled with the excitement and spirit of the city. The fact of her cross-dressing serves only to emphasise the crude theatricality of her exploits, in a crude and theatrical setting. In her life, however, the emphasis clearly shifts from beggary to criminality. The historians of the subject, led astray by contemporary pamphleteers, often fail to distinguish between vagrants and villains, thus compounding the original misperceptions which labelled every beggar a potential criminal.

The fact that not all beggars were villains, however, is suggested by the available records of the parish registers. "To a poore woman and her children, almost starved . . . For a shroude for Hunter's child, the blind beggar man . . . given to a poore wretch, name forgot . . . to Mr. Hibb's daughter, with childe, and likely to starve . . . to William Burneth in a sellar in Ragged Staff-yard, being poore and verie sicke." On a statistical, as well as a personal, level the poverty and beggary of London "reached crisis proportions" in the 1690s. So the beggars filled the streets. It was no longer a question of "brotherhoods," with sanctuaries in Cold Harbour or Southwark or White Friars, but something altogether more basic and desperate. A seventeenth-century report, *A Discourse of Trade*, noted that the poor were "in a most sad and wretched condition, some famished for want of bread, others starved with cold and nakedness."

It has been suggested that the industrial expansion of the eighteenth century materially helped to lessen the number of beggars; more specifically, in the latter part of the century, changes in parish systems and the diminution of gin-drinking after the 1750s are supposed to have thinned their numbers. But there is no real evidence of this. There was simply a change in the nature of beggary itself. In the sixteenth and early seventeenth centuries the characteristic pattern was of beggars forming crowds, or groups, or settlements. In their place emerged the solitary or individual beggar, of which one fictional example was Moll Flanders. "I dress'd myself like a Beggar Woman, in the coarsest and most despicable Rags I could get, and I walk'd about peering, and peeping into every Door and Window I came near." But Moll learns the lesson which is imparted in time to every beggar, that "this was a Dress that every body was shy, and afraid of; and I thought every body look'd at me, as if they were afraid I should come near them, least I should take something from them, or afraid to come near me, least they should get something from me." What should they get from her? Abuse? Spittle? Or, more likely, disease? Beggars were the representatives of the city's depths and the city's dirt.

So although in the early nineteenth century there were still reports of bands or gangs of beggars roaming within the metropolis, particularly after the ending of the Napoleonic Wars, the general focus of interpretation was upon the individual figure. It is a strange reversal of the dominant mood, when "classes" were emerging from the heterogeneity of eighteenth-century London and when the whole emphasis came to rest upon the "systems" of the city; yet this process itself rendered the individual beggar more isolated and in a literal sense déclassé.

In 1817 J.T. Smith published *Vagabondiana: or, Anecdotes of Mendicant*

Wanderers through the streets of London; with Portraits of the most Remarkable drawn from the life, which emphasised the postures and expressions of the blind and the crippled. One example is that of "A Legless Jewish Mendicant of Petticoat Lane," in which an aged patriarch with a battered hat sits in a kind of wooden cart upon wheels. Behind him is a wall with a graffito of a grinning man, or skeleton. A hundred years before, the hordes of vagrants would have defied individual representation.

Four years later the French painter Théodore Géricault depicted two scenes of poverty and beggary on the streets; it was the year after he had exhibited *The Raft of the Medusa* in the Egyptian Hall off Piccadilly, and all the tenderness of his nature found expression in *Pity the Sorrows of a Poor Old Man whose Trembling Limbs have Born him to Your Door* and *A Paraleytic Woman*. In the first of them the helpless old man leans against a wall; he is accompanied by a dog, with an old twisted rope for a lead. The dog, the "bufe" in beggars' cant, has always been the companion of the London outcast; its presence not only suggests a wandering life, but also marks a type of friendlessness and isolation. The dog is the beggar's only companion in this world of need; it has connotations, too, of blindness and general affliction. In Géricault's second sketch a young mother and child look back at the paralysed old woman, with a gaze both of pity and of apprehension. Once more her solitude is being emphasised, quite different from the solidarity and conviviality of the "beggar brotherhoods." There is another aspect of this isolation, in the sense that no one wishes to come too close. The fear of contagion proves too strong; it is not just the contagion of disease, however, but that of fear and anxiety. What if I were to become like you?

The records of nineteenth-century street-life are filled with memories and recollections of these phantoms. "Perhaps some of my readers," Mayhew once wrote, "may remember having noticed a wretched-looking youth who hung over the words "I AM STARVING" chalked on the footway on the Surrey side of Waterloo Bridge. He lay huddled in a heap, and appeared half-dead with cold and want, his shirtless neck and shoulders being visible through the rents in his thin jean jacket; shoe or stocking he did not wear." The author of *Highways and Byways of London* recalled an old man who had a particular corner along Oxford Street—"feeble, pitiful, wizened, who carried an empty black bag, and stretched it out to me appealingly. The contents, if any, of the black bag I never discovered; but I often gave him a penny, simply because he was so unutterably pathetic. He is gone now, and his place knows him no more. But he always haunts my dreams." There was a crippled beggar who always sat under the picture gallery in Trafalgar Square, his "frail body propped on a padded crutch" and his "lean long fingers fluttering the keys of an old accordion."

Joanna Schopenhauer, the mother of the philosopher, published her account of London in 1816, and left her description of one remarkable beggar who was supposed to be the sister of Mrs. Siddons the actress. She had been brought low by misfortune, and perhaps madness, but was always greeted with a curious reverence on the streets of London where she preferred "to live on the charity of strangers. We often saw this curious apparition. She always wore a black silk hat, which left her face and features clearly visible, a green woollen dress, a large snow-white apron and a kerchief also white." She was supported by two crutches, and never begged or asked for anything, yet still those who passed her felt "obliged, even driven, to give her something." She was a native of the streets, a tutelary presence to which offerings had to be made.

Charles Lamb wrote an essay in the 1820s, entitled "A Complaint of the Decay of Beggars in the Metropolis," which remarked upon one of those sporadic and inconclusive attempts by the civic authorities to "clear the streets"; there have through the centuries been proclamations and policies, but the beggars always return. Lamb in elegiac mood, however, anticipated their passing. "The mendicants of this great city were so many of her sights, her lions. I can no more spare them than I could the cries of London. No corner of the street is complete without them. They are as indispensable as the ballad-singer, and in their picturesque attire as ornamental as the signs of old London." The beggar somehow embodies the city, perhaps because he or she is an eternal type; like the games and songs of children, endlessly recurrent. As Lamb suggests, the beggar "is the only man in the universe who is not obliged to study appearances. The ups and downs of the world concern him no longer." Beyond the fleeting appearances of the world he represents unchanging identity. So beggars became "the standing morals, emblems, mementoes, dial-mottos, the spital sermons, the books for children, the salutary checks and pauses to the high and rushing tide of greasy citizenry—look upon that poor and broken bankrupt there." The example of the bankrupt is apposite; in a city devoted to the pursuit of money there is a dignity to be derived from complete impoverishment, and in his rags the beggar was a standing reproach to those intent upon "appearances."

By the mid-century, when all forms of urban existence were under intense scrutiny, the beggar became the object of research and record. The growth of social control and system in mid-Victorian London, for example, covered the phenomenon of beggary. A "Mendicity Society" was established in Red Lion Square, where all the beggars of the metropolis were classified and described. Charles Dickens was in many respects a generous benefactor to the poor, but he was never slow to "report" an apparently shamming beggar, or begging-letter writer, to the society.

Charles Babbage, the inventor of the Analytic Engine and "father of the computer" as well as the author of *Tables of Logarithms*, made a systematic study of London beggars. He records that, walking home "from the hot rooms of an evening party" he was often followed "through a drizzling rain" by "a half-clad miserable female, with an infant in her arms and sometimes accompanied by another just able to walk" begging for a little charity. He asked for details of their circumstances, and discovered that they lied to him. He was once introduced, in a dense fog, to "a pale emaciated man" who in the words of the owner of a common lodging house "has tasted nothing during the last two days but water from the pump on the opposite side of the street." Babbage gave him some clothes and a little money, and the young man said that he was about to accept a situation "of steward in a small West Indiaman." But again he was lying. "He had been living riotously at some public-house in another quarter, and had been continually drunk." So Charles Babbage brought him before the magistrates. He was remanded for a week, duly lectured and discharged.

What are we to make of these examples of London beggars? They were the outcasts of the city, first seen in drizzling rain or dense fog like exhalations of the lead and stone. They lived upon the margins of existence and, in all cases, seemed doomed to an early death. The stages of emaciation and drunkenness, in the young man, followed quickly upon one another. They were persistent cheats and liars because they had no connection with the ordered and comfortable society which Babbage represented; their reality was so precarious that they had nothing left to lose. They were living in a different state of human existence. Only London could harbour them.

One fear behind these attempts at survey and statistic was that which touched upon the most primitive impulse. What if the beggars were multiplying out of control? "The crop," one late nineteenth-century writer put it, "has kept pace with the increase of the population." That was the great fear, the engendering of a species clinging so closely to London that it could not be distinguished or removed from it. It was also feared that the changes in urban society would reproduce themselves in the nature of beggary itself, so that, as

Blanchard Jerrold put it, "the cheat has developed, the vagrant has become a systematic traveller, the beggar has a hundred stories . . . which the rascal of old could not employ." There were "disaster beggars," for example, which included "shipwrecked mariners, blown up miners, burnt out tradesmen, and lucifer droppers." The unfortunate mariner "is familiar to the London public in connection with rudely executed paintings representing either a ship wreck, or more commonly the destruction of a boat by a whale in the North Seas. This painting they spread upon the pavement, fixing it at the corners, if the day be windy, with stones." There were generally two men in attendance, and in most cases one of them had lost an arm or a leg. Curiously enough, the nineteenth-century handbooks on beggary are very much like their sixteenth-century counterparts; there is the same emphasis upon the dramatic ability of the beggar, together with the repertoire of his or her favourite tricks and dodges. It is almost as if a separate race had indeed perpetuated itself.

Like any native population they had their particular beats or districts, and were identified by such. There were the "Pye street beggars" and the "St. Giles beggars" while individuals did their own particular "runs." "I always keep on this side of Tottenham Court Road," a blind beggar confided to an investigator in the 1850s. "I never go over the road; my dog knows that. I am going down there. That's Chenies-street. Oh, I know where I am; next turning to the right is Alfred-street, the next to the left is Francis-street, and when I get to the end of that the dog will stop." So London can be mapped out through routes of supplication.

The beggars also learned the temperament of their fellow dwellers in the city. The rich and the middle class gave nothing at all, on the assumption that all beggars were impostors; this was of course the theme of official and quasi-official reports, which they willingly and gladly accepted. In a city beginning to be ruled by system, systematic prejudice also emerged. "If the power of reasoning were universally allotted to mankind," wrote John Binny, the author of *Thieves and Swindlers*, "there would be a poor chance for the professional beggar." The more affluent sort of tradesmen were also immune to appeal. But beggars were successful "amongst tradesmen of the middle class, and among the poor working people." Their particular benefactors were the wives of working men, which corresponds to the testimony of others that the London poor were charitable to the poor whose need was greater than their own. It suggests also that, contrary to public opinion, not all beggars were impostors; there were some who summoned up fellow feeling.

By the end of the nineteenth century the beggars complained that their lives and careers were being threatened by the twin forces of the new police and the Mendicity Society, but there is no sure way of discovering whether their numbers were significantly diminished. Certainly contemporary statistics and descriptions would suggest that they were still "swarming," to employ a favourite term, over the metropolis. Indeed it would be sensible to suggest that, the larger the population, the greater the number of beggars.

Memoirs of the early twentieth century do not report bands or troupes of beggars, but specific individuals who customarily made a pretence of selling matches or lozenges as a cover for begging. They were required to own a "hawker's licence," which cost five shillings a year, and then they selected their "patch." One, on the corner of the West End Lane and Finchley Road, used to wind up a gramophone; another used to wander along Corbyn Road with a single box of matches; there was an organ-grinder called "Shorty" who used to "work" Whitechapel and the Commercial Road; there was Mr. Matthewman who used to sit outside Finchley Road Underground Station with a "pedlar's pack" and a tin mug. These are all stray cases, but they impart the flavour of London begging between the wars. The author of *London's Underworld*, Thomas Holmes, remarks: "it is all so pitiful, it is too much for me, for sometimes I feel that I am living with them, tramping with them, sleeping with them, eating with them; I become as one of them." It is the sensation of vertigo, of being drawn to the edge of the precipice in order to throw oneself down. How easy it must be to become one of them, and willingly to go under. This is the other possibility which the city affords. It offers freedom from ordinary cares, and all the evidence suggests that many beggars actually enjoyed their liberty to wander and to watch the world.

The sellers of bootlaces and matches have gone and in their place, in the twenty-first century, have come "the homeless" who sleep in doorways; they carry their blankets with them as a token of their status. Some of them have all the characteristics of their predecessors; they are slow-witted, or drunken, or in some other way disabled from leading an "ordinary" existence. Others are shrewd and quick-witted, and not unwilling to practise the old arts of shamming. But such cases, perhaps, form the minority. Others find that they are genuinely unable to cope with the demands of the city; they fear the world too much, or find it difficult to acquire friends and form relationships. What will the world of London seem to them then? It becomes a place which the dispossessed and homeless of all ages have experienced: a maze of suspicion, aggression and small insults.

The vagrants have always had to accommodate themselves to the hardness and incuriosity of Londoners. In his poem "The Approach to St. Paul's" James Thomson is jostled by anxious crowds whose

> heart and brain
> Were so absorbed in dreams of Mammon-gain
> That they could spare no time to look upon—

To look upon what? Those who had fallen along the way. It happens "only in so large a place as London," Samuel Johnson suggests, "where people are not known."

This unseen world exists still in the early twenty-first century, although it has changed its outward form. The close-packed tenements of Stepney have gone, but the high-rise estates have taken their place. The "hereditary casuals" have been replaced by those seeking "benefit." The shelters of London have become the homes of the dispossessed, marked by what Honor Marshall describes in *Twilight London* as "mental disorder, family disruption, in particular the broken marriage; chronic ill health, recidivism, prostitution, alcoholism." In Wellclose Square there was a mission designed to harbour "the people nobody wants," the rejected and the discarded who would otherwise simply fade into the streets. They fade because nobody sees them. There are certain busy places of London, like the forecourt of Charing Cross Station, where lines of people queue for soup from a Salvation Army mobile canteen; but for the crowds hurrying past them, it is as if they were not there at all. A beggar can lie immobile among happy crowds of people drinking outside a pub, unacknowledged and unregarded. In turn these dispossessed people gradually lose all contact with the external world; and in London it is easier to go under than in any other part of the country. A recent survey of a night shelter in central London, reported in *No Way Home* by S. Randall, revealed that "four fifths of young people . . . were from outside London and most were recent arrivals"; the city is, as ever, voracious. A quarter had been "in care," half had already "slept rough," and nearly three-quarters "did not know where they were going next." They were characteristically in ill health, with inadequate clothing and no money. This night shelter was at Centrepoint, beside the site of the old rookery of St. Giles where previous migrants to London had lived in rags.

CHAPTER 66

They Outvoted Me

L ondon drives some of its citizens mad. A psychiatric survey in the 1970s revealed that cases of depressive illness were three times higher in the East End than in the rest of the country. Schizophrenia was also a common condition.

As early as the fourteenth century the hospital of St. Mary of Bethlem had begun to care for those sick in mind. "Pore naked Bedlam, Tom's a-cold." "God Almighty bless thy five wits—Tom's a-cold!" Their cries might also have been heard in St. Mary, Barking, "a hospital for priests and inhabitants of London, both male and female, who were inflicted with insanity." Yet it is through Bethlem that London has always been associated with insanity. Thomas More asked if the city itself were not a great madhouse, with all its afflicted and distracted, so that Bethlem became the epitome or little world of London. In 1403 the records suggest that there were nine inmates supervised by a master, a porter and his wife, as well as a number of servants. But the number of patients steadily increased. In the *Chronicles of London*, dated 1450, there is a reference to "A Church of Our Lady that is named Bedlam. And in that place be found many men that be fallen out of their wit. And full honestly they be kept in that place; and some be restored unto their wit and health again. And some be abiding therein forever, for they be fallen so much out of themselves that is incurable to man."

Some were allowed to leave the "madman's pound," as it was known, in order to wander the streets as mendicants; a tin badge on the left arm signified their status, and they were variously known as "God's minstrels" or "anticks." There was dread and superstition, as well as pity, surrounding them; in the streets of the city they might be regarded as tokens of the city's madness. They were wandering spirits—sometimes abject and sometimes prophetic, sometimes melancholy and sometimes denunciatory—calling attention to the naked human condition in a city that prided itself upon its artifice and civilisation.

Early sixteenth-century maps show "Bedlame Gate" beside the highway of Bishopsgate. You opened this gate and walked into a courtyard with a number of small stone buildings; here was a church and a garden. There were thirty-one of the insane crowded into a space designed for twenty-four, where "the cryings, screechings, roarings, brawlings, shaking of chains, swearings, frettings, chafings are so many, so hideous, so great; that they are more able to drive a man that hath his wits rather out of them." The usual treatment was the whip and the chain. In an inventory are mentioned "six chains with locks and keys belonging to them, four pairs of iron manacles, five other chains of iron, and two pairs of stocks." Thomas More writes in that century of a man who had "ben put uppe in bedelem, and afterward by betyinge and correccyon gathered hys remembraunce to hym," so it can be assumed that punishment or "correction" was considered efficacious. You had to be brave to be mad.

By the early seventeenth century Bedlam had become the only hospital used for the incarceration of "lunaticks." The preponderance of them were "vagrants, apprentices and servants, with a sprinking of scholars and gentlemen. Of the fifteen vagrants, eleven were women." There were many wandering the streets of London who might be deemed mad, and could be thrown into the compter for the night, but they generally remained at liberty. The large proportion of female vagrants among the inmates of Bedlam, approximately one in three, also throws a suggestive light on the life of the London streets.

One inmate was Lady Eleanor Davis who was confined in the winter of 1636 for proclaiming herself a prophet; she was kept in the steward's house, rather than in the ordinary ward, but she later complained that Bedlam itself was "like hell—such were the blasphemies and the noisome scenes." It was "the house of such restless cursing," and she complained that the steward and his wife abused her when they were "very farre gone in drincke." So Bedlam represented an intensification of the worst aspects of London life. That is why, in the early years of the seventeenth century, it was put on stage. In a number of dramas the madhouse became the scene of violence and intrigue, where the inmates act

> Such antic and such pretty lunacies,
> That spite of sorrow they will make you smile.

These lines are from Thomas Dekker's play of 1604, *The Honest Whore*, which was the first to include scenes within Bedlam itself.

The fact that London contained the only madhouse in the country was in itself suggestive to dramatists. In Webster's *The Duchess of Malfi* madness is associated with various urban professions, such as that of a tailor "crazed i' the brain with the study of new fashions," intimating once more that life in the city can render you insane. It is the most important point of contact between London and lunacy. There was another important association manifested in John Fletcher's *The Pilgrim* of 1621, where the drama is concerned with the mental stability of the keepers rather than the patients. If the custodians and gaolers are mad, then so is the society that bestowed their status and responsibilities upon them.

The old madhouse was, by the middle of the seventeenth century, in such a squalid and ruinous condition that it had become a civic scandal. So in 1673 it was decided that a great modern building, situated in Moorfields, would take its place. Designed upon the model of the Tuileries Palace, and decorated with gardens and columns, it took three years to complete. Above its entry gate the sculptor, Cibber, created two bald-headed and semi-naked figures called "Raving Madness" and "Melancholy Madness"; they became one of the great sights of London, rivalling the fame of those earlier guardians of the city Gog and Magog. From this time forward Bethlem Hospital acquired its true renown; visitors, foreign travellers and writers flocked to its apartments in order to see the mad confined within them. It was of great importance to the city, and to the civic authorities, that lunacy should be seen to be managed and restrained. It was part of the great movement of "reason" after the Great Fire and the plague, when the city itself had become the scene of madness and unreason on an enormous scale. Daniel Defoe had narrated the events of 1665 when so many citizens were "raving and distracted, and oftentime laying violent hands upon themselves, throwing themselves out of their windows, shooting themselves, mothers murdering their own children in their lunacy—some dying of mere grief as a passion, and some of mere fright and surprise without any infection at all, others frightened into despair and melancholy madness." Londoners had a propensity for mania; perhaps that was the condition for their very existence in the city.

Yet, as if to point the moral that lunacy is undignified and absurd, the inmates were on display like so many wild beasts in a zoo; they were ravening creatures that had to be manacled or tied. There were two galleries, one above the other; on each floor a corridor ran along a line of cells, with an iron gate in the middle to divide the males from females. Outside it seemed to be a palace; inside, it closely resembled a prison. The price of admission was a penny and it has been reported that the "distempered fancies of the miserable patients most unaccountably provoked mirth and loud laughter in the unthinking auditors; and the many hideous roarings, and wild motions of others, seemed equally entertaining to them. Nay so shamefully inhuman were some . . . as to provoke the patients into rage to make them sport." This "familiar letter" from Samuel Richardson provides a mid-eighteenth century picture of desolation which is fully documented by other sources.

One other commentator, on witnessing these scenes, remarked "that the maddest people in this kingdom are not *in* but *out* of Bedlam." Here was the most curious thing: the building in Moorfields provoked irrational behaviour in its visitors as well as in its inmates, the whole scene of "wild motions" (which can be deemed to be sexual) and "hideous roarings" creating an unimaginable confusion of types and roles. Prostitutes used to linger in the galleries, looking for custom, on the principle that lustfulness might be excited by the antics of the mad. It was suggested, only half seriously, that another asylum be built to house those who came to mock and make sport of the insane. So it might seem that the contagion of madness spread from Moorfields across the whole city.

Thus, in the literature of the period, "Bedlam" becomes a potent metaphor for all the evils of London. In Pope's verses it casts its shadow over Grub Street, where poverty and lack of accomplishment have driven many mad. Traherne wrote that

The World's one Bedlam, or a greater Cave
Of Mad-men, that do alwaies rave.

John Locke compared temporary madness to being lost in the streets of a strange city, a suggestive analogy which was taken up by many observers of London. In Smollett's *Humphry Clinker*, for example, Matt Bramble remarks of Londoners that "All is tumult and hurry; one would imagine that they were impelled by some disorder of the brain, that will not suffer them to be at rest . . . How can I help supposing they are actually possessed by a spirit, more absurd and pernicious than anything we meet within the precincts of Bedlam?" So the building at Moorfields rears over a city which is infected with the same disorder. The citizens of London live in a state of unnatural energy and uproar; they live in foul houses with no light or air; they are driven by the whip of business and money-making; they are surrounded by all the images of lust and violence. They are living in Bedlam.

By the end of the eighteenth century Bethlem Hospital had acquired its own patina of decay and desolation. In 1799 a commission described it as "dreary, low and melancholy" as if the material fabric had been infected by the melancholy madness of its inhabitants. The neighbourhood was itself suffused with dreariness; the hospital was "surrounded by squalid houses" as well as a number of shops dealing in old furniture. So in 1807 it was agreed that the institution should move across the river to Southwark. The third Bedlam in London's history rose within appropriate surroundings, since Southwark had always been the nursery of prisons and other institutions.

The new building was as grand as its predecessor, with a portico decorated with Ionic columns and surmounted by a great dome. Yet the conditions of the interior were as sparse as before, as if once again the whole purpose of the building was a theatrical display designed to depict the triumph over lunacy in London. The two sculpted giants of madness, known popularly as "the brainless brothers," were kept in the vestibule.

Methods of treatment remained severe, and were largely dependent on mechanical restraint; one patient lay in chains for fourteen years. It was not until the mid-nineteenth century that a more "enlightened" policy was developed; after two inquiries had been severely critical of the hospital regime, a "moral medical" treatment was instituted with the patients being given jobs or occupations as well as medical therapy with drugs such as chloral and digitalis.

It was a world within a world. Its water came from an artesian well within the grounds, so that the patients remained free of the cholera and dysentery which raged around them. And there was a monthly ball, where the patients danced with one another; many observers commented on this moving and somewhat bizarre occasion. Yet still the persistent question about madness remained. Charles Dickens walked past the hospital one night, and was moved to reflect: "Are not all of us outside of this hospital, who dream, more or less in the condition of those inside it every night of our lives?"

The rate of insanity in London had tripled by the middle of the nineteenth century, and other institutions for the mentally ill were established; those of Hanwell and Colney Hatch were perhaps the best known. Bethlem moved to the country, near Beckenham, in 1930, but by that time the capital was well stocked with asylums. These in turn have become known as mental health units or "trusts," where patients are "service users."

In more recent years, too, the mentally ill have been released on medication "into the community." On the streets of London it is not uncommon to see passers-by talking rapidly to themselves and sometimes gesticulating wildly. On most main thoroughfares you will see a lone figure huddled in a posture of despair, or staring vacantly. Occasionally a stranger will shout at, or offer violence to, others. There was once a famous saying of London life,

Go thy way! Let me go mine

to which may be added,

I to rage, and you to dine.

THE MUD-LARK.

[From a Daguerreotype by BEARD.]

An etching of a "mud-lark," one of those small children who searched the banks of the Thames for pieces of coal, wood or metal, which could be sold in the streets. They comprised one of those small communities, separate and apart, which made up the sum of London's heterogeneous life.

CHAPTER 67

The Feminine Principle

It is generally supposed that London is, or was, a male city. Phallic symbols of copper alloy have been found beneath Leadenhall Street and Cheapside, and phallic sculpture in Coleman Street. The great phallus-like erection, Canary Wharf Tower, now dominates all of London; it is also a symbol of successful commercial speculation, thus displaying the twin poles of London's identity. The buildings close to that tower have "wrap-around sheaths" of sandstone, yet another example of the penis in stone. London has always been the capital of masculine fashion, its structures of power characteristically dominated by men. Rivers are normally feminine deities, but London's river is known as "Old Father Thames." Yet there is a strange ambiguity in all this imagery. The Monument rises erect by London Bridge, and upon its base London is depicted as a weeping woman. In its fall, through fire, it changes its gender.

In the early written records women acquire status and identity only through their commercial dealings. The role of medieval London widows, for example, is indicative of a world in which trade, matrimony and piety were thoroughly mingled. On the death of her husband, the widow was allowed a half-share in his goods and, unlike civic law in the rest of the country, was permitted to occupy their joint house until the time of her own death. She could become a freewoman of the city, and was expected to continue her husband's old trade or business. In the fourteenth and fifteenth centuries, the known widows of artisans, for example, all continued with their husbands' businesses. The continuity of trade was important to the civic authorities, but these arrangements also suggest the formidable position which women could assume in the city. They could also join the guilds or fraternities and there is a record, from the fraternity of the Holy Trinity in St. Stephen's, Coleman Street, of a charity box "to whiche box eche brother & sister schal paie eche quarter a peny." There were also rich widows who played a large part in city life, but they were in the minority. In another context there are references in fourteenth-century records to "the female practitioners of surgery." Certainly there were "wise women," who fulfilled a role as doctors within certain London parishes, but we may also find women in the trades of haberdasher and jeweller, spice merchant and confectioner. For every twenty or thirty men paying tax, however, only one woman appears in the fourteenth-century records.

The general images of order and subordination, of decency and seemliness, were of course applied to the women of the city. For many centuries unwed women went bareheaded, while married women wore hats or hoods. Wife-beating was acceptable, while the ducking of "scolding" wives was on occasions deemed a fit punishment. The ecclesiastical authorities often condemned women for wearing red antimony and other "make-up" upon their faces, for curling their hair with tongs of iron, and for wearing finery; they had, as it were, taken on the unnatural colours of the city. In contrast, the presence of the great convents in London, up to the time of the Dissolution, offered an image of women who had retired from the world; theoretically, at least, they were part of the city of God rather than the city of men. A general portrait of London women might, therefore, be constructed along familiar lines as the subordinate elements of a hierarchical and patriarchal society; in a city of power and of business, they retain a supportive invisible presence.

Yet the women of London were also distinguished by other characteristics. The daughters of wealthier households, together with some of those from the merchant class, were sent to elementary schools; we may presume that a significant number of women could read and write, or owned manuscripts, and might deal with the males of the household on terms of practical if not theoretical equality. A study of wills and testaments, *Medieval London Widows, 1300–1500*, edited by C.M. Barron and Anne F. Sutton, describes them as "verbose, bossy, disorganised, affectionate and anecdotal" with a concern for distant relatives and distinct expressions of affection for household servants. They also reveal "networks of female friendships and loyalties" which stretched across London.

Most of the early descriptions of London women, then, suggest that they were very much part of the city. One German traveller of the fifteenth century entered a London tavern and a woman, presumably the landlady, kissed him fully on the lips and murmured: "Whatever you desire, that we will gladly do." This is not quite the docility and propriety expected of women of a patriarchal culture, but it supports evidence from other sources of women who seem to be filled with all the energy and licentiousness of the city.

Representations of women in drama, from the scold to Noah's wife, display characteristics of aggression and violence. As mentioned earlier, in the *Chronicles of London* for 1428, there is recorded the fate of a Breton in London who murdered a widow "an as he wente hys wey where as he hadd i-do this cursed dede, women of the same parissh come owte with stonys and canell dong, and there made an ende of hym in the hyghe strete, so that he wente no ferther notwithstondynge the constables and othere men allso, the wiche hade hyum undir gouernans to condite hym forwarde; ffor ther whas a gret manye of them, and no mercy ne no pity." This scene, which was "without Algate" and thus on the site of the present Whitechapel High Street, is of some interest. A large party of women, aroused by the murder of one of their own, overpower or intimidate a group of men surrounding the murderer; then they stone him to death. This is not a city of order and subordination, but one in which some communal or egalitarian feminine spirit seems to be at work. The women were also without "mercy ne no pity," which in turn suggests that they were in some sense brutalised or rendered callous by their existence in London.

In an early sixteenth-century account it is revealed that "the women have much more liberty than perhaps in any other place." The same foreign observer reports that "they also know well how to make use of it, for they go dressed out in exceedingly fine clothes, and give all attention to their ruffs and stuffs, to such a degree indeed that, as I am informed, many a one does not hesitate to wear velvet in the streets, which is common with them, whilst at home perhaps they have not a piece of dry bread." There was a sixteenth-century proverb that England, for which we may safely substitute London, was hell for horses, purgatory for servants but a paradise for women. One of the central images of the age is that of Dame Alice More berating her husband, Thomas More, for his stupidity in resisting the king's will. Her remarks to him were often sharp and occasionally sarcastic, but he received them cheerfully enough. Perhaps only in London could that intense spirit of equality be sustained.

Of course such treatment was the prerogative of rich or well-connected families; the notions of liberty, on the streets, meant different things. So the same foreign observer suggested that "many witches are found in London, who frequently do much mischief by means of hail and tempest"; he seems here to be invoking an irrational fear of women, a disturbance which the experience of the city itself appears to engender. Records of the seventeenth century suggest that the troubling spirit was not curbed. One stranger to London wrote that he had sometimes met in the streets "a woman carrying a figure of straw representing a man, crowned with very ample horns, preceded by a drum and followed by a mob, making a most grating noise with tongs, grid-irons, frying pans and saucepans. I asked what was the meaning of all this: they told me, that a woman had given her husband a sound beating, for accusing her of making him a cuckold." That example of violence can be followed by another, when "some of our party saw a wicked woman in a rage with an individual supposed to belong to the Spanish embassy. She urged the crowd to mob him, setting the example by belabouring him herself with a cabbage stalk." And, again in another report, "the English seem to fear the company of women." The women of London "are the most dangerous women in the world." This may or may not be accurate, but for all the harshness there was also gaiety. Another traveller noted "what is particularly curious is that the women as well as the men, in fact more often than they, will frequent the taverns or ale-houses for enjoyment. They count it a great honour to be taken there and given wine with sugar to drink: and if one woman only is invited, then she will bring three or four other women along and they gaily toast each other."

There were less happy circumstances. For every engraving of a matron, or merchant's wife, there are pictures of women who are almost literally slaves of the city.

It was the tradition that women sold perishable goods, such as fruit and milk, whereas men customarily sold durable or solid articles; perhaps it was an obscured representation of the fact that, in the city, the women themselves were more perishable. The street-sellers depicted by Marcellus Laroon in the 1680s form a remarkable collection of urban types. A seller of strawberries, wearing a loose hood, looks curiously pensive. A crippled woman selling fish has an unutterably weary face, although Laroon's editor and commentator, Sean Shesgreen, remarks that she is "dressed in an eccentrically stylish way . . . careful and even fastidious about her appearance"; it is a curiously London mixture of theatricality and pathos. The seller of "great Eeles" is lively and more alert, with an expression so quizzical and yet so wary that she might be ready to see, or hear, anything as she made her way through the streets. Single women were certainly vulnerable to every kind of attention and even molestation. The female seller of wax is "a study in melancholy, she wears an impassive almost stupid look and walks with a wooden gait." Her clothes are "tattered and run-down, patched in various places and eaten away at the sleeves." Here is a woman brutalised by the city into a state of indifference and neglect. The seller of apples has a peculiar sneer upon her face, as if demonstrating her contempt either for her customers or for her calling. The "merry Milk Maid" is anything but merry. The female mackerel-seller, an ancient creature with palsied face and puckered eye, is a definite urban type, the image of London marked upon her visage. So too is the seller of cherries whose intelligent expression suggests that she manoeuvres successfully through the streets and markets of London.

Another urban type, endlessly displayed in chapbooks and upon the stage, was the female innkeeper immortalised by Mistress Quickly but endlessly renewed ever since. "At every review in Hyde Park these trollops are certainly in a hackney, will stop the coach to drink pint glasses with 'em at Phillips, yet wonder at the liberties some women take, and tho' they are ready to eat every fellow they see, can't believe any of their sex virtuous but themselves." This is entirely characteristic, and in the writing of the sixteenth and seventeenth centuries there seems to be a consensus that the city tends to harden, or sharpen, female perceptions.

London wreaks transformations—the angry become docile, the querulous resigned—but in terms of women it was generally believed that there was a downward draught. London was not a suitable place for women. Those who made a pact, or compact, with it were regarded as fallen; the earliest actresses upon the stage, for example, were considered as "brazen and tarred." Certainly this was true of Eleanor Gwynn whose "pert vivacity," to use Macaulay's phrase, recommended her to Charles II. She was a genuine London type, "frank, unsentimental," according to the *Dictionary of National Biography*. Her behaviour was considered "unedifying," while her remarks were often "sharp and indecent." "I am the Protestant whore," she once declared and there is a famous scene of her cursing upon the stage at the spectacle of an almost empty house. She was "indiscreet" and "wild," and "her eyes when she laughed became almost invisible." And she, a seller of perishable goods like other women, herself perished young.

Mary Frith, otherwise known as Moll Cutpurse, again became a figure symbolic of London itself; she was born in the Barbican in 1589, and quickly acquired a reputation for violent eccentricity. Her portrait became the frontispiece of Middleton's and Dekker's *The Roaring Girle*, a true story of city life, and depicts her in male clothes complete with pipe and sword. In fact she generally dressed as a man, and was well known for her stentorian voice. In the twenty-first century this might be seen as a token of sexual identity; in fact it was a token of urban identity, her behaviour manifesting one of the most complicated but significant aspects of female life in the city. By dressing in male clothes she understood where the power of London lay; that is why she became more ostensibly masculine than any male. Yet there may be anxiety, or misery, involved in that pursuit. Mary Frith declared that "when viewing the Manners and Customs of the Age, I see myself so wholly distempered, and so estranged from them, as if I had been born and bred in the Antipodes." This strangely reflects the words of Aphra Behn, who died in a garret in 1689 not far from where Mary Frith was born, and who declared that "All my life is nothing but extremes." She is now considered to be a harbinger of feminist consciousness in literature, having written novels, plays, pamphlets and poems on an heroic scale, but, as the *Dictionary of National Biography* suggests, "She attempted to write in a style that would be mistaken for that of a man." Hence she was accused of "uncleanness," "coarseness" and "indecency." But there was no alternative; it was the style of the city. They had to become "unruly women," in the phrase of the period, in order that their identities or gifts might survive.

The fate of ruly women in London did not materially alter during the eighteenth century. They were servants of the city in an almost literal sense, since it has been estimated that approximately one-quarter of all women in work were engaged in domestic service. Others were employed in clothing and in hawking, in shopkeeping or in laundry work. They were overworked and underpaid. There was also a certain pattern to their urban exploitation; as they grew older, they descended still lower into poverty and distress. The city hardened those whom it did not kill. Yet single women, among them widows and deserted wives, still flocked into the city as the only market for their unskilled labour. It is no coincidence that this was also the period of London's great commercial unfolding; as business and industry grew, the male presence of the city was rendered more powerful. So women were commercial objects, wearing such-and-such an amount of material at such-and-such a price, or they were rendered "feminine" and "pretty." The more straightforward and forlorn images of the late seventeenth century give way to idealised representations of the feminine by the middle of the succeeding century. There was a vogue for advice books, beginning in 1750 and reaching its peak in the 1780s, with titles such as *An Unfortunate Mother's Advice to her Absent Daughters* and *An Enquiry into the Duties of the Female Sex*, in which the virtues of humility and obedience are continually encouraged. The purpose was to restrain or curb the natural power or instincts of women, all the more overtly displayed in the city; a distinction was often drawn between the city wife and the country wife, for example, the latter manifesting all the characteristics of docility and faithfulness which the former notably lacks.

During the eighteenth century the prejudice against actresses had faded; they were no longer considered "coarse" or "degraded" but, like Kitty Clive and Mrs. Pritchard, were allowed into the society of men such as Horace Walpole. There were many eminent women throughout the century—Lady Mary Wortley Montagu, Theresa Cornelys, Hannah More and Mary Wollstonecraft among them—but although the pieties of Hannah More raised her above any disapprobation, and indeed she exercised an influence not unlike that of an abbess in early medieval London, the careers of other celebrated women were beset by scandal and obloquy. Walpole wrote of Lady Mary Wortley Montagu, for example, that "she is laughed at by the whole town. Her dress, her avarice, and her impudence must amaze anyone . . . she wears a foul mop, that does not cover her greasy black locks, that hang loose never combed or curled; an old mazarine blue wrapper, that gapes open and discovers a canvas petticoat. Her face swelled violently on one side, and partly covered by white paint, which for cheapness she had brought so coarse that you would not use it to wash a chimney." Mary Wollstonecraft, whose ingenious and suggestive *A Vindication of the Rights of Women* was written in Store Street off the Tottenham Court Road, was disparaged as a blasphemer and a whore; her demands for female equality were dismissed as the tirade of an "amazon," and her life was marked by isolation and unhappiness. As William St. Clair has written in *The Godwins and the Shelleys*, "At the end of the entry [in the *Anti-Jacobin Review*] for 'Mary Wollstonecraft' the reader is cross-referred to 'Prostitution,' but the single entry under that heading is '*see* Mary Wollstonecraft.' "

It will perhaps come as little real surprise that the desire to control women occurred at times of panic and low financial confidence. It ought also to be recalled that there was a sense of impending change and disturbance in the air, and that the first intimations of revolution in France and America threatened the very existence of the state polity or "Old Corruption." Mary Wollstonecraft's *A Vindication of the Rights of Women* was itself an aspect of that fervour, which may explain why females were never more derided than in the latter decades of the eighteenth century. It was another method of urban control.

The women of nineteenth-century London were also marginalised and restricted. They were given roles, in other words, to which they were forced to adapt. The culture of the period is permeated by images of saint and sinner, angel and whore, pure and fallen, but this is only one aspect of a fixed network of expression. Fictional representations, for example, often concentrate upon the innocent fragility of milkmaids or flower-sellers treading the hard streets of the city; yet the obsessive interest in innocence, particularly in the middle decades of the nineteenth century, was based upon the understanding that it would be destroyed. When the narrator of Dickens's *Master Humphrey's Clock* meets the pre-pubescent girl, Little Nell, wandering through the streets of London he is filled with anxieties "of all possible harm that might happen to the child." No Londoner reading this, in 1841, would have the least possible doubt that the most likely harm was that of being literally forced "upon the streets." The trade in child prostitution was thriving. The city of that period had nurtured, if not created, that trade; we might say that it prospered upon it. So all the tears at the death of Little Nell, and all the pity and sympathy at the spectacle of transient innocence, were instigated by a context and by a city which the Victorians themselves created. They wept over young women who were being betrayed by the great metropolis, so in this depiction of innocence there is also a kind of necessary cruelty or hardness. Innocence has to be destroyed if the city itself is to survive and prosper.

London was the arena for "the battle of life" or "the struggle for life," to use two characteristic Victorian expressions, and its women were not soldiers. That is why the role generally imposed upon the middle-class and non-working woman was that of the angel of the hearth, a domestic deity whose role as wife and mother was pre-eminent and inevitable. She tended her husband when he returned home from the battlefield, and protected her children from the depredations of the city. The London house became a zone of privacy and segregation. In Victorian homes the exterior world seems literally to be kept at bay by a whole artillery of protective forces; it was screened by thick curtains and by lace inner curtains, muffled by patterned wallpaper, held off by settees and ottomans and whatnots, mocked by wax fruit and wax candles, the metaphorical and literal darkness of London banished by lamps and chandeliers. This was the home of the feminine principle.

Those who were not protected from the life of the nineteenth-century city were obliged to work very hard in order to survive. They became part of the "sweating" industries, where "sweating" means long days and nights of sewing and stitching in overcrowded attics or small rooms. Many were confined within the drudgery of domestic service, while other categories of employment were cooking and laundering. Some could not withstand the pressures upon them. In the 1884 list of the inmates of Bethlem Hospital for the mad are listed thirty-three servants, seven needlewomen, four milliners and sixty "wives, widows and daughters of tradesmen."

There were other forms of escape. The women of what the Victorians called "the lower classes" were reported to "drink to excess more than men. They take to it largely to carry them through their work . . . The women are worse than the men, but their drinking is largely due to their slavery at the wash tub." Alcohol was the curse of working women precisely because they were consigned to a life of unremitting labour. If the "soakers" smelled of gin or of beer, it was also the smell of the city.

Verlaine wrote of the behaviour of certain girls, perhaps prostitutes, that "you can't imagine what charm there is in the little phrase 'old cunt' addressed every evening to old gentlemen." Swearing and blasphemy were everywhere apparent but, in a thoroughly pagan city, what else was to be expected? Close observers of the streets, such as Charles Dickens and Arthur Morrison, also noticed the propensity of poor women for violent argument and assault. The photographs of females in late nineteenth-century London show them staring suspiciously at the camera. One of the most familiar and suggestive of these images, particularly at the turn of the century, is that of the flower-seller. Instead of the painterly image of innocence and fresh-faced exuberance, no longer to be found on the streets, the photographs show glum and elderly women, each wearing a straw hat or a man's cap, transfixed by a hat-pin, together with a shawl and an apron. They congregated around the fountain of Eros, in Piccadilly Circus, with their baskets of violets and carnations spread around them. They were always known as "flower-girls," never "women," and in that linguistic transference there is contained a great deal of London lore. One observer of the city regarded them as "Cockney vestal virgins," although virgins they probably were not. These female emblems of London, as they soon became, were grouped around the statue of desire; yet they themselves were old and withered. They sold flowers, images of perishable beauty, when they themselves had dropped into the sere leaf of age. This contrast of youth and desire with age and poverty, at the very heart of the city, is a potent reminder of the wastefulness and weariness of urban life. They continued at their post until the early 1940s, before disappearing in one of London's great silent transitions.

Throughout the early decades of the twentieth century the prevailing image of women is still one of work and labour. For every description of glamorous and affluent society women, there are others of the hotel restaurant "slavey," of the shop assistant, of the typing pool. There is a sequence, in a film entitled *Every Day Except Christmas*, of a real character known as "Old Alice," the last of the women porters in Covent Garden Market, pushing a barrow of flowers; the film was made in 1957, which suggests the longevity of certain trades.

Some female occupations were quite new, however, and the period of both world wars fundamentally changed the nature of labour. When the young men were despatched to the trenches and battlefields of the First World War, women were for the first time accepted within previously male reserves. They began to do "war work" in heavy industry, particularly in munitions and in engineering. The number of women employed at Woolwich Arsenal rose from 125 to 28,000, while the old workhouse at Willesden was used as lodgings for the women working at factories in Park Royal. There were female bus- and tube-drivers, with a steady admission of women into clerical or commercial work. Although women were not continually employed in the heavier industries after the First World War, their counterparts in office life remained. This was complemented by another great transition. By the end of the First World War the number of women in their once traditional occupations, dress-making and domestic service, had dropped quickly and significantly. Instead women found work in banking and commerce, local government and retailing, shops and businesses, public administration and the civil service.

. . .

One distinct type had been the "factory girl," whose token moment of emancipation arrived in the summer of 1888 when 1,500 "girls," working in the Bryant & May match factory in Bow, walked out of their jobs in a demand for higher wages; they were to a certain extent organised by the Fabian militant, Annie Besant, and their success had significant consequences. In that year also women were allowed to vote in local London elections, and of course the movement of the suffragettes found its source and purpose in London. For the first time in the city's history, women were able to engage its egalitarian spirit in pursuit of their own interests.

In 1913 Sylvia Pankhurst founded the East London Federation of the Women's Social and Political Union (the WSPU itself was established by her mother ten years earlier); the federation's birthplace was a baker's shop along the Bow Road, not far from the Bryant & May factory. Sylvia wrote later that "I regarded the rousing of the East End as of utmost importance . . . The creation of a woman's movement in that great abyss of poverty would be a call and a rallying cry to the rise of similar movements in all parts of the country." So through the efforts of women London reacquired its destiny as the home of radical dissent; it was a suitable response, kindling a spirit in all those women who had been written off as "soaks" or worse.

The history of the suffragettes connected with Sylvia Pankhurst was associated very closely with that of the East End, and became a genuine expression of the area's concerns. Meetings were held in Poplar, Bromley and Bow; processions began, or ended, in Victoria Park; the printer of suffragette literature was in premises along Roman Road, while the Women's Hall opened on the Old Ford Road. The significance of the topography of the women's movement has never adequately been analysed, but it has become clear that the eastern areas of London lent power and authority to it. During the First World War, a Distress Bureau was opened on the Old Ford Road for women who, with their husbands' income gone, had been threatened with eviction. A co-operative factory, organised by Sylvia Pankhurst, was established in Norman Road with a day nursery within it. A free clinic and nursery was opened on the corner of Old Ford Road and St. Stephen's Road; it had once been a public house, known as the Gunmaker's Arms but was renamed the Mother's Arms. It was this double movement, of caring feminism and the female adoption of male working roles, which steadily advanced the moral and social position of women in the city.

. . .

There are still women wrestlers in Shoreditch; the inmates of Holloway Prison have been characteristically convicted of cruelty to children, prostitution, or drug trafficking. There are still many poor women whom the city has beaten into submission. From the latter half of the twentieth century there are records of hostels and refuges for "sick women and battered women." There is a truth about London here; the pattern of relative misery remains recognisable and unaltered, while surging above it are broad general movements of change. So, for example, the latest statistics suggest that female labour in London has increased by over 6 per cent in the ten years from 1986, while that of men has declined. It is now estimated that 44 per cent of the women in London are in paid employment. So the city has become friendlier to women, and they permeate all of its structures and institutions; there are female taxi-drivers and female executives. Just as the early twenty-first-century city is becoming lighter and more open, so after two thousand years it is discovering its feminine principle.

CHAPTER 68

Boys and Girls Come Out to Play

he history of children in London affords much material for contemplation. Whether in their mortality, in their savagery, or in their instinct for game, the great forces of the city are revealed. The first evidences are brief and elusive: fragments of small leather shoes and slippers, as well as bronze toys and bone whistles. The delight in game, or play, is profound and eternal. The tombstones of children from the Roman era still also survive; one is inscribed to Onesimus, the "helpful" child and "well-deserving" son, and another to "good Dexius, son of Diotimus." The death of children is a constant thread in the history of London. In more than one sense, youth is a stuff which will not endure within the confines of the city.

Deep beneath the level of Poultry has been found the golden statuette of a baby and that small image represents all those ideas of holiness or sacredness which surround the child. There are accounts of children as prophets and visionaries; one young Londoner "was imbued, to the glory of God, with a knowledge which the master had not taught him." We read of another who "had the job, along with two boys from the cathedral school," of guarding the abbey at Westminster. There are accounts of children carrying baskets of sand and gravel to Smithfield in the early twelfth century in order to help Rahere in the building of St. Bartholomew's great church there.

This connection of children with the protection, and even erection, of London's sacred sites is a highly significant one; the city is acquiring the energy and innocence of its children, in an activity not far removed from that of child-sacrifice in the foundations of temples or of bridges. Certainly children were at the centre of civic and ecclesiastical ceremonies. It has been noted that "upon St. Nicholas, St. Katherine, St. Clement and Holy Innocents Day, children were wont to be arrayed in chimers, rockets, surplices, to counterfeit bishops and priests and to be led with songs and dances from house to house, blessing the people." As late as the sixteenth century, just before the Reformation, "a boy habbited like a bishop in *pontificabilis* went abroad in most parts of London, singing after the old fashion." In the Lord Mayor's Show of 1516 the great procession was accompanied by "16 naked boys," and children were an integral feature of all the city and guild pageants that were carried along Cornhill and Cheapside. We may also note here the curious and yet consistent pattern of superstition which surrounded children. During the Commonwealth "the prophesies of children were listened to intently," and astrologers employed children as "scryers" or visionaries. "When a spirit is raised," one book of magic suggests, "none hath power to see it but children of eleven or twelve years of age or such as are true maids." Here the idea of innocence, in a corrupt and corrupting city, is powerfully effective.

The status of the child as a legal and commercial entity was also quickly established. Of William the Conqueror's charter to Londoners in 1066, the second of the three precepts was "I will that every child be heir after his father's death," thus confirming a tradition of primogeniture. A complex system of wardship was also in place, so that there was no possibility that the children of the deceased might be fraudulently deprived of their inheritance. The commercial importance of the child in London is emphasised by the words of an ancient ballad, in which a married couple send their boy "away to fair London, an Apprentice for to find," while the first extant record of a young London apprentice can be dated to 1265. Another commercial activity undertaken by children was that of begging, while children themselves were robbed, kidnapped and murdered for profit. One Alice de Salesbury was condemned to stand in the pillory because "she had taken one Margaret daughter of John Oxwyke, Grocer . . . and had carried her away and stripped her of her clothes that she might not be recognised by her family, that she might go begging with the said Alice, and a gain might be made thereby." This activity of child-stealing continued upon the streets of London well into the nineteenth century, when it was called a "kinching lay"; the children of the affluent were a particular prey since they could be decoyed, and their clothes and jewellery sold. Many of them were killed upon the spot, to prevent their crying out or afterwards identifying their assailants. London could be a perilous place for the young.

William Fitz-Stephen preferred to emphasise the energy and vivacity of the youthful citizens, how they delighted in cockfighting and in "the well-known game of foot-ball" with an inflated pig's bladder used as a ball. On the holy days of summer, the children engaged in leap-frogging, wrestling and "slinging javelins beyond a mark"; in winter, they indulged in snowballing and ice-skating, using the long shin bones of animals rather like the skate-boards of the late twentieth century. Fitz-Stephen is at pains to emphasise the elements of competition and aggression in these games, to complement his description of the valiant spirit which marked out London from other cities. The "lay sons of the citizens rush out of the gate in crowds . . . and there they get up sham fights, and exercise themselves in military combat." Young children were often given bows and arrows with which to practise their skills, since one day they might be required to defend their city. They were already "Londoners," with a strong sense of civic identity and pride. In similar fashion schoolboys were taught how to engage in dispute and rhetorical combat one with another, while "the boys of the different schools wrangle with each other in verse, and contend about the principles of grammar or the rules of the perfect and future tenses." In well-known public areas, such as the churchyard of St. Bartholomew the Great in Smithfield, the children would mount upon makeshift stages and compete in "rhetorical harangues" or recitations. Here lies one of the origins of London drama but aptly, in Fitz-Stephen's account, the elements of combat and aggression are compounded with spectacle and theatricality. In this respect the children of London are faithful images of the city itself.

One fourteenth-century bishop reproved "impudent youths" who scribbled in the margins of books, while Robert Braybroke in his "Letter of Excommunication" on 9 November 1385 complained of boys "good for nothing in their insolence and idleness, instigated by evil minds and busying themselves rather in doing harm than good." They "throw and shoot stones, arrows and different kinds of missiles at the rooks, pigeons, and other birds nesting in the walls and porches of the church. Also they play ball inside and outside the church and engage in other destructive games there, breaking and greatly damaging the glass windows and the stone images of the church."

A baker's boy was carrying a basket of loaves up the Strand; he passed the bishop of Salisbury's palace, and one of the bishop's servants stole a loaf. The boy raised a "hue and cry" and a crowd of children, apprentices and other citizens engaged in what almost became a full-scale riot. Children were, in other words, part of the turbulent life of the turbulent city. The administrative reports of the fourteenth century record "a boy climbing up to a gutter to retrieve his lost ball; of others playing on a heap of timber when one fell and broke his leg; and of another, a schoolboy returning over London Bridge after dinner, who must needs climb out and hang by his hands from a plank on the side of the bridge, and fell in and was drowned." They played "hoodman blind," now known as blind man's buff, and "cobnutte," which is the present game of "conkers."

There were rule-books for schoolboys which by indirection preserve the essence of a London childhood in the medieval city, with injunctions concerning "no running, jumping, chattering, or playing, no carrying of sticks, stones or bows, no tricks upon passers by; no laughing or giggling if anyone were to read or sing *minus bene*, rather less than well." In turn there survive doggerel poems by schoolboys about their masters:

I would my master were an hare . . .
For if he were dead I would not care.

In a city where everyone was competing for notice, the children also clamoured. But they also seemed drawn to the forbidden places of London, as if in defiance against its threat. It is the spirit of impudence, or mockery, which has always been noticeable among London children. In the 1950s and 1960s they played a game called "Last Across" in which they would run across the road in imminent danger of being knocked down by cars. It is a question of meeting, and beating, the city on its own terms.

When the young Thomas More walked in the 1480s from his house in Milk Street to St. Anthony's School in Threadneedle Street, the city pressed upon him in ways which he never forgot. He passed the Standard in Cheapside, for example, where public and bloody executions took place; children were not spared the spectacle of violent death. He passed churches, painted images of the saints, and the "pissing conduit" as well as the stalls of the fishmongers and butchers; he would have seen the beggars, some of his own age, as well as the prostitutes and the thieves or loiterers set up in the stocks. Like an adult he went dressed in doublet and hose because children were not considered "different" from their elders but simply younger versions of the same thing. At school he learned music and grammar, as well as useful proverbial phrases. "O good turne asket another . . . Many handes maken lite werke . . . The more haste, the werse spede." He was also educated in rhetoric, and was one of those children who competitively exercised their talents in St. Bartholomew's Churchyard. But the important point is, simply, that he was being trained for a career in the legal administration of London. It was undoubtedly and principally a civic education; he was taught to celebrate order and harmony, and much of his public career was devoted to introducing that order and harmony within the streets which he had known since childhood. Yet those same streets hardened him, as they hardened all their children. His own writing is filled with their slang and demotic; the hardness and theatricality of his own nature, as well as his wit and aggression, sprang from a characteristic London childhood.

London children, therefore, confronted harsh realities. If they were poor they were put out to hard service, working hours as long as their adult companions, but if they were the offspring of affluent families they were enlisted within the households of richer or more eminent citizens; the young Thomas More, for example, entered the household of the archbishop of Canterbury. It was necessary to work, or be punished. The records of Bridewell show that nearly half of its inmates were boys accused of nothing but vagrancy; they were "packte up and punnyshed alyke in Brydewell with rogues, beggers, strompets and pylfering theves." This harshness is reflected in the commentaries of two Londoners, the late fifteenth-century William Caxton, and the early sixteenth-century Roger Ascham. Caxton complained that "I see that they that ben borne within [the city of London] encrease and prouffyte not lyke theys faders and olders," while Ascham maintained that "Innocence is gone: Bashfulnesse is banished; moch presumption in yougthe." These sentiments might be considered as the perpetual rage of age against youth, in the context of the changing generations, but it is interesting to note that they were made at a time when the city was expanding. Between 1510 and 1580 the population rose from 50,000 to 120,000, and it suffered from an excess of turbulence, unrest and energy; it seems likely that the children embodied that spirit in the most obvious and, to the older citizens, alarming way.

The image of the unruly young apprentice was a potent one within the city, for example, and as a result the civic authorities drew up tightly regulated and organised statutes of labour and discipline. Nothing could be allowed to disrupt commercial harmony. The apprentice was bound "and must obey. Since I have undertook to serve my Maister truly for seven years My duty shall both answer that desire And my Old Maister's profite every way. I prayse that City which made Princes tradesmen." By the latter comment the speaker meant that even those of noble birth could be enrolled as apprentices of a trade. The commercial instinct was very strong. Apprentices were forbidden to muster in the streets, drink in the taverns, or wear striking apparel; they were, in addition, allowed only "closely cropped hair." In a similar spirit it was still the custom for children to kneel before their father to acquire his blessing before proceeding with the day's events. They often dined at a separate, smaller table, and were served after the adults; then they might be questioned about their activities, or their learning at school, or asked to recite a verse or a proverb. Recalcitrant children were often whipped with "the juice of the birch" which is "excellent for such a cure if you apply it but twise or thrice."

The songs, as well as the calls and cries, of children are part of the general sound of the city. "Home againe home againe market is done" must rival for antiquity "On Christmas night I turn the spit" or "Matthew, Mark, Luke and John, bless the bed that I lie on." In 1687 John Aubrey wrote that "Little children have a custome when it rains to sing, or charme away the raine; thus they all join in a chorus and sing thus, 'Raine, raine, go away, come againe a Saterday.' " There are a great many songs and rhymes set specifically in London; this is perhaps not surprising, since the city had the largest congregation of children in the nation and, eventually, in the world. It has been stated by those authorities on childhood matters, Iona and Peter Opie, that most of these rhymes can be dated after 1600; certainly they emanated from London printer-publishers of the period, one of whom was jocularly known as "Bouncing B, Shoe Lane."

But there are more significant urban features of these songs. They emanate from the street cries and ballads of London; their context is that of an oral culture. Some rhymes relate indirectly to wars or to political matters, while others refer to urban events such as an "Ice Fair" upon the Thames, or the burning "of a bridge of London town" in February 1633. Other songs came from the London theatres, such as "There was a jolly miller" and "When I was a little boy, I washed my mammy's dishes." "The house that Jack built" was originally the title of a London pantomime. In fact there were so many pantomimes and harlequinades—*Old Mother Hubbard and her Dog, Harlequin and Little Tom Tucker*, and a host of others—that it could be presumed that Londoners themselves had become like little children.

The printers of Shoe Lane, Paternoster Row and elsewhere issued a stream of story-books and song-books, catching the young with their usual commercial spirit, and again the presence of London filled their pages. "O was an oyster girl, and we went about town," from an eighteenth-century spelling book, is only the plainest of a number of verses or songs which celebrated London trades and tradespeople. There are children's songs on the milkmaids of Islington and the sweeps of Cheapside, as well as the tailors, the bakers and the candlestick-makers. Some of them begin "As I was going o'er London Bridge" as a great metaphor for the highway of life, but of course the most ancient and familiar is the mysterious song

> London Bridge is broken down,
> Broken down, broken down,
> London Bridge is broken down,
> My fair lady.

In its twelve verses it evokes a bridge that is continually being destroyed and rebuilt. Thus "Wood and clay will wash away . . . Bricks and mortar will not stay . . . Iron and steel will bend and bow . . . Silver and gold will be stolen away." Why should such strange sentiments issue from the mouths of London children, unless it be a reference to the ancient belief that only the sacrifice of a child can placate the river and preserve the bridge unnaturally set across it? The Opies themselves suggest that the song "is one of the few, perhaps the only one, in which there is justification for suggesting that it preserves the memory of a dark and terrible rite of past times"; they then describe the connection of child-sacrifice with the building of bridges. So the singing child is alluding to a dreadful destiny within the city, and perhaps there is also an intimation that London itself can only be reared and protected by the sacrifice of children.

There is some element of this fatal relationship in that other great London song, "Oranges and Lemons," where the invocation of old London churches reaches a climactic moment with the lines

> Here comes a candle to light you to bed,
> Here comes a chopper to chop off your head.

Again the origins of this verse are mysterious. It has been suggested that they allude to the journey of a condemned man to the scaffold, when the bells of London rang out to mark the stages of his progress, or that in some way the song commemorates the bloody marital career of Henry VIII. Yet its power resides in its almost magical invocation of sacred places, with their names ringing out like an incantation. "Ring ye Bells at Whitechapple . . . Ring ye Bells Aldgate" as well as those at St. Catherine's, at St. Clement's, at Old Bailey, at Fleetditch, at Stepney and at Paul's. A sacred as well as ferocious city is being invoked. It could be suggested, then, that death was often in the minds of London children.

"Pray, do tell me the time, for I have let my watch run down."
"Why, 'tis half an Hour past Hanging-time, and time to hang again."

In one of those silent patterns of oral mnemonics "hanging" became "kissing," although of course the halter was known as "the kiss" or "the cheat."

The point of rhymes and riddles was to train the perceptions of small children, so that they might learn how to survive in a difficult environment. That is why there is a tradition of sharpness and impertinence among young Londoners. When Winston Churchill met a boy outside Downing Street and asked him to stop whistling, the child replied: "Why should I? You can shut your ears, can't you?" Aubrey and Swift collected examples of wit and sallies from street children, as have other compilers from Dickens and Mayhew to the Opies. The "artful dodger" is perhaps only a slightly dramatised version of any "street-wise" London child, that imp of the perverse who seems somehow to have inherited all the levelling and egalitarian spirit of the city in his or her own small person.

There was a film made just after the Second World War, entitled *Hue and Cry*, in which a boy's quick-witted observations thwart a criminal gang. He is asked, "So you're the boy who sees visions in the streets of London?" It is a question which might have been posed in the early medieval city. In a climactic scene of the same film the criminals are pursued by a gang of children across the bomb-sites and ruined buildings of the Blitz; here again is an eternal image of urban childhood. There are many pictures and descriptions of the London child against a background of flames, of the child carried to safety during the incursions of Boudicca or the depredations of the Great Fire, yet somehow the image of children clambering over ruins is more poignant. Whether it be Saxon children playing among the vestiges of Roman London, or twentieth-century children leaping among the bomb-sites of the Second World War, it summons up associations of eternal renewal and invincible energy which are precisely the characteristics of London itself.

Boys and girls come out to play,
The moon doth shine as bright as day.
Leave your supper and leave your sleep,
And join your playfellows in the street.

This mysterious image of streets filled with play is amplified by Zechariah VIII: 5—"And the streets of the city shall be full of boys and girls playing in the street thereof." Children can be found clustering in certain areas for play, among them Exmouth Market, the Commercial Road, south and east of the Elephant and Castle, along the Goswell Road, and of course the scores of small parks and recreation grounds which echo across the capital. Certain areas seem to draw them towards games, as if the presence of the children will soften them and render them inhabitable. Children, for example, always congregated east of Aldgate Pump.

In 1931 Norman Douglas published a scholarly volume entitled *London Street Games*, perhaps in order to preserve the memory of a world which he sensed to be in some kind of transition. But it is also a vivid memorial to the inventiveness and energy of London children, and an implicit testimony to the streets which harboured and protected their play. There were girls' games such as "Mother I'm Over the Water" or "Turning Mother's Wringer" and skipping-rope games such as "Nebuchadnezzer" and "Over the Moon." Their voices rose to the tapping of their feet upon the pavement.

Charlie Chaplin, meek and mild,
Stole a sixpence from a child,
When the child began to cry,
Charlie Chaplin said goodbye.

The texture of the city itself can create opportunities for play. Marbles were rolled in the gutters, and the paving stones were marked with chalk for a hopping game. Children made use of walls, against which "fag-cards" were flicked in games such as "Nearest the Wall Takes" or "Nearest the Wall Spins Up." It was remarked that these games "make the boys uncommonly nimble with their hands, and this must help them later on, if they go in for certain trades like watch-making." Then there were the "touch" games, one entitled "London." The game of "Follow My Leader" was popular in the streets of London, particularly in the suburbs: it included crossing the road at precarious moments, following the route of railway lines, or knocking upon street-doors. And there was an evening game called "Nicho Midnight" or "Flash Your Light"; as one Cockney boy put it, "You have to play in the dark because torches are no good in the daytime." Street games can be played in the darkness of London because "sport is sweetest when there be no spectators." That is why old tunnels, disused railways lines, dilapidated parks and small cemeteries have become the site of games. It is as if the children are hiding themselves from London. From that secluded vantage, the boisterous may jeer or throw missiles at passing adults, or shout insults such as "I'll punch your teeth in!" An instinctive savagery and aggression often seem to be at work in the city air.

Some of the most poignant memorials of children date from the seventeenth and eighteenth centuries. Carvings of charity children, for example, are still to be seen in Holborn and Westminster. There were statuettes of schoolchildren by St. Mary, Rotherhithe, where a "Free School for eight sons of poor seamen" was established in 1613. Two children of Coade stone were placed outside St. Botolph, Bishopsgate, with badges numbered "25" and "31." Those belonging to St. Bride's School were three feet six inches in height, which is a token of the average size of the London child. There are children in Hatton Garden and Caxton Street and Vintner's Place; some of them wear the costume dating back almost three hundred years, with blue coat and yellow stockings (apparently worn to ward off rats), and are a perpetual reminder of an otherwise forgotten aspect of London childhood. They can be associated with all the other stone or wooden representations of children within the city. The "fat boy" in Giltspur Street, the pannies boy in the Bread Market near St. Paul's, the boys playing a game of marbles above a doorway on Laurence Pountney Hill, the child brandishing a telephone in Temple Place, all are images of the child living within the city but now, as it were, taken out of time. In that sense they embody the eternal nature of childhood itself.

Yet the city of time could still degrade them. A late sixteenth-century writer noted that "manye lytle prettie children, boyes and gyrles, doe wander up and downe in the stretes, loyter in Powles, and lye under hedges and stalles in the nights." In the spring of 1661 Pepys records that "In several places I asked women whether they would sell me their children; that they denied me all, but said they would give me one to keep for them if I would." Samuel Curwen, another seventeenth-century diarist, was walking down Holborn when he noticed a crowd of people around a coach filled with children. They were aged between six and seven, "young sinners who were accustomed to go about in the evenings stealing, filching and purloining whatever they could lay their little dirty claws on, and were going to be consigned into the hands of justice." Most of such children had been abandoned by their masters, or by their parents, to fall upon the mercy of the streets. Benjamin and Grace Collier, as reported in the County Records of the late seventeenth century, "privately made away with their goods and run away, leaving their children destitute." Sara Rainbow served in an alehouse in Long Alley, Little Moorfields, for nine years "with very much hardship and of late a month's causeless imprisonment in Bridewell, and other great cruelties, which she could not endure." In 1676 she ran away, together with her two brothers; one boy sold himself for five shillings to a clipper bound for Barbados, while the other was never seen again.

There are pictures of such children selling, or begging, or stealing, upon the streets, "almost *naked* and in the last degree *miserable*, eaten up with Vermin, and in such nasty Rags, that one could not distinguish by their *Clothes* what *Sex* they were of." Contemporary illustrations verify this unhappy condition. One image of a street child shows him wearing the ragged clothing of an adult with a tattered greatcoat and pitifully torn breeches; his hat and shoes are much too large, and by his side he carries a tin bowl to be used both for drinking and for cooking. He seems to be of no age and of every age, the acquisition of cast-off adult clothing serving to emphasise this ambiguous status. These wandering children are as old, and as young, as the city itself.

The records of parish children in the eighteenth century are filled with images which provoke sorrowful contemplation. Foundling children were often named after the part of London where they were taken up; the registers of Covent Garden parish are replete with names such as Peter Piazza, Mary Piazza and Paul Piazza. The phrase for those dropped or abandoned was "children laid in the streets," which itself is sufficiently evocative. The parish officers were given ten pounds for each child brought into their care, on which occasion there was a feast known as "saddling the spit"; it was assumed "that the child's life would not be long, and therefore the money might be spent on jollification." Once more it is the pagan nature of these urban rituals which requires emphasis. A general opinion prevailed "that a parish child's life is worth no more than eight or nine months purchase," and it seems likely that their deaths were hastened by unnatural means. A parliamentary report of 1716 revealed that "a great many poor infants and exposed bastard children are inhumanly suffered to die by the barbarity of nurses." In one Westminster parish, only one child survived out of five hundred "laid in the streets."

If they lived, the poor children were lodged in the parish workhouses. These were essentially primitive factories where, from seven in the morning until six in the evening, the little inmates were set to work spinning wool or flax and knitting stockings; an hour a day was spent upon the rudiments of learning, and another hour for "dinner and play." These workhouses were generally filthy and overcrowded places. That in the parish of St. Leonard's, Shoreditch, for example, was "obliged to put thirty nine children into three beds." It combined the aspects of both factory and prison, thus confirming its identity as a peculiarly urban institution; many of the children infected one another with "disorders" and contagious diseases, and were then despatched to hospitals. The quartet of London confinement—workhouse, factory, prison and hospital—is complete.

Children were confined precisely because, in their natural and liberated state, they were considered to be wild. They were still "half-naked or in tattered rags, cursing and swearing at one another . . . rolling in the dirt and kennels, or pilfering on the wharfs and keys." These were the "ill natured cattal" with which "our prisons are daily filled and under the weight of which Tyburn does so often groan." Very few social observers chose to discuss whether the conditions of London itself brutalised or dehumanised these small children; the reality was too overwhelming, and too palpable, to elicit any cogent analysis beyond the imagery of bestiality and savagery. Once the vagrant children had been trained to labour in the parish workhouse, for example, they are "as much distinguished from what they were before as is a tamed from a wild beast." But that imagery can be applied elsewhere in the commercial jungle of London. "The master may be a tiger in cruelty, he may beat, abuse, strip naked, starve or do what he will to the poor innocent lad, few people take much notice, and the officers who put him out the least of anybody." The reference here is to the "parish child" being sold off as an apprentice; although that condition has been immortalised in *Oliver Twist* in 1837, the cruelties and hardships associated with this trade in children have a particular eighteenth-century emphasis.

Consider the plight of chimney-sweeps, apprentices known as "climbing boys." They were usually attached to their masters at the age of seven or eight, although it was also common for drunken or impoverished parents to sell children as young as four years old for twenty or thirty shillings. Small size was important, because the flues of London houses were characteristically narrow and twisted so that they became easily choked with soot or otherwise constricted. The young climbing boy was prodded or pushed into these tiny spaces; fearful or recalcitrant children were pricked with pins or scorched with fire, to make them climb more readily. Some died of suffocation, while many suffered a more lingering death from cancer of the scrotum known as "sooty warts." Others grew deformed. A social reformer described a typical climbing boy at the close of his short career. "He is now twelve years of age, a cripple on crutches, hardly three feet seven inches in stature . . . His hair felt like a hog's bristle, and his head like a warm cinder . . . He repeats the Lord's prayer." These children, blackened by the soot and refuse of the city, were rarely, if ever, washed. They were coated in London's colours, an express symbol of the most abject condition to which it could reduce its young. A familiar sight, they wandered about, shouting out in their piping voices "to sweep for the soot, oh!" It was known as "calling the streets."

In the harsh condition of London, however, they were rarely the objects of compassion. Instead, they were condemned as thieves, part-time beggars and "the greatest nursery for Tyburn of any trade in England." Yet in one of those astonishing displays of theatrical ritual, of which the city was always capable, once a year they were allowed to celebrate. On the first of May, they were painted white with meal and hair-powder and as "lilly-whites," to use the contemporaneous expression, they flocked through the streets where they called "weep weep." They also banged their brushes and climbing tools as they paraded through the city. In this reversal we recognise both the hardness and gaiety of London: they had very little to celebrate in their unhappy lives, yet they were allowed to play, and become children again, for one day of the year.

But there are other connotations here, which reach deep into the mystery of childhood in the city. The climbing boys were characteristically dressed in foil, gold leaf and ribbons just as were the children in the pageants of the medieval city; in that sense they came to represent once more holiness and innocence, in however vulgarised a fashion. Yet, banging the instruments of their trade along the thoroughfare, they also become lords of misrule for the day; thus their wildness is being emphasised, itself a threat to the city unless it were formalised and disciplined within ritual patterns. All these elements converge—playfulness, innocence, savagery—to create the child in the city.

Peter Earle, in *A City Full of People*, has noted that early eighteenth-century London "offered many enticements" for young people. In particular the city offered "the lure of bad company, gambling, drink, idleness, petty theft and 'lewd women.' " So London children were, from the beginning, at a disadvantage. In the spirit-shops lurked "children, who drink with so much enjoyment that they find it difficult to walk on going away." In the engravings of Hogarth, too, children are often characterised as malevolent or mischievous tokens of the city; their faces are puckered up in misery or derision, and they tend to mock or imitate the conduct and appearance of their elders. In the fourth plate of *A Rake's Progress* a young boy can be seen sitting in the gutter; he is smoking a small pipe, and reading with attention a newspaper entitled *The Farthing Post*. The sign of White's gambling house can be seen in the distance, down St. James's Street, and in the foreground five other children are engaged with dice and cards. One boy is a bootblack who has literally lost his shirt; another is a seller of spirits, while a third is a newspaper vendor known as a "Mercury." Of nineteenth-century street-boys, too, it was noticed that "gambling was a passion with them, indulged in without let or hindrance." In the early decades of the twentieth century, also, quite young children were still being arrested for street-gambling in games such as "Buttons." So for at least two centuries London children have been associated with, or identified by, gambling. And why should they not be gamblers, faced with the general uncertainty of life in the city? Another boy, away from the foreground in the Hogarth engraving, is stealing a handkerchief from the rake himself. Here in miniature is the image of the eighteenth-century London child, busily engaged in all the adult life and activity of the streets. Their features are also stamped with greed and acquisitiveness, like tutelary spirits of place. In the series of engravings, "Morning," "Noon," "Evening" and "Night," children play a significant role. Some of them wear exactly the same clothes as their elders, so that they have all the appearance of dwarf-like or deformed citizens; others are ragged street urchins, fighting for food in the gutter or huddled together for warmth beneath wooden street stalls.

The ragged children of the streets have a vivid emblematic quality, therefore, but in the photographs of nineteenth-century London they become more recognisable and more sorrowful. These are no longer characters or caricatures, but somehow familiar human faces, soft or plaintive, sorrowful or bewildered. It has been suggested that the philanthropic instinct had changed by the end of the eighteenth century, towards a more benign dispensation, but the actual conditions of London had not altered. "The amount of crime, starvation and nakedness or misery of every sort in the metropolis," Dickens told a journalist in the mid-nineteenth century, "surpasses all understanding." It surpassed understanding because that starvation and misery affected the very youngest and most vulnerable. In 1839 almost half the funerals in London were of children under the age of ten, and it was a pretty

conceit of early photographers to pose small children among the tombstones
of the city graveyards; it represents the brutality of Victorian naïveté.

In another genre of photograph three little girls sit in the street, their feet
in the gutter and their bodies upon the flat stone pavement; one girl looks
round with surprise at the camera, but the most striking impression is of their
dark and faded clothes. It is as if they were mimicking the dark and cracked
stone all around them, so that they might become almost invisible. It is often
forgotten how drab and dirty the Victorian capital was; the thoroughfares
were always filled with litter, and there was a general air of grime and grease.
As Dickens wrote: "How many, who, amidst this compound of sickening
smells, these heaps of filth, these tumbling houses, with all their vile contents,
animate and inanimate, slimily overflowing into the black road, would believe that they breathe this air?"

There is another photograph, of seven little boys who have obviously
been arranged in a tableau by the photographer; but it is a tableau of want. All
of them are barefoot; one child is wearing a battered hat but his trousers are
in rags and falling off at the knee. How they managed to live is something of
a mystery still; they look careworn, but they are not starving. There is a famous picture of a boy selling Bryant & May matches; he holds up a box with
an air of solemn defiance, as if to say—Take it or leave it, I shall survive.

In the early part of the century, Prince Herman Pückler-Muskau saw a
child of eight driving his own vehicle, in the middle of a whirlpool of carriages, and commented that "such a thing . . . can only be seen in England,
where children are independent at eight and hanged at twelve." There is indeed the famous description by a traveller in 1826 of a group of twelve-year-
olds, sitting in the condemned cells in Newgate, "all under the sentence of
death, smoking and playing very merrily together." In 1816 there were 1,500
inmates of London gaols who were under the age of seventeen. "Some were
barely nine or ten," according to the *Chronicles of Newgate*. "Children began
to steal when they could scarcely crawl. Cases were known of infants of
barely six charged in the courts with crimes." Children formed regular gangs,
"each choosing one of their number as captains, and dividing themselves into
reliefs to work certain districts, one by day and by night." Their favourite
tricks were those of picking pockets, or shop-lifting, smash and grab where a
young thief would "starr" a window pane, and robbing drunkards. In this last
occupation, "The girls attacked him, and the boys stripped him of all he had."

The street children of the nineteenth century were known as "little
Arabs," a title that indicated in jingoistic terms their propensity for savagery.

It is perhaps appropriate to note in this context that the recalcitrant children of more affluent families were known as "little radicals," as if to identify the source of social unrest in the energy of the young. Three different books were published in the 1870s and 1890s, each with the title *The Cry of the Children*, confirming the prevalence of that anxious note; it could be interpreted as a cry of battle as much as a cry of woe. Tolstoy visited London in 1860, and remarked that "When I see these dirty tattered children, with their bright eyes and angels' faces, I am filled with apprehension as if I were seeing drowning people. How to save them? Which to save first? That which is drowning is that which is most valuable, the spiritual element in these children." Charles Booth came across a group of "cockney arabs," "small rough-looking children"—"I suggested they would be better at home and in bed at this time of night; to which a girl of about eight (and little at that) replied in saucily precocious style, speaking for herself and a companion, "Garn, we're ahrt wiv ahr blokes; that's my bloke." "Yus," says the other girl, "and that's mine." At this there was a general shout of laughter, and then came a plaintive plea. "Give us a penny, will you, Guv'nor?'"

London children were a paying proposition. "No investment," wrote the author of *The Children of the Poor* in 1892, "gives a better return today on the capital put out than work among the children of the poor." Some young children became "errand boys" or the carriers of beer; others donned a red uniform and were employed to clean up the horse manure in the busy streets. They held horses for those who wished to make a purchase; they carried trunks to and from the railway, or parcels for omnibus passengers; they stood at the doors of theatres and public places ready to call a cab, especially when the night "turned out wet"; and they helped porters whose duties had become too onerous, or cab-men who were befuddled with drink. It is possible to envisage a city of children—the number occupied in street-work was estimated between ten and twenty thousand—watching for work and taking it up with eagerness and alacrity when it was offered. They were the true progeny of London.

Others became street-sellers, and were recognisable figures with nicknames such as the Cocksparrow or the Early Bird. They were envied by "unemployed little ones, who look upon having the charge of a basket of fruit, to be carried in any direction, as a species of independence." This is an interesting vision which these children possessed; to have even the smallest means of earning a living allowed you to become master or mistress of the streets, to wander as you will. Small boys and girls, known as "anybody's children," were hired by costermongers or small tradesmen to sell stock upon commission. Each child would undertake to bring back an amount for the wares he or she had been given, and could keep as "bunse" anything earned beyond that figure. At first light the children would assemble in the various street-markets. A boy would run up to the barrows of costermongers with the plea, "D'you want me, Jack?" or "Want a boy, Bill?" They waited all day to "see if they're wanted" and, if they were fortunate, became the favourites of certain costermongers. A boy was often employed at "crying" the goods which he and his master were pushing in a barrow. This might appear to be a charming custom, except that "we find the natural tone completely annihilated at a very early age, and a harsh, hoarse, guttural, disagreeable mode of speaking acquired." Here the physical effects of living in the city are clearly delineated; London wearied even the voices of the young, and turned high notes into harsh ones.

Another occupation for the children of London was to provide light entertainment for the citizens. Many small boys, for example, used to keep pace with the trams "not merely by using their legs briskly, but by throwing themselves every now and then on their hands and progressing a few steps (so to speak) with their feet in the air." The favourite locale for this energetic activity was Baker Street, where the children cartwheeled "to attract attention and obtain the preference if a job were in prospect; done, too, in hopes of a halfpenny being given the urchin for his agility." This display in the streets is an aspect of theatrical London, too, but the spectacle had its consequences. Mayhew examined the hands of one "urchin" and noticed that "the fleshy parts of the palm were as hard as soling-leather, as hard, indeed, as the soles of the child's feet, for he was bare-footed." So the city hardened its street children in every sense. The unhappy process is complemented by the description of their "stolid and inexpressive" countenances.

When the children worked "on their own hook" there were certain items which they could not sell. No child could master the sale of patent medicines because they did not have the experience to gull the public, nor were they skilful at selling "last dying speeches." More curious, however, is the evident fact that these street juveniles did not sell such childish items as marbles or spinning tops. The reason here may be more profound. Who would wish to purchase items of childhood innocence and play from those who had always been denied such things?

Street children had their penny gaffs, commonly known as "low" theatres, where amateur dramatic representations were performed for an audience which also came from the street. They became a byword for filth and indecency. There were other forms of drama for more affluent London children, however, principal among them the toy theatre. It was sold with characters "penny plain and two pence coloured" which were cut out, pasted on to cardboard, glued to wires or sticks, and then pushed upon a wooden or cardboard stage. Play-acting was essentially a London pastime crucially combining the tradition of the caricature or satirical print, to be seen in the windows of every print-seller, with that of the London drama or pantomime.

The earliest of these childhood spectacles was manufactured in 1811, and they soon became immensely popular. When George Cruikshank was dilatory in their publication "the boys used to go into his shop and abuse him like anything for his frequent delays in publishing continuations of his plays." The toy theatre was part of the history of London spectacle, in other words, emerging from the gothic and the phantasmagoric. It imitated the humour and heterogeneity of the London stage, also, with burlesques and buffooneries: *The Sorrows of Werther* became *The Sorrows of Water, or Love, Liquor and Lunacy*.

It was a city of melodrama in many respects, where the young loved to act and to recite. One of the daily reading lessons at London schools was taken from the drama, and there was a perfect "itch for acting" among the young boys and girls. In *Vanity Fair* (1847–8) Thackeray depicts two London boys as having a pronounced "taste for painting theatrical characters." Another Londoner, writing of the early 1830s, stated that "nearly every boy had a toy theatre."

There is a picture, composed in 1898, of "Punch By Night" which depicts a group of tiny children looking up in wonder at a Punch and Judy booth illuminated by oil-light. Some are barefoot, and some in rags, but as they stand on the rough stones their eager attentive faces are bathed in light; yet it may be that the illumination is emerging from them on this dark London night. A similar sense of the numinous emerges in descriptions of children at play in the streets of the city. Theodore Fontane, the German author, wrote of spring in the rookeries of St. Giles when "The children have taken their one, pitiful toy, a home-made shuttlecock, into the street with them and while, wherever we look, everything is teeming with hundred of these pale children grown old before their time with their bright, dark eyes, their shuttlecocks fly up and down in the air, gleaming like a swarm of pigeons on whose white wings the sunlight falls." There is a sense of wonder, and mystery, vouchsafed in the

wave of happiness and laughter emerging from the foul and squalid tenements of the poor. It is not a question of innocence contrasted with experience, because these children were not innocent, but somehow a triumph
of the human imagination over the city. Even in the midst of filth, they have
the need and the right to be joyful.

That sense, that human aspiration, is also present in the many descriptions of children dancing in the street. In A.T. Camden Pratt's *Unknown
London* there is an account of Holywell Street in the late nineteenth century
with "the curious sight of the children in lines across the roadway at either
end of the row, dancing to the music of a barrel organ that never seems to go
away ... It is noticeable that they all dance the same simple step; but the grace
of some of these unkempt girls is remarkable." It is as if it were some ritual
dance, the dance of the city, to a music that never seems to fade. Evelyn
Sharp, in *The London Child*, records how "sometimes, they danced in unison,
sometimes as a kind of chorus to a little *première danseuse* in whirling pinafore
and bare feet; and always they betrayed their kinship with the motley crowd
that dances in wild abandonment to the jingle of the street organ." Once more
the street organ betrays its persistent presence, as if it were the music of the
stones, but the simple ritualised step of the children has made way for wildness and "abandonment"; they are giving themselves up to forgetfulness and
oblivion because in the savage dance they can ignore the conditions of their
ordinary existence. Implicitly they are defying the city. If we can dance like
this, what harm can you do us?

A poem of 1894 depicts "a City child, half-girl, half elf . . . babbling to
herself" while playing hopscotch on the steps of St. Paul's Cathedral.
London "roars in vain" to catch "her inattentive ear" and she does not bestow
one glance upon the great church rising above her. Here the dignity and self-
sufficiency of the "City child" are being celebrated, quite removed from all
the demonstrations of power and business around her. She would appear to
have been created out of the very conditions of the streets, and yet there is
something within her which is able to ignore them. It is a mystery vouchsafed
to the late nineteenth-century poet Laurence Binyon, who depicts two
children in an alley once more dancing to the sound of a barrel organ—"face
to face" they gaze at each other, "their eyes shining, grave with a perfect pleasure." Their mutual enjoyment and understanding rise above the sordid
material world that surrounds them. In George Gissing's novel *Thyrza*
(1887), Gilbert Grail turns into Lambeth Walk and as "he did so, a street organ began to play in front of a public house close by. Grail drew near; there

were children forming a dance, and he stood to watch them. Do you know that music of obscure ways, to which children dance . . . a pathos of which you did not dream will touch you, and therein the secret of hidden London will be revealed." It is the great secret of those who once existed in the dark heart of the city. It is defiance, and forgetfulness, compounded. It is the London dance.

Lambeth is now, like much of London, quieter than once it was. There seem to be no children on the streets, but a small green named Pedler's Park in Salamanca Street has been classified as a "children's play area"; where once all London was a "play area" now zones have been segregated for that purpose. Lambeth Walk, once the centre of Old Lambeth, is now pedestrianised with three-storey council houses of dark brick along it. It leads to a shopping mall, albeit a dilapidated one, down which staggers a drunken man cursing to himself; shops are boarded up, and some are derelict. But above the mall itself have been painted murals of children. One shows Lambeth Ragged School, in Newport Street, and is dated 1851. Another is of children, with their legs bare, exuberantly dancing after a watering cart; the image is taken from a photograph by William Whiffin, dated *c.* 1910, which showed some small boys playing in the spray. And then suddenly, on 1 July 1999, four young girls bring out a skipping rope and begin to play in the middle of Lambeth Walk.

Continuities

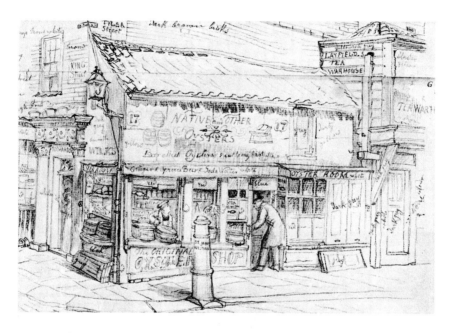

George Scharf's drawing of "The Original Oyster Shop" in
Tyler Street; the shop itself has gone but all the buildings on the
same site have followed its contours.

CHAPTER 69

Have You Got the Time?

The nature of time in London is mysterious. It seems not to be running continuously in one direction, but to fall backwards and to retire; it does not so much resemble a stream or river as a lava flow from some unknown source of fire. Sometimes it moves steadily forward, before springing or leaping out; sometimes it slows down and, on occasions, it drifts and begins to stop altogether. There are some places in London where you would be forgiven for thinking that time has come to an end.

In medieval documents ancient London customs were declared to be "from time out of mind, about which contrary human memory does not exist"; or an object might be classified as standing "where it now stands for a longer time than any of the jurors can themselves recall." These were ritualised, or standardised, phrases suggesting that the earliest measure of time was human memory itself. In an anonymous medieval poem on the life of St. Erkenwald there are verses which concern the masons rebuilding St. Paul's Cathedral in the fourteenth century; they discover a great tomb within the ancient foundations of the church, in which rests the unblemished corpse of a pagan judge who speaks thus: "How long I have lain here is from a time forgotten. It is too much for any man to give it a length," although even in that distant period London was "the metropolis and the master town it evermore has been." The corpse is baptised, its soul saved, and at the close "all the bells of London rang loudly together."

Beyond the time measured by human memory there exists, therefore, sacred time invoked by the sound of these bells. The visions of Our Lady in the church of St. Bartholomew, or the miracles surrounding the shrine of Our Lady of Willesden, suggest that London was also the harbour of eternity. The bells provided that sonority where sacred and secular time met. Yet for many centuries a form of communal memory was also commonplace—"In the great hard frost . . . in the late dreadful storme . . . ever since the sicknesse yeare . . . two or three dayes after the great high wind"—when the events of London mark out an imprecise but useful chronology. Public gatherings also measured London time, in "sermon time" or "at Exchange time when the merchants meet at the Royal Exchange." There was a human scale, also, in the measurement of light and shadow in the city as an index of time: "about candlelighting in the evening" or "when it was duskish."

The spirit of the city lives, too, in the emblems which adorn it. There were four "wall dials" in the Inner Temple, one of which bore the inscription "Begone About Your Business," which is a true London apothegm. On the sundial in Pump Court are etched the words, "Shadows we are and like Shadows Depart," and in Lincoln's Inn two emblems of sacred time were installed. On the southern gable of the Old Buildings was the motto *Ex Hoc Momento Pendet Aeternitas*, or "On This Moment Hangs Eternity," and, beside it, *Qua Redit Nescitis Horam* or "We Do Not Know the Hour of his Return." These emblems are the written equivalent of the church bells, resounding through the streets of the city. In the Middle Temple another sundial reasserts the actual nature of London with complementary mottoes. *Time and Tide Tarry For No Man* and *Vestigia Nulla Retrorsum* or "No Moment Is Backward." So even the sun, and the light, are mastered by the urgent rhythm of city activity.

In this context the dominance of clock time in the city can be understood. Wren's London churches have clocks designed within them; no doubt the dials are a substitute for the bells which once rang out, but there is also a suggestion that time itself has somehow become a deity to be venerated. When in the early eighteenth century Bennett's Clock Shop, at 65 Cheapside, set up images of Gog and Magog above its frontage the shop's owner was expressing a general truth; these tutelary deities of London were used to strike the hour, confirming the identity of time and the city. For a city based upon work and labour, upon power and commerce, time becomes an aspect of mercantilism.

That is why the city became famous for its clocks, from that upon St. Paul's to that of "Big Ben" on St. Stephen's tower at Westminster, and renowned for its clock-makers. Artificers such as Charles Gretton and Joseph Antram of Fleet Street, John Joseph Merlin of Hanover Place and Christopher Pinchbeck of St. John's Lane, were often visited by foreign travellers and were themselves notable London figures; Pinchbeck opened a clock-making and clock-work gallery to display his skills, while Merlin had his own Mechanical Museum. The measurement of time, and the ingenuity of its artificial instruments, fascinated Londoners; in a city always moving and always making, the attention to the process of measuring was also an attention to its own energy and greatness. That is why London also became the world centre of watch-making. By the end of the eighteenth century, for example, there were more than seven thousand workmen in Clerkenwell assembling watches at a rate of 120,000 a year, 60 per cent of which were exported. It is almost as if London was manufacturing time itself, and then distributing it to the rest of the world. The nature of its manufacture, with different artisans in different districts making one small part of the assembly, means that Clerkenwell itself could be seen as a clockwork mechanism with its face to the sky.

The position of Greenwich upon the meridian is well known but on this famous site was also erected the time signal ball, a wood or leather sphere five feet in diameter, which was raised and dropped by a galvanic motor clock; this device was considered to be "the most wonderful clock in the world" regulating "the time of all the clocks and watches in London." In particular "a very small outlay . . . will secure true Greenwich time to every City establishment." So time and trade ran together. Another great clock was established at the post office of St. Martin's le Grand in the 1870s; it was known as the "chronopher" and by means of a "time current" running along the electric telegraph it controlled the time of "sixteen of the most important cities in the kingdom." London set up and dominated the time of the entire country. With the central position of Greenwich, it might even be said to have controlled the time of the world. There was also the phenomenon of "railway time," so that the locomotives speeding out of London set the time for the provincial stations through which they passed.

In twenty-first-century London too, time rushes forward and is everywhere apparent; it hangs upon neon boards, and is illuminated on the front of office buildings. Clocks are everywhere, and most citizens have the image of time strapped to their wrists. It might even be suggested that the general and characteristic obsession of London is with time itself. That is why all of its commercial operations are designed to be conducted and monitored in the shortest possible time, just as information is only important when it is of instantaneous access. The faster an action or a dealing can be reported, the more significance it acquires. The affluent Londoners of the fourteenth century who first displayed the counterpoise clock in their households were at the beginning of a process in which London would capture and market time. The city oppresses its inhabitants, and the evidence of that oppression can be found in the time it imposes; there is a time for eating, a time for working, a time for travelling to work, a time for sleeping. It represents the great triumph of materialism and commerce within the city.

The consequences emerge in the activity and imagery of London over a long period. One eighteenth-century observer remarked that in London they "talk little, I suppose, that they may not lose time." Similarly there is no bargaining, and the custom of having fixed prices "is not the product solely of competition and confidence, but also of the necessity of saving time." It has often been noted how quickly Londoners walk. If there is a cause for this anxious speed it may lie in the deeply inherited instinct that time is also money.

There is an old London inscription: "As every thread of Gold is valuable / So is every minute of Time." Time must not be "wasted." Chateaubriand noticed that Londoners were impervious to art and general culture precisely because of this obsession; "they chase away the thought of Raphael as liable to make them *lose time* and nothing more." Significantly he associates this with the need to work; they are "for ever on the brink of the abyss of starvation if for a moment they forget work." Time and work are indeed intimately mingled within the consciousness of London; they cannot be separated, not even for a moment, and out of this conflation emerges frantic and continuous activity. Like automata, the citizens become the components of the monstrous clock that is London. Then time indeed becomes a prison. A riddle in a London chapbook asked the question, What am I?

Close in a cage a bird I'll keep
That sings both day and night,
When other birds are fast asleep,
Its notes yield sweet delight.

And the answer? "I am a clock." Even the gallows was wreathed with the implication of time. One victim of the rope declared in his last speech: "Men,

Women, and Children, I come hither to hang like a Pendulum to a Watch, for endeavouring to be Rich too Soon." The clock of Holy Sepulchre, Newgate, in turn regulated the times of hanging.

It is of course possible to control time; Ned Ward noticed an assistant, in an early seventeenth-century "Musick-shop," "beating Time upon his Counter" while his customers danced to the sound of pipes and fiddles. This is an ancient yet still familiar scene, of course, and suggests that the permanent refuge of Londoners from the claims of clock-time may lie in song and dance; that is one way, at least, to "beat Time." And there are also places where time may cease to exist. Among the prison inmates of London, for example, "day after day rolled on, but their state was immutable . . . every moment was a moment of anguish, yet did they wish to prolong that moment, fearful that the coming period would bring a severer fate." During the Second World War, Harold Nicolson noted, "one lives in the present. The past is too sad a recollection and the future too sad a despair. I go up to London. After dinner I walk back to the Temple." He is walking through a timeless city, abandoned to darkness during the black-out, and there are still areas of London where time seems to have come to an end or ceaselessly to repeat itself.

The phenomenon can be particularly noted in Spitalfields, where the passing generations have inhabited the same buildings and pursued the same activities of weaving and dyeing. It may be noticed that by the market of Spitalfields archaeologists have recovered successive levels of human activity dating back to the time of the Roman occupation.

But time also moves slowly in Shoreditch and Limehouse; these areas have acquired a finality, in which nothing new seems able to prosper. The time of Cheapside and Stoke Newington is rapid and continuous, whereas that of Holborn and Kensington is fitful. Jonathan Raban, in *Soft City*, has noted that "Time in Earl's Court is quite different from time in Islington," by which he is suggesting that the rhythms imposed upon the inhabitants of these areas are particular and identifiable. There are streets in which the presence of old time is familiar; the area of Clerkenwell, and the passages off Maiden Lane, are notable in that respect. But there are other places, such as Tottenham Court Road and Long Acre, which seem to exist in a continual state of novelty and unfamiliarity.

There are also forms of timelessness. Neither vagrants nor children are on the same journey as those whom they pass on the crowded thoroughfares.

CHAPTER 70

The Tree on the Corner

꙰

onsider the plane tree at the corner of Wood Street and Cheapside. No one knows how long it has existed on that spot—once the old churchyard of St. Peter's, which was destroyed during the Great Fire of 1666—but in extant documents it is termed "ancient," and for centuries it has been a familiar presence. In 1799, for example, the sight of this tree in the centre of London inspired Wordsworth to compose a poem in which the natural world breaks through Cheapside in visionary splendour:

> At the corner of Wood Street, when daylight appears,
> Hangs a Thrush that sings loud, it has sung for three years:
> Poor Susan has pass'd by the spot, and has heard
> In the silence of morning the song of the Bird.

Then enchantment holds her, and she witnesses

> A mountain ascending, a vision of trees;
> Bright volumes of vapour through Lothbury glide,
> And a river flows on through the vale of Cheapside.

This might be construed as an example of Wordsworth's disenchantment with the city, and his wish to obliterate it in the interests of "nature," but it might also represent his vision of a primeval past. The tree conjures up images of its distant predecessors. Everything about this corner of Wood Street suggests continuity. Even its name is connected with the tree; wood was indeed once sold here, but the tree itself is protected and can never be cut down. In the spring of 1850 rooks came to rest in its branches, re-establishing the ancient association between London and those dark birds. The London plane flourishes in the smoke and dust of London, and the tree at the corner of Wood Street has become an emblem of the city itself. It has now reached a height of approximately seventy feet, and is still thriving.

Beneath it nestle the small shops which have been an aspect of this corner for almost six hundred years. In 1401 a shop known as the Long Shop was first built here against the churchyard wall, and others followed; after the Fire, they were rebuilt in 1687. The site is only a few feet in depth, and each small shop still consists of a single storey above and a box-front below. The trades which have passed through them were various—silver-sellers, wig-makers, law stationers, pickle- and sauce-sellers, fruiterers—all of them reflecting the commercial life of the capital. Appearances may change, but form remains constant. In more recent years there was a shirt-maker and a music warehouse, a sweet-shop and a gown-maker. A florist, Carrie Miller, who was born in St. Pancras, and had never left London, was interviewed here in the years immediately following the Second World War: "I was fortunate enough to find this little shop under the famous tree in Wood Street. Before I came it was a toy shop. The City is in my blood now. I would not be anywhere else in the whole world." So this tiny spot, this corner, provides evidence of continuity on every level, human, social, natural, communal. There exists on the site today a shirt-maker's, L. and R. Woodersen, which advertises itself as "under the tree," a newsagent's with the shop sign "Time Out. London's Living Guide," and a sandwich bar called "Fresh Options."

Such lines of continuity are to be found everywhere within London, some of great antiquity. The fact that Heathrow Airport is built upon the site of an Iron Age camp is suggestive, with the evidence of a neolithic track or *cursus* extending two miles on the western side of the "runways" of the present airport. The original Roman street pattern of London has survived, unchanged, in certain parts of the city; Cheapside, Eastcheap and Cripplegate still follow the ancient lines. In Milk Street and Ironmonger Lane, seven successive waves of building have employed exactly the same sites, despite the fact that during this period the street-level itself rose some three feet three inches.

There is a spiritual, as well as a physical, continuity. One historian of the parish of St. Andrew, Holborn, C.M. Barron, has noticed that "along the Roman road leading westwards from Newgate there was a kind of funerary ribbon development," which in turn coincides with the fatal route taken by the condemned from Newgate to Tyburn; the line of death seems to have been prepared in advance. In a similar spirit we may note that at the same church of St. Andrew, there is evidence of pagan cremation burials, Roman sepulchral building and remnants of early Christian worship; the layers of sacred activity radiate from one to another within what is undoubtedly an holy area. An archaeological investigation of the graveyard of St. Katherine Cree, between Leadenhall Street and Mitre Street, offers interesting evidence of continuous occupation. Here were a series of "patchy Roman surfaces," according to the *London Archaeologist*, into which were cut "burials in stone and mortar cists, probably a continuation of the late Saxon graveyard excavated to the east . . . The area continued to be used as a graveyard to the present day, with burials being made in wooden and lead coffins and the ground level rising steadily."

Londoners seem instinctively aware that certain areas have retained characteristics or powers. Continuity itself may represent the greatest power of all. The coinage of early tribes in the area of London, particularly that of the Iceni, carried the image of a griffin. The present City of London uses the same miserly and rapacious birds as its emblem. More than two thousand years after their appearance, the griffins still guard the boundaries of the City.

Within that City, the administrative network of the wards is of ancient date; these units of local government can be traced back to the early ninth century, and their exact alignments are still employed at the beginning of the twenty-first century. This is perhaps so familiar a concept that its striking singularity is often missed. There is no other city on earth which manifests such political and administrative continuity; its uniqueness is one of the tangible and physical factors that render London a place of echoes and shadows.

The texture of the city is also remarkably consistent. Peter's Hill and Upper Thames Street were laid out in the twelfth century. Other street-surfaces and frontages have a similar history, with property divisions remaining intact for many hundreds of years. Even the devastation of the Great Fire could not erase the ancient lanes and boundaries. In a similar pattern of continuity those streets which were newly laid out after the Fire also showed tenacity of purpose. Ironmonger Lane, for example, has had the same width for almost 335 years. That width was and is fourteen feet, originally sufficient to allow two carts to pass each other without hindrance or blockage. It is another aspect of this continuous London history that its structure can accommodate itself to quite different modes of transport.

When George Scharf drew an early nineteenth-century oyster-shop on the corner of Tyler Street and King Street, just east of Regent Street, its shallowness was explained by Scharf's latest editor, Peter Jackson—"all the houses on the north side of Tyler Street followed a medieval building line which ran at an angle making them progressively shallower." The streets have been renamed as Foubert's Place and Kingly Street but even now "the building on this spot still has the same proportions."

An even more remarkable physical token of the past lies a little further west in Park Lane. The lower end of that street, from Wood's Mews down to Stanhope Gate, is marked by irregularity; the streets are set back a few feet from each other, so that the "front" is never in a straight line. This is not an accidental or architectural arrangement, however, since the "map or plott of the Lordship of Eburie" reveals that those streets were in fact laid down upon the pattern of the old acre strips of the farmland which once covered the site. These acre strips belonged to the village community system of the Saxon period, and the irregularity of Park Lane is a token of their continuing presence and influence. Just as the Saxon wards maintain their energy and power within the city, so the Saxon farming system has helped to create the structure and topography of the modern city. In similar fashion the curve of West Street, where the Ivy restaurant is now situated, exactly imitates the curve of the country lane which once existed there.

A sixteenth-century surveyor named Tiswell drew up a map of the land which is now occupied by the West End. At that time it consisted of farmland with lanes winding between the villages of St. Giles and Charing. Yet a modern map superimposed upon the Elizabethan plan coincides with its principal thoroughfares and most notable topographical features. It may be a cause of surprise, but it should be one of wonder. Once the city is seen in this light, then it begins to reveal its mysteries. The persistent echoic effect can be recognised everywhere. Thus one of the great twentieth-century writers upon London, Steen Eiler Rasmussen, has noted of standard London dwellings in *London: The Unique City* that the "little house, of which there have been thousands and thousands, is only sixteen feet broad. It has probably been the ordinary size of a site since the Middle Ages." He adds that "the uniformity of the houses is a matter of course, and has not been forced upon them." These houses emerge as a matter of instinct, therefore, deriving from some ancient imperative; it is as if they were similar to the cells that cluster in a human body. When in 1580 Elizabeth I declared by edict that one house should belong to one family, she was giving expression to another great truth about London life; and, as Rasmussen suggests, her proclamation or programme "has been repeated over and over again through the centuries." The names of the streets, in which many of these houses are to be found, also prove to be of ancient provenance. In similar fashion the squares of London can be associated with the courtyards of the medieval city. The so-called "ribbon development" along the Western Avenue in the 1930s obeys the same process of growth as the ribbon development along Whitechapel High Street in the 1530s. The passage of four hundred years means very little in the workings of London's inexorable laws.

A recent study of London demography, *London: a New Metropolitan Geography* by K. Hoggart and D.R. Green, concluded that "several of London's population characteristics have been present for five hundred years or more," among them the creation of suburbs, the "over-representation of adolescents and young adults" as well as "the presence of a marginalised and destitute under-class" and "the exceptional representation of overseas migrants, and religious, cultural and ethnic minorities." Any slice or slide of London life, in other words, would broadly mirror that of previous and succeeding centuries. There has been no fundamental change.

The work of London is also consistent. The preponderance of finishing trades and what have become known as the service industries affords one example, while another continuity is to be found in the reliance upon small workshop, rather than factory, production. In the fifteenth and sixteenth centuries aldermen complained about lack of public money; the complaint has been repeated in almost every decade of every century. Stephen Inwood, in *A History of London*, has remarked that "For a city that is the home of national government, London has often been a surprisingly poorly governed place." Perhaps it is not a surprise, after all; it may be part of its nature and organic being.

These are all large concerns with which to demonstrate the essential continuities of the city's life. But they can also be glimpsed in local and specific ways, where a stray object or perception can suddenly manifest the deep history of London being. It was in the early fifteenth century that Richard Whittington built near the mouth of the Walbrook in the Vintry the huge public privy that was known as "Whittington's Longhouse." John Schofield, in *The Building of London*, has noted that "centuries later the offices of the Public Cleansing Department now cover the site."

In Endell Street there was once found an "ancient bath" of unknown date "fed by a fine spring of clear water, which was said to have medicinal qualities." In the nineteenth century the lower parts of the bath-house were filled with lumber and rubbish so that "the spring no longer flows." But it did not disappear; it simply emerged in different form. There is a sauna in Endell Street, and on the corner a public swimming bath known as "The Oasis."

The site of the curative wells in Barnet, where people gathered for healing in the seventeenth century, is now occupied by a hospital. At the foot of Highgate Hill, where it inclines gently into Holloway, a great lazarhouse or leper hospital was established in the 1470s. It had fallen into decay by the middle of the seventeenth century. But the spirit of the place was not diminished. In 1860 the Small Pox and Vaccination Hospital was erected there. The site is now the Whittington Hospital. Almshouses for the frail or feeble were erected in Liquorpond Field; the Royal Free Hospital now covers the area. There was an old poorhouse on Chislehurst Common, erected in 1759; it is now the site of St. Michael's Orphanage.

Once a famous maypole was set up at the crossing of Leadenhall Street and Gracechurch Street; it towered above the city, and in the fifteenth century the church of St. Andrew Cornhill was rededicated as St. Andrew Undershaft because it was, physically, under the shaft. The great maypole itself was stored along the side of Shaft Alley. This might seem an exercise in medieval nostalgia, were it not for the fact that on this very same spot now rises the tall and glittering Lloyds Building.

The history of a structure on the corner of Fournier Street and Brick Lane is also curiously suggestive; it was built in 1744 as a church for the Huguenot weavers of the period, but was used as a synagogue for the Jewish population of Spitalfields between 1898 and 1975; now it is a mosque, the London Jamme Masjid, for the Muslim Bengalis who succeeded the Jews. Succeeding waves of immigrants have chosen to maintain this place as a sacred spot.

It is possible, too, that an unpleasant or unhappy atmosphere may persist like some noisome scent in the air. It has been noted of certain streets such as Chick Lane, Field Lane or Black Boy Alley, all in the vicinity of the present Farringdon Road, that "a curious fact about these places is that their bad character began so early and persisted so long." Of Coventry Street, off Piccadilly, it was stated in 1846 that "there is a considerable number of gaming houses in the neighbourhood at the present time, so that the bad character of the place is at least two centuries old, or ever since it was built upon." The act of building may itself determine the character of an area for ever, in other words; it is as if the stones themselves carried the burden of their own destiny. So we may see the passage of time through stone, but that vision of unbroken continuity is essential to the vision of London itself. This is not the eternity vouchsafed to the mystic, who ascends from the body to glimpse the soul of things, but one immured in sand and stone so that the actual texture or process of life is afforded a kind of grace. The continuity of London is the continuity of life itself.

East and South

An etching of Billingsgate by James McNeill Whistler, executed in 1859; it
shows something of the animation of the docksides, with many boats
engaged in trade upon the ever commercial Thames.

CHAPTER 71

The Stinking Pile

It has often been suggested that the East End is a creation of the nineteenth century; certainly the phrase itself was not invented until the
1880s. But in fact the East has always existed as a separate and distinct entity. The area of Tower Hamlets, Limehouse and Bow rests upon a
separate strip of gravel, one of the Flood Plain gravels which were created at
the time of the last glacial eruption some 15,000 years ago. Whether this
longevity has played any part in creating the unique atmosphere of the East
End is open to question, perhaps, but the symbolic importance of east versus
west must not be ignored in any analysis of what became known in the late
nineteenth century as "the abyss." The Roman burials of Londinium, some
of them within the very area now known as the East End, were so conducted
that the heads of those interred were inclined towards the west; the same
practice can be found in early Christian burial rituals, again in the territory of
London, which suggests some profound affinity. It seems also to have been
an instinctive one, part of a territorial spirit that emerges in the earliest
recorded periods of London's history. Archaeological evidence suggests, for
example, that the invading Saxons of the fifth and sixth centuries settled to the
west of the River Walbrook while the defeated and demoralised Romano-

British natives dwelled upon the east bank. This pattern of habitation has been consistent and profound.

There is one interesting and significant feature of the eastern area which suggests a living tradition stretching back beyond the time of the Romans. In the late nineteenth and early twentieth centuries there was found evidence of a great "wall" running along the eastern portion of the Thames, down the river bank and along the Essex shores, to protect the land from the depredations of the tidal river; it was constituted of timber banks and earthworks. At the end of the wall in Essex, close to the area now known as Bradwell Waterside—which may plausibly be translated, even after two thousand years of transition, as Broad Wall—were discovered the earthworks of a Roman fortress as well as the ruins of a later chapel, St. Peter-on-the-Wall, which had become a barn. Other local antiquarians have also found small churches or chapels placed beside what might be called this great eastern wall. It is quite forgotten, save by a few local historians, but by keeping at bay the water, and by helping to drain the marshland of the eastern areas, it created the East End or London's dark side. Every city must have one.

And where does the "East" begin? According to certain urban authorities the point of transition was marked by the Aldgate Pump, a stone fountain constructed beside the well at the confluence of Fenchurch Street and Leadenhall Street; the existing pump lies a few yards to the west of the original. Other antiquaries have argued that the real East End begins at the point where Whitechapel Road and Commercial Road meet. The taint of poverty, already apparent in the late medieval period, was in any case gradually extended. Stow observed that between 1550 and 1590 there was "a continual street or filthy strait passage with alleys of small tenements or cottages built . . . almost to Ratcliffe." The road from the pump of Aldgate to the church at Whitechapel was by this date also lined with shops and tenements, while the adjoining field to the north was "pestered with cottages and alleys." In similar manner there was "a continuous building of small and base tenements for the most part lately erected" from Bishopsgate to Shoreditch, and even beyond that there were mean buildings "a good flight shot" as far out as Kingsland and Tottenham. By the end of the sixteenth century the eastern portions of the city were being defined as "base" and "filthy," their squalor and stench emerging despite proclamations and parliamentary Acts. The area of Spitalfields, laid out along more regular lines between 1660 and 1680, also soon acquired a reputation for poverty and overcrowding. The houses were

small and narrow, while the streets themselves were often only fifteen feet
wide. That sense of diminution, or of constriction, exists still. As the houses,
so their inhabitants. A report of 1665 described the overcrowding created by
"poor indigent and idle and loose persons." So the "filthy cottages" of Stow's
report were being filled with "filthy" persons. It is the story of London.

The industries of the eastern neighbourhood gradually became filthy,
too. Much of its trade and commerce came from the river, but in the course
of the seventeenth century the region became steadily industrialised. In the
vicinity of the Lea mills, malodorous manufactories were introduced. In 1614
a local court records that "The jury present Lancelot Gamblyn, lately of
Stratford Langthorne, starchmaker, because by unlawful making of starch
such a stink and ill favour continue and daily arise." Less than fifty years
later Sir William Petty was lamenting "the fumes, steams, and stinks of the
whole Easterly Pyle," and indeed for hundreds of years after that the "Easterly Pyle" became the home of what were known as "the stink industries"; all
forms of corruption and noisomeness were fashioned there. It represented the
focus for London's fear of corruption and disease. Nor were these fears entirely ill-founded, either; demographic surveys revealed a remarkably high
incidence of consumption and "fever" in the eastern reaches of London.

So the flight westward continued. From the seventeenth century onward
the laying out of streets and squares moved inexorably in that direction; the
wealthy and the well-born and the fashionable insisted upon dwelling in what
Nash called "the respectable streets at the West end of the town." The topographical divide, or rather the obsession with the West over the East, could
be seen in minute particulars. When Jermyn Street was completed in the
1680s, the *London Encyclopaedia* observes that "the west end of the street was
more fashionable than the east." Another line of demarcation ran through
Soho Square, where "every minute longitude east is equal to as many degrees
of gentility *minus*," as an American visitor put it, "or towards west, *plus*." Of
the newly fashioned Regent Street it was noted that "there are many squares
on the eastern side of this thoroughfare, and some good streets, but rank and
fashion appear to avoid them."

It has been observed that the West End has the money, and the East End has
the dirt; there is leisure to the West, and labour to the East. Yet in the early
decades of the nineteenth century it was not singled out as being the most
desperate source of poverty and violence. It was known principally as the
centre of shipping, and of industry, and thus the home of the working poor.

In fact the industry and the poverty steadily intensified; dye works and chemical works, manure factories and lamp-black factories, manufacturers of glue and of paraffin, producers of paint and bonemeal, all clustered in Bow and Old Ford and Stratford. The River Lea for centuries had been the site of industry, and of transport, but throughout the nineteenth century it was further exploited and degraded. A match factory on its banks lent the water a urinous taste and appearance, while the smell of the whole area became offensive. In all this, of course, we see the condition of the sixteenth and seventeenth centuries being expanded and intensified; it is as if the process continued with a momentum of its own. The industrial districts of Canning Town, Silvertown and Beckton were created between the Lea and Barking Creek, Beckton becoming particularly well known for its sewage dispersal system. All the filth of London crept eastwards.

But then, at some point in the 1880s, it reached what might be called critical mass. It imploded. The East End became "the abyss" or "the nether world" of strange secrets and desires. It was the area of London into which more poor people were crammed than any other, and out of that congregation of poverty sprang reports of evil and immorality, of savagery and unnamed vice. In his essay "On Murder, Considered as One of the Fine Arts," Thomas De Quincey apostrophised the area of the Ratcliffe Highway Murders of 1812 as one of the "most chaotic" and "a most dangerous quarter," a "perilous region" replete with "manifold ruffianism." It is perhaps important that a writer should inscribe the East End in this manner, since its subsequent and lurid reputation was to a large extent established upon the work of journalists and novelists who felt almost obliged to conjure up visions of darkness and horror as a way of describing the shadow which London itself cast. And of course the defining sensation which for ever marked the "East End," and created its public identity, was the series of murders ascribed to Jack the Ripper between the late summer and early autumn of 1888. The scale of the sudden and brutal killings effectively marked out the area as one of incomparable violence and depravity, but it was equally significant that the crimes should have been committed in the darkness of malodorous alleys. The fact that the killer was never captured seemed only to confirm the impression that the bloodshed was created by the foul streets themselves; that the East End was the true Ripper.

All the anxieties about the city in general then became attached to the East End in particular, as if in some peculiar sense it had become a microcosm of London's own dark life. There were books written, the titles of which represented their themes—*The Bitter Cry of Outcast London, The People of the Abyss, Ragged London, In Darkest London, The Nether World.* In that last novel George Gissing provides a description of "the pest-stricken regions of East London, sweltering in sunshine which served only to reveal the intimacies of abomination; across miles of a city of the damned, such as thought never conceived before this age of ours; above streets, swarming with a nameless populace, cruelly exposed by the unwonted light of heaven." This is a vision of the East End as the Inferno, the city as hell, and it is not one confined to the novelist. The autobiographical narrative of "John Martin, School Master and Poet" was partly set in the purlieus of nineteenth-century Limehouse. "A mind is needed—black, misanthropic in its view of things, used to fearful visions of the night, to look with comprehensive and unflinching eye upon these scenes of sickly horror and despair."

When Jack London first wished to visit the East End in 1902 he had been told by the manager of Thomas Cook's Cheapside branch that "We are not accustomed to taking travellers to the East End; we receive no call to take them there, and we know nothing whatsoever about the place at all." They knew nothing about it, perhaps, and yet everyone knew of it. In *Tales of Mean Streets* (1894) Arthur Morrison declared that "There is no need to say in the East End of what. The East End is a vast city, as famous in its way as any the hand of man has made. But who knows the East End?"

The presence of 100,000 Jewish immigrants, in Whitechapel and in Spitalfields, only served to emphasise the apparently "alien" quality of the neighbourhood. They served also to reinforce that other territorial myth which clung to the East End. Because it did indeed lie towards the east, it became associated with that larger "east" which lay beyond Christendom and which threatened the borders of Europe. The name given to the dispossessed children of the streets, "street-Arabs," offers some confirmation of this diagnosis. The East End was in that sense the ultimate threat and the ultimate mystery. It represented the heart of darkness.

Yet there were some who came as missionaries into that darkness. As early as the 1860s men and women, impelled by religious or philanthropic motives, set up halls and chapels in the East End. The vicar of St. Jude's in Whitechapel, Samuel Barnett, was instrumental in what was called "settlement work" where generally idealistic young men and women tried materially to assist the straitened or precarious lives of the East Enders. Arnold Toynbee declared in one of his lectures to the inhabitants of Bethnal Green: "You have to forgive us, for we have wronged you; we have sinned against you grievously . . . we will serve you, we will devote our lives to your service, and we cannot do more." Partly as a result of his example, and his eloquence, various "missions" were established, among them Oxford House in Bethnal Green and St. Mildred's House upon the Isle of Dogs. The tone of supplication in Toynbee's remarks might also be construed as one of anxiety that those, who had been so grievously treated, might react against the "sinners" who betrayed them.

There was indeed much radical activity in the East End, with the members of the London Corresponding Society in the 1790s and the Chartists in the 1830s meeting in the mug houses and public houses of Whitechapel and elsewhere, in order to promote their revolutionary causes. A radically egalitarian and anti-authoritarian spirit has always been rising from the area, in terms of religious as well as political dissent (if in fact the two can be distinguished). In the eighteenth century the Ancient Deists of Hoxton espoused millennarian and generally levelling principles, and there is evidence of Ranters and Muggletonians, Quakers and Fifth Monarchy men, contributing to the general atmosphere of dissent. In the early decades of the twentieth century, the political ethic of the East End was dominated by "municipal socialism." George Lansbury in particular became associated with the movement known as "Poplarism," a variant of populism whereby in 1919 the local Labour Party in control of the borough set unemployment relief at a level higher than the central government permitted. There was a confrontation, and the councillors of Poplar were briefly imprisoned, but the central demands of Lansbury were eventually met.

It was a characteristic episode, in the sense that the East End never "rose up," as the civic authorities feared. It was always considered a potent ground for insurrection, as Oswald Mosley and his followers demonstrated in the 1930s, but like the rest of London it was too large and too dispersed to create any kind of galvanic shock. A more important revolutionary influence came, in fact, from the immigrant population. The communist and anarchist movements among the German and Russian populations have borne significant witness to the effect of the East End upon human consciousness. There was the celebrated Anarchists Club in Jubilee Street, among whose members were Kropotkin and Malatesta; opposite the London Hospital along Whitechapel High Street, a hall accommodated the fifth congress of the Russian Social Democratic Labour Party which ensured the preeminence of the Bolshevik Party. In a hostel in Fieldgate Street, Joseph Stalin was a welcome guest. Lenin visited Whitechapel on numerous occasions, and attended the Anarchists Club, while Trotsky and Litvinov were also frequent visitors to the area. The East End can in that sense be considered one of the primary sites of world communism.

No doubt the presence of political exiles from Europe is largely responsible for that eminence, but the prevailing atmosphere of the place may also have been suggestive. Blanchard Jerrold, in the 1870s, had remarked upon the fact that "the quaint, dirty, poverty-laden, stall-lined streets are here and there relieved by marts and warehouses and emporiums, in which rich men who employ the poorest labour, are found." Already the startling contrast between the "rich" and the "poorest," standing upon the same ground, is being revealed. The East End was also the image of the whole world, with "the German, the Jew, the Frenchman, the Lascar, the swarthy native of Spitalfields, the leering thin-handed thief . . . with endless swarms of ragged children." International communism sprang from an international context.

But other visitors saw other realities. The Czechoslovakian playwright Karel Čapek, observing the East End at first hand in the early twentieth century, suggested that in "this overwhelming quantity it no longer looks like an excess of human beings, but like a geological formation . . . it was piled up from soot and dust." It is an impersonal force of dullness, the total aggregate of labour and suffering among the soot of ships and factories. It is a "geological formation," perhaps, to the extent that the area itself seems to emanate waves of frustration and enervation. At the turn of the nineteenth century Mrs. Humphry Ward noticed the monotony of the East End in terms of "long lines of low houses—two storeys always, or two storeys and a basement—of the same yellowish brick, all begrimed by the same smoke, every door-knocker of the same pattern, every window-blind hung in the same way, and the same corner 'public' on either side, flaming in the hazy distance." George Orwell noticed it, too, in 1933 when he complained that the territory between Whitechapel and Wapping was "quieter and drearier" than the equivalent poor areas of Paris.

This is a familiar refrain, but it tends to come from those upon the outside. The autobiographical reminiscences of East Enders themselves do not dwell upon monotony or hardship, but upon the sports and clubs and markets, the local shops and local "characters," which comprised each neighbourhood. As one old resident of Poplar put it in a recent history of the area, *The East End Then and Now*, edited by W.G. Ramsey, "It never occurred to me that my brothers and sisters and I were underprivileged, for what you never have you never miss." This is the experience of the East End, and of all other impoverished parts of London, for those who live in them; the apparent deprivation and monotony are never realised, because they do not touch the inner experience of those who are meant to be affected by them. Any emphasis upon the uniformity or tedium of the East End has in any case to be seriously modified by the constantly remarked "merriment" or "cheerfulness" of its inhabitants. There was "a valiant cheeriness full of strength," Blanchard Jerrold remarked after reciting a litany of sorrowful mysteries to be found upon the eastern streets, "everywhere a readiness to laugh." He also observed that "The man who has a ready wit will employ his basket, while the dull vendor remains with his arms crossed."

Thus emerged the figure of the Cockney, once the native of all London but in the late nineteenth and twentieth centuries identified more and more closely with the East End. This was the character heard by V.S. Pritchett with "whining vowels and ruined consonants" and "the hard-chinned look of indomitable character." The creation of that chirpy and resourceful stereotype can in some measure be ascribed to another contrast with East End monotony, the music hall. The conditions of life in Whitechapel, Bethnal Green and elsewhere may have predisposed their inhabitants to violent delights; the penny gaffs and the brightly illuminated public houses are testimony to that, as well as the roughness and coarseness which were intimately associated with them. But it is also significant that the East End harboured more music halls than any other part of London—Gilbert's in Whitechapel, the Eastern and the Apollo in Bethnal Green, the Cambridge in Shoreditch, Wilton's in Wellclose Square, the Queen's in Poplar, the Eagle in the Mile End Road, and of course the Empire in Hackney, are just the most prominent among a large number which became as characteristic of the East End as the sweatshops or the church missions. By the mid-nineteenth century, the area roughly inclusive of the present borough of Tower Hamlets harboured some 150 music halls. It is perhaps appropriate that Charles Morton, universally if inaccurately known as "Father of the Halls" because of his establishment of the Canterbury in 1851, was born in Bethnal Green. In one sense the eastern region of the city was simply reaffirming its ancient identity. It has been mentioned before that two of the earliest London theatres, the Theatre and the Curtain, had been erected in the sixteenth century upon the open ground of Shoreditch; the whole region outside the walls became a haven for popular entertainment of every kind, from tea-gardens to wrestling matches and bear-baiting. So the music halls of the East End represent another continuity within the area, equivalent to its poor housing and to its "stink industries."

Yet in another sense the halls represented the extension and intensification of East End life in the nineteenth century. Many emerged and prospered in the 1850s—the Eagle Tea Gardens, the Effingham and Wilton's are of that period—by including burletta performances as well as variety acts and orchestral music. Among those who played here were the "*lions comiques*," Alfred Vance and George Leybourne, who sang such Cockney songs as "Slap Bang, Here We Are Again" and "Champagne Charlie." Vance in particular was known for his "coster" songs written in a "flash" or Cockney dialect, among them "Costermonger Joe" and "The Chickaleary Cove" where humour and bravado are easily mingled. Such songs as these became the folk songs of the East End, animated by all the pathos and diversity of each neighbourhood, charged with the circumstances and realities of the entire area. They remain powerful because they are filled with a real sense of place, as tangible as Artillery Lane or Rotherhithe Tunnel. When Charles Coborn sang "Two Lovely Black Eyes" at the Paragon in Mile End, he recalled "parties of girls and lads of the coster fraternity, all of a row, arm in arm, shouting out my chorus at the top of their voices." The identification of performer and audience was paramount, so that when Lively Lily Burnand sang about the housekeeping of the poor at the Queen's in Poplar she was touching upon a familiar subject:

> Don't forget the ha'penny on the jam jar . . .
> The landlord's comin' in the mornin'
> An he's so par-ti-cu-lar . . .

In this instance, it was the importance of earning the halfpenny on the return of the jam jar to the shop. The common elements of privation, and poverty, were lifted into another sphere where they became touched by universal comedy and pity; thus, for a moment at least, was misery transcended. It would not be too much to claim, in fact, that the halls provided a boisterous and necessary secular form of the Mass in which the audience were themselves identified and uplifted as members of a general community.

In early twentieth-century memoirs of the East End that life is recorded with what, in retrospect, looks like the precision of all lost things. Along Poplar High Street there were, Horace Thorogood wrote in *East of Aldgate*, once "little shops of various shapes and heights and sizes" interspersed with small houses "with polished brass numbers on the doors." Here might be found "a parrot-cage shop, a musical instrument shop," and, characteristically, "rows of little one-storeyed houses standing a few feet back from the pavement behind iron railings." In Shadwell the children went barefoot and wore rags but "that was just Irish slovenliness, they never wanted for food." In the East End, in the first decades of the twentieth century, the public houses "were open from early morning till half-past midnight" with gin at fourpence halfpenny a quartern and "beer a penny for a half-pint. Women would come in at seven in the morning and stay till three in the afternoon." The East End was also famous for its markets—Rosemary Lane, Spitalfields, Chrisp Street, Watney Street—when the thoroughfares "swarmed with people, and at night flared with naphtha light . . . you could have walked on the people's heads all the way from Commercial Road to Cable Street."

A fierce and protective sense of identity marked out the East End in these decades. The inhabitants of Limehouse called the people to the west those "above the bridges," and there was a great deal of "inbreeding" which sprang from territorial loyalties. One isolated corner of Poplar, beside the Leamouth Road, in the 1920s had a population "numbering about 200 men, women and children," according to *The East End Then and Now*, who were "members of no more than six families, among whom the Lammings, the Scanlans and the Jeffries were the most numerous. These families tended to marry within their own circle . . . the community had its own school, two pubs and a small general store." It was noticed, too, that the Chinese residents of Pennyfields married girls from Hoxton rather than those from Poplar. "Poplarites were against mixed marriages," according to one observer in the 1930s. It might be surmised that since Hoxton is closer to the City, and to the rest of London, it has avoided that peculiar sense of territoriality or insularity.

When East Enders became more affluent, they moved out. The clerks of the nineteenth century, for example, took advantage of the burgeoning transport system to migrate into the more salubrious areas of Chingford or Forest Gate. The population of Middlesex grew 30.8 per cent in ten years; Wembley grew by 552 per cent and Harrow by 275 per cent. Only the poor remained in the old centres of the East End, their numbers increasing as their fate grew more desperate. This in turn established precisely the sense of separation and grievance which has not yet been dissipated.

The cost of labour, in human terms, was very high. The East End tended to wake up earlier than the rest of the city, and at dawn the area became a great plain of smoking chimneys. The factories kept on coming, in search of

cheap labour, and by 1951 it contained almost 10 per cent of the city's working population. In the early years of the twentieth century, Horace Thorogood came upon one East End "cottage" under a railway where he "found a
family of six living in one upper room, the window of which had to be kept
closed, otherwise sparks from the trains flew in and set light to the bed-
clothes."

The effect of the Second World War surpassed those few disagreeable
sparks, and great swathes of the East End were destroyed; approximately 19
per cent of the built areas of Stepney, Poplar and Bethnal Green were razed.
Once more the East End was adversely affected by its industrial history; the
German bombers sought out the ports, and the factory areas close to the Lea
Valley, as well as using the inhabitants of the East End as an "example." It
suggests the importance of the East, in the whole process of the war, that the
king and queen visited Poplar and Stepney immediately after the celebrations
of VE Day in May 1945. It was, perhaps, one method of controlling or ascer-
taining the mood of a populace which since the nineteenth century had been
considered mysterious.

Even as late as 1950 whole areas were still characterised only as "bomb-
sites" where strange weeds grew and where children played. A temporary
housing programme authorised the construction of Nissen huts and prefabri-
cated single-storey dwellings, but many of these prefabs were still in use
more than twenty years later. There were other schemes to house the residents of the East End, not least the "Greater London Plan" of Professor
Abercrombie who wished to relocate many city dwellers in satellite towns beyond the newly established Green Belt. The proposal was to disperse a large
number of residents from Hackney and Stepney and Bethnal Green, yet the
whole history of London suggests that such exercises in civic engineering are
only partially successful. An equivalent emphasis was placed on the rebuilding and replanning of the devastated East, as if its character might be thoroughly changed. But it is impossible to destroy three hundred years of human
settlement.

For all the redevelopments of the East End in the 1950s and 1960s, you
had only to turn a corner to encounter a row of terraced housing erected in
the 1880s or the 1890s; there were still Georgian houses, as well as laid-
out "estates" from the 1920s and the 1930s. The postwar East End was a
palimpsest of its past. For those who cared to look for such things, there were
the dark canals and the gasworks, old pathways and rusting bridges, all with
the exhalation of forgetfulness and decay; there were patches of waste ground

covered with weeds and litter, as well as deserted factories and steps seeming to lead nowhere. The old streets of tiny yellow-brick houses were still to be found, with their characteristic pattern of a small front parlour and a passage leading past it from the street door straight into the kitchen, which looked out upon a small yard; two small bedrooms above, and a cellar beneath. Along the Barking Road were scores of side-streets—Ladysmith Avenue, Kimberley Avenue, Mafeking Avenue, Macaulay Road, Thackeray Road and Dickens Road form one sequence—in which row upon row of suburban villas, albeit one grade higher than the terraces of Bethnal Green or Whitechapel, effortlessly retained into the 1960s the atmosphere of the late nineteenth century.

The borough of Hackney epitomises sprawl and heterogeneity. One account, evocatively titled *A Journey Through Ruins: The Last Days of London*, published in 1991, took Dalston Lane as its centre of enquiry; here the author, Patrick Wright, discovered "a street corner of forgotten municipal services" as a token of civic neglect. Yet its old energies remain, and "Dalston Lane is a jumble of residential, commercial and industrial activities" with factories, clothiers, shops and small businesses.

One of the most surprising aspects of the contemporary East End is the extent to which it has maintained its economic life in the equivalent of the nineteenth-century small workshop; a number of the main thoroughfares, from the Hackney Road to the Roman Road and Hoxton Street, are populated by store-front businesses ranging from television repairers to newsagents, upholsterers to fruiterers, cabinet-makers to money-exchangers. In the East, where historically land and property have been less valuable than in the West, the relics of lost decades linger and are commonly allowed to decay.

There are curious regions of the East End where other continuities may be glimpsed. In Walthamstow, just beyond the High Street to the east, some spectral image or atmosphere of the countryside suddenly pervades Church Hill; this is indeed a peculiar sensation since all the streets close to it, including the High Street, Markhouse Road and Coppermill Road, embody the characteristic patterns of the East End suburbs. Nevertheless the old presence of a once rural neighbourhood seems to issue from the territory itself. Many areas in that sense preserve their identity. There is a harshness about Barking, for example, which makes it dissimilar from Walthamstow; here a native population seems to have maintained its presence, with a kind of bleakness or hardness of attitude. The survival of part of the ancient abbey in no way diminishes that atmosphere, which is powerfully sustained by the presence of the old creek from which the majority of the population once earned their living. It remains a strangely isolated or self-communing neighbourhood, where the London accent seems peculiarly thick. In Pennyfields, where the Malays and Chinese dwelled more than a century before, there is now a large population of Vietnamese. Second-hand pornography is sold in Sclater Street, Shoreditch, in what has always been a red-light district. The market of Green Street, in East Ham, recalls the energy and spirit of medieval London itself. In fact the ancient mercantile life of the city has been reawakened (if indeed it ever really slept) in areas as diverse as West Ham and Stoke Newington, Spitalfields and Leytonstone.

A typical journey around an East End neighbourhood will disclose one or two Georgian houses with perhaps some large mid-Victorian establishments, now turned into council offices or social security centres; there will be remnants of late nineteenth-century housing together with council housing of the 1920s and 1930s; pubs and betting offices, together with the ubiquitous small general store and newsagent; mini-cab offices, as well as shops specialising in long-distance telephone calls to Africa or India; a variety of council blocks, the oldest estates alongside low-rise estates of the 1980s and the nineteen-storey tower blocks of the same period. There will be an open space, or a park. In some parts of the East, the arches beneath the innumerable railway bridges will be used for car-maintenance or for storage.

Yet there have of course been changes. Poplar High Street was a crowded thoroughfare, with a plethora of shops and stalls and grimy buildings on either side; now it is an open street bordered by five-storey council-house estates, pubs and shops of yellow brick. The sound of people thronging, buying and selling has now been replaced by the intermittent noise of traffic. Much of the East End has followed that example. Where there was once a collection of shops and houses in a variety of styles, there will now be a "block" of uniform texture and dimensions; as a substitute for rows upon rows of terraced houses, there are major roads. The altered neighbourhoods seem somehow lighter, perhaps because they have lost touch with their history. At the extreme western end of Poplar High Street, just beyond Pennyfields, Joseph Nightingale's coffee rooms, with signs for steak and kidney or liver and bacon, used to adjoin the horseflesh shop of James McEwen which in turn was next to George Ablard the hairdresser; the buildings had different frontages and were of varying height. In recent years that corner has been taken up by three-storey red-brick council dwellings and a small thoroughfare, Saltwell Street, runs by it. The opium quarter of Limehouse is now represented by a Chinese take-away. Here was once a street known as Bickmore Street and an extant photograph, taken in 1890, shows crowds of children posed outside a number of bow-windowed shopfronts; in its place today stands part of a recreation ground.

It might be concluded that the clutter and clatter of life have gone from these areas, even if they exist elsewhere in the East End. It could also be suggested that the rebuilt or renovated neighbourhoods resemble those within other areas of London; the council estates of Poplar, for example, are not so very different from those of Southall or Greenford. So the aspiration towards civic contentment has led to a diminution of local identity. The greatest contrast of all, evinced in photographs taken from 1890 to 1990, lies in the diminution of people in the streets. The life of the East End has gone within. Whether the telephone or television has effected this change is not the question; the salient fact remains that the human life of the streets has greatly diminished in exuberance and in intensity. Yet it is important not to sentimentalise this transition. If the East seems a more denuded place, it is also a less impoverished one; if it is more remote, or less human, it is also healthier. No one would willingly exchange a council flat for a tenement slum, even if the slums were filled with a communal spirit. You cannot go back.

CHAPTER 72

The South Work

🜚

hat was how Southwark received its name, from the "south work" of a river wall to match its northern counterpart. Its origins, however, remain mysterious. Along the Old Kent Road, at the junction with Bowles Road, were discovered the remnants of an ancient settlement which manufactured flint tools. "Within the weathered sands," reported one investigator in the *London Archaeologist*, "were many finds associated with the activities of prehistoric people." No doubt it would be fanciful to connect this long history of human settlement with the air of exhaustion, of spent life, which seems to pervade the vicinity. There is, after all, another explanation: the roads of the south were decorated with funereal monuments, and the memory of these important emblems may in part account for the sense of transience associated with the neighbourhood. Three inhumation burial sites have been found close to each other, the first along the present Borough High Street. Their significance lies in their rarity, the only other burial of an equivalent date being close to the Tower of London, but also in the fact that two Roman burials of a similar nature were found a few yards to the south-east. The whole area of Southwark is in fact rich in Roman burial sites, with a cluster of inhumations in the area where Stane Street and Watling Street once diverged from what is now Borough High Street; the lines of the streets still exist under the names of Newington Causeway and the Old Kent Road. Another cluster of burial sites can be found to the north-west, beside another great Roman road leading from the bridge across the river. That is why travellers met in Southwark, in order to continue their journeys southward, and of course it represents the starting point of the Canterbury pilgrimage narrated by Chaucer. There have always been taverns and inns here for the welfare of those passing through; hospitals congregated here, also, perhaps in some atavistic homage to transitoriness.

The Roman settlement left another legacy. A gladiator's trident was discovered in Southwark, prompting speculation that an arena may have been constructed in the vicinity where, in the late sixteenth century, the Swan and the Globe theatres flourished. The South Bank has always been associated with entertainment and pleasure, therefore, and its most recent incarnations encompass the newly thriving Globe Theatre as well as the whole area dominated by the Royal Festival Hall, the National Theatre and the Tate Modern.

St. Mary Overie, later St. Saviour, later Southwark Cathedral, became a favoured place of sanctuary for those fleeing from the city's justice. So Southwark acquired an ill-favoured reputation. There were seven prisons in the area by the seventeenth century (its most famous, the Clink, gave its name literally to other such institutions) and yet there was continual riot and disorder. The neighbourhood was owned by various religious authorities, among them the archbishop of Canterbury and the Cluniac Order which inhabited the priory at Bermondsey, and yet it was known for its licentiousness. The prostitutes of the Bankside, practising their trade within the "Liberty" of the bishop of Winchester, were known as "Winchester Geese." So there existed a strange oscillation between freedom and restraint which is, perhaps, not so strange after all, in the general pattern of contraries which covers the whole of London.

In Wyngaerde's map of 1558 the area south of the Thames is intimately connected with that of the north by various lines of harmony, rather like the contemporary map of the Underground, flowing towards and over the bridge. A continuous row of houses stretches for almost a mile along the southern bank of the Thames, from Paris Garden Stairs to the great "Beere Howse" just east of Tooley Street beside Pickle Herring Stairs. It is perhaps worth noting that over a century before Shakespeare's Falstaff appeared at the Globe, a short distance away, his namesake Sir John Falstolfe owned "four messuages called beer houses here." In similar fashion Harry or "Herry" Bailey of the

Tabard Inn was a real and familiar Southwark figure before he entered Chaucer's *Canterbury Tales*; perhaps there is something in the air of Southwark which encourages the transaction between reality and imagination. On the "Agas map" of the 1560s are shown ponds, water mills, smoky industries, bear pits, pleasure gardens and "stewhouses" like the celebrated "Castle upon the Hope Inn" which still survives as the Anchor.

The city, in a sense, feared the contagion of these pleasurable haunts. A civic edict of the sixteenth century ordered the wherrymen, who were customarily employed to row citizens across the river to the brothels, to moor their boats at night by the northern stairs in order to ensure that "thieves and other misdoers shall not be carried" to the southern bank. Another form of civic displeasure is exemplified in the fact that although "Bridge Without" had become the twenty-sixth ward of the city "its inhabitants were not allowed to elect their own aldermen" who were in effect imposed upon them. Southwark had become a kind of satrapy, thus ensuring that almost to the end of the twentieth century it remained a relatively undeveloped and ill-regarded place. Yet it was not necessarily poorly administered. The rich or "middling class," as always, superintended the poor and ensured that travelling paupers were discouraged. The parish vestry collected the rates and distributed poor relief, while the local court supervised all aspects of trade. These suggestions of a relatively self-sufficient community have been amplified in a recent historical survey which concludes that the population of this particular suburb, and by extension of others like it, was relatively stable. The inhabitants of Southwark maintained residence in the same houses and intermarried in the same neighbourhood, as was characteristic of the city in general.

These conclusions tend to support the notion that, throughout the whole of London and its outlying districts, there was a vital and recognisable communal spirit. This spirit has survived over so many centuries that the present neighbourhood of Rotherhithe, for example, is still distinct from those of Deptford and Bermondsey. There is an indigenous or native spirit which animates a particular area. In contemporary south London there are a number of different areas, among them Lambeth and Brixton, Camberwell and Peckham, which have developed beside one another and by some form of symbiosis make up a recognisable atmosphere.

Yet the South remained relatively unknown to other Londoners, except as a source of disquiet. The southern bank fulfilled some of the functions of the "Eastern pyle," as a boundary zone to which London could consign its dirt and its rubbish. Hence in the early eighteenth century it became the repository for some of the "stink industries" which had been banished from the City proper. The tanneries were consigned to Bermondsey, for example, while Lambeth became the site for noisy timber yards, vinegar-makers, dye manufactories and the makers of soap and tallow. It was reported in the local press that "a society of persons did exist at Lambeth . . . who made a trade of digging up the bodies of the dead: they made candles of the fat, extracted volatile alkali from the bones, and sold the flesh for dog's meat." This sounds sufficiently alarmist to be apocryphal, but there is no doubt that south London already had a difficult reputation. One market gardener of the area decided in 1789 to set up his business elsewhere because "the smoke . . . constantly enveloped my plants . . . the obscurity of the situation, the badness of the roads leading to it, with the effluvia of surrounding ditches being at times highly offensive." South London, or at least those parts of it which were in immediate relation to the rest of the city and could be seen from it, was considered as a poor and disreputable appendage. There was always a form of urban discrimination.

That is why there were so many prisons in the vicinity, as well as institutions for female orphans and asylums for the poor; Bethlem, too, was erected in Lambeth (1815). London was consigning all its difficult or problematic citizens to the South. The area also acquired a reputation for dubious taverns and doubtful pleasure gardens. Establishments such as the Apollo Gardens were under civic scrutiny, and were on occasions closed down by the authorities for "disorderliness." The whole of Lambeth became known as a "louche and even disreputable quarter." The Temple of Flora and the Dog and Duck Tavern, situated where the path across St. George's Fields met the Lambeth Road, was "certainly the most dreadful place in or about the metropolis . . . the resorts of women, not only of the lower species of prostitution, but even of the middle classes." South London had once more manifested its ancient status as a haven of sexual freedom. The philanthropist Francis Place recalled highwaymen of the 1780s claiming their horses in these southern fields where "flashy women come out to take leave of the thieves at dusk and wish them success." It is known that radical insurrectionaries were hunted down in the area, since they were believed to plot and plan in various decaying public houses; just as the music-hall stars of the mid-nineteenth century moved south to Brixton, so those of dubious public reputation like the transvestite Chevalier d'Eon had moved to Lambeth a century before. It was, in every sense, a dumping ground.

. . .

But the prospect of dirt, or dilapidation, did not materially affect the growth of London in that direction; like the beetle which lives upon dung, the "offensive" smells and sounds might even arouse its powers into further expenditures of energy. The erection of Westminster Bridge in 1750, and the completion of Blackfriars Bridge nineteen years later, marked the real development of south London. Highways led from the newly established bridges, and moved towards Kennington and the Elephant and Castle; in addition roads were laid across open fields to join these major thoroughfares. The new roads led to fresh industrial development, so that the vinegar- and dye-works were complemented by potteries, lime kilns and blacking factories. By 1800, Lambeth had assumed all the characteristics of a slum.

Yet the area still grew; it expanded and developed, acquiring its shape along with the other ribbon developments which snaked southwards. The process acquired resistless momentum in the first decade of the nineteenth century when three toll bridges were completed. Southwark Bridge, Waterloo Bridge and Vauxhall Bridge opened the way for the extensive building programmes which created south London in its present form. The increase in London's population, and the exertion of the new industrial forces, drew the city over the Thames at an ever increasing rate. The streets around St. George's Circus were soon thickly inhabited, with houses covering all the adjacent fields, but soon the shops and houses and businesses began to travel down the roads which radiated from that neighbourhood. Newington, Kennington and Walworth were directly affected and by the 1830s the whole area of the present South was being covered in roads and houses. The suburban development soon expanded to include Peckham and Camberwell, Brixton and Clapham, even so far as Dulwich and Herne Hill. It was not long before Sydenham and Norwood, Forest Hill and Honor Oak, became part of the same urban diaspora.

Those who have recorded their impressions of coming into London by the railway from the south, have remarked upon the apparently endless vista of red and brown roofs, dead walls, and little streets which flashed by. The prospect has been compared to that of a sea, or a desert, both images invoking the power of some remorseless force which cannot be withstood. A character in H.G. Wells's *Tono Bungay* travelling in the early 1900s on the South-Eastern Railway, "marked beyond Chislehurst the growing multitude of villas, and so came stage by stage through multiplying houses . . . the congestion of houses intensified and piled up presently into tenements: I mar-

velled more and more at this boundless world of dingy people." One of the
principal sensations was also that of fear. It was the instinctive fear of uniformity, as well as fear of the approaching capital which had engendered it.

As the railway carriage travelled closer to its destination at Cannon
Street, "whiffs of industrial smell, of leather, of brewing" circulated like the
odours of sulphur from some unseen inferno. Since the colonisation of the
southern bank was entirely driven by the need for industrial expansion and
exploitation, it is appropriate that the smell of industry itself should permeate
the territory. There were glue factories and wool warehouses, while Charles
Knight's *Encyclopaedia of London* notes that "chimneys shot up at intervals of
a few yards, towering above a very maze of red roofs, and furnishing their
contribution to the smoky atmosphere of the neighbourhood." The district,
once characterised by its priory, was now celebrated for its protean quality; it
"may be regarded as a region of manufacturers, a region of market-gardeners, a region of wholesale dealers, and a maritime region, according to
the quarter where we take our stand." Just as there were various trades in
Bermondsey, so there were heterogeneous odours. "In one street strawberry
jam is borne in upon you in whiffs, hot and strong; in another, raw hides and
tanning; in another, glue; while in some streets the nose encounters an unhappy combination of all three." Between 1916 and 1920 the London novelist and essayist V.S. Pritchett worked for a leather manufacturer; he also
recalled the odours of Bermondsey. "There was a daylight gloom in this district of London. One breathed the heavy, drugging beer smell of hops and
there was another smell of boots and dog dung . . . the stinging smell of vinegar from a pickle factory; and smoke blew down from an emery mill . . . from
the occasional little slum houses, the sharp stink of poverty." That last is of
course the most penetrating and significant odour of them all, compounding
the noisome reputation of south London in general.

The similarities between the East and the South are apparent, but there
were also significant disparities. The East End offered a more intense kind of
community than the South; it possessed more open markets, for example, and
more music halls. In the South, also, there was less contact with the rest of
London. By sheer proximity the East End could share some of the energy and
animation of the old City; it had, after all, existed against its walls for many
centuries. But the great swathe of the river had always isolated the South,
lending it a somewhat desolate quality. It is reflected in those comments
about south London which render it a distinct and alien place.

George Gissing, for example, depicted Southwark in terms of its unpleasant odours. "An evil smell hung about the butchers' and the fish shops. A public-house poisoned a whole street with alcoholic fumes; from sewer-grates rose a miasma that caught the breath." A London reporter, writing in 1911, remarked that to pass over London Bridge was to cross "that natural dividing line of peoples"; it is an interesting remark, suggesting an almost atavistic reverence for the natural boundary of the river which changes the essence of the territory on either bank. He then asked whether, having crossed that significant line, "the very streets changed in some subtle and unconscious manner, to a more sordid character; the shops to a more blatant kind—even the people to a different and lower type?"

If London contains the world, then there is a world of meaning here. The distinction between the "northern" and "southern" races is of ancient date, the North being considered more ascetic and more robust than the effete and sensual South. It was a distinction emphasised by Darwin who, in the context of that theory of natural selection which he developed in London, declared that "the northern forms were enabled to beat the less powerful southern forms." The "southern forms" may be weaker because they come from too attenuated an origin, perhaps stretching back to the great tracts of mesolithic and neolithic time. Those noisome smells may in part include the odour of ancient history. And what of their pleasures? According to the London reporter of 1911, "even the dramatic tastes of the people 'over the water' are now supposed to be primitive; and 'transpontine' is the adjective applied to melodrama that is too crude for the superior taste of northern London." Yet the sensational and spectacular aspects of the theatre of the South may be a refraction of those sixteenth-century tastes which the South Bank once satisfied.

If you stand on Bankside today you will see in alignment the 1963 power station of Sir Giles Gilbert Scott transformed into the new Tate Modern, opened in 2000, beside the seventeenth-century house on Cardinal's Wharf reputed to have been the lodging of Christopher Wren in the 1680s while he superintended the construction of St. Paul's Cathedral across the river; beside that, in turn, is the Globe recreated in its sixteenth-century form. A short distance away, in Borough High Street, the remnants of the George Inn evoke the atmosphere of Southwark during those centuries when it was a staging post and haven for travellers on their journeys towards or away from the great city. Close by, in St. Thomas's Street, an old operating theatre has been discovered in the attic of the eighteenth-century parish church. An account of this strange relic, dating from 1821, notes that "many of the surgical instruments were still very similar to those used in Roman times." Trepanning, a procedure in use three thousand years ago, was still one of the most common operations on this site. So when the patients were brought in blindfolded, and strapped to the small wooden table, and when the doctor raised his knife, perhaps they were participating in rites which had taken place on the same ground since the time of the neolithic and Roman settlements.

These tokens or emblems of the past have retained their power as a consequence of the relative isolation or insularity of south London; even in the 1930s according to A.A. Jackson's *Semi-Detached London*, "it was rare for a Londoner to cross the river" because it remained "foreign territory, with a quite unfamiliar, distinctively different transport system." Of course much has been demolished—a row of Elizabethan houses in Stoney Street, Southwark, was torn down in order to make way for the bridge into Cannon Street Railway Station—but much survives in a different aspect. Where once in the seventeenth century Thomas Dekker observed so many taverns that the high street became "a continued ale house with not a shop to be seen," the public houses still cluster together on the way leading to London Bridge. Even in the early nineteenth century the Talbot Inn, once called the Tabard, could still be inspected by the curious antiquarian as well as the nightly visitor; above its gateway was the inscription "This Is The Inn Where Geoffrey Chaucer, Knight, And Nine and Twenty Pilgrims, Lodged in Their Journey to Canterbury in 1383." Neither fashion nor pressing commercial need affected the fabric of South London. This accounts for its charm, and its desolation.

Yet the revival of the South Bank in particular, with a new footbridge erected in 2000 in order to span the river from St. Peter's Hill to Bankside, will lead to a great change. South London has been underdeveloped, in past centuries, but this neglect has allowed it effortlessly to reinvent itself. The point can be made by looking at the stretch of the Thames where much redevelopment is taking place. On the northern bank the streets and lanes are filled to bursting with business premises, so that no further alteration in its commercial aspect or direction is possible without more destruction. The relatively undeveloped tracts south of the Thames are in contrast available for a spirited and imaginative transformation.

To walk along the north bank of the river between Queenhithe and Dark House Walk is an experience in isolation; there is no sense of any connection with people, or with the city, along the "Thameside Walk" which winds between the old quays and jetties. These wharves exist as little more than the disconnected riverside terraces of various company headquarters, including one bank and a depot of the corporation of London. The northern bank of the Thames, to use a contemporary expression, has been "privatised." To the south, however, there is interchange and animation; from the new Tate Modern to the Globe, and then to the Anchor public house, the broad walkway is commonly filled with people. The ancient hospitality and freedom of the South are emerging once more; in the twenty-first century it will become one of the most vigorous and varied, not to say popular, centres of London life. So the South Bank has been able triumphantly to reassert its past. The restored Bankside Power Station, with its upper storey resembling a box filled with light, is aligned with Cardinal's Wharf and the newly constructed Globe in a triune invocation of territorial spirit. This is surely a cause for wonder, when five centuries are embraced in a single and simple act of recognition. It is part of London's power. Where the past exists, the future may flourish.

A detail from Hogarth's *A Harlot's Progress* showing a small black servant;
black slaves were often employed in the more affluent London
households of the eighteenth century.

CHAPTER 73

Maybe It's Because I'm a Londoner

London has always been a city of immigrants. It was once known as "the city of nations," and in the mid-eighteenth century Addison remarked that "when I consider this great city, in its several quarters, or divisions, I look upon it as an aggregate of various nations, distinguished from each other by their respective customs, manners, and interests." The same observation could have been applied in any period over the last 250 years. It is remarked of eighteenth-century London in Peter Linebaugh's *The London Hanged* that "here was a centre of worldwide experiences" with outcasts, refugees, travellers and merchants finding a "place of refuge, of news and an arena for the struggle of life and death." It was the city itself which seemed to summon them, as if only in the experience of the city could their lives have meaning. Its population has been likened to the eighteenth-century drink "All Nations," made up of the remains at the bottoms of various bottles of spirit; but this is to do less than justice to the energy and enterprise of the various immigrant populations who arrived in the city. They were not dregs or leftovers; in fact the animation and enterprise of London often seemed to invade them and, with one or two exceptions, these various groups rose and prospered. It is the continuing and never-ending story. It has often been remarked that, in other cities, many years must pass before a foreigner is accepted; in London, it takes as many months. It is true, too, that you can only be happy in London if you begin to consider yourself as a Londoner. It is the secret of successful assimilation.

Fresh generations, with their songs and customs, arrived at least as early as the time of the Roman settlement, when London was opened up as a European marketplace. The working inhabitants of the city might have come from Gaul, from Greece, from Germany, from Italy, from North Africa, a polyglot community all speaking a variety of rough or demotic Latin. By the seventh century, when London rose again as an important port and market, the native and immigrant populations were thoroughly intermingled. There was also a more general change. It was no longer possible to distinguish Britons from Saxons and, after the northern invasions of the ninth century, the Danes entered the city's racial mixture. By the tenth century the city was populated by Cymric Brythons and Belgae, by the remnants of the Gaulish legions, by East Saxons and Mercians, by Danes, Norwegians and Swedes, by Franks and Jutes and Angles, all mingled and mingling together to form a distinct tribe of "Londoners." A text known as IV Aethelred mentions that those who "passed through" London, in the period before the Norman settlement, were "men from Flanders, Pontheiu, Normandy and the Ile de France" as well as "men of the emperor: Germans."

In fact London has always been a hungry city; for many centuries it needed a permanent influx of foreign settlers in order to compensate for its high death-rate. They were also good for business, since immigration has characteristically been associated with the imperatives of London trade. Foreign merchants mingled here, and intermarried, because it was one of the principal markets of the world. On another level, immigrants came here to pursue their trades when denied commercial freedom in their native regions. And, again, other immigrants arrived in the city ready and able to take on any kind of employment and to perform those tasks which "native Londoners" (given the relative nature of that phrase) were unwilling to perform. In all instances immigration corresponded to employment and profit; that is why it would be sentimental and sanctimonious to describe London as an "open city" in some idealistic sense. It has acquiesced in waves of immigration because, essentially, they helped it to prosper.

There were, however, occasions of criticism. "I do not at all like that city," Richard of Devizes complained in 1185. "All sorts of men crowd there from every country under the heavens. Each brings its own vices and its own customs to the city." In 1255 the monkish chronicler Matthew Paris was bemoaning the fact that London was "overflowing" with "Poitevins, Provençals, Italians and Spaniards." It is an anticipation of late twentieth-century complaints that London was being "swamped" by people from Africa, the Caribbean, or Asia. In the case of the thirteenth-century chronicler there is an atavistic and incorrect notion of some original native race which is being displaced by others. Yet other forces are at work in his attack upon the foreigners; he was not wholly sympathetic to the commercial instincts of the capital, and felt himself alienated or removed from its heterogeneous life. Thus to single out foreign merchants was a way of neutralising or challenging the city's commercial nature. Those who attacked immigrants were in effect attacking the business ethic which required the constant influx of new trade and new labour. The attack did not succeed; it never has succeeded.

The immigrant rolls of 1440–1 provide an absorbing study in ethnicity and cultural contrast. An essay by Sylvia L. Thrupp in *Studies in London History*, "Aliens in and around London in the Fifteenth Century," offers interesting parallels with other periods. Some 90 per cent were classified as *Doche*; this was a generic term including Flemish, Dane and German, but more than half in fact came from Holland. The evidence of their wills suggests that their common characteristics were "a striving towards piety and economic advancement through honest work and mutual help within the group," an observation which could equally be applied to more recent immigrants from, for example, South Asia. These fifteenth-century immigrants tended to settle into defined trades such as goldsmithery, tailory, haberdashery, clock-making and brewing. They were also celebrated as printers. Others mingled within the broader urban community as beer-sellers, basketmakers, joiners, caterers and servants within London households or at London inns. Evidence from the guilds and from extant wills also "indicates that English became the means of communication within this group," again a characteristic and often instinctive response of any immigrant community. In the city wards the Italians comprised "a commercial and financial aristocracy," although there were differences within the group. There were Frenchmen, and a number of Jews; and "Greek, Italian, and Spanish physicians," but the underclass of that period seems to have been Icelanders who were commonly employed as servants.

There was a period of sustained suspicion in the 1450s, when Italian merchants and bankers were condemned for usury. But the imbroglio passed, leaving only its rumours as confirmation of the fact that Londoners were particularly sensitive to commercial double-dealing. The "Evil May Day" riots of 1517, when the shops and houses of foreigners were attacked by a mob of apprentices, were dispelled with equal speed and without any permanent effect upon the alien population. This has been the custom of the city over many centuries; despite violent acts inspired by demagoguery and financial panic, the immigrant communities of the city have generally been permitted to settle down, engage with their neighbours in trade and parish work, adopt English as their native language, intermarry and bring up their children as Londoners.

A wave of immigration in the mid-1560s, however, when the Huguenots sought refuge from Catholic persecution, provoked a general alarm. On 17 February 1567, there was "a great watch in the City of London . . . for fear of an insurrection against the strangers which were in great number in and about the city." The Huguenots were accused of trading secretly among themselves and of engaging in illicit commercial practices such as hoarding. They "take up the fairest houses in the city, divide and fit them for their several uses [and] take into them several lodgers and dwellers"; thus they were held directly responsible for London's overcrowding. Even if the children of these immigrants "born within this realm are by law accounted English," they remained foreigners by "inclination and kind affection." Once more it is a familiar language, adopted by those who were uneasy at the presence of "aliens" in their midst. There were also charges that they pushed up the prices of London properties.

It was perhaps inevitable that, at times of financial recession or depression, the onus fell upon the supposedly unfair or restrictive commercial practices of the "aliens." In similar manner, at times of growth and expansion, the presence of the same traders was greeted as an indication of the city's munificence and varied wealth. Addison, on viewing the polyglot assembly at the Royal Exchange, remarked that it "gratifies my Vanity, as I am an *Englishman*, to see so much an Assembly of Country-men and Foreigners consulting together upon the private Business of Mankind, and making this Metropolis a kind of *Emporium* for the whole Earth." There is no Jew-baiting or Francophobia in this account.

In 1850 William Wordsworth, writing of his earlier residence in London, reflected upon the fact that within the city crowd he had found

every character of form and face:
The Swede, the Russian; from the genial south,
The Frenchman and the Spaniard; from remote
America, the Hunter-Indian; Moors,
Malays, Lascars, the Tartar and Chinese
And Negro Ladies in white muslin gowns.

He also mentions the "Italian . . . the Turk . . . the Jew" and can thus be said to provide a comprehensive survey of the immigrant population. It provides a now familiar insight into the character of a city which contains many nations within itself, but in the nineteenth century there came a fresh movement of political as opposed to religious refugees. Carlyle noticed their presence in London when he observed that "one might mark the years and epochs by the successive kinds of exiles that walk London streets and, in grim silent manner, demand pity from us and reflections from us." The Russian revolutionary Kropotkin celebrated London as the haven for political refugees from all over the world, and indeed it has been claimed that by the close of the nineteenth century the city had become the most significant arena for the dissemination of political ideas, for the creation of political ideologies, and for the promulgation of political causes. So there were Spanish refugees in Somers Town—"you could see a group of fifty or a hundred stately tragic figures, in proud threadbare coats; perambulating, mostly with closed lips, the broad pavements of Euston Square and the regions about St. Pancras New Church." They became conspicuous in 1825 and then, like many other such groups, vanished almost as suddenly as they had first arrived. In the spring of 1829, according to a diarist of the period, "there was an abrupt increase in the numbers of French in London"; as political agitation and civic uprisings fluctuated in intensity, so did the numbers of the French. London became the political barometer for the whole of Europe. Garibaldi and Mazzini came, as did Marx and Engels; in 1851 Herzen and Kossuth arrived, the one a Russian, the other a Hungarian; so did political refugees from Poland and Germany. England, and in particular London, was the place most welcoming to exiles.

The history of any one group is filled with profound interest. There were Jews, Africans, and representatives of most of the European races, at the time of the Roman settlement. It is not too much to claim that their lives have haunted London ever since. The mystery of difference and of oppression has been played out over the centuries, touching upon the need to define oneself or one's race and implicated in the pride or susceptibility of a "native" population. This narrative has been largely conceived in terms of acceptance and assimilation, but no known human history is without its victims.

The Jews suffered early from prejudice and brutality. Refugees from the Rouen pogrom arrived in the city in 1096, but the first documentary evidence for a Jewish quarter emerges in 1128. They were not permitted to engage in ordinary commerce but were allowed to lend money, the "usury" from which Christian merchants were barred; then of course they were blamed or hated for the very trade imposed upon them by the civic authorities. There was a murderous assault upon their quarters in 1189 when "the houses were besieged by the roaring people . . . because the madmen had not tools, fire was thrown on the roof, and a terrible fire quickly broke out." Many families were burned alive, while others fleeing into the narrow thoroughfares of Old Jewry and Gresham Street were clubbed or beaten to death. There was another pogrom in 1215, and on certain occasions the Jews took refuge in the Tower in order to escape the depredations of the mob. They suffered from the noble families who were indebted to them, also, and in strange anticipation of a later destiny they were obliged to wear a sign upon their clothes in recognition of their race. It was not the Star of David, but a *tabula* or depiction of the stone tablets upon which the Ten Commandments were supposed to have been miraculously inscribed.

In 1272 hundreds of Jews were hanged on suspicion of adulterating the coinage, and then eighteen years later—their usefulness at an end after the arrival of Italian and French financiers—all were expelled, beaten, spat upon or killed in a mass exodus from the city. It would have seemed that the wandering race could find no permanent haven even in the cosmopolitan and commercial city of London. London, instead, had become the very pattern of urban exploitation and aggression. But some returned, quietly and almost invisibly, over the next two or three centuries under the guise of Christians; in the seventeenth century Charles I made use of their financial skills and resources but it was Cromwell who, with a more profound biblical knowledge, allowed the right of settlement after a "Humble Petition of the Hebrews at Present Residing in this city of London." They requested that "wee may therewith meete at our said private devotions in our Particular houses without feere of Molestation either to our persons famillys or estates." These were Sephardic Jews who, like Isak Lopes Chillon, one of the signatories to the petition, came out of Spain and Portugal; but in the latter part of the seventeenth century, from central and eastern Europe, arrived the Ashkenazi Jews who

were less affluent, less well educated, and variously depicted as "down-trod-
den" and "poverty-stricken." Charles Booth has described how "the old settlers held aloof from the newcomers, and regarded them as a lower caste, fit
only to receive alms."

And here emerges the other face of the immigrant population. The newcomers were not necessarily the accepted and acceptable, not merchants and
doctors, but the wandering alien, the lowly refugee, the poor unskilled migrant fit only for the "sale of old clothes or in peddling goods such as fruit,
jewellry and knives." The Ashkenazim were representative of an entire impoverished and wandering population, alternately exploited and abused by
the native residents.

More Ashkenazi Jews arrived at various notable occasions in the eighteenth century; there were persecutions, and partitions, and sieges, which
sent them flocking to their co-religionists already in London where the first
Ashkenazi synagogue had been established in Aldgate in 1722. But they were
not welcomed, principally because they were poor. It was suggested that they
would "deluge the kingdom with brokers, usurers and beggars"; once more
emerges the irrational but instinctive fear of being "swamped." They were
also accused of taking jobs from native Londoners, although, since they
could not be apprenticed to Christian masters, the fear of their usurping available employment was a false one. But, in London, such fears have always
been widely advertised and believed; in a society where financial want and insecurity were endemic among the working population, any suggestion of unfair labouring practices could arouse great discontent. Thus in the 1750s and
1760s Jew-baiting became a "sport, like cock-throwing, or bull-baiting, or
pelting some poor wretch in the pillory."

There is another problem, evinced as early as the seventeenth century,
whereby immigrants are lent distinct and opprobrious identities. "As the
Frenchmen love to be bold, Flemings to be drunken," Thomas Dekker wrote
in 1607, so "Irish [love] to be costermongers" or street pedlars. It is a
question, in the modern term, of "stereotyping" which afflicts all migrant
populations. The irony, of course, is that certain groups seem unable to escape this matrix of false expectations and misperceptions. The London Irish,
for example, had always been typecast as the poorest of the poor. By 1640
parish records note the presence of "a poor Irishman . . . a poore distressed
man from Ireland . . . a shroude for an Irishman that dyed . . . a poore gentleman vndone by the burning of a cittie in Ireland . . . his goods cast away
comeing from Ireland . . . four poore women and six children that came oute

of Ireland . . . poor plundered Irish." All these instances, and more, come from the registers of St. Giles-in-the-Fields and evoke the first steps in a sad history of migration. Yet it was not quite the beginning. Eleven years before, an edict had declared that "this realm hath of late been pestered with a great number of Irish beggars, who live here idly and dangerously, and are of ill-example to the natives." This has always been one of the cries against the immigrants of London: that they are lazy, living off hand-outs like beggars, and thus demoralising the resident population. The assumption here must be that immigrants are a threat because they undermine the will to work, and provide examples of successful idleness; they are also receiving help or charity which, paradoxically, the native population claims by right to itself. The same complaints have been levelled in recent years against the Bangladeshi population of Whitechapel, and of Tower Hamlets in general.

There were riots against the Irish, too, once more on the prevailing assumption that they were allowing themselves to be used as cheap employment—"letting themselves out to all sorts of ordinary labour," Robert Walpole wrote, "considerably cheaper than the English labourers have." There were masters who took them in "for above one-third less per day." Few observers stopped to consider the measure of poverty and desperation which would encourage them to accept almost starvation wages; instead there was open hostility and violence directed against them, committed by mobs which "arose in Southwark, Lambeth and Tyburn Road." There were assaults upon the Irish in Tower Hamlets, Clare Market and Covent Garden. During the Gordon Riots, in 1780, under the lambent cry of "No Popery!," Irish dwellings and public houses were indiscriminately attacked and pulled down. Another familiar component of these actions against the immigrants was the prevailing belief that many of them were criminals come to prey upon unsuspecting Londoners. One city magistrate, in 1753, argued that "most of the robberies, and the murders consequent upon them, have been committed by these outcasts from Ireland." Just as the Jews were receivers, so the Irish were thieves. London was "the refuge" where dangerous or depraved immigrants "seek shelter and concealment." The meaning of "refuge," then, can subtly change from haven to lair.

Among these riots and alarms there was another group of immigrants who, if they stirred little outrage, excited even less sympathy. They were the Indians, the forgotten ancestors of the twentieth-century arrivals, who came to London as servants or slaves; some remained in employment, while others were summarily dismissed or ran away to a vagrant life. There were "hue and cry" advertisements in the public prints—a guinea for the recapture of "a black boy, an Indian, about thirteen years old run away the 8th ins. from Putney with a collar about his neck with this inscription, 'The Lady Bromfield's black, in Lincoln's Inn Fields.' " Other advertisements were placed to discover an "East India Tawney Black" or a "Run-away Bengal Boy." Other Asian servants were "discharged" or "dumped," having attended their employers on their passage from India, so that they were reduced to a life upon the streets. One Indian visitor wrote to *The Times* in order to complain about the presence of Indian beggars who were "a great annoyance to the Public, but more so to the Indian gentlemen who visit England." The *Public Advertiser* in 1786 observed that "those poor wretches who are daily begging for a passage back, proves that the generality of those who bring them over leave them to shift for themselves the moment they have no further occasion for their services." These were the unwilling immigrants.

Although the general number of European immigrants increased throughout the nineteenth century, the Jews and the Irish remained the targets of public opprobrium. They were the object of derision and disgust because they lived in self-contained communities, popularly regarded as squalid; it was generally assumed, too, that they had somehow imported their disorderly and insanitary conditions with them. Philanthropic visitors to the Irish rookeries discovered such scenes "of filth and wretchedness as cannot be conceived." Somehow these conditions were considered to be the fault of the immigrants themselves, who were accustomed to no better in their native lands. The actual and squalid nature of London itself, and the social exclusion imposed upon the Irish or the Jews, were not matters for debate. The question—where else are they to go?—was not put. Similarly the fact that immigrants were willing to accept the harshest and most menial forms of employment was also used as another opportunity for clandestine attack, with the implied suggestion that they were good for nothing else. Yet the Jews became part of the "sweated" system, in order to make enough money to move out of the unhappy situation in which they were placed. They no more appreciated the noisome conditions of Whitechapel than did philanthropic visitors. Their poverty became the object of pity and disgust, while their attempts to transcend it were met with hostility or ridicule.

The popular prejudice against another Asian group is representative. By the late nineteenth century the Chinese, of Limehouse and its environs, were considered to be a particular threat to the native population. In the newspapers they were portrayed as both mysterious and menacing, while at a later

date the dangerous fumes of opium rose in the pages of Sax Rohmer, Conan
Doyle and Oscar Wilde. A cluster of associations was then reinforced. These
particular immigrants were believed to "contaminate" the surrounding urban
population, as if the presence of aliens might be considered a token of disease.
Throughout the history of London there has run an anxious fear of contagion, in the conditions of an overpopulated city, and that fear simply changed
its form; the fear of pollution had become moral and social rather than physical or medical. In fact the Chinese were a small and generally law-abiding
community, certainly no more lawless than the residents by whom they were
surrounded. They were also disparaged because of their "passivity"; the
spectre of the eastern habit of opium-smoking was resurrected, but in fact the
Jews had also been characterised as the "passive" recipients of scorn and insult. It was as if the native London tendency towards violence were somehow
provoked or inflamed by those who eschewed violence in their daily intercourse. The enclosed nature of the Chinese community in turn provoked a
sense of mystery, and suspicions of evil; there was particular concern about
the possibility of sexual licence in their "dens of iniquity." Once more these
are characteristic of more general fears about immigration and resident
aliens. They emanate in hostile attacks upon Russian Jews at the start of
the twentieth century, against Germans during the world wars, against
"coloureds" in 1919. These anxieties were directed against Commonwealth
immigrants in the 1950s and 1960s, and were in turn followed by hostility
against Asian and African migrants in the 1980s and 1990s. The pattern
changes its direction, but it does not change its form.

Yet with fear, on certain occasions, comes respect. This is nowhere more
evident than in the sometimes grudging attention paid to the fact that a
variety of immigrants retained their fidelity to a particular religion or ortho-
doxy. Their imported faith was in such contrast to the generally disaffiliated
or frankly pagan inclinations of London's native population that it was often
a matter of remark. The faith of the Jews, for example, was regarded as providing a strong moral presence and continuity in the East End; ironically it
was seen as one method with which they withstood assault and opprobrium
from other Londoners. The Protestant faith of the Huguenots, the Catholic
faith of the Irish and of the Italians in Clerkenwell, the Lutheran faith of the
Germans: such religious practices were also considered a redeeming feature.
"Then he would catch sight of one of the old, Jewish black garbed men, venerable and bearded"—so runs one narrative of the East End, *The Crossing
Point* by G. Charles—"now so few in the quarter but occasionally to be seen,

and his heart would lift with a kind of passionate nostalgia as if through such men he could still touch the certainty, the vitality, the rough, innocent, ambitious, swarming life of those early immigrants with so much before them of promise." This passage evokes those other aspects of immigrant life which, in the context of great and overwhelming London, are often disregarded; there is "nostalgia" for the certainties of an old faith, but also a fascinated attention to that "vitality" and "ambition" which have helped to create the contemporary multiracial city.

The Notting Hill Carnival, of Trinidadian origin, takes place in mid to late August, exactly as the old Bartholomew Fair at Smithfield did. It is an odd coincidence which emphasises the equally curious continuities of London life, but it throws into relief one of the strangest stories of urban immigration when black and white confronted the mystery of each other's identity within the context of the city. In sixteenth-century drama "the Moor," the black, tends to be lascivious, prone to irrational feeling, and dangerous. His appearance upon the stage is of course a consequence of his entry into London, where colour became the most visible and most significant token of difference. There were Africans during the long existence of Roman London, and no doubt their successors by intermarriage continued to live in the city during its Saxon and Danish occupations. But sixteenth-century trade with Africa, and the arrival of the first black slaves in London in 1555, mark their irruption into the city's consciousness. If they were heathen, did they possess souls? Or were they somehow less than human, their skin the mark of a profound abyss which set them apart? That is why they became the object of fear and curiosity. Although relatively few in number, most of them watched and controlled as domestic slaves or indentured servants, they were already a source of anxiety. In 1596 Elizabeth I despatched a letter to the civic authorities complaining that "there are of late diverse blackamoores brought into these realms, of which kinde there are already here too manie," and a few months later the queen reiterated her sentiment "that these kinde of people may be well spared in this realme, being so populous." Five years later a royal proclamation was announced, in which "the great number of begars and Blackamoores which are crept into this realm" were ordered to leave.

Yet, like all such proclamations touching upon London and London's population, it had little effect. The imperatives of trade, particularly with the islands of the Caribbean, were more powerful. Africans arrived as the slaves of plantation owners, or as sailors free and unfree, or as "presents" for affluent Londoners. In addition the increase of traffic with Africa itself afforded open access to the ports of London where many black crews found temporary homes in the eastern suburbs. Black servants also became popular, and fashionable, in the households of the nobility. So the population grew and, by the mid-seventeenth century, blacks had become unremarkable if still unfamiliar members of the urban community. Most of them were still indentured or enslaved and, according to James Walvin's *The Black Presence*, "consigned to the status of sub-human property"; the evidence of their existence in London is thereby confined to "decaying headstones, crude statistics in crumbling parish registers, cryptic advertisements." This of course is also the destiny of most Londoners, and it might be said that these black immigrants—seen, as it were, by a reverse image—represent in emblematic form the inflictions of London itself.

On 11 August 1659, an advertisement in *Mercurius politicus* concerned "A Negro boy, about nine years of age, in a gray Searge suit, his hair cut close to his head, was lost on Tuesday last, August 9, at night, in St. Nicholas Lane, London." Those who were "lost," or ran away, found themselves upon the mercy of the streets. One German observer noted, in 1710, that "there are in fact such a quantity of Moors of both sexes . . . that I have never seen so many before. Males and females frequently go out begging." The most significant abuses occurred, however, among those who were in more orthodox employment; until a famous trial in 1772, the Somerset case, established that the English courts would not recognise slave status, they were still slaves labouring for their masters. The London Sessions reported a case, in 1717, of a black immigrant, John Caesar, who with his wife had worked as a slave "without wages for fourteen years" for a company of printers in Whitechapel. As late as 1777 an advertisement appeared concerning a "black servant man about twenty-four years of age named William of a brown or tawney complexion" wearing "a parson's great coat, blue breeches, white Bath flannel waistcoat, yellow gilt shoe buckles, and a beaver hat with a white lining." He had run away and, although his appearance seemed fashionable and exemplary, the advertisement noted that "He is also the property of his master, and has a burnt mark L.E. on one of his shoulders." This was the brand not of infamy but of inhumanity; it was a way in which the blacks could be marked out as something less than human. In a commercial city, they became part of its movable property. Thus in the eighteenth century there were a large number of notices advertising their sale—"To be sold a negro boy aged eleven years Enquire at the Virginia Coffee House in Threadneedle Street . . . his price is

£25, and would not be sold but the person he belongs to is leaving off business."

And yet the condition of London bears another witness to their fate. These commercial transactions were undertaken by the wealthy or the well connected; there can be little doubt that the "gentlemen" who purchased and sold their little slaves would have been quite happy to see the "lower orders" of London generally consigned to such servitude. In that sense the fate of the black slave was representative of civic and administrative oppression on a larger scale. That is why the London crowd treated the black population with a certain amount of sympathy and fellow-feeling. It is a manifest expression of that native egalitarianism which has already been defined as one of the moving spirits of London life. That egalitarianism, to be seen at its most profound among the poor and wretched, is evinced in the life of a "black one-legged violinist" named Billy Walters who was nicknamed "the King of the Beggars." It was said that "every child in London knew him." It has often been observed how the prophets of racial conflict in London have been proved false; the voices crying doom, in the late 1960s and early 1970s, have since fallen quiet. We may find the causes of that relative harmony and tolerance, between black and white, in the general urban sympathy for the mistreated black immigrants of the eighteenth century.

Yet as their presence grew, even very slightly, so did the anxieties about the "blackness" in the midst of London. John Fielding, a London magistrate in the mid-eighteenth century, suggested that they became a subversive element almost as soon as they arrived in the city, particularly when they realised that white servants performed the same functions as themselves. To be black, in other words, was not a unique or an inalienable mark of servitude. So "they put themselves on a footing with other servants, became intoxicated with their liberty, grew refractory . . . so as to get themselves discharged." And when they were "discharged" into London, what then? They "corrupt and dissatisfy the mind of every black servant that comes to England." Others made their way to the retired streets and alleys where a black community had established itself. So for the civic authorities "the black presence," as it has been called, posed a double threat. Those in habitual servitude were being aroused to anger or complaint, while small clusters of immigrants were to be found in the "low" districts of Wapping, St. Giles and elsewhere.

The number of "destitute negroes" had also increased by the end of the eighteenth century; in particular black recruits who had fought for the English during the American War of Independence fell into dereliction on their arrival. This was another aspect of immigration, where the influx was the direct result of the actions of the host country; in that sense these black ex-soldiers created a recognisable line of descent to those twentieth-century migrants who left the ruins of empire. A pamphlet issued in 1784 stated that thousands of blacks "traversed the town, naked, pennyless, and almost starving." As a result they were believed to threaten social order. The African, Afro-American or West Indian—as long as his or her skin was of the appropriate hue—was always and instinctively considered a "threat." With that fear came also the prospect of miscegenation, since mixed marriages were not unusual in the poorer areas of London. Here the sixteenth-century connection of the "Moor" with lasciviousness was once more revived, as if a black skin were a token of "black" desires lying just beneath the surface of the human order. "The lower classes of women in England are remarkably fond of the blacks," it was reported, "for reasons too brutal to mention." A Committee for Relieving the Black Poor was set up with the sole purpose of assisting in expatriation. It was not a success. Less than five hundred, out of a population estimated between 10,000 and 20,000, embarked upon the emigrant ships—an indication, perhaps, of the fact that London remained their chosen city. However dolorous or impoverished their lives, the majority of black immigrants wished to remain in a place which in its daily commerce remained one of opportunity and diversion.

That population became acclimatised and, although still subject to racial taunts, a familiar presence in the streets of nineteenth-century London. They had become part of the "underclass" and were scarcely to be differentiated from it; as crossing-sweepers, as vagrants, or as beggars, they had become almost invisible. In the vast city they did not exist in numbers large enough to command public attention or concern; they were not competing for employment and so did not threaten anyone's livelihood. They rarely appear in novels or narratives, except as occasional grotesques, and their general fate seems to have been one of settlement among the urban poor.

Yet the beginning of immigration from the Caribbean islands in the late 1940s set off a litany of familiar fears, among them the prospect of white unemployment, of intermarriage, and of general over-population. In the summer of 1948 the SS *Empire Windrush* brought 492 young migrants from Jamaica. It marked the beginning of a process which would alter the demography of London and affect all aspects of communal life. The West Indians were in turn followed by immigrants from India, Pakistan and East Africa so that, at the beginning of the twenty-first century, it is estimated that London harbours almost two million non-white ethnic minorities. Despite occasional racially motivated attacks, and despite the anxiety felt by certain minorities at the behaviour of the police, there is striking evidence that the egalitarian and democratic instincts of London have already marginalised fear and prejudice. Immigration is so much part of London that even its latest and most controversial manifestations eventually become a settled part of its existence. This became clear even in the aftermath of the Notting Hill riots of 1958, and in particular after the murder of a young Antiguan carpenter named Kelso Cockrane. An essential element of London life returned. "Normally, in the early days, you know," one young West Indian informed the authors of *Windrush*, a study of twentieth-century immigrants from the Caribbean, "whenever something appeared in the papers, you could always test the temperature by going on the bus. People would be very hostile. And in this instance, after that funeral, there was a turning point. You could sense a change. People were more friendly. People began to react and respond in a different way." There have been riots, and murders, in the course of the last twenty years but no one can doubt that the central and essential movement within London has been one of absorption and assimilation. It is an intrinsic aspect of its history.

The city itself, in the process, has also changed. The authors of *Windrush*, Michael and Trevor Phillips, provide an interesting context for this alteration. They suggest that workers from Jamaica, Barbados and elsewhere, were not simply "migrating to Britain." They were in effect migrating to London because "it was the life of the city which called to them and which they had begun to crave." In the twentieth century the city had effectively created the conditions of modern industrial and economic life; thus for the new settlers the journey to London was the only way "to engage with the broad currents of modernity." It is a significant observation in itself, and one that throws a suggestive light upon all immigrant transactions over the last thousand years. They were drawn to the city itself. London called them. To settle there was, in some oblique and intuitive way, to be part of the present moment moving into futurity. The importance of time within the city has already been outlined but, for the first generations of the immigrant population, the city represented the movement of time itself.

Yet their vitality and optimism in turn brought energy back into the city. Throughout the 1960s, for example, it is claimed that the immigrants themselves assisted the "process of remodelling and modernising" the streets and houses in which they lived. Areas like Brixton and Notting Hill had been "declining and rundown since the nineteenth century," but the new arrivals "revalued huge swathes of the inner city." The use of the word "revalued" suggests the economic effectiveness of the settlers, but the transition from black immigrant to black Londoner also called upon different resources. Caribbeans "had to go through a fundamental series of changes in order to live and flourish in the city"; like the Jews or the Irish before them, they had to acquire an urban identity which maintained their inheritance while at the same time allowing its smooth passage into the huge, complex but generally welcoming organism of London. That urban environment might have seemed anonymous, or hostile, or frightening, but in fact it was the appropriate arena for the Caribbeans and other immigrants to forge a new identity.

So it is that the authors of *Windrush* suggest that "the instinct of the city was to . . . equalise choices" and "to level out differences between consumers and producers." This is the new egalitarianism which in turn equalises the differences between the various races which comprise it, since "the essential job of the city was to put people together." Yet in turn "the character of the city . . . came to define the identity of the nation," and the existence of a various and heterogeneous London has helped to redefine the notion or nature of Englishness itself. Now there are Montserratians in Hackney and Anguillians in Slough, Dominicans in Paddington and Grenadians in Hammersmith. Where once there were Swiss in Soho, and Cypriots in Holborn, there are now Barbadians in Notting Hill and Jamaicans in Stockwell. There are Punjabis in Southall and Bangladeshis in Tower Hamlets, Turks in Stoke Newington and Pakistanis in Leyton. Each community has replicated its independence within the larger context of London, so that once more the city takes on the aspects of a world in itself. The city, that "globe of many nations," acts as a paradigm and forerunner in the great race of life.

CHAPTER 74

Empire Day

*B*y the last decades of the nineteenth century London had become the
city of empire; the public spaces, the railway termini, the hotels,
the great docks, the new thoroughfares, the rebuilt markets, all
were the visible expression of a city of unrivalled strength and immensity. It
had become the centre of international finance and the engine of imperial
power; it teemed with life and expectancy. Some of its gracefulness and variety
had now gone; its Georgian compactness and familiarity had also disappeared,
replaced by the larger scale of neo-classical or neo-Gothic architecture which
somehow matched the aspirations of this larger and more anonymous city. Nelson's Column in Trafalgar Square, erected in 1843, was conceived upon the
model of a column in the temple of Mars the Avenger, in imperial Rome, while
a revised classicism was employed for the new buildings along Whitehall; the
architecture of London, according to Jonathan Schneer in *London 1900*, celebrated "British heroism on the battlefield, British sovereignty over foreign
lands, British wealth and power, in short, British imperialism." If it was a more
public and more powerful city, it had also become a less human one. Tower
Bridge, which took some thirteen years to build and was eventually completed
in 1894, was a representative emblem; it was an extraordinary feat of engineering, but it seems deliberately to have been built upon an impersonal and some-

what forbidding scale. In its immensity and complexity, it reflected the work-ings of the city itself.

Late nineteenth-century London was established upon money. The City had acquired the historic destiny that it had been pursuing for almost two thousand years. It had become the progenitor of commerce, and the vehicle of credit, throughout the world; the City maintained England, just as the riches of the Empire rejuvenated the City. The sea trade of the earliest set-tlers had over the centuries borne unexpected fruit since by the turn of the century almost one half of the world's merchant shipping was controlled, di-rectly or indirectly, by the institutions of the City. In the early decades of the twentieth century new office blocks became a familiar presence; new banks, company headquarters, insurance offices were built upon a massive scale, with intense and dramatic architectural effects. The latest edition of Pevsner's *Buildings of England* for the City of London notes, for example, how the Bank of England acted as a field of force for other commercial enterprises. "Around it are clustered the headquarters and major branches of the main clearing banks, many of which had grown enormously by merger and acqui-sition at the end of the 1910s. They were built to impress, inside and out." Here the element of London's essential theatricality once more emerges, but strangely mingled with the principles of profit and of power. The tendency towards "merger and acquisition" among banking institutions was reflected in a general movement towards the creation of greater and greater organisa-tions; the newspaper industries, the enormous growth of the Post Office, the vast expansion of insurance companies, all contributed to the sense of a city growing quickly and almost unnaturally.

It was unnatural in other respects. The advent of electric light in the 1890s—its first interior use occurred, in 1887, in the premises of Lloyds Bank along Lombard Street—inevitably meant that natural light was no longer nec-essary to work indoors. So arrived those great waves of City workers who in-deed might have been dwelling beneath the sea; they came to work in the darkness of a winter morning, and departed in the evening without once seeing the sun. So London helped to instigate one of the great disasters for the human spirit. In addition the use of new building technologies, particularly those of re-inforced concrete and steel, and the introduction of passenger lifts, led inex-orably to the erection of ever higher buildings. By that strange symbiotic process which has always marked the development of London, the expansion of the available space was matched only by the increase of the number of people ready to inhabit it. It has been estimated that the working population of the city numbered 200,000 in 1871, but 364,000 in 1911. Charles Pooter, of "The Laurels," Brickfield Terrace, Holloway, is a fictional variant of one of the thousands of clerks who comprised what one guidebook terms "a very city of clerks." "My boy, as a result of twenty-one years' industry and strict attention to the interests of my superiors in office, I have been rewarded with promotion and a rise in salary of £100." The fact that the Grossmiths' comic creation has endured in public affection for more than a hundred years is testimony, perhaps, to the instinctive accuracy of their account; the ordinariness of Pooter's life was seen as emblematic of the new type of urban, or suburban man. In his loyalty, and in his naïveté, he was the kind of citizen whom London needed in order to sustain itself.

But it was not only a city of clerks. London had become the workplace of the new "professions," as engineers and accountants and architects and lawyers moved ineluctably towards the city of empire. In turn these affluent "consumers" created a market for new "department stores" and new restaurants; there arose a revived and more salubrious "West End" of theatres under such actor-managers as Irving and Beerbohm Tree. There were also more refined delights. The parks, the museums and the galleries of mid-Victorian London were discovered by a new and more mobile population of relatively affluent citizens. There were better libraries, and a plethora of distinguished or specialised exhibitions to satisfy a new urban taste for instruction compounded by enjoyment. It was also the city of Fabians, and of the "new woman"; it was the home of the *fin-de-siècle*, most readily associated in the public mind with the spectacular London career of Oscar Wilde.

But the old city never went away. In the 1880s approximately four hundred people of both sexes used to sleep in Trafalgar Square among the fountains and the pigeons. As H.P. Clunn noted in *The Face of London* (1932), "only about one-third of these people had any regular calling or occupation, and the rest simply lived from day to day as best they could from childhood, and could hardly explain how they had managed to exist for so long." In any one year of that decade approximately "twenty-five thousand people were charged with being drunk and disorderly in the streets," in part because the public houses were allowed to remain open all night; perhaps the strain of being the richest and most powerful city in the world had some effect upon the citizens themselves. It was a city of contrast. Until the late 1870s, Leicester Square was littered with "tin pots, kettles, old clothes, cast-off shoes, dead cats and dogs."

The streets were filled with the ceaseless and incessant stream of horse-drawn, motor-driven and steam-propelled traffic; the average speed of the hansoms and the growlers and the vans and the "bumpers" or buses remained approximately twelve miles per hour. Old women squatted in the streets selling herbs, apples, matches and sandwiches. There was a floating population of ragged barefoot children who slept in alleys or beneath bridges. There were costermongers with their carts selling anything from coals to flowers, fish to muffins, tea to crockery. There were also epidemics of surprising speed and savagery which passed through the floating urban population. But somehow, perhaps only with the benefit of hindsight, the lives and roles of the poor seem diminished within the immensity and complexity of late nineteenth-century London; their voices are heard less easily amid the incessant traffic, and their struggles are lost among the army of clerks and "professions" and the whole multiplying population of the city.

This immensity and complexity, the emanations of so much wealth and power, created problems for the authorities themselves. How could the Metropolitan Board of Works, together with all the vestries and parishes, supervise or control the largest and most important city in the world? As a result, in 1888, the London County Council (LCC) was established to administer an area of approximately 117 square miles. It covered the whole of London, inner and outer, from Hackney in the north to Norwood in the south. There had always been unstated fears concerning an over-mighty and overweening city, so the LCC was granted no powers over the police or the public utilities: yet even at the time its inauguration was considered an event of great significance in the development of London. Sidney Webb described it as a movement towards a "self-governing community," which indirectly aroused memories of the medieval "commune" with its wall and its army. The great constitutional historian of London, Laurence Gomme, became Clerk of the LCC which for him represented "the reincarnation of the democratic spirit of the medieval charters, and traditions of citizenship as ancient as the Saxon and Roman origins of the city." In 1899, in a further act of reorganisation, twenty-eight Metropolitan Boroughs were created out of the vestries and district boards of the preceding century; although these were designed to impede any centralising impulses of the LCC they, too, had a somewhat atavistic air. At a "royal review" in the summer of 1912, each borough mustered a battalion to march before King George V; it may have been a harbinger of the Great War but the troops from Fulham and Wandsworth, Stepney and Camberwell, Poplar and Battersea, were a reminder of old territorial loyalties issuing from the earliest days of the *burg* and the *soke*.

The LCC embarked upon its municipal duties with enthusiasm and animation. The earliest priority was that of slum clearance and the development of public housing. What might seem, in retrospect at least, a symbolic gesture claimed the area of the "Jago" in Bethnal Green; the squalid alleys and tenements immortalised by Arthur Morrison were swept away in the late nineteenth century, and in their place was erected the Boundary Green Estate. Other areas of inner London were cleared but, in deference to the prevailing taste for "expansion" as a physical and mental imperative, "cottage estates" were erected in places like East Acton and Hayes.

In 1904 the county council assumed control of elementary education in London, and funded a system of scholarships whereby clever children might move on from board schools to grammar schools. Such innovations directly affected the lives of Londoners. A city government impinged upon the citizens for the first time in living memory. The administration of London was no longer some distant and almost unrecognisable presence, characterised by what Matthew Arnold described in another context as a "melancholy, long, withdrawing roar"; it had become a force for change and improvement.

London once more embodied a young and energetic spirit, with a curious acquisitive atmosphere which floods the pages of urban chroniclers such as H.G. Wells. The laborious and intricate city of the *fin-de-siècle* seems to have vanished, together with that heavy and lassitudinous atmosphere so peculiar to the memoirs of the period; it is as if the city had come alive with the new century. It was the first age of the mass cinema, too, with the advent of the Moving Picture Theatre and the Kinema. The Underground lines had abandoned their steam trains, and the whole network was electrified by 1902. Motor buses, tram-cars, lorries and tricycles added to the general momentum. London was, in a phrase of the period, "going ahead." Where in the late nineteenth century, wrote the author of *The Streets of London*, "it had been rich and fruity, it was becoming slick and snappy." One of the permanent, and most striking, characteristics of London lies in its capacity to rejuvenate itself. It might be compared to some organism which sloughs off its old skin, or texture, in order to live again. It is a city which has the ability to dance upon its own ashes. So, in the memoirs of Edwardian London, there are accounts of *thés dansants*, tangos and waltzes and Blue Hungarian bands. There were twelve music halls and twenty-three theatres in the central area, with another forty-seven just outside. The shops and restaurants grew in size, while the tea shops became "corner houses" and "maisons." There were picture domes and prizefights and soda fountains and cafés and revues, all compounding the atmosphere of a "fast" city.

The Great War of 1914–18 cannot be said to have impeded the city's growth or its essential vitality. London has always been energetic and powerful enough to buttress itself against distress and disaster. Herbert Asquith heard a "distant roaring" on the final day of peace at the beginning of August 1914. He wrote that "War or anything that seems likely to lead to war is always popular with the London mob. You remember Sir R. Walpole's remark, 'Now they are ringing their bells; in a few weeks they'll be wringing their hands.' " London was accustomed to violence and to latent savagery, not least in the manifestations of the mob, and for many the vision of chaos and destruction acted as a restorative. The inhabitants of a large city are always the most sanguineous. It is true, also, that London expanded during the years of war. Just as in earlier centuries it had killed more than it cared for, so in the present conflict it seemed to thrive upon slaughter. The city's economy was fuelled by full employment, with so many of its young males detained elsewhere, and as a result the standard of living improved. Of course there were local hazards and difficulties. Building work was suspended, and at night the city was only partly illuminated by lamps which had been painted dark blue as a precaution against the raids of Zeppelin warships. Parks and squares were used as kitchen-gardens, while hotels became government offices or hostels. But there were more foreign restaurants and *pâtisseries* than ever, as a result of the presence of émigrés, while the dance halls and music halls were full. There was a loss of life in the capital—it is still not unusual to find plaques upon the walls of long-since renovated buildings, commemorating a Zeppelin raid upon the site—with approximately seven hundred killed in the four years of war. In contrast it has been estimated that almost 125,000 Londoners died in battle. Yet London is prodigal of life.

The close of the war in November 1918 was greeted with scenes of revelry and enthusiasm which have always punctuated the city's history. Stanley Weintraub has depicted the occasion in *A Stillness Heard Around the World: The End of the Great War*. "The street was now a seething mass of humanity. Flags appeared as if by magic. Streams of men and women flowed from the Embankment . . . Almost before the last stroke of the clock had died away, the strict, war-straitened, regulated streets of London had become a triumphant pandemonium." This is a description of the city stirring into life again, with the "streams" of its citizens like the blood once more racing through its arteries. Pedestrians "were dancing on the sidewalks" and vast crowds gathered in all the public places in order to experience that inchoate sense of collective feeling which is one aspect of urban identity on these occasions; the citizens do indeed become one body and one voice. George V drove "through waves of cheering crowds," with the image of the sea once more invoking the strange impersonality and inexorability within this expression of mass emotion. Osbert Sitwell recollected that the last time he had seen such a crowd "was when it was cheering for its own death outside Buckingham Palace on the evening of August 4, 1914; most of the men who composed it were now dead."

Here the exultation comes very close to savagery, and a kind of barbaric triumph is let loose upon the streets of London. "The God of Herds" had taken over as the people "sometimes joining up, sometimes linking hands, dashed like the waves of the sea against the sides of Trafalgar Square." The celebrations there would continue for three days without ceasing. Paradoxically there was a certain amount of violence and riot to celebrate this peace, while one observer described it "as a sort of wild orgy of pleasure: an almost brutal enjoyment. It was frightening. One felt that if there had been any Germans around, the women would have advanced upon them and torn them to pieces." The same cruelty had of course been visible in the crowd's delight at the beginning of the war. In one novel relating these events, James Hilton's *Random Harvest*, the scenes represent "a common earth touch—a warm bawdy link with the mobs of the past." The frenzy spread in unexpected directions. There is the story of the famous parrot in the Cheshire Cheese Public House who with his beak "drew a hundred corks without stopping amid the din of Armistice Night 1918 and then fell down in a faint." It may seem perverse to pay more attention to the celebrations of a few days in winter than to the whole course of a war, but in that shorter period the city became more intensely itself.

Out of that conflict, too, emerged dynamic movement and a fresh sense of purpose. By 1939 the population of Greater London had risen to 8,600,000; it was the largest level it had ever attained, and is perhaps ever likely to attain. One in five of the British population had become a Londoner. The city had expanded in every sense, with new dual carriageway roads and radial highway schemes which reached out to Cheshunt and Hatfield, Chertsey and Staines. Just as it grew outwards, so its interior fabric was renewed. New banks and office blocks arose in the city, while the Bank of England itself was rebuilt. A new Lambeth Bridge was being constructed. With new initiatives in education and welfare, as well as schemes for the redevelopment of housing and of parks, the London County Council sustained the momentum of the city's development. H.P. Clunn, writing *The Face of London* in 1932, suggested that "the new London is rising, with irresistible energy, on time-honoured sites." It was not the first, nor the last, period of restoration; London is perpetually old, but always new. It was an appropriate sign of renovation, however, that in the autumn of 1931 the most significant public and commercial buildings of the capital were for the first time illuminated by floodlighting.

Its novel brightness attracted powerful forces; the process of what has often been called "metropolitan centralisation" attracted politicians, trade unionists and broadcasters; thus the BBC, ensconced in the heart of London, also became the "voice of the nation." The film and newspaper industries, together with the myriad advertising companies, migrated to the metropolis, in the process helping to spread images and visions of the capital throughout the entire country. Industry, too, was part of this mass migration. The authors of the *County of London Plan* noted that many commercial leaders were attracted by "the sight of numerous flourishing factories and the general air of prosperity associated with Greater London." Once more London had reverted to type and become Cockaigne or the city of gold.

The 1930s have in particular been anatomised as the age of anxiety, when economic depression, unemployment and the prospect of another world war materially affected the general disposition of the city. Yet the historians and reporters bring their own preoccupations to the subject; London is large enough, and heterogeneous enough, to reflect any mood or topic. It can hold, or encompass, anything; in that sense it must remain fundamentally unknowable.

J.B. Priestley, for example, saw evidence of a giant transition. He described a new urban culture, growing up all around him, as one "of arterial and by-pass roads, of filling stations and factories that look like exhibition buildings, of giant cinemas and dance halls and cafes, bungalows with tiny garages, cocktail bars, Woolworths, motor coaches, wireless." The familiar London sensation, of everything growing too large, once more emerged. It was reported in 1932 that Dagenham, for example, had within ten years increased its population by 879 per cent. In 1921 it had been a small village, complete with cottages and fields of corn; within a decade 20,000 houses had been erected to sustain a working-class population. George Orwell had mentioned Dagenham in his account of a new city where the citizens inhabit "vast new wildernesses of glass and brick," where "the same kind of life . . . is being lived at different levels, in labour-saving flats or council houses, along the concrete roads." He was describing the same reality as Priestley, with "miles of semi-detached bungalows, all with their little garages, their wireless sets." They were both reacting to the single most important change in London life within the last 150 years. They were talking about the suburbs.

One of many posters from the London Underground—this one dates from 1929–extolling the virtues of suburbia or "Metroland." The retreat into suburbia in fact marked the greatest change in London's topography since the estates of the eighteenth century.

CHAPTER 75

Suburban Dreams

he suburbs are as old as the city itself; they were once the spillings and scourings of the city, unhappy and insalubrious. The "subarbes" contained precisely that which had been banished from the town—the "stink" industries, brothels, leper hospitals, theatres—so that the area beyond the walls was in some way deemed threatening or lawless. It was neither city nor country; it represented London's abandoned trail across the earth.

Nevertheless by the sixteenth century such diverse extramural areas as Wapping and Holborn, Mile End and Bermondsey, began to manifest all the signs of burgeoning population, trade and housing. The author of *Londinopolis* wrote, in 1657, that " 'tis true that the suburbs of London are much broader than the body of the city, which make some compare her to a Jesuit's hat whose brims are far larger than the block." In the same period the Spanish ambassador remarked, "I believe there will be no City left shortly, for it will all have run out of the gates to the suburbs." Yet the process was as inevitable as it was inexorable. London could no more cease growing than a lava flow can stop its irruption.

But the process was complex and unpredictable. London did not extend itself ever outwards in all directions, like some blocked-in mass perpetually extending its perimeter; it spiralled out in various directions, making use of existing roads or trade routes and testing the capacity of various villages or parishes to sustain its weight. The south of Stepney, for example, seemed like a "city by the river," one of the earliest industrial suburbs, but to its north still "this Parish has the face of the country." London moved organically, in other words, always finding the right ecology in which it might exist and flourish. Spitalfields expanded fivefold in less than sixty years, and the derivation of these fields of spittle might have been taken from the fluffy white excreta of the spider continually expanding its web.

Yet of course this natural glut of buildings and of people provoked sensations of disgust or dismay. It seemed to threaten the identity of the city itself. On a technical level the authorities could no longer supervise trade, or working practices, or prices; in a less palpable sense the guardians of law and of authority were gradually losing control. That loss of power induced anxiety. So, for example, Charles I blamed mob riots in Whitehall upon "the meane and unrulie people of the suburbs," and the suburbs themselves have been described in Stephen Inwood's *A History of London* as "a nether world of dung heaps, stinking trades, bloodsports, gallows, low taverns, prostitutes, foreigners, thieves, the poor and the mob."

Yet for a while it still seemed possible to escape from the blight of the city. By the end of the eighteenth century there were in Peckham "many handsome houses . . . most of which are the country seats of wealthy citizens of London." In Kentish Town "the air being exceedingly wholesome, many of the citizens have built houses; and such whose circumstances will not admit of that expense, take ready furnished lodgings for the summer." In Fulham, also, were "many good buildings belonging to the gentry and citizens of London." The process here was not one of confused inchoate growth, but one of deliberate colonisation of the surrounding countryside. Villages such as Clapton and Hampstead and Dulwich became, in the nomenclature of a later period, "suburban villages."

As early as 1658, beside Newington Green, terraced houses appeared on the model of London terraces. Thirty years later Kensington Square was similarly laid out, while according to Chris Miele in *Suburban London*, "making no apparent concession to the rural character of the place." By some strange alchemy the city had reassembled itself in a distant spot, as a silent token of that which was to come. By a similar process suburban estates emerged in previously rural areas, closely modelled upon the estates which had already been constructed in the western quarters of London; Kensington New Town, Hans Town and Camden Town were cities in miniature, laid down at conve-

nient and profitable sites beside the main roads. The suburbs, like the rest of
London, were established upon the principles of commercial gain.

Just as areas such as Hammersmith and Camberwell could no longer be
described as either town or country, but were now something partaking of
both, so their inhabitants were mixed and ambivalent. Defoe had already noticed the emergence of "the Middle sort of Mankind, grown Wealthy by
Trade, and who still taste of London; some live both in the City, and the
Country at the same time." Hybrid forms of architecture, too, began to
emerge in these mingled landscapes. In the 1750s and 1760s, for example, villas emerged as standard suburban dwellings. They were soon visible in Islington and Muswell Hill, Ealing and Clapham, Walthamstow and South
Kensington. It has been said that their example directly affected the appearance of a later and more extensive suburbia, with what John Summerson
described as "the flood of Victorian house-building, that torrent of 'vil-
ladom.' " This description may itself be said to partake of the somewhat
dismissive attitude still adopted towards the suburbs of the nineteenth
and twentieth centuries, yet the villas of the mid-eighteenth century anticipated the atmosphere and texture of later suburban life in more than an architectural sense. They embodied, for example, that privacy which was
instinctive to the London character but which the city could no longer provide. One of the motives behind the movement towards the suburbs, both in
its early and late forms, was to escape the sheer proximity of other people and
other voices; the quietness of a modern suburban street may not equal the silence of villa grounds in Roehampton or Richmond, but the principle of exclusion remains the same. The villas were originally designed as dwellings
for one family, of course, surrounded and protected from the depredations of
the city. The notion of one unit as one family is indeed central to the later development of suburban life, where the yearning for safety and the relative
anonymity of isolation have been equally powerful. The villas were "detached." Cheaper versions for the more populous areas were in turn established upon semi-detachment.

There are social, and aesthetic, consequences attendant upon what some
might see as retreat or regression. The original villas were a highly visible token of respectability—"of cheerfulness, elegance and refinement," to quote a
brochure of the period—and this vision of respectability sustained the suburbs for the next two centuries. The phrase "keeping up appearances" might
have been coined for suburban living. But the original villas themselves introduced a form of artifice; they were not "villas" in any classical sense (cer-

tainly nothing like the Roman variant which would once have been seen all over southern England), and the illusion of country living was sustained only with a great amount of determination and ingenuity. The nineteenth- and twentieth-century suburbs were also involved in an elaborate game of make-believe, with the implicit assumption that they were not part of the city at all. In reality they were as much an aspect of London as Newgate or the Tottenham Court Road, but their principal attraction was still based on the assumption that they were free of the city's noxious and contaminating influences.

This happy fiction could not be sustained for long, however, with the emergence of mass transport expediting the greatest exodus in London's history. Soon the pattern became clear, with the more prosperous citizens moving further out to more extensive grounds and eminences even as they were being displaced by new arrivals. The phenomenon is as old, and as new, as the city itself. Charles Manby Smith in *The Little World of London*, observed the progress over the 1820s to 1850s of one fictional street, which he named Strawberry Street, in suburban Islington. It was two or three years in building, with "a double row of two-storied dwellings," and at first "clung with considerable tenacity to rural associations and characteristics" in order to avoid "being swallowed up in Babylon's bosom." It was genteel, the abode of professional gentlemen and their families, "clerks, managers, and responsible persons employed in the city." But then it began to change. "The professional ladies and gentlemen moved by degrees further north, and their places were supplied by a new class—by tradesmen's clerks, by foremen, and overseers of workshops" who worked all hours and who "let lodgings to help pay the rent." Soon enough "long ranks of cottages, not twenty feet apart, sprang up like mushrooms in the waste ground on the eastern side. They were inhabited as soon as built." A saw-mill was erected in the vicinity, and in the street itself there appeared a variety of shops; a carpenter, a joiner, a greengrocer joined the older residents so that "in a couple of years . . . the whole street on both sides of the way, with the exception of a very few houses, was transformed into a third-rate business street." The saw-mill itself prospered and "gathered round it a host of industrial processors." Beer-shops and public houses and coffee shops emerged, alongside workshops and work-yards. So within thirty years the street had been transformed "from the abode of quiet and ease-loving competence to that of the toiling and struggling mass."

There was another characteristic urban process, too, with development along the lines of the main roads followed by a consolidation of the areas between the thoroughfares so that, as *The Builder* of 1885 put it, "the growth of the solid nucleus, with but few interstices left open, has been nothing less than prodigious." By the 1850s the city began to lose its population to areas such as Canonbury to the north, and Walworth to the south. The advent of cheap "workmen's fares" meant that areas close to a railway station could be quickly inhabited; thus there emerged "working-class" suburbs such as Tottenham and East Ham. The drift was gathering pace and by the 1860s the clerk and the shopkeeper desired nothing but a little villa "out of town." An observer perched on top of Primrose Hill, in 1862, noted that "the metropolis has thrown out its arms and embraced us, not yet with a stifling clutch, but with ominous closeness." The metaphors here suggest some alien threat or invasion, and of course they represent a familiar if unimaginative attitude towards London. The city's expansion over the countryside was noisy, noxious and destructive. Yet it could equally be argued that the city brought energy and activity to those areas which it covered, and that in the creation of suburbia it fashioned a new kind of life. It brought prosperity and, for those who settled on the new estates, a kind of contentment.

In the middle decades of the nineteenth century, therefore, there was endless building activity in all the environs of London. "Let as fast as built" was one slogan, yet it would be a mistake to characterise all suburbs as examples of shoddy architecture or improvised planning. The informal St. John's Wood Estate and those of Wimbledon Common or Hampstead Garden Suburb, for example, were quite distinct from the working-class terraces of Walthamstow or Barking. The rows of small houses that comprised Agar Town differed from the more genteel avenues of Brixton. The Eton College Estate, covering the district known as Chalk Farm, was very different from the Seven Sisters Estate. Dreary Islington was not the same as leafy Crouch End. H.G. Wells reacted with dismay to the suburbia of Bromley, where he had grown up, and denounced its "jerry built unalterable houses" as well as the "planlessness of which all of us who had to live in London were the victims." Yet only a decade after the young Wells was unhappily ensconced in Bromley, the young W.B. Yeats was enjoying the relatively sylvan delights of Bedford Park. Both were London suburbs.

The broadest view, however, might identify three separate types of suburb. There were those still on the very outer limits of the city; areas like Surbiton, Sidcup and Chislehurst were characterised by the grander villas with large gardens built on high ground. There was a sprinkling of "cottages" and shops by the nearest railway station, but the rural illusion could still be maintained. In the second degree of suburbs, in areas such as Palmers Green and

Crouch End, dwelled the "middle managers, supervisors and better paid clerks" who benefited from the low fares of the surface railways to find a safe and relatively quiet retreat from the roar of "Babylon." The third level catered for the working class and, in estates like Leyton and East Ham, undistinguished and indistinguishable terraces of low-cost housing covered every available open space. These latter were generally located in the east of the city. The ancient territorial imperatives were, after all, also a determining factor in the character and quality of the suburbs, those to the east and north-east being obviously inferior to those of the west. The suburbs to the south were more expansive, and more sedate, than those to the north.

By the 1880s it was agreed that London was "as to its greater part, a new city." It had become, in the words of *Building News* in 1900, a "huge overgrown Metropolis" largely comprised of a "tide of small houses." This was the paradox—that a vast capital could be constructed out of small individual units. It was almost as if London had, by some strange act of intuition, taken on the visible shape of burgeoning social democracy. New forms of mass transportation, such as the deep-level Underground system, had helped to create a new city; in turn that city was now creating the context for evolutionary social change. "Where will London end?" asked *The Builder* in 1870, to which the only reply was, "Goodness knows." The question might have been asked at any time over the last six centuries, and received a similar answer. In 1909 C.F.G. Masterman also described the growth of the suburbs—as a London topic, it was on everyone's mind—as "miles and miles of little red houses in little silent streets, in numbers defying the imagination." For him it represented "a life of Security, a life of Sedentary Occupation; a life of Respectability." At a later date, in *Homage to Catalonia*, George Orwell in similar vein remarked upon "the huge peaceful wilderness of outer London . . . sleeping the deep, deep sleep of England."

Yet the denigration and the tone of limited contempt, implicit in these descriptions, were not shared by those who lived in the suburbs. Sleep and respectability may have been precisely the conditions required by succeeding generations of new Londoners; the population of the city had for many centuries been characterised by its violence and impetuosity, its drunkenness and ill health. The suburbs represented a new urban civilisation which would flourish without any of the familiar urban attributes. When Ilford was developed in the 1900s as a middle-range suburb for clerks and skilled workers, the speculators refused to permit the construction of any pubs in the vicinity.

Their concern was to render the new suburb as little like London as possible. In the same period the London County Council shifted its emphasis from the refurbishment or redevelopment of "inner-city" areas to the erection of "cottage estates" on the fringes of London. The idea of the cottage was itself much abused in the process, but the introduction of two-storey terraced houses with small rear gardens changed the reputation of council housing and in fact changed the image of the Londoner. The Cockney need not necessarily be a product of the slums.

In the mid-1930s it was estimated that, each day, two and a half million people were on the move in London. That is why there was a large increase in private, as well as public, suburbia. It was the age of "Metroland," which began life with the Cedars Estate in Rickmansworth and spread outwards to include Wembley Park and Ruislip, Edgware and Finchley, Epsom and Purley. The importance of transport in effecting this mass dispersal is emphasised by the fact that the very notion of Metroland was created by the Metropolitan Railway Company, and heavily endorsed by the London Underground. Their booklets and advertisements emphasised the resolutely non-urban aspects of what were effectively great housing estates.

"Metroland beckoned us out to lanes in beechy Bucks," according to John Betjeman who had a tenacious if ambiguous affection for the suburban terrain—for "gabled gothic" and "new-planted pine," for the "Pear and apple in Croydon gardens" and "the light suburban evening" where a vast and welcoming security is so much to be hoped for. In a poem entitled "Middlesex" Betjeman invoked another form of permanence—"Keep alive our lost Elysium—rural Middlesex again"—and the advertisers of the Metropolitan Railway and the Underground exploited this ache, or longing, for continuity and predictability. According to the brochures—displaying, once more according to Betjeman, "sepia views of leafy lanes in Pinner"—the new inhabitant of the suburbs will dwell beside "brambly wildernesses where nightingales sing." One advertisement prepared by the London Underground showed three rows of grey and mournful terraces, with the words "Leave This and Move to Edgware." A sylvan scene presents itself accompanied by a quotation from the seventeenth-century poet Abraham Cowley, who himself retired to Chertsey after the Restoration in 1660. In a single sentence he expresses the wish that "I might be Master of a small House and a Large Garden, with moderate conveniences joined to them." Once more the new suburban vision, in accordance with the implicit antiquarianism of London itself, took refuge in an appeal to an ill-defined and ill-explained past.

The same form of cultural nostalgia was evident in the architectural style of the new suburbs, the dominant model being "mock Tudor" or what became known as "Stockbroker Tudor" or "Tudorbethan." The desire was to combine the sense of continuity with the satisfaction of traditional workmanship and design. It was a way of conveying substantiality, and a measure of dignity, to these new Londoners who had exiled themselves from the central core of the city. The city can transform and regenerate itself in unanticipated ways. Thus the suburban Gardens, Drives, Parks, Ways and Rises are now as much a part of London as the old Rents and Lanes and Alleys.

London had created, and harboured, a new kind of life. Once more it happened unpredictably, with no concerted or centralised planning, and was directed by short-term commercial demands. So the suburbs became the home of shopping parades and imposing cinemas, of aesthetically pleasing Underground stations and ornate railway stations. It was the age of the Morris and the Ford. The factories which lined the new dual carriageways were now manufacturing the domestic items of this new civilisation—the washing machines and the refrigerators, the electric cookers and the wirelesses, the processed food and the vacuum cleaners, the electric fires and the leatherette furniture, the "reproduction" tables and the bathroom fittings.

In a novel entitled *Invisible Cities* (1975), the Italian writer Italo Calvino reflects upon the nature of the suburbs under the assumed names of the cities of Trude and Penthesilea. We may substitute Acton and Wembley Park. The narrator is told that he may travel wherever he chooses "but you will arrive at another Trude, absolutely the same, detail by detail. The world is covered by a sole Trude which does not begin and does not end." But this was always the definition of London, that it had no beginning and no ending. In that sense its suburbs simply partake of its endless nature. The gin palaces of the old city gave way to the glittering cinemas of the 1930s, the hostelries were replaced by "roadside inns" or mock-Tudor pubs located on significant crossroads, and the street-markets by shopping parades and department stores. The suburbs of the inter-war years significantly extended the life and reach of London, but essentially they elaborated upon it. In Calvino's novel the narrator asks for the location of Penthesilea, and the inhabitants "make a broad gesture which may mean 'Here' or else 'Farther on' or 'All around you' or even 'In the opposite direction.' " So for Calvino the visitor begins to ask "whether Penthesilea is only the outskirts of itself. The question that now be-gins to gnaw at your mind is more anguished: outside Penthesilea does an outside exist? Or, no matter how far you go from the city, will you only pass from one limbo to another, never managing to leave it?"

London is so ubiquitous that it can be located nowhere in particular. The extraordinary growth of its suburbs emphasised the fact that, since it has no defined or definite centre, its circumference is everywhere.

A famous photograph of St. Paul's cathedral; miraculously the church
survived the depredations of the bombs of the Second World War, but it
rose over a blasted and wasted city.

CHAPTER 76

War News

※

It began with attacks upon outer London. Croydon and Wimbledon were hit and, at the end of August, there was a stray raid upon the Cripplegate area. Then, at five p.m. on 7 September 1940, the German air force came in to attack London. Six hundred bombers, marshalled in great waves, dropped their explosive and high incendiary devices over east London. Beckton, West Ham, Woolwich, Millwall, Limehouse and Rotherhithe went up in flames. Gas stations, and power stations, were hit; yet the Docks were the principal target. "Telegraph poles began to smoke, then ignite from base to crown, although the nearest fire was many yards away. Then the wooden block road surface ignited in the searing heat." The firemen had to race, through fire and perpetual explosion, to reach conflagrations which were almost "out of hand." "The fire was so huge that we could do little more than make a feeble attempt to put it out. The whole of the warehouse was a raging inferno, against which there were silhouetted groups of pigmy firemen directing their futile jets on walls of flame." These reports come from *Courage High*, a history of London fire-fighting by Sally Holloway. One volunteer was on the river itself where "half a mile of the Surrey shore was ablaze . . . burning barges were drifting everywhere . . . Inside the scene was like a lake in Hell." In the crypt of a church in Bow "people were kneeling and crying and praying. It was a most terrible night."

The German bombers came back the next night, and then the next. The Strand was bombed, St. Thomas's Hospital was hit together with St. Paul's Cathedral, the West End, Buckingham Palace, Lambeth Palace, Piccadilly, the House of Commons. Truly to Londoners it seemed to be a war on London. Between September and November almost 30,000 bombs were dropped upon the capital. In the first thirty days of the onslaught almost six thousand people were killed, and twice as many badly injured. On the night of the full moon, 15 October, "it seemed as if the end of the world had come." Some compared London to a prehistoric animal, wounded and burned, which would disregard its assailants and keep moving massively onward; this was based on the intuition of London as representing some relentless and ancient force which could withstand any shock or injury. Yet other metaphors were in use—among them those of Jerusalem, Babylon and Pompeii—which lent a sense of precariousness and eventual doom to the city's plight. When in the first days of the Blitz Londoners saw the ranks of German bombers advancing without being hindered by anti-aircraft fire, there was an instinctive fear that they were witnessing the imminent destruction of their city.

The earliest reactions were, according to the reports of Mass Observation and other interested parties, mixed and incongruous. Some citizens were hysterical, filled with overwhelming anxiety, and there were several cases of suicide; others were angry, and stubbornly determined to continue their ordinary lives even in the face of extraordinary dangers. Some tried to be jovial, while others became keenly interested spectators of the destruction all around them, but for many the mood was one of spirited defiance. As one anthologist of London history, A.N. Wilson, has put it, the records of the time reveal "the perkiness, the jokes, the songs" even "in the immediate and garish presence of violent death."

It is difficult fully to define that particular spirit, but it is of the utmost interest in attempting to describe the nature of London itself. In his definitive study, *London at War*, Philip Ziegler has suggested that "Londoners made a deliberate effort to seem nonchalant and unafraid," but this self-control may have been a necessary and instinctive unwillingness to spread the contagion of panic. What if this city of eight million people were to regress into hysteria? It was precisely that fate which Bertrand Russell had predicted in a pamphlet, *Which Way to Peace?*, in which he anticipated that London would become "one vast bedlam, the hospitals will be stormed, traffic will cease, the homeless will shriek for peace, the city will be a pandemonium." It is possible that ordinary citizens, with instincts finer than those of their erstwhile "betters," knew that this could not be allowed to happen. So the "calmness, the resigned resolution of the Londoner" was the quality which impressed those coming from outside. In all of its periodic crises, and riots, and fires, London has remained surprisingly stable; it has tipped, and tilted, before righting itself. This may in part be explained by the deep and heavy presence of trade and commerce within its fabric, the pursuit of which rides over any obstacle or calamity. One of Winston Churchill's wartime phrases was "Business as usual," and no slogan could be better adapted to the condition of London.

Yet there was another aspect of the calmness and determination of Londoners in the autumn and winter of 1940, springing from some deep sense that the city had suffered before and had somehow survived. Of course nothing could equal the fury and destruction of the Blitz, but the sheer persistence and continuity of London through time lent an intimate yet perhaps at the time unidentifiable reassurance. There was always the intimation of eventual renewal and reconstruction. The poet Stephen Spender, in north London in the aftermath of one raid, related: "I had the comforting sense of the sure dark immensity of London." Here is another source of consolation; the city was too large, too complex, too momentous, to be destroyed. Then he recognised that "The grittiness, stench and obscurity of Kilburn suddenly seemed a spiritual force—the immense force of poverty which had produced the narrow, yet intense, visions of Cockneys living in other times." This has the "spiritual force" of revelation, since Spender seems to have concluded that poverty and suffering had somehow produced a kind of invulnerability to even the worst onslaughts which the world can unleash. "We can take it" was one of the often recorded comments by those who had been bombed out of their homes, with the unspoken addition that "we have taken everything else."

The attitude of self-sufficiency was often accompanied by an element of pride. "Every one absolutely determined," one observer, Humphrey Jennings, wrote, "secretly delighted with the *privilege* of holding up Hitler." There was, according to Ziegler, "a strange lightness of heart . . . Londoners felt themselves an elite." They were proud of their own sufferings, in the same way that earlier generations of Londoners claimed an almost proprietorial interest in their noxious fogs, in the violence of their streets, in the sheer anonymity and magnitude of their city. In a sense Londoners believed themselves to be especially chosen for calamity. This may in turn help to explain the evident fact that "macabre exaggeration became a hallmark of many Londoners' conversation," particularly on the numbers of the dead and the wounded. The innate theatricality of London life affords one explanation; it has been said that there "was never any conflict in the city's history to match the drama of the Second World War." London firemen claimed that half their time was spent in dispersing crowds of interested spectators rather than fighting the conflagrations. If it were not for the sheer blank monotony of tiredness and suffering, suffused with the horror of the bombs, one might almost sense a gaiety or delight in destruction itself.

There are other images of these early months. One was of the blackout which plunged one of the most brilliantly illuminated cities of the world into all but total darkness. It became once more the city of dreadful night, and aroused in some inhabitants sensations of almost primitive fear as once familiar thoroughfares became lost in blackness. One of Evelyn Waugh's characters notes that "Time might have gone back two thousand years to the time when London was a stockaded cluster of huts"; urban civilisation had been established upon light for so long that, in its absence, all customary certainties fell away. Of course there were some who took advantage of the darkness for their own purposes, but for many others the predominant sensation was one of alarm and insufficiency. The lure of shelter under the ground has already been discussed, together with the fear of administrators that London would breed a race of "troglodytes" who would never wish to come to the surface. The reality, however, was both more stark and more prosaic. Only 4 per cent of the city's population ever used the London Underground for night shelter, largely on account of the overcrowded and often insanitary conditions which they would have found there. In implicit compliance to the tradition of London as a city of separate family dwellings, most citizens elected to stay in their own houses.

And what might they have seen when they emerged at daybreak? "The house about 30 yards from ours struck at one this morning by a bomb. Completely ruined. Another bomb in the square still unexploded . . . The house was still smouldering. There is a great pile of bricks . . . Scraps of cloth hanging to the bare walls at the side still standing. A looking glass I think swinging. Like a tooth knocked out—a clean cut." Virginia Woolf's description registers the sensation of almost physical shock, as if the city were indeed a living being which could suffer hurt. "A vast gap at the top of Chancery Lane. Smoking still. Some great shop entirely destroyed: the hotel opposite like a shell . . . And then miles & miles of orderly ordinary streets . . . Streets empty. Faces set & eyes bleared." It might seem that nothing could obliterate these "miles & miles" of streets, that London could as it were "soak up" any punishment, yet its citizens were not so sturdy; fatigue, and weariness, and anxiety passed over them in waves. In the following month, October 1940, Woolf visited Tavistock and Mecklenburg Squares where she had lived. She passed a long line of people, with bags and blankets, queuing at eleven thirty that morning for a night's shelter in Warren Street Underground Station. In Tavistock Square she found the remnants of her old house—"Basement all rubble. Only relics an old basket chair . . . Otherwise bricks & wood splinters . . . I cd just see a piece of my studio wall standing: otherwise rubble where I wrote so many books." And then there was the dust, like the soft residue of obliterated experience. "All again litter, glass, black soft dust, plaster powder."

It was remarked at the time that upon everything lay a fine coat of grey ash and cinders, prompting further comparison between London and Pompeii. The loss of personal history was another aspect of the city bombings; the wallpaper, and mirrors, and carpets were sometimes stripped bare and left hanging in the air of a ruin as if the private lives of Londoners had suddenly become public property. This encouraged a communal feeling and became one of the principal sources of the evident bravado and determination.

The Second World War also created a climate of care. It became a question of saving the children, for example, by a process of mass evacuation from the city to the country. In the months preceding the outbreak of hostilities on 3 September 1939, a policy of voluntary evacuation was drawn up to deal with the movement of approximately four million women and children, yet the curious magnetism of London then began to exert itself. Less than half the families wished, or decided, to leave. Those children about to be sent to reception areas in the country departed reluctantly. The children of Dagenham were despatched on boats and John O'Leary, author of *Danger over Dagenham*, has recorded "awful silence. The children did not sing." One of a childhood contingent from Stepney, the writer Bernard Kops, recalled that "this was the place where we were born, where we grew up, where we played and sang, laughed and cried. And now all the grey faces as we passed were weeping. It was strangely quiet." When they arrived in the country they seemed, and were, quite out of place. A minority were unwashed, lice-ridden and disruptive. Here the old image of the savage rises forcefully. Others "would not eat wholesome food but clamoured for fish and chips, sweets and biscuits" and "would not go to bed at reasonable hours." They were the unnatural progeny of an unnatural city. And there "were children who refused new clothes and who fought and clung desperately to old and dirty things." The image of the London child as somehow "dirty" and woeful is here reinforced. Then, within a few weeks, they began to return home. By the winter of 1939 approximately 150,000 mothers and children had come back; by the early months of the following year, half of the evacuees had made their way back to the city. "London was, for me, like a return from exile," one is reported as saying in Ziegler's history. "My pet cat met me at the gate, the neighbours welcomed me and the sun shone." Here is a palpable sense of belonging, of being part of the city, which is the strongest sentiment among Londoners.

In the summer of 1940, when the German forces began to conquer Europe, another attempt was made to remove the children, those of the East End in particular. One hundred thousand children were evacuated but, two months later, 2,500 children were coming back each week. It represents the strangest, and perhaps most melancholy, instinct—the need to get back to the city, even if it becomes a city of fire and death. The curious fact, even during the air-raids themselves, was that the children proved "more resilient" than the adults. Like their predecessors over many eras, like the children depicted by Hogarth in the eighteenth century, they seemed to revel among all the suffering and privation, and in part reclaimed that state of semi-savagery which had been the mark of the street-Arabs of the previous century. One visitor to Stepney after a raid noted that the children were "wild-looking and grimy outwardly, but full of vitality and enthusiasm. One child said, 'Mister, let me take you to see the last bomb round the corner.' "

In Watson's Wharf, off Wapping, a gang of children congregated under the name of the "Dead End kids." Their story is told in *East End Then and Now*, edited by W.G. Ramsey. They were the unofficial fire-fighters of the East End. "Some of these children were very poor, and dressed in cheap clothes . . . They were split into sections of four. Each section was responsible for a district on Wapping Island." They had iron bars and a hand-truck as well as sand buckets and spades to assist them in their work. They roped in time bombs, and tossed them into the Thames; they carried the wounded away from incendiary scenes. One intense night of bombing in Wapping brought them out and, in the words of one witness, "In a moment ten boys rushed up the stairs, ready, as it seemed, to *eat* fires." They entered a burning building in order to lead out some horses trapped within, and emerged "with the clothes of some of those boys . . . smouldering." Some of them were killed in the fires and explosions but, when casualties depleted their ranks, others willingly filled their places. It is a most extraordinary story which emphasises in vivid and poignant detail the hardiness and self-reliance bred within London children. A little girl from the Elephant and Castle, when asked if she wished to return to the country, said, "No fear." No fear—that is the key to their self-containment or recklessness.

There was also a different kind of community. Elizabeth Bowen, in her novel of wartime London, *The Heat of the Day*, suggested that those who had died in the fire and destruction were not forgotten. "These unknown dead reproached those left living not by their own death, which might only be shared, but by their unknownness, which could not be mended now." The war had revealed the essence of the city's conditions of solitude and anonymity. "Who had the right to mourn them, not having cared that they had lived?" As a result there was an attempt by the citizens "to break down indifference," and in some sense to ignore or mitigate the usual restrictions of life in London. "The wall between the living and the living became less solid as the wall between the living and the dead thinned." So strangers would say, "Good night, good luck" as they passed each other in the evening.

There was also a marked and pervasive sense of unreality, as if the familiar outlines of the city had suddenly changed their aspect and become unknown or intangible. "Everybody and all familiar things and jobs seemed so unreal," one recalled, "we even spoke differently to each other as if we should soon be parted." This sense of fragility or transitoriness helped to form the atmosphere in what was called "a besieged city," and one Londoner who made a brief visit to the countryside professed himself surprised "at buildings unthreatened, at mountains that could not be overthrown." As a result of his experience "All permanence was astonishing. So unnatural had his own life been, that Nature seemed not to belong to him nor he to Nature." The city had always been deemed "unnatural" by atavistic moralists, but now that sense was shared by its citizens. It was unnatural to be congregated in a place where bombs would fall; it was unnatural to be part of so vast and manifest a target. Yet this was the condition of their lives; perhaps it was the condition of being human.

The bombings of 1940 culminated in the most celebrated and notorious of all raids, that of Sunday 29 December 1940. The warning was sounded a little after six in the evening, and then the incendiaries came down like "heavy rain." The attack was concentrated upon the City of London. The Great Fire had come again. The area from Aldersgate to Cannon Street, all of Cheapside and Moorgate, was in flames. One observer on the roof of the Bank of

England recalled that "the whole of London seemed alight! We were hemmed in by a wall of flame in every direction." Nineteen churches, sixteen of them built by Christopher Wren after the first Great Fire, were destroyed; of the thirty-four guild halls, only three escaped; the whole of Paternoster Row went up in flames, destroying some five million books; the Guildhall was badly damaged; St. Paul's was ringed with fire, but escaped. "No one who saw will ever forget," William Kent wrote in *The Lost Treasures of London*, "their emotions on the night when London was burning and the dome seemed to ride the sea of fire." Almost a third of the city was reduced to ash and rubble. By curious coincidence, however, the destruction was largely visited upon the historical and religious aspects of the old City; the thoroughfares of business, such as Cornhill and Lombard Street, remained relatively unscathed while none of the great financial centres was touched. The deities of the city protected the Bank of England and the Stock Market, like the City griffins which jealously guard its treasure.

One who walked through the ruins the day after the raid recalled that "The air felt singed. I was breathing ashes . . . The air itself, as we walked, smelt of burning." There are many accounts of the craters, the cellars opened to the outer air, the shattered walls, the fallen masonry, the gas-mains on fire, the pavements covered with dust and broken glass, the odd stumps of brick, the broken and suspended stairs. "For some days the church walls steamed and smoked," according to James Pope-Hennessy in an account entitled *History Under Fire*. Yet the workers, the temporary inhabitants, of the City came back. After the raids, "the whole City seemed to be on the tramp" as the clerks and secretaries and office boys all took circuitous ways through the ruins to their destinations. Many had arrived to find their places of employment "gutted" or absolutely destroyed, and then returned on the following morning "simply because they had nothing better to do." The power of the City then became manifest in their behaviour; they resembled the prisoners of Newgate who, after it had been fired by the Gordon rioters, returned to wander among the ruins of their cells.

The City had become unfamiliar territory. The area between St. Mary le Bow in Cheapside and St. Paul's Cathedral reverted to wasteland, where the long grass was crossed by beaten paths bearing the names of Old Change, Friday Street, Bread Street and Watling Street. Signs were nailed up, with the names of these streets and others, to prevent people from losing their way. Even the colours of the city had changed; concrete and granite had "been scorched umber" while church ruins were "chrome yellow." There are some remarkable photographs, taken by Cecil Beaton in the aftermath of the December raid. Paternoster Row is a mound of broken rubble with odd pieces of ironwork sticking out among the brick and stone; the premises of thirty publishers were destroyed. In the last Great Fire the Row was similarly struck and, according to Pepys, "all the great booksellers almost undone." Outside the church of St. Giles, Cripplegate, the statue of Milton had been blown off its plinth by the blast of a bomb but the tower and walls of the church survived as they had done almost four hundred years before. It was recorded on 12 September 1545 that "Sant Gylles was burned, alle hole, save the walles, stepall, and alle, and how it came God knoweth"; now, almost by a miracle, they were saved again. There are photographs of many ruined church interiors, with monuments tumbled down, screens fallen into fragments, and cherubs' heads scattered across the floor; there are photographs of the ruined Guildhall, of the bombed Middle Temple, of craters and falling roofs. It seemed to many that the tangible and textural history of London was without meaning, if its glory could disappear in a night; it was too fragile, and frail, to be relied upon. It was the invisible and intangible spirit or presence of London that survived, and somehow flourished, in the period of devastation.

There were, however, unexpected discoveries. A section of the Roman Wall, hidden for many hundreds of years, was uncovered by the bombing of Cripplegate. An underground chamber paved with tiles emerged below the altar of St. Mary le Bow, and a "Gothic blocked-up doorway" was recovered in St. Vedast's, Foster Lane, after its bombardment. Roman relics were found by Austin Friars, one of them a tile with the paw-marks of a dog in pursuit of a cat. Behind the organ of All Hallows Church, hitherto concealed by panelling which the bombs destroyed, was found a seventh-century arch formed out of Roman tiles. The parish priest described how "out of the wall adjacent to the arch great fragments fell which had for at least eight hundred years been embedded as the capstones in the strong Norman pillars of that date. Some of these stones were most remarkable . . . They represent a school of craftsmanship whereof we have no other evidence. They form a portion of a noble Cross which once upreared its head on Tower Hill, before the Norman William conquered London." The emblematic significance of the discovery was not in doubt; the German bombs had fortuitously uncovered a Saxon cross representing defiance before an invader. So those who believed that the city's history could be easily destroyed were mistaken; it emerged at a deeper level with the implicit assurance that, like the ancient cross, London itself would rise again. There was even a natural analogy. Air damage to the herbarium in the Natural History Museum meant that certain seeds became damp, including mimosa brought from China in 1793. After their trance of 147 years, they began to grow again.

Yet there was also a curious interval when the natural world was reaffirmed in another sense. One contemporary has described how "many acres of the most famous city in the world have changed from the feverish hum and activity of man into a desolate area grown over with brightly coloured flowers and mysterious with wild life." The transformation was "deeply affecting." In Bread Street and Milk Street bloomed ragwort, lilies of the valley, white and mauve lilac. "Quiet lanes lead to patches of wild flowers and undergrowth not seen in these parts since the days of Henry VIII." The connection here with the sixteenth century is an appropriate one, when this part of London was laid out with gardens and pathways, but the bombed city travelled further back to the time when it was prehistoric marshland. The author of *London's Natural History*, R.S. Fitter, suggested after the war that "the profusion of wild flowers, birds and insects to be seen on the bombed sites of the city is now one of the sights of London"; he mentioned "269 wild flowers, grasses and ferns, 3 mammals, 31 birds, 56 insects and 27 kinds of other invertebrates" which had appeared since 1939. Pigs were kept, and vegetables cultivated, in wasteland beside the bombed Cripplegate Church; this earth had been covered with buildings for more than seven centuries, and yet its natural fertility was revived. It is indirect testimony, perhaps, to the force and power of London which kept this "fertility" at bay. The power of the city and the power of nature had fought an unequal battle, until the city was injured; then the plants, and the birds, returned.

After the great fire-raid at the end of December 1940, the attacks were more sporadic but no less deadly. There were raids in January 1941, with a brief cessation in February, but they began again in earnest in March. On 16 April the city was visited by what the Germans described as "the greatest air-raid of all time"; the bombers returned again three nights later. More than a thousand people were killed on each night of the bombardment, which hit areas as diverse as Holborn and Chelsea. London became confused and misshapen, while anxiety and loss of sleep marked the faces of Londoners. It was the crushing sense of unreality, and meaninglessness, which now weighed heaviest; the weariness combined with the destruction to create a light-headedness among the population. "So low did the dive-bombers come," one witness recalled, "that for the first time I mistook bombers for taxi-cabs." The heaviest and most prolonged raid of all occurred on Saturday 10 May 1941, when bombs fell in Kingsway, Smithfield, Westminster and all over the City; almost 1,500 were killed. The Law Courts and the Tower of London were attacked, the House of Commons reduced to a shell. The church of St. Clement Danes was destroyed, so devastated that its rector died "from the shock and grief" in the following month. His wife died four months later. This perhaps represents a small amount of suffering, compared to the totality of misery endured during these years, but it marks one pertinent aspect of London's destruction; certain individuals can become so attached to, or associated with, certain buildings that their destruction provokes death itself. The city and its inhabitants are intertwined, for better or for worse. On the following day "the smell of burning was never so pronounced as on that Sunday morning." It seemed then that the city could not withstand the onslaught for much longer. An American journalist, Larry Rue, noticed that male workers in the City were travelling to their offices unshaven. "I began to realise," he wrote, "to what deep depths of their being the 10 May raid had shocked and shaken the people of London. It was just one raid too much." Yet it was to be the last significant attack upon London for three years.

The German invasion of Russia had indirectly saved the city from more destruction, and there succeeded a relative peace. Then "life" went on. The city seemed to resume its normal course, with its postmen and bus-drivers and milkmen and errand boys, but there was the strangest feeling of ennui or despondency after the spectacular damage of the Blitz. Philip Ziegler in *London at War* has described it as an "enervating lull." With the conflict taking place in other cities and over other skies, "Londoners felt that they had been left on the sidelines, they were bored and dejected." Those who still used the Underground shelters had established a network of friendship and camaraderie but this subterranean spirit was an odd token of London's general condition, in what Elizabeth Bowen called "the lightless middle of the tunnel," enduring the discomforts and disadvantages of a war over which it had no control. The citizens were frustrated at, and bored by, the privations of life. And this in turn affected the very atmosphere and character of London itself. The people were shabbily dressed and, in instinctive and intimate sympathy, their houses became shabby. The windows were cracked, the plaster was flaking away, the wallpaper manifested signs of damp. The public buildings of the city were also showing signs of fatigue and depression, as their façades became more grimy and decayed. The atmosphere was woebegone, with a strange symbiosis between the city and its inhabitants which suggests—as Defoe had discovered during the Great Plague—the presence of a living, suffering organism.

Then, at the beginning of 1944, the bombs returned. But the "little blitz," as it was called, was the unhappy end of unfinished business; there were fourteen raids in all, the heaviest in February and March, directed against a city which had been wearied and to a certain extent demoralised by the prolonged and uncertain conflict. "London seems disturbed by the raids and less ebullient than in 1940–1," Jock Colville noted.

Then something else happened. In June of that year pilotless jet planes carrying a bomb known as the V1, alias doodlebug, alias flying bomb, alias buzz bomb, alias robot bomb, began to appear in the skies above London. They were recognised by the sharp buzzing of the engine followed by sudden silence, as the engine cut out and the bomb fell to earth. They came in daylight, with infrequent intervals between them, and were perhaps the hardest to bear. "One listens fascinated to the Doodle Bugs passing over," one contemporary wrote, "holding one's breath, praying that they will travel on . . . The atmosphere in London has changed. Back into the Big Blitz. Apprehension is in the air. Buses half empty in the evening. Marked absence of people on the streets. Thousands have left, and many go early to the shelters." The novelist Anthony Powell was on fire duty and watched the V1s travelling through the air to their unknown targets, "with a curious shuddering jerky movement . . . a shower of sparks emitted from the tail." He saw them as "dragons" and "In imagination one smelt brimstone," so that the city under threat becomes once more a place of fantasy and myth. Almost two and a half thousand flying bombs fell upon the capital within ten months—"droning *things*, mercilessly making for you, thick and fast, day and night." It was the impersonality of the weapons, often compared with giant flying insects, which compounded the fear. The intended victims themselves became depersonalised, of course, so that the condition of living in the city was the condition of being less than human. Londoners, according to Cyril Connolly, "grow more and more hunted and disagreeable; like toads, each sweating and palpitating under his particular stone." The general mood was one of "strain, weariness, fear and despondency." "Let me get out of this" was the unspoken wish visible upon every tired and anxious face, while at the same time the inhabitants of London carried on with their customary work and duties. The mechanism continued to operate, but now in a much more impersonal manner; the whole world had turned into a machine, either of destruction or of weary survival.

Just as the frequency of the flying bombs began to diminish, in the early autumn of 1944, Vengeance Two—the V2—was targeted upon the capital. For the first time in the history of warfare, a city came under attack from long-distance rockets which travelled at approximately three thousand miles per hour. No warning could be sounded; no counter-attack launched. The first one hit Chiswick and the explosion could be heard at Westminster about seven miles away. Their power was so great that "whole streets were flattened as they landed." One resident of Islington recorded: "I thought the end of the world had come." That phrase has been repeated before in the history of London, at moments of crisis or terrible conflagration. Almost a thousand rockets were aimed at the capital, with a half reaching their targets. There were open spaces where streets had been. One rocket hit Smithfield Market, and another a department store in New Cross; the Royal Hospital in Chelsea was struck. "Are we never to be free of damage or death?" one Londoner complained. "Surely five years is long enough for any town to have to suffer?"

It was the coldest winter for many years, and the bombs continued to fall. Illness was in the air, as it has been throughout London's troubled history, along with rumours of epidemics and mounting deaths. Yet there was also a certain insouciance abroad; the V2s were so unpredictable and random that they revived the gambling spirit of Londoners who now retired to bed without knowing if they were necessarily going to rise on the following morning.

And then, suddenly, it was all over. At the end of March 1945 a rocket fell upon Stepney, and another on Whitefield's Tabernacle on the Tottenham Court Road. But then the raids ceased; the rocket-launching sites had been captured. The skies had cleared. The Battle of London was finally won. Almost 30,000 Londoners had been killed, and more than 100,000 houses utterly destroyed; a third of the City of London had been razed.

On 8 May 1945 there were the usual celebrations for victory in Europe, VE Day, although by no means as garish or as hysterical as those of 1918. The participants were more weary, after five years of intermittent bombing and death, than their predecessors on the same streets twenty-seven years before; and the war against Japan was continuing (VJ Day was 15 August 1945). Yet something had happened to London, too. In the phrase of the period the "stuffing" had been "knocked out of it," the metaphor suggesting a thinner and more depleted reality. Certainly it had lost much of its energy and bravura; it had become as shabby as its inhabitants and, like them, it would take time to recover.

New homes rise from London's ruins....

A poster extolling the virtues of the Lansbury council estates in Poplar, built upon the ruins of the old East End. Some of the energy and the animation of the original tenements had gone but the East End was a safer and healthier place.

CHAPTER 77

Fortune not Design

*H*ow Shall We Rebuild London? This was the title of a book, by C.B. Purdom, which described the postwar city "dulled by such extensive drabness, monotony, ignorance and wretchedness that one is overcome by distress." That drabness or "greyness," so characteristic in recollections of London in the 1950s, was a matter of privation; in the years immediately after the Second World War, most commodities were rationed. But in another sense it was the greyness of twilight. If one natural reaction after the war lay in the desire to create a "new world," as the urban planners wished, then another was to reconstruct the old world as if nothing particular had happened. So when Roy Porter in *London: A Social History* invokes the 1950s in terms of a "knees-up at the pub" and "contented commuters," he is remarking upon the atavistic tendency of London to go on doing all the things which it had been doing before the unhappy interruption of hostilities. Yet it could not, and did not, succeed. The desire to impose a set of familiar conditions, in changed circumstances, led only to a vague atmosphere of oppression or constriction.

The two great set-pieces of London theatre were the Festival of Britain in 1951 and the Coronation of Elizabeth II in 1953. This sense of London as a successful and enthusiastic community, miraculously reassembled after the war, was subtly reinforced by the resurgence of orthodox values and conventional activities. Youth organisations, like the Scouts and the Cubs, flourished; it was a great period for Boys Clubs in east and south London. Attendance at football matches rose once again to prewar levels; the cinemas were also crowded, perhaps because, as one Londoner of the period recalled, "there was practically nothing else to do." This air of mild oppression, like a hangover after the excitement of war, was intensified by a concerted if unspoken desire to redefine sexual and social mores which had been considerably relaxed during the conflict. The relative sexual freedom of women, and the chummy egalitarianism of enforced contact between the classes, were phenomena strictly of the past. And that in turn led to further if ill-defined unease, especially among the younger population. The standards of the 1930s were being reintroduced within a quite different society. The imposition of two years of compulsory military service, known as "National Service," only served to emphasise the atmosphere of general constriction. It was a less advantageous aspect of the newly formed "welfare state."

So London, then, was drab. Compared with other great cities, such as Rome and Paris and New York, it was ugly and forlorn; for the first time in its history it had become something of an embarrassment. And yet there were already stirrings of change, arriving from unexpected quarters. The Teddy boys of Elephant and Castle, and other parts of south London, were joined by the bright young things of the Chelsea set and the beatniks of Soho, as objects of moral outrage. It is perhaps significant that these various groups were closely associated with certain areas of the city, as if local historical forces were also at work. They were all intent upon breaking free from what they considered to be the dreary uniformity of urban life still modelled on outdated systems of class and belief. The dead areas of Walworth or of Acton, of Islington or of Stoke Newington, were a standing reproof. Their territorial spirit, too, was manifest in what they wore; the clothes of the Teddy boy, as well as his successor the Mod, were the single and often only mark of identity. The Teddy boys had in fact borrowed their "look" from the more respectable tailors of Savile Row and Jermyn Street who were trying to promote the images of "Edwardian" refinement among their male customers. Edward became "Teddy," and a new hybrid was created. Instead of those images of working-class youth in the late nineteenth and early twentieth centuries, shabbily dressed and with the uniform cloth cap perched upon their heads, there emerged a picture of boys in velvet jackets and drainpipe trousers. The recklessness and freedom, already evinced by the children of the Blitz, were still apparent. In the eighteenth and nineteenth centuries clothes were "handed down" from class to class in the spiral of trade, but on this occasion the disadvantaged actively promoted the transaction. It was another feature of native London egalitarianism accompanied by a self-possession and aggression which have been evident in London since the days of the medieval apprentices. In fact many Teddy boys were themselves apprentices.

But these attitudes were reinforced by the fact that London was becoming once more a young city. The rising birth rate and accelerating prosperity of London in the 1950s helped to create a younger society which wished to divest itself of the limitations and restrictions of the postwar capital. There was no sudden transition, in other words, to the "Swinging Sixties." There were cafés and coffee bars and jazz-clubs in Soho; there were clothes-shops and small bistros in Chelsea some years before the efflorescence of boutiques and discothèques. London was slowly being rejuvenated, and by the mid-1960s it was suggested that 40 per cent of the general population were under twenty-five. This is approximately the condition of Roman London, when only 10 per cent of the population survived after forty-five, and we may infer a similar sexual energy. It also corresponds to the ratio of the city's population in the sixteenth century, where all the evidence suggests an earlier resurgence of the London appetite for fashion. If the conditions are approximately the same, then urban attitudes will be repeated.

"Before the Blitz," Rasmussen has written in *London: The Unique City*, "Londoners took their dingy streets as a matter of fact, an unavoidable act of fate." But when whole terraces could be levelled with one bomb, they came to believe that even London was susceptible to destruction and could be changed. It was dirty, and seedy; it was part of the civilisation which had created two world wars. A London newspaper, the *Evening Standard*, asked for more dynamite. Even before the war was over a regional planner, Patrick Abercrombie, had prepared two proposals, the *County of London Plan* and the *Greater London Plan*, which would lend London "order and efficiency and beauty and spaciousness" with an end to "violent competitive passion." It is the eternal aspiration, or delusion, that somehow the city can be forced to change its nature by getting rid of all the elements by which it had previously thrived.

Yet, in topographical terms, the Abercrombie plans were immensely influential. They required a significant shift of population within the city itself in order to "create balanced communities each comprising several neighbourhood units"; the reconstruction of bombed London would proceed on the basis of "density zones" which would disperse hitherto overcrowded neighbourhoods. There would be a balance of housing, industrial development and "open space" with key highways connecting variously integrated communities. Three examples may represent many. Much of the population of Bethnal Green was rehoused in LCC "low-density" estates such as Woodford in Essex; the bombed areas of Poplar were rebuilt as the great Lansbury Estate with a mixed style of block and single dwellings. Within inner London the Loughborough Estate rose in Brixton, its main edifices eleven storeys high. The elements of London were being redistributed, to create more light and air. The old streets, which were variously considered "obsolete" or "outworn," "narrow" or "confined," were erased in order to make room for modern, larger and neater estates. The advent of municipal control over large swathes of the city was not, however, without disadvantages. It altered the reality of London, damping down its natural laws of growth and change. Small businesses, the life and blood of the city, could no longer thrive. The "inner London councils" were attempting to ignore, or reverse, the natural tendencies of the city which had been in operation for almost a thousand years. It was inevitable that the old City of London would promote other ideas and in its own plan the planners suggested "the conservation wherever possible of features which are of traditional and archaeological significance" as well as maintaining "the romance and history which the very street names breathe." But their proposals for careful redevelopment were not in accordance with the modern spirit of innovation and large-scale urban planning; they were rejected by the national administration, and the LCC was invited to redevelop areas around St. Paul's, the Tower and the present Barbican.

Other elements of Abercrombie's plans were also implemented, most notably in the Town and Country Act of 1947. He proposed that London become a "circular inland city" composed of four rings—the Inner Urban Ring, the Suburban Ring, the Green Belt Ring and the Outer Country Ring. It was a way of containing the "inner city," as if it were some dangerous or threatening organism which could not be permitted to grow. On most maps it is painted black. It was also important to remove industry and people from this inner darkness as if the act of so doing would render it less dangerous. In order to expedite the migration of a million people another part of Abercrombie's report suggested the development of new "satellite towns" in the Outer Country Ring. Eight of these were built, and prospered, but the effects upon London itself were not exactly as had been anticipated and planned. As any historian of London might have told the various urban boards, neither schemes nor regulations would be able to inhibit the city. It had been proposed to check its industrial and commercial growth, by siting new industries in the "satellite towns," but London's commercial prosperity revived after war. The manufacture of cars, buses, trucks and aeroplanes rose to unprecedented levels; the Port of London handled record numbers of goods, and employed 30,000 men; the "office economy" had restored the City of London so that it experienced a property boom. The population of the capital had dipped slightly, after the dispersal of many of its inhabitants to the suburbs and to the new towns, but the effect was mitigated by sudden and unexpectedly high fertility. Nothing could withstand the ability of the city to rejuvenate itself, and continue its growth.

The new "satellite towns," such as Stevenage and Harlow and Basildon, became part of an historical process which was also too powerful—too instinctive—to be "reversed." London has always grown by taking over adjacent towns or villages and cradling them in its embrace. It has been a feature of its development since the eleventh century. And so it overtook the newly created towns.

So powerful is the historical imperative that Patrick Abercrombie and his colleagues were instinctively creating just the same patterns of habitation as the seventeenth-century builders of Bloomsbury and Covent Garden. The "new towns" ineluctably became as much part of London as their predecessors; instead of restricting the size of the city, the postwar planners immeasurably expanded it until the whole south-eastern area became "London." The Outer Metropolitan Area represented the latest manifestation of urban life, characterised by endless movement. But that was always the condition of London. Whenever the opportunity and location are offered, it replicates its identity. It is a blind force in that sense, not susceptible to the blandishments of planners or politicians—except, as we have seen, when they offer further prospects of growth.

The Green Belt did not then act as a barrier or inhibitor of urban life; in certain respects it simply became a large open space fortuitously situated within the outer Metropolitan Region. But it did have one effect, in checking the physical development of the inner city and its immediate suburbs which had to leap over the greenness in order to continue their ineluctable life. Yet as part of this phenomenon there was also a curious sense in which the city recoiled upon itself. It fed back into itself. Deprived of any room for immediate local extension, it began to re-explore its own patterns and possibilities. The construction of the great Inner London estates, the resurgence of interest in restoring old dwellings, the process of "gentrification," the growth of "loft" living, the whole emphasis upon renewal, are the direct consequences of the Green Belt which forced London and Londoners to look inwards rather than outwards.

The imperatives of London's history had one further consequence. The postwar planners had also envisaged a great network of orbital and ring roads, with much the same intent and significance as the wide avenues proposed for London by Wren and Evelyn after the Great Fire. But, like the earlier designs, they came to nothing; they were defeated by political pressure, economic constraints, and vehement local opposition. London, almost alone of English cities, has withstood the edicts of rational planners and "highway management"; it was part of its ability successfully to frustrate any general or grandiose plan. General structural change did not, and could not, occur. The city has preserved its character ever since the first Tudor proclamations concerning "town planning" were ignored.

Yet this was not generally understood at the time and, in London, the 1960s were particularly charged with forgetfulness. The American weekly *Time* proclaimed on its front cover "LONDON—THE SWINGING CITY." Its affluence was visible enough; real earnings had risen by approximately 70 per cent in the twenty years since the war, and the high birth rate in the first years of peace certainly gave the impression of a city dominated by youth. The fact that National Service had been abolished in 1960 itself represented a literal and emblematic lifting of restrictions upon young males in particular. So music, and fashion, returned on an unprecedented scale. One designer, Mary Quant, has suggested that she wished to create clothes that "were much more for life—much more for real people, much more for being young and alive in." So there was an efflorescence of boutiques in well-defined areas of London; Carnaby Street became the centre for young men who wore Mod fashions, with the familiar London emphasis upon what was "new" or "in the news," while the King's Road in Chelsea became the destination for young women who wished to be trendy. Music, too, emanated from London with groups such as the Who, the Kinks, the Small Faces and the Rolling Stones, many of their members having come from London art schools and colleges. Those groups from outside the city, like the Beatles, necessarily migrated to it. Designers had also caught the prevailing mood. Terence Conran recollected that "I'd always believed that well-designed things should be available to the whole population, that it shouldn't be an elitist thing. And I think this coincided with a lot of people who'd had further education coming through who were discontented with the way things were." So broader access to higher education played its part in what Conran called "the atmosphere of discontentment." It was discontent, primarily, with the postwar world of hierarchy and repression but also with the perceived shabbiness and dreariness of London. It was a way of lightening the surroundings. The actual nature and identity of the city were no longer of any consequence. For a few years instead it became the "style capital" where music and fashion attracted the ancillary industries of magazine publishing, photography, advertising, modelling, broadcasting and film-making to create a bright new city.

But of course "Swinging London" was not "new" at all. The city's familiar instincts had never ceased their operation. The commercial imperative of the city's life, for example, had identified a "market" among the newly resurgent youth which could be in turn exploited by intelligent entrepreneurs. The commercial infrastructure of the music business, for example, was already in place. In all areas of this teenage revolt, in fact, the youths themselves were exploited by a vast commercial project. It was a thoroughly London undertaking. The phenomenon of the 1960s was essentially theatrical and artificial in nature, too; like so many London displays, it glided over the fundamental underlying life in the capital. To see the decade clearly it is important to see it steadily, and as a whole, encompassing all of its realities.

It is significant, for example, that the age of the boutique and the discotheque was also the age of the tower block, of public vandalism, and of increased crime. They are not unconnected. Of the tower blocks of the 1960s, much has been written. They had become the resort of planners and architects motivated by aesthetic, as well as social, reasons. They seemed to offer the vision of a new kind of city; many Georgian and Victorian terraces were razed by the civic authorities to make way for an experiment in urban living in which a new kind of vertical community might be forged. The popularity of the tower blocks—some four hundred were erected in London during the late 1960s—was also animated by economic principles. They were standardised, and therefore could be quickly and cheaply assembled. There were so many people on housing lists, or living in parts of the "inner city" which were deemed unfit for human habitation, that the "high-rise estates" seemed at the time to be the only efficient and affordable means of translating citizens from relative squalor into relative comfort.

It was the age of the property developer when great fortunes could be made, trading off development land to the LCC for permission to build on sensitive sites. Their names were legion—Centrepoint, London Wall, Euston Centre, Elephant and Castle, all of London seemed to have been changed out of scale and out of recognition. It was a form of vandalism in which the government and civic authorities were happy to acquiesce. Vast swathes of London disappeared in the process—Printing House Square, Caledonian Market, St. Luke's Hospital, parts of Piccadilly, stretches of the City, were all demolished in order to make way for what became known as "comprehensive redevelopment." What it represented was a deliberate act of erasure, an act of forgetting, not so dissimilar in spirit to the mood and ambience of the "Swinging Sixties" elsewhere in London. It was as if time, and London's history, had for all practical purposes ceased to exist. In pursuit of profit, and instant gratification, the past had become a foreign country.

Three examples from the 1960s may suffice. Londonderry House in Park Lane was dismantled, in 1962, to make way for the London Hilton; the Georgian streets of the Packington Estate in Islington were demolished in 1966 to make room for a council estate; in 1963 the great Euston Arch, the portico of Euston Station, was pulled down as part of a scheme of "modernisation." Just as the excitement of the "trendy" had animated the worlds of music and fashion, so the same denial or rejection of the past determined architectural and civic planning. "Swinging London" was all of a piece, and much of the swinging was done by the implements of the demolition teams.

London has always been an ugly city. It is part of its identity. It has always been rebuilt, and demolished, and vandalised. That, too, is part of its history. The ancient creed—"Cursed be he that removeth old landmarks"—has never been observed in the city. In fact one of the characteristics of London planners and builders, over the centuries, has been the recklessness with which they have destroyed the city's past. There were even songs on the subject from previous centuries:

> O! London won't be London long
> For 'twill all be pulled down
> And I shall sing a funeral song . . .

It might have been sung by Victoria Station, or Knightsbridge, or St. Giles Circus, in the 1960s.

> The haunts we revelled in today
> We lose tomorrow morning,

As one by one are swept away
In turn without a warning . . .

In the 1260s all the old "ruinated" work of past ages was swept away in the entire redevelopment of Bridge Ward. In the 1760s the medieval gates of the city walls were demolished on the grounds that they "obstructed the free current of air"; in the same decade of "improvement," houses were demolished to make way for new streets in no fewer than eleven wards. It was the greatest single change in London since the Great Fire a hundred years before. Then in 1860 the Union of Benefices Act expedited the destruction of fourteen city churches, some of them erected by Wren after that Fire. The 1860s were in fact the great period of destruction when, in the words of Gavin Stamp in *The Changing Metropolis*, "half of London was being rebuilt . . . the city must have been a nightmare of dust, mud, scaffolding and confusion." Queen Victoria Street and the Holborn Viaduct were being constructed, causing massive destruction to the oldest parts of London, while the various railway networks were defacing the cityscape with tracks and stations; the London Chatham & Dover Railway passed across Ludgate Hill, for example, and obscured the view of St. Paul's Cathedral. This disfigurement of the cathedral was once more the charge levelled against property developers of the 1960s, so it would seem that there is no pause in the destruction of London.

It can be no more than coincidence that these great waves of vandalism occurred in the 60s of each century, unless you were to believe that some theory of cyclical recurrence can be applied to the city's development. In that case we might expect the 2060s to mark the destruction of much twentieth-century building.

Other aspects of the 1960s seem, in retrospect, aligned to each other. There was an extraordinary and indeed unprecedented rise in crime, which tripled in the twelve years after 1955 and showed no signs of diminution in the late 1960s. The culture of instant gratification, and of youthful power, must have played a large part in inciting less affluent youths to theft and house-breaking. But the tower blocks, and the property speculators, and the garish fashions, all contributed to a mood of implicit or explicit aggression. "Controls" had been removed from office-building and from planning applications, but controls had also been removed from all aspects of London's existence. The later waves of youthful protest, from the "hippies" and "flower children" of the late 1960s to the "punks" of the 1970s, manifested only confusion and anxiety in a highly unsettled urban society.

The civic existence of London, like some Behemoth below the water, continued ineluctably to expand. In 1965 the Greater London Council, comprising thirty-two boroughs and some 610 square miles of territory, was established; as has always been the case with London's government it represented a political compromise and a division of powers between different levels of urban government. The confusion can be exemplified, perhaps, in the decision that the GLC should be responsible for "metropolitan roads," the Ministry of Transport for "trunk" roads and the boroughs for "local" roads. Yet confusion is, perhaps, the wrong word for the fundamental condition of London's administration. The competing road authorities were remarkably similar to the competing vestries and parishes and metropolitan authorities which in the early decades of the nineteenth century were responsible for lighting and sanitation. London has always been a muddle; that is, perhaps, why it has survived. The GLC, however, was given responsibility for a new "Development Plan" for London including the distribution of population, employment, transport and redevelopment in the continuing delusion that the city could somehow be made to serve the will of civil servants, politicians and planners. Even at the time of its inception, however, the Greater London Council was not great enough to control or supervise the expansion of a city which, in terms of planning for population and employment, now took in the entire south-east of England. Its administrative area was already anachronistic, and its planning purposeless. It could not have been otherwise.

But something else was happening, over which no one had any control. Trade was being lost. Manufacturing industries moved out, or closed down; unemployment rose very quickly. The most important transition occurred upon the river where in quick succession London's docks were deemed redundant and irrelevant. They were no longer large enough to handle the new container ships and, in any case, trade with the Commonwealth was rapidly decreasing. The East India Dock ceased activity in 1967, followed by St. Katherine's Dock and London Dock two years later. The Surrey Commercial Docks were closed in 1970, and there were further closures until the banks of the Thames were bare and empty, with echoing warehouses and waste ground the only visible remnant of what had once been one of the city's glories. The Queenhithe Dock, which had a continuous history since the time of Saxon London, was destroyed in the spring of 1971 to make way for a luxury hotel. In a sense it epitomises the movement of London, where one trade must give way to another. But the wasteland of the dockside area, once the centre and principle of the city's commerce, was in a larger sense an emblem of London in the 1970s.

The 1960s have been described by some commentators as a time of "innocence" (although their levels of crime and vandalism may serve to alter that impression), but whatever "innocence" still existed fell away in the succeeding decade when all the old problems of London reasserted themselves. An economic boom in the late 1960s was followed by a bust in the mid-1970s. London lost its vivacity, and much of its energy. The sudden decay of trade and commerce, in a city devoted to them, provoked considerable dismay and anxiety. For a while it seemed that its life was being stopped. This in turn led to concern among those who administered the city. London was sick, and needed a fresh access of life and trade.

The long experiment with high-rise tower blocks, on borough housing estates, came to an end; it had been effectively destroyed by a structural accident at Ronan Point in 1968, in which several people were killed, but the spirit of the time—and indeed the spirit of London—turned against it. The emphasis would now rest upon "high-density" and "low-rise" estates which would, in a sense, attempt to reproduce the atmosphere of the old terraced streets. At the same time measures were introduced to revive the central areas of London with schemes designed to protect the environment and expedite public transport. In particular the policy of demolishing Victorian or Georgian housing was reversed, and grants were instead made available for "improvements" in older and more dilapidated dwellings. The city, once more, was being comforted and consolidated rather than destroyed. There ensued a process of what became known as "gentrification" when generally middle-class and professional couples moved into run-down houses or areas in order to refurbish and renew them. Islington and Spitalfields were two previously "deprived" areas which benefited from this change of ownership and direction. The Green Belt turned the city in upon itself. The edges of Greater London were now so distant that Londoners began to reclaim those parts of the city closer to home. The city was solidifying; perhaps it was about to realise its potential.

At a time of recession, and falling expectations, there were also fears that it might become the terrain of social conflict. It became the task of administration, therefore, to preserve and heal the fragile city; thus, in the late 1970s, the Greater London Council funded new community projects, with the emphasis resting upon the vulnerable or the marginal; ethnic and sexual minorities, in particular, were afforded assistance. Here was an affirmation of London's democratic and egalitarian instincts, but it was also a necessary remedy for difficult times. The real needs of the city, having been ignored or exploited for some years, were being met. It is significant, too, that in the period of improvement grants and gentrification the conservation of London became a matter of great and growing public concern. A scheme for the "Motorway Box" around London was dropped; proposals to refit Covent Garden, in accordance with principles of traffic flow and pedestrian decks, were abandoned after strenuous local opposition. By the mid-1970s there were some 250 "conservation areas" located in all parts of the city, testifying to a new awareness of London's textural fabric and social history. Hostilities against the city had finally come to an end. The abolition of the Greater London Council in 1986 left it without a unified authority, but it did not seem to notice; in effect London resumed its ancient life, with the separate boroughs affirming distinct and different identities. The city, in the process, acquired its old momentum. The election of a mayor, and assembly, for London will not materially affect its nature or direction. It does not respond to policy committees or to centralised planning. It would be easier to control the elements themselves.

This was nowhere more evident than in the conception and creation of "Docklands." The Docklands Development Corporation was established in 1981 to restore or renew the wasteland left by the closure of the London Docks; Wapping, Rotherhithe, the Isle of Dogs, Silvertown, north Woolwich and Beckton were within its boundaries and a number of enterprise zones—rate-free and tax-free catchment areas—were marked out for especial attention. The London City Airport, the Docklands Light Railway, and an extended Jubilee Line, were the designated means of transport. But, as in most London developments, the results were largely unplanned and unpredictable. The fate of Canary Wharf was in that sense emblematic. Its central feature was an 800-foot tower surmounted by a pyramid (which might provoke thoughts of imperial destiny) with approximately ten million square feet of office space. The original developers withdrew from the scheme and their replacement, the firm of Olympia & York, was reduced to bankruptcy even as the tower was nearing completion. A third consortium took over the project, even though a surplus of office space in the rest of the capital mitigated against early success. And yet, somehow, it worked. Tenants were found, and the whole of Canary Wharf flourished.

Docklands itself experienced a similar fate. Wild fluctuations in the urban economy left it balancing between triumph and disaster on a number of occasions; its apartment blocks were fashionable one year, and unfashionable the next; there were complaints about rudimentary transport facilities as well as the absence of shops, but nevertheless there was continual development. Michael Hebbert, in *London*, has remarked that there were "few preconceptions as to what should occur," and that this "hands-off approach produced a curiously piecemeal environment." Yet in that respect it followed the pattern of most London growth, which is no doubt the reason for its success. Docklands "had no overall philosophy for the massing and scale of buildings, or for the layout of public spaces," but that is why it has become a natural and recognisable extension of London. The entire area was accused of "aesthetic incoherence" and a "market-driven disregard of social policy" but these are precisely the conditions and circumstances in which the city has expanded and flourished; it understands no other principles of life.

That is the context in which the great tower of Canary Wharf, which dominates the London skyline, has won in Hebbert's words "immediate acceptance and affection." This great shaft, so in tune with the alignment of the city, now rivals the Monument and Big Ben as the symbol of London. It represents, too, the single most important shift in urban topography for many centuries; the commercial and social pressures had always edged westwards, but the development of Docklands has opened up what has been called London's "eastward corridor" which in historical and structural terms offers passage and access to Europe at a time when London's economy is becoming more closely associated with the continent. There is a suspicion that the City of London—as well as the banks and brokers newly moved to Docklands—will come to dominate the financial markets of the European Community. Here, in this steady progress eastwards, we may be able to sense London's instinctive and almost primordial reaching towards money and trade.

It is appropriate to mention here the "Big Bang" which transformed the City in the autumn of 1986; that explosion turned the Stock Exchange into the International Stock Exchange, enabled the merger of banking and brokerage houses, finished the system of fixed commissions and introduced "electronic dealing." It was not the beginning of the City's triumphalism; the phenomenon of young urban professionals named "yuppies" had been first noticed in 1984: a group who, in the phrases of the period, wished to "get rich quick" before "burn-out." But the events of 1986 heralded a sea-change in the position of the City of London. Its foreign exchange market is now the most advanced and elaborate in the world, handling approximately one-third of the world's dealings; with 600,000 employed in banking and allied services it has become the largest exchange in the world. Once more London was fulfilling its historical destiny, and recovering the pre-eminence which it had achieved in the eighteenth and nineteenth centuries. It is an historical achievement in more than one sense since, as Hebbert has explained, "The compactness of a 2000-year old urban core is fortuitously well suited to the operation of a globalised financial service centre." Whether it is entirely "fortuitous" is another matter, however, since the actual nature of that square mile seems uniquely possessed by the spirit of commerce. There have been booms and busts, but it has maintained its ascendancy.

A new type of commercial activity, however, demanded new forms of building. That is how the City changes, while keeping its identity intact. The demand was for large open spaces which could accommodate the miles of cables attached to electronic activity and which could harbour thousands of employees working under consistent pressure. There was, after all, a human cost to this fresh access of trade. In the late 1980s some four million square metres of office space were added to the stock of the City, not least with the development of the Broadgate complex. Light-sensitive blinds and prismatic blue-green glass shielded the devotees of finance as they continued, night and day, with their dealings and transactions. All the gods and griffins of the City protected them.

What gods were these? Who can say? In 1986 *Faith in the City*, a report sponsored by the archbishop of Canterbury, noted that it was "the poor who have borne the brunt of the recession, both the unemployed and the working poor. Yet it is the poor who are seen by some as 'social security scroungers,' or a burden on the country, preventing economic recovery. This is a cruel example of blaming the victim." It is one of the great and continuing paradoxes of London life that the rich global city contains also the worst examples of poverty and deprivation. But perhaps that comprises the "meaning" of London. Perhaps its destiny is to represent the contradictions of the human condition, both as an example and as a warning.

The report also described those council estates which "have a quite different social and economic system, operating almost entirely at subsistence level, dependent entirely on the public sector . . . the degeneration of many such areas has now gone so far that they are in effect 'separate territories' outside the mainstream of our social and economic life." These sentiments will be familiar to those who have studied the social topography of London over the centuries; Charles Booth's "Poverty Map" of 1889 might provoke a similar analysis, for example, with the proviso that there was then no public sector to support the indigent and the unfortunate. Once more it is the condition of London itself which is being described. If the city had a voice it might be saying: There will always be those who fail or who are unfortunate, just as there will always be those who cannot cope with the world as presently constituted, but I can encompass them all.

The decade which saw the emergence of the "yuppies," for example, also witnessed the revival of street-beggars and vagrants sleeping "rough" upon the streets or within doorways; Lincoln's Inn Fields was occupied once more by the homeless, after an interval of 150 years, while areas like Waterloo Bridge and the Embankment became the setting for what were known as "cardboard cities." The Strand, in particular, became a great thoroughfare of the dispossessed. Despite civic and government initiatives, they are still there. They are now part of the recognisable population; they are Londoners, joining the endless parade. Or perhaps, by sitting upon the sidelines, they remind everyone else that it is a parade.

And yet what is it, now, to be a Londoner? The map of the city has been redrawn to include "Outer Metropolitan Areas" as well as "Greater" and "Inner" London; the entire south-east of England has—willingly or unwillingly—become its zone of influence. Is London, then, just a state of mind? The more nebulous its boundaries, and the more protean its identity, has it now become an attitude or set of predilections? On more than one occasion, in its history, it has been described as containing a world or worlds within itself. Now it has been classified as a "global city," and in Hebbert's words as "a universe with its own rules, which has genuinely burst out of national boundaries." So it does truly contain a "universe," like some dense and darkly revolving cloud at its centre. But this is why so many millions of people describe themselves as "Londoners," even if they are many miles from the inner city. They call themselves Londoners because they are pervaded by a sense of belonging. London has been continuously inhabited for over two thousand years; that is its strength, and its attraction. It affords the sensation of permanence, of solid ground. That is why the vagrant and the dispossessed lie in its streets; that is why the inhabitants of Harrow, or Croydon, call themselves "Londoners." Its history calls them, even if they do not know it. They are entering a visionary city.

Cockney Visionaries

A fantastical "tribute to Christopher Wren" outlining the spires and vistas of
the great and powerful city which he helped to create. Much of
his work has gone but the power and energy remain.

CHAPTER 78

Unreal City

It has always been a city of vision and prophecy. It is supposed to have been founded after a prophetic dream vouchsafed to Brutus, and the vision of a great city in "a strange yet greener country" haunts the imaginations of the classical poets. As Ovid wrote in his *Metamorphoses*,

> Even as I speak I see our destiny
> The city of our sons and sons of sons,
> Greater than any city we have known,
> Or has been known or shall be known to men.

Its visionary or mythic status has rendered it provisional and impalpable. It has become an "Unreal city," in the phrase of T.S. Eliot, which throughout its history has been populated by the creatures of mythology. Nymphs have been seen along the banks of its rivers, and minotaurs within its labyrinths of brick. It has been aligned with Nineveh and Tyre, Sodom and Babylon, and at times of fire and plague the outlines of those cities have risen among its streets and buildings. The city's topography is a palimpsest within which all the most magnificent or monstrous cities of the world can be discerned. It has been the home of both angels and devils striving for mastery. It has been the seat of miracles, and the harbour of savage paganism. Who can fathom the depths of London?

Chaucer's prophetic dream in the *House of Fame*—"I dreamt I was within a temple made of glass" with "many a pillar of metal"—has been applied to many of London's edifices but the most formidable prophecies are of revelation and apocalypse. On the north side of Aldersgate were inscribed the words: "Then shall enter into the gates of the city kings and princes sitting upon the throne of David . . . and the city shall remain forever." Even to its inhabitants, it was a biblical city; its history, "beyond the memory of man," verified its sacredness. Yet its inhabitants have also been touched by other forms of vision. Of Chaucer's pilgrims, on their way to Canterbury along Borough High Street, William Blake said that they "compose all ages and nations." Every race or tribe or nation, every faith or form of speech, have been comprehended within the city. The whole universe may be found within a grain of London's life. The "gate of heaven," in St. Bartholomew the Great, was located beside the shambles of Smithfield. But if it is a sacred city, it is one which includes misery and suffering. The bowels of God have opened, and rained down shit upon London.

The most abject poverty or dereliction can appear beside glowing wealth and prosperity. Yet the city needs its poor. What if the poor must die, or be deprived, in order that the city might live? That would be the strangest contrast of all. Life and death meet and part; misfortune and good fortune shake hands; suffering and happiness inhabit the same house. "Without Contraries," Blake once wrote, "is no progression." He reached this truth by steady observation of the city. It is always ancient, and forever new, that disparity or disjunction itself creating a kind of ferment of novelty and inventiveness. It may be that the new protects the old, or the old guards the new, yet in the very fact of their oneness lies the secret of London's identity shining through time.

Yet wherever you go in the city you are continually being assaulted by difference, and it could be surmised that the city is simply made up of contrasts; it is the sum of its differences. It is in fact the very universality of London that establishes these contrasts and separations, it contains every aspect of human life within itself, and is thus perpetually renewed. Yet do the rich and the poor inhabit the same city? It may be that each citizen has created a London in his or her own head, so that at the same moment there may exist seven million different cities. It has sometimes been observed that even native Londoners experience a kind of fear, or alarm, if they find themselves in a strange part of the city. It is partly the fear of becoming lost, but it is also the fear of difference. And yet is a city so filled with difference, also, therefore filled with fear?

This vision of totality, of fullness of life, may be cast in an optimistic sense. Boswell suggested that "the intellectual man is struck with London as comprehending the whole of human life in all its variety, the contemplation of which is inexhaustible." It is the vision which was imparted to him as he was driven along the Haymarket in the early days of 1763: "I was full of rich imagination of London . . . such as I could not explain to most people, but which I strongly feel and am ravished with. My blood glows and my mind is agitated with felicity." It is the fullness of London which prompts his happiness; the congregation of people, of all races, of all talents, of all fortunes, releases a massive air of expectancy and exhilaration.

London manifests all the possibilities of humankind, and thus becomes a vision of the world itself. Steele was a "great Lover of Mankind"; and by Cornhill "at the sight of a prosperous and happy Multitude . . . I cannot forbear expressing my Joy with Tears that have stoln down my Cheeks." A century later Charles Lamb wrote that "I often shed tears in the motley Strand, for fulness of joy at such a multitude of life." The multitudes induce wonder; they are not an incoherent mass, or a heap of irreconcilable elements, but a flowing and varied multitude.

English drama, and the English novel, spring out of the very conditions of London. In Jonson, and Smollett and Fielding, the poetry of the streets finds its fulfilment. Theirs is a visionary imagination as rich as that of Chaucer or of Blake, but it is a peculiarly London vision filled with images of the theatre and the prison-house, of commerce and of crowds, of fullness and rapacity and forgetfulness.

From a London vision springs a distinctive sensibility. All of these writers—and many more are numbered with them—were preoccupied with light and darkness, in a city that is built in the shadows of money and power. All of them were entranced by the scenic and spectacular, in a city that is continually filled with the energetic display of people and institutions. They understood the energy of London, they understood its variety, and they also understood its darkness. So they tended to favour spectacle and melodrama. As city artists they are more concerned with the external life, with the movement of crowds, with the great general drama of the human spirit. They have a sense of energy and splendour, of ritual and display, which may have very little to do with ethical judgement or the exercise of moral consciousness. In part they share the sublime indifference of London, where the multitudes come and go. However hard and theatrical it may seem, it is a true vision of the world. In the famous phrase, London made me. But then it cannot be altogether hard; it reduced Steele and Lamb to tears.

It is appropriate, then, that there should also have been visions of disaster; of London in ruins or choked to death upon its own smoke and dirt. The French writer Mirbeau invoked a city "of the nightmare, of dream, of mystery, of the conflagration, of the furnace, of chaos, of floating gardens, of the invisible, the unreal . . . this special nature of the prodigious city." An image of the furnace often emerges in London visions. In Blake's *Jerusalem* "Primrose Hill is the mouth of the Furnace & of the Iron Door," and in Arthur Machen's "When I Was Young in London" there was a moment when, "looking back one could see all the fires of London reflected dimly in the sky, as if far away awful furnace doors were opened." It has been known as "the Oven," as if that sense of unnatural heat provokes strange images of its inhabitants being cooked and eaten. Yet it has also been called "a temple of Fire-worshippers," so perhaps the citizens venerate the agents of their destruction.

A nineteenth-century observer of the fog noticed the sun as a "mysterious and distant gleam which seemed to be trying to penetrate to this immobile world." This is another true vision of the city, when all its noise and bustle have disappeared; when it lies silent and peaceful, all of its energy momentarily suspended, it seems like some natural force that will outlast all the activity of humankind. It is gigantic, monstrous, and, by the very fact of its enormity, somehow primeval. The poet, Tom Moore, had a refrain:

Go where we may, rest where we will,
Eternal London haunts us still.

Eternity may have many aspects. One is that of eternal recurrence, so that the people of the city will say the same things or use the same gestures upon the same streets. Since no one may watch a corner or a stretch of thoroughfare over hundreds of years, the truth of this will never be discovered. Yet perhaps it has become clear that certain activities seem to belong to certain areas, or neighbourhoods, as if time itself were moved or swayed by some unknown source of power. Yet if this seems too fanciful, there may be another aspect of "Eternal London." It is permanent. It is unceasing. Of its essence, it is unchanged. It is a condition of the universe. As the author of *London Nights* has put it, "London is every city that ever was and ever will be." Thus Wordsworth saw by Ludgate Hill

> A visionary scene—a length of street
> laid open in its morning quietness,
> Deep, hollow, unobstructed, vacant, smooth . . .

The silence is the silence of permanence. When all the passing generations have sung their songs and departed, the city continues its quiet life. To see London without its inhabitants is indeed a "visionary scene," because another presence then reveals itself. That is why there have been so many visions of London in ruins. In drawings and in engravings—even in images of film—it resembles some lost continent, or a city lately risen from the sea. These are not the ruins of Babylon or Rome, but of Atlantis or some other mythological landscape. They are emblems of some undying need or aspiration.

It is possible, however, to see among them the passing generations. London is "eternal" because it contains them all. When Addison visited the tombs of Westminster Abbey he was moved to reflect that "When I read the several dates of the tombs, of some that died yesterday, and some six hundred years ago, I consider that great day when we shall all of us be contemporaries and make our appearance together." It may be that London, uniquely among cities, prompts such considerations since the dead seem to be pursuing at the heels of the living. For some this is a hopeful vision; it suggests reconciliation where all the manifest differences of the city, riches and poverty, health and sickness, will find their quietus. One cannot be separated from the other. So Turner saw "the most angelic beings in the whole compass of the London world" in the squalor and filth of the London Docks.

There are those who have been possessed by a different vision. According to Geoffrey Grigson, London "stood for *doing*, at least, it stood for *beginning*." Branwell Brontë, in the parsonage at Haworth, collected all the maps of London he could find depicting "its alleys, and back slums and short cuts"; according to Juliet Barker in *The Brontës* he "studied them so closely that he knew them all by heart" so that he appeared to be an "old Londoner" who "knew more about the ins and outs of the mighty Babylon than many a man who had passed his life within its walls." This intense reading of London was, for him, a form of liberation; the maps represented all the hopes for, and aspirations towards, a new life. It was as if he were studying his own destiny. But for others the dream may become feverish, when the whole weight of London presses down. At the end of *Bleak House*, that threnody among the labyrinths of London, Richard Carstone towards the close of his wretched life asks, "It was all a troubled dream?" For many, that is also a true vision of the city.

The elements of innovation and of change are subtly mingled, together with the sheer exhilaration of being one among a numerous company. One could become anybody. Some of the great stories of London concern those who have taken on new identities, and new personalities; to begin again, to renew oneself, is one of the great advantages of the city. It is part of its endlessly dramatic life. It is possible, after all, to enter if only for a moment the lives and emotions of those who pass by. This collective experience can, in turn, be a source of exhilaration. It was what Francis Thompson perceived in his vision of

> the traffic of Jacob's ladder
> Pitched between Heaven and Charing Cross.

It is the enchantment of a million golden souls moving back and forth between heaven and the city, all singular and all blessed. It is the same vision vouchsafed to those who have heard the music of London, a pattern of notes rising and falling in some great melody to which all the streets and avenues move in unison. The city then forms "a geography passing beyond the natural to become metaphysical, only describable in terms of music or abstract physics": thus writes Michael Moorcock in *Mother London*. Some inhabitants hear the music—these are the dreamers and the antiquarians—but others perceive it only fitfully and momentarily. It may be in a sudden gesture, in a sentence overheard, in an instant of memory. London is filled with such broken images, laughter which has been heard before, a tearful face which has been seen before, a street which is unknown and yet familiar.

CHAPTER 79

Resurgam

If you were to walk across the Isle of Dogs, where the Canary Wharf tower itself is to be found, past the enamel panels and the jet mist granite, past the silver cladding and the curved glass walls, you might come across other realities. Here and there still stand late Victorian pubs, marking the corners of otherwise shattered roads. There are council blocks from the 1930s, and council-house estates from the 1970s. Occasionally a row of nineteenth-century terraced houses will emerge like an apparition. The Isle of Dogs represents, in other words, the pattern of London. Certain of the new developments are themselves decked out as if they were Victorian warehouses, or Georgian terraces, or twentieth-century suburban dwellings, thus intensifying the sense of heterogeneity and contrast. This, too, is part of London. This is why it has been said that there are in reality hundreds of Londons all mingled.

There are different worlds, and times, within the city; Whitehall and West Ham, White City and Streatham, Haringey and Islington, are all separate and unique. Yet in the last years of the twentieth century they participated in the general brightness of London. If light travels in waves then it may be described as a rippling effect, as the renovation or rejuvenation of the inner core has spread outwards. London has opened up; there seems to be more space and more air. It has grown in lightness. In the City towers are clad in silver-blue reflective glass, so that the difference between the sky and the building is effaced; in Clapton and Shepherd's Bush, houses are being repaired and repainted.

If London were a living thing, we would say that all of its optimism and confidence have returned. It has again become "the capital of all capitals" in every cultural and social sense. The world flocks to it and once more it has become a youthful city. That is its destiny. *Resurgam*: "I will arise." It was the word found upon a piece of stray and broken stone just when Wren began his work upon St. Paul's Cathedral; he placed it at the centre of his design.

In Exchange Square of the Broadgate Development, in the last autumn of the twentieth century, a calypso band was playing in an open space designed for performance; some City workers, before their journey homewards, were drinking in a public house close by. A man and woman were dancing, to the rhythm of the music, in the shadow of the great arch of Exchange House. In an area below them a shallow cascade of water ran continually, while to one side reclined a statue entitled "The Broadgate Venus." Below the square I could see the platforms of Liverpool Street Station, with the trains moving inwards and outwards, while on the horizon behind Exchange House the spire of St. Leonard, Shoreditch, could plainly be discerned. It was a matter of conjecture how many different times inhabited this small area; there was a nineteenth-century railway time, but also the time of the music. There was the endless movement of water, but also the rhythm of the dancing. The great statue of the reclining nude seemed almost preternaturally still amid all this activity, enjoining a quietness not unlike that of St. Leonard in the distance. And then there were the office-workers with glasses in their hands who were, at that moment, like their ancestors, wandering out of time. So Broadgate, in the early evening, contained many times, like currents of air invisibly mingling.

On that same evening, I walked perhaps two hundred yards to the east, and I came across another London site. Just beyond the old market of Spitalfields archaeologists have discovered an area where the medieval hospital of St. Mary Spital once stood. On this small spot were found the stone sarcophagus of a fourth-century Roman female; a fourteenth-century charnel house and graveyard; a fifteenth-century gallery from which civic dignitaries listened to the "Spital sermon"; evidence of a sixteenth-century artillery ground; London fortifications of the seventeenth century; eighteenth-century dwellings; and part of a nineteenth-century street. More will emerge in time, although time itself has a thicker and more clouded atmosphere in such a place. The levels of the centuries are all compact, revealing the historical density of London. Yet the ancient city and the modern city literally lie beside each other; one cannot be imagined without the other. That is one of the secrets of the city's power.

These relics of the past now exist as part of the present. It is in the nature of the city to encompass everything. So when it is asked how London can be a triumphant city when it has so many poor, and so many homeless, it can only be suggested that they, too, have always been a part of its history. Perhaps they are a part of its triumph. If this is a hard saying, then it is only as hard as London itself. London goes beyond any boundary or convention. It contains every wish or word ever spoken, every action or gesture ever made, every harsh or noble statement ever expressed. It is illimitable. It is Infinite London.

An Essay on Sources

If London is endless and illimitable, so are the books and essays devoted to it. *The Bibliography of Printed Works on London History*, edited by Heather Creaton (London, 1994), lists 21,778 separate publications from London History Periodicals to Service War Memorials. No scholar of the city, however eager or ambitious, can hope to assimilate all this material. My own thread through the labyrinth has been twined out of enthusiasm and curiosity, coarse enough in the circumstances but serviceable.

Of the general studies I can recommend *The Future of London's Past* by M. Biddle and D. Hudson (London, 1977); *The Stones of London* by J.V. Elsden and J.A. Howe (London, 1923); *The Soul of London* by F.M. Ford (London, 1905); *Street Names of the City of London* by E. Ekwall (Oxford, 1954); *The Lost Language of London* by H. Bayley (London, 1935); *London in Song* by W. Whitten (London, 1898); *London Echoing* and *The London Perambulator*, both by James Bone (London, 1948 and 1931); *Historians of London* by S. Rubinstein (London, 1968); *Memoirs of Extraordinary Popular Delusions* by C. Mackay (London, 1841); *The Synfulle Citie* by E.J. Burford (London, 1990); *London Mystery and Mythology* by W. Kent (London, 1952). Note that these books are in no particular order, chronological or thematic, and in that sense they act as an image of the city itself where stray impressions leave their mark. In turn we have *The Streets of London Through The Centuries* by T. Burke (London, 1940); *They Saw it Happen* edited in four volumes by W.O. Hassall, C.R.N. Routh, T. Charles-Edwards, B. Richardson and A. Briggs (Oxford, 1956–1960); *The Ghosts of London* by J.A. Brooks (Norwich, 1982); *Characters of Bygone London* by W. Stewart (London, 1960); *The Quack Doctors of Old London* by C.J. Thompson (London, 1928); *London As It Might Have Been* by F. Barker and R. Hyde (London, 1982); *Queer Things About London* by C. Harper (London, 1923). *The Geology of London and South-East England* by G.M. Davies (London, 1939) is matched by *London Illustrated Geological Walks* by E. Robinson (Edinburgh, 1985); *The Curiosities of London* by J. Timbs (London, 1855) can similarly be placed beside *Literary and Historical Memorials of London* by J.H. Jesse (London, 1847), *London Rediscoveries* by W.G. Bell (London, 1929), and *Old Customs and Ceremonies of London* by M. Brentnall (London, 1975).

The *Londoner's Almanac* by R. Ash (London, 1985) contains peculiar and sometimes interesting facts such as "Twenty Slang Words Used by London Taxi-Drivers"; W. Kent's *London in The News Through Three Centuries* (London, 1954) contains astonishing stories of hauntings, body-snatchings and deaths by lightning. *The Aquarian Guide to Legendary London* edited by J.M. Matthews and C. Potter (Wellingborough, 1990) is indispensable reading for those who are interested in the occluded aspects of the city's history, while *London Bodies* by A. Werner (London, 1998) is a fascinating exercise in comparative physiology. *The Building of London* by J. Schofield (London, 1984) offers many valuable perceptions into the fabric and texture of the developing city while *The City of London* by C.H. Holden and W.G. Holford (London, 1947) is concerned with the task of reconstruction after the Second World War. *Lost London* by H. Hobhouse (London, 1971) is necessary if poignant reading on all that has been destroyed or vandalised by generations of London's builders, and it is complemented by G. Stamp's *The Changing Metropolis* (London, 1984) which contains many fascinating photographs of the vanished or forgotten city. *Studies in London History* edited by A.E.J. Hollaender and W. Kellaway (London, 1969) is a collection of essays which has the virtue of appealing to every literate Londoner, with articles ranging from the real Richard Whittington to the pre-Norman London Bridge. Invaluable, too, is *London in Paint* edited by M. Gallinou and J. Hayes (London, 1996) which moves from the earliest oil painting of London to the latest emanation of what might loosely be termed "The School of London." In a similar spirit *The Image of London: Views by Travellers and Emigrés*

1550–1920 edited by M. Warner (London, 1987) collects the compositions of, among others, Whistler, Monet and Canaletto to provide a pictorial synopsis of the city. *London on Film* by C. Sorensen (London, 1996) performs a similar feat with the cinema. *Curious London* by R. Cross (London, 1966) is filled with, well, curiosities; and with a sigh we may finish this intricate selection with *Where London Sleeps* by W.G. Bell (London, 1926).

It would be out of place here to list the literature of London, simply because to a large extent it also represents the literature of England; few novelists, poets or dramatists have not been touched or moved by London. I might also name Chaucer, Shakespeare, Pope, Dryden, Johnson and the myriad other writers who comprise a distinct and distinctive London world. That is the matter for another book. All I can do here is list specific debts and allegiances, especially to those writers and books which emerge in the course of my narrative. I feel of course an obligation to T.S. Eliot, Thomas More, William Blake and Charles Dickens who have helped to fashion my vision of London; to Thomas De Quincey, Charles Lamb, George Gissing, Arthur Machen, and the other urban pilgrims, I owe an especial debt. I have alluded in this biography particularly to Virginia Woolf, Henry James, Aldous Huxley, Joseph Conrad, George Orwell, H.G. Wells and G.K. Chesterton; from other centuries, the urban works of Tobias Smollett, Daniel Defoe, Ben Jonson and Henry Fielding have been a perpetual comfort and reward. Specific references are made to Samuel Selvon's *The Lonely Londoners* (London, 1955), Michael Moorcock's *Mother London* (London, 1988), Iain Sinclair's *Downriver* (London, 1991), Arthur Morrison's *A Child of the Jago* (London, 1896) and Elizabeth Bowen's *The Heat of the Day* (London, 1949). Certain literary studies have also been immensely helpful. There are many general works, such as W. Kent's *London for the Literary Pilgrim* (London, 1949), Andrew Davies's *Literary London* (London, 1988), W.B. Threshshing's *The London Muse* (Georgia, 1982) and *The Book Lover's London* by A. St. John Adcock (London, 1913). Of more specific import are *Henry James and London* by J. Kimmey (New York, 1991) and *Virginia Woolf's London* by D. Brewster (London, 1959). *London Transformed* by M. Byrd deals primarily with the literary territory of the eighteenth century. I owe an especial debt to J. Wolfreys's *Writing London* (London, 1998), particularly for his perceptive remarks on Carlyle and Engels.

The early history of London is marked by speculation and controversy. Much of it is veiled in myth or legend, and the enchantment can be glimpsed in *Legendary London: Early London in Tradition and History* by L. Spence

(London, 1937) and *Prehistoric London: Its Mounds and Circles* by E.O. Gordon (London, 1914). *The Holy Groves of Britain* by F.J. Stuckey (London, 1995) is also of absorbing interest. A more sober account is provided by N. Merriman in *Prehistoric London* (London, 1990) which is complemented by F.G. Parsons's *The Earlier Inhabitants of London* (London, 1927). The great antiquarian and scholar, Laurence Gomme, a true successor of John Stow, has written *The Governance of London* (London, 1907) and *The Making of London* (London, 1912) as well as *The Topography of London* (London, 1904). For the deeper background I recommend *Celtic Britain* by C. Thomas (London, 1986) and *The Druids* by S. Piggott (London, 1968). For the city of later date, *London: City of the Romans* by R. Merrifield (London, 1983) is essential reading together with a shorter study by R. Merrifield and J. Hally entitled *Roman London* (London, 1986); a more speculative account can be found in *The London That Was Rome* by M. Harrison (London, 1971). Then, later still, *The Anglo-Saxons* edited by J. Campbell (London, 1982) is the best general account. The essays and articles in *The Journal of the London Society* are of great importance in the study of early London, but the major source of archaeological information remains *The London Archaeologist*. The articles and site reports in that periodical are invaluable.

The medieval city has been the object of much study, and all general histories of England survey its conditions. Contemporary documents sometimes provide haunting detail, and they can be found in *The Chronicles of London* edited by C.L. Kingsford (Oxford, 1905), *The Chronicles of Richard of Devizes* edited by J.T. Appleby (London, 1963), *Fifty Early English Wills* edited by F.J. Furnivall (London, 1882), *The London Eyre of 1244* edited by H.M. Chew and M. Weinbaum (London, 1970), *Calendar of Pleas and Memoranda Rolls of the City of London* edited by A.H. Thomas and P.E. Jones, (London, 1924–1961) and *Liber Albus of 1417* edited by H.T. Riley (London, 1861). Later historical studies include G.A. Williams's indispensable *Medieval London: From Commune to Capital* (London, 1963), E. Ekwall's *Studies on the Population of Medieval London* (Stockholm, 1956), S. Thrupp's *The Merchant Class of Medieval London* (London, 1948), *London 800–1216: The Shaping of a City* by C.N.L. Brooke (London, 1975), *London Life in the Fourteenth Century* by C. Pendrill (London, 1925) and G. Home's *Medieval London* (London, 1927). Especial mention must be made of L. Wright's *Sources of London English: Medieval Thames Vocabulary* (Oxford, 1996) which brings the reader right down to the reeking waterside.

Accounts of sixteenth-century London are of course dominated by

Stow's *A Survey of London*; the edition by C.L. Kingsford (London, 1908) is still the most authoritative. More recent studies include *Elizabethan London* by M. Holmes (London, 1969), *Worlds Within Worlds: Structures of Life in Sixteenth-Century London* by S. Rappaport (Cambridge, 1989), *Trade, Government and Economy in pre-Industrial England* edited by D.C. Coleman and A.H. John (London, 1976), *London and the Reformation* by S. Brigden (Oxford, 1989) and *The Pursuit of Stability: Social Relations in Elizabethan London* by I.W. Archer (Cambridge, 1991).

The diaries of John Evelyn, and of Samuel Pepys, are of course essential for any understanding of seventeenth-century London. And Macaulay's *History of England from the Accession of James II* is still immensely readable. But there are specific volumes of great interest, among them *London and the Civil War* edited by S. Porter (London, 1996), and *The Rebuilding of London After the Great Fire* by T.F. Reddaway (London, 1940). P. Earle's *A City Full of People: Men and Women of London, 1650–1750* (London, 1994) is a fascinating quarry. L. Picard's *Restoration London* (London, 1997) provides a detailed synopsis of daily living; it is complemented by the images within *The Cries and Hawkers of London: The Engravings of Marcellus Laroon*, edited by S. Shesgreen (Aldershot, 1990), which provide direct access to the streets and people of the late seventeenth century. I have also made use of *Wenceslaus Hollar* by R. Godfrey (New Haven, 1994) which provides different, but no less interesting, images. E. Ward's *The London Spy* (London, 1697–1703) comes at the end of the century, but not at the end of a rich tradition of London "low life" sketches.

Eighteenth-century London is replete with source material, from the poems and plays of John Gay to the engravings of William Hogarth. Any biography of Samuel Johnson or William Blake will provide a vision of the city in its general and particular circumstances. Specific mention, however, might be made of J. Boswell's *London Journal 1762–1763* edited by F.A. Pottle (London, 1950). The world of Addison and Steele can be discovered within the pages of *Selections from the Tatler and the Spectator* edited by A. Ross (London, 1982). The best general survey of the period is M.D. George's *London Life in the Eighteenth Century* (London, 1925) while J. Summerson's *Georgian London* (London, 1945) will clarify the reader's mind on architectural matters. George Rudé's *Hanoverian London, 1714–1808* (London, 1971) remains a very important study. Of more specific interest is *London in the Age of Industrialisation* by L.D. Schwarz (Cambridge, 1992), while M. Waller's *1700: Scenes from London Life* (London, 2000) provides an intimate picture of ordinary life. Crime, death and punishment seem to emerge as objects of attention in eighteenth-century London; among the books devoted to them are P. Linebaugh's *The London Hanged: Crime and Civil Society in Eighteenth-Century London* (London, 1991), and *Death and the Metropolis* by J. Landers (Cambridge, 1993); of related interest is I. McCalman's *Radical Underworld* (Cambridge, 1988). *John Gay's London* by W.H. Irving (Cambridge, 1923) is precise and informative, as is J. Uglow's *Hogarth: A Life and a World* (London, 1997). The latter biography can be read alongside the edition of *Hogarth's Graphic Works* edited with a commentary by R. Paulson (London, 1989). *The Godwins and the Shelleys* by W. St. Clair (London, 1989) provides more interesting source material on radical London, and S. Gardner's *The Tyger, the Lamb and the Terrible Desart* (London, 1998) provides an approximation of the Blakean vision.

The nineteenth-century city has been the object of fascinated enquiry ever since the nineteenth century itself. Major texts are of course those of Henry Mayhew and Charles Booth. Mayhew's *London Labour and the London Poor*, taken from articles in the *Morning Chronicle* and published in four volumes between 1851 and 1862, mingles anecdote with statistic in a characteristically mid-nineteenth century style. Yet it remains the single most important source for the manner and speech of the nineteenth-century poor, enlivened by Mayhew's eye for detail which can truly be described as Dickensian. The seventeen volumes of Booth's *Life and Labour of the People of London* (1891–1902) are perhaps less colourful but no less sympathetic. This was also the century for the great compilations of London's history by enthusiasts and antiquarians. Principal among them are the six volumes of *Old and New London* edited by W. Thornbury and E. Walford (London, 1883–1885), which moves from area to area like some great eagle-eyed observer, and C. Knight's *London* in six volumes (London, 1841) which provides a series of long essays ranging in subject from prisons to beer-making to advertisements. *London: A Pilgrimage* by Blanchard Jerrold and Gustave Doré (London, 1872) contains haunting images of the savagery and industry of imperial London. An edition of *George Scharf's London*, with a text by P. Jackson (London, 1987), offers images of early nineteenth-century London in a different tone and mode from those of Doré. There are many books upon the Victorian poor, but those I have found most useful include *The Rookeries of London* by T. Beames (London, 1850), *People of the Rookery* by D.M. Green (London, 1986) and J. Hollingshead's *Ragged London in 1861* (London,

1986). F. Sheppard's *London 1808–1870: The Infernal Wen* (London, 1971) is also highly instructive in this context. For a more romantic picture of the city, it is worth looking at *Grandfather's London* by O.J. Morris (London, 1960) while *Dickens's London: An Imaginative Vision* (London, 1991) contains many rare and distinctive photographs of the period. More can be discovered in *Old London* by G. Bush (London, 1975), part of the Archive Photograph Series. There are also general histories. *The Victorian City*, edited by H.J. Dyos and M. Wolff (London, 1973) is invaluable, together with D.J. Olsen's *The Growth of Victorian London* (London, 1976); the latter is particularly interesting for its account of the building work of the period, culminating in the partial destruction of Georgian London and the growth of the great new estates. *Tallis's London Street Views, 1838–1840*, (London, 1969) helps to complete the picture. *London World City 1800–1840*, edited by Celina Fox (London, 1992), contains a valuable series of essays from science to architecture. *The Making of Modern London, 1815–1914* by G. Weightman and S. Humphries (London, 1983) should also be studied.

There are also many nineteenth- and early twentieth-century memoirs, now practically forgotten but still an impressive and comprehensive account of the city known and unknown. There are anecdotes, and walks, and rambles, with titles like H.V. Morton's *The Spell of London* (London, 1926), C.W. Heckthorne's *London Memories* and *London Souvenirs* (London, 1900 and 1891), *Bygone London Life* by E.L. Apperson (London, 1903) and *London Revisited* by E.V. Lucas (London, 1916). The two volumes of A. Hare's *Walks in London* (London, 1883) are charming as well as erudite while W.G. Bell's *Unknown London* (London, 1919) is a repository of secret urban knowledge. From an earlier date come C.M. Smith's *The Little World of London* (London, 1857) and Aleph's *London Scenes and London People* (London, 1863); E.T. Cook's *Highways and Byways in London* (London, 1906) affords similar nostalgic pleasures. A.T. Camden-Pratt's *Unknown London* (London, 1897) covers among other subjects Newgate and the Wool Exchange, while *The West End of Yesterday and Today* by E.B. Chancellor (London, 1926) speaks for itself. R. Nevill's *Night Life in London and Paris* (London, 1926) is in a similar category. A.V. Compton-Rickett's *The London Life of Yesterday* (London, 1909) covers many centuries with a very light touch. But particular mention should be made of another great London historian, Walter Besant, who published a number of volumes on the life and history of the city. His *South London* (London, 1899), *East London* (London, 1901), *London* (London, 1904), *Medieval London* (London,

1906) and *London North of the Thames* (London, 1911) provide a diorama of urban history; his bust is to be found beside the Thames opposite Northumberland Avenue.

It is perhaps appropriate that, at the beginning of the twentieth century, there should also be a concentration of books on the occluded or darker aspects of the city. *London in Shadow* by B. Kennedy (London, 1902) is complemented by *London's Underworld* by T. Holmes (London, 1912), one of the many studies devoted to the vagrant and the dispossessed at the turn of the century. The atmosphere is deepened by S. Graham's *London Nights* (London, 1925), a highly evocative study, and rendered poignant by P. Norman's *London Vanished and Vanishing* (London, 1905). C.H. Rolph's *London Particulars* (London, 1980) provides a detailed and not at all nostalgic memoir of the early decades, while J. Schneer's *London 1900* (New Haven, 1999) offers an "over-view" of social and cultural developments at that time of transition. A more optimistic version of urban commentary emerged in *The Face of London* by H.P. Clunn (London, 1932), *The Wonderful Story of London* edited by H. Wheeler (London, 1949), and A. Bush's *Portrait of London* (London, 1950). One of the greatest of twentieth-century accounts, however, remains *London: The Unique City* by S.E. Rasmussen (London, 1934) which seems to prove the familiar adage that foreign observers view London matters with a clear eye. *A Guide to the Structure of London* by M. Ash (Bath, 1972) is good on the intricacies of post-War planning. *Docklands in the Making* by A. Cox (London, 1995) is a lively introduction to the phenomenon of the resurgent banks of the Thames, and takes its rightful place as part of the great Survey of London which has been compiled over a period of one hundred years. In a similar spirit *Focus on London 97* (London, 1996), published by the Office of National Statistics, is a source of reliable information. *The Making of Modern London* by S. Humphries and J. Taylor (London, 1986) is required reading, and is particularly good on the growth of the suburbs. *London* by S. Harding (London, 1993) can be recommended together with *London: a New Metropolitan Geography* edited by K. Hoggart and D.R. Green (London, 1991). H. Marshall's *Twilight London* (Plymouth, 1971) is one of a number of studies devoted to the problems of contemporary poverty and homelessness; others include B. Mahony's *A Capital Offence* (London, 1988) and *No Way Home* by G. Randall (London, 1988). *The London Nobody Knows* by G. Fletcher (London, 1962) is a highly readable account of the more arcane aspects of London life, and P. Wright's *A Journey Through Ruins: The Last Days of London* (London, 1991) opens up the purlieus of Dalston and Hackney to public gaze. V.S. Pritchett's urban memoir, *London Perceived* (London, 1974) is recommended, together with J. Raban's *Soft City* (London, 1974).

There are several late twentieth-century studies of London, among the best of which are S. Inwood's *A History of London* (London, 1998), a truly comprehensive and scholarly account of the city from its earliest times, and R. Porter's *London: A Social History* (London, 1994) which is more polemical in intent but no less readable. *Landlords to London: the Story of a Capital and its Growth* and *The Selling of Mary Davies* by S. Jenkins (London, 1975 and 1993) are invaluable. F. Sheppard's *London: A Social History* (Oxford, 1998) is concise and serious, while M. Hebbert's *London* (Chichester, 1998) is colourful and idiosyncratic. The most important guide to City architecture remains the Pevsner series; *London 1: The City of London*, edited by Simon Bradley and Nikolaus Pevsner (London, 1997) has brought it up to date. And then of course there is *The London Encyclopaedia*, edited by B. Weinreb and C. Hibbert (London, 1983), which is a prodigy of research and reference. There are also urban anthologies, among them *The Oxford Book of London* edited by P. Bailey (Oxford, 1995) and *The Faber Book of London*, edited by A.N. Wilson (London, 1993) in which appear passages of prose and verse which might otherwise have languished in obscure and forgotten places. *The Pride of London*, edited by W. and S. Scott (London, 1947) is also useful. An especial mention must be made of the three volumes, *London 1066–1914, Literary Sources and Documents*, edited by X. Baron (London, 1997). Here are Lamb and De Quincey, Engels and Dostoyevsky, Dekker and Gay, together with a hundred other observers and chroniclers of the city; these volumes are an important and indeed indispensable guide to London through the centuries.

I have devoted some space in this biography to the observations of foreign travellers, some of which are derived from secondary sources. Since it would be laborious and otiose to keep on creating footnotes for the same material, I include it here. There are the three volumes, *London 1066–1914*, which have already been mentioned. Together with these come *England as Seen by Foreigners* edited by J.W.B. Rye (London, 1865), *Strange Island: Britain Seen through Foreign Eyes, 1395–1940*, edited by F.M. Wilson (London, 1955), *Mine Host London* by W. Kent (London, 1948), *As The Foreigners Saw Us* by M. Letts (London, 1935) and *Coming to London* by various hands (London, 1957). *English Interludes* by C. Mackworth (London, 1956) is primarily concerned with the residence of nineteenth-century French poets in London, and can be compared with *Voltaire: Letters Concerning the English Nation*, edited by N. Cronk (Oxford, 1994). There is *Tolstoy in London* by V. Lucas (London, 1979), *Monet in London* by G. Sieberling (Seattle, 1988), *Berlioz in London* by A.W. Gaaz (London, 1950), *Arthur Rimbaud* by E. Starkie (London, 1938), *Fyodor Dostoyevsky: Winter Notes on Summer Impressions* translated by R.L. Renfield (London, 1985), *The Life of Olaudah Equino* (New York, 1971), *A Japanese Artist in London* by Yoshio Markino (London, 1911), *The Letters of Henry James*, edited by L. Edel (London, 1987) and *Revolutionists in London* by J.W. Hulse (Oxford, 1970). The memoirs of earlier travellers are collected in *The Diary of Baron Waldstein* translated and edited by G.W. Groos (London, 1981), *The Journals of Two Travellers in Elizabethan and Early Stuart England* edited by P. Razzell (London, 1995), *A Tour of London* by P.J. Grosley (Dublin, 1772), *German Travellers in England 1400–1800* by W.D. Robson-Scott (Oxford, 1953), *London in 1710 from the Travels of Zacharias Conrad von Uffenbach*, edited by W.H. Quarrell and M. Mare (London, 1934), *A Foreign View of England in the Reigns of George I and George II: The Letters of Cesar De Saussure*, edited by Madame van Muyden (London, 1902). So is unrolled a wealth of comment.

On London paganism, the most important study is *Magic in Modern London* by E. Lovett (Croydon, 1925).

On matters of sound and silence there is nothing more appropriate or interesting than the arresting *The Acoustic World of Early Modern England* by B.R. Smith (Chicago, 1999).

On the question of maps and general topographical matters there are *The Times London History Atlas* edited by H. Clout (London, 1991) and *The History of London in Maps* by F. Barker and P. Jackson (London, 1990). There is also a wonderful series of old maps, published in association with the London Topographical Society and the Guildhall Library, under the general rubric of "A to Z" of Elizabethan, Restoration, Georgian, Regency and Victorian Londons.

There are several studies on the Cockney dialect; *London's Dialect* by M. Macbride (London, 1910), W. Matthews's *Cockney Past and Present* (London, 1938), *Cockney Phonology* by E. Sivertsen (Oslo, 1960) and, most importantly, P. Wright's *Cockney Dialect and Slang* (London, 1981).

The history of St. Giles is revealed in *St. Giles-in-the-fields* by L.C. Loveless (London, 1931) and *Some Accounts of the Hospital and Parish of St. Giles-in-the-fields* by J. Parton (London, 1822). Volume III of the *Survey of London* on that district (London, 1912) was also important.

On other penal and criminal matters there are many volumes. Those consulted include *The Beggars' Brotherhood* by R. Fuller (London, 1936), *Crime within The Square Mile* and *The Triple Tree* by D. Rumbelow (London, 1971 and 1982), *The Underworld* by D. Campbell (London, 1994), *Body Snatchers* by M. Fido (London, 1980), and *Crime in England 1550–1800* edited by J.S. Cockburn (Princeton, 1977). On London prisons, and on Newgate in particular, there are several important works. *The English Bastille* by A. Babbington (London, 1971) is the most recent, but *London Prisons Today and Yesterday* by A. Crew (London, 1933) and *The London Prisons* by H. Dixon (London, 1850) are valuable. *The Chronicles of Newgate* by A. Griffiths (London, 1884) and *The Newgate Calendar* edited by N. Birkett (London, 1951) are of course necessary records.

For horrible murders M. Fido's *Murder Guide to London* (London, 1986) is a handy Baedeker which should be consulted beside *The Murder Club Guide to London* edited by B. Lane (London, 1988). *Jack the Ripper: A Summing Up and Verdict* by C. Wilson and R. Odell (London, 1987) is a convenient summary of that bizarre history. P. Haining's *The Legend and Bizarre Crimes of Spring-Heeled Jack* (London, 1977) is, as might be expected, the definitive account.

On the food of London, G. Dodd's *The Food of London* (London, 1856) is enough, at least when combined with nineteenth- and twentieth-century memoirs.

On questions of refuse and sanitation the most authoritative modern study is *The Great Stink of London* by S. Halliday (London, 1999). Other works consulted have been *Garbage in the Cities* by M.V. Melosi (Texas, 1941), J.L. Horan's *The Porcelain God: A Social History of the Toilet* (London, 1996) and *The Disposal of Refuse from the City of London* by G.L. Sutcliffe (London, 1898). H. Jephson's *The Sanitary Evolution of London* (London, 1907) is equally self-explanatory.

On the Great Fire and accompanying fires, A. Hardwick's *Memorable Fires in London* (London, 1926) is informative, while W.G. Bell's *The Great Fire of London* (London, 1923) is an accurate account. G. Milne's *The Great Fire of London* (London, 1986) is the most recent, however, and the most authoritative. *London in Flames, London in Glory* edited by R.A. Aubin (New Brunswick, 1943) is a very interesting anthology. Another important study is *Courage High: A History of Fire Fighting in London* by S. Holloway (London, 1992).

On Fetter Lane I have consulted *The Parish of St. Andrew, Holborn*, by

C.M. Barron (London, 1974) as well as the many references in other biographical and historical works.

For the birds and bees of the city my principal sources have been *London's Natural History* by R.S.R. Fitter (London, 1945), *The Natural History of the City* by R.S.R. Fitter and J.F. Lousley (London, 1953), *Bird Watching in London* by E.M. Nicholson (London, 1995), *London Green* by N. Braybrooke (London, 1959), *Birds in London* by W.H. Hudson (London, 1924), *London Birds and Beasts* by J.T. Tristram-Valentine (London, 1895) and *Familiar London Birds* by F. Finn (London, 1923).

On the weather of London, the most significant account is contained in *The Big Smoke: A History of Air Pollution in London* by P. Brimblecombe (London, 1987) while *London's Hurricane* by M. Davison and I. Currie (Tonbridge, 1989) blew some fresh air into the subject.

The nature and history of Clerkenwell are covered in several volumes, the most important being *The History of Clerkenwell* by H.J. Pinks (London, 1865). J. Adlard's *In Sweet St. James's Clerkenwell* (London, 1984) can be recommended, together with *Islington* by C. Harris (London, 1974) and *Smithfield Past and Present* by A. Forshaw and T. Bergstrom (London, 1980).

For all subterranean contemplations I owe a debt to *London Under London* by R. Trench and E. Hillman (London, 1985), *Buried London* by W.T. Hill (London, 1955) and *The Lost Rivers of London* by N. Barton (London, 1962).

On the madness of London it is worth consulting M. Byrd's *Visits to Bedlam* (Columbia, 1974) and R. Reed's *Bedlam on the Jacobean Stage* (Cambridge, 1952); the most significant work, however, is D. Russell's *Scenes From Bedlam* (London, 1997).

On the subject of children there are all the volumes composed by I. and P. Opie, particularly *The Lore and Language of Schoolchildren* (Oxford, 1959) and *Children's Games in Streets and Playgrounds* (Oxford, 1969). Other sources include *London Street Games* by N. Douglas (London, 1931), *The Young Londoner Through the Ages* by D.M. Stuart (London, 1962), *Children's Literature: An Illustrated History* edited by P. Hunt (Oxford, 1995), *The London Child* by E. Sharp (London, 1927), and *The Cries of Banbury and London* by J. Rusher (London, 1820). *Growing Up in London* by M. Chamberlain (London, 1989) is a wonderful memoir, while no account of London childhood would be complete without mentioning the important work of G. Speaight. I have made particular use of his *The History of the English Puppet*

Theatre (London, 1955), *The History of the English Toy Theatre* (London, 1946) and *A History of the Circus* (London, 1980).

On graffiti three works, as well as the walls of London, have been scrutinised: *Graffiti* by R.G. Freeman (London, 1966), *The Handwriting on the Wall* by E. Abel and B. Buckley (London, 1977) and the extraordinary *The Merry Thought or the Glass Window and Bog House Miscellany* by Hurlo Thrumbo (London, 1732).

On immigration I have consulted I. MCauley's *Guide to Ethnic London* (London, 1993), *Indians in Britain 1700–1947* by R. Viscram (London, 1986), *Exiles of Erin* by L.H. Lees (Manchester, 1979) and *Windrush* by M. and T. Phillips (London, 1999).

For my chapter on the suburbs I am indebted to *London Suburbs*, with an introduction by A. Saint (London, 1999), *Semi-Detached London* by A.A. Jackson (London, 1973), *London in the Country* by G.R. Williams (London, 1975) and *Something in Linoleum* by P. Vaughan (London, 1994).

For my chapter on the Second World War I am indebted to *London at War* by P. Ziegler (London, 1995), *The Lost Treasures of London* by W. Kent (London, 1947) and *History Under Fire* by J. Pope-Hennessy (London, 1941).

On the subject of illustrations, I would like to acknowledge the invaluable assistance of Richard Shone. On illustrative, and general editorial matters I am indebted to Penelope Hoare and Stuart Williams.

Index

A Note About the Author

Peter Ackroyd is a bestselling writer of both fiction and nonfiction. His most recent books include the award-winning biography *The Life of Thomas More* and the novel *The Plato Papers*. He has won the Whitbread Award, the Royal Society of Literature's William Heinemann Award, the James Tate Black Memorial Prize, and the *Guardian* fiction prize. He lives in London.

a   note   about   the   type

London: A Biography is set in Fournier, a digitized version
of the original font cut that was part of the Monotype
Corporation historical typeface revivals in the 1920s.

Fournier was created by the typographer and printing
historian Stanley Morison (1889–1967) and grew out of
his admiration for the type cuts of Pierre Simon Fournier
(1712–1768).